MEXICO

THE COLONIAL ERA

This book is the second in a three-volume history of Mexico, a major work that conveys the full sweep of Mexican history in all its social, economic, and political diversity, from the first human settlement of Mesoamerica down to the post-PRI politics of our day.

Focusing on the period from 1521 to 1821, Volume 2 offers a comprehensive narrative and analysis of colonial Mexico following the Spanish conquest. In explaining colonial patterns of development, Alan Knight pays particular attention to the political economy of the colony: the formation and growth of the hacienda and its impact on the Indian peasantry; the dynamics of the colonial state and its relationship to the church; the role of trade, demography, warfare and taxation; and contrasting patterns of regional development, of class and ethnic conflict, and of popular protest in both city and countryside. Global comparisons and theoretical perspectives inform the analysis. The author also addresses the processes of ethnic formation, religious conversion, and acculturation which gave New Spain its distinct and diverse identity. The book concludes with an analysis of the accumulating tensions of the Bourbon era and of the bloody struggle for Mexican independence.

Alan Knight is Professor of the History of Latin America at Oxford University. He is the author of the two-volume *The Mexican Revolution* (Cambridge, 1986), which was awarded the Beveridge Prize by the American Historical Association and the Bolton Prize by the Conference on Latin American History.

MEXICO

THE COLONIAL ERA

ALAN KNIGHT

St. Antony's College, Oxford University

CAMBRIDGE
UNIVERSITY PRESS

PUBLISHED BY THE PRESS SYNDICATE OF THE UNIVERSITY OF CAMBRIDGE
The Pitt Building, Trumpington Street, Cambridge, United Kingdom

CAMBRIDGE UNIVERSITY PRESS
The Edinburgh Building, Cambridge CB2 2RU, UK
40 West 20th Street, New York, NY 10011-4211, USA
477 Williamstown Road, Port Melbourne, VIC 3207, Australia
Ruiz de Alarcón 13, 28014 Madrid, Spain
Dock House, The Waterfront, Cape Town 8001, South Africa

http://www.cambridge.org

© Alan Knight 2002

First published 2002

Printed in the United States of America

Typeface New Aster 10/13.5 pt.   *System* LaTeX 2_ε [TB]

A catalog record for this book is available from the British Library.

Library of Congress Cataloging in Publication Data

Knight, Alan, 1946–
Mexico. The colonial era / Alan Knight.
   p. cm.
Includes bibliographical references and index.
ISBN 0-521-81475-8 – ISBN 0-521-89196-5 (pb.)
1. Mexico – History – Spanish colony, 1540–1810.   I. Title.
F1231 .K65   2002
972′.02 – dc21   2001052625

ISBN 0 521 81475 8 hardback
ISBN 0 521 89196 5 paperback

For Florence

Contents

Preface

I should like to thank the three anonymous readers of this book (then manuscript), who did their job scrupulously, sensitively, and with remarkable speed. I should also like to thank the people of Cambridge University Press – Frank Smith, Alia Winters, Camilla Knapp and Susan Greenberg – who helped bring this book to fruition. Needless to say, any faults are of my making, not theirs.

It is usual in these prefaces to list a roll call of individuals and institutions who made it all possible. In fact, the trend within British higher education – faithfully, even enthusiastically, repeated in my own university, Oxford – has been towards a narrow (and misconceived) utilitarianism, a diminution of real resources dedicated to research, and relentless bureaucratic overload (evident in the endless round of evaluation, assessments, management gimmicks, reforms of 'governance', etc.). All of this – horribly reminiscent of the ill-fated Bourbon Reforms of the late eighteenth century (see this volume) – served, certainly in my experience, to impede rather than to advance research and scholarship.

However, I would like to acknowledge the supportive camaraderie of three groups, who in their different ways have all helped counteract this institutional drag: my colleagues in (or associated with) the Oxford Latin American Centre: the handful of Mexican historians based in the U.K. who have kept the flame alight in far from easy times (Professors Brading, Hamnett and Thomson in particular); and, last but not least, the many Mexicans – scholars, students, librarians, archivists and many others – who have helped me along the way, as I have tried to learn about their fascinating country.

Series Introduction

This is one volume in a three-volume series which charts the history of Mexico from the beginning – that is, from the initial human settlements in North America – down to the present. It is, therefore, a sort of 'national' history: it takes what is now – notwithstanding certain internal and external challenges – a clearly constituted nation-state, Mexico, and treats the history of that entity: the geographical space in which Mexico sits and the thousand or so generations of 'Mexicans' who have lived since the first settlers crossed the Bering land bridge from Asia and headed south. Of course, the nation-state of Mexico came into being only in 1821 (the concluding point of my second volume), and, even then, it was a fragile entity, destined for severe mutilation at the hands of the United States some twenty-five years later. Nevertheless, the Mexican nation-state (whose post-1821 history will be the subject of a third volume, now in preparation) was created on the foundations of the colony of New Spain, which in turn had been built on the detritus of the Mesoamerican polities (above all, the Aztec empire) which flourished prior to 1519. 'Mesoamerica' – the cultural-cum-chronological entity which embraced what would later become 'Mexico' (as well as some of Central America) – was, of course, no nation-state; rather, it was a congeries of empires, city-states and stateless peoples. But by virtue of historical processes which involved both deep continuities and sharp ruptures, Mesoamerica metamorphosed into colonial New Spain; and New Spain provided the foundation of the independent republic of Mexico. Those continuities and ruptures form the basis of this study.

National histories are not the staple of historiography that they once were. True, scholars may make a killing with a successful 'national' textbook; but, in doing so, they garner no critical acclaim from their peers. Textbooks, by definition, are succinct and synthetic, uncontentious and undemanding. (That may not stop them being more influential than most works of history, of course.) This book is not a textbook, although it was first conceived as a succinct, synthetic survey of Mexican history, from the beginning to the present (a present that is now quite a few years in the past). With time the survey grew, and I became aware that I was not up to writing a textbook. The result is this three-volume study. Volume I covers the history of Mesoamerica/Mexico from 'the beginning' – that is, from the first human entry into the Americas, c. 20,000 B.C., to the Spanish Conquest in 1519–21. (The first twenty thousand years or so are, however, peremptorily despatched in a matter of pages.) Volume II deals with the colonial period, from Conquest to Independence (1821), and Volume III tells the story of Mexico since Independence.

If national histories are at a discount these days, why hazard this grand and perhaps quixotic survey? A personal justification is that I wanted to educate myself about pre-Independence Mexican history, thus to emancipate myself from the narrowly modernist view I had acquired on the basis of my previous work (which focused on the Mexican Revolution of 1910). Because of the heavy pall of history which hangs over modern Mexico, it seemed to me both necessary and interesting for a historian of modern Mexico to retreat in time, to note the continuities and ruptures previously mentioned and thus to prime oneself against those vendors of historical snake oil who – be they politicians, social scientists, journalists, 'organic intellectuals' or cheapskate historians – exploit and traduce the past in the narrow interests – personal, political or pecuniary – of the present.

While this may offer a (personal) reason for writing these books, it does not justify anyone's reading them. Here, I think, two justifications can be entered. The first is obvious: Mexico, like Mount Everest, is there; hence it is worthy of study, not least by those who may visit the country or who may nurture some nugget of historical information – Cortés's meeting with Moctezuma in 1520; Juan Diego's meeting with the Virgin of Guadalupe eleven years later – which they wish to contextualize. While it would be overly subjective and invidious to compile league tables of national histories, it cannot be denied that Mexico's history is – like the history of Greece or Italy, China or Iran – unusually 'long', rich and culturally diverse, as well as being particularly violent and at times tragic. It is littered with arresting episodes and images (like the two meetings just mentioned). 'May you live in interesting times', says the Chinese curse; the Mexicans/Mesoamericans have had more than their fair share of 'interesting times'. Thus, to the extent that history embodies a genuine 'romantic' appeal – by which I mean the appeal of presenting momentous events and processes, located in radically unfamiliar and intellectually challenging contexts[1] – Mexico/Mesoamerica is a prime candidate for historical study.

The second justification is that Mexico offers ample scope for 'scientific' history, by which I mean history which engages with the social sciences – history which, some would say, is 'nomothetic' as well as 'idiographic', which is concerned with generalities (e.g., processes of religious conversion) as well as with particularities (like the apparition of the Virgin of Guadalupe). 'Scientific' – or, if you prefer, 'analytical' or 'reasoned'[2] – history involves comparing and contrasting, assembling data and marshalling arguments, drawing upon relevant theory for useful explanatory concepts. While narrative, particularist ('idiographic') history and scientific/analytical/reasoned ('nomothetic') history employ different 'rhetorics' and may appeal to different intellects, they are, in my view, complementary and not antithetical. They both depend, for their cogency, on similar rules of evidential inquiry and presentation;[3] and, taken together, they capture

---

[1] Mexico may be, for me, a foreign country; but, as the old adage says, 'the past is a foreign country', hence modern Mexicans, too, face an intellectual challenge when they grapple with their own remote (and maybe not so remote) history.

[2] Stephen Haber, 'Anything Goes: Mexico's "New" Cultural History', *Hispanic American Historical Review*, 79/2 (1999), pp. 310–11, following Fogel and Elton (a decidedly odd couple), contrasts, I think excessively, 'social science' and 'traditional' history; Pierre Vilar, *Iniciación al vocabulario del análisis histórico* (Barcelona, 1980), pp. 9, 11, favours 'reasoned' (*razonada*) history, although he goes on to recall how, when asked 'do you believe that history is a science?', he 'replied, irritated, that if I did not so believe I would not devote myself to teaching it'.

[3] I mention this in part to join together what others might wish to put asunder; in part to rebut, should rebuttal be required, the whimsical notion that history involves free-floating texts, detached from any 'reality', hence incapable of reasoned debate on the basis of empirical evidence: a notion which, if less prevalent than some positivistic scaremongers would have us believe, does nevertheless have its proponents, especially among the Lotophagi of literary criticism: see Richard J. Evans, *In Defence of History* (London, 1997), ch. 4.

two powerful justifications of historical research – the (idiographic) interest in compelling narrative and the (nomothetic) concern for understanding broad processes of social change.

'National' histories, even though they seem *passé* in the eyes of many historical professionals,[4] offer perfectly adequate vehicles for these complementary rhetorics. It is a mistake to believe that a focus on national history precludes comparison or ensures superficiality: not only can 'nations' be compared to each other but also, more importantly, 'nations' (not to mention grand non-national entities like 'Mesoamerica') are themselves composites which have to be disaggregated so that the parts can be analysed comparatively. Thus, historians of Mexico largely agree that there are and always have been 'many Mexicos' and that to understand the loose aggregate 'Mexico' (again, not to mention 'Mesoamerica') we have to disaggregate – not only by region or locality, which, given Mexico's huge size and corrugated landscape, is often crucial, but also by class (e.g., landlord or peasant), ethnicity (Indian, mestizo or creole), ideology (Catholic, 'syncretic' or 'pagan') and sector (market or subsistence; mining, agriculture or manufacturing). Thus, national history requires comparison and – today at least – in no sense implies the contemplation of a flawless national monolith. In this respect, the difference between 'national', 'regional' and 'local' history is purely one of degree and should not be elevated to a ruling shibboleth. Regional and local history, which has rightly proliferated and prospered in recent years, also involves a good deal of aggregation and may, despite its narrower focus, still display superficiality. Furthermore, national history offers a potential context for regional and local histories (plural), hence may help to sort out the typical from the aberrant, just as global or continental history offers a potential context for national studies.

Mexico is also fertile terrain for 'scientific' history. Many of the most weighty questions which historians (and other social scientists) confront have their distinctive Mexican embodiments: the Neolithic revolution and the origins of 'civilization'; the formation of states

---

[4] Hence this argument is directed primarily at the professionals (including budding students of history); the lay reader may see nothing archaic in national history, hence little of relevance in this argument.

and class societies; empire-building, both European and extra-European; the expansion of Europe and the onset of Latin American 'dependency'; the role of religion – again, both European and extra-European; the rationale of ritual practices (including sacrifice) and religious conversion; the dynamics of colonial government, 'native' resistance and accommodation, ethnic miscagenation, migration and cultural syncretism; the genesis of nationalism and the conquest of independence, within the broad context of the 'Atlantic Revolution' of 1776–1821.

Thus, the study of Mexico should shed light on much wider processes of historical change, and therefore without, I hope, losing sight of the specificity of the Mexican experience, I have paid some attention to those processes and to the concepts and explanations which help make sense of them. This has involved some theoretical detours which, in this day and age, may also seem *passé* and even quaint. I have, for example, reprised the old argument about the 'feudal' or 'capitalist' character of Spain and the Spanish empire: an argument which was, in a sense, shelved long before it either achieved resolution or lost all utility. Historians, social scientists and others readily talk about the triumph of capitalism – today more triumphant and triumphalist than ever – and such usage must imply something or (better) somethings (plural) which went before which were not capitalist. Elucidating the difference is therefore a matter of some importance, which cannot be left to mere intuition or common sense. It is particularly important in a broad synthetic study such as this since, as a general rule, the broader the historical sweep is, the more crucial are the 'organizing concepts' used to make sense of the sweep. As Voltaire queried: 'If you have nothing to tell us except that one barbarian succeeded another on the banks of the Oxus and Jaxartes, what is that to us?'[5] Or, we could echo, on the banks of the Lerma and the Usumacinta?[6] Gibbon, of course, told the story of riverside barbarians (*inter alia*), but he linked his magisterial narrative to 'philosophical' inquiries – concerning, for example, the rationale of Christian conversion.[7] Braudel, too, linked specific stories

[5] Quoted in E. H. Carr, *What Is History?* (Harmondsworth, 1964), p. 88.
[6] Not that I mean to suggest that those living on the banks of the Lerma and Usumacinta were 'barbarians'.
[7] Peter Burke, *History and Social Theory* (Cambridge, 1992), p. 5.

and other 'idiographic' particularities to a grand vision and quasi-theory of history. Without claiming to scale the heights of Gibbonian or Braudelian history, I would plead the legitimacy of asking big questions and trying to marshal the big concepts necessary to make sense of them.

Of course, big concepts are a matter of subjective choice. We can all agree that Cortés made landfall on the Gulf of Mexico in 1519 and entered the smoking ruins of Tenochtitlán as a conqueror in 1521. When it comes to explaining why that happened – why Cortés overcame Moctezuma and not vice versa[8] – interpretations will differ and will not be easily adjudicated according to shared criteria. Was the religious conversion of Mexico's Indians in the sixteenth century a glorious 'spiritual conquest' or a sordid story of oppression, coercion and dissimulation? Was Mexican independence the result of endemic social, ethnic and nationalist tensions, or an almost accidental by-product of the Napoleonic invasion of Spain in 1808 – without which the colony would have remained in Spanish hands, content with a modicum of 'home rule'? Did the Aztecs slaughter prisoners *en masse* because they were avid for protein? Did the Classical Maya cities fall victim to war, revolution, disease or starvation? Was New Spain feudal or capitalist?

When it comes to asking – and tentatively answering – these big questions, personal inclinations cannot be avoided. I find these questions interesting, even if they are in some cases old (but nonetheless unresolved). Some historians find them irrelevant or tedious, and there is nothing I can do about that. Meanwhile, there are questions – of a somewhat different sort – which, I concede, are neglected in these pages. These might be loosely summed up as 'cultural' questions: a catch-all category which includes both traditional historical themes, such as 'high' culture (e.g., painting, literature, architecture), and 'new', and certainly fashionable, themes, such as popular culture (religion, ritual, recreation), gender, signs and signifiers. To put it bluntly, this history may seem overly materialist, concerned more with the Mexican political economy than with the Mexican psyche.

---

[8] This question is a complex one, involving not only superior Spanish technology, logistics, morale, or luck but also Spanish motivation – why, in other words, did a Spanish fleet sail to Mexico, rather than an Aztec fleet to Spain?

Beyond pleading subjective inclination – which is a plea of limited validity[9] – I would enter three modest considerations.

First, it should be recognized that some of the supposedly 'new' cultural history involves a semantic repackaging of older ideas and topics. 'Subalterns', for example, were once called workers and peasants (among other things). I have tried to give a good deal of attention to 'subalterns', even though I have not used the term, at least not systematically. So I think I write 'subaltern history' just as I write prose, but I do not make an issue of it. At any rate, there is a fair amount of 'bottom-up' (popular) history in these pages, not least because 'top-down' (elite) history cannot be understood in isolation; the two are dialectically related. It is true, however, and quite deliberate, that my 'subalterns' are seen more at work than at play, more in acts of protest than in moments of recreation, more on the streets and in the fields than in their own homes. Subjective inclination and constraints of space aside, there are a couple of reasons for this, which have to do with the availability, status and relevance of the evidence.

Second, some of 'new cultural history' is still incipient (it is contesting for acceptance in the 'market-place of ideas'), and anyone who tries to write a general synthetic history should beware of the dictates of fashion. I have therefore stitched this story together from fairly traditional material, not the latest fashionable fabrics, however eye-catching. Caution is particularly in order when, given the novelty of some themes, there is – as yet – no conclusive evidence, no sign of scholarly consensus. For example, the impact of the Spanish Conquest on Mesoamerican gender relations appears to

---

[9] 'Subjective inclination' is of limited, but not negligible, validity. All historians – irrespective of whether they work on national, regional, local or thematic topics – have to select themes, facts and arguments from a huge range of possibilities. The bigger the topic, roughly speaking, the greater the range of possibilities and the problems of selection. The process of selection, in turn, will reflect the historian's own interests and priorities. The finished work is therefore open to criticism on two fronts: sins of commission (getting the facts, argument or internal logic of the work wrong) and sins of omission (leaving out important topics which deserve attention). The first criticism, being more focused, is more conducive to objective debate; the second is necessarily more subjective. Yet – as readers of academic reviews, regular seminar-goers and doctoral candidates will attest – the second is often the easiest and commonest form of criticism: 'the author/paper/candidate neglected...'. While this criticism can sometimes be substantiated in terms of the overt claims and logic of the book/talk/thesis, it is often just a countersubjective claim: it means, 'if I had written this book/paper/thesis I would have done it differently and would have said more about...'; and, in turn, it begs the question, 'given that time and space are finite, what would you have left out instead?'

be a matter of considerable disagreement, but disagreement based,
it seems, on a scarcity, rather than a surfeit, of hard data and mature
debate.[10] In comparison, we know a lot about the make-up of the
colonial hacienda or the character of the Bourbon Reforms; and,
while knowledge does not guarantee consensus, it does provide the
national historian with the material with which to attempt an informed synthesis.[11] I do not doubt that, in the years to come, as recent research is consolidated and incorporated into synthetic studies
they will mutate accordingly, and for the better.

Finally, the relevance of some 'cultural' themes is not always clear.
I work on the assumption that a history of Mexico/Mesoamerica
ought to explain the main dynamics of change in a large and complex
society. Necessarily, this means heroic (or stupid) aggregation, and
the omission of much that might be interesting in itself, but which
is of limited relevance to the big story. For example, I have paid relatively little attention to elite culture (literature, 'high' art and architecture), save where it seemed to me that elite culture clearly intertwined with economics or politics, broadly defined. Thus, the lay-out
of the sacred city of Teotihuacan or the severe neoclassical architecture of the late Bourbon period clearly carried powerful sociopolitical significance. But this is not true of all products of 'high culture';[12]
and I did not want to go the way of some textbooks, which, within the

[10] Compare Arthur J. O. Anderson, 'Aztec Wives', pp. 77, 84–5, for whom 'the Aztec world, after
the conquest as well as before, was a man's world', hence, 'nothing in the position of Aztec
wives had altered much' as a result of the Conquest, and Susan Kellogg, 'Tenochca Mexican
Women, 1500–1700', pp. 133, 139, who sees an 'eventual and marked decline in the status of
Mexican women': both in Susan Schroeder, Stephanie Wood, and Robert Haskett, eds., *Indian
Women of Early Mexico* (Norman, Okla., 1997).

[11] Hence, by way of explanation and apology, the colonial volume in this series is heavily foot-
noted: in order (a) to point the reader to relevant sources and (b) to engage in debates, qualifi-
cations and clarifications which would clutter the text but which are important for conveying
the scope and complexity of colonial scholarship.

[12] Some might wish to make a tight, even deterministic, conection between high culture and
social, political and economic forces, which they see marching in lockstep through defined
historical stages or periods. Recent literary criticism (again) inclines to this view; as did Harry
Lime (*The Third Man*), with his famous association between, on the one hand, Renaissance
political violence and high artistic achievement, and, on the other, Swiss sociopolitical stability
and – the cuckoo clock. Such a view probably exaggerates Swiss sociopolitical stability and
(more important) assumes that high culture is a reflex of social forces, whereas I would see
it – as some choose to see the state – as 'relatively autonomous' of those forces. And, since
those forces are my chief concern in this book, it follows that high culture need make only an
occasional appearance in its pages. A similar argument can be made for popular culture, if
narrowly defined to denote *aesthetic* practices (music, dance, textile and ceramic styles) rather
than broader *collective* activities (e.g., fiestas, drinking, riots).

grand structure of national history, create tiny token compartments for 'poetry', 'music', 'architecture' and so on. This is not a history of Mexican poetry, music or architecture. The same is true, *mutatis mutandis*, for popular, as opposed to elite, culture: I introduce the industrious Indian potters of Tonalá (Jalisco), or the exalted religious insurgents of Cancuc (Chiapas), both of them exemplary cases of broad trends in colonial society; but I do not claim to present a thorough analysis of, say, popular artisan styles and ritual practices throughout New Spain.

Indeed, critics might say, and they might be right, that this is a mainly materialist history, concerned with forms of economic production and exchange, as well as with the political structures which made those forms possible. Thus, its primary themes are population, agrarian production and labour systems; villages and haciendas, mines and cities; political and clerical authority; state- and empire-building; warfare, rebellion and repression. The Mesoamericans/Mexicans, having lived in 'interesting times' for a good two millennia, have yielded a vast body of evidence under these diverse headings. Hence, in seeking to do them – both the themes and the people – historiographical justice, I have necessarily neglected some other themes, whose omission, whole or partial, may be lamented by those less tarred with the brush of materialism. In conclusion I would ask: given the story told in these pages, what is omitted that is crucial to explaining its course and outcome? There are no doubt plenty of possible answers, and plenty of historians capable of filling the blanks.

ONE. The Habsburg Colony

I. Military and Material Conquest

Following the fall of Tenochtitlán a small force of Spaniards[1] usurped the political hegemony of the Aztec state, which had dominated a million and a half Indians in the Valley of Mexico and as many as twenty millions in its tributary provinces. This demographic imbalance did not inspire caution; on the contrary, the conquistadors at once pressed ahead with further explorations and conquests. They sought, first, to incorporate the outlying reaches of the empire they had overthrown (one of Cortés's first acts was to appropriate the Aztec tribute rolls); second, to find fresh sources of bullion, those of Tenochtitlán having been seized and squandered; and, third, to provide gainful employment for those many conquistadors who felt deprived of sufficient spoils.

Thus, even before the final victory of 1521, Spanish expeditions had penetrated southwards to Oaxaca and the Gulf coast of the

---

[1] Concerning the chapter title, it is sometimes objected that New Spain was a kingdom (*reino*) under the Habsburg Crown; part, therefore, of a 'composite monarchy', along with the kingdoms of South America and the Peninsula; hence not strictly a colony (see Colin M. MacLachlan and Jaime E. Rodríguez O., *The Forging of the Cosmic Race: A Reinterpretation of Colonial Mexico* [Berkeley, 1980], p. 96). Some (idealistic) contemporaries said as much (e.g., Peter of Ghent: Peggy K. Liss, *Mexico under Spain, 1521–1556: Society and the Origins of Nationality* [Chicago, 1975], p. 72). Although the argument has some relevance to the final collapse of the empire in 1808–21, it is, for most purposes, a narrowly juridical, excessively formal and therefore potentially misleading point of view. During the three preceding centuries, it is clear, Mexico – New Spain – was subject to Spanish control, was exploited in the (perceived) interest of Spain, and experienced a regime different from that which prevailed in the peninsula.

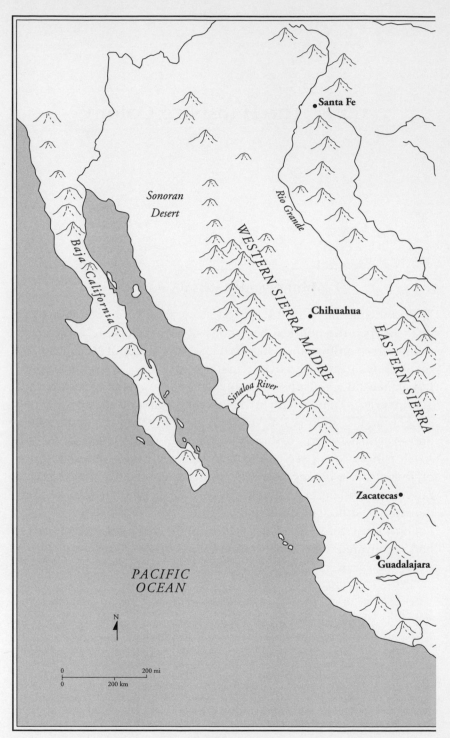

Map 1

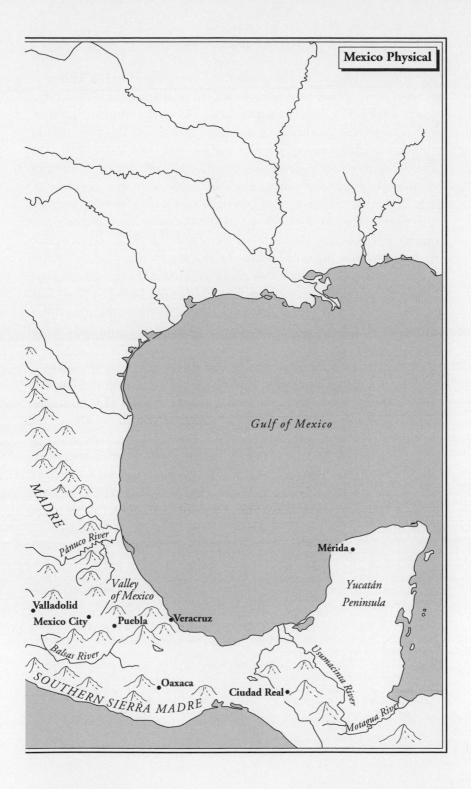

Mexico Physical

Gulf of Mexico

MADRE

Pánuco River

Valley of Mexico

Valladolid

Mexico City

Puebla

Veracruz

Mérida

Yucatán Peninsula

Balsas River

SOUTHERN SIERRA MADRE

Oaxaca

Ciudad Real

Usumacinta River

Motagua River

Isthmus, as well as to the Huasteca, northeast of the Valley of Mexico – both zones of relatively recent and insecure Aztec hegemony. After 1521, the conquistadors – Cortés included – ranged farther, asserting Spanish control over Moctezuma's erstwhile dominions and, before long, penetrating beyond their loose perimeter. Like the Aztecs before them, the Spaniards were drawn to the rich and densely populated zones of southern Mesoamerica. During the early 1520s the Mixtecs and Zapotecs of Oaxaca were overcome: once again, internal divisions aided the conquerors; some *caciques* treated with the Spaniards, rather than resist; and, in consequence, the conquest was briefer, less bloody and traumatic, than the defeat of the Aztecs.[2] But it was also more conditional and uncomplete. Further south, a Spanish expedition to Chiapas failed in 1524, but, four years later, a second effort succeeded – despite strenuous opposition – and the Spaniards established a partial and contested control over Chiapas.[3]

Such conquests – facilitated by Indian divisions – were also complicated by Spanish dissensions. Having initially defeated the Huastec Indians of the Province of Pánuco to the northeast (1522), Cortés had then to confront the challenge of Francisco Garay, newly arrived from Cuba; Garay's expedition collapsed, but Cortés now faced a major Huastec revolt, which resulted in hundreds of Spanish casualties. This, the worst Spanish reverse since the Noche Triste, was overcome and bloodily revenged. The Huastec elite was decimated, and the now pacificied province was given over to the callous rule of Nuño de Guzmán.[4] In the south, meanwhile, Pedro de Alvarado penetrated

---

[2] Especially in lowland Oaxaca – the Valley of Oaxaca and the Isthmus – and in the Mixtec highlands (western Oaxaca). However, the northern sierra – rough country, inhabited by simpler and more egalitarian communities – offered both fewer incentives and stiffer resistance to Spanish domination (in which respect Oaxaca constituted a kind of microcosm of Mexico as a whole): see John K. Chance, *Race and Class in Colonial Oaxaca* (Stanford, 1978), pp. 30–1; and John K. Chance, *Conquest of the Sierra: Spaniard and Indian in Colonial Oaxaca* (Norman, Okla., 1989), pp. 16–20.

[3] Victoria Reifler Bricker, *The Indian Christ, the Indian King: The Historical Substrate of Maya Myth and Ritual* (Austin, 1981), pp. 43–6.

[4] Donald E. Chipman, *Nuño de Guzmán and the Province of Pánuco in New Spain (1518–1533)* (Glendale, 1967), pp. 59–82. Not that Guzmán's abuses were unique. Compare those of Luis de Berrio in Oaxaca (1529–31): Chance, *Conquest of the Sierra*, p. 18; or of Gaspar Pacheco in Yucatán: Diego de Landa, *Yucatán Before and After the Conquest* (New York, 1978; first pubd. 1937, translated by William Gates from the 1566 original), pp. 24–5.

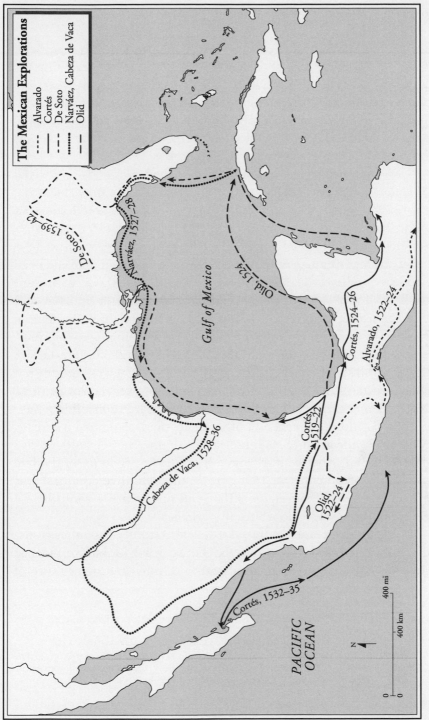

The Mexican Explorations

- Alvarado
- Cortés
- De Soto
- Narváez, Cabeza de Vaca
- Olid

De Soto, 1539–42

Narváez, 1527–28

Gulf of Mexico

Olid, 1534

Cortés, 1524–26

Alvarado, 1522–24

Cabeza de Vaca, 1528–36

Cortés, 1519–22

Olid, 1522–24

Cortés, 1532–35

PACIFIC OCEAN

N

400 mi

400 km

0

Map 2

Guatemala and Salvador, carving out an independent captaincy; and Cristóbal de Olid, sent to conquer Honduras, repudiated Cortés's authority – much as Cortés had Diego de Velázquez's five years before – and obliged Cortés to mount a punitive mission, complete with Indian auxiliaries, which involved prodigious losses and privations.[5] Among the casualties was the Aztec prince Cuauhtémoc, taken as hostage and executed for alleged rebellion.[6]

To the southeast, the Spaniards established footholds on coastal Yucatán. But Maya society, lacking the 'overarching imperial structure' of the Aztecs, was less vulnerable to a concentrated knock-out blow; furthermore, it proved capable of limiting – and at times reversing – the Spanish advance.[7] Maya literature therefore lacked the 'grief-stricken anguish of the Aztec elegies for a world that had been suddenly and irrevocably shattered'; indeed, the Maya, with their cyclical view of the world and their old experience of external conquest, nurtured hopes that Spanish dominion would prove temporary.[8] For a generation the Spanish settlements, clinging to the coast, enjoyed a precarious existence, threatened by Maya counterattack. A major revolt shook the incipient colony in 1546–7; it was bloodily put down, eastern and southern Yucatán suffering severe devastation. Not until mid-century, therefore, did the Spaniards consolidate their coastal position (even then, 'Lutheran corsairs' remained a threat). Meanwhile, the great Maya hinterland remained largely under Maya control for a further century and a half (the last redoubt of the Itzá kingdom was defeated in 1697); Yucatán's definitive conquest was an achievement of the eighteenth – and nineteenth – centuries, of Bourbon rather than Habsburg imperialists.[9]

The Spanish advance to the west was also stoutly, though less successfully, resisted. Here, where the Tarascan kingdom had blocked Aztec expansion, the Spaniards were motivated by the old lure of

[5] Bricker, *The Indian Christ*, ch. 3; Hugh Thomas, *The Conquest of Mexico* (London, 1993), p. 596; Liss, *Mexico under Spain*, p. 125.

[6] Liss, *Mexico under Spain*, p. 121; Inga Clendinnen, *Aztecs* (Cambridge, 1991), p. 273.

[7] Nancy M. Farriss, *Maya Society under Colonial Rule: The Collective Enterprise of Survival* (Princeton, 1984), p. 12; Bricker, *The Indian Christ*, ch. 2; Inga Clendinnen, *Ambivalent Conquests: Maya and Spaniard in Yucatán, 1517–1570* (Cambridge, 1987), ch. 2.

[8] Farriss, *Maya Society*, pp. 20–5, 70.

[9] Bricker, *The Indian Christ*, p. 19; Clendinnen, *Ambivalent Conquests*, pp. 40–1; Farriss, *Maya Society*, pp. 16, 18.

Asia: Cortés himself envisaged reaching the Pacific and kitting out an expedition to sail to the Moluccas (indeed, a fleet finally sailed in 1527, inaugurating the trans-Pacific trade which would play a significant role in New Spain's mercantile economy).[10] Old enemies of the Aztecs, the Tarascans were fully acquainted with the fate of Tenochtitlán; they, too, were smitten by smallpox, alarmed at the supernatural powers of the Spaniards and wracked by internal political dissensions. The invaders, soldiers and priests, soon penetrated the Tarascan dominions, imposing their new secular and religious authorities. Tarascan resistance was sporadic rather than sustained, and it was met by repression and enslavement.

Late in the 1520s, as Nuño de Guzmán sought to carve out a personal satrapy in the west and northwest of New Spain, Spanish repression increased and abuses mounted. The Tarascan king, Cazonci, accused of fomenting sedition, was seized, tried, tortured, garroted and burned. Guzmán – 'a natural gangster' – cut a swathe through Michoacan and penetrated beyond Sinaloa before his egregious actions forced his recall (1533).[11] But the province of New Galicia, which he had helped establish, lived with the legacy of its founder. In 1540 the Cascan Indians, who inhabited the northern borderlands of New Galicia, rose in revolt, provoked by Spanish abuses. Fiercely independent nomadic people, inspired by the cult of Tlatol, the Cascanes had never submitted to either the Tarascan or the Aztec yoke; now they halted the Spaniards' advance and began to roll back their scattered settlements. Three successive Spanish expeditions were defeated in this, the Mixtón War (1540–2). Finally, Viceroy Mendoza himself led a large army of Spaniards and Indian auxiliaries against the Cascanes and ensured their defeat.[12] But the Chichimec frontier, which demarcated the dense, sedentary,

---

10 J. Benedict Warren, *The Conquest of Michoacán: The Spanish Domination of the Tarascan Kingdom in Western Mexico, 1521–1530* (Norman, Okla., 1985), pp. 116, 118–19.

11 Warren, *Conquest of Michoacan*, pp. 47, 69, 211–34; J. H. Parry, *The Audiencia of New Galicia in the Sixteenth Century* (Cambridge, 1948), p. 19 ('gangster').

12 Nathan Wachtel, *The Vision of the Vanquished: The Spanish Conquest of Peru through Indian Eyes, 1520–1570* (Hassocks, 1977), pp. 184–6, sees the Mixtón War as a millenarian movement, analogous to contemporaneous Peruvian rebellions. Certainly the Cascanes were religiously inspired and repudiated Catholicism; whether they were 'millenarians' is another matter. We will note later that such root-and-branch, religious-cum-political resistance to the Spaniards was much rarer in Mexico than in Peru.

Spanish-ruled society of central and southern Mexico from the scattered, mobile Indians of the north, remained fragile and porous.

Not until the mining discoveries of the mid-sixteenth century
would the Spaniards mount a sustained – though still patchy and
selective – colonization of the north. For the first thirty years after
the initial conquest, however, the north remained *terra incognita*,
penetrated only by intrepid – and foolhardy – explorers who probed
its remote expanses in search of fabled cities and mythical treasure.
The old dreams which had motivated the first conquistadors still cast
their spell (even Cortés, advanced in years, volunteered to fight the
infidel in Algiers), and there were plenty amid the restless, mobile society of New Spain who succumbed; indeed, continued immigration
from Spain, coupled with miscegenation in the new colony, created
a swelling class of 'white vagabonds', covetous of the privileges of
hidalguía.[13] Since central Mexico itself could not satisfy their aspirations, they looked elsewhere (even as far afield as Peru); they joined
the veteran captains in their expeditions south or west; or they followed northwards the great explorers of the 1530s and 1540s – men
whose celebrated individual feats were seconded by an 'infinite number of wanderers' of lesser fame and rank.[14]

Pánfilo de Narváez, cheated of his glory in New Spain, explored
Florida and the Gulf, losing his life in a storm off the Mississippi delta
(1528). But his lieutenant, Alvar Núñez Cabeza de Vaca, survived, fell
in with friendly Indians and eventually trekked overland across Texas
to the Pacific coast, where he encountered the new Spanish outpost
of Culiacán (1536). The vague reports of rich northern cities brought
back by Cabeza de Vaca and his men stimulated further efforts,
now of a more official kind. In 1540 the governor of New Galicia,
Francisco Vázquez de Coronado, crossed New Mexico – where the
mythic city of Cíbola failed to live up to expectations – and penetrated
Kansas, where the mythic land of Quivira proved entirely elusive. At
the same time, Hernando de Soto chased similar chimaeras in the
southeast. From Florida he advanced up to the Appalachians, then
doubled back and died on the banks of the Mississippi. The remnants

---

[13] Thomas, *Conquest of Mexico*, pp. 599–600 (Cortés); J. I. Israel, *Race, Class, and Politics in
Colonial Mexico, 1600–1670* (Oxford, 1975), p. 11 (vagabonds).

[14] François Chevalier, *Land and Society in Colonial Mexico* (Berkeley, 1970), p. 28, quoting Martín
Cortés, son of Hernán.

of his expedition sailed down the great river back to the familiar Gulf coast.[15]

For all their daring and heroism, none of these expeditions achieved material gain or permanent conquest. Myths were punctured; reports of 'shaggy cows' (buffalo) did not compensate for the lack of gold. And the northern Indian peoples – though they cohered in dense, complex communities in regions like New Mexico – did not constitute rich empires, ripe for looting (though they were looted nonetheless).[16] Thus, although the Crown of Spain laid claim to extensive regions to the north of New Spain, effective control was lacking. For centuries, these vast tracts were crossed – if they were crossed at all – as if they were oceans, by tiny forces whose wagon-trains resembled fleets of sea-going ships (they were even termed *flotas*), and whose ports of call were the isolated mining and mission settlements, strung out like scattered, archipelagian islands: Monterrey, founded in the 1570s, Sante Fe (New Mexico) in 1609.[17]

We will resume the story of this slow northern advance later. Around 1550, a generation after the Conquest, the advance had barely begun. At this time, Mexico consisted of a three-tier entity: the old Aztec heartland of the central highlands, securely held and governed (the means of government will be discussed shortly); recently conquered peripheral provinces, some still threatened by Indian rebellion (New Galicia, Oaxaca, Chiapas, Yucatán); and a yet vaster outer periphery, ranging from the forests of the Petén to the high expanses of northern mountain, desert and prairie, where independent Indian populations survived, defiant yet respectful of Spanish power. As this sketch suggests, the Spaniards' Mesoamerican empire was squarely built on Aztec foundations, just as the new Spanish churches were constructed upon – and even with – the rubble of native temples. Conquest correlated with proximity and civilization: it was the more developed, central and *centralized* Indian polities (chiefly, Aztec, Tlaxcalan, Tarascan and Totonac; to a lesser degree, Mixtec, Zapotec and Huastec) which were most fully and firmly

[15] David J. Weber, *The Spanish Frontier in North America* (New Haven, 1992), pp. 41–55, offers a good summary of the northern expeditions; on the Cíbola myth, see Luis Weckman, *La herencia medieval de México* (Mexico, 1996; first pubd. 1984), pp. 51–4.

[16] Ramón A. Gutiérrez, *When Jesus Came the Corn Mothers Went Away: Marriage, Sexuality and Power in New Mexico, 1500–1846* (Stanford, 1991), pp. 41–5.

[17] Chevalier, *Land and Society*, p. 8; Philip Wayne Powell, *Soldiers, Indians and Silver: The Northwards Advance of New Spain, 1550–1600* (Berkeley, 1952), p. 65.

incorporated into the new empire and which yielded the most numerous, docile and profitable subjects; conversely, acephalic, scattered societies – atomized in bands, tribes or chiefdoms – resisted with greater success, in the Maya south or the vast Gran Chichimec of the north. Even where modest states existed – for example, in New Mexico – they were protected by the intervening distance and a *cordon sanitaire* of inhospitable terrain and peoples. And, until these remote societies were shown to possess desirable resources (chiefly, precious metals), the Spaniards lacked the incentive to embark on what could only prove costly campaigns of conquest.

Given the marked numerical imbalance in the early colony, Spanish rule depended on the exploitation of existing Indian rulers, communities and resources. Indian auxiliaries served in their thousands in campaigns of conquest and repression: the Tlaxcalans, pioneers of such tactical collaboration, fought against Tenochtitlán, followed Alvarado in his Central American expedition and played an important role in the later conquest and colonization of the Gran Chichimec.[18] The Otomíes, the supposedly boorish butts of Aztec ethnocentrism, celebrated their new role as martial conquerors.[19] Indian *caciques*, in particular, not only figured as military auxiliaries (Don Carlos Ixtlilxochitl of Texcoco was a key ally) but also served as vital intermediaries between Spanish rulers and Indian subjects. And those subjects, in their tens of thousands, laboured to support New Spain's new elite: 'la tilma del indio a todos cubre', as a Spanish priest later put it – 'the Indians' cloak covers us all'; or, as Viceroy Juan de Ortega baldly stated: 'while the Indians exist the Indies will exist'.[20] Indeed, the ethic of *hidalguía* required nothing less. Had not one errant conquistador, prematurely setting himself up as a planter

---

[18] Chevalier, *Land and Society*, pp. 197, 218–19; Charles Gibson, *Tlaxcala in the Sixteenth Century* (Stanford, 1967), pp. 182–9. Farriss, *Maya Society*, p. 230, notes a (probable) Tlaxcalan diaspora as far afield as Yucatán; however, these migrants were Mayanized, whereas the northern settlers clung to their Tlaxcalan identity: Gibson, *Tlaxcala*, pp. 187–8.

[19] Serge Gruzinski, *The Conquest of Mexico* (Cambridge, 1993), pp. 133–5.

[20] William B. Taylor, *Drinking, Homicide and Rebellion in Colonial Mexican Villages* (Stanford, 1979), p. 120; R. Douglas Cope, *The Limits of Racial Domination: Plebeian Society in Colonial Mexico City, 1660–1720* (Madison, 1994), p. 11. Variations on this theme are common: 'let no one make your majesty believe that the mines can be worked without Indians', wrote Viceroy Luis Velasco to the king, 'rather, the moment they raise their hands from labour the mines will be finished': James Lockhart and Enrique Otte, *Letters and People of the Spanish Indies: The Sixteenth Century* (Cambridge, 1976), p. 191; note also Mercedes Olivera, *Pillis y macehuales. Las formacione sociales y los modos de producción de Tecali del siglo XII al XVI* (Mexico, 1978), p. 125.

at Tuxtepec (Oaxaca), incurred Cortés's wrath for thus sinking to 'breeding birds and planting cocoa'?[21]

The Spaniards' objection was not simply to manual labour but also to direct farm management. Their aim was to be supported – in comfortable if not lavish style – by the direct producers, chiefly Indian peasants, and thus to be released, like Aristotle's slave-owning Athenian citizens, for the good life of luxury and culture, warfare and public service. The good life usually meant urban life. 'No-one can be found', a Spaniard lamented in 1599, 'who wishes to go to the country'; the rustic immobility of the English colonists of North America amazed their Spanish counterparts in Mexico.[22] Thus, in the mid-seventeenth century, 57 per cent of Mexico's Spaniards lived in ten cities, each of which was laid out, according to the architectural fashion of the day, in gridiron fashion, with cental plaza, rectilinear streets and outlying (often Indian) barrios.[23]

Eschewing the countryside – and, above all, direct cultivation in the countryside – the Spaniards conceded a measure of rural autonomy to the Indian population, at least so long as the Indians rendered tribute and obedience. Thus, while the Aztec imperial state was decapitated – and the priestly caste was entirely eliminated – the remaining organs of Indian society survived, albeit traumatized. Collaborators in Tlaxcala or Oaxaca were guaranteed their lands and native rulers; the Maya of Yucatán, displaying a 'creative optimism' and faith in their old and tested powers of assimilation, proved capable of Mayanizing the new Spanish invaders as they had the Spaniards' Toltec predecessors.[24] Neither the Tlaxcalans nor the

---

[21] Bernal Díaz, *The Conquest of New Spain* (Harmondsworth, 1981; first pubd. 1963), p. 269.

[22] D. A. Brading, *Miners and Merchants in Bourbon Mexico, 1763–1810* (Cambridge, 1971), p. 6; Chevalier, *Land and Society*, pp. 41–2, citing Gage. The Spaniards 'had not come to Yucatán to farm...they had come to subjugate the Indians and find riches': Clendinnen, *Ambivalent Conquests*, p. 24; see also Farriss, *Maya Society*, p. 30.

[23] George C. Kubler, *Mexican Architecture of the Sixteenth Century* (New Haven, 1948), vol. 1, pp. 75, 92–4. One architect, Alonso García Bravo, was responsible for the lay-out of Mexico City, Veracruz and Antequera (Oaxaca): Chance, *Race and Class*, p. 34; Thomas, *Conquest of Mexico*, p. 51, which notes the rigour of García Bravo's plan for Mexico City (houses were 'built so regularly and evenly that none varies a finger's breadth'). This model of town-planning did not, of course, represent European urban reality – which was cluttered and chaotic – but rather European neoclassical fashion, which could now be deployed in a compliant colonial context, especially in places, like Mexico/Tenochtitlán, where the previous settlement had been razed to the ground.

[24] Gibson, *Tlaxcala*, pp. 62–3, 161ff.; Taylor, *Landlord and Peasant in Colonial Oaxaca* (Stanford, 1972), p. 36; Farriss, *Maya Society*, pp. 96–7.

Maya were typical. But, like any ramblng pre-industrial empire, that of Spain required extensive use of collaborators and systems of 'indirect rule': 20 leagues outside Mexico City, a Spaniard reported in 1545, the king's writ scarcely ran; the Indians were subject to Spanish *encomenderos* and Indian *caciques*.[25] *Caciques* were vital cogs in the imperial machinery. They governed, taxed and administered justice; at the same time, many learned Spanish, dressed in European style and acquired special (even noble) privileges. Some intermarried; at Tecali they drank chocolate and carried swords; one high-living *cacique* in Puebla went preceded by a Spanish page who carried his gloves.[26]

Caciques also creamed off a significant economic surplus. Responsible for tribute collection, they could take a slice (some even acquired formal rights to tribute); they received rent, in labour and kind, from Indian commoners (*macehuales*); they were also to be found, active and entrepreneurial, 'in whatever branch of the Spanish economy impinges on their area, whether *obrajes* (workshops) in Tlaxcala, pig raising in Toluca, or petty commerce in Texcoco'.[27] Like their subjects, they did not abjure the money economy. The Conquest thus had a significant impact on Indian political society, even where it left it formally intact. Processes already under way before 1519 were briskly accelerated: the expropriation of communal land by *caciques*/aristocrats probably quickened, and, in some cases, the power of the Indian elite/aristocracy was enhanced by the opportunities which the new Spanish state afforded for the accumulation of power, at least on a local level and in

[25] Liss, *Mexico under Spain*, p. 126; note also Robert W. Patch, *Maya and Spaniard in Yucatán, 1648–1812* (Stanford, 1993), pp. 45–6.

[26] Olivera, *Pillis y macehuales*, pp. 162–4 (Tecali); Chevalier, *Land and Society*, p. 208; for the Valley of Mexico, see Charles Gibson, *The Aztecs under Spanish Rule: A History of the Indians of the Valley of Mexico, 1519–1810* (Stanford, 1964), pp. 155–6, 198; for Morelos, Robert Haskett, *Indigenous Rulers: An Ethnohistory of Town Government in Colonial Cuernavaca* (Albuquerque, 1991), pp. 161–2; and for Oaxaca, Taylor, *Landlord and Peasant*, pp. 46–8; Joseph Whitecotton, *The Zapotecs: Princes, Priests, and People* (Norman, Okla., 1984), pp. 185–8, 202; and Ronald Spores, *The Mixtec Kings and Their People* (Norman, Okla., 1967), pp. 178–9.

[27] James Lockhart, 'Introduction', in Ida Altman and James Lockhart, eds., *Provinces of Early Mexico: Variants of Spanish American Regional Evolution* (Los Angeles, 1976), p. 21. Arij Ouweneel, *Ciclos interrumpidos. Ensayos sobre historia rural mexicana, siglos XVIII–XIX* (Toluca, 1998), pp. 285, 294, 304–5, 317, stresses *cacical* power to the extent of depicting colonial (central) Mexico as a quasi-feudal society comparable to medieval Europe, in which 'siegneurial *caciques*' lorded it over their Indian 'vassals'. This, for reasons that will be given, remains unconvincing.

the short term.[28] At the same time, however, the chief beneficiaries may have been smart, upwardly mobile parvenus – even a few go-getting plebeians – rather than blue-blooded magnates. For, although the Conquest preserved Indian elites and self-government, it did so in conditions of unprecedented flux and upheaval, which affected old practices. The endemic warfare of pre-Conquest Mesoamerica was brought to an end, bringing derogation of the old warrior/noble ethos; traditional noble privileges were either ended (e.g., polygamy), or generalized (eating meat and drinking pulque). In this new Darwinian world, elites were constituted more on the basis of opportunism and struggle than of ancient legitimacy.[29]

The initial upheaval of the Conquest was soon compounded by demographic collapse. By the late sixteenth century, many Indian *caciques* had fallen on hard times, especially in regions (like lowland Puebla) where Spanish settlement and control were strongest. They lost control of land and – perhaps more important – of labour; their prestige declined; they were eclipsed by new officials (such as the *gobernador*, who, though usually an Indian, occupied a position created and controlled by Spaniards).[30] So, too, in the Valley of Mexico years of colonial rule exerted a levelling effect on Indian society, such that the late colonial *cacique* was 'hardly distinguishable from the mass of the Indian population'.[31] In contrast, in regions of lesser Hispanization, such as Oaxaca or the Puebla highlands, *caciques* survived, some in sumptuous style.[32] Either way – elevated

---

[28] Chevalier, *Land and Society*, pp. 207–8; Israel, *Race, Class, and Politics*, pp. 42–3.

[29] On social mobility: Gibson, *Aztecs under Spanish Rule*, p. 156; Gruzinski, *Conquest of Mexico*, p. 64; Cheryl English Martin, *Rural Society in Colonial Morelos* (Albuquerque, 1985) p. 50; James Lockhart, *The Nahuas after the Conquest: A Social and Cultural History of the Indians of Central Mexico, Sixteenth Through Eighteenth Centuries* (Stanford, 1992), pp. 111–12. On changing mores (which will be further analysed later): Farriss, *Maya Society*, p. 174; Gruzinski, *Conquest of Mexico*, pp. 95 (food), 216 (polygamy).

[30] Gibson, *Aztecs under Spanish Rule*, pp. 165, 168–72, 177; Whitecotton, *The Zapotecs*, pp. 188–91; Lockhart, *The Nahuas*, pp. 31–5; Bernardo García Martínez, *Los pueblos de la sierra. El poder y el espacio entre los indios del norte de Puebla hasta 1700* (Mexico, 1987), pp. 203–4.

[31] Gibson, *Aztecs under Spanish Rule*, p. 165.

[32] Chevalier, *Land and Socety*, p. 214; Olivera, *Pillis y macehuales*, p. 124; Taylor, *Landlord and Peasant*, pp. 49–55, which sees the derogation of Oaxaca's *caciques* as a post-1650 phenomenon. In the remote Mixteca of Oaxaca, Indian *caciques* survived relatively successfully throughout the seventeenth century; their old theocratic authority waned (as the new Catholic dispensation demanded), but, in the absence of a powerful Spanish presence, they acquired economic assets (land and control of labour), while playing the role of political mediators within a system of indirect colonial rule: Rodolfo Pastor, *Campesinos y reformas: La Mixteca, 1700–1856* (Mexico,

or ground down – the Indian *cacique* was a vital agent of Spanish hegemony, who mediated between state and people, who chan-nelled surpluses from producers to consumers and who sustained the structure – while also sometimes alleviating the burdens – of colonial rule.

As their hopes of immediate bonanzas faded, the Spaniards had to look to their own sustenance in a strange land. Hardly had they been founded when the new Spanish towns faced the threat of dearth and began to clamour for guaranteed food supplies.[33] Guaranteeing the urban food supply was, after all, one of the chief functions of early modern government.[34] The principal device to which the Spaniards resorted was an import from the Antilles, which traced back to Reconquista policy: the *encomienda*. Under this system, groups of Indians were assigned to Spanish *encomenderos* who were required to protect and convert their charges; in return, the Indians would provide labour and tribute (tribute being payable in goods as well as in cash).[35] In addition, it should be noted, some Indians, located in 'Crown towns' paid tribute directly to the Crown, thus to the colonial bureaucracy.[36] Though forms of Indian slavery existed (after the 1540s illegally), *encomienda* Indians were not chattel slaves: they more resembled European serfs, especially those Russian serfs who, by imperial decree, owed labour dues to a servitor aristocracy.[37] They remained in their communities as direct producers, yielding up goods, money or labour to their supposed paternalist overlords. The *encomenderos* therefore enjoyed quasi-seigneurial rights rather than direct ownership of land; what is more, *encomiendas* were not heritable, unless so stipulated by the Crown.

1987), pp. 81–5. In Yucatán, in contrast, the Maya *caciques* were more rapidly reduced to 'agents of colonial rule (and) not even junior partners': Farriss, *Maya Society*, pp. 101, 176–7, 235.
33 Taylor, *Drinking, Homicide and Rebellion*, pp. 17–18; Leslie Byrd Simpson, *The Encomienda in New Spain: The Beginnings of Spanish Mexico* (Berkeley, 1982), p. 149, quoting the viceroy to Charles V in 1553 on the continued provisioning problems of Mexico City.
34 Charles Tilly, 'Food Supply and Public Order in Modern Europe', in Tilly, ed., *The Formation of National States in Western Europe* (Princeton, 1975), pp. 380–455.
35 Simpson, *The Encomienda*; Gibson, *Aztecs under Spanish Rule*, ch. 4; Chance, *Conquest of the Sierra*, pp. 23–4.
36 Enrique Semo, *The History of Capitalism in Mexico: Its Origins, 1521–1763* (Austin, 1993), pp. 38–9.
37 Cf. Perry Anderson, *Lineages of the Absolutist State* (London, 1979), p. 330ff.

The *encomienda* represented a means to support the Spanish conquistadors – who clamoured for reward and livelihood[38] – while exploiting, but not destroying, existing Indian communities, lands and
social practices. For tribute, of course, had been the basic means of
transferring surplus under Mesoamerican regimes. Indian *caciques*
could now be charged to deliver up tributary payments to new masters.[39] The *encomienda* was thus a contrived, convenient response
to circumstances – the first of many such adaptations of old institutions to new Mexican realities. It was also a reluctant reponse,
in that Cortés, who had witnessed the destruction wrought by the
encomenderos in the Antilles, was initially unenthusiastic; so, too,
were the Crown and – we shall note – the clergy. But for the moment there was no viable alternative. Within a few years of the fall of
Tenochtitlán, therefore, the *encomienda* was well established as the
chief exploitative device of the new colony, with Cortés's compan-
ions figuring as the principal beneficiaries – albeit within a stretched
hierarchy ranging from the modest to the lavish. Chief within this
hierarchy was Cortés himself who, his initial scruples overcome, became the privileged overlord of a vast tributary population centred
upon Oaxaca, which made him 'the wealthiest person in the entire
Spanish world'.[40] In addition to such tributary rights, Cortés and
his heirs were invested with ample lands and jurisdictional powers,
which together constituted 'a distant replica of the Duchy of Bur-
gundy in the heart of New Spain'.[41] Even this munificence, however,
did not satisfy the Great Captain's princely ambitions; nor, we shall
see, were his offspring content with their lot.

Initially concentrated in the old Aztec heartland, where the Indian
population was densest, the *encomienda* soon spread to newly

---

[38] As early as 1521 Cortés's lieutenants were grumbling about the Great Captain's supposed fortune, which contrasted with their own slim pickings; graffiti to this effect appeared on the
whitewashed walls of Cortés's palace in Coyoacán, to which Cortés replied in kind, writing:
'a blank wall is the paper of fools': Thomas, *Conquest of Mexico*, pp. 544–5.

[39] Olivera, *Pillis y macehuales*, pp. 163–4; Farriss, *Maya Society*, p. 271; Gibson, *Aztecs under
Spanish Rule*, pp. 195–6; James Lockhart, 'Capital and Province, Spaniard and Indian: The
Example of Late Sixteenth–Century Touca', in Altman and Lockhart, *Provinces of Early Mexico*,
pp. 102–4.

[40] Charles Gibson, *Spain in America* (New York, 1966), p. 55. See also Chance, *Race and Class*,
pp. 36–9; G. Michael Riley, *Fernando Cortés and the Marquesado in Morelos, 1522–1547*
(Albuquerque, 1973).

[41] Chevalier, *Land and Society*, pp. 127–8.

conquered provinces like New Galicia and Yucatán – wherever, in fact, a settled Indian peasantry could be subjugated. For the essence of the *encomienda* was its exploitation not of land but of labour: labour which could either directly serve the Spanish rulers or, more often, yield up a quota of goods; labour, too, which was usually mediated and organized through the authority of Indian *caciques*. Thus it was Indian labour which cultivated the land and fed the cities, which built both the massive convents of the friars and the ornate town houses of the conquistadors and which made possible the Herculean transformation of Mexico City from a city of causeways and canals to one of streets, plazas and aqueducts.[42]

Though technically hedged about with restrictions and obligations, the *encomienda* became – especially in the chaotic and piratical years which immediately followed the Conquest – a licence for robbery and extortion, unredeemed by paternalist solicitude and accentuated by the fall in Indian numbers. Indian collaborationism was, at times, strained to the limit, while the Spaniards justified their extreme conduct in terms of dire necessity.[43] Those who settled in remote zones – such as Compostela, on the far frontier of New Galicia – lamented the lack of Indians, which condemned them to hard work and poverty.[44] During these initial, chaotic years, too, thousands of Indians (200,000 according to Motolinía's estimate, which was not the highest) were reduced to outright slavery; many were shipped great distances, even to the Antilles, where they were traded for the cattle and horses which New Spain needed.[45] Nuño de Guzmán

---

[42] Gibson, *Aztecs under Spanish Rule*, p. 119 (clerical use of forced labour); according to Motolinía, the rebuilding of Tenochtitlán/Mexico City represented 'the seventh plague' in terms of Indian mortality: Nicolás Sánchez-Albornoz, 'The Population of Colonial Spanish America' in Leslie Bethell, ed., *Cambridge History of Latin America*, vol. 2, *Colonial Latin America* (Cambridge, 1984), p. 9; see also Thomas, *Conquest of Mexico*, pp. 560–2, and Serge Gruzinski, *Histoire de Mexico* (Paris, 1996), pp. 226–7.

[43] Gibson, *Aztecs under Spanish Rule*, pp. 77–8, sees 'generalized abuse and particular atrocities' and, p. 196, demands which 'strained to the full the native capacity to pay'. Simpson, *The Encomienda*, p. 63, quotes a contemporary view that maltreatment reflected the *encomenderos'* uncertain status; the Indians were 'borrowed goods', to be exploited to the full while the opportunity remained.

[44] Parry, *The Audiencia of New Galicia*, p. 44.

[45] Enrique Florescano, 'La formación de los trabajadores en la época colonial, 1521–1750', in Florescano *et al.*, *La clase obrera en la historia de México*, vol. 1, *De la colonia al imperio* (Mexico, 1980), pp. 52–3; Warren, *Conquest of Michoacan*, pp. 134–5, 182, 195, 200–2; Simpson, *The Encomienda*, p. 69.

rounded up slaves for export from the conquered Huasteca (for each change of masters, the slave acquired a new facial brand: the Spanish chronicler Diego Durán, writing in the 1570s, recalled as a boy seeing such branded Indians in the streets of Mexico City); and by the 1540s the conquistadors of Yucatán had begun slave shipments to the islands of the Caribbean, inaugurating an odious commerce which would again flourish three centuries later.[46]

This resort to *de facto* – but illicit – Indian enslavement was further encouraged by the growth of legal *de jure* black slave imports. Black slaves, though expensive, guaranteed a work force for the early, labour-intensive enterprises of the colony, chiefly the mines and the sugar plantations.[47] These required a permanent and, to a degree, skilled labour force which *encomienda* Indians could not adequately provide; so, between 1521 and 1594 some 36,500 black slaves were shipped to Mexico, the first batch of 200,000 who would be imported throughout three centuries of colonial rule. Many – perhaps 40 per cent in the 1570s – lived in Mexico City, where they graced rich households as servants and drivers; others became hacienda and mining foremen; while in coastal Veracruz and Guerrero, black and mulatto communities sprang up, where they have remained to this day.[48] This repertoire of colonial coercion was completed by the system of forced labour – of blacks, mestizos and Indians – which served the *obrajes* (workshops) and *presidios* (forts), of which more later.[49]

The *encomienda*, however, enjoyed only a brief supremacy. It faced three challenges; those of church, crown and demographic collapse. First, the Church denounced it as an instrument of conquistador exploitation (the *encomendero's* reciprocal duty of evangelization, the clergy noted, was rarely fulfilled). This attack formed part of a broader clerical campaign against conquistador abuses, a campaign which antedated the Conquest of Mexico but for which the Conquest

[46] Chipman, *Nuño de Guzmán*, pp. 198–9, 209–10; D. A. Brading, *The First America: The Spanish Creole Monarchy and the Liberal State, 1492–1867* (Cambridge, 1991), p. 284; Farriss, *Maya Society*, pp. 24–5.

[47] Liss, *Mexico under Spain*, pp. 136–9; Patrick J. Carroll, *Blacks in Colonial Veracruz: Race, Ethnicity and Regional Development* (Austin, 1991), p. 28ff.

[48] Lesley B. Rout, Jr., *The African Experience in Spanish America: 1502 to the Present Day* (Cambridge, 1976), pp. 77–8, 279–82; Cope, *Limits of Racial Domination*, pp. 13–14; Carroll, *Blacks in Colonial Veracruz*; Gonzalo Aguirre Beltrán, *Población negra de México* (Mexico, 1972).

[49] See pp. 87, 98, 164–5.

provided fresh ammunition. Tales of Spanish rapacity, retailed especially by Bartolomé de Las Casas, prompted reform, while providing the raw material for the *leyenda negra*, the black legend of abuse
and obscurantism, which Spain's Protestant enemies would trumpet
to the world.[50] Second, clerical critics found an ally in the Crown.
The Conquest had joined public and private interests in uneasy collaboration. Once triumphant, the conquistadors successfully staked
a claim to rewards which, in the absence of spectacular hauls of
bullion, had to take the form of *encomiendas*, or comparable royal
favours, such as *mercedes* (land grants). As yet, *mercedes* were of secondary importance: tribute counted for more than mere territory. In
conferring such favours, the Crown followed the old tradition of the
Reconquista, awarding lands and rights in return for services rendered. But the Crown's unhappy experiences with insurgent feuda-
tories were recent and vivid, and it recoiled from the prospect of
fostering a new feudalism ('feudalism', that is, in a strictly political
sense) on the other side of the Atlantic. As it soon became clear that
the Conquest had given birth to 'an encomienda class bent on making of itself a hereditary colonial aristocracy', a clash between Crown
and conquistadors was inevitable.[51]

Cortés's own grand pretensions were therefore cut down to
size: showered with honours, he was progressively deprived of the
seigneurial status he craved, and he died an embittered hero.[52] His
heirs, too, had their seigneurial rights and sprawling acres clipped
back.[53] The first two viceroys (Antonio de Mendoza, 1535–50, and
Luis de Velasco, 1550–64) strove to curb *encomendero* power, and,
even as the number of *encomiendas* rose, so their individual value declined, and their recipients increasingly became docile clerics and officials rather than freewheeling conquistadors. With the 'New Laws'
of 1542, the Crown made a bold attempt to limit all *encomienda*
grants to a single lifetime and to abolish Indian personal service.[54]

[50] Brading, *First America*, pp. 58, 63–8. See also Charles Gibson, *The Black Legend: Anti-Spanish Attitudes in the Old World and the New* (New York, 1971).
[51] Gibson, *Aztecs under Spanish Rule*, p. 59 (quote); Brading, *First America*, pp. 71–2; John H. Elliott, 'The Spanish Conquest and Settlement of America', in Leslie Bethell, ed., *Cambridge History of Latin America*, vol. 1, *Colonial Latin America* (Cambridge, 1984), p. 157 (*reconquista*).
[52] Chevalier, *Land and Society*, pp. 128–31; Liss, *Mexico under Spain*, pp. 52–9; Thomas, *Conquest of Mexico*, p. 600, on Cortés's final years.
[53] Chance, *Race and Class*, pp. 36–9; Riley, *Fernando Cortés*, pp. 88–91.
[54] Simpson, *The Encomienda*, ch. 10.

This proved provocative as well as unattainable; in Mexico, the viceroy prevaricated; in Peru, disaffected conquistadors rebelled; in Spain, they lobbied, bribed and enlisted the services of the celebrated Aristotelian scholar Juan Ginés de Sepúlveda, who argued that the innate inferiority of the Indians justified their subjection. Las Casas, in reply, argued for an alternative Spanish imperialism, based on royal paternalism and peaceful conversion.[55] The Crown compromised, easing the lifetime restriction on *encomiendas* and introducing a new form of coerced labour, the *repartimiento*. Nevertheless the conquistadors' formal defeat of the New Laws was a Pyrrhic victory. What the Crown failed to do by instant fiat it achieved, in typical Habsburg fashion, by long-term bureaucratic attrition. The heritability of *encomiendas* was largely limited to two generations (recipient and son); personal services were suppressed; tributary rights were confined to goods (increasingly, cash and basic foodstuffs); and Indian labour was placed under separate royal control, via the *repartimiento*. Since, in addition, Indian slavery was progressively eliminated, the coercive bases of both Indian exploitation and conquistador supremacy were severely weakened.[56]

In other respects too, we shall note, royal authority shouldered aside the emergent feudal aristocracy of New Spain, who, for their part, increasingly looked to freehold land rather than to *encomienda* dues as their chief source of livelihood. Over time, and despite *encomendero* protests, the initial lavish grants of the 1520s – and the derogation of royal authority which they implied – were clawed back by the Crown, aided by clerics, officials and town councils. *Encomiendas* which survived into the 'third life' tended to resemble state pensions rather than seigneurial privileges; some remained important sources of income (notably in Yucatán, a remote backwater, where the *encomendero* class thrived as nowhere else), but many *encomiendas* yielded only a paltry return and the endebted *encomendero* became a stock colonial figure.[57] Meanwhile, the Crown continued to levy its own Indian tribute, which came to constitute

[55] Brading, *First America*, pp. 67–8, 79–93.
[56] Simpson, *The Encomienda*, ch. 11; Gibson, *Aztecs under Spanish Rule*, pp. 62–3, 81–2, 154, 223–4.
[57] Chevalier, *Land and Society*, pp. 118–19; Gibson, *Aztecs under Spanish Rule*, p. 219; cf. Farriss, *Maya Society*, p. 88; Patch, *Maya and Spaniard*, pp. 96–100.

a *de facto* poll tax. With the progressive monetization of the economy, tribute was increasingly rendered in cash rather than kind.[58] As this outcome exemplified, the threat of a rampant transatlantic feudalism was conjured; by the 1570s, 'the victory of the Crown over the encomenderos had been won'; and the *encomenderos*, shaking their heads at the ingratitude of the Crown and the injustice of the friars, set to justifying their families' heroic role in the Conquest, thus planting the first seeds of a distinctive 'creole patriotism' in the colony.[59]

The Crown won not least because inexorable demographic trends worked to its advantage. The Spanish Conquest of America caused a demographic collapse of globally unprecedented proportions. According to the figures of Cook and Borah (which may exaggerate), the population of Central Mexico (that is, Mexico from the Chichimec frontier to the Isthmus of Tehuantepec), fell from some 20 to 25 million in 1519 to perhaps 6 million in 1548 and to less than 2 million in 1580, reaching a nadir of 750,000 around 1630.[60] The Valley of Mexico was particularly affected: its population of 1.5 million in 1519 had slumped to some 70,000 (Indians) in the mid-seventeenth century.[61] Outlying provinces also experienced demographic collapse, albeit the tempo varied. The Indian population of Yucatán fell from 2.3 million in 1519 to 170,000 in the mid-seventeenth century; that of Oaxaca declined less dramatically, from 350,000 to 150,000 between

---

[58] Semo, *History of Capitalism*, p. 40; Ross Hassig, *Trade, Tribute, and Transportation: The Sixteenth–Century Political Economy of the Valley of Mexico* (Norman, Okla., 1985), pp. 226–8. Lockhart, *The Nahuas*, p. 180, argues persuasively that the shift from tribute in kind to a cash payment reflected not only Spanish official policy but also Indian preferences, indicating a progressive monetization of the Indian economy; Matthew Restall, *The Maya World: Yucatec Culture and Society, 1550–1850* (Stanford, 1997), pp. 182–3, ventures a similar conclusion for the Maya, although the evidence is hardly overwhelming.

[59] Gibson, *Aztecs under Spanish Rule*, pp. 62–3; Brading, *First America*, pp. 53–4.

[60] There is a huge literature surrounding the demographic debate. Sherburne F. Cook and Woodrow Borah, *The Indian Population of Central Mexico, 1531–1610* (Berkeley, 1960), argued for a high initial population and a massive drop. Recent research has tended to modify both estimate: for a balanced review, Sánchez–Albornoz, 'The Population of Colonial Spanish America', pp. 4–5, 13–14. Francis J. Brooks, 'Revising the Conquest of Mexico: Smallpox, Sources and Population', *Journal of Interdisciplinary History*, 24/1 (1993), pp. 1–29, offers a more sweeping critique; William T. Sanders, 'The Population of the Central Mexican Symbiotic Region, the Basin of Mexico, and the Teotihuacan Valley in the Sixteenth Century', in William M. Denevan, ed., *The Native Population of the Americas in 1492* (Madison, 1976), pp. 85–150, is a detailed revisionist analysis, which suggests a slower demographic decline up to 1540, then a more rapid fall (agreeing broadly with Borah).

[61] Gibson, *Aztecs under Spanish Rule*, p. 141.

1519 and 1570.[62] As these figures attest, Mexico's Indian population suffered a dramatic collapse, associated with three successive epidemics: the initial wave of smallpox, begun in 1519, during which the Indians 'died in heaps, like bedbugs'; the *cocolitzli* epidemic of 1545–8 and the *matlazahuatl* (typhus?) epidemic of 1576–7.[63]

Although war, maltreatment and, it has been suggested, an erosion of the very will to live all contributed to this catastrophic decline in Indian population,[64] disease was clearly the crucial factor. It could strike down populations even in regions – like Oaxaca – where fighting and social dislocation had been much less severe than in the Valley of Mexico. And it lingered endemically, preventing any swift demographic revival: yellow fever invaded the tropical lowlands, and recurrent epidemics afflicted the highlands, aggravated, it seems, by declining natality.[65] Everywhere, Mexico's Indians paid for the 'dangerous privilege of longest isolation from the rest of mankind'.[66] Everywhere, too, the result was the diminution of the colony's basic resource, Indian labour. In the Valley of Mexico, for example, where rich *encomiendas* had been staked out within the orbit of the new colonial capital, the tributary population fell from some 1.5 million in 1519 to 350,000 in 1570, after which it slumped further; in the Guadalajara region of New Galicia the tributary population fell at

[62] Farriss, *Maya Society*, pp. 59, 79–80, 83; Taylor, *Landlord and Peasant*, p. 170; note also Olivera, *Pillis y macehuales*, pp. 131–2; Martin, *Rural Society in Colonial Morelos*, p. 14.

[63] The exact dating and identification of these diseases are open to debate: Brooks, 'Revising the Conquest', even questions the common attribution of smallpox. Noble David Cook, *Born to Die: Disease and the New World Conquest, 1492–1650* (Cambridge, 1998), the best recent synthesis, is in no doubt (pp. 64–70); Cook equates *cocolitzli* with typhus or pulmonary plague (pp. 100–1) and sees the mortality of the late 1570s as the result of a 'compound epidemic' of typhus, smallpox and other diseases (pp. 120–1). See also Sánchez-Albornoz, 'The Population of Colonial Spanish America', p. 13; Liss, *Mexico under Spain*, p. 119; Olivera, *Pillis y macehuales*, p. 131. Lists of the main epidemics are given by: Peter Gerhard, *A Guide to the Historical Geography of New Spain* (Cambridge, 1972), p. 23; Hassig, *Trade, Tribute, and Transportation*, p. 156; and Cook, *Born to Die*, p. 132.

[64] Nathan Wachtel refers to suicides and abortions 'betraying a mood of despair and serving as a form of protest': 'The Indian and the Spanish Conquest', in Bethell, ed., *Cambridge History of Latin America*, vol. 1, *Colonial Latin America*, p. 213; for accounts of suicide and infanticide, Gruzinski, *Conquest of Mexico*, p. 97; Semo, *History of Capitalism*, p. 34. The wounded Moctezuma, who 'seems either to have refused to be treated, or to have had no wish to live longer', may have been an early example: Thomas, *Conquest of Mexico*, p. 402.

[65] Whitecotton, *The Zapotecs*, notes a 'tremendous decrease' in population of the Valley of Oaxaca, which had not experienced much fighting. On endemic disease and natality: Sánchez-Albornoz, 'The Population of Colonial Spanish America', pp. 11–12.

[66] Alfred W. Crosby, *The Columbian Exchange: Biological and Cultural Consequences of 1492* (Westport, 1972), p. 37.

the rate of around 5 per cent per year during the mid-sixteenth century.[67] The economic consequences were profound. Church tithes declined; *encomienda* income dried up; the royal tribute fell from a third of a million pesos to less than two hundred thousand pesos in the century 1560–1660.[68] As food production fell, prices rose, alarming urban consumers; and as Indian communities shrank or disappeared altogether, the supply of labour became constricted, costly and unreliable, again prejudicing the interests of the new Spanish cities and mines.

The Spanish response was threefold. First, the state assumed direct coercive control of labour through the system of *repartimiento*, whereby Indians were compelled to work for Spaniards on a rotational basis and at fixed wage rates. From the mid-sixteenth century the *repartimiento* replaced the *encomienda* as the chief source of Indian labour in the colony.[69] Second, the authorities began to 'congregate' the dispersed and declining Indian population in communities, the better to control and convert them.[70] Third, the Crown encouraged the growth of private landholding, using royal land grants (*mercedes, composiciones*) to reward its servants and populate its thinly inhabited realm. Here (we shall see) lay the origin of New Spain's great estates. By these measures, the Crown, through its burgeoning bureaucracy, established itself as the fount of the two fundamentals of the colonial agrarian economy: private land and forced labour; the Crown alone could bring together these two necessities of Spanish well-being.

Denied the rich pickings they had hoped for from plunder or tribute, Spanish immigrants now turned to the direct acquisition and

---

[67] Gibson, *Aztecs under Spanish Rule*, pp. 137–8; Eric Van Young, *Hacienda and Market in Eighteenth-Century Mexico: The Rural Economy of the Guadalajara Region, 1675–1820* (Berkeley, 1981), p. 37.

[68] John Frederick Schwaller, *Origins of Church Wealth in Mexico: Ecclesiastical Revenues and Church Finances, 1523–1600* (Albuquerque, 1985), pp. 150–60; Semo, *History of Capitalism*, pp. 41–3.

[69] The introduction of the *repartimiento* was staggered, beginning in the Valley of Mexico in the 1560s, evident in Oaxaca in the 1570s, reaching New Galicia in the last quarter of the century: Van Young, *Hacienda and Market*, pp. 238–9. For regional examples, see Gibson, *Aztecs under Spanish Rule*, pp. 226–8, 249–50; García Martínez, *Pueblos de la Sierra*, pp. 248–58; Chance, *Race and Class*, pp. 76–80; Agueda Jiménez Pelayo, 'Condiciones del trabajo de repartimiento indígena en la Nueva Galicia en el siglo XVII', *Historia Mexicana*, 38/3 (1989), pp. 455–70.

[70] See below, pp. 27–8, 42.

exploitation of the land – that is, if they did not strike lucky with mining (which few did), nor, as merchants, batten on to the lucrative urban and international markets. This turn to the land did not imply a Spanish commitment to manual labour: direct exploitation did not mean family farming. It was still expected – and contrived – that Indians, sometimes supplemented by black slaves, would till the soil. But it did mean that elite Spaniards relinquished tributary income in favour of the more direct – 'European' – exploitation of land and labour.[71] This shift involved partially by-passing Indian intermediaries (the *caciques* who rendered tribute payments) and also brought greater direct pressure to bear on the Indian communities themselves, whose land and labour now entered a productive network organized by Spaniards for Spaniards. One consequence was an accelerated acculturation of the Indians, who now entered more deeply into the Hispanic economy and society.[72] The *repartimiento* system, however, embodied a complex division of powers. Individual Spaniards acquired extensive landholdings, but the labour drafts were provided by Spanish officials, still acting in collaboration with Indian *caciques*, who now delivered up workers rather than goods.[73] Though the pressures on the Indian community increased, the system still depended on the continued existence of the community, and its indigenous authorities, in order to function. Landlord and Indian existed in a tense, unequal symbiosis; the system perpetuated, even as it slowly eroded, the ancient peasant community.

Erosion of the Indian community occurred partly as a result of the Spaniards' biological impact – epidemic disease – and partly as a result of their less dramatic but still significant agricultural innovations. Although Spaniards soon set about cultivating the Indian staple of maize, the Spanish preference was for wheat and bread

---

[71] P. J. Bakewell, *Silver Mining and Society in Colonial Mexico: Zacatecas, 1546–1700* (Cambridge, 1971), p. 225. I would not agree, however, that this new system 'was plainly of a capitalist nature'. The matter is discussed in the final section of this chapter.

[72] Lockhart, *The Nahuas*, pp. 427–36, which convincingly designates this period as the second in a three-stage process of acculturation.

[73] Communities were expected to deliver some 2–4% of their active labour force, rising to 10% during the peaks of the agricultural season, on the basis of weekly shifts: Enrique Florescano, 'The Formation and Economic Structure of the Hacienda in New Spain', in Bethell, ed., *Cambridge History of Latin America*, vol. 2, *Colonial Latin America*, p. 165; Gibson, *Aztecs under Spanish Rule*, pp. 226–7, 231–2, notes a progressive increase in *repartimiento* demands, reflecting the fall in population, throughout the later sixteenth century and into the seventeenth.

rather than maize and tortillas. Wheat rapidly became an important crop, suitable for cultivation in the temperate valleys of Central Mexico (Puebla, Toluca, Mexico) and actively encouraged by the viceregal government (vines and olives, the two other staples of Iberian agriculture, were less favoured, either by climate or policy, and New Spain continued to import wine and olive oil from Spain). Sugar, too, was successfully transplanted from the Atlantic islands to the warm valleys south of Mexico City (Cortés, having disdained cacao production, was a pioneer of the Morelos sugar plantations); indigo, cochineal and cacao were lesser cash crops, often cultivated by Indian peasants.[74]

But the most striking innovation was stock raising. Like Spain, the colony displayed a voracious demand for meat, hides and tallow – especially as the mining industry developed after mid-century. In addition to the horses which had given them a decisive edge in combat, the Spaniards had brought pigs, goats and cattle which, herded along with the early expeditions, constituted a 'commissariat on the hoof', a mobile supply of provisions.[75] When Coronado set off to scour the plains of North America he took with him fifteen hundred animals – horses, mules, cattle, pigs and sheep.[76] Further south, the new animal population of Mexico, favoured by both ecology and policy, multiplied prodigiously. Cattle, already a staple industry in the Antilles, flourished in Mexico; within ten years of the Conquest bullfights were being held in the capital; by the 1540s the supply of meat was glutted in many regions and Indians (reduced in numbers) ate meat as never before.[77] Newcomers to the the colony were astonished at the size of Mexico's herds. By the later sixteenth century,

[74] Florescano, 'Formation and Economic Structure', p. 155; Chevalier, *Land and Society*, pp. 59–66, 71–82, 193; Taylor, *Landlord and Peasant*, p. 14; Gibson, *Aztecs under Spanish Rule*, p. 323 (wheat); Martin, *Rural Society*, pp. 12–13 (sugar).

[75] Crosby, *Columbian Exchange*, p. 77.

[76] Weber, *The Spanish Frontier*, p. 46; William H. Dusenberry, *The Mexican Mesta: The Administration of Ranching in Colonial Mexico* (Urbana, 1963), pp. 32–4, which points out that, legend notwithstanding, those iconic animals of the southwest, the Texas longhorn and the Plains mustang, did not descend from Coronado's strays; they were, instead, a product of a later, seventeenth-century, faunal diaspora. The Arkansas razorback, however, may descend directly from the 'ambulatory larder' which De Soto took to Florida in 1539: Weber, *The Spanish Frontier*, p. 51.

[77] Chevalier, *Land and Society*, ch. 3; Gruzinski, *Conquest of Mexico*, p. 95; John C. Super, *Food, Conquest, and Colonization in Sixteenth-Century Spanish America* (Albuquerque, 1988), pp. 28–32, 85.

as the prairies of the north were opened up, herds running into the tens of thousand were common: a French observer gazed in awe at 'great level plains, stretching endlessly and everywhere covered with an infinite number of cattle'.[78] Sheep now numbered some eight million; annually, three hundred thousand sheep were herded from the central highlands to the pastures of Nuevo León in the northeast – a Mexican version of the ancient transhumance of medieval Spain.[79] Spanish tradition also conspired with Mexican circumstances to create a distinctive cowboy (*vaquero*) culture which, with its rodeos, lassos and mustangs, later became part of the folklore of the American West.[80]

But in the New World, as in the Old, the expansion of stock raising had a marked impact on arable farming. Sheep and cattle cut a swathe through Indian – and some Spanish – agriculture, trampling crops, polluting streams and deforesting hillsides.[81] In the Valley of Mexico the old processes of soil erosion were further accelerated by stock raising. Farmers from Cholula, near Puebla, petitioned against the 'many cattle estancias [ranches] which are ruining [them] and putting poor *macehuales* [Indian peasants] to flight'.[82] The authorities, seeking to stem this bovine tide, legislated to protect farming communities, banned stock raising in some valleys (such as Oaxaca) and even built walls – in the Valley of Toluca, for example – which demarcated Spanish and Indian landholdings. The sheer reiteration of such measures, however, attested to their inadequacy and also to the power of the stock raisers who, in New as in Old Spain, possessed a powerful representative guild, the Mesta.[83] Thus, as in Europe, sheep 'ate men': the peasant farmer could not withstand the inroads of commercial stock raising. Over time, Darwinian pressures culled the herds; after some forty years of 'irruptive oscillation', some measure of stabilization was achieved, matching herds to pasture.[84] But

---

[78] Chevalier, *Land and Society*, p. 94.
[79] Chevalier, *Land and Society*, p. 95. See the excellent study by Eleanor G. K. Melville, *A Plague of Sheep: Environmental Consequences of the Conquest of Mexico* (Cambridge, 1994).
[80] Dusenberry, *The Mexican Mesta*, pp. 67, 136–8 (rodeos and lassos).
[81] Melville, *A Plague of Sheep*.
[82] Chevalier, *Land and Society*, p. 100.
[83] Chevalier, *Land and Society*, pp. 99–101; Melville, *A Plague of Sheep*, p. 136; Dusenberry, *The Mexican Mesta*, pp. 174–6.
[84] Melville, *A Plague of Sheep*, pp. 6–7, 47–8; Chevalier, *Land and Society*, pp. 102–5.

by then the damage was done: once verdant regions (such as the Mezquital Valley) had been reduced to barren scrubland.[85]

Pastoral farming, moreover, was only the most obvious and dynamic threat which Indian communities faced in the early colony. Arable farmers, townspeople and clergy all coveted Indian land and labour (the two went together). Especially in the choice, watered valleys, where ecological conditions were favourable and where urban consumers were clustered, Spanish landlords advanced at the expense of Indian communities: in the Valleys of Mexico, Puebla, Toluca and Cuernavaca; soon, in the rolling, fertile hinterland of Guadalajara and the temperate plains of the Bajío (where the indigenous population was fewer and politically weaker). Despite frequent recourse to 'paternalist' colonial law, the Indians could not easily resist, the more so as epidemic disease shrank their numbers and sapped the vitality of their communities.[86]

Thus during the sixteenth century was born that quintessential Mexican institution, the hacienda, or great estate. Recent research has stressed the complexity of the hacienda's origins, the variety of forms which it assumed and the divergent regional patterns associated with its development. Though the hacienda, as a piece of freehold property, was legally quite distinct from the *encomienda* (thus to equate the two is incorrect), nevertheless there was a clear continuity in the transition from an *encomienda-* to an hacienda-based agrarian economy.[87] *Encomenderos* were foremost among those who sought and acquired royal land grants (*mercedes*) or royal confirmation of *de facto* land occupations (*composiciones*), often in the same region where earlier *encomienda* grants had conferred upon them power, wealth and jurisdiction. Though the legal norms changed, and with them the mode of exploitation of the dependent population, nevertheless astute or lucky families weathered the change, parlaying *encomienda* privileges into hacienda titles and tribute collection

---

[85] Melville, *A Plague of Sheep*, pp. 157–63.

[86] Examples of hacienda expansion: Chevalier, *Land and Society*, p. 213; Gibson, *Aztecs under Spanish Rule*, p. 289; Chance, *Race and Class*, pp. 56, 58; D. A. Brading, *Haciendas and Ranchos in the Mexican Bajío: León, 1700–1860* (Cambridge, 1978), p. 17.

[87] James Lockhart, 'Encomienda and Hacienda: The Evolution of the Great Estate in the Spanish Indies', *Hispanic American Historical Review*, 49 (1969), pp. 411–29, remains a good overview. See also Florescano, 'Formation and Economic Structure', pp. 166–8.

into direct exploitation.[88] Not for the last time in Mexican history, important socioeconomic changes were masked by a degree of familial continuity.

Despite royal misgivings, officials – especially lower-level officials – connived at the creation of the *hacendado* class, and their usurpation of Indian lands. Often, indeed, officials – rather than *encomenderos* – were the chief beneficiaries of this trend. And the Crown, even the king's deputy, the viceroy himself, could not exercise close control over the dynamic forces that were shaping colonial society. The Crown, too, saw several advantages in the establishment of flourishing private estates: their legalisation raised revenue; their output fed the cities; and their operations gave employment to the army of footloose vagrants whose presence alarmed the authorities.[89]

In addition, from the mid-sixteenth century, the Crown adopted a policy of *congregación*, whereby the dwindling Indian population was gathered in certain new approved communities, the better to be controlled, taxed and moralized.[90] This, too, facilitated Spanish landed expansion. (It also tended to encourage village endogamy, which was probably greater after the Conquest than before.)[91] Indian *caciques*, falling on hard times, connived at the alienation of Indian land, especially on the central plateau: they personally sold up to Spaniards or tried to meet excessive tribute demands (excessive in view of population loss) by selling or renting out community land.[92] The policy of congregation, undertaken in successive bursts, at the instigation of both lay and clerical authorities, had mixed results. Although many new communities – equipped with fields, pasture, church and nucleated settlement – took root, thus facilitating

---

[88] Lockhart, 'Encomienda and Hacienda', p. 418; Chevalier, *Land and Society*, pp. 123–4, 138–9, 143; Martin, *Rural Society*, p. 12; Patch, *Maya and Spaniard*, p. 105.

[89] Chevalier, *Land and Society*, pp. 217, 266; Israel, *Race, Class, and Politics*, p. 12.

[90] The process, advocated by both lay and clerical authorities, came in two main spurts: the 1550s and 1590s. See Gruzinski, *Conquest of Mexico*, pp. 118–19, 122; Peter Gerhard, 'Congregaciones de indios en la Nueva España antes de 1570', *Historia Mexicana*, 26/3 (1977), pp. 347–95; Howard Cline, 'Civil Congregations of the Indians in New Spain, 1598–1606', *Hispanic American Historical Review*, 29 (1949), pp. 349–69; Taylor, *Landlord and Peasant*, pp. 26–7; Gibson, *Aztecs under Spanish Rule*, pp. 282–3; García Martínez, *Pueblos de la sierra*, pp. 151, 163–4.

[91] Olivera, *Pillis y macehuales*, pp. 138–9.

[92] Chevalier, *Land and Society*, pp. 213–14; Martin, *Rural Society*, pp. 52–3; Olivera, *Pillis y macehuales*, p. 133.

colonial control, others failed – especially in regions, like Yucatán, where dispersed settlement was the ancient norm.[93] For many Indian communities, already reeling from the impact of conquest and disease, *congregación* meant another gratuitous upheaval: the desertion of old fields and shrines, forcible resettlement, fresh border disputes with new neighbours.[94] Some Indians took to their heels: *congregación* paradoxically resulted in flight and dispersal.[95] And the newly congregated populations proved more vulnerable not only to Spanish exploitation but also to disease.[96]

The story of hacienda expansion – a story which would span four centuries – varied from region to region. The hacienda[97] – in its various guises, both arable and pastoral – came to dominate the warm valleys of central Mexico, the plains of the Bajío and the vast expanses of the north. But the Indian village survived vigorously in highland zones in Central and, even more, in southern, Mexico: in Oaxaca and Yucatán, for example, which remained bastions of Indian peasant farming. In these regions, the incentives for hacienda production and expansion were weak: urban and mining demand was feeble; and the village could display its corporate strength – litigating, politicking, occasionally violently resisting – and thus successfully fend off Spanish encroachments. In Yucatán, where the 'colonial siesta' was particularly somnolent, haciendas were little more than collections of Maya communities, loosely supervised and

[93] Farriss, *Maya Society*, p. 207; Patch, *Maya and Spaniard*, pp. 48–52; Restall, *The Maya World*, pp. 172–3.

[94] García Martínez, *Pueblos de la sierra*, pp. 175–9; Gibson, *Aztecs under Spanish Rule*, pp. 284–5. Pastor, *Campesinos y reformas*, p. 75, gives the example of Nochixtlán, Oaxaca, which experienced forced relocation twice in twenty years.

[95] Farriss, *Maya Society*, pp. 206–8; García Martínez, *Pueblos de la sierra*, p. 175; Taylor, *Landlord and Peasant*, p. 27.

[96] Brading, *First America*, p. 125.

[97] The term 'hacienda' is general and fairly vague. Haciendas came in various shapes and sizes (Patch, *Maya and Spaniard*, p. 120, compares the 'Lilliputian' haciendas of Yucatán with the 'Brobdinagian' estates of northern Mexico); they are conventionally distinguished from the smaller rancho. Roughly, the hacienda may be defined as a large private landholding (Brading, *Haciendas and Ranchos*, p. xvi, calls it a 'large landed estate'); the rancho corresponds to a smallholding (Brading, p. xvii: 'a small landed property, a subordinate section of an hacienda'; see also Taylor, *Landlord and Peasant*, pp. 122–3). 'Estancia' usually denotes a stock-raising hacienda. I have tended to avoid the term 'latifundio' (a very large hacienda), and I occasionally use 'plantation' – without implying any rigid conceptual dichotomy (hacienda/plantation) – to denote an hacienda tightly articulated with the market, usually producing tropical products (e.g., sugar).

mildly exploited by landlords who still relied on the archaic mechanism of *encomienda* tribute to maintain their modest station. Here,
too, many Spanish settlers absorbed Maya ways: they learned the
Maya tongue and ate Maya food; even the clergy delegated parish
organization to the Indian elite.[98] In peripheral Mexico, therefore,
as in peripheral Spanish America more generally, the long-term survival of the *encomienda* (and, the other side of the coin, the feeble
development of the hacienda) depended on the maintenance of a
dense, self-governing Indian population, upon which the Spaniards
imposed a rickety superstructure of government and culture.

At the other extreme, the vigorous growth of the hacienda in the
Valleys of Mexico, Puebla, Toluca or Cuernavaca, or in the environs
of Guadalajara, ground down the villages, wrested from them their
land and autonomy, and in some cases created circumscribed pueblos which eked out a dependent existence in the interstices of the
hacienda system. By the 1570s many villages in the Valley of Mexico
were so constituted: 'estates had crept up to the very threshold of
huts in villages like Tenayuca'.[99] By 1620 Spaniards owned half the
Valley arable land, and the city relied on haciendas for its basic grain
supply.[100] In such areas, too, Indian 'acculturation' (or, some would
say, 'de-Indianization') proceeded apace. In the temperate valleys, in
the booming mining towns or along the royal roads, the commercial and administrative arteries of the colony, which carried people, goods, news and rumours, Indians rapidly acquired Spanish
ways. They laboured for Spanish masters, earned cash, intermarried,
dressed in European garb, ploughed with oxen, ate meat and drank
wine as well as the native pulque.[101] They abandoned polygamy and
adopted Christian rites of passage (baptism, marriage, last unction);
they wrote wills which displayed not only Christian sentiments but

[98] Farriss, *Maya Society*, pp. 9, 33, 112.

[99] Chevalier, *Land and Society*, p. 212.

[100] Cope, *Limits of Racial Domination*, p. 13.

[101] For a good overview of Indian acculturation (discussed more fully later) see Murdo MacLeod,
'Forms and Types of Work and the Acculturation of the Colonial Indians of Mesoamerica:
Some Preliminary Observations', in Elsa Cecilia Frost, Michael C. Meyer and Josefina Zoraida
Vázquez, eds., *El trabajo y los trabajadores en la historia de México* (Mexico, 1979), pp. 75–91,
which, p. 80, notes the acculturating impact of the Mexico City–Acapulco *camino real*.
See also Lockhart, *The Nahuas*, pp. 198–9 (dress), Gruzinski, *Conquest of Mexico*, p. 95
(food).

also individualist values.[102] They even began to display something of the swaggering machismo which became a staple of Mexican society.[103] Such Indians thus came to form part of a Hispanized, market-oriented, colonial society. Yet, even where these trends were most marked, the peasant village did not disappear, nor did the Indian culture which accompanied it (though we must except regions, such as the Bajío, where both had been weak to start with and where rural society was formed around an hacienda-rancho axis, rather than the more common hacienda-village polarity).[104]

Indeed, it was not in the interest of the Spaniards that the village should disappear. The Crown, which assumed a moderately paternalist and protective role towards the Indians, needed Indian tribute; and, in accordance with the unwritten principle of colonial macroparasitism, tribute demands were 'finely tuned' to compel required forms of Indian labour or production without either destroying the Indian communities or creating an independent class of Indian entrepreneurs.[105] The cities, too, depended to a degree on peasant production of basic staples. Though the old Mesoamerican staple of maize receded somewhat before the challenge of European grains, especially wheat, the highland Indian village remained committed to the traditional triad of maize, beans and chile, surpluses of which could be channelled to the urban population. Some well-placed peasant communities – in Oaxaca, Puebla, the Valley of Mexico – also engaged in profitable truckfarming.[106]

[102] Louise Burkhart, *The Slippery Earth: Nahua–Christian Moral Dialogue in Sixteenth-Century Mexico* (Tucson, 1989), offers a perceptive analysis of rival cosmologies/ethics, and their interaction (pp. 112–13: baptism; p. 154: polygamy). On wills: Gruzinski, *Conquest of Mexico*, pp. 236–7; Taylor, *Landlord and Peasant*, p. 75; S. L. Cline, *Colonial Culhuacan, 1580–1600: A Social History of an Aztec Town* (Albuquerque, 1986), p. 14 and ch. 3; Restall, *The Maya World*, pp. 155–7.

[103] Taylor, *Drinking, Homicide and Rebellion*, pp. 82–3; Steve J. Stern, *The Secret History of Gender: Women, Men, and Power in Late Colonial Mexico* (Chapel Hill, 1995), pp. 53, 66–7, illustrates how – in the late colonial period – violent machismo crossed ethnic boundaries.

[104] Brading, *Haciendas and Ranchos*, p. 17. Likewise the highlands of Jalisco: Celina Guadalupe Becerra, 'Rancheros en Los Altos de Jalisco en la época colonial', in Esteban Barragán López *et al.*, *Rancheros y sociedades rancheras* (Zamora, 1994), pp. 125–40.

[105] MacLeod, 'Forms and Types of Work', pp. 78–9 ('fine-tuning').

[106] Gibson, *Aztecs under Spanish Rule*, pp. 322–3, on the Valley of Mexico Indians' (rational) aversion to wheat as a crop (it yielded less than maize and was subject to the tithe); on truck farming: Taylor, *Landlord and Peasant*, pp. 91, 103, 105; apart from foodstuffs, Indians sold salt, soap, fish and other products in the markets of Mexico City: Gibson, *Aztecs under Spanish Rule*, pp. 338–41, 349.

Though peasants thus competed with commercial landowners, the latter had ways to cirumvent the competition quite effectively (as we shall see); meantime, the hacienda needed supplies of village labour, especially at peak times in the harvest cycle, when temporary workers supplemented the hacienda's core of permanent resident workers. Such workers were drawn, by incentive or obligation, from neighbouring villages: thus the village carried many of the costs of reproducing the labour force, enabling the hacienda to respond to long- and short-term market fluctuations. Market production rode on the back of pre-capitalist forms and lacked either the vigour or the agility to dismount. The total dispossession of the peasant village would have been economically irrational, as well as socially dangerous. Thus, even in the Valley of Mexico, hacienda and village coexisted in a symbiotic relationship, albeit a relationship which was shifting, dynamic and responsive to periodic renegotiation, as economic and demographic trends changed. The nature of that relationship, established in the early colony and surviving down to the twentieth century, will be the subject of further analysis later.

II. Spiritual Conquest

The Spanish military conquest was accompanied – and facilitated – by a parallel 'spiritual conquest',[107] in which the mendicant orders played a crucial role. In addition, during the post-Conquest battles of rival philosophies and interests (Crown versus conquistador, bureaucracy against feudalism) the Church broadly threw its weight behind the Crown, enabling it to claw back some of its early concessions and thus to conjure the threat of a transatlantic feudalism. Any analysis of the early colony must therefore give due attention to the role of the Church. The Spanish Church in general and the mendicant

---

[107] The term is taken from Robert Ricard, *The Spiritual Conquest of Mexico* (Berkeley, 1966; first published in Paris, 1933): a seminal, but at times simplistic, work, which celebrated the success of Catholic proselytization. By way of reaction, recent historians have tended to stress both the coercive and the incomplete character of conversion – some tending to see Catholicism as a thin veneer covering a still pagan Indian people. Stafford Poole, 'Some Observations on Mission Methods and Native Reactions', *The Americas*, 50/3 (1994), pp. 337–50, reviews the debate (and reacts against the revisionists); William Taylor, *Magistrates of the Sacred: Priests and Parishioners in Eighteenth-Century Mexico* (Stanford, 1996), pp. 51–62, offers an excellent overview.

orders in particular were especially well-suited to play a prominent colonial role. Like Castilian society as a whole, the Church was a crusading institution, newly invigorated by the heady triumph over Moorish Granada, which instilled a mood of 'jingo exuberance'.[108] It was also a Church undergoing a pervasive renaissance, by virtue of which a new Erasmian humanism – a common feature of Western Christendom in the early sixteenth century – combined with a revived medieval chiliasm to heighten spiritual ardour and expectations. The discovery of the New World, pioneered by the great secular mystic Columbus, now opened up 'dazzling vistas': the prospect of mass conversions (to complement those of the Jews and Moors in Spain), spiritual triumph over Islam, perhaps the end of the world itelf.[109] Even the initial trauma of the Reformation stimulated more than it depressed Catholic proseltyization: for would not the souls lost to the heretic Luther be more than offset by the teeming millions to be converted in the New World?

Thus, the first Franciscans who journeyed to Mexico – the famous twelve of 1524 – saw themselves as epigones of the Apostles, engaged on a mighty task of global conversion. Not all these Franciscan pioneers were Spanish (several, like their leader, Peter of Ghent, were Flemings), and their exalted, supra-national and at times Utopian sentiments accorded with the neo-medieval imperialist philosophy which pervaded the court of the new emperor Charles V. For some, indeed, Charles was the secular Messiah foretold in the prophecies of Joachim of Fiore.[110] In spiritual terms as well as political, the Conquest of Mexico was, as we have suggested, more a product of the late Middle Ages than of the Early Modern era of (supposedly) capitalism and nationalism.[111]

The disciplined and ascetic Observant Franciscans were well-suited to the great task which fell to them. Their champion, Archbishop Cisneros, primate of Spain, was influential at court; the Crown appreciated that, thanks to the Patronato Real, which gave it control over clerical appointments in the Americas, it could deploy

[108] Brading, *First America*, pp. 19, 25, 46–7.
[109] John L. Phelan, *The Millennial Kingdom of the Franciscans in the New World* (Berkeley, 1956), p. 18; Brading, *First America*, pp. 14, 82, 108.
[110] Weckmann, *La herencia medieval*, pp. 212–18.
[111] Brading, *First America*, p. 104.

mendicant efforts to royal advantage; and conquistadors like Cortés (who personally summoned the friars to Mexico and keenly supported their efforts) grasped that the mendicants would make better pioneer missionaries than would fat prelates, given to 'vices and profanations'.[112] True enough, the poverty and simplicity of the first friars deeply impressed Indian populations accustomed to defer to an ascetic priesthood. And the mendicants supplied a stream of important figures: the Franciscan Juan de Zumárraga, the first bishop of Mexico; the Dominican Las Casas and the Franciscan Toribio de Benevente ('Motolinía' – 'poor' in Nahuatl), both, in their different ways, powerful advocates of Indian rights; Andrés de Olmos and Bernardino de Sahagún, who pioneered the historical and anthropological study of Indian society; and Ramírez de Fuenleal, the president of the second Audiencia, an astute political servant of the Crown.[113]

For a generation the mendicants – Franciscans, Dominicans, Augustinians – provided the shock troops of the spiritual conquest, surprising even themselves by their successes.[114] They preached, converted, baptised, built, educated, wrote, researched and administered. By 1559, although the mendicants numbered fewer than one thousand, they had established 160 convents; cynical *encomenderos*, vexed by mendicant criticism, observed that 'in the Indies it rains friars'.[115] The Franciscans dominated the centre, west and northwest of the colony, the Dominicans the south, notably Oaxaca (though neither this rough geographical demarcation nor common Christian charity was sufficient to prevent some virulent intra-mendicant feuds).[116] While the densest concentration of missions was to be found, logically, in the pacified heartland of the Valley of Mexico (these were 'missions of occupation', in Ricard's words), convents were also built – necessarily sturdy and defensible – in outlying regions; here, 'missions of penetration' often preceded and facilitated

---

[112] Liss, *Mexico under Spain*, pp. 69–70; Ricard, *Spiritual Conquest*, p. 21; Anthony Pagden, ed., *Hernán Cortés, Letters from Mexico* (New Haven, 1986), pp. 332–3.

[113] Brading, *First America*, pp. 58–101 (Las Casas), 104–10 (Motolinía), 119–24 (Sahagún); Liss, *Mexico under Spain*, pp. 52–4 (Ramírez de Fuenleal), 77–83 (Zumárraga).

[114] Israel, *Race, Class, and Politics*, p. 8.

[115] Brading, *First America*, p. 42, quoting Gonzálo Fernández de Oviedo. On mendicant figures, see Gruzinski, *Conquest of Mexico*, p. 146.

[116] Ricard, *Spiritual Conquest*, pp. 75–7, 242ff.; Gibson, *Aztecs under Spanish Rule*, pp. 105, 111.

later secular conquest.[117] In the north particularly, the Franciscans hatched bold plans of spiritual conquest which – to the extent that the friars relied more on example and persuasion, leading, perhaps, to 'charismatic' domination – brought them into conflict with secular Spaniards who preferred more direct, violent and lucrative methods of colonization.[118] In general, however, spiritual and secular conquest proceeded in tandem and proceeded quicker and more effectively in regions where Indian realms had been swallowed whole and where existing Indian authorities could be harnessed to the work of conversion (the old Aztec heartland, Tarascan Michoacan, and to a lesser degree Oaxaca). In peripheral zones, where nomads roamed or stateless ('tribal') societies predominated, the Indians resisted conversion or displayed a 'sly inertia' in the face of Christian proselytization.[119] The Aztec Mexica or Tarascans were thus more thoroughly and expeditiously converted than, say, the Maya of Yucatán, the Zapotecs of Oaxaca, or even the 'brutish' Otomí of Central Mexico.[120] No doubt the perceived correlation between conversion and civilization gratified missionary sensibilities.

Throughout the colony, however, conversion was so rapid as to raise questions concerning its character and efficacy. By 1524 a million Indians were reported baptised, by 1540, four million. Motolinía himself was said to have baptised 300,000 new converts; in one five-day session, with the help of one other friar, he baptised 14,200 Indian converts.[121] Throughout, elements of coercion entered into the work of conversion. The Spaniards, it has been suggested, were more prepared than other European imperialists to 'impose

---

[117] Ricard, *Spiritual Conquest*, pp. 77–8; Kubler, *Mexican Architecture*, vol. 1, p. 71.

[118] Gutiérrez, *When Jesus Came*, p. 55.

[119] Ricard, *Spiritual Conquest*, p. 267.

[120] Gibson, *Aztecs under Spanish Rule*, p. 116. Spanish friars thus picked up and perpetuated the old Aztec myth of Otomí inferiority (now further reinforced by the environmental degradation created by Spanish sheep in the Otomí region): Melville, *A Plague of Sheep*, pp. 32, 115.

[121] Ricard, *Spiritual Conquest*, p. 91; Brading, *First America*, pp. 105–6. Assuming Motolinía and his partner worked a ten-hour day, shared the work and got the Indians to move along with assembly-line precision, they baptised at the rate of 142 an hour, or one every 40 seconds: a productive, if perfunctory, baptismal procedure. The assembly-line metaphor is not inappropriate: one friar allegedly baptised between 4,000 and 6,000 Indians in a day, 'switching the jar of holy water from arm to aching arm, while callouses thickened on his hands and the Mexican sun burned his tonsured head raw': Clendinnen, *Ambivalent Conquests*, p. 48. The question obviously arises: what did the mass Indian converts make of this breakneck ritual (Burkhart, *Slippery Earth*, pp. 112–13)?

their culture on their colonial subjects by force"[122] – an attitude nurtured in the Reconquista and indicative of the more inclusionary, as well as the more martial, character of Iberian Catholicism, as compared with Anglo-Saxon Protestantism. The Franciscans, in particular, were zealous proselytizers; they were prepared to win souls by brandishing the secular sword and to keep them by using the stocks and the whip; thus, from Yucatán to New Mexico, stories of Franciscan brutality abounded.[123] The Dominicans, in contrast, preferred a more cautious and gradual strategy of conversion (Las Casas's Augustinian theology advised caution in the matter of mass baptism);[124] they were skeptical of Franciscan Utopianism and condemned the Franciscans for conniving – naively or maliciously – at the abuses and extortions which had accompanied conversion. The Franciscans, for their part, saw the Dominicans as carping latecomers, overconcerned for Indian material well-being at the expense of Indian mortal souls. However, inasmuch as the Franciscans pioneered the first great wave of Mexico's spiritual conquest, they set their stamp on the process, while the Dominicans, adopting their more gradual approach, prevailed in Spain's Andean colonies.[125]

Soon, the Mexican landscape was dotted with churches, built by Indian labour, proclaiming the glory of the faith and possessing capacious open courtyards (*atrios*) which could accommodate mass Indian congregations.[126] The latter, by their sheer numbers and apparent amenability to conversion, won them the praise and protection of their mendicant mentors. In the eyes of the friars, especially the Franciscans, the Indians were spiritual children, special wards, blessed with human rationality (as yet untapped) and pristine virtues

---

[122] Farriss, *Maya Society*, p. 91.

[123] Jorge Klor de Alva, 'Spiritual Conflict and Accommodation in New Spain: Toward a Typology of Aztec Responses to Christianity', in George A. Collier *et al.*, eds., *The Inca and Aztec States, 1400–1800: History and Anthropology* (New York, 1982), p. 357; Bricker, *The Indian Christ*, p. 20; Farriss, *Maya Society*, p. 92; David Sweet, 'The Ibero-American Frontier Mission in Native American History', in Erick Langer and Robert H. Jackson, eds., *The New Latin American Mission History* (Lincoln, 1995), pp. 21–2; Gutiérrez, *When Jesus Came*, pp. 76, 80, on Franciscan coercion in New Mexico, which included 'a clerical technique occasionally used to render an obdurate and cocksure [*sic*] Indian submissive' – that is, 'grab[bing] him by the testicles and . . . twist[ing] them until the man collapsed in pain'.

[124] Brading, *First America*, pp. 63–4.

[125] Klor de Alva, 'Spiritual Conflict and Accommodation', pp. 346–7.

[126] Ricard, *Spiritual Conquest*, pp. 165–6. See also Kubler, *Mexican Architecture*, vol. 1, pp. 23–8, 65–72.

(as yet untainted). They seemed meek, decorous, docile and industrious; they were like 'soft wax' ready to be moulded, as the Franciscan chronicler Gerónimo de Mendieta put it.[127] But this happy state was threatened by a rapacious secular colonialism. The friars therefore took it upon themselves to convert and educate the Indians, while sustaining the Indian social order, which seemed to them gratifyingly non-materialistic.[128] The aim was optimistic and contradictory: to uproot Mesoamerican religion in favour of Catholicism but to preserve the pristine – and somewhat idealized – Indian community; to effect a neat split in what had been a unitary, socioreligious whole. To this end, the friars assiduously learned Indian tongues (one mastered ten languages, it was said); they encouraged Indian music and crafts, fiestas and sodalities (under Catholic auspices, of course); and they looked forward to the eventual consecration of Indian priests. Even as they promiscuously destroyed Indian temples, idols and codices, they also carefully researched Indian history and customs – indeed, Las Casas has been termed the first comparative ethnographer.[129] In Mexico City the Franciscans started an elite school for young Indians (Santa Cruz de Tlatelolco, 1536), stocking its library with Virgil, Cicero, Aristotle and Erasmus; its pupils proved capable of confounding pretentious European clerics in debate.[130] In Michoacan, Bishop Vasco de Quiroga briefly established model communities inspired by Thomas More's *Utopia*.[131] Meanwhile, the friars condemned – both individually and institutionally – the abuses perpetrated by Spanish laymen. The Franciscan Zumárraga denounced and helped halt the rapacious career of Nuño de Guzmán; at the Spanish court the Dominican Las Casas took up

---

[127] Israel, *Race, Class, and Politics*, p. 15; see also Brading, *First America*, pp. 86, 113; Burkhart, *Slippery Earth*, p. 18.

[128] On Indian virtue, simplicity and non-materialism: Phelan, *Millennial Kingdom*, p. 49; Liss, *Mexico under Spain*, pp. 75, 79; Brading, *First America*, pp. 92, 111. However, the friars were not of one mind; a gratifying lack of material cupidity could also be construed as bestial stupidity: Liss, *Mexico under Spain*, p. 86.

[129] Ricard, *Spiritual Conquest*, chs. 8, 14; Brading, *First America*, p. 107 (codices), p. 89ff. (Las Casas). Diego Durán and Bernardino de Sahagún were also notable pioneers of the study (and critique) of Indian society, culture and history: Tzvetan Todorov, *Conquest of America* (New York, 1995), pp. 202–41.

[130] José María Kobayashi, *La educación como conquista (empresa franciscana en México)* (Mexico, 1985), p. 207ff.; Georges Baudot, *Utopia and History in Mexico: The First Chronicles of Mexican Civilization* (Niwot, Colo., 1995) pp. 111–15; Ricard, *Spiritual Conquest*, pp. 219–20.

[131] Brading, *First America*, p. 104.

cudgels for the Indians, eliciting royal concern and reform. Thus the friars earned the cordial dislike of many Spanish laymen.[132]

The Franciscans, in particular, sought to constitute themselves as a thin grey (or brown) line, separating Indian from Spaniard. Thus, they claimed, Indian society could best be protected; thus, their lay critics countered, the Franciscans could better exploit their Indian charges spiritually and materially.[133] Certainly the ultimate mendicant objective was a separate Indian realm – a *república de indios* – organized along quasi-medieval corporatist lines, under theocratic rule sanctioned by the Crown; a realm from which Spaniards and Spanish ways (money-grubbing, wine-bibbing and horse-riding) would be paternalistically excluded.[134] But it is certain, too, that mendicant rule displayed less benevolent features in practice. Corporal punishment was used to discipline the new Indian converts: 'we... whip them as children', Mendieta explained, 'and, seeing that we do it in love and for their own good, they not only endure it patiently but thank us for it'.[135] In Yucatán, Diego de Landa, provincial of the Franciscans, instituted a 'reign of terror' against Maya idolaters in the 1560s; in New Mexico, the Franciscans flogged, shackled and humiliated their Pueblo parishioners.[136] Meantime, massive amounts of Indian labour were deployed in construction: not just of churches but also of new houses, plazas, even aqueducts. Las Casas, the great critic of Spanish oppression and champion of Indian rights, was free with his own appropriation of Indian labour (and, we should recall, he initially advocated African slavery as an antidote to the exploitation of the Indians).[137] His fellow Dominican, Peláez de Barrio,

[132] Warren, *Conquest of Michoacan*, p. 222; Brading, *First America*, pp. 41–2, 60–1, 291; Chevalier, *Land and Society*, p. 302.

[133] Brading, *First America*, pp. 114–15; similar charges and countercharges would later become common in the north too: Gutiérrez, *When Jesus Came*, pp. 108–9.

[134] Farriss, *Maya Society*, pp. 91–2; Chevalier, *Land and Society*, p. 199; Phelan, *Millennial Kingdom*, pp. 53, 66, 83–4.

[135] Charles S. Braden, *Religious Aspects of the Conquest of Mexico* (Durham, 1930), p. 170; Brading, *First America*, pp. 113, 190–1.

[136] Brading, *First America*, p. 103; Clendinnen, *Ambivalent Conquests*, pp. 75–7; Gutiérrez, *When Jesus Came*, pp. 73, 76, 80.

[137] Kubler, *Mexican Architecture*, vol. 1, pp. 28, 65, 117, 135–51, 227–8; Gibson, *Aztecs under Spanish Rule*, pp. 118–19 (churches); MacLachlan and Rodríguez O., *Forging of the Cosmic Race*, p. 124 (aqueduct); Brading, *First America*, p. 75 (slavery). Motolinía acidly pointed out that Las Casas 'had forced an unconscionable number of native bearers to carry his huge collection of documents denouncing the employ by Spaniards of Indian carriers': Liss, *Mexico under Spain*, p. 75.

acquired a reputation in Oaxaca as 'a prototype conquistador at his rapacious and greedy worst'.[138]

The Indians' submission to the spiritual conquest, and the burdens and benefits it involved, was a complex phenomenon. Direct coercion played a part – a part underestimated in some versions[139] – but the spiritual conquest responded to several other factors, three of which should be stressed. First, the old prudential – one might say pragmatic – theology of Mesoamerica encouraged ready acceptance of a triumphant faith. If the old gods had failed, they should at least be supplemented – not necessarily supplanted – by the new: by Jesus Christ, by his Mother and by the army of saints whom the Spaniards revered and invoked, who had brought the conquistadors victory in battle (while protecting them from smallpox), and whose power was proclaimed by the pioneer mendicants – shabby, barefoot ascetics who impressed the Indians, and to whom even the great Cortés humbly deferred.[140] Conversion did not therefore mean the outright denial of the old pantheon. Now as in the past, new gods could be assimilated; old and new religious calendars could coexist.[141] As Frans Blom empathized the reasoning of the Maya: 'there might be cases where the new gods might help. It was best to play safe'.[142] Throughout Mesoamerica, Pascal's wager was played out on a mass, collective basis.

In particular, the conversion of Indian *caciques* – whose prudential, pragmatic motives were strongest of all – often led to the mass conversion of their subjects; conversely, where *caciques* resisted, conversion came slowly.[143] The friars perceived the utility of bolstering cacical authority, in the face not only of Spanish attacks but also

[138] Chance, *Race and Class*, p. 40.

[139] Notably Ricard, *Spiritual Conquest*: see the comments of Poole, 'Some Observations'.

[140] On prudential conversion: Fernando Cervantes, *The Devil in the New World* (New Haven, 1994), pp. 42–3; Lockhart, *The Nahuas*, p. 203ff.; and Gruzinski, *Conquest of Mexico*, p. 104, citing an Indian primordial (i.e., land) title of 1531: 'I have decided to set up a sanctuary where we shall place the new god that the Castilians have brought us. They want us to adore him. What should we do, my sons? We must be baptised, give ourselves up to the men of Castile to see if in this way they will spare us'. There is, of course, nothing new in prudential conversion: since the time of Constantine the Great (if not before), 'the proof of a god is best found in his protection': Robin Lane-Fox, *Pagans and Christians* (New York, 1987), p. 618.

[141] Farriss, *Maya Society*, p. 24; Gruzinski, *Conquest of Mexico*, pp. 88–9 (calendrical syncretism).

[142] Frans Blom, *The Conquest of Yucatán* (New York, 1971; first pubd. 1936), p. 108.

[143] Gibson, *Aztecs under Spanish Rule*, p. 112; Taylor, *Landlord and Peasant*, p. 37; cf. Olivera, *Pillis y macehuales*, p. 130.

of popular challenges. The Dominicans of Oaxaca worked in close collusion with the native *caciques*, to mutual advantage: spiritual conquest did not mean social subversion.[144] It could, however, bring generational conflict. The missionaries appealed, with apparent success, to Indian youth, even to the extent of turning them against their orthodox (i.e., pagan) parents. Indian youths were enlisted as interpreters by the missionaries; they denounced their parents' heresies to the friars; they collaborated in the destruction of pagan idols; in Tlaxcala, they stoned to death a recalcitrant pagan priest.[145] Such juvenile insolence reflected a generational split – of which Christian conversion was the most obvious and overt emblem – which sundered families and which formed part of the more general social upheaval of the Conquest.

Conversion was further facilitated by the many points of ostensible similarity between Mesoamerican religion and Catholicism. Elements such as sacrifice, confession, asceticism, divine intercession (and, in Yucatán, baptism) were common to both, at least in the eyes of heterodox Indian converts. Gods and saints were readily conflated: Tonantzin was equated with the Virgin; Quetzalcóatl with Saint Thomas; the Zapotec rain god, Cocijo, with Saint Peter.[146] Such assimilation was encouraged – largely unwittingly – by Spanish ecclesiastical policy. The sites of old cults became new Catholic shrines, like that of the Christ of Chalma. The Basilica of Guadalupe, eventually Mexico's greatest shrine, and a cynosure of Mariolatry, was built on a hill once sacred to Tonantzin (the Virgin even inherited from her Precolumbian predecessor a divine association with pulque).[147]

---

[144] Robert Wasserstrom, *Class and Society in Central Chiapas* (Berkeley, 1983), p. 20; Taylor, *Landlord and Peasant*, pp. 37–8; Serge Gruzinski, *Man-Gods in the Mexican Highlands: Indian Power and Colonial Society, 1520–1800* (Stanford, 1989), p. 34.

[145] Ricard, *Spiritual Conquest*, pp. 98, 100; Braden, *Spiritual Aspects*, pp. 156, 167; Wachtel, 'The Indian and the Spanish Conquest', p. 228.

[146] Jacques Lafaye, *Quetzalcóatl y Guadalupe. La formación de la conciencia nacional en México* (Mexico, 1991), pp. 260–327; Whitecotton, *The Zapotecs*, p. 213.

[147] Ricard, *Spiritual Conquest*, p. 192 (Chalma); Brading, *First America*, pp. 343–6, Lockhart, *The Nahuas*, pp. 246–7, and Gruzinski, *Conquest of Mexico*, pp. 190–3 (Virgin of Guadalupe); Taylor, *Drinking, Homicide and Rebellion*, pp. 31, 59 (pulque). Stafford Poole, *Our Lady of Guadalupe: The Origins and Sources of a Mexican National Legend, 1531–1797* (Tucson, 1995), pp. 9, 78–81, questions the conventional equation of Tonantzin, Tepeyac, and the Virgin of Guadalupe. Gordon Brotherston, *Book of the Fourth World: Reading the Native Americas through Their Literature* (Cambridge, 1992), pp. 16, 98, suggests a somewhat subtler continuity: the Virgin's symbol of the crescent new moon (in Nahutla, *meztli*) denotes the Mexica, or Nahua.

Thus, many – not all[148] – of the Mesoamerican shrines which had played so important a role in pre-Conquest society metamorphosed into centres of Catholic pilgrimage; and, more generally, Indian communities swapped their old *lares et penates* (*calpulteotl*) for new Catholic patron saints, who took on the task of supernatural protection.[149] Mesoamerican tradition conspired with the equally venerable tradition of Spanish/Byzantine santolatry to produce a society suffused with saints: at Patambán, a Franciscan parish in Michoacan, the local Church boasted twenty-five statues or pictures dedicated to fourteen saints, including five Saint Francises and five Saint Antonies (not to mention several Christs, Magi and Stigmata).[150] Saints were not merely decorative; they were expected to work for their living. According to the old tradition of Mesoamerican religion, sacrifice and mortification earned divine intercession – that is, practical help; but negligent saints – those who failed to intercede – were beaten, buried and blasphemed against.[151] Meanwhile, in similar syncretic fashion, Spanish church-builders appropriated the stones of old temples with such abandon that ancient glyphs and symbols could be seen staring from the walls of new Catholic churches.[152] Comforting continuities were established, too, by the friars' encouragement of Indian crafts, music and fiestas. Thus, while the early missionaries sought a decisive break with the past in the religious – not the social – sphere, they connived at maintaining important cultural continuities which speeded conversion and eased the trauma of conquest.

[148] Some remained 'pagan' shrines, where the cult of the old gods survived clandestinely: Gibson, *Aztecs under Spanish Rule*, p. 101; Gruzinski, *Conquest of Mexico*, pp. 231, 259.

[149] Gibson, *Aztecs under Spanish Rule*, p. 154; Gruzinski, *Conquest of Mexico*, p. 240; Lockhart, *The Nahuas*, pp. 237–9.

[150] Gruzinski, *Conquest of Mexico*, pp. 238–9; Lockhart, *The Nahuas*, p. 235, notes how 'saints leap out of wills, municipal decrees, sales, leases, annals, primordial titles, indeed almost everything the Nahuas wrote'. For Yucatán, see Restall, *The Maya World*, pp. 152–3. On European parallels and origins: Brading, *First America*, pp. 349–50; William A. Christian, Jr., *Local Religion in Sixteenth-Century Spain* (Princeton, 1989).

[151] Gruzinski, *Conquest of Mexico*, pp. 230, 246–7.

[152] Kubler, *Mexican Architecture*, vol. 1, pp. 163–4; Whitecotton, *The Zapotecs*, p. 212. Just as there were European parallels for this syncretic sacred architecture, so, too, were there pre-Conquest precedents (see the discussion concerning Olmec San Lorenzo in Tatiana Proskouriakoff, 'Olmec and Maya Art: Problems of Their Stylistic Relation. Discussion', in E. P. Benson, *Dumbarton Oaks Conference on the Olmec* [Washington, D.C., 1968], pp. 131–3). On the general question of syncretism – the blending of diverse religious traditions – see Taylor, *Magistrates of the Sacred*, pp. 53–9.

Closely linked to this conservative cultural strategy was the friars' more general sociopolitical role, which helped them win souls and influence people. True, the Indians did not universally accept the mendicants' self-styled role as their spiritual mentors; hence there were occasional revolts, and, with time, a pervasive tendency towards backsliding and apostasy. Nevertheless, the friars proved the most consistent Spanish allies of the Indians during the harsh initial years of the colony, and the Indians were aware of the utility of this alliance. (Indians were also aware that conversion offered some guarantee of royal protection, which no doubt spurred the process of conversion.)[153] Prudential theology was therefore seconded by a form of prudential sociopolitical reasoning: in the here-and-now, as well as in the afterlife, conversion offered tangible benefits. The friars, we have seen, fostered Indian education, even to the level of university studies based on European humanistic learning; they sponsored plays and processions; they organized public works – hospitals, aqueducts, irrigation dams; and they offered Indians jobs – as gardeners, porters, sacristans, choristers and musicians.[154] They also encouraged Indian agriculture and artisanry, often in very practical this-worldly fashion: silk in the Mixteca of Oaxaca, orchards in Michoacan.[155] In the broadest sense, too, mendicant policy helped counteract the anomie which – insofar as so intangible a phenomenon can be inferred from the evidence – afflicted Indian society in the wake of the Conquest.[156] In place of the old, overthrown ways the friars offered new certainties, social and spiritual, to a people whose lives had traditionally been suffused by religious ritual.

This solace was all the more important as Indian numbers slumped. By the 1540s, as we have seen, the missionaries had begun

---

[153] Wasserstrom, *Class and Society*, p. 20.

[154] Ricard, *Spiritual Conquest*, chs. 8–13; Chevalier, *Land and Society*, p. 238 (public works); Gruzinski, *Conquest of Mexico*, pp. 65–6, and Lockhart, *The Nahuas*, p. 133 (jobs).

[155] Chevalier, *Land and Society*, p. 193.

[156] Klor de Alva, following León-Portilla, puts forward the notion of 'nepantlism' ('that situation in which a person remains suspended in the middle between a lost or disfigured past and a present that has not yet been assimilated or understood'), which he considers 'abundantly documented' from the 1520s. I take this to represent – roughly – a variant of anomie. Thanks partly to the mendicants' efforts and partly to the creative efforts of the Indians themselves 'nepantlism' was – usually and eventually – resolved into a form of syncretism, a blend of old and new, at both the individual and the collective level: Klor de Alva, 'Spiritual Conflict and Accommodation', pp. 353–5; see also Cervantes, *Devil in the New World*, pp. 57, 61.

to pioneer new Indian settlements (*congregaciones*), communities designed both to speed and to consolidate conversion and also to impose firmer social control on a dwindling, traumatized population (indeed, the friars had to wrestle with the problem of an inscrutable providence which consigned tens of thousands of new converts to early graves).[157] The product, in the main, of colonial self-interest, these new Indian communities sometimes offered social niches within which Indian society could reconstitute itself amid the up-heaval and mortality of the post-Conquest years. Some, indeed, were quasi-theocratic communities, in which 'missionaries . . . became the true local political authorities and overseers of economic life'; the best example – the work of a secular bishop, not a mendicant – was the (literally) Utopian community founded by Vasco de Quiroga in Michoacan, where the bishop took it upon himself to reorder a Tarascan population traumatized by the callous rule of Nuño de Guzmán.[158]

These practical embodiments of Renaissance Christian humanism did not survive long in their pristine form. Missionary zeal faded, and secular rapacity took its toll. Some *congregaciones* failed, as the Indians upped and fled.[159] But the constructive social role of the early friars could not be undone. Communities survived, as did the lay organizations – *cofradías* (sodalities) – set up by the friars within many villages. These served – manifestly – to support saints' cults and fiestas. But their latent function, once again, was that of restoring the cohesion and solidarity of Indian society, albeit by means of new symbols and rituals. The *cofradías*, born in the sixteenth century and fully flowering in the seventeenth, offered foci of community alle-giance, practical forms of 'ecclesiastical insurance',[160] avenues of mo-bility, and, perhaps, a means whereby community affairs were grad-ually and modestly democratized, within a prevailing patriarchy.[161]

[157] Brading, *First America*, pp. 109–10.
[158] Liss, *Mexico under Spain*, pp. 83–4, 90; García Martínez, *Pueblos de la sierra*, pp. 276–7, de-scribes the integrating work of the Church in the more remote and anonymous Sierra de Puebla.
[159] Taylor, *Landlord and Peasant*, p. 27; García Martínez, *Pueblos de la sierra*, p. 175; Farriss, *Maya Society*, pp. 206–8.
[160] Gibson, *Aztecs under Spanish Rule*, p. 129.
[161] Though patriarchy prevailed, women did play a part in many *cofradías*. For the latter's role and organization, see: Asunción Lavrín, 'Cofradías novohispanas: Economías material y

That is, the *cofradía* and the cargo system into which it matured tended to distribute power and prestige within the community, inhibiting the development of narrow, entrenched oligarchies.[162] In its classic form, the *cofradía* integrated the community by fostering common rituals and – to an extent – sharing out wealth and office, at least among village males; and it did so autonomously, often independent of Church and *cura*.[163] Such social functions were not universal, nor did they represent the friars' conscious objectives. Nevertheless, such religiously inspired communities and associations gave the Indian population a solid corporate niche within colonial society. By 1585, Mexico City boasted 300 *cofradías*; at the obsequies held for King Philip IV in 1665, 82 Indian *cofradías* participated along with

espiritual', in Pilar Martínez López-Cano, Gisela Von Wobeser, and Juan Gullermo Muñoz, *Cofradías, capellanías y obras pías en la América colonial* (Mexico, 1998), pp. 49–64; Clara García Ayluardo, 'A World of Images: Cult, Ritual and Society in Colonial Mexico City', in William H. Beezley, Cheryl English Martin, and William E. French, eds., *Rituals of Rule, Rituals of Resistance: Public Celebrations and Popular Culture in Mexico* (Wilmington, Del., 1994), pp. 77–94; Gibson, *Aztecs under Spanish Rule*, pp. 127–32; García Martínez, *Pueblos de la sierra*, pp. 273–4; Farriss, *Maya Society*, pp. 265–6; Taylor, *Magistrates of the Sacred*, ch. 12; Ernesto de la Torre Villar, 'Algunos aspectos acerca de las cofradías y la propiedad territorial en Michoacan', *Jahrbuch für Geschichte von Staat, Wirtschaft, und Gesellschaft Lateinamerikas*, 4 (1967), pp. 410–39; Lockhart, *The Nahuas*, pp. 218–29, which (pp. 220–1) notes the democratic (as well as theocratic) potential of the *cofradía*, but discerns – in what is a cloudy picture – some 'room ... for indigenous people to assert themselves', hence some measure of 'direct community participation'.

[162] Although drawing inferences from recent anthropological research is risky (see Taylor, *Magistrates of the Sacred*, pp. 321–2), it is worth noting the lively debate over the function in modern Mesoamerican communities of the cargo system – a relative-cum-descendant of the colonial *cofradía*, which in turn may have had Precolumbian roots (see Lockhart, *The Nahuas*, p. 217; Farriss, *Maya Society*, pp. 348, 527, n. 86). According to some analysts, the cargo system serves to bolster the community's solidarity, define its borders, conserve its resources and inhibit its internal stratification: Frank Cancian, *Economía y prestigio en una comunidad Maya. El sistema religioso de cargos en Zinacantan* (Mexico, 1976), p. 190 and ch. 12; but cf. Jan Rus and Robert Wasserstrom, 'Civil-Religious Hierarchies in Central Chiapas: A Critical Perspective', *American Ethnologist*, 7 (1980), pp. 466–78. Kevin Gosner, *Soldiers of the Virgin: The Moral Economy of a Colonial Maya Rebellion* (Tucson, 1992), pp. 75–85, offers a useful review; see also Chance, *Conquest of the Sierra*, pp. 137–46, which captures the tension between 'the opposing principles of hierarchy and egalitarianism' evident in the cargo system. Given that tension, it seems to me quite plausible that both *cofradía* and cargo systems performed different functions at different times in different communities; however, the notion that they could – and quite often did – reinforce community solidarity while inhibiting community stratification retains some validity.

[163] Hence the 'theocratic' outcome was unusual: *cofradías* were usually run by villagers, not priests. See Gibson, *Aztecs under Spanish Rule*, pp. 236, 240–1, 247. Taylor, *Magistrates of the Sacred*, p. 322, sees (Central Mexican) priests exercising authority over *cofradía* income and expenditure, while leaving ritual activity to the laity; in general, cofradías were 'local institutions maintained by local people', which afforded 'a locus of more or less independent religious expression'.

19 Spanish and 16 black and mulatto sodalities.[164] In most communities, too, the parish church became a key symbol of collective life: its very construction, during the great church-building efforts of the 1530s and 1540s, could help generate a 'sense of community' during troubled times; and, thereafter, the church figured not only as the focus of social life but also as the necessary criterion for the establishment of full corporate status.[165] A churchless community was an incomplete, adolescent, vulnerable community.

However much these factors encouraged conversion, they did not require a doctrinaire acceptance of the faith. The friars, pursuing the literally Utopian objective of revolutionizing Indian religious life, while conserving the main lineaments of Indian society, were aware of the risks they ran. For all their destruction of idols and codices, the missionaries could not extirpate the old ways; occasionally they turned a blind eye, or they connived at pagan survivals by designating the old gods as devils – who had survived – rather than as figments who had vanished.[166] Thus, the social continuities which the friars approved were reflected in religious continuities which they abominated. Rapid, mass, conversion left a legacy of ingrained Indian idolatry, backsliding and indifference to Catholic doctrine: 'they *believed* in God', complained the Dominican Diego Durán, 'and at the same time *practised* their old rites and customs of the devil'.[167]

New converts happily mingled the old and the new in a hybrid ritual and theology which was shot through with heresy. The old gods were eclectically merged into new saints' cults, or they survived, *sub rosa*, with their acolytes worshipping – or boozing – in secret; the drunken Indian binges condemned by censorious Spaniards were sometimes bibulous traditional fiestas now given an incongruous Christian veneer.[168] Codices depicting the old gods were hidden away

[164] Gibson, *Aztecs under Spanish Rule*, p. 241; Brading, *First America*, p. 376.

[165] Gibson, *Aztecs under Spanish Rule*, pp. 120–1; Lockhart, *The Nahuas*, p. 55.

[166] Burkhart, *Slippery Earth*, p. 3,(not unreasonably) considers the mendicant project 'hopelessly quixotic'. See also: Gibson, *Aztecs under Spanish Rule*, p. 116 (blind eye); Cervantes, *Devil in the New World*, p. 15 (gods-as-devils). Turning a blind eye – construing Indian heterodoxy as petty superstition rather than major idolatry – was facilitated by the friars' infantilization of the Indian; children might be naughty, but they were not fundamentally evil: Taylor, *Magistrates of the Sacred*, pp. 18–19, 153, 174.

[167] Gruzinski, *Conquest of Mexico*, p. 178.

[168] Taylor, *Drinking, Homicide and Rebellion*, pp. 40, 59; Gruzinski, *Conquest of Mexico*, pp. 85, 152. Lockhart, *The Nahuas*, p. 112, cautions against taking Spanish moral outrage at Indian

and preserved. *Curanderos* (healers), sorcerers and midwives kept alive the old rites, beliefs and magical vocabularies. At the same time, respectable Catholic rituals were appropriated and – priests believed – perverted by atavistic Indian excesses: flagellation, fasting, lavish Noche Buena bonfires, the prodigal burning of *copal* (incense).[169] At Tayasal, Yucatán, a sick black horse became the object of Indian veneration; when – hurried along by Indian ministrations of meat, flowers and honey – the animal died, its image was represented in stone and 'worshipped as the principal deity of Tayasal' until an outraged friar smashed it in 1618.[170] More than two centuries later, the Maya continued to revere pagan gods, and to find in them inspiration for sustained revolt against alien rule; but they also appropriated Catholic roles and rituals, creating Indian popes and bishops and claiming that the Indians were better Christians than the backsliding Spaniards.[171] The Maya south was exceptional: superficially conquered, it possessed an enduring culture and cosmology which Hispanic Catholicism could influence but not extirpate. More generally, the outer periphery and remote highlands of New Spain witnessed recurrent idolatry ('idols behind altars', to cite the usual cliché): stories abound of Indians making covert offerings in sacred caverns or occasionally rallying to prophetic leaders and shamans.[172]

drinking too seriously, since it was probably premised on a stereotyped and exaggerated notion of pre-Conquest sobriety. Caution is also advisable given that colonial Spaniards started (or continued) a tradition of elite advocacy of temperance which, combining misconception and hypocrisy, would endure through generations, even centuries: e.g., Moisés González Navarro, *Historia moderna de México. El Porfiriato, La vida social* (Mexico, 1970), p. 72. Apart from drink, Indian hallucinogens (such as peyote) provoked Spanish concern; they, too, had strong religious and ritualistic associations: Gruzinski, *Conquest of Mexico*, pp. 215–16; Taylor, *Drinking, Homicide and Rebellion*, p. 69; Cervantes, *Devil in the New World*, p. 47.

[169] Gruzinski, *Conquest of Mexico*, ch. 4, offers a rich panorama.

[170] Blom, *Conquest of Yucatán*, p. 50. Indian receptions of and reactions to the horse have been examined by William Taylor, 'Santiago's Horse: Christianity and Colonial Indian Resistance in the Heartland of New Spain', in William B. Taylor and Franklin Pease, eds., *Violence, Resistance and Survival in the Americas* (Washington, D.C., 1994), pp. 157–8. For a variant on this theme, note the treatment meted out to the Spaniards' dogs and pigs by the Tarascan king of Michoacan (Cazonci Zinchicha) in 1520: 'what are these?', he asked, 'are they rats?'; after which he ordered them to be slaughtered: Thomas, *Conquest of Mexico*, p. 473.

[171] Bricker, *Indian Christ*, pp. 20–1; Gosner, *Soldiers of the Virgin*, ch. 6. Devout Spaniards were naturally appalled at Indian appropriations of Catholic ritual and symbols (holy communion, the crucifixion); these were monstrous inversions, which smacked of diabolism: Cervantes, *Devil in the New World*, pp. 30, 38, 51.

[172] Gruzinski, *Conquest of Mexico*, pp. 87, 92–3, 183; Gruzinski, *Man-Gods*; Cervantes, *Devil in the New World*, pp. 14, 50.

And the entire colony – including the cities and populated valleys – was familiar with everyday 'magic', the work of Indian *curanderos*, magicians and witches: people who ministered at rites of passage, who could harm enemies or bring rain, good health or success in the hunt.[173] Familiar enough in Europe, such powers and practices elicited the interest and custom of Spaniards and mestizos, for whom Indian magic exerted the dark appeal of the unknown.[174]

In the main, therefore, Indian 'paganism' took the form of mute, discrete, religious backsliding rather than militant political resistance.[175] If this offered some consolation to the Spaniards, it did not satisfy the early missionaries. From the outset, the friars were aware of the danger of rapid conversion; the Dominicans warned their Franciscan brothers against *trop de zèle*. Franciscans like Bishop Zumárraga responded not by curtailing conversion, but by channelling their zeal toward the material destruction of paganism. By 1531, Zumárraga proudly claimed, five hundred temples and twenty thousand idols had been destroyed.[176] So had many irreplaceable

---

[173] Gruzinski, *Conquest of Mexico*, pp. 153–8, 170–1. Thus we find, *mutatis mutandis*, all the repertoire of 'cunning men and popular magic' which Keith Thomas has analysed in the English context: Keith Thomas, *Religion and the Decline of Magic* (Harmondsworth, 1973), chs. 7, 8. One apparent – and odd – omission (according to Gruzinski, *Conquest of Mexico*, p. 155) is the Mexican mine where, Gruzinski states, idolatry was absent – in stark contrast to the common practices in Andean mines (see Michael Taussig, *The Devil and Commodity Fetishism in South America* [Chapel Hill, 1980]). Assuming this is not a false conclusion, possibly derived from the bias of the sources, it may reflect the predominance of mestizo and mulatto free wage labourers in the (northern) Mexican mines, compared to the Indian draft labourers (*mitayos*) of the Andes: see D. A. Brading and Harry E. Cross, 'Colonial Silver Mining: Mexico and Peru', *Hispanic American Historical Review,* 52/4 (1972), pp. 557–9.

[174] Gruzinski, *Conquest of Mexico*, p. 177; Richard Boyer, *Lives of the Bigamists: Marriage, Family and Community in Colonial Mexico* (Albuquerque, 1995), pp. 175–6, on Spanish fascination with 'the shadowy terrain of Indian wisdom, lore and magic', typified by one Spaniard obsessed with the notion that an Indian shaman might 'show him where money was buried'.

[175] Compare Spain's Andean realms, where pre-Conquest religion survived more lustily, sometimes linked to a more radical 'nativist' project and sustained by influential Indian elites and shamans: Taylor, *Drinking, Homicide and Rebellion*, p. 126n; Kenneth R. Mills, *Idolatry and Its Enemies: Colonial Andean Religion and Extirpation, 1640–1750* (Princeton, 1997), p. 253.

[176] Brading, *First America*, pp. 62–3, 73 (Dominican caution); on Zumárraga: Israel, *Race, Class, and Politics*, pp. 7–8; Cervantes, *Devil in the New World*, pp. 13–14. Diego de Landa, ruthlessly repressing idolatry in Yucatán, consigned stacks of Maya books and other sacred objects to the flames: a holocaust which, he noted, almost in surprise, the Maya 'regretted to an amazing degree and which caused them great affliction': Clendinnen, *Ambivalent Conquests*, p. 70. Striving for empathy, we might indulge for a moment in the counterfactual: a Maya fleet makes landfall in Galicia and – having slaughtered numerous inhabitants, thrown some to ravenous jaguars and introduced lethal disease – puts Santiago de Compostela to the torch.

codices. The friars also ferreted out witches and sorcerers. When, in 1539, drought threatened a revival of the old cult of Tlaloc, Zumárraga – a veteran of witch-hunts in the Basque country, now Inquisitor as well as bishop of Mexico – ordered the burning for heresy of Don Carlos Chichimecatecuhtli, ruler of Texcoco and one of the first Christian converts.[177] Suspicious of heterodoxy, the friars frowned on the new cult of the Virgin of Guadalupe, which centred on the hill of Tepeyac, near Mexico City, a spot once held sacred to the goddess Tonantzin, where the Virgin allegedly appeared to an Indian convert in 1531.[178] In consequence, the Guadalupe cult was soon taken up by the secular clergy in their battle with the mendicants, and it developed into a potent source not only of religious inspiration but also of proto-national sentiment.[179]

By the mid-sixteenth century, a reaction to early mendicant millenarianism had set in. The high hopes of the early missionaries had been partly fulfilled, partly dashed: millions of souls had been won for the faith, yet paradoxically this new flock had been decimated by disease (Motolinía blamed the Indians' past 'sins and idolatries'; his fellow-Franciscan Gerónimo de Mendieta ingeniously argued that the Indian hecatomb represented 'an otherworldly reward for the Indians and a thisworldly punishment for the Spanish laymen' – who lost their abundant supply of labour).[180] Perhaps in consequence – as the prudential imperatives of conversion waned – the Indians' initially eager embrace of Christianity weakened. Even when Indians attended Church (which they did under compulsion) they chatted

---

[177] Brading, *First America*, p. 106; Cervantes, *Devil in the New World*, pp. 45–6; on the context, Gibson, *Aztecs under Spanish Rule*, p. 117; Gruzinski, *Man-Gods*, pp. 33–4.

[178] On the origins of the Marian cult in Mexico: Brading, *First America*, ch. 16; Gruzinski, *Conquest of Mexico*, pp. 190–3; Taylor, *Magistrates of the Sacred*, pp. 282–3; and, the fullest account, Poole, *Our Lady of Guadalupe*. Poole justifiably questions the traditional association of the Virgin, Tonantzin and Tepeyac, and shows that the cult's diffusion was (a) slow rather than immediate and (b) initially associated with creoles rather than Indians. Over time, however, it flourished dramatically and extensively (other Marian apparitions, which were common enough, left no such legacy), and by the eighteenth century it certainly came to exercise a powerful appeal to popular – including Indian – groups. How far that appeal depended on a syncretic association of old and new divinities it is hard to say; certainly the evidence is not conclusive.

[179] Brading, *First America*, p. 361; Taylor, *Magistrates of the Sacred*, pp. 285–7.

[180] Lockhart and Otte, *Letters and People*, p. 239; Phelan, *Millennial Kingdom*, p. 94; Brading, *First America*, pp. 109–10.

and sidled out during services; friars and officials alike began to
lament the loss of the stern social discipline of the Aztecs.[181] They
lamented, too, the survival of idolatry, which, as the years went by,
could no longer be dismissed as a doomed vestige of the past. Rather,
churchmen became aware that the initial, euphoric spiritual conquest had been neither as pervasive nor as profound as the early
missionaries had hoped – or as some later historians, such as Ricard,
have suggested.[182]

With time, therefore, the exalted chiliasm of the early spiritual conquest inevitably dissolved. The world had not come to an end, no
Garden of Eden had been found. As the colonial economy developed,
too, the hermetic separation of Spaniard and Indian, which the friars had advocated, proved unattainable. The friars did not abandon
their struggle, but inexorable economic pressures made for increased
social intercourse, for Indian 'accculturation', hence for the erosion
of the initial ethnic barriers and the mendicant Utopia which they
circumvallated. In the ecclesiastical sphere, these trends were accompanied by the formation of the secular clergy – theoretical allies,
but practical rivals, of the regulars. The early mendicant monopoly
of the colonial church was now challenged (even though mendicant
numbers continued to rise).[183] Secular bishops and newly installed
parish priests laid claim to the diminished Indian flock, criticizing

181 Israel, *Race, Class, and Politics*, p. 14; Burkhart, *Slippery Earth*, p. 18; Phelan, *Millennial Kingdom*, p. 83; Brading, *First America*, pp. 121–2, on the decline of Indian morals, with which
Indian (elite) observers concurred: Alonso de Zorita, *The Lords of New Spain* (London, 1973),
pp. 120–52. By the mid–sixteenth century, when 'relations between friars and Indians came
everywhere to be marked by estrangement', there were already signs of an emerging gendered
response: 'Indian men were reported to be less concerned with church attendance than Indian
women' (Gibson, *Aztecs under Spanish Rule*, p. 111). Like plebeian drinking, the superior religiosity of women would become an enduring stereotype of Mexican cultural history, down
to the present. It might repay synthetic long–term analysis.
182 Klor de Alva, one of Ricard's most telling critics, offers a sophisticated typology of Aztec
reactions to Christianity, ranging from accommodation to conflict, and embracing several
combinations of overt compliance, partial conversion, active and passive resistance: 'Spiritual Conflict and Accommodation', pp. 351–2; Poole,'Some Observations', provides a simpler
matrix.
183 There were 800 mendicants in 1559, 1,500 in 1580 and 3,000 by 1650; the secular clergy,
who were outnumbered more than two-to-one by their mendicant counterparts in 1580, had
reached 2,000 by 1650: Gruzinski, *Conquest of Mexico*, pp. 146, 197; Schwaller, *Origins of
Church Wealth*, pp. 6–7. On the ratio of priests to people (which increased with demographic
decline), see Gibson, *Aztecs under Spanish Rule*, pp. 112–14, which also illustrates a key trend:
in the Valley of Mexico, there was a growing concentration of priests in Mexico City, and
relatively few in the Indian countryside: 'only about one cleric in seventy had anything to do
with Indians in the late colonial period'.

the political, religious and even architectural arrogance of the friars, as well as their supposed material cupidity.[184] As Mexican dynamics conspired with the grander global policy of Rome, signalled by the Council of Trent (1545–63), the seculars became spokesmen of the Spanish laity (whom the friars allegedly neglected) and, more generally, of the culturally and economically Hispanized sector of colonial society. The Crown encouraged this process: the Ordenanza del Patronato of 1574 set limits to the regular orders and subordinated them to episcopal authority – a clear victory for the secular clergy.[185] By the later sixteenth century, bitter conflicts and even pitched battles were fought between the regulars on the one side and the seculars and their lay allies on the other. The chief prize was control of the Indians. As for the Indians themselves, their opposition to the ouster of the friars was sometimes violent: when secular clergy were sent to one of the Indian barrios of Mexico City 'the entire Indian congregation rose up against them', hurling stones and demanding the return of the Franciscans, which they got.[186] But reactions varied. Around Puebla, for example, the Indians seemed indifferent to the battle being fought between the regulars and seculars for control of their souls; the ousted friars left Puebla without popular protest.[187]

The friars, too, were changing. Some, like Las Casas, had questioned the initial policy of mass conversions. Others tempered their millennial hopes or were supplanted by a second generation of regulars, products of the Counter-Reformation and of the established colony. The friars, whose simple poverty had won the praise of Cortés and – as late as 1550 – of Viceroy Velasco, increasingly acquired goods and land and thus approximated to the Spanish norm; by the seventeenth century there were complaints of friars riding in carriages, wearing 'beaver hats . . . and silken hose'.[188] Parish priests,

---

[184] Ricard, *Spiritual Conquest*, ch. 15; Brading, *First America*, pp. 114–15; Spores, *Mixtec Kings*, p. 87

[185] Schwaller, *Origins of Church Wealth*, pp. 161–6.

[186] Gibson, *Aztecs under Spanish Rule*, p. 110; on regular-secular conflict, see also Israel, *Race, Class, and Politics*, p. 47, and Schwaller, *Origins of Church Wealth*, pp. 99–101.

[187] Brading, *First America*, p. 236.

[188] Chevalier, *Land and Society*, pp. 232, 251; J. Eric S. Thompson, ed., *Thomas Gage's Travels in the New World* (Norman, Okla., 1985; first pubd. in this edition, 1958; first pubd. 1648), pp. 43–4, describes a friar in Jalapa 'riding . . . a goodly gelding . . . with his habit tucked up to his girdle, making shew of a fine silk orange-color stocking upon his legs and a neat Cordovan shoe upon his foot, with a fine holland pair of drawers, with a lace three inches broad at the knee'. Gage, a

too, now paid more attention to their flocks of sheep than to their parishioners; reports of clerical profiteering and peculation became commonplace.[189] Meanwhile, the friars' great educational drive petered out. Not for the last time in Mexican history, erstwhile idealists despaired of changing society by transforming men's minds. Society proved recalcitrant, and the wellsprings of idealism dried up. The Tlatelolco college failed (one of its most distinguished alumni, Don Carlos, perished at the stake for heresy); the archbishop of Mexico decided that it was impolitic for mere Indians to study Latin, rhetoric and philosophy; Sahagún's massive scholarly investigations of Indian life and history incurred official clerical displeasure and had to wait two centuries for publication.[190] The encouragement of Indian art and music was abandoned and the development of an Indian priesthood aborted.[191] By then, a 'violent, anti-native reaction' was evident, even among the formerly Indophile Franciscans, and the Indians reciprocated: by the seventeenth century the friars had become objects less of Indian veneration than of Indian indifference or even resentment.[192]

Such trends conspired with a more general decline in Indian social mobility, evident in the political as well as religious sphere. The social fluidity of the post-Conquest years gave way to glacial caste hierarchies; once mighty Indian nobles were reduced to poverty and impotence, their 'apparently wretched plight contrast[ing] with their magnificent names'.[193] Meanwhile, sniffing out Indian heresy became *de rigueur*. In this, however, the Indians were not the sole

British Catholic and friar, who lived and travelled extensively in Mexico and Guatemala in the 1620s and 1630s, is a well-informed but – in view of his later turn to Protestantism – a far from disinterested source; though compared to the editor of his memoirs, J. E. S. Thompson, he is a model of sober objectivity (see, for example, Thompson, 'Editor's Introduction', p. xvii, on the 'sanctimonious bigotry' of 1640s Puritanism, contrasted with 'the free–speaking tradition of Spain').

[189] Gruzinski, *Conquest of Mexico*, p. 147; Schwaller, *Origins of Church Wealth*, pp. 99–101; Gibson, *Aztecs under Spanish Rule*, pp. 123–4.

[190] Brading, *First America*, pp. 118–20; Gibson, *Aztecs under Spanish Rule*, pp. 382–3.

[191] Gruzinski, *Conquest of Mexico*, pp. 67, 251, 264, which notes, however, clandestine officiating by Indian 'priests' (cantors and sacristans) in the seventeenth century; and, by the mid-eighteenth, the existence of 'about 50 indigenous priests' in Mexico.

[192] Ricard, *Spiritual Conquest*, p. 35; Burkhart, *Slippery Earth*, p. 18, captures the shift in Franciscan attitudes towards the Indians who, previously seen as 'good but errant children', became 'subtle, conspiratorial, stubborn (and) intractably carnal'.

[193] Chevalier, *Land and Society*, p. 213; Farriss, *Maya Society*, pp. 99–100.

or even the principal victims. As the Inquisition's role in colonial life grew, Indians suffered less than did Spaniards and mestizos (in 1571 Indians were formally exempted from the attentions of the Holy Office, on grounds of their 'rude character and incapacity'; women, too, being of weaker moral fibre, were indulged by the tribunal of the Holy Office).[194] In Mexico as in Spain, it was moriscos (converted Moslems), conversos (converted Jews) and Erasmians – groups whose participation in colonization had been more readily tolerated in the optimistic and cosmopolitan climate of Charles V's reign – whom the Inquisition chiefly targeted, and who were now rooted out and persecuted.[195] For now a different climate prevailed: a harsh, post-Tridentine authoritarianism came to prevail; the virtues of 'ceremony and conformity' were paramount; Europe's paranoid fear of diabolism began to infiltrate the colony.[196] In 1555 strict censorship was established in New Spain; in 1571 the Jesuits, the shock troops of the Counter-Reformation, arrived in the colony.[197] The century of the Conquest thus concluded with heresy-hunting and baroque scholasticism dominating Mexican high culture.[198] Cultural change mirrored changes in colonial personnel – as well as shifts in European thought. As the conquistador elite and their *encomiendas*, products of the heroic early colony, faded into history, so, too, did

[194] Brading, *First America*, p. 222; Solange Alberro, *Inquisición y sociedad en México, 1571–1700* (Mexico, 1988), pp. 22, 73, 218, 581.

[195] Richard E. Greenleaf, *The Mexican Inquisition of the Sixteenth Century* (Albuquerque, 1969), pp. 19–20, 27, 34, 48, 53; Alberro, *Inquisición y sociedad*, p. 148. The latter offers a scholarly corrective to the *leyenda negra* of the Holy Office, discounting its sanguinary repression and stressing its legalism, lack of resources, nepotism and corruption; MacLachlan and Rodríguez O., *Forging of the Cosmic Race*, p. 135, tend to agree. In part because the Inquisition lacked the money to mount them, *autos da fe* were rare spectacles (only 56 were held in the 125 years between 1574 and 1699: Alberro, *Inquisición y sociedad*, pp. 77–8); nevertheless, some were grandiose 'baroque fiestas', in which the crowd – 30,000 at the *auto da fe* of 11 April 1649 – could experience 'the rare satisfaction of relishing the dishonour of some of the principal personalities of the Viceroyalty' who, wont to travel in fine carriages, now rode, half-naked, on mules, towards the flames (pp. 581–2). See also n. 699 below.

[196] Liss, *Mexico under Spain*, pp. 93, 100–1; Cervantes, *Devil in the New World*, pp. 19–20. Alberro, *Inquisición y sociedad*, persuasively links cycles of inquisitional activity to political events (e.g., the union of the Spanish and Portuguese Crowns in 1580, which aggravated Spanish fears of crypto-Jews penetrating the colonies: pp. 148, 153); however, the supposed correlation between inquisitional activity and silver production, p. 211, seems less convincing.

[197] Brading, *First America*, pp. 167, 171, 176–9.

[198] Irving Leonard, *Baroque Times in Old Mexico: Seventeenth-Century Persons, Places, and Practices* (Ann Arbor, 1966), pp. 22–7; see also MacLachlan and Rodríguez O., *Forging of the Cosmic Race*, p. 140.

their most effective early collaborators and critics – the mendicants and their missions. Conquistador and friar, *encomienda* and convent, were shouldered aside – though not entirely displaced – by bureaucrat and *hacendado*, by bishop, *cura* and Jesuit.

III. Political Conquest

If, in the economic sphere, this transition was typified by the rise of the hacienda, in the political realm it meant the assertion of royal control over the centrifugal tendencies of early Spanish colonialism. This assertion was almost coeval with the Conquest itself, and it was closely bound up with the process and politics of religious conversion; mendicants like Zumárraga 'assumed that royal and religious purposes were identical and this threw their considerable weight behind the Crown and its lay officials'.[199] An assertion of royal power was required since the Conquest – by virtue of its chaotic, decentralized, free enterprise character – had conferred ample *de facto* power on the conquistadors, now *encomenderos* and, in some exalted cases, governors of provinces;[200] and this power provoked justifiable royal fears of a fractious transatlantic feudalism. In addition, the Crown sought to maximize returns from the new colony, as well as to live up to its proclaimed legal, political and religious responsibilities. The Habsburgs did not intend to let the broad expanse of the Atlantic render them *rois fainéants*. In its bid for control, however, the Crown was constantly inhibited by financial contraints, which in turn encouraged further reliance on Spanish private enterprise and a renewed delegation of authority. Colonial history was therefore marked by a constant tussle – usually covert, sometimes threateningly overt – between the Crown and its over-mighty colonial subjects. But, although the Crown made necessary retreats and concessions, the inexorable trend was towards greater royal control made possible by the 'astonishingly rapid' growth during the sixteenth century of colonial bureaucracy, in which priests served alongside the ubiquitous Spanish

[199] Liss, *Mexico under Spain*, p. 83.
[200] J. H. Elliott, 'Spain and America in the Sixteenth and Seventeenth Centuries', in Leslie Bethell, ed., *Cambridge History of Latin America*, vol. 1, *Colonial Latin America* (Cambridge, 1984), pp. 292–3.

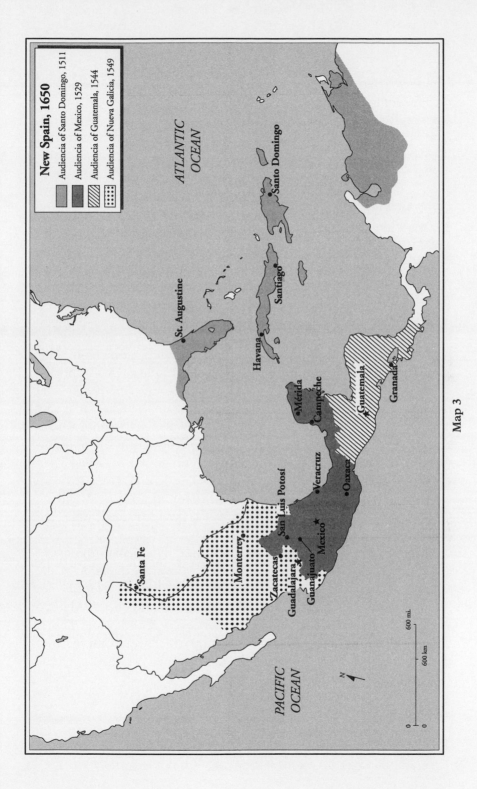

New Spain, 1650

Audiencia of Santo Domingo, 1511
Audiencia of Mexico, 1529
Audiencia of Guatemala, 1544
Audiencia of Nueva Galicia, 1549

ATLANTIC OCEAN

Santo Domingo

Santiago

St. Augustine

Havana

Mérida
Campeche
Guatemala
Granada

Veracruz
Oaxaca

Santa Fe

Monterrey
San Luis Potosí
Zacatecas
Guadalajara
Guanajuato
Mexico

PACIFIC OCEAN

N

600 mi.

600 km

Map 3

lawyers.[201] Here, the Crown's control of ecclesiastical appointments – the Patronato Real, transferred from Spain to the New World, proved a potent weapon.[202] The clerical and forensic agents of royal centralization, recently and successfully active in the peninsula, now turned their attention to the distant colony.

The first step towards the consolidation of colonial government came with the creation of the First Audiencia, a royal court whose authority went beyond the strictly judicial. During its brief life (1528–30) the First Audiencia successfully countered the power of Cortés and his clients; but it remained a creature of the conquistadors – notably, of its first president, Nuño de Guzmán – hence it reflected conquistador factionalism more than it furthered royal power. The Second Audiencia (1530–35), however, was made up of more statesmanlike and legalistic figures, like Bishop Vasco de Quiroga, who loyally executed royal policy, encouraging the missionary efforts of the friars and striving to protect the Crown's Indian subjects from their predatory Spanish masters. The *oidores* – Audiencia judges – whittled away at conquistador and *encomendero* power; they appointed local officials – *corregidores* – who had already proved to be useful agents of centralization in Spain, and who now performed a similar role in New Spain. European precedent was also followed in the appointment of a viceroy (since the thirteenth century, viceroys had been entrusted with the overseas provinces of Aragon's Mediterranean empire). The first two viceroys of New Spain, Antonio de Mendoza (1535–50) and Luis de Velasco (1550–64), were dogged, able and diplomatic in their furtherance of the Crown's interests. They weathered Indian rebellion in the early 1540s and conquistador conspiracy in the 1560s. They encouraged the northward expansion of the colony and asserted royal control over the Indian population, not least by a judicious display of viceregal paternalism: Luis de Velasco received delegations of Indian petitioners every Monday and Thursday morning, thus inaugurating a tradition which would survive into the twentieth century.[203] Above all, the viceroys presided over the

---

[201] Israel, *Race, Class, and Politics*, p. 5.

[202] N. M. Farriss, *Crown and Clergy in Colonial Mexico, 1759–1821: The Crisis of Ecclesiastical Privilege* (London, 1968), pp. 6–7.

[203] Elliott, 'Spain and America in the Sixteenth and Seventeenth Centuries', pp. 294–8; on viceregal paternalism, see Woodrow Borah, *Justice by Insurance: The General Indian Court of Colonial Mexico and the Legal Aides of the Half-Real* (Berkeley, 1983), pp. 65–6, 84–109.

creation of a complex and durable administrative structure, which linked the Crown and the royal Council of the Indies to the viceroy and Audiencia, who in turn governed through local officials, *corregidores* and *alcaldes mayores* (the two being largely indistinguishable). The latter represented the Crown on town councils (*ayuntamientos* or *cabildos*), which, following an old and vigorous Iberian urban tradition, enjoyed extensive powers of local government, involving self-defence, policing, provisioning, market regulation and public health. Increasingly monopolized by small, rich, self-recruiting oligarchies (initially conquistadors and *encomenderos*, later landlords and merchants), the town councils embodied no more than vague notions of democracy and representation, which were occasionally and fitfully stirred into life by the Crown's fiscal demands.[204]

As the colonial frontier advanced, new provinces were incorporated into this administrative framework: Nueva Vizcaya, 1562; Nuevo León, 1579; New Mexico, 1598. The viceroyalty of New Spain thus became a skein of disparate provinces, ultimately stretching from Central America in the south to Florida, New Mexico and California in the north, and even embracing the distant Philippines. Its political and demographic heart, however, was located in Central Mexico, which was governed directly by the viceroy and the Mexico City Audiencia; outlying provinces such as New Galicia acquired their own Audiencias, whose members – legally trained career officials – kept a close watch on their provinces, cementing royal control while, at the same time, channelling the grievances and wishes of the province – usually of the provincial elite – back to the metropolis. The Crown was at pains to enforce its will, even across the expanse of the Atlantic. Periodically, special 'visitors' – hand-picked royal officials – were despatched from Spain to observe the machinery of colonial government first-hand: to detect and eliminate faults, to punish offenders and to report back to the Council of the Indies.[205] Outgoing

[204] Gerhard, *Guide to the Historical Geography of New Spain*, pp. 10–14, and MacLachlan and Rodríguez O., *Forging of the Cosmic Race*, pp. 101–12, offer good summaries of Spanish administrative structures in Mexico; on the *cabildos*, see Elliott, 'Spain and America in the Sixteenth and Seventeenth Centuries', pp. 298–9; and, for more detailed analysis of Puebla, José F. de la Peña, *Oligarquía y propiedad en Nueva España (1550–1624)* (Mexico, 1983), pp. 162–71, and Guy P. C. Thomson, *Puebla de los Angeles: Industry and Society in a Mexican City, 1700–1850* (Boulder, 1989), pp. 190–1.

[205] Parry, *The Audiencia of New Galicia*; Liss, *Mexico under Spain*, p. 130; Israel, *Race, Class, and Politics*, p. 19.

viceroys, too, were subjected to a careful review of their steward-ships. Such mechanisms could not guarantee efficiency. But then, large pre-industrial empires, beset by insuperable logistical prob-lems, were never noted for their efficiency.[206] Habsburg colonial ad-ministration was, as the familiar stereotype suggests, a creaking, cumbersome engine, which consumed quantities of paper, energy, legal casuistry and 'illegal' cash payments.[207] Indeed, the lubricant of 'corruption' – bribes and the sale of offices – was essential if the ma-chine was not to seize up for want of officially dispensed remunera-tion; 'corruption' was, in this sense, integral to the system rather than a deviation from the norm. Much like traders in today's commodity markets, speculators bought future office; paying for office was seen, in fact, as a sign of 'taking it seriously', of ensuring that 'the best men', those with a genuine stake in the community, should come to occupy positions of command.[208] Despite its deviations from Weberian-style bureaucracy, the machine endured, and it worked. Gradually, the triple alliance of royal official, friar and Indian *cacique* was able to confront, contain and roll back the frontiers of conquistador power.

But not without a fight. On the economic front, we have seen, the *encomienda* declined in importance; Indian slavery was curtailed (though it lingered on the northern frontier); Indian labour tribute was abolished. Protection of the Indian thus legitimized royal con-striction of conquistador power.[209] As the Crown came to monopolize tribute payment, so the tributary system became an important vehi-cle for the extension of royal power into the provinces.[210] Politically,

---

[206] Anthony Giddens, *The Nation-State and Violence* (Berkeley, 1987), pp. 3–4, 38–9; Michael Mann, *The Sources of Social Power*, vol. 1, *A History of Power from the Beginning to A.D. 1760* (Cambridge, 1986), pp. 141–5ff.

[207] Paper was certainly expensive and in short supply: Lockhart and Otte, *Letters and People*, p. 199; Cheryl English Martin, *Governance and Society in Colonial Mexico: Chihuahua in the Eighteenth Century* (Stanford, 1996), p. 81. This is not surprising when one discovers that a single *visita* – a one-off investigation of a viceroy's stewardship – could consume 49,555 sheets of paper: Elliott, 'Spain and America in the Sixteenth and Seventeenth Centuries', p. 303. On corruption: Borah, *Justice by Insurance*, pp. 282–6; Rebecca Horn, *Postconquest Coyoacán: Nahua-Spanish Relations in Central Mexico, 1519–1650* (Stanford, 1997), pp. 73–4; Chance, *Conquest of the Sierra*, p. 103.

[208] Patch, *Maya and Spaniard*, pp. 127–8; Martin, *Governance and Society*, p. 88, which also notes how (in the early eighteenth century) municipal posts were not only sold, but openly adver-tised: 'vacancies were advertised first in Guadalajara and then in San Felipe (Chihuhuahua), and candidates were invited to submit their bids'.

[209] Borah, *Justice by Insurance*, pp. 20–1, 123.

[210] Liss, *Mexico under Spain*, p. 130.

too, as the *corregidor* system was extended throughout the country, royal authority penetrated and dissolved the private fiefs of the early *encomenderos*. The *encomenderos* grumbled and even flirted with rebellion; in the 1560s a desperate cabal conspired to make Martín Cortés, son of the Great Captain, king of an independent Mexico. They planned 'to make a great fire in the plaza of all the papers and writings that were in the archives and offices so that there should remain no written memory of the name of the King of Castile'.[211] But the plotters were betrayed, their ringleaders were executed, and Martín Cortés was exiled. The dour King Philip II, who liked paperwork almost as much as he disliked rebellion, sent Alonso de Muñoz to tighten the screws on New Spain's dissident aristocracy, which he did with considerable zeal.[212] By the end of the century, with *encomienda* income fast declining in relation to other sources of colonial profit, the *encomendero* class was also politically subdued, 'well and truly cowed' by royal officialdom.[213] The 'old elite of conquest' had failed to establish a true aristocracy and had, indeed, dwindled to 'a small and largely impoverished group'.[214]

Royal officialdom was – along with the new mining and merchant elites – the chief beneficiary of colonial consolidation. In the great territorial hand-out which created the haciendas of New Spain, officials were prominent, both giving and receiving. *Oidores*, *corregidores* and *alcaldes mayores* all amassed property, thanks in part to their official positions. Hopes that *oidores* would serve as disinterested 'Platonic guardians, judging and governing without the distraction of local ties and pressures', proved illusory.[215] Officials enjoyed further advantages through their control of labour (both *repartimiento* Indians and coerced criminal labour), through their regulation of trade and their involvement in the collection and sale of tribute-in-kind. Thus,

---

[211] Anthony Pagden, 'Identity Formation in Spanish America', in Nicholas Canny and Anthony Pagden, eds., *Colonial Identity in the Atlantic World, 1500–1800* (Princeton, 1987), p. 55.

[212] MacLachlan and Rodríguez O., *Forging of the Cosmic Race*, pp. 100–1, refer to a royal 'reign of terror'.

[213] Israel, *Race, Class, and Politics*, p. 16. Doris M. Ladd, *The Mexican Nobility at Independence, 1780–1826* (Austin, 1976), pp. 14–15, notes that only three noble titles survived from 'the epic phase of the sixteenth century'; and one of these – the Condes de Moctezuma – belonged to descendants of the Aztec emperor.

[214] Brading, *First America*, pp. 2–3, 53–4.

[215] Elliott, 'Spain and America in the Sixteenth and Seventeenth Centuries', p. 297.

'a royal official in the capital could expect a regular, preferential
and inexpensive supply of necessary goods – a canoe load of fod-
der each day, two loads of firewood per week, and food and service
to supply his needs'.[216] By the seventeenth century, royal officials
had also established a profitable business through the forced sale of
Spanish goods to the Indians (the *repartimiento de comercio*: a system which combined elements of tax farming, fiscal exaction and the
subsidy of Spanish commercial interests). Official profiteering now
outstripped official paternalism, especially at the local level, guaranteeing a stream of abuses and protests.[217]

In consequence, the local oligarchies which sprang up throughout
the colony contained a powerful official element, while the Audiencias became nests of nepotism. In one (extreme) case, a sixteen-year-
old, son of the Audiencia president, held five *corregimientos* in New
Galicia – while still a student in Mexico City.[218] Positions on town
councils, too, were put up for sale, so that by the seventeenth century most had become narrow, self-perpetuating and even hereditary
institutions. The phenomenon of the irremovable *alcalde* (mayor)
emerged.[219] Both Spaniards and creoles collected the political spoils;
castes were excluded; and Indian officialdom was confined to the
república de indios, where (theoretically) elected governors were responsible for maintaining law and order and for collecting tribute.
Indian officials, too, succumbed to the temptations of office, but for
them the rewards were less, the risks greater. Jammed between colonial government and colonial governed, they faced reprisals from
above if they failed in their duties (if, for example, they fell short
on tribute collection) and protests from below if they displayed

[216] Gibson, *Aztecs under Spanish Rule*, p. 231. See also Chevalier, *Land and Society*, pp. 161–4,
180.
[217] Israel, *Race, Class, and Politics*, pp. 34–5; Gibson, *Aztecs Under Spanish Rule*, pp. 94–6, which
reports the forced sale to Indians of cows, mules, liquor, silk stockings and wax candles
(especially for All Souls Day – the Day of the Dead – on 1 November). An alternative *repar-
timento* involved the forced purchase of Indian goods, especialy textiles, which flourished
in Yucatán and Oaxaca: Patch, *Maya and Spaniard*, pp. 83–91; Brian Hamnett, *Politics and
Trade in Southern Mexico, 1750–1821* (Cambridge, 1971), pp. 13–14. For complaints against
officials, see Borah, *Justice by Insurance*, pp. 86, 148–61. Contrasting interpretations of the
repartimiento are cited in n. 584 below.
[218] Chevalier, *Land and Society*, p. 164. The Inquisition, too, was steeped in nepotism: Alberro,
Inquisición y sociedad, p. 65.
[219] Martin, *Governance and Society*, p. 93.

excessive administrative zeal (for, we will see, the Indians had some sanctions at their disposal). By the mid-seventeenth century, the bishop of Puebla noted, 'few Indians now aspire to be gobernador or alcalde'.[220]

In government, as in so many areas of colonial life, theory and practice sharply differed. The Crown willed a different outcome – bans on official profiteering and property acquisition came thick and fast – but it did not provide the material means to achieve it. On the contrary, the poverty of official salaries encouraged peculation and profitable side-lines; in addition, from the late sixteenth century, the Spanish Crown – like most of its European counterparts – resorted to the profligate sale of offices to bolster its shaky finances.[221] The rot set in at the top: under Charles II (1665–1700), a nine-year-old inherited a seat on the Council of the Indies.[222]

Meanwhile, in the colony itself, money bought office and office made money. In the north, where the Crown perforce repeated its earlier policy of conferring broad administrative powers and generous material grants upon those who performed the spadework of colonization, the result was a regime of landed oligarchs (a few of them genuine aristocrats, for the sale of office was, especially in the later seventeenth century, seconded by the sale of titles, albeit on a more modest scale).[223] Such oligarchs combined landed, mercantile and sometimes mining wealth with extensive political powers, some the *de jure* result of royal appointments, some the *de facto* consequences of pioneer colonization. Thus, even as the Crown clawed back political power in central Mexico, it partially surrendered it in the north, allowing the creation of oligarchic establishments, centred on the new mines and latifundia. A second generation of go-getting adventurers, notably the Basque pioneers of colonization in Zacatecas and Durango, the Ibarras and Oñates, now amassed large estates, political powers, commercial interests and quasi-feudal clienteles (it is this

[220] Gibson, *Aztecs under Spanish Rule*, p. 193.

[221] On salaries: Gibson, *Aztecs under Spanish Rule*, p. 95; Hamnett, *Politics and Trade*, p. 5. On sale of offices: Israel, *Race, Class, and Politics*, p. 35; Chevalier, *Land and Society*, pp. 34, 126; Borah, *Justice by Insurance*, pp. 270–1.

[222] MacLachlan and Rodríguez O., *Forging of the Cosmic Race*, pp. 142–3.

[223] Chevalier, *Land and Society*, ch. 5, remains the classic study. On the sale of noble titles, which accelerated in the eighteenth century, see Ladd, *Mexican Nobility*, pp. 15–17.

mix of interests which leads Chevalier, in his seminal work, to qualify these northern magnates as both capitalists and feudal seigneurs;
we will address this problem of categorization later).[224]

From the Crown's point of view, however, the game was well worth
the candle. Without delegation and decentralization of power –
which in some cases verged on outright local autonomy[225] – there
could be no colonization, certainly not colonization on the cheap;
hence there could be no further mining bonanzas, no fiscal returns
to the Crown and no secure northern frontiers. Spanish colonization
could never proceed as a simple, state-run exercise. Like the initial
Conquest, colonization was a blend of dynamic private initiative and
loose public control. So long as the new conquistadors of the north
remained broadly loyal (which, after the lesson of the 1560s, they
did), so long as they governed in the name of the king and made
possible the annual shipment of Mexican bullion, their patrimonial
status could be tolerated. Initially lavish grants of authority could
be gradually, patiently, recovered (recall the progressive derogation
of *encomendero* privileges). For, above all, the Crown had time on
its side. Habsburg administration ground slowly, but it ground ex-
ceeding small. Legal cases and administrative disputes could drag
on for years (sometimes with innocent victims languishing in foetid
gaols),[226] but they were ultimately attended to – during Philip II's
long reign, by the painstaking workaholic king himself, cloistered
in his gloomy, paper-strewn study in the Escorial. Royal commands
might be flouted for a time, but, by dint of administrative tenacity,
and by virtue of the pervasive legalism of Hispanic society, the royal
will eventually prevailed over egregious offenders. Even those who
offended against lowly Indians could be hauled before the *juzgado de*

---

[224] Chevalier refers to the 'big capitalists' of the north, who were 'something like powerful feudal
lords', endowed with 'feudal habits': *Land and Society*, pp. 150, 158, 163.

[225] Chevalier, *Land and Society*, pp. 156–7. In remote New Mexico 'many a governor imposed his
will as law, silencing opposition by prohibiting travel and censoring mail': Gutiérrez, *When
Jesus Came*, p. 100; see also Andrew L. Knaut, *The Pueblo Revolt of 1680* (Norman, Okla.,
1995), pp. 89, 95.

[226] Farriss, *Crown and Clergy*, p. 49, recounts the (eighteenth-century) case of an innocent friar,
deported from Mexico and thrown into gaol in Cádiz, where he languished for ten years
because of delayed paperwork. The representative of the Inquisition in Yucatán in the 1620s
complained that correspondence with Mexico City could take four years or more: Alberro,
Inquisición y sociedad, pp. 23–4 (see also p. 224 on gaol conditions). On judicial delay and
backlogs: Borah, *Justice by Insurance*, pp. 229, 286.

indios, established in the 1590s to hear complaints against corrupt or oppressive officials – which, since it was no mere cypher, it did to some good effect.[227]

As a result, no major or concerted challenge to the Crown emerged during two hundred years of Habsburg colonial rule. Despite – or, perhaps, because of – its creaking inefficiency, the Habsburg regime enjoyed a definite legitimacy. No insurgent aristocratic *fronde* challenged the Crown, no mass rebellion shook the colony. Revolts – we will note – were sporadic; more important, rebels habitually rebelled in the name of the Crown, uttering the familiar slogan of 'naive monarchism': 'long live the King and death to bad government'.[228] Of course, ample abuses could be perpetrated and dissimulated – hence the constant reiteration of royal measures against official corruption, clerical interference in secular affairs and the enslavement and exploitation of Indians. Royal officials took refuge in the famous motto of colonial government: *obedezco pero no cumplo* ('I obey but do not carry out'). So, too, did bishops.[229] A display of formal obedience could mask a multitude of sins, and the gulf between administrative theory and practice often gaped, in colonial as in modern Mexico. But while individual and even family interests were subject to biological and economic vicissitudes, the Crown – and its frequent, though sometimes fickle ally, the Church – were virtually immortal institutions, which could take the long view. The early *encomenderos* were brought to heel; the powerful oligarchs of the north served royal interests even as they served their own; royal officialdom triumphed over an emergent aristocracy. The result was two centuries of comparative stability, premised on a degree of genuine political legitimacy. But by the eighteenth century things began to change: as new

---

[227] Borah, *Justice by Insurance*, p. 108ff.

[228] Cope, *Limits of Racial Domination*, pp. 142, 146. On 'naive monarchism', see Eric Van Young, 'Quetzalcóatl, King Ferdinand and Ignacio Allende Go to the Seashore; or Messianism and Mystical Kingship in Mexico, 1800–1821', in Jaime Rodríguez O., ed., *The Independence of Mexico and the Creation of the New Nation* (Los Angeles, 1989), pp. 111–12, which, like a good deal of the new social history, owes a debt to E. J. Hobsbawm's seminal *Primitive Rebels* (Manchester, 1974; first pubd. 1959), pp. 112, 117–21. For a skeptical critique, see James Scott, *Domination and the Arts of Resistance: Hidden Transcripts* (New Haven, 1990), pp. 96–103.

[229] Elliott, 'Spain and America in the Sixteenth and Seventeenth Centuries', p. 303; Farriss, *Crown and Clergy*, p. 56. Viceroy Velasco, writing to the king in 1595, complained of 'the difficulty that attends all affairs in the Indies: that is, slackness in execution': Borah, *Justice by Insurance*, pp. 109–10.

sources of income burgeoned, office-holding no longer offered the road to riches it once had; wealth and office began to diverge; town councils had to press reluctant citizens into service. In this changing climate, the Crown emerged from its musty Habsburg chrysallis and took flight in its new, more flamboyant, Bourbon form. The metropolis now imposed a more thorough, greedy and centralized regime upon its neglected colony. Private, patrimonial appropriation of the colony's wealth gave way to official, bureaucratic appropriation – at least in theory, to a lesser extent in practice. The spoils of this long, Fabian campaign of royal centralization now began to flow, in unprecedented volume, from colony to metropolis, Mexico to Madrid.

IV. The 'Conquest' of the North

We will resume the story of eighteenth-century Bourbon policy later. For the moment, we must return to the century of the Conquest. The late sixteenth-century sale of offices coincided, ironically, with a boom in transatlantic trade and colonial revenue, associated with new mining discoveries. The quest for bullion had been coeval with the Conquest. But the accumulated bullion of centuries had soon been pillaged and the initial mining strikes had disappointed. Shipments of bullion to Spain fell off after a brief peak in the 1520s. Subsequent modest strikes – in Guerrero, Oaxaca and Jalisco – kept hopes alive through the 1530s and 1540s, but they far from satisfied expectations. At mid-century, however, the discovery and rapid exploitation of Zacatecas's silver deposits dramatically changed the geopolitical profile of the colony. Hitherto, Spanish rule and settlement correlated, often very precisely, with Mesoamerican populations and political centres: in the old Aztec heartland, the Aztec dominions to the south, and, to the west, the Tarascan and Cascan confederations (the latter recently subdued in the Mixtón War). To the northwest, the Santiago River remained the rough boundary of Spanish rule, as it had of Toltec and Aztec power; to the north, Querétaro, founded in 1531, stood as a frontier post, guarding the route from Mexico City to the precariously held settlements and missions of the Bajío.[230]

---

[230] Van Young, *Hacienda and Market*, pp. 15–16, 19; John C. Super, *La vida en Querétaro durante la Colonia, 1531–1810* (Mexico, 1983), pp. 11–13.

Beyond this line lay the Gran Chichimec, where the Spanish presence was limited to occasional expeditions mounted by would-be
conquistadors or intrepid friars, who penetrated the sierras of Sichú
and Mextitlán. The first viceroy, however, chastened by the Mixtón
War and drawn by that familiar viceregal mirage, the secure frontier
(which was as seductive in Mexico as in British India), was keen to
push further; hence, through the 1540s he licensed several *entradas*,
whose leaders were sufficiently attracted by the certainty of land and
the possibility of bullion to venture north, where they were supposed
to confer with and convert the fierce Chichimec Indians.[231] Gradual
probes gave way to full-scale advance after 1546, with the discovery –
by a typical expedition of Spanish troops, friars and Indian auxiliaries – of major silver deposits at Zacatecas, in the territory of the
Zacateco Indians. The town of Zacatecas was founded, and, after a
precarious start – while its inhabitants lived in constant fear of Indian
attack – migrants flowed in, population rose and a secure, defensible community was established. The new amalgamation method of
smelting silver, introduced in the 1550s, boosted production, and by
the end of the century Zacatecas rivalled Puebla as the second city
of New Spain.[232]

The discovery of silver, principally at Zacatecas but also at other
northern sites (Sombrerete, Mazapil, Parral), as well as at Pachuca
and Guanajuato further south, had decisive effects on the development of the colony. A handful of miners and merchants amassed
fabulous fortunes, parlaying their mineral and mercantile wealth
into landed property.[233] The Crown, as recipient of the *quinto* – the
royal fifth – had a direct interest in encouraging and regulating mining production, and the annual flow of bullion, mediated through
the famous *flota* system of regular transatlantic sailings, tightened
the colonial nexus and sustained the grandiose foreign policy of

---

[231] 'Chichimec' (literally, 'sons of dogs' – or, presumably, 'sonsofbitches'?) is a loose, portmanteau,
(obviously) pejorative term, used by contemporaries – both Spaniards and Aztecs – to denote
a wide range of ethnic groups, some nomadic, all stateless, who occupied the vast expanses of
northern Mexico (the Gran Chichimeca) and were, in Cortés's words, 'very barbarous people
and not so intelligent': see Charlotte M. Gradie, 'Discovering the Chichimecs', *The Americas*,
51/1 (1994), pp. 67–88.

[232] Powell, *Soldiers, Indians and Silver*, pp. 4–10; on the amalgamation method: Pierre Vilar, *A
History of Gold and Money* (London, 1984), pp. 117–18; Bakewell, *Silver Mining*, pp. 130, 138,
140–4.

[233] Brading, *Miners and Merchants*, p. 13.

the Habsburgs.[234] Spanish merchants, too, took their cut: altogether, perhaps 80 per cent of New Spain's burgeoning bullion production found its way to the metropolis. But, if silver reinforced colonial dependency, both political and economic, it also served as a powerful stimulus to the internal development and economic integration of the colony. Zacatecas and the other principal mines were no mere enclaves, or peninsular appendages. They demanded goods and labour from the populous regions of central Mexico; they remitted bullion which, if its ultimate destination was Europe (and Asia),[235] nevertheless massaged colonial trade and production en route and somewhat eased the shortage of capital from which the colony chronically suffered.[236] The grand Zacatecas–Mexico axis thus represented, writ large, the symbiotic relations which linked lesser mining centres to their commercial partners (e.g., Sichú and Querétaro) or to their agricultural suppliers (e.g., Pachuca and the Hueyapán Valley).[237]

The new northern mines were established in a region where sedentary Indian communities were fewer, and chiefdoms rather than states prevailed. Spanish state-building had to start *de novo*. The process involved military forays, slave raids and depredations, unredeemed by any official paternalism; the Indians – dispersed, sometimes nomadic, and accustomed to local warfare – strenuously resisted. Given that no local labour supply could be tapped (Chichimec prisoners proved refractory), workers had to be brought up from the south. Initially, during the 1550s, this meant coercion, as slaves,

[234] As early as 1520, Mexican bullion – the first fruits of conquistador looting – had found its way into the pockets of the viceroy of Majorca and the bey of Tunis: Thomas, *Conquest of Mexico*, p. 353. Fernand Braudel, *The Mediterranean and the Mediterranean World in the Age of Philip II* (London, 1972), vol. 1, p. 479, maps the disbursement of Spanish 'political silver' c. 1600. Good overviews of Spain's transatlantic system are provided by Murdo J. MacLeod, 'Spain and America: The Atlantic Trade, 1492–1720', in Leslie Bethell, ed., *Cambridge History of Latin America*, vol. 1, *Colonial Latin America* (Cambridge, 1984) (see pp. 364–70), and Carla Rahn Phillips, 'The Growth and Composition of Trade in the Iberian Empires, 1450–1750', in James D. Tracey, ed., *The Rise of the Merchant Empires* (Cambridge, 1990), pp. 74–100.

[235] Mexican silver, shipped on the Manila galleon in exchange for silk and porcelain, came to play an important role in Asian commerce: Fernand Braudel, *Civilization and Capitalism, Fifteenth-Eighteenth Centuries*, vol. 3, *The Perspective of the World* (London, 1985), pp. 217, 491; Vilar, *History of Gold and Money*, pp. 202–3.

[236] On the colony's shortage of coin: Cope, *Limits of Racial Domination*, p. 109; Martin, *Governance and Society*, p. 71; Chevalier, *Land and Society*, p. 276; Semo, *History of Capitalism*, p. 89.

[237] John C. Super, 'The Agricultural Near North: Querétaro in the Seventeenth Century', in Altman and Lockhart, *Provinces of Early Mexico*, pp. 234–5; Edith Boorstein Couturier, *La hacienda de Hueyapán, 1550–1936* (Mexico, 1976), pp. 35–7.

black and Indian, met the miners' demand.[238] By the 1560s, however, workers were being lured north by cash incentives and by the promise of freedom from tribute payments and personal service. Almost from the beginning, therefore, the northern Mexican mining sector differed from its Peruvian counterpart, where the coercive *mita* delivered labour drafts on a rotating basis. (In central Mexico, too, forced labour continued, with the *repartimiento* system supplying the needs of the mines of Taxco and Pachuca; as late as 1756 the labour draft for the Pachuca mines provoked a serious revolt in the Actopan region of present-day Hidalgo.)[239] Whatever the causes of this significant divergence, the labour system of the northern mines set a pattern – of cash incentives and broadly free wage labour – which the north would more generally follow.[240] Furthermore, although the northern colonizers, with Franciscans and Jesuits in the van, also used promises of land and privileges to lure Indian migrants from the south in sufficient numbers to create new sedentary communities – of Tlaxcalans, for example, in the Saltillo region, or of Otomíes in the Bajío – these could never achieve a density of population comparable to that of central Mexico.[241]

Thus, while the human geography of Mesoamerica determined the pattern of Spanish settlement and urbanization in Central Mexico, often very precisely,[242] from the Bajío north the demographic

---

[238] About 15% of the early mining labour force were slaves: Brading, *Miners and Merchants*, pp. 7–8.

[239] Peter Bakewell, 'Mining in Colonial Spanish America', in Leslie Bethell, ed., *Cambridge History of Latin America*, vol. 2, *Colonial Latin America* (Cambridge, 1984), pp. 123–9; Brading and Cross, 'Colonial Silver Mining', pp. 557–9; Ignacio del Río, 'Sobre la aparición y desarrollo del trabajo libre asalariado en el norte de Nueva España (siglos XVI y XVII)', in Frost *et al.*, eds., *El trabajo y los trabajadores*, pp. 92–114, is a valuable analysis, which notes, p. 113, the contrast with central Mexico, which experienced 'a long-term though far slower movement in the direction of permanent paid labour'. On central Mexican coercion of mine workers, see García Martínez, *Pueblos de la sierra*, pp. 252–4; Brading, *Miners and Merchants*, p. 8; Gibson, *Aztecs under Spanish Rule*, p. 230; Taylor, *Drinking, Homicide and Rebellion*, pp. 124–5; and Robert S. Haskett, '"Our Suffering with the Taxco Tribute": Involuntary Mine Labor and Indigenous Society in Central Mexico', *Hispanic American Historical Review*, 71/3 (1991), pp. 447–76.

[240] Del Río, 'La aparición'; Lockhart, 'Introduction', p. 22; Martin, *Governance and Society*, pp. 47–9.

[241] Chevalier, *Land and Society*, pp. 218–19; John Tutino, *From Insurrection to Revolution in Mexico: Social Bases of Agrarian Violence, 1750–1940* (Princeton, 1986), pp. 50, 53; Gibson, *Tlaxcala*, pp. 185–9.

[242] On the post-1519 continuity of the Precolumbian altepetl: Horn, *Postconquest Coyoacán*, ch. 1; Lockhart, *The Nahuas*, pp. 28–30, 47–8, 55; and the same author's *Nahuas and Spaniards:*

determinants were reversed: colonization was patterned primarily by the hazards of mining and – with exceptions, like the Yaquis, which will be discussed later – Indian settlement followed this emerging pattern. Northern colonial society was thus created from scratch – not in a complete social vacuum, but at least in a more rarefied atmosphere, where the Indian ('Chichimec') presence was notable more for its negative impact (the threat it posed and the military response it elicited) than for any positive, creative influence, of the kind exerted by the sedentary Indian population of the centre. Northern New Spain was, in consequence, a European creation, characterized by Hispanic features: mining, stock raising, wheat farming and viticulture, all involving significant market activity and free labour recruitment.[243] Migrant Indians played a role in this process of colonization and even successfully transported to the north certain features of central Mexican society (Nahuatl provided place names as well as certain mining terms; Indian barrios, *cofradías* and even town councils sprang up and conducted their business in Nahuatl). Nevertheless, they did so in a different environment, where, compared with central Mexico, mobility was greater and caste divisions less entrenched, where Spaniards and *déraciné* Indians (*naborías*) confronted each other in the absence of powerful Indian communities and *caciques*, and where relations between Spaniards and pacified Indians were accordingly more direct and characterized less by outright coercion than by ostensible collaboration, mediated through the cash nexus.[244]

Postconquest Central Mexican History and Philology (Stanford, 1991), p. 23; a similar argument can be made for the Maya *cah* and the Totonac *chuchutsipi*: Restall, *The Maya World*, chs. 2, 3; Ouweneel, *Ciclos interrumpidos*, p. 23.

[243] Bakewell, *Silver Mining*, p. 225, discerns, by the seventeenth century, 'an economy that was in its general outline of contemporary European design'. In this sense, northern Mexico roughly played the part that Western Europe would in Brenner's grand scheme (the market was broadly associated with free wage labour); central Mexico more resembled southern Europe (where tenancy, sharecropping and peasant smallholdings coexisted with *latifundia*); while southern Mexico would – eventually, as market demand grew in the eighteenth and nineteenth centuries – repeat some of the characteristics of labour-coercive Eastern Europe: see Robert Brenner, 'Agrarian Class Structure and Economic Development in Pre-Industrial Europe', *Past and Present*, 70 (1976), pp. 30–75.

[244] Lockhart, 'Introduction', p. 19; Martin, *Governance and Society*, pp. 42, 48–9. This applies to *naborías* and miners – i.e., *déraciné* Indian, mestizo, and mulatto wage labourers (who were relatively numerous: Chevalier, *Land and Society*, pp. 169, 279); it is less applicable either to settled Indian farming communities, such as the Yaquis of Sonora or the Pueblos of New Mexico, or, *a fortiori*, to independent northern Indian 'tribes', such as the Apaches and Comanches, whose relations with the Spanish elite involved greater coercion and overt conflict.

The typical settlement, too, was not the peasant community, but the private estate (smaller in the Bajío, sprawling in the more distant north), upon which Indians – and others – were congregated under Spanish masters. Northern society was also one in which the necessary resort to self-defence – not to mention unilateral aggression – bred a certain marcher independence and belligerence.[245] On occasion, the armed citizenry (such as that of Nombre de Dios) had to defend their new communities. Landlords looked to their workers-cum-retainers to fight as well as to labour; warrior leaders achieved local office on the basis of their military prowess.[246] And certain northern Indian groups, such as the Opata and Pima of Upper Sonora, became loyal auxiliaries of the Spanish Crown.[247] Again, the result was a blurring of caste lines and the creation of some perceived, reciprocal interest between landlord and worker-retainer, notwithstanding the great social and material gulf separating them. Chevalier's ready use of feudal labels in his classic description of the north may be misleading in strictly economic or theoretical terms, but it suggests something of the social relations which developed in this rough, open, warlike region, where landlord and labourer, patron and client, captain and soldier, joined in loose alliance against the forces of nature, of the Chichimecs, and even of Mexico City.[248]

Small though it was, this new northern population required active provisioning, if only to ensure the continued flow of silver bullion. This meant the development of either local production or long-distance trade. In the first instance, local haciendas soon sprang up, operating in close symbiosis with the new mining centres. Indian

---

[245] 'Presidial captains conducted themselves as feudal lords and treated their troops as their personal vassals': Max L. Moorehead, *The Presidio: Bastion of the Spanish Borderlands* (Norman, Okla., 1975), p. 269. I discuss the feudal analogy below, n. 248.

[246] Powell, *Soldiers, Indians and Silver*, pp. 127, 130; Martin, *Governance and Society*, pp. 24, 75–6; Chevalier, *Land and Society*, pp. 296, 301–2.

[247] Edward H. Spicer, *Cycles of Conquest: The Impact of Spain, Mexico and the United States on the Indians of the Southwest, 1533–1960* (Tucson, 1981), pp. 87, 98–9.

[248] Chevalier, *Land and Society*, pp. 148–50, 158. Indeed, Chevalier's image of the north – characterized by powerful warlords ('men rich and powerful'), heading large clienteles, and relatively independent of central authority – carries all the hallmarks of 'feudal society' as (narrowly) defined by some non-Marxist scholars, such as Joseph Strayer: 'fragmentation of authority, public power in private hands, and a miltary system in which an essential part of the armed forces is secured through private contracts' (quoted in Norman F. Cantor, *Inventing the Middle Ages*, Cambridge, 1991, pp. 279–80). A balanced review of Chevalier and his critics is provided by José Cuello, 'El mito de la hacienda colonial en el norte de México', in Arij Ouweneel y Cristina Torales Pacheco, eds., *Empresarios, indios y estado. Perfil de la economía mexicana (siglo XVIII)* (Amsterdam, 1988), pp. 186–205; and see n. 684 below.

colonists, too, farmed staple crops. But the mining population, possessed of a high per capita income (and, probably, a high marginal propensity to consume), craved goods which only Mexico City – or Europe shipping through Mexico City – could adequately supply. As early as the 1550s north-bound caravans were transporting consignments of guns, swords, machetes, horseshoes, kettles, hoes, nails and thimbles; barrels of wine, olives, sardines, figs and tuna; rope, soap, gloves, boots and axles; silk from Granada, leather goods from Castile, shirts from Rouen.[249] Since northern consumers were willing and able to pay high prices, and since the authorities had a strong interest in fostering the northern mines (was not the *quinto* 'the royal barometer of good administration'?),[250] the new settlements in the north exercised a disproportionate influence on the colonial political economy. New roads were laid out north from Mexico City and northeast from Guadalajara; existing towns, such as Guadalajara and Querétaro, hitherto frontier outposts, became entrepôts and points of departure for the north (initially a source of prosperity, this role could – and, in the case of Guadalajara, it did – lead to a subsequent loss of dynamism and population); and new towns were called into existence either as defensive way stations (e.g., Celaya, San Miguel and San Felipe) or fortified frontier outposts (Jerez, Saltillo and San Luis Potosí).[251] And with roads and settlements came haciendas, small farms and inns (some owned and run by Indians), which catered to the through traffic of migrants, soldiers and merchants.

The multiplier effect of northern mining upon the colonial money economy was particularly pronounced because lines of communication were long and transport was slow and costly. Goods and people travelled across the vast northern expanses – it was some

---

[249] Powell, *Soldiers, Indians and Silver*, pp. 25–6; Martin, *Governance and Society*, pp. 23, 29, 61, illustrates northern consumer taste and imports for the eighteenth century; Ignaz Pfefferkorn, *Sonora: A Description of the Province* (Tucson, 1989; first pubd. 1794–5), pp. 44, 310–15, gives details of the 'enormous' prices which had to be paid at the end of this sprawling commercial network.

[250] Originally – as its name suggests – a fifth of production, the *quinto* was reduced by the Crown, in an effort to stimulate production, from the mid–sixteenth century; it stabilized at a tenth (*diezmo*): see Bakewell, 'Mining in Colonial Spanish America', p. 134, and the same author's *Silver Mining*, pp. 181–5; the quote is from Parry, *The Audiencia of New Galicia*, p. 12.

[251] Super, *La vida en Querétaro*, p. 12; Chevalier, *Land and Society*, p. 40; Powell, *Soldiers, Indians and Silver*, pp. 2, 5–6.

seven hundred miles from Mexico City to the mines of Parral – in convoys of lumbering wooden carts, whose physical and functional resemblance to the caravels of Spain's Atlantic fleet was enhanced by the machicolated wooden walls which they carried as defence against Indian attack. Convoys could include over a hundred of such waggons, loaded with goods and people, drawn by mules or oxen (the demand for draught animals was prodigious). Both beasts and humans had to be fed and watered during trips which – as with the Mexico City to Parral journey – could take up to four months.[252] If, for northern consumers, the inordinate transport costs meant high prices, they also brought profit and employment to a horde of hucksters and middlemen, to *hacendados*, farmers, merchants, innkeepers, soldiers, muleteers, carters and whores.

Problems of supply were compounded by the 'Chichimec' threat.[253] While the complex societies of central Mexico had been rapidly subdued in 1519–21, the nomads of the north presented a greater military challenge, a challenge which Spain's Aztec predecessors had understood and which initial Spanish slave raids only exacerbated. The Chichimec tribes – especially the Zacatecos and Guachichiles who occupied the north-central zone between the Santiago River and the Sierra Madre Occidental – were rightly suspicious of the Spaniards, even when they came bearing gifts; Spanish diplomacy (never particularly sincere) soon gave way to Spanish coercion; and, during the 1550s, a brand of warfare developed which would continue for nearly half a century. The Chichimecs, it was generally agreed, were formidable warriors, highly mobile, rashly brave and no less fond of violent reprisals than their Spanish enemies. While the Spaniards launched *entradas* against Chichimec zones and settlements, devastating, killing, enslaving and (by way of practical precaution) amputating the thumb and fingers of Indian bowmen, the Chichimecs in turn abducted, raped and tortured, enabling several Spanish friars to win a martyr's crown. Moreover, the Chichimecs had the time and wit to respond to the Spanish challenge in a manner

---

[252] Powell, *Soldiers, Indians and Silver*, p. 65; Chevalier, *Land and Society*, p. 8; Semo, *History of Capitalism*, p. 17. European travellers made comparisons with trans-Saharan caravans: Ouweneel, *Ciclos interrumpidos*, p. 162.

[253] Readers are reminded that 'Chichimec' is a loose (and, in its day, pejorative) label for a number of Indian groups: see n. 231 above.

the Aztecs had not (in this, they prefigured the long struggle of the Plains Indians). Some were, like their Spanish adversaries, veterans of the Mixtón War, and they had acquired a familiarity with Spanish battle tactics. Over time, they acquired horses, steel weapons, even a few arquebuses; they sank their ethnic differences and, by 1561, had formed a loose, anti-Spanish Chichimec confederation (here, as in North America, European pressure encouraged a process of political and military centralization, sometimes loosely referred to as 'tribalization').[254] Belligerent Indians received covert help from nominally pacified Indians, like the Cascanes, and they even made common cause – the Spaniards alleged – with runaway black slaves, thus aggravating the Spaniards' chronic fear of combined Indian and black insurrection.[255] And in this, as in later examples of Indian resistance, leadership often fell to 'Ladinized' Indians, those who had acquired a familiarity with Spanish ways. Acculturation, in other words, could facilitate resistance as well as docility.

For a generation Chichimec war parties raided Spanish towns and trade routes, sometimes making off with lavish booty. Sixty waggons and 30,000 pesos worth of cloth, silver and mules were seized at Ojuelos Pass in 1554. The Spaniards, backed by their usual numerous Indian auxiliaries (Tlaxcalans, Mexica, Tarascans and Otomíes) established defensive towns, walled villages, forts (*presidios*) and

[254] Inverted commas are essential because 'tribe' is a slippery and promiscuously used term; it carries (by my somewhat amateur reckoning) at least two different meanings: (1) an anthropological category in the ascending hierarchy band-tribe-chiefdom-state, which Jared Diamond, *Guns, Germs, and Steel: A Short History of Everybody for the Last 13,000 Years* (London, 1997), p. 270, calls a 'political definition'; and (2) a loose description of an enduring ethnic group, as in Prescott's 'numerous and rude tribe' of the Chichimecs (*Conquest of Mexico*, p. 6); compare Diamond, p. 270, 'a group that shares language and culture'. Category (1) is usually much smaller than category (2). And category (2) is complicated by the fact that 'tribal' associations fluctuate, particularly in response to external challenges: the Iroquois, for example, comprised several 'tribes' (sharing a related language and, to some extent, a common culture), who came together to create a formidable coalition – the League of the Five (later Six) Nations – which by the eighteenth century acted as a magnet to other 'tribes' (e.g., Tuscaroras, Shawnees, Delawares): Eric Wolf, *Europe and the People without History* (Berkeley, 1982), pp. 165–70; Daniel K. Richter, *The Ordeal of the Longhouse: The Peoples of the Iroquois League in the Era of European Colonization* (Chapel Hill, 1992), pp. 238–9. The Chichimecs – to a much lesser extent – appear to have been nudged towards such 'tribal' confederation by Spanish aggression.

[255] Powell, *Soldiers, Indians and Silver*, p. 62; Cope, *Limits of Racial Domination*, pp. 17–18 on Spanish fears of black subversion. However, as the Spanish settlers of Zacatecas observed, concerning their black slaves, while 'their presence is an evil, . . . their absence is a much greater one': Chevalier, *Land and Society*, p. 113.

even rock-ribbed churches;[256] they launched punitive raids against Chichimec camps; and, in the 1580s, under Viceroy Enríquez, they stepped up their campaigns, with no quarter asked or given. But the Spaniards' efforts were chronically inhibited by both administrative infighting and the Crown's customary parsimony. Funds were denied or were granted sparingly; hence the task of pacification in the north, like the original conquest of the centre, depended largely on private initiative and resources, which in turn required the private incentive of Chichimec enslavement to be forthcoming. With Chichimec males reaching up to 100 pesos in the market, slaving spread throughout the north, from the Gulf to the Pacific: it was warmly advocated by northern colonists (for whom the only good Indian was an enslaved Indian); and it was even condoned by clerics who, however solicitous they might be for the docile Indians of central Mexico, readily justified slavery for the recalcitrant, 'sexually licentious' savages of the north.[257] Thus, in contrast to Cortés's brief, brave conquest of Anáhuac, northern pacification was long and laborious. In 1567 the viceroy recorded his 'shame' that 'enemies having neither property nor arms, unshod and naked, without religion and ordered life' should so effectively resist Spanish power.[258] Yet, fifteen years later, as Spanish governmental and military commitments were increased (the war now called into being the first regular Spanish soldiery in the colony), Chichimec resistance continued: as noxious as the infidel Turk, Gerónimo de Mendieta lamented, and as impudent as Sir Francis Drake.[259]

By the late 1580s, however, some Chichimec groups had come to terms with the Spaniards and even enlisted as auxiliaries against their old confederates. War-weariness and, perhaps, the ravages of disease, induced a readiness to treat, which the Spaniards, relaxing

[256] Powell, *Soldiers, Indians and Silver*, p. 61; a few Dominicans, in the Las Casas tradition, spoke out against the enslavement of the northern Indians, but the Franciscans aligned themselves with the secular colonists, not least because conversion required some coercive back-up: Powell, *Soldiers, Indians and Silver*, p. 106; Knaut, *The Pueblo Revolt*, pp. 24–5. On the *presidios*, of which some 50 were established, see Moorehead, *The Presidio*, chs. 1, 6.

[257] Powell, *Soldiers, Indians and Silver*, p. 107; Israel, *Race, Class, and Politics*, p. 18; similar justifications for enslavement were voiced a generation later, among the Pueblo communitiies of New Mexico: Gutiérrez, *When Jesus Came*, p. 104.

[258] Powell, *Soldiers, Indians and Silver*, pp. 97–8.

[259] Powell, *Soldiers, Indians and Silver*, pp. 107, 136.

their previous counterproductive policy of *guerre à outrance*, now sought to encourage. Slave-raiding was banned; gifts of food and clothes were offered; diplomatic clerics replaced bellicose soldiers. During the 1590s cartloads of corn and blankets rolled north, in accordance with this new 'peace by purchase' policy.[260] Chichimec chiefs, in particular, succumbed to Spanish blandishments, to the appeal of horses, weapons and privileges. The process of co-option which had cemented colonial rule in central Mexico was found also to work – belatedly, after much preliminary pummelling – in the savage north as well; and it was cheaper than repression. The Chichimecs were given title to land (land which had been theirs at the outset, of course), they received Christian instruction, and they were confronted by the example of migrant Indian settlers from the south – an example many were disposed to follow. By the end of the sixteenth century a fragile peace prevailed, at least on the northern plains; while in the sierras, still-independent tribes – Tepehuanes and Tarahumara in the western Sierra Madre, fugitive Pames and Jonaces in the Sierra Gorda further south – held out against Spanish rule. Further conflicts would soon ensue, in which, according to the familiar logic of imperialism, recently pacified groups (Zacatecos and Guachichiles) would enlist as auxiliaries of the advancing Spanish power.

V. Hacienda and Village

The Spaniards' bloody northward advance was necessitated, above all, by the growth of northern mining, which was crucial in determining the shape and character of the late sixteenth-century colony. The colony, we may say, rested on four supportive pillars: mine and city, village and hacienda. Each of these was, to a degree, interdependent and mutually supportive. But it is analytically valid to take the village and the hacienda (or, we should say, private rural landholding) as central to the socioeconomic development of New Spain. Government, industry and commerce resided in the gridiron towns, where

---

[260] Powell, *Soldiers, Indians and Silver*, pp. 218–19. On the impact of disease, see Daniel T. Reff, *Disease, Depopulation, and Culture Change in Northwestern New Spain, 1518–1764* (Salt Lake City, 1991), p. 124ff.

Spaniards could live the kind of civilized urban existence to which they aspired; the mines made a few fortunes and afforded the rationale of the transatlantic imperial economy; but the foundations – the central pillars – of the colony were provided by the twin institutions of village and hacienda. For, despite the growth of towns, New Spain remained an essentially rural and agrarian economy.[261] Furthermore, while the resilience of New Spain's peasant villages (numbering some 4,000) was remarkable, they tended to assume defensive roles, conserving resources and responding opportunistically to the challenges which impinged on them from outside.[262] Often, these challenges emanated from the hacienda, which now took up and furthered the task of Hispanization which the *encomienda* had begun.[263]

[261] On urban culture and Spanish aspirations, see the useful symposium edited by Louisa Schell Hoberman and Susan Migden Socolow, *Cities and Society in Colonial Latin America* (Albuquerque, 1986). Though the opening declaration – 'the civilization that the Iberian nations implanted in the New World was profoundly urban' (Socolow, 'Introduction', p. 3) – may be true in cultural-cum-aspirational terms, it is open to quantitative quibble: at the end of the colonial period, when cities had grown substantially beyond the levels of the Habsburg period, the percentage of each intendancy (roughly, province) resident in the capital city was, with the exception of Zacatecas (22%), 10% or less (e.g., Mexico City 10%; Puebla 9%; Guanajuato, 8%; Tlaxcala, 6%; Oaxaca, 5%): Alexander Von Humboldt, *Political Essay on the Kingdom of New Spain* (Norman, Okla., 1988; first pubd. in this edition, abridged by Mary Maples Dunn, 1972; first pubd. in English, 1811), p. 33, citing census figures of 1794. In the first half of the seventeenth century, Mexico City may have had a population of 100,000, but it dwarfed other cities: Puebla, 10,000; Guadalajara, 3,000; Oaxaca, 2,000; Guanajuato and Querétaro, about 1,500. In short, the urban population could not have exceeded 150,000, out of a total population of perhaps 1.5m (i.e., <10%): B. H. Slicher Van Bath, 'Dos modelos referidos a la relación entre población y economía en Nueva España y Perú durante la época colonial', in Ouweneel and Torales Pacheco, *Empresarios, indios y estado*, p. 20; Israel, *Race, Class, and Politics*, pp. 21–2; Socolow, 'Introduction', p. 5. In eighteenth–century Europe, by way of very rough comparison, the urban population stood at 50% in Holland, 30% in England and around 16% in France: Braudel, *The Perspective of the World*, pp. 305–6.

[262] The figure – a rough guess – refers to the Mexican heartland (from Oaxaca north to Zacatecas) at the end of the colonial period (Semo, *History of Capitalism*, p. 37, citing Miranda); but it also roughly tallies with the pueblos enumerated in Gerhard's compendious *Guide to the Historical Geography of New Spain*. By stressing the *defensive* role of peasant villages, I do not mean to imply the inertia, rural idiocy or 'prepolitical' status of Mexico's colonial peasantry (as the rest of my analysis should make clear). I refer, rather, to what Steve Stern has called 'a kind of insular militance that set village insider, identity, and customary right against ethnocommunal outsiders' (although I would not use quite those terms): see Stern, *Secret History of Gender*, p. 29; and I echo Taylor, *Drinking, Homicide and Rebellion*, p. 142, which notes that 'the peasants' primary conscious motive for collective violence [was] the *defence* of relationships that were threatened'. The point has to be laboured somewhat, in order to avoid both the old disdain for peasant agency (which oddly united both conservatives and Marxists) and the new celebration of subaltern resistance, which sometimes seems to inflate (voluntarist) resistance at the expense of (structural) subalternity: see, for example, Sweet, 'The Ibero–American Frontier Mission', pp. 41–6.

[263] Lockhart, *The Nahuas*, pp. 18–19; Gibson, *Aztecs under Spanish Rule*, pp. 292–9.

Though institutionally quite different, *encomienda* and hacienda formed a sequential progression in the process of colonial consolidation and Indian acculturation.

Thus, the hacienda – often portrayed as a sluggish institutional equivalent of Thomas Carlyle's Anglo-Saxon, 'waddling about in potbellied equanimity' – was in fact the chief single determinant of New Spain's pattern of development. By the late eighteenth century – when mining and commerce had grown substantially – the hacienda still rivalled the peasant village as the hub of economic life; it contributed the greater part of New Spain's domestic product, outstripping the mines; and its resident communities surpassed some provincial towns not only in population but also in the 'diversity of [their] social, religious and economic functions'.[264] Apart from bullion, the bulk of goods circulating in urban markets were products of the hacienda. The hacienda thus 'had the power to set the pattern according to which the rest of rural life was organized', in a society which was still overwhelmingly rural.[265]

This brief analysis of the political economy of the colony will therefore begin with the hacienda; it will proceed to the related question of Indian and peasant resistance and acculturation;[266] then, it will return to the hacienda, to consider its productive rationale and the implications of this rationale for colonial society, including the

[264] Richard B. Lindley, *Haciendas and Economic Development: Guadalajara, Mexico, at Independence* (Austin, 1983), p. 11. Lindley's study, it should be made clear, deals with a region (the later state of Jalisco) of relatively rich haciendas.

[265] Lindley, *Haciendas and Economic Development*, p. 211.

[266] Some experts dislike the term 'acculturation', not least because (they say) it implies a one-way process, whereby Indians assume non–Indian characteristics, while Europeans remain doggedly European (for a good critique of this 'narrow' concept of 'acculturation', see Farriss, *Maya Society*, pp. 110–13). Some prefer 'transculturation', which seems more even-handed and has the added merit of sounding like a subtle neologism (which it isn't: see Manuel Carrera Stampa, *Los gremios mexicanos* [Mexico, 1954], p. 254). I do not find this argument persuasive. Scholars eminently sensitive to the dialectical subtleties of this process are happy to use 'acculturation' (e.g., Gruzinski, *Conquest of Mexico*, p. 146). Furthermore, an excessive emphasis on even–handed, two-way, 'transculturation' tends to overlook the fact of colonialism: these were not equal encounters but (very often) impositions by one culture on another; and the resulting amalgam was skewed in favour of the colonial master-culture, politically, culturally and linguistically. More Indians learned Spanish than Spaniards learned Nahuatl, Maya or Otomí; and while New Spain was certainly a complex and peculiar hybrid, it probably had more in common with Old Spain than Old Anáhuac. A two-way view is therefore appropriate; but it is no less appropriate to focus on the ways in which subject Indians responded to the threats, pressures and opportunities of Spanish colonial rule (= 'acculturation', by way of shorthand).

expanding cities; finally, it will review the dynamics of the entire ensemble over time (roughly, over the 'long' seventeenth century; the Bourbon era will be treated separately), addressing the questions of imperialism (the significance of New Spain's colonial status) and of mode of production (was New Spain 'feudal', 'capitalist', both, or neither?).

With the decline of the *encomienda*, the private estate emerged as the principal form of Spanish rural enterprise. Through the later sixteenth and into the seventeenth century, royal land grants (*mercedes*) and confirmations (*composiciones*) augmented the holdings not only of big *hacendados* but also of lesser landowners, such as *rancheros*, some of whom were dependently linked to the haciendas because of their need for credit, storage or transport facilities.[267] Private landholdings thus diverged in size: the giant estates of the north or the tropical coastlands contrasted with the smaller enterprises of the central highlands; nevertheless, the general trend was towards an increasingly uniform system of private freehold land tenure.[268] In some cases, land concentration was bolstered by the legal device of the entail (*mayorazgo*), which ensured primogeniture and averted the fractioning of estates; however, entails were too few to determine the general character of Mexican landholding which – in its private, lay form – was determined more by economic than by institutional factors.[269]

Church landholdings were another matter. They grew apace: first, with the mendicants, especially the Augustinians and Dominicans (the Dominicans pioneered the classic sugar and slave plantations of central Mexico); then, with the secular clergy, notably the cathedral chapters, who combined individual, private property with extensive corporate, institutional landholdings.[270] Above all, the Jesuits acquired a reputation – perhaps exaggerated – for their 'marvellous skill' at estate management, which was evidenced in their rapid

---

[267] Van Young, *Hacienda and Market*, pp. 108–9; Gibson, *Aztecs under Spanish Rule*, pp. 274–5, 289; Chevalier, *Land and Society*, pp. 266–9; Martin, *Rural Society*, pp. 28–9, 40–4.

[268] Chevalier, *Land and Society*, pp. 217, 276.

[269] Lindley, *Haciendas and Economic Development*, pp. 31–2, and Van Young, *Hacienda and Market*, pp. 124–6, offer somewhat different interpretations of the *mayorazgo*; on which, see also de la Peña, *Oligarquía y propiedad*, ch. 6.

[270] Chevalier, *Land and Society*, pp. 237–8; Martin, *Rural Society*, pp. 32, 38; Schwaller, *Origins of Church Wealth*, p. 107.

accumulation of profitable enterprises.[271] In fact, both the Church's progressive acquisition of land (which the Crown sought in vain to arrest) and the Jesuits' reputation for ruthless efficiency stemmed from similar institutional – rather than attitudinal – features: that is, the immortality of ecclesiastical institutions, as compared to lay individuals and families; the Church's fiscal and legal privileges; its role as the colony's chief banker; and its accumulation over decades and centuries of bequests and donations from the faithful (which especially benefited the Jesuits, who educated many of the colony's elite).[272] Through gifts, bequests and foreclosed mortgages the Church accumulated property which did not face the fissiparous pressures which affected lay landlords. There were no sons clamouring for their inheritances, no daughters needing dowries.[273] Once acquired, land tended to remain in the 'dead hands' of the Church: disbursements (such as charity and education) were more than met by income. The Church could take the long view, successfully avoiding the generational vicissitudes which afflicted lay landlords (indeed, it could benefit from them, by snapping up bankrupt haciendas at bargain prices).[274]

In the process, the Church built up the capital which, in a capital-poor colony, provided either direct investment on Church estates or loans – especially long-term loans – to *hacendados*. Thus, even in regions where Church lands were few, Church capital was vital for the agrarian sector in general.[275] Here, rather than in any supposedly superior business ethic, lay the secret of Jesuit success. To the extent that the Jesuits resembled 'modern' businessmen (Chevalier's description of Jesuit business operations is classically Weberian), it

271 Bishop Palafox, quoted in Hermes Tovar Pinzón, 'Elementos constitutivos de la empresa agraria jesuita en la mitad del siglo xviii en México', in Enrique Florescano, ed., *Haciendas, latifundios y plantaciones en América Latina* (Mexico, 1975), p. 133; see also pp. 206–8, which offers a good resumé.

272 Chevalier, *Land and Society*, p. 244; Van Young, *Hacienda and Market*, p. 183; Enrique Florescano, *Origen y desarrollo de los problemas agrarios de México, 1500–1821* (Mexico, 1976), pp. 62–7.

273 Church estates were also exempted from paying the tithe, although the Jesuits' exemption gave rise to bitter disputes between secular and regular clergy: D. A. Brading, *Church and State in Bourbon Mexico: The Diocese of Michoacán 1749–1810* (Cambridge, 1994), pp. 11–14.

274 Van Young, *Hacienda and Market*, p. 188; Chevalier, *Land and Society*, p. 254.

275 Schwaller, *Origins of Church Wealth*, pp. 144–5; and, on the tithe as a source of working capital, *ibid.*, pp. 19–82; see also Arístides Medina Rubio, *La iglesia y la producción agrícola en Puebla, 1540–1795* (Mexico, 1983), ch. 3.

was less because of their profit-seeking attitudes (which they shared with lay *hacendados*) than because of the stable, institutional organization which they enjoyed over more than two centuries.[276] The Church was a 'corporation' – and the Jesuits were a 'company' – in more than just the original senses of these terms, and they enjoyed corresponding advantages which were denied private, family enterprises, for whom (like peasant households writ large) private and business operations were inextricably mixed.

The initial expansion of the hacienda, we have seen, was closely associated with the sixteenth-century boom in stock raising. A small Spanish minority, organized in its powerful and official corporate lobby, the Mesta,[277] soon began to flood the colony with herds of sheep and cattle, taking advantage of the decline of the Indian population, the favourable ecological conditions and the abundant land which – being either empty or imperfectly titled – they could appropriate. By the later sixteenth century, meat glutted the market, and the cities' supply of grain (which meant Indian corn as well as Spanish wheat) became precarious, especially in the wake of the 1576 epidemic and the depopulation which it provoked. The colonial authorities had to act. If, in nineteenth-century Argentina, to govern was to populate (*gobernar es poblar*), in colonial Mexico to govern was to feed: the state had to play an active role in provisioning, especially provisioning the cities, and it could not rely upon the workings of a highly imperfect market to achieve that end. 'Although anyone may do as he likes with his own property', observed a Crown attorney, 'in the things necessary for the sustenance of life sellers should not be at liberty to set and raise prices

---

[276] Note that Jesuit management could be lacklustre (Taylor, *Landlord and Peasant*, p. 183); some Jesuit enterprises went bust (Martin, *Rural Society*, p. 73); and some haciendas flourished *after* leaving Jesuit control: Silvia González Marín, 'Chapingo', in Enrique Semo, coord., *Siete ensayos sobre la hacienda mexicana, 1780–1880* (Mexico, 1977), pp. 20–1. On Jesuit operations: Chevalier, *Land and Society*, pp. 242, 246–50; Herbert J. Nickel, *Morfología social de la hacienda mexicana* (Mexico, 1988), pp. 69, 72; Brading, *First America*, p. 179; Tovar Pinzón, 'Elementos constitutivos' and James D. Riley, 'Santa Lucía: desarrollo y administración de una hacienda jesuita en el siglo XVIII', in Florescano, *Haciendas, latifundios y plantaciones*, pp. 132–222, 242–72; P. L. G. van der Meer, 'El Colegio de San Andrés y la producción del azúcar en sus haciendas de Xochimancas y Barreto (1750–1767)', in Ouweneel and Torales Pacheco, *Empresarios, indios y estado*, pp. 138–64; Pilar González Aizpuru, 'La influencia de la compañía de Jesús en la sociedad novohispana del siglo XVI', *Historia Mexicana*, 32 (1982–3), pp. 262–81.
[277] Dusenberry, *The Mexican Mesta*, pp. 48–9.

freely'.[278] Accordingly, the authorities pressed for tribute payments in maize; in consequence, a once diverse inventory of tribute gave way to a more simple duality of cash and grain, and the old polyculture of Mesoamerica, with its rich variety of complementary crops, began to shift towards a maize monoculture.[279]

But, despite official pressure, the declining Indian population could not meet the colony's growing demand for grain. The authorities therefore turned to Spanish landlords to make up the deficit. The wholesale land grants of the later sixteenth century were thus designed to create a Spanish landowning class capable of supplying the colony's demand for grain. And they succeeded: between 1580 and 1630 Spanish grain production forged ahead, and, especially in regions of growing population (like Querétaro), arable farming rapidly supplanted stock raising.[280] In the first half of the seventeenth century, as the Indian population reached its nadir and a powerful class of Spanish landlords consolidated their position in the colony, the structural problems of food supply were solved. Indeed, the old pattern was now reversed: meat prices rose once again, while those of grain declined; landlords sometimes had difficulty selling grain at a profit, especially when they competed with Indian producers of corn.[281] Thus, while aggregate supply balanced demand (the 'structural' problem was solved), this did not rule out – indeed it may even have encouraged – the possibility of recurrent dearths, the result partly of the vagaries of nature, partly of the profiteering of man. Then, in particular regions and particular years, a shortfall in grain brought sharply rising prices and profits, urban deprivation, popular unrest and occasional, violent protest.[282]

[278] Van Young, *Hacienda and Market*, p. 43 (the quote derives from the eighteenth century but is no less valid for the early colonial period). On shortages, see *ibid.*, p. 24, and Cope, *Limits of Racial Domination*, pp. 128–30.

[279] Murdo J. MacLeod, 'Forms and Types of Work', pp. 78–9; Van Young, *Hacienda and Market*, pp. 24–5.

[280] Gibson, *Aztecs under Spanish Rule*, pp. 326–7; Super, 'The Agicultural Near North', p. 236. De la Peña, *Oligarquía y propiedad*, p. 31, lists Spanish wheat-growing zones: Puebla, Valladolid, Zamora, Guadalajara and the Bajío.

[281] The classic study is Enrique Florescano, *Precios del maíz y crisis agrícolas en México (1708–1810)* (Mexico, 1969), especially ch. 8. Van Young, *Hacienda and Market*, pp. 86–7, illustrates the scale of Indian provisioning of (eighteenth-century) Guadalajara; de la Peña, *Oligarquía y propiedad*, pp. 46–7, notes the high returns accruing to seventeenth-century stock raising.

[282] Florescano, *Precios del maíz*, ch. 10; Cope, *Limits of Racial Domination*, pp. 125–38, offers a sophisticated analysis of one major case, the Mexico City riot of 1692, which is discussed later.

Along with the cities, the hacienda's second external link was to the mines, especially the mines of the north. These required not only imported foodstuffs but also draught animals, which supplied the motive power for the amalgamation process, the hides and leather which were the raw materials of mining technology, and the tallow candles which lit the dim underground galleries. Certain agricultural zones thus established close symbiotic ties with the mines, their fortunes fluctuating in tandem with mineral production. However, the aggregate demand of the mines should not be exaggerated. During the booming 1590s, the mining labour force did not exceed ten thousand.[283] The chief importance of the mines derived from another factor: the generation of capital, which either greased the wheels of commerce or was poured into landed investment. For a key feature of the colonial economy was the capacity of the rural sector to soak up fortunes made in mining and commerce, as *nouveaux riches* bought land, and occasionally titles: first for reasons of prestige and social advancement; second (and more importantly) for reasons of economic rationality. For although the mines could occasionally yield spectacular profits, they were also very risky enterprises. Failures outnumbered successes. Land, in contrast, while it offered no bonanzas, was a safer, less stochastic, form of investment, epecially over the long-term. In particular, it provided a refuge for mercantile or mining fortunes threatened with dissolution at the moment of their makers' deaths. In a pre-industrial economy of very limited technological innovation and highly imperfect markets, capital tended to circulate sluggishly, achieving only modest accumulation and displaying a recurrent tendency to revert to the land.[284]

In amassing land – and, of course, water – the Spanish elite partially and progressively dispossessed their Indian subordinates. The rate of dispossession varied according to time and place. Central Mexico set the pace in the sixteenth and seventeenth centuries, notably in the Valleys of Mexico, Cuernavaca, Toluca and Puebla. Here,

[283] Bakewell, *Silver Mining*, p. 222; Florescano, 'Formation and Economic Structure', p. 156, provides an illustrative map, the work of West and Augelli.
[284] Brading, *Miners and Merchants*, pp. 103, 127; Van Young, *Hacienda and Market*, p. 141; Tovar Pinzón, 'Elementos constitutivos', p. 204. Compare northwestern Europe, where more varied investment opportunities presented themselves: trade, manufacturing, government and mortgage debt, and, by the eighteenth century, joint-stock companies: Jan de Vries, *The Economy of Europe in an Age of Crisis, 1600–1750* (Cambridge, 1976), pp. 219–22.

despite the massive fall in Indian population, population began to press on landed resources. By the 1620s, two-thirds of the arable land in the Valley of Mexico was held by private Spanish landowners.[285] By the eighteenth century, west-central Mexico (the Guadalajara region) was in the van, with similar processes of estate expansion and peasant dispossession taking place. Now, the southern Valley of Oaxaca also experienced a phase of accelerated commercialization. In general, however, the Indian communities of the south and southeast (Oaxaca, Yucatán, Chiapas) retained much of their landed patrimony down through the colonial period and well into the nineteenth century.[286] Thus, while images of strict linear progression should be regarded skeptically, it would be broadly true to see Mexican rural history in terms of successive, geographically shifting waves of agrarian commercialization, hacienda expansion and peasant dispossession. The Valley of Toluca, *circa* 1580, roughly foreshadowed the Valley of Oaxaca, *circa* 1750.[287] Later, we will argue, eighteenth-century agrarian commercialization laid the groundwork for the great insurrection of 1810, especially in the centre-west; a century later, a similar process generated the 1910 Revolution, chiefly in the centre and parts of the north. Arguably, these were the fundamental social changes which determined Mexico's pattern of development, first as a colony, then as an independent nation.[288]

But within such broad processes and patterns there were important variations and exceptions.[289] Peasant farming survived even in

[285] Gibson, *Aztecs under Spanish Rule*, pp. 277–9, 289; see also Martin, *Rural Society*, p. 52; Tovar Pinzón, 'Elementos constitutivos', p. 143; Chevalier, *Land and Society*, pp. 222–3.

[286] Patch, *Maya and Spaniard*, pp. 67–8, 75, on the weakness of Yucateco haciendas and Maya control of the maize supply. For Oaxaca, see Taylor, *Landlord and Peasant*, ch. 3.

[287] Lockhart, 'Introduction', p. 6.

[288] Tutino, *From Insurrection to Revolution*, is a good overview, stronger on the earlier period.

[289] We encounter here a familiar methodological problem, especially acute when it comes to general, synthetic history: the historian tries to highlight important trends, differentiating, over time and place, the 'typical' from the 'untypical'; but these tend to be somewhat subjective judgements, at best supported by 'impressionistic' examples. The kind of rigorous, quantitative, 'falsifiable' evidence which we would need in order to reach categorical conclusions (and which some commentators urge us to rely upon: Stephen Haber, 'Introduction: Economic Growth and Latin American Economic Historiography', in Haber, ed., *How Latin American Fell Behind: Essays on the Economic History of Brazil and Mexico, 1800–1914* [Stanford, 1997], pp. 1–33) are simply not available. We fall back on (informed) hunches, *a priori* theory, unspoken prejudices, and – a technique which should not be disdained – a 'feel' for the literature. This emphatically does not mean, however, that the process of historical inquiry is random and unrelated to criteria of 'truth'. It simply means that truth is elusive, and absolute truth is unattainable.

areas of hacienda hegemony. (Chevalier, sometimes taken to task for exaggerating the hacienda's predominance, clearly recognized the tenacious and ubiquitous survival of the village community.)[290] Often, haciendas controlled the irrigated valleys, leaving Indian peasants to eke out a chancey existence on *temporal* (rainfed) uplands.[291] Conversely, even in the remoter, less commercialized regions of Mexico, the hacienda made its mark, albeit more faintly. In Oaxaca, a bastion of Indian peasant farming, haciendas soon developed pockets of commercial farming in the valleys.[292] The strength of the market, the proximity of cities or mines, the degree of Indian resistance, all helped determine the nature of local patterns. And Indian resistance depended crucially on Indian numbers. Where population collapse was most complete, the hacienda advanced into vacant land; it pushed against an open door. In much of central Mexico the nascent hacienda established itself – with ambitious borders, encompassing untilled acres – as the Indian population fell to its mid-sixteenth-century nadir and, at the same time, underwent *congregación*. Subsequently, as the Indian population recovered, the pressure on hacienda land increased; but by then hacienda titles were well established and the resurgent Indian population faced an uphill legal battle.[293] Where demographic collapse and hacienda expansion had been relatively less pronounced (Yucatán, Oaxaca and many mountain regions, such as the Sierra Norte de Puebla) the potential for subsequent landlord-peasant conflict was diminished.[294] In the north, too, the sparsity of peasant settlement and the dominance *ab initio* of the hacienda made such conflict less likely and less extensive. Similarly, in the coastal hot country, large 'rudimentary' estates were carved out of underpopulated territory; scattered sugar and cacao plantations, worked by slaves, stood amid sheep and cattle pastures; here, too, the classic confrontation of Indian village and Spanish landlord was less acute.[295]

---

[290] Chevalier, *Land and Society*, pp. 219–20.

[291] Gibson, *Aztecs under Spanish Rule*, p. 310.

[292] Taylor, *Landlord and Peasant*, ch. 4; Whitecotton, *The Zapotecs*, pp. 197, 208.

[293] Nickel, *Morfología social*, p. 193ff., gives examples.

[294] Even sierra regions had their landlord-village conflicts, however: García Martínez, *Pueblos de la sierra*, pp. 238–9.

[295] Chevalier, *Land and Society*, pp. 279–80. De la Peña, *Oligarquía y propiedad*, pp. 66–71, depicts coastal Colima as a remarkably early example of (cacao) monoculture.

The partial dispossession of the Indian peasantry was crucial in view of the hacienda's need for labour. With demographic decline, labour became more precious than land. Some landowners – notably those engaged in the highly capitalized and profitable production of sugar – bought black slaves. But for the majority of Mexico's landowners – and even miners – slave prices were too high, profits were too low and alternative sources of labour were (population decline notwithstanding) too tempting: in Mexico slavery never assumed the fundamental role that it did in export and plantation colonies like Brazil or the West Indies.[296] With the exception of the sugar plantations, slaves provided at most a small nucleus of permanent hacienda workers, often overseers and foremen. After 1640, futhermore, the slave trade to Mexico halted, and slave numbers went into steady decline: from perhaps eighty thousand in the mid-seventeenth century to a mere ten thousand in the late eighteenth.[297] African-born slaves (*bozales*) declined in numbers relative to American-born *negros criollos*; the latter intermarried, adding a black dimension to Mexico's complex caste system. Thereafter, the only new slaves were Indian prisoners – Apaches, in particular – reduced to servitude during the long Indian wars of the northern frontier: but these captives were neither numerous nor reliable.[298]

The bulk of rural labour therefore had to be extracted from the Indian villages. Since the initial *encomienda* proved inadequate, the authorities developed the *repartimiento* as a means to supply private landlords, lay and clerical, with forced Indian labourers. Local officials organized labour drafts for landlords who, in turn, were required to pay the draftees a fixed wage. The *repartimiento* system, which flourished between the 1550s and 1630s, achieved several

---

[296] Carroll, *Blacks in Colonial Veracruz*, pp. 34–6, illustrates relative prices in Jalapa, c. 1620: a horse cost 15 pesos, a small town house 200, a slave between 300 and 400. For comparative (Spanish–American) prices, see Rout, *The African Experience*, pp. 323–7.

[297] Carroll, *Blacks in Colonial Veracruz*, pp. 30–9; Martin, *Rural Society*, pp. 25, 122–3, 131–2; Cope, *Limits of Racial Domination*, pp. 95–7. The story of Mexico's black population is told by Aguirre Beltrán, *La población negra de México*, (Mexico, 1946), and Colin A. Palmer, *Slaves of the White God: Blacks in Mexico, 1570–1650* (Cambridge Mass., 1976). The rapid decline of the slave population was accelerated by a high rate of manumission, particularly in the cities, where grateful – or conscience-stricken – owners freed their (usually elderly) slaves, or allowed slaves to purchase their freedom: Frederick Bowser, 'Africans in Colonial Society', in Bethell, *Cambridge History of Latin America*, vol. 2, *Colonial Latin America*, pp. 375–6.

[298] Weber, *The Spanish Frontier*, pp. 127–9; Martin, *Governance and Society*, pp. 43, 48.

results, not all of them necessarily conscious goals: it guaranteed a labour supply during the period of heaviest population loss; it ensured that fields would be tilled and cities would be fed (above all, fed with the wheaten bread which Spanish palates preferred); it provided labour for public works, such as Mexico City's massive drainage canal, for church-building and for some central Mexican mines;[299] and it gave the royal authorities a useful lever in their efforts to control the Spanish elite, at the same time as it afforded limited paternalistic protection to the Indians themselves. Over the long term, too, the *repartimiento* familiarized the Indians with temporary wage labour: with the patterns of hacienda production and with the demands and opportunities of the labour market. As such, it acted as an engine of acculturation.[300] Since wage rates on the free market were higher than *repartimiento* rates, and since, with demographic decline, they tended to rise, Indians began to seek out 'free' labour contracts, thus evading *repartimiento* obligations.[301] Like other colonial corvées, therefore, the *repartimiento* system indirectly helped prepare the way for freer forms of proletarian labour.[302]

Under the *repartimiento* system the authorities – and their Indian *cacique* collaborators – served as intermediaries between Spanish employers and Indian workers. Both Crown and *cacique* benefited from this mediating role, which required the maintenance of the Indian population as a distinct stratum (a 'reserve army of labour'?), from which labour – and tribute – could be extracted at regular, controlled rates, without these demands bringing social upheaval or disintegration. Being seasonal and revolving, *repartimiento* labour drafts did not fundamentally threaten the viability of the Indian community. The system may be seen, retrospectively and theoretically,

[299] On the desagüe (drainage canal): Gibson, *Aztecs under Spanish Rule*, p. 224–42; Richard E. Boyer, *La gran inundación. Vida y sociedad en la ciudad de México (1629–1638)* (Mexico, 1975), p. 38ff. Kubler, *Mexican Architecture*, vol. 1, pp. 135–6 (churches); García Martínez, *Pueblos de la sierra*, pp. 252–3 (mines).

[300] Lockhart, *The Nahuas*, pp. 428, 431.

[301] Gibson, *Aztecs under Spanish Rule*, pp. 248–52. Gruzinski, *Conquest of Mexico*, pp. 64–5, notes that servile Indians (*macehuales*) also took advantage of population decline and labour shortage to evade the authority of Indian *caciques* and nobles, thus accelerating the latter's decline.

[302] 'Officials [in Africa] sometimes admitted [that colonial tax policy] was intended less to collect revenue than to require each household to make a minimum contribution to the cash economy': Frederick Cooper, 'Africa and the World Economy', in Cooper *et al.*, eds., *Confronting Historical Paradigms: Peasants, Labor, and the Capitalist World System in Africa and Latin America* (Madison, 1993), p. 124.

as an organized articulation of modes of production: the community provided labour and assumed much of the burden of reproducing the labour force; the hacienda drew upon community labour without destroying the community (indeed, it would have been counterproductive, politically as well as economically, for the *hacendado* to expropriate the community and proletarianize its inhabitants). Successful parasitism meant preserving the exploited host. At the same time, the system represented a vague secular version of the earlier mendicant vision: that of carefully preserved Indian communities, required to conform only to certain preferred Spanish norms (religious norms for the mendicants, economic for lay authorities and landlords). Considerations of social responsibility and economic rationality thus led the authorities to espouse literally conservative and paternalistic policies, which in turn guaranteed a real measure of Indian landholding, self-government and fiscal autonomy.[303]

Logically, the regular clergy endorsed this approach. Logically, too, Spanish landowners, especially the bigger, richer landlords, questioned it. Like their mercantile colleagues, they sought to penetrate the Indian community, to gain unqualified access to its land, labour and market. And they resented the barriers which, from the earliest days of the colony, the mendicants sought to erect around these coveted human and material resources. For Spanish landlords, the *repartimiento* was a mixed blessing. *Repartimiento* labour was better than no labour at all; hence in the short term it was essential. But better still, especially for richer landlords, was a system which allowed direct access to Indian labour on the basis of either permanent or temporary hacienda work: a system which, to succeed, required sufficient 'push' factors to impel the Indians towards such hacienda employment (e.g., population growth, tribute demands, landlessness, *caciquista* oppression). Permanent hacienda workers (*gañanes, peones acasillados*) would be lodged on the newly formed estates, providing reliable, amenable, 'acculturated' workers, whose communities, though established within hacienda boundaries as *de facto* hacienda labour compounds, would nevertheless replicate many of

---

[303] The heyday of the *repartimiento* system – roughly, the century beginning in the 1540s – corresponds to Lockhart's 'stage 2', 'during which Spanish elements came to pervade every aspect of Nahua life, but with limitations, often as discrete additions within a relatively unchanging indigenous framework': *The Nahuas*, pp. 428–9ff.

the features of the old Indian communities: compact residential patterns, central churches, corporate fiesta cycles and, in some cases, subsistence farming plots. The institutional strengths of the ancient corporate village could thus, to an extent, be plagiarized by the new hacienda. At the same time, temporary workers (*eventuales*) could be drawn from the villages, on the basis either of *repartimiento* drafts or of cash incentives, as hacienda requirements demanded; these workers would supplement – and, especially at harvest-time, outnumber – the permanent work force. A third variant, particularly evident in the Bajío, where indigenous villages were few, involved labour service tenancies: here, in a system characteristic of such newly settled, non-Indian zones, tenants received plots of land in return for which they provided labour on the hacienda demesne.[304]

As this – very rough – schema suggests, the emergent hacienda came to rely on forms of labour recruitment and control which, because of their diversity and flexibility, offered the *hacendado* a certain basic security. Over time, they enabled the hacienda to emancipate itself, to a great extent, from its initial reliance on official – 'extra-economic' – coercion.[305] For this to occur, the necessary 'push' factors (pressures on peasant communities) had to conspire with 'pull' factors (cash or other incentives, such as the 'tributary sponsorship and protection' which landlords offered Indians who quit their communities).[306] Such 'pull' factors depended partly on the landlords' political power, but even more on their economic muscle, and thus on hacienda profits which, in a cash-starved economy like that of New Spain's, were often scant.[307] Logically, therefore, it

---

[304] Nickel, *Morfología social*, p. 74ff., and Ouweneel, *Ciclos interrumpidos*, pp. 112–14, 130–7 (hacienda organization); García Martínez, *Pueblos de la sierra*, pp. 237–8, and Van Young, *Hacienda and Market*, pp. 246, 265 (hacienda replicates village); Florescano, 'Formation and Economic Structure', pp. 168–71 (regional variations).

[305] This remains a contentious question. A traditional view of the hacienda stresses its reliance on coerced labour, initially *encomienda* and *repartimiento* labour drafts, later debt-peonage (see, for example, Semo, *History of Capitalism*, pp. 117–34, especially p. 133). A revisionist view, to which I incline, plays down the coercive elements of hacienda labour: see below, section VIII, 'The Political Economy of New Spain'. There are, as usual in these debates, many intervening shades of emphasis, and the 'truth' would vary according to time and place.

[306] MacLeod, 'Forms and Types of Work', p. 79. Martin, *Rural Society*, p. 122, illustrates how, from around the 1620s, 'haciendas [in Morelos] became increasingly powerful magnets attracting Indians dissatisfied with the quality of their lives in their native villages'.

[307] On the shortage of currency, see the references gathered under n. 236. On low hacienda profits: Brading, *Miners and Merchants*, p. 219; Nickel, *Morfología social*, p. 72; Van Young, *Hacienda*

was the richer landlords, farming profitable haciendas in the more prosperous, market-oriented zones of the colony, who were keenest to establish the two-tier free labour system, combining both permanent and temporary wage workers, *gañanes* and *eventuales*, and by-passing the cumbersome *repartimiento*. Such zones were to be found in central Mexico, where the cities cried out for food and where Indian dispossession had proceeded furthest, and in parts of the north where, even if the local labour supply was scant, mining generated healthy profits which in turn made long-distance labour recruitment feasible.

The shift to wage labour was far from uniform. In central Mexico *repartimiento* labour shrank to the status of a minor corvée: the Sysiphean labour of the *desagüe* of the Valley of Mexico in the early seventeenth century was something of an exception: more typical was the ancillary harvest work required in the Guadalajara region down through the early eighteenth.[308] However, *hacendados* in Oaxaca or Yucatán operated within sluggish economies, bereft of mines, amid large landholding Indian peasantries, whose labour could not be elicited at the low wage rates which (relatively impecunious) landlords were prepared to pay. As a result, forced labour remained of central importance in Yucatán, where Indians were required to furnish labour for public works, for communal projects and – most hated of all – for the 'personal service' of their Spanish masters, that is, as household servants, artisans, day-labourers, as well as field workers.[309] Roughly between these two extremes – the more fully proletarianized Valley of Mexico and the coercive southeast – stood New Galicia, in the centre-west of the colony.[310]

The range of rural labour systems (which, of course, were the dominant forms) had their urban counterparts: city air did not necessarily make a man free, as it did in medieval Europe.[311] Seventeenth-century Mexico City had a dense, if declining, slave population,

and Market, p. 224, which gives an average annual net return on landed property of 5%; this figure, however, derives from the late eighteenth century when cheap labour and growing demand had 'improved the margins of profit which might reasonably be expected' (p. 141). Low profits did not, of course, mean that profits were disdained; they were simply hard to ratchet up.

[308] Gibson, *Aztecs under Spanish Rule*, pp. 236–42; Van Young, *Hacienda and Market*, pp. 240–1.

[309] Farriss, *Maya and Spaniard*, pp. 47, 53; for Oaxaca, see Taylor, *Landlord and Peasant*, pp. 144–7.

[310] Van Young, *Hacienda and Market*, pp. 238–40.

[311] Anderson, *Passages*, p. 206.

including household servants and skilled artisans.[312] The colony's primitive woollen textile workshops, the *obrajes*, also relied heavily on coerced labour: convicts, endebted workers and bonded apprentices.[313] Indeed, conditions of work in the *obraje* were generally worse than those of the hacienda; profits were often low and uncertain, discouraging competitive bidding for free wage labour; and the very physical structure of the enterprise – compact and four-walled – facilitated tight control over the work force. Even more than the hacienda, the *obraje* relied on coercive labour, especially in regions, like the Bajío, where the demand for labour outstripped supply.[314]

Throughout the colony, therefore, forms of free and unfree labour coexisted, even under the same roof. In the southeast, particularly, the old tribute and *repartimiento* systems flourished down to the end of the colonial period: here, the Spanish and Indian sectors – modes of production, perhaps – articulated, under official control and manipulation; the arena of the market, in which goods and labour were traded as mobile commodities, remained tightly circumscribed. In consequence, the Indian sector and the Indian community which was its constitutive element were preserved largely intact, albeit periodically squeezed by the arbitrary and coercive demands of the Spaniards. If, in central and northern Mexico, capitalism was *at best* embyronic, in the south it had not been conceived.[315] Indeed, the predominance of official exactions (of labour and goods) over private appropriation of surplus by landlords distanced Yucatán and its analogues from feudalism too. If anything, the southeast retained elements of the old Mesoamerican tributary system (which we have roughly compared to the Marxist Asiatic mode), which survived as the basis of production, now under Spanish rather than Mesoamerican overlords.[316]

---

[312] Cope, *Limits of Racial Domination*, pp. 13–14, 95–6.

[313] Richard J. Salvucci, *Textiles and Capitalism in Mexico: An Economic History of the Obrajes, 1539–1840* (Princeton, 1987), ch. 4; Manuel Miño Grijalva, *La protoindustria colonial hispanoamericana* (Mexico, 1993), ch. 4; Cope, *Limits of Racial Domination*, pp. 98–105.

[314] Gibson, *Aztecs under Spanish Rule*, p. 253; Salvucci, *Textiles and Capitalism*, pp. 114–15; John C. Super, 'Querétaro Obrajes: Industry and Society in Provincial Mexico, 1600–1810', *Hispanic American Historical Review*, 56/2 (1976), pp. 206–7.

[315] See below, section VIII, 'The Political Economy of New Spain'.

[316] For interpretations along these lines, see Semo, *History of Capitalism*, ch. 2; Olivera, *Pillis y macehuales*, p. 155.

New Spain thus witnessed no more than a partial and patchy transition to wage labour during the first two centuries of the colony. The
transition was pioneered by the early mines and commercial haciendas; it was first evident in the valleys of central Mexico (where private, free labour had triumphed over official, *repartimiento* labour by
about 1630) and in certain pockets of the north; during the later colonial period the rest of central as well as west-central Mexico was gradually affected. In the south, however, the transition was stretched
down to the twentieth century. Throughout the colony, this transition was slow, halting and far from unilinear. It was opposed by officials, friars and *caciques*, who resisted the seepage of Indians from
village to hacienda, from the official, tribute/*repartimiento*, system
to the private, free labour/market, system. But it had powerful supporters, too: market-oriented landlords, who, in some highly commercialized regions, had outbid and undermined the *repartimiento*
as early as 1600; the secular clergy, who, roughly, identified with
the Spanish market sector (and who had their own estates to worry
about); and, not least important, the Indians themselves, for whom
the market could offer advantages and freedoms (or, we should say,
a form of exploitation, through the market, that was often preferable to the 'extra-economic' exploitation of the *repartimiento*). Not
surprisingly, market wage rates were higher than coerced labour
rates, both on the hacienda and in the *obraje*;[317] and *repartimiento*
labour became more onerous from the late sixteenth century, especially as work on the Mexico City *desagüe* generated a massive
demand for labour drafts throughout central Mexico.[318] Furthermore, work on the *desagüe*, like work in the *obrajes*, was arduous,
risky and – in terms of its rhythms and rationale – very different
from the seasonal agricultural work with which Indian peasants
were familar. For this kind of dangerous drudgery, voluntary workers were hard to find, and employers, unable or unwilling to pay the
market rate, resorted to coercion. *Hacendados*, of course, were not
protagonists of Manchesterite economics, and they were quite prepared to resort to coercion when it proved necessary, profitable or

[317] Salvucci, *Textiles and Capitalism*, pp. 44, 55.
[318] Reaching as far as the Sierra de Puebla: García Martínez, *Pueblos de la sierra*, pp. 256–7; see
also Boyer, *La gran inundación*, pp. 40–4.

feasible;[319] but, on balance, and for reasons of rational self-interest, they tended to shift towards voluntary labour recruitment. They were helped by the fact that, even as official *repartimiento* demands lessened and were finally curtailed in the 1630s, village Indians remained subject to the requirements of community work (the *coatequitl*) and, sometimes, to the arbitrary powers of Indian cacical rule which over time tended increasingly to resemble its Spanish official counterpart in terms of exploitation and repression.[320] Indians who quit the village for the hacienda were not necessarily fleeing happy bucolic communities. Indeed, there were some positive incentives for those who made the break, especially the minority of Indians who – notwithstanding the discouragement of the colonial authorities – set up as successful traders, pulque producers, artisans, muleteers and innkeepers.[321]

Indians themselves thus contributed to the major socioeconomic changes which affected the colony during its first two centuries of maturation. As population fell, they bid up wages (most obviously in Mexico City); they strove to achieve greater control over their own and their families' economic destinies by exploiting, as well as by shunning, the opportunities of the market; they took advantage of the policy of *congregación* to seek out better land and livelihood; and, in distinct cases, they fled from community and *repartimiento* obligations, exchanging the arbitrary political will of *cacique* and *corregidor* for the – perhaps – more predictable economic authority of the landlord.[322] For, as both specific and comparative studies suggest, arbitrariness was probably the feature of oppression which most galled and threatened peasant communities, living as they were on the narrow shelf of subsistence.[323] A regular, predictable level of

---

[319] For example: Nickel, *Morfología social*, pp. 74–5, 82–3; Martin, *Governance and Society*, pp. 49, 63; Susan M. Deeds, 'Rural Work in Nueva Vizcaya: Forms of Labor Coercion on the Periphery', *Hispanic American Historical Review*, 69/3 (1989), pp. 440–1.

[320] Coatequitl: Lockhart, *The Nahuas*, p. 431; Gibson, *Aztecs under Spanish Rule*, pp. 222, 227. Exploitative *caciques*: García Martínez, *Pueblos de la sierra*, p. 199; Martin, *Rural Society*, p. 50; Taylor, *Landlord and Peasant*, pp. 53–4; Ouweneel, *Ciclos interrumpidos*, pp. 285–6.

[321] Taylor, *Landlord and Peasant*, pp. 36–7; MacLeod, 'Forms and Types of Work', p. 79; Cope, *Limits of Racial Domination*, p. 90.

[322] Martin, *Rural Society*, p. 50; Whitecotton, *The Zapotecs*, p. 209; Farriss, *Maya Society*, pp. 215–17.

[323] Farriss, *Maya Society*, pp. 49, 205; Scott, *Moral Economy*, pp. 179, 189. Tutino, *From Insurrection to Revolution*, p. 28, defines his third explanatory variable as 'security...[that is] the

exploitation could be tolerated; sudden, arbitrary demands pushed the peasant family or community into the abyss of destitution. At the same time, peasants sought to maximize security by diversifying income (in this they behaved like little *hacendados*: both super- and subordinate classes were conditioned by the constraints of an insecure, cash-starved, agrarian economy).[324] By their dogged evasion of arbitrary exactions and their sometimes ingenious pursuit of economic security, Indians played a significant part in moulding the contours of colonial society: they were not simply instruments of elite control and manipulation. It is clear, for example, that in central Mexico the *repartimiento* system began to break down – well in advance of its formal abolition (1633) – in part because of Indian noncompliance. In west-central Mexico, too, where the *repartimiento* lingered into the early eighteenth century, Indian recalcitrance similarly spurred a transition to free wage labour.[325] Seepage from village to hacienda thus depended as much on Indian connivance as on landlord contrivance.

This deserves a passing comment. Scholarly battle has periodically been joined between, on the one hand, scholars who tend to see the spread of the market and free labour as heightening peasant exploitation (hence, they suggest, peasants cling to older, paternalistic or pre-capitalist forms, expressive, perhaps, of a 'moral economy' and resist the capricious and pernicious penetration of market relations) and, on the other hand, scholars who regard the market, which peasants enter as sellers of both goods and labour, as emancipatory,

ability to attain subsistence consistently', which, he says, can 'at times [become] an apparent obsession among rural poor people'. The classic image is that of Tawney's Chinese peasant, 'standing up to his neck in water, so that even a ripple is sufficient to drown him': R. H. Tawney, *Land and Labor in China* (Boston, 1966), p. 77.

[324] Cf. Donald N. McCloskey, 'The Economics of Choice: Neoclassical Supply and Demand', in Thomas G. Rawski *et al.*, eds., *Economics and the Historian* (Berkeley, 1996), pp. 148–9. Another way of putting it would be to say that *hacendados* displayed distinctly Chayanovian tendencies: that is, they sought diversification, avoided risk and maximized security; however, for them, the penalty of failure was (at worst) bankruptcy, while for the peasant it might be starvation.

[325] Van Young, *Hacienda and Market*, p. 243. As noted earlier, Lockhart, *The Nahuas*, p. 180, followed by Restall, *The Maya World*, pp. 182–3, further argues that it was Indian acquisition of money (via wage labour and market activity) which induced the authorities to commute tribute payments in kind to payments in cash, rather than commutation (from above) compelling Indians to seek wage labour or enter the market, as has often been assumed. In both cases, it will be noted, Indian agency is stressed over non-Indian compulsion.

as freeing peasants from coercive, paternalistic authority, and as permitting them economic advancement, even cultural liberation.[326]

Neither side, of course, has a monopoly of the truth: instances of both patterns can be found. As a lady once said of the Mexican weather: 'no hay reglas fijas' (there are no fixed rules).[327] In some cases, in fact, both sides may be right: certain peasants may benefit from market involvement, while others suffer.[328] The reasons are obvious: market penetration tends to break up communities, dissolving old hierarchies, creating new ones; in the process, some individuals and families benefit, some fall by the wayside. If, taking a broad and general perspective, we relate this process to the genesis of agrarian capitalism, we may discern a familiar pattern: under the impact of the market, the peasantry tends to polarize, as an upper stratum (not necessarily the pre-existing upper stratum) takes advantage of market opportunities, combats whatever egalitarian inhibitors the community may possess and embarks on a course of profit-making and accumulation. Thus, England's yeomen farmers arose from the ranks of the medieval peasantry, and Russia's kulaks – the 'strong and sober' upon whom Stolypin placed his famous wager – broke away from the constraints of the peasant commune.[329]

These, the most obvious protagonists and beneficiaries of peasant commercialization, were small minorities. But there were other peasant groups – notably migrant and temporary labourers – who also took advantage of market opportunities and, no less important, combined individual betterment (however modest) with collective

---

[326] The classic debate pitted Scott, *Moral Economy*, against Samuel L. Popkin, *The Rational Peasant: The Political Economy of Rural Society in Vietnam* (Berkeley, 1979). McCloskey, 'The Economics of Choice', p. 146, weighs in for Popkin and berates 'the baleful influence' of Scott, Polanyi and Chayanov; his contribution, characteristically bullish but unconvincing, is based on the dubious notion that a rational (neoclassical) economic actor, parachuted into a feudal society (as described by the baleful trio) would make a killing ('buy[ing] low from one set of fools in order to sell high to another') rather than be killed.

[327] Charles Macomb Flandrau, *Viva Mexico!* (New York, 1938), p. 20.

[328] For a a good (eighteenth-century) example of how market demand – for maize and maguey fibre – benefited some while prejudicing others within a hitherto stable peasant community, see Tutino, *From Insurrection to Revolution*, pp. 160–3, describing San Miguel Mezquitic. Here, however, as usually happened in such cases, beneficiaries were outnumbered by victims: a telling point in favour of Scott's thesis.

[329] Christopher Hill, *Reformation to Industrial Revolution* (Harmondsworth, 1969), pp. 64–6, 70–1; Teodor Shanin, *Russia as a 'Developing Society'* (2 vols., New Haven, 1985), vol. 2, pp. 55–6, 236ff.

survival: thus, their market activity did not, like that of yeomen and kulaks, tend to dissolve the peasant community but rather served to reinforce it, by channelling resources from the market sector back to the village. By thus 'raiding the cash economy', market-oriented peasants might sustain, rather than subvert, the corporate community.[330] Plenty of Mexican peasant communities survived – even prospered – by combining subsistence farming with agrarian or artisan specialization: cochineal, tomatoes, onions, ceramics, furniture, firewood.[331]

Here, of course, we renew our acquaintance with the 'articulation of modes of production'. Now whether the market encourages such 'articulation' between coexisting modes – or, rather, the trituration of one mode by another – will depend on circumstances. It is probably true that, as the theorists of the moral economy have argued, the logic of the unfettered market is inimical to the survival of corporate peasant communities, hence the long-term consequence of market penetration is likely to be the destruction of those communities (unless peasant resistance – whether violent and spectacular or covert and anonymous – halts the process). However that is a long process. En route, some individual peasants and even some collective peasant communities may derive real benefits from market participation. They may tactically embrace the market (the creation, in a sense, of non-peasant elites), much as they tactically embrace other 'elite' creations, such as the Catholic religion or Hispanic law. The Tarahumara of northern Mexico – scattered, independent sierra Indians – showed themselves to be 'addicted to bartering' when Spanish goods entered their local economy.[332] Thus,

[330] The phrase is Scott's: *Moral Economy*, p. 212. On Indian migrant labour, see Van Young, *Hacienda and Market*, pp. 261–3; Martin, *Rural Society*, pp. 144–5. Ouweneel, *Ciclos interrumpidos*, p. 33, presents some suspiciously sweeping figures of migration ('about half the inhabitants of every village or city were born elsewhere'), an opinion which seems to be unduly influenced by the particular case studied by D. J. Robinson and C. G. McGovern, 'La migración regional yucateco en la época colonial. El caso de San Francisco de Umán', *Historia Mexicana*, 30/1 (1980), pp. 99–125 (compare Restall, *The Maya World*, p. 176, which gives a wide range of patterns for Yucatán, including some 'fully native' communities, untouched by migration). It is certain, however, that the traditional image of a static and immobile rural society is wrong.

[331] García Martínez, *Pueblos de la sierra*, p. 146; Whitecotton, *The Zapotecs*, pp. 197, 199; Horn, *Postcolonial Coyoacán*, pp. 87–9.

[332] The words of a Spanish missionary, quoted by Susan M. Deeds, 'Indigenous Responses to Mission Settlement in Nueva Vizcaya', in Langer and Jackson, eds., *The New Latin American Mission History*, p. 91.

even though the market, religion and the law may generally serve elite, non-peasant interests, they also offer opportunities which peasants may selectively and creatively seize upon to their own advantage. This, perhaps obvious, point is clear in the case of colonial Mexico: plenty of peasants (not, to be a sure, a majority) perceived benefits in quitting the community, temporarily or permanently, in favour of hacienda, mine and city; and benefits accrued, for individuals and, sometimes, communities, though at the cost of incurring new risks and forms of exploitation. The task of balancing beneficiaries against victims, and of trying to plot the broad trends contained within this process, is a difficult one, demanding careful spatial and temporal distinctions. It will be tackled, all too briefly and tentatively, over the next few pages.

Towns, mines and haciendas all came to depend to a degree on voluntary wage labour, as well as on Indian production for the market. Indians thus contributed both labour and goods to the commercial sector. The genesis of the northern mines offers a clear example. More generally, colonial cities came to depend on the services of déraciné Indians who, drawn by economic opportunity, quit their pueblos – periodically if not permanently – in order to find work as muleteers, bakers, pedlars, painters, potters, brickmakers, tailors, saddlers, blacksmiths, weavers, even innkeepers.[333] Mexico City began to acquire Indian barrios specializing in particular crafts and trades.[334] Individual communities also responded to the lure of commerce: the potters of Tonalá, Jalisco, for example, catered to extensive markets in the late colonial period; and the vigorous markets of pre-Conquest Mexico survived, notably in regions like Oaxaca, where Indian petty traders abounded.[335] Indians also produced and

[333] Gibson, *Aztecs under Spanish Rule*, pp. 397–400 (blacksmiths, tailors, saddlers, glass-workers, sword-, bell-, lace-, and glove-makers); Lockhart, *The Nahuas*, pp. 194–5 (muleteers and traders), 198 (painters and weavers). Cope, *Limits of Racial Domination*, p. 90, recounts how, when 50 Indian families were found 'living in ruined buildings near the Alameda' in central Mexico City in 1706, 'the Indian men proved to be nearly all skilled craftsmen; fully half were bricklayers or blacksmiths, and only a handful worked as common laborers'.

[334] For example: Cimatlan specialized in painting and metalwork; San Francisco Tequipec in stonemasonry; Atenco in spinning; Apahuascan in shoe- and button-making: Gibson, *Aztecs under Spanish Rule*, pp. 398–9, which notes that this represented, in part, a continuation of pre-Conquest residential-cum-occupational patterns.

[335] Tonalá's pottery ('the best the kingdom has to offer', in the words of a Spanish official) was worth 30,000 pesos a year in the 1790s: William B. Taylor, 'Banditry and Insurrection: Rural Unrest in Central Jalisco, 1790–1816', in Friedrich Katz, ed., *Riot, Rebellion, and Revolution: Rural Social Conflict in Mexico* (Princeton, 1988), p. 241. The English traveller Thomas Gage

sold cash crops: fruit and vegetables from the *chinampas* of Lake Xochimilco fed Mexico City (here, the old Mesoamerican tradition of polyculture lived on, sustained by the demands of the colonial capital); Puebla and Guadalajara were fed, in part, by Indian suppliers; cochineal from Oaxaca, cultivated by Indians, became a significant export crop; in central Mexico, Indians sold corn, pulque and even sugar, which they refined in small trapiches, alongside the big plantations of Morelos.[336] As a local *cacique* commented, expressing a common opinion, 'before the Spanish conquest, everyone had worked hard; by 1580 people spent far less time at work and much more time in trade'.[337]

Corn and pulque, of course, both represented subsistence products, only a fraction of which was usually marketed, the rest being locally consumed. Peasant participation in the market was therefore strictly limited and ancillary to subsistence production: market involvement seconded and did not subvert the subsistence rationale of most village farmers (there are useful analogies to be found among some twentieth-century Indian communities).[338] Among the Maya of colonial Yucatán, money was scarce and market participation

described the Indian merchants of the Mixteca, dealers in wax, honey and silk, 'who traffic to Mexico and about the country with twenty or thirty mules of their own, chopping and changing, buying and selling commodities': Thompson, *Thomas Gage's Travels*, p. 110; see also p. 147.

[336] Gibson, *Aztecs*, p. 321; Lockhart, *The Nahuas*, pp. 187–8, 191; Horn, *Postcolonial Coyoacán*, pp. 204–6; Van Young, *Hacienda and Market*, pp. 24–5; Haskett, *Indigenous Rulers*, pp. 177–83. Horst Pietschmann, 'Agricultura e industria rural indígena en el México de la segunda mitad del siglo XVIII', in Ouweneel y Torales Pacheco, *Empresarios, indos y estado*, pp. 81–2, and Juan C. Garavaglia and Juan C. Grosso, *Puebla desde una perspectiva microhistórica. Tepeaca y su entorno agrario: Población, producción e intercambio (1740–1870)* (Mexico, 1994), p. 109, illustrate the continued importance of Indian provisioning of Mexico City and Puebla through the eighteenth century. On cochineal: MacLeod, 'Forms and Types of Work', pp. 85–7; Whitecotton, *The Zapotecs*, pp. 198, 205; Hamnett, *Politics and Trade*, pp. 9–10, 25, 30–2. Olivera, *Pillis y macehuales*, pp. 158–9, also notes cochineal production in Puebla.

[337] Martin, *Rural Society*, p. 19. The notion that Indians had worked harder in the old days – under Aztec rule – is recurrent: see Gruzinski, *Conquest of Mexico*, pp. 84, 89. Given the demographic collapse of the sixteenth century (whch radically changed the man–land ratio), and the influx of European crops and animals, it is entirely likely that productivity increased, thus raising consumption and/or diminishing labour inputs. It may also be (though this would be much harder to ascertain) that the Spaniards, for all their colonialist whipcracking, were less effective at exacting surplus from the subject population than their Aztec predecessors had been. The contrast may be less clearcut for regions, such as Oaxaca, where the Aztec yoke had been lighter and, perhaps, the demographic collapse less severe and sudden: Chance, *Race and Class*, pp. 20, 69.

[338] Sol Tax, *Penny Capitalism: A Guatemalan Indian Economy* (Chicago, 1963), pp. 186–206.

limited.[339] When Indians entered the market, furthermore, they did so primarily to promote their own subsistence, not to turn themselves into commercial specialists: Spanish 'emphasis on the accumulation of surplus clashed with indigenous custom which, while not eschewing petty trade, embraced more immediate uses for agricultural production in consumption, gift-giving, and supernatural offerings'.[340] Such peasants did not become capitalists (employers of wage labour who sought rational profit-maximization and capital accumulation), although some became proletarians (free wage workers, lacking means of subsistence, hence obliged to sell their labour).

A few peasant producers, however, rose above the common ruck, setting themselves up as independent merchants, relatively emancipated from communal and subsistence ties. The spiky agave, for example, could be succesfully grown on arid rainfed fields in highland central Mexico, and nearby cities – Mexico City above all – had an unquenchable thirst for the pulque which it produced. Several villages in the immediate orbit of the capital came to specialize in pulque production; by the late colonial period even fertile irrigated zones like Cuauhtitlán were given over to endless rows of maguey plants. Some individuals prospered enough to acquire extensive property: one eighteenth-century Indian owned ten thousand maguey plants, four houses and an hacienda.[341] Indian traders commuted into the capital, marketing the fresh pulque. Many were women, Mexican equivalents of West Africa's mercantile mammies: the pulque trade offered a rare oportunity for female Indians to enter the market and achieve a degree of mobility; pulque-trading and rioting were the two urban activities in which Indian women particularly distinguished

---

[339] 'The ordinary Maya rarely had any cash': Farriss, *Maya Society*, p. 45. Restall, *The Maya World*, pp. 55–6, 107, 182–3, seeks to depict a more moneyed Maya, but the evidence is thin and, such as it is, seems to derive from the later years of the colony; furthermore, a society in which a machete or a door could become a valued heirloom hardly seems to be teeming with brisk market activity (see pp. 106, 115, 179).

[340] Deeds, 'Indigenous Responses', p. 82.

[341] On pulque production and trade, with particular reference to Indian participation: Gibson, *Aztecs under Spanish Rule*, pp. 318–19; Horn, *Postcolonial Coyoacán*, p. 205; Cope, *Limits of Racial Domination*, pp. 13, 35; Taylor, *Drinking, Homicide and Rebellion*, pp. 30–2, 36–8; Garavaglia and Grosso, *Puebla*, p. 118; Humboldt, *Political Essay*, p. 65, draws attention to an 'old Indian woman' who, at her death, bequeathed agave plants worth £15,000 in the Cholula region.

themselves.[342] Like all colonial commerce, the pulque trade was regulated (vigorous markets did not necessarily mean free markets). In this case, however, the authorities saw a threat in untrammelled Indian trading, and their attempts to tax and regulate the pulque trade led to recurrent conflict between Indian bootleggers and Spanish tax collectors.[343]

Pulque acted as a magnet to migrants – and as a source of potential unrest in a more general sense too. Male Indians regularly gathered in the city to meet, drink and carouse: 'the city was a time-out setting, an island of temporary personal liberty' for hedonistic visitors, perhaps two thousand of whom – by the later colonial period – daily quit their austere communities for the delights of the metropolis, where they added to Spanish concern over city crime.[344] The metropolis, as Simmel put it, became the 'locale of freedom'.[345] If, in this respect, Mexico City was the main attraction, lesser towns, like Oaxaca and Querétaro, also pulled in their temporary – and permanent – migrants from surrounding villages. Indeed, had they not done so, urban populations would have shrunk or stagnated, for urban growth (gradual in the seventeenth century, more rapid in the eighteenth) depended heavily on in-migration rather than natural reproduction.[346]

The hacienda was no garden of earthly delights. But it, too, offered an escape (temporary or permanent) from the village and an

[342] Taylor, *Drinking, Homicide and Rebellion*, pp. 37–8, 53 ('the important role of women in the pulque trade'), 116 (riots involving 'nasty mobs of hundreds of women brandishing spears and kitchen knives or cradling rocks in their skirts').

[343] Gibson, *Aztecs under Spanish Rule*, p. 318.

[344] Taylor, *Drinking, Homicide and Rebellion*, pp. 37, 66–7; Israel, *Race, Class, and Politics*, p. 57.

[345] George Simmel, in Richard Sennett, ed., *Classic Essays on the Culture of Cities* (New York, 1969), pp. 5–6. It was a different story, of course, for the dragooned workers of the city *obrajes*: see pp. 87, 164–5.

[346] There was no census of Mexico City until the 1790s; estimates of population vary considerably and, indeed, the actual population probably fluctuated a good deal in response to disease, flood and migration. From around 100,000 in the mid-sixteenth century, the city declined to perhaps 50–60,000, c. 1600; then recovered (irregularly) to 100,000 at the end of the seventeenth century, reaching perhaps 135,000 by the 1800s: Gibson, *Aztecs under Spanish Rule*, pp. 377–81; Gruzinski, *Histoire de Mexico*, pp. 240, 262, 294. Querétaro, meantime, grew from 1,000 in 1590 to 5,000 in 1630 and 26,000 in 1746: Super, *La vida en Querétaro*, pp. 16–17. A clear case of growth by in-migration was the Indian town of Jalatlaco, near Oaxaca (Antequera), which grew from less than 1,000 in the late sixteenth century to over 3,000 in the 1720s, 'primarily [as a result of] the in-migration of Indians from the Valley and the surrounding region': Chance, *Race and Class*, pp. 112–14.

opportunity to make a living. It therefore served, over time, as the chief engine of Indian acculturation, drawing Indians out of their pueblos, sometimes eroding local villages as much by its subtle elicitation of labour as by its more obvious expropriation of land. Eventually, village leaders complained of the hacienda's control of the hearts and minds, as well as the bodies, of their people, who now spurned community authority, tradition and ritual.[347] Certainly the hacienda community acquired a collective life which rivalled that of the village. Haciendas possessed their resident peon quarters, their chapels, garden plots, patron saints and fiestas.[348] Such organic ties redounded to the benefit of the *hacendado*, who had a strong interest in fostering them: rewarding loyalty, providing credit, offering political protection, forming networks of fictive kinship (*compadrazgo*) with peasant families, sponsoring – and even participating in – fiestas (witness the landlord-bishop who joined in bullfights).[349] Chapels were particularly important in constituting autonomous hacienda communities: they 'severed the last connection between nearby Indian towns and peasants residing on hacienda lands'.[350]

Haciendas were therefore more than simple units of economic production (even though production was their *raison d'être*). They were self-reproducing residential communities, possessed of distinctive characters and traditions. Hence their marked durability and longevity. They were also political enclaves, in the sense that the landlord enjoyed many of the powers conventionally associated with functionaries of the state. Sometimes, of course, landlords enjoyed such powers *de jure*: they actually held formal office; often, however, these were *de facto* powers, derived from the exploitation of private assets (land, capital, prestige, clienteles). With the elimination of the *encomienda*, Florescano observes, the hacienda acquired direct

---

[347] Van Young, *Hacienda and Market*, pp. 264–5. In eighteenth-century Yucatán we find Maya villagers opting to work on Spanish *estancias* in order to avoid the heavier taxes and collective work obligations of the pueblos: Patch, *Maya and Spaniard*, p. 197.

[348] Nickel, *Morfología social*, pp. 91–3; Chevalier, *Land and Society*, pp. 288–99; Lindley, *Haciendas and Economic Development*, pp. 11, 29; Martin, *Rural Society*, pp. 136, 144.

[349] Chevalier, *Land and Society*, p. 306; Ouweneel, *Ciclos interrumpidos*, p. 115; Nickel, *Morfología social*, p. 88, rightly points to the difficulty of evaluating hacienda 'paternalism'.

[350] Taylor, *Landlord and Peasant*, p. 123. Nickel, *Morfología social*, p. 227, notes that hacienda chapels – and their liturgical paraphernalia – frequently exceeded hacienda tools and machinery in value.

control over its dependent population: 'the owners progressively became masters, legislators, judges and magistrates over the hacienda residents'.[351]

Peons and their families were therefore bound to their masters by multiple ties. If economic dependence was the most obvious and pervasive, social, political and ideological dependence also underwrote the hacienda. Direct coercion – emphasized in some analyses of colonial society – was sporadic and probably not a *sine qua non*: hacienda peons were not corralled slaves, itching to escape. This raises the important and contentious question of debt peonage. According to the old *leyenda negra* of Hispanic colonialism, hacienda peons were tied to the estate by debts which converted them into surrogate slaves. Outright chattel slavery might have been rare in Mexico, the legend goes, but quasi-slavery existed throughout the colony, justified by peon debts. Certainly there were cases – some haciendas, a good many *obrajes* – of genuinely servile peonage, whereby peons, nominally free, were in fact held in bondage, subject to physical detention and corporal punishment.[352] Here, debt was a mere entrapment; it served as the figleaf of servitude. In other cases, however, debts represented perks or incentives, designed to attract, retain and reward workers. Far from indicating coercion, debts reflected the bargaining power of the worker and the (calculating) paternalism of the hacienda. Both systems – that is, both coercive and voluntary peonage – involved debts, which historians can read off from surviving hacienda account books. But debts in themselves prove little: it is the context within which debts were incurred which counts. And, obviously, debts-as-bonds and debts-as-perks operated within different contexts, with different results: a bonded labour force implied a very different kind of hacienda, both socially and economically, as compared to a voluntary labour force.[353]

---

[351] Florescano, 'Formation and Economic Structure', p. 167.

[352] Chevalier, *Land and Society*, p. 69, expresses the traditional view that 'serfdom through debt became a full-fledged institution in the seventeenth century under the hacienda economy'. For further examples of this view, see Van Young, *Hacienda and Market*, pp. 248–9. Examples of employer coercion, in both haciendas and *obrajes*, are given by Nickel, *Morfología social*, pp. 85–7; Martin, *Rural Society*, pp. 147–8; Taylor, *Landlord and Peasant*, p. 152; Borah, *Justice by Insurance*, p. 181; Cope, *Limits of Racial Domination*, pp. 98–101.

[353] Barrington Moore Jr., *Social Origins of Dictatorship and Democracy: Lord and Peasant in the Making of the Modern World* (Harmondsworth, 1969), pp. 433–5.

Late colonial evidence, which is quite abundant, shows that debt
peonage was not a fundamentally coercive system of servitude; that
endebted peons could and did move around, changing employers;
that, in several cases, haciendas owed peons more than peons owed
them.[354] Debt thus figured as an item in a relatively 'free' (but, of
course, highly unequal) bargaining relationship. Peons threatened
to quit estates if their demand for credit was refused; conversely,
some eighteenth-century landlords sought to eliminate debts, on the
grounds that they were inefficient and loss-making. And the royal
authorities did not consider it their task to chase up defaulting peon
debtors.[355] Furthermore, it does not seem that this was a wholly novel
situation in the eighteenth century. Indians who demanded a monetary advance before working on haciendas claimed that they did so
by 'ancient custom'.[356] Of course, peasants regularly and imagina-
tively invoke 'ancient customs',[357] but in this case there would seem
to be some basis to the claim. In the seventeenth century, labour
was in shorter supply than in the eighteenth, thus peon bargaining
power was greater. While this *could* have made for pervasive coercion of labour, it does not seem that it actually did. Indian complaints
against abusive *curas*, officials, mine-owners and *obraje*-bosses appear to greatly outnumber complaints against *hacendados*.[358] In the
Guadalajara region, 'the system of credit advances to workers was
a manifestation not of the weakness of their position in the free-
labor market, but of their strength. Rural laborers could and did
demand substantial advances of cash and goods, as well as the payment on credit of tithes, ecclesiastiacal fees, legal fines, and other
obligations'.[359] In a sense, the peon's debt paralleled the *hacendado*'s,

---

[354] Taylor, *Landlord and Peasant*, pp. 151–2; Gibson, *Aztecs under Spanish Rule*, pp. 254–5; Martin,
Rural Society, p. 73; Ouweneel, *Ciclos interrumpidos*, p. 112. The existence of peon 'savings'
raises the question of whether these were 'forced' savings (which redounded to the benefit of
the landlord) or voluntary savings, which workers chose to 'bank' with their employer: Nickel,
Morfología social, p. 87, prefers the former; but the evidence is hardly conclusive either way.

[355] Taylor, *Landlord and Peasant*, pp. 148–9; Gibson, *Aztecs under Spanish Rule*, p. 253.

[356] Gibson, *Aztecs under Spanish Rule*, p. 255.

[357] Gruzinski, *Conquest of Mexico*, p. 101; compare Juan Martínez Alier, *Haciendas, Plantations
and Collective Farms* (London, 1977), p. 51.

[358] Borah's analysis of Indian litigation suggests that victims were more often villagers than peons,
and that the alleged perpetrators of abuses were more often colonial officials and clerics
than landlords (*Justice by Insurance*, p. 126ff.). However, this may partly reflect the fact that
hacendados effectively screened their properties from the prying eyes of royal justice.

[359] Van Young, *Hacienda and Market*, p. 249.

often owed to church or merchant money-lender: both peon and *hacendado* operated within a cash-starved economy, in which pay- ments either in kind or on credit were ubiquitous.

Peons' debts – advances – thus figured among a range of incentives which, in the prevailing circumstances, made hacienda employment either tolerable or desirable for a large section of the rural popula- tion. Of course, 'prevailing circumstances' is a major qualifier, includ- ing progressive dispossession of villages, fiscal demands (taxes, tithe and tribute), ethnic discrimination and the gradual monetization of the agrarian economy. Without these pressures, villagers would not have sought *hacienda* employment, and *hacendados* would have had to meet their labour requirements either by resorting to outright co- ercion (as, for example, *obraje*-owners often did), or by paying hefty wage increases, which they were certainly unwilling to do, and (given the marginal productivity of labour) they were perhaps unable to do, without risk of bankruptcy.[360] As it was, prevailing circumstances cast the hacienda in an ostensibly more benign role. The hacienda offered security and succour; hence the landlord's authority, espe- cially where it was exercised with a certain paternalist solicitude, acquired legitimacy, for the landlord appeared to contribute to a rela- tionship which, however unequal, was at least reciprocal and which allowed some mutual bargaining. Such ostensible reciprocity has rightly been seen as the basis of stable landlord-peasant relations, just as its breakdown has been seen as signalling the onset of peas- ant protest and revolution (of which more shortly).[361] While coercion was necessary to provide sugar plantations with slaves, *obrajes* with weavers and some northern mines with underground toilers, many haciendas could rely on non-coercive mechanisms to recruit their workers. Similar paternalist relations, revolving around the provi- sion of credit, appear to have characterized the Mexico City labour market too.[362]

---

[360] Martin, *Rural Society*, p. 73, notes that the Morelos landlords faced 'crippling labor shortages' even when they offered daily wages of two and a half reales (that is, about 25% above average: see Nickel, *Morfología social*, p. 80). For an interesting theoretical discussion, see Evsey D. Domar, 'The Causes of Slavery or Serfdom: A Hypothesis', *The Journal of Economic History*, 30 (March 1970), pp. 18–32.

[361] Scott, *Moral Economy*, ch. 6, and Barrington Moore, Jr., *Injustice: The Social Bases of Obedience and Revolt* (London, 1979), pp. 20–2, 26–7, 440–4, offer perceptive analyses of reciprocity as a social norm.

[362] Cope, *Limits of Racial Domination*, pp. 38–9, 112–14.

As regards resident workers, a battery of positive factors, many of them non-economic, reinforced peon dependency: security, paternalism, preaching, seigneurial prestige. But economic pressures – the need to subsist, the 'dull pressure of economic relations' – were paramount.[363] Such pressures also served to draw temporary labourers from the villages to the haciendas where, during the busy months of the agricultural cycle, they supplemented the permanent workers.[364] While the quasi-industrial sugar plantations required a large permanent work force (which in turn made coercion more feasible and cost-effective), most haciendas needed to recruit gangs of temporary labourers (*eventuales*), and many developed stable, symbiotic relations with local villages in order to meet their needs. Again, such relations tended to be – 'in the prevailing circumstances' – voluntaristic. For, as I suggested earlier, villagers derived not only individual but also, sometimes, collective benefits from temporary hacienda work. Haciendas needed villages and, in a roundabout way, sustained them, at least so long as they served as reliable sources of labour.

Thus, compared with chattel slavery, *encomienda* and *repartimiento* – the three labour systems of the early colony – the hacienda of the mature colony was a relatively non-coercive institution. For that reason it could exist – and did so well into the eighteenth century – despite the absence of a standing army or equivalent coercive institutions.[365] The Habsburg hacienda was not the target of sustained violent peasant resistance. Its expansion took advantage of a declining, disorganized peasantry, and its subsequent development offered employment opportunities which were, to a degree, negotiable. Furthermore, hacienda expansionism was severely constrained by the limits of the market, as we will analyse later. The prospective economic returns which would accrue from a

---

[363] Marx, quoted by Pierre Bourdieu, *The Logic of Practice* (Stanford, 1990), p. 41; see also Nicholas Abercrombie, Stephen Hill, Bryan S. Turner, *The Dominant Ideology Thesis* (London, 1984). pp. ix, 163.

[364] Nickel, *Morfología social*, pp. 74–5; Gibson, *Aztecs under Spanish Rule*, p. 254, which contrasts the flexible labour regime of the hacienda with the more draconian *obraje*.

[365] Prior to the eighteenth century Spanish justice – though sporadically harsh, especially in moments of crisis (such as the 1692 riot in Mexico City, discussed later) – was civilian, inefficient and lacking both reach and resources. Indian communities, meanwhile, largely policed themselves: Colin M. MacLachlan, *Criminal Justice in Eighteenth-Century Mexico: A Study of the Tribunal of the Acordada* (Berkeley, 1974), pp. 25–36.

thorough-going expropriation – that is to say, proletarianization – of the peasantry did not justify the potential political risks. (Even the proletarianization of miners – turning them from freelance 'artisans' into a disciplined wage labour force – proved difficult and contentious.)[366] So the village was allowed its place, albeit a constricted place, at least so long as agrarian markets remained sluggish. Both Habsburg paternalism and Habsburg social stability were therefore products of inexorable economic and demographic forces, rather than of any high-flown Christian idealism.

VI. Acculturation and Resistance: Central Mexico

If the economic incentives for hacienda expansion and peasant dispossession remained quite limited, at least till the eighteenth century, the associated political risks were apparent throughout. Despite immigration, miscegenation and disease, the Indian subordinate mass always outnumbered the Spanish superordinate elite; the latter lived with a lurking fear, occasionally reinforced by chilling experience, that the feckless Indian would turn ferocious savage, perhaps in unholy alliance with the black slave.[367] For the Church, too, the superficial Christian meekness of the Indian often masked idolatry and diabolism.[368] Lacking sizeable, permanent military forces, the Spanish elite had to govern with some regard to the wishes of the governed. That raises a crucial but difficult question: the place of the Indians – and, increasingly, the castes – in the colonial order. Conquered by Cortés, the Indians of central Mexico had to come to terms with a radically new society. How did they react? What part did the Indian mass play in colonial society? This elusive question is perhaps best tackled under the dual heading of acculturation and resistance.[369]

---

[366] Doris Ladd, *The Making of a Strike: Mexican Silver Workers' Struggles in Real del Monte, 1766–1775* (Lincoln, 1988), p. 14ff.; Martin, *Governance and Society*, pp. 49–56.

[367] Cope, *Limits of Racial Domination*, pp. 11, 15–16, 21, 25. See also Lockhart and Otte, *Letters and People*, pp. 185–6, on Viceroy Velasco's intemperate scaremongering and stereotyping.

[368] Gruzinski, *Conquest of Mexico*, pp. 146–7ff.

[369] As already mentioned in n. 266 the notion of 'acculturation' raises some academic hackles, since it is sometimes assumed to mean a 'one–directional' process whereby Indians were 'acculturated' (or 'decultured'): Farriss, *Maya Society*, p. 110. Cynthia Radding, *Wandering Peoples: Colonialism, Ethnic Spaces, and Ecological Frontiers in Northwestern Mexico, 1700–1850* (Durham, 1997), pp. 110–11, further criticizes the concept for implying 'a state of social and ecological equilibrium prior to the conquest' (which would clearly be wrong). I do not think such narrow and skewed perspectives are necessarily inherent in the term, which I take

For the Aztec regions of central Mexico the Conquest was a traumatic experience. Old rulers and old gods were suddenly confounded and cast down. New forms of art, communication and calendrical reckoning replaced the old.[370] Ancient rituals – human sacrifice, the ballgame – were eliminated. The martial ethic of the Aztec warrior class was extinguished. While the conquered Maya could derive some comfort from their cyclical view of history, and from their own record of assimilating – Mayanizing – previous waves of conquerors, the defeated Aztecs found no such cultural solace.[371] Some Indians – the Otomí of central Mexico, the Zapotecs of Oaxaca – tried to blot the Conquest from their collective memory.[372] Contemporaries described (in so many words) a condition of anomie: Indian society, having lost its social and religious bearings, appeared to disintegrate in a welter of drink, suicide, idleness and vagrancy.[373] Certainly the harsh, Catonist ethic of the Aztec regime was relaxed; and Spanish officials and clerics, like Zorita, who lamented its passing (and, perhaps, exaggerated its efficacy) proved incapable of reviving it.[374] In the 1520s – as again in the 1820s and 1920s – war, upheaval and mortality left a legacy of rootless people (including the first generation of mestizos), cut off from community, subsisting as best they could in a newly fluid environment.[375]

to denote a multidirectional blending of cultural items and representations (including, for example, 'Mayanization' of Spaniards as well as 'Hispanization' of the Maya). Furthermore, it is difficult to know what alternative portmanteau term should be preferred: Gruzinski, *Conquest of Mexico*, p. 282, claims to prefer 'Europeanization' but nevertheless uses 'acculturation' (e.g., pp. 96, 146, 150). 'Resistance' is, in my view, even more slippery: see the perceptive analysis of Lockhart, *The Nahuas*, pp. 442–6. I therefore put forward these terms less as major analytical categories than as simple pegs on which to hang a discussion.

370 Gruzinski, *Conquest of Mexico*, ch. 1.

371 Farriss, *Maya Society*, pp. 20, 25, 70. The difference is not absolute. Gruzinski, *Conquest of Mexico*, pp. 127–8, describes the Nahua's mental wrestling with Spanish notions of time (before and after Christ, the last judgement and resurrection), noting points of congruence and assimilation, as well as points of contradiction and incomprehension.

372 Gruzinski, *Conquest of Mexico*, pp. 132–7.

373 Gibson, *Aztecs under Spanish Rule*, 149–50; Taylor, *Drinking, Homicide and Rebellion*, pp. 28, 40, 45; Gruzinski, *Conquest of Mexico*, p. 97.

374 Zorita, *Lords of New Spain*; Brading, *First America*, p. 113.

375 Cope, *Limits of Racial Domination*, p. 15; Padden, *Hummingbird and the Hawk*, p. 232, describes how the 'camp children ... conceived and born during the conquest' were, by the early 1530s, 'roaming in packs like wolves ... feared for their depredations against organized society'. While this may capture something of contemporary anxieties – Spanish and Indian – it should be taken with a pinch of salt. Inter-generational stereotypes are poor guides to social reality. Lockhart, 'Introduction', p. 15, considers the 'mestizo vagabond' to be largely mythical. Furthermore, even if Mexico's first mestizos were – in Cope's phrase – 'quintessential outsiders',

Social anomie had its spiritual counterpart in the pervasive condition of *nepantlism*: that is, a midway hovering between the blasted
faith of old, and the new, as yet poorly understood and assimilated,
Catholicism of the Spaniards, which in turn bred a hybrid ritual,
'a confused participation in both types of rites'.[376] And, in general
terms, the realm of religion shrank. In Precolumbian Mesoamerica religion had pervaded society and nature; it had been inseparable from 'secular' activities such as work and government. The
Conquest introduced the Spanish/European duality of religion and
nature, spirit and flesh, thus justifying a more instrumental attitude toward nature, as well as a more puritanical attitude towards
sexuality; Indians had to wrestle with new notions of 'sin', asceticism, heaven and hellfire.[377] Now, 'mundane' activities, such as work
and government, lost much of their religious aura and, perhaps,
much of their legitimating rationale. Thus desacralized, work became a means – to survival – and government a power to be reckoned with but not revered. The 'merry', hard-working Indians of the
early sixteenth century soon became the lazy natives of the colony,
the object of incessant Spanish complaint.[378] Old beliefs and rituals lived on covertly, as we have noted; in their daily lives the
Indians still invested supernatural significance in familiar places
and things: caves, hills, streams, wells, trees, plants, arrows, gourds,

this was a conjunctural, historical condition, not some permanent mark of Cain. I stress this
point because there has been a tendency to impute virtually timeless characteristics to these
broad and shifting 'racial' categories: e.g., Eric Wolf, *Sons of the Shaking Earth* (Chicago,
1972), pp. 238–41 (on which, see also Cope, p. 6); and, more egregiously, José Vasconcelos,
The Cosmic Race (Baltimore, 1997; transl. Didier Jaen).

[376] Klor de Alva, 'Spiritual Conflict and Accommodation', p. 355; see also Cervantes, *Devil in the
New World*, pp. 57, 61.

[377] Gruzinski, *Conquest of Mexico*, pp. 165–6; Burkhart, *Slippery Earth*, pp. 28–34, 53–7, which
describes mendicant efforts to convey the notion of hellfire to puzzled Indians: one friar
'acted out the torments of hell upon his own body: walking on hot coals; washing in boiling
water; and having his Indian assistants choke him, whip him, and drip burning pine resin into
his wounds'. Another, less given to masochism or self-mortification, hit on a better idea: he
organized 'the burning alive [of] small animals in an oven; their cries of pain were to represent
the anguish of sinners in hell'. On Catholic/European dualism, see Perry Anderson, *Passages
from Antiquity to Feudalism* (London, 1978), pp. 133, 188.

[378] Gibson, *Aztecs*, p. 220 ('merry' Indians); cf. Gruzinski, *Conquest of Mexico*, p. 85; Deeds, 'Indige-
nous Responses', pp. 77, 95 (Indians as 'vain, sneaky, faithless, cheating thieves and drunks').
Mestizos – especially lower-class mestizos – were similarly seen as 'lazy [and] parasitic': Cope,
Limits of Racial Domination, pp. 19–20. The colonial parallels are many and obvious: see Syed
Husein Alatas, *The Myth of the Lazy Native* (London, 1977).

baskets.[379] But the totality of Mesoamerican religion was shattered. And neither the new Spanish priests nor the Indian converts who supplanted the pre-Conquest *papas* as mediators between God and Man were able to restore that totality.

It has been suggested that the social upheaval of the Conquest represented a kind of collective psychological trauma, inducing an Indian mentality comparable to the supposed 'Sambo' stereotype of the North American black slave: depressed, irresponsible, childish, feckless, self-destructive.[380] Even today, students of Indian society sometimes lapse into murky Jungian discourse, imputing to the Indian a kind of traumatized collective unconscious, dating to the Conquest and transmitted down the generations.[381] In fact, to the extent that 'Sambo-like' features were discerned in colonial society, they were the consequence of the Indians' social, political and economic subordination. They represented a mask rather than a soul.[382] Or, changing the metaphor, they numbered among the 'weapons of the weak': irresponsibility, fecklessness, ostensible childishness were means to contest the power of superiors, in a situation where overt resistance was likely to be risky and counterproductive.[383] As Humboldt (who subscribed to the familiar stereotype) acutely observed, Mexico's Indians 'suffer the vexations to which they are frequently exposed from the whites. They oppose to them...a cunning veiled under the deceitful appearance of apathy or stupidity'.[384] Another, related, Spanish lament concerned Indian alcoholism, which was seen as further proof of Indian degeneration. 'If our sources may be believed', writes Gibson, 'few peoples in the whole of history were more prone

[379] Gruzinski, *Conquest of Mexico*, pp. 92–3, 153, 171, 231–2; Marcelo Carmagnani, *El regreso de los dioses* (Mexico, 1988), pp. 27–31.

[380] Taylor, *Drinking, Homicide and Rebellion*, p. 2 (criticizing this stereotype); compare Stanley M. Elkins, *Slavery: A Problem in American Institutional and Intellectual Life* (Chicago, 1959).

[381] Alan Knight, 'Racism, Revolution and *Indigenismo*: Mexico, 1910–1940', in Richard Graham, ed., *The Idea of Race in Latin America, 1870–1940* (Austin, 1990), p. 94

[382] Sweet, 'The Ibero–American Frontier Mission', pp. 39–40, makes the point with respect to northern Indians and their relationship to the missions; see also Farriss, *Maya Society*, p. 93.

[383] Compare James C. Scott, *Weapons of the Weak: Everyday Forms of Peasant Resistance* (New Haven, 1985).

[384] Humboldt, *Political Essay*, p. 57.

to drunkenness than the Indians of the Spanish colony'.[385] Intoxicated by adulterated drink, a Mexico City priest complained, Indians 'commit heathen idolatries and sacrifices, fall into disputes and kill each other, and engage in carnal abominations and incestuous sexual acts'.[386] In fact, the Spaniards exaggerated both pre-Conquest abstinence and post-Conquest excess (not least because they feared that drink stoked the fires of Indian belligerence). They also overlooked the self-regulation of drinking habits by Indian communities. Drink, the curse of the Indian, in fact figured prominently in community fiestas, collective work and day-to-day relations; it reinforced rather than destroyed the bonds of community.[387] The same was true of the hallucinogens (notably the peyote mushroom) which played an important part in Indian ritual, alarming the Spaniards with its supposed association with religious deviance and diabolism.[388] Alcohol, however, was more pervasive, and possessed one signal social virtue, apart from those just mentioned: it offered a valid excuse for violence – even homicide – in colonial courts.[389] Indian 'alcoholism' had a forensic, as well as a festive, purpose.[390]

Furthermore, the consequences of the Conquest for Indians were not wholly negative; the Conquest not only brought downfall and depression but also stimulated creative iniatives which belied the Sambo-like stereotype. In the sixteenth century, as in later centuries, Indians could rise, prosper and innovate, given propitious social circumstances. The Conquest toppled ruling dynasties and shook up Indian social hierarchies. The latter, like geological strata shaken by earthquakes, slipped, crumbled and were compressed. To put it crudely, Indian society emerged from the Conquest more egalitarian within itself, with kings cast down, nobles demoted and

---

[385] Gibson, Aztecs under Spanish Rule, p. 409. See also Sonia Corcuera de Mancera, El fraile, el indio y el pulque. Evangelización y embriaguez en la Nueva España (1523–1548) (Mexico, 1991), pp. 116–25.

[386] Cope, Limits of Racial Domination, p. 35.

[387] Taylor, Drink, Homicide and Rebellion, p. 57–62; Lockhart, The Nahuas, p. 112; Deeds, 'Indigenous Responses', p. 84, discusses Tarahumara tesguinadas (social drinking bouts) in northern Mexico. Humboldt, Political Essay, p. 51, agreed that (late colonial) Spaniards exaggerated Indian bibulousness.

[388] Gruzinski, Conquest of Mexico, pp. 153, 215–18; Cervantes, Devil in the New World, pp. 14, 47.

[389] Taylor, Drink, Homicide and Rebellion, pp. 64–5; Stern, Secret History of Gender, p. 51.

[390] The notion that 'no man is guilty of an act of rage (coraje)' – a condition frequently associated with drink – continues to inform modern Mexican practice: Paul Friedrich, The Princes of Naranja (Austin, 1987), pp. 8, 15.

serfs (*mayeques*) eliminated.[391] (Of course, this egalitarianism was a function of the imposition, over all Indian strata, of a new, alien, Spanish elite; as Patch puts it, 'one of the tragedies of European colonialism in America was the transformation of great civilizations into peasantries'.)[392] Such an upheaval, of course, produced winners and losers, even among the conquered. Don Carlos, son of King Nezahualpilli, was not idly imagining the good old days when he complained that 'in the time of our forefathers the *macehuales* (commoners) did not sit on straw mats and seats; now, everyone says and does whatever comes into his head'.[393] As Don Carlos implied, old norms and practices had been subverted by the Conquest. Patterns of marriage and (especially male) dress changed; consumption patterns shifted, as new foodstuffs entered the Indian diet; coin replaced (or supplemented) the cacao 'currency' of pre-Conquest Mesoamerica.[394] Indians learned new trades – pedlar, muleteer, chorister, weaver of wool or silk – and worked with new tools and animals. Some believed that Indians worked less (and ate more).[395] Certainly they fought less: the Conquest ended the endemic warfare of the Postclassic period and ushered in three centuries of peace.[396] Although the economic burdens of tribute could be heavy and (what

---

[391] Gibson, *Aztecs under Spanish Rule*, pp. 153–7; Lockhart, *The Nahuas*, pp. 96–7, 99–100, 111; Padden, *Hummingbird and the Hawk*, pp. 225, 233–4; Horn, *Postconquest Coyoacán*, p. 53. Change, though roughly comparable, was slower in the south (Oaxaca, Yucatán), where Indian nobles retained greater power, prestige and property: see Taylor, *Landlord and Peasant*, pp. 41, 49–50; Whitecotton, *The Zapotecs*, p. 186; Patch, *Maya and Spaniard*, pp. 24–5; Farriss, *Maya Society*, ch. 8.

[392] Patch, *Maya and Spaniard*, p. 67.

[393] Gruzinski, *Man-Gods*, p. 35.

[394] Gruzinski, *Conquest of Mexico*, p. 27; Lockhart, *The Nahuas*, pp. 177–9, notes both the speedy introduction of Spanish coinage into Indian (Nahua) society and the survival of cacao – chiefly for 'small transactions', i.e., as 'small change' – throughout the colonial period, a survival encouraged by the colony's acute shortage of metal currency (see, for example, Farriss, *Maya Society*, pp. 154, 266; though cf. Restall, *The Maya World*, p. 183, who finds 'no evidence of the continued use of cacao beans as small change' in Yucatán).

[395] Gruzinski, *Conquest of Mexico*, pp. 84, 95; Martin, *Rural Society*, p. 19. The English traveller Thomas Gage commented on the abundance of food in early seventeenth-century Mexico; but, with characteristic English disdain for foreign gastronomy, he felt obliged both to disparage the fruit ('most fair and beautiful to behold', he conceded, yet lacking the 'inward virtue or nourishment' of a Kentish pippin [apple]) and to draw tendentious human parallels: 'as in meat and fruit there is this inward and hidden deceit, so likewise the same is to be found in the people that are born and bred there, who make fair outward shews, but are inwardly false and hollow-hearted': Thompson, *Thomas Gage's Travels*, pp. 59–60.

[396] This generalization applies to the old Mesoamerican heartland, including the Tarascan, Aztec and Maya regions; it does not apply to the Gran Chichimec of the north, which neither suffered the intense inter-state warfare of the Postclassic nor enjoyed the Pax Hispánica of the colony.

was often worse) capricious, they were not necessarily more extreme than they had been before the Conquest – especially, it would seem, in the heartland of the old Aztec empire. Paradoxically, while the Aztecs suffered the greatest fall from dominion to servitude, the living standards of their people may have benefited most from the Conquest.[397]

Once the Conquest was complete, Mexico's Indians were able to set their own stamp on the evolving colony. Indian *caciques*, we have noted, enjoyed power and privilege; the old Mesoamerican *altepetl* – the city-state and its immediate hinterland – frequently formed the basis for the new Spanish *municipio*; Aztec *calpulli* became Spanish barrios, or residential districts; the relations between head towns (*cabeceras*) and their satellite communities (*sujetos*) also mirrored Mesoamerican precedent.[398] Within the Indian towns a vigorous form of self-government prevailed, involving elections which impressed Spanish observers.[399] The maintenance of a separate, though subordinate, Indian culture was advocated by the regular clergy, by Indian *caciques*, and (with necessary tergiversations) by the colonial authorities. Against this 'united bureaucratic front' (which was not always so united), stood the Spanish landlords, miners and merchants who needed Indian labour and encouraged the seepage of Indians from their communities into the mines, haciendas and cities. And in this, they often enjoyed the sympathy and support of the

[397] References to Indian idleness and good living (see n. 395) appear to derive chiefly from the Valley of Mexico, seat of the overpopulated and disciplinarian Aztec empire. Here, following the Conquest, dramatic demographic decline occurred in a region of high productivity (higher still thanks to the introduction of European crops and animals). Elsewhere – in Chiapas or Yucatán, for example – the contrast was less clearcut; possibly Spanish exactions – of goods and labour – exceeded those of pre-Conquest elites.

[398] Lockhart, *The Nahuas*, pp. 28–58; Gibson, *Aztecs under Spanish Rule*, pp. 152, 182, 190; Horn, *Postcolonial Coyoacán*, ch. 1; Spores, *The Mixtec Kings*, pp. 106–7.

[399] Gibson, *Aztecs under Spanish Rule*, pp. 175–8; Lockhart, *The Nahuas*, pp. 30–40; Taylor, *Landlord and Peasant*, pp. 48–51; Carmagnani, *Regreso de los dioses*, pp. 190–4; Haskett, *Indigenous Rulers*, especially ch. 2. Electoral procedures varied from place to place; electorates also varied but appear usually to have been the elite males of the community (though in at least one case [Santa Fe, in the Valley of Mexico, 1790] the electorate came to include all married males: Gibson, *Aztecs under Spanish Rule*, p. 177; Taylor, *Landlord and Peasant*, p. 50). Ouweneel, *Ciclos interrumpidos*, p. 279, offers several [eighteenth-century] examples, ranging from 7% to 27% of the population, with an average of 13% [$N = 5$]. Factionalism was rife (the Indian community was no happy consensual Utopia); and, in defiance of formal rules, Indian officials – *gobernadores*, *alcaldes* and *regidores* – were often re-elected time after time. This was not popular democracy, but it afforded a limited degree of representation, competition and, perhaps, accountability.

secular clergy.[400] In simple and schematic terms: Spanish laymen sought to make of the Indians a subordinate class, free from royal and clerical paternalism, available for exploitation, yet condemned by their Indianness to perpetual subordination and debarred from competing with Spaniards as rural producers or urban traders and artisans. The Spaniards wanted the advantages of the free market within the constraints of strict ethnic segregation: the parallel with apartheid South Africa or the Old South is striking. The Crown and religious orders, in contrast, sought to maintain caste and ethnicity in a purer form, permitting a degree of mobility *within* the *república de indios* but strictly controlling and limiting both the seepage of Indians into the Spanish sector and the brusque invasion of Spaniards (and mestizos and blacks) into the Indian 'republic'. Friars were accused not only of insulating the Indian community but even of enticing Indians from the haciendas and back to their villages.[401] The Spanish lay vision was of a vertically layered society, Spaniards atop Indians; the Crown and mendicant alternative was of two parallel but unequal hierarchies, with contact between the two curtailed and regulated. In the first case, the servants lived below stairs; in the second, they were billeted in separate quarters.

Given this conflict, the Indians themselves were far from powerless or passive. Indian *caciques* took advantage of both royal privileges and hacienda needs; Indian labourers (*naborías*) could play *cacique* against hacienda; Indian communities litigated tirelessly over land, treasuring their land titles, beating their bounds, claiming their patrimony 'from time immemorial' until 'the Day of Judgement'.[402] In the same litigious spirit – 'the conquerors were amazed that subjects so meek showed such ferocity and tenacity in litigation' – Indians ceaselessly lobbied the royal bureaucracy, taking advantage of whatever opportunity royal paternalism offered to offset the structural ethnic bias of the colony.[403] The outcome was complex and fluid, but

---

[400] Israel, *Race, Class, and Politics*, pp. 49–50, 52, 86.

[401] Israel, *Race, Class, and Politics*, p. 50.

[402] Taylor, *Landlord and Peasant*, pp. 37–40; Martin, *Rural Society*, pp. 48–9; Gruzinski, *Conquest of Mexico*, pp. 100–1, 120–1.

[403] Borah, *Justice by Insurance*, pp. 40–1. Thus, Susan Kellogg, *Law and the Transformation of Aztec Culture, 1500–1700* (Norman, Okla., 1995), pp. 2–3ff., plausibly sees the legal system as a crucial means to 'channel and defuse Nahua discontent'. On litigiousness – which, in Spanish eyes, figured along with drink and sexual incontinence as the salient vices of the

certain broad features – both structural characteristics and shifting trends – can be discerned.

Over the years, strict caste barriers tended to erode. Women formed a small minority of the early Spanish settlers, perhaps no more than one-seventh in the 1520–40 period. Spanish men soon followed Cortés's example in taking Indian wives and mistresses. Prior to the economic needs of the hacienda, therefore, it was the sexual needs of the Spaniards which spurred Indian acculturation and ladinization. In addition to the basic Indian/Spanish dichotomy, African slaves formed a significant minority, especially in the sixteenth and seventeenth centuries. The result was a spectrum of racial types, which the colonial regime sought to classify with bureaucratic precision. Each type represented a particular conjugation of the original triad Indian/Spaniard/African; each had its slang variant, too.[404] But certain basic categories predominated: Spaniard (*español*), that is, European, either Spanish-born (*peninsular*) or American-born (criollo/creole: though the term was rarely used); caste or mestizo (a category denoting Spanish/Indian miscegenation which in turn contained many subcategories); black and mulatto; and 'pure' Indian.[405] The colony was thus formed on the basis of four basic ethnic types (Spaniard, Indian, caste and black); with the decline of the black population in the seventeenth century, a tripartite system emerged (Spaniard, Indian and caste).[406]

In the mid-seventeenth century, Indians still represented the majority of New Spain's population, notwithstanding the post-Conquest demographic collapse. They numbered perhaps 1.3 million, or three-quarters of New Spain's total population; American-born Spaniards (creoles) now represented 10 per cent (169,000), mulattos 7 per cent (117,000), mestizos 6 per cent (109,000), blacks 2 per cent (35,000), and *peninsular* Spaniards – the commercial and administrative

---

Indian population – see also Zorita, *Lords of New Spain*, p. 125; Haskett, *Indigenous Rulers*, pp. 79–82. Taylor, *Magistrates of the Sacred*, pp. 363, 378, 440, shows that litigiousness did not fade with time; eighteenth-century Indians litigated even more than their ancestors had.

[404] Israel, *Race, Class, and Politics*, pp. 60–6; Leonard, *Baroque Times*, p. 51; Pastor, *Campesinos y reformas*, p. 124.

[405] Cope, *Limits of Racial Domination*, p. 24, notes 40 potential racial categories and 7 actual categories: Spaniard; castizo (i.e., the offspring of a Spaniard-mestizo union); morisco (Spaniard-mulatto); mestizo (Spaniard-Indian); mulatto (Spaniard-black); Indian; and black.

[406] Cope, *Limits of Racial Domination*, p. 83.

elites – less than 1% (14,000).[407] Even in Mexico City, the cynosure of Spanish society, European-born Spaniards (*peninsulares*) comprised only two per cent of the population; while about half of the city's inhabitants were classed as Indian.[408]

Increasingly, however, these simple racial determinants were overridden by social attributes and allegiances.[409] True, physical ('phenotypical') attributes counted: white skin was an advantage; 'cariblancos' (white faces) inspired trust; 'indio' and 'mulato' became pejorative terms.[410] Parish priests, when they classified marriage partners, relied on phenotypical criteria, as well as local reputation.[411] But perceptions of race were fluid and increasingly subject to social, economic and cultural filtering: achieved status, in other words, competed with ascriptive. Ethnic labels were earned, not merely inherited. 'Indians' were defined in terms of their Indian life-style (language, domicile, dress, custom, religion); Indians who settled on haciendas and in cities entered upon a process of *mestizaje* ('mestization'), which involved social rather than strictly biological transformation. Conversely, mestizo families which integrated into Indian villages risked becoming Indians.[412] Supposedly rigid, ascriptive statuses were thus softened and warped by social and economic pressures.[413] Socioeconomic differences cut across caste lines: black slaves sometimes tyrannized over 'free' Indian workers; some rich Indians and mestizos stood – in terms of material

---

[407] MacLachlan and Rodríguez O., *Forging of the Cosmic Race*, p. 197, following Aguirre Beltrán.

[408] Cope, *Limits of Racial Domination*, pp. 20, 64.

[409] Cope, *Limits of Racial Domination*, pp. 18–19, 22, 83.

[410] Martin, *Governance and Society*, pp. 129, 135; note also Cope, *Limits of Racial Domination*, p. 25.

[411] Hence parents who objected to their son's proposed marriage partner could invoke racial inequality: as in one (1759) case, where Spanish parents sought to prevent their son marrying a servant girl whom they claimed – in the face of their son's denials – was a *mulata*; the proof being that 'the face of her mother did not appear Spanish': Patricia Seed, *To Love, Honor and Obey in Colonial Mexico: Conflicts over Marriage Choice, 1574–1821* (Stanford, 1988), p. 154.

[412] On achieved ethnicity (which could turn Indians into mestizos and vice versa): Cope, *Limits of Racial Domination*, p. 54. It is harder to trace 'Indianization', especially in the absence of anthropological studies: Farriss, *Maya Society*, p. 110, refers to a broad process of 'Mayanization' which, presumably, could include the absorption of mestizos into Indian communities; Gibson, *Aztecs under Spanish Rule*, pp. 145, 147, notes how mestizos were readily categorized as Indians, probably 'in order to render them liable in [*sic*] tribute payment and other kinds of obligation'.

[413] Gibson, *Aztecs under Spanish Rule*, pp. 144–7; Ouweneel, *Ciclos interrumpidos*, pp. 245–6; Patricia Seed, 'Social Dimensions of Race: Mexico City, 1756', *Hispanic American Historical Review*, 62/4 (1982), pp. 569–606.

wealth – far above the common ruck of Spaniards (it was not unknown for a rich mestizo to have Spanish servants); and poor, propertyless Spaniards, mestizos, mulattos and Indians worked side by
side on haciendas, in *obrajes*, or down the mines. Facing the competition of Indian craftsmen in Mexico City, some Spanish artisans
allowed the Indians to join their guilds; both thus joined in collusion against the city consumer.[414] Indeed, in the teeming metropolis of Mexico City, Spaniards, castes, Indians and blacks defied efforts at segregation and lived in close proximity, often in the same
building (Spaniards usually at the top, castes in the dark, damp,
basements); they wove dense webs of economic collaboration and
sexual dalliance across ethnic barriers.[415] When riot broke out, a
common plebeian solidarity appears to have overridden strict ethnic
identity.[416]

Although ethnic barriers were permeable, and individuals, families and even communities could over time shift from one category to another (especially from Indian to mestizo), these barriers remained important, especially prior to the eighteenth century.
The formal transfer from one status to another was a complex
and sometimes costly business. Priests, when writing marriage cer-
tificates, might take individual declarations at face value, might
hazard their own opinion or might take local soundings. While
'passing' between different castes, and even moving from 'Indian'
to 'caste', was feasible (because the respective ethnic identities
were less clearly demarcated and less jealously defended), achieving
Spanish status – with all that it implied about honour, *calidad* and
'limpieza de sangre' (pure blood) – was another matter altogether.[417]
Here, the ancient Spanish concern for lineage, nurtured during the
Reconquista and reinforced in the colonial context, imposed major
barriers.[418]

---

[414] Brading, *Miners and Merchants*, pp. 21–3; Gibson, *Aztecs under Spanish Rule*, pp. 400–1.

[415] Cope, *Limits of Racial Domination*, pp. 22, 32; see also the evocative sketch in Gruzinski, *Histoire de Mexico*, ch. 10.

[416] Cope, *Limits of Racial Domination*, p. 147 (though compare p. 152).

[417] Cope, *Limits of Racial Domination*, pp. 53–6, 121; Robert McCaa, 'Calidad, Clase, and Marriage in Colonial Mexico: The Case of Parral, 1788–90', *Hispanic American Historical Review*, 6/3 (1984), p. 477–501, which forms part of a complicated debate, briefly addressed in the next chapter.

[418] Martin, *Governance and Society*, pp. 125–32.

Furthermore, informal prejudice remained powerful, and ethnic identity – blurred and changeable though it was – constituted a key determinant of status and opportunity. Even the poorest Spaniard was a gentleman, possessed, if not of wealth, at least of status. Conversely, even the richest Indian was subject to ethnic discrimination – Indians paid tribute (but not excise or tithe payments); could be whipped (hence the beating of a youth was deemed wrong 'his being white, Spanish to look at'); could not (in theory) carry firearms; were subject to special laws and separate jurisdiction (but, unlike blacks, were exempt from the authority of the Holy Office); and, of course, were targets of common derogatory ethnic stereotypes.[419] Indians were reckoned to be idle, feckless, dissolute and brutish, overfond of drink and resistant to hard work.[420] Hence they would work only under compulsion, and coercion was necessary: 'the Indian only hears through his backside', as the Yucateco saying went.[421] Beneath their ostensibly adult visages lurked an infantile psyche: Indians were 'children with beards', who required paternalist supervision, lay and clerical. Worst of all were ladinized Indians, who uniquely combined Indian and Spanish vices.[422] Blacks, too, were subject to stereotyping (Viceroy Gelves entertained a 'visceral hatred of blacks and mulattos'); if they worked harder than Indians, they were, by the same token, more assertive and restive (*mulatas*, for similar reasons perhaps, made the best lovers).[423] A spate of slave

---

[419] Brading, *Miners and Merchants*, pp. 21–2, 109; Martin, *Governance and Society*, pp. 128–9, 131 (quotation); Alberro, *Inquisición y sociedad*, pp. 26–7. Castes were also obliged to pay tribute and disqualified from bearing arms: Cope, *Limits of Racial Domination*, p. 16.

[420] Examples are legion: Deeds, 'Indigenous Responses', pp. 77, 95; Gibson, *Aztecs under Spanish Rule*, pp. 91–2; Taylor, *Magistrates*, pp. 172, 183, 369.

[421] Gilbert M. Joseph, *Revolution from Without: Yucatán, Mexico and the United States, 1880–1924* (Durham, 1988), p. 76; Patch, *Maya and Spaniard*, p. 125, quoting an egregious governor of Yucatán (1678), illustrates the long lineage of this self-justifying association of Spanish coercion with Indian idleness; note also p. 164.

[422] Taylor, *Drinking, Homicide and Rebellion*, p. 42 (quotation); Israel, *Race, Class, and Politics*, pp. 56–7 (ladinized Indians). The Spaniards' fear and loathing of ladinized Indians – such as the 'dangerously talented, uppity, betwixt-and-between' Maya *cacique*, Fernando Uz – were not wholly misplaced: many of the major Indian rebellions were led by Indians of this sort, who had had some direct experience of Spanish society: for example, Jacinto Canek of Yucatán (1761) or the Tarahumara leader Tepórame (1648): Farriss, *Maya Society*, pp. 99–100; Spicer, *Cycles of Conquest*, pp. 30–1.

[423] Cope, *Limits of Racial Domination*, pp. 21–2; Boyer, *La gran inundación*, p. 33, and Leonard, *Baroque Times*, pp. 19–20, recount how at Eastertime 1612 rumours of a black uprising made Mexico City tremble; Holy Week processions were cancelled; and, when, on the night of Good Friday, a herd of pigs entered the city, squealing and grunting, 'the inhabitants took them to be

rebellions and marronnage in the 1600s reinforced Spanish fears and prejudices, which only slowly subsided as the revolts were put down and both slave trade and slave population declined during the century.[424] In addition, *peninsular* Spaniards looked down on American-born creoles in whom – they alleged – the enervating ambience of the New World engendered idleness and decadence.[425] Such intra-Spanish prejudice, fostered by New Spain's colonial status and justifying *peninsular* monopoly of major office, would later help nurture sentiments of proto-nationalism among the creole elite.

If over time ethnic caste divisions began to blur, especially in central and northern Mexico, this process depended above all on economic pressures. Linguistic analysis, pioneered by James Lockhart, reveals a clear progression, as the Nahuatl-speakers of central Mexico acquired Spanish words, names and concepts: prior to *circa* 1550 (that is, during the era of the *encomienda*), language changed little, since surplus was rendered according to old tributary principles; between roughly 1550 and 1650, while the *repartimiento* flourished, nouns were borrowed, Spanish names were acquired and religious art displayed a syncretic Indian/Hispanic quality; after 1650, with the hacienda established as the dominant rural institution, directly recruiting Indian workers, bilingualism became common and art, architecture and songs assumed clearly European forms.[426] The Spanish sector's demand for Indian labour and goods thus stimulated Indian acculturation, as migrants quit their villages for

wild negroes (*negros bozales*) and locked themselves, terrified, in their houses'. Farce turned to tragedy when, after Easter, 33 blacks were 'barbarously executed', their severed heads being 'conspicuously displayed on pikes until the stench of decomposition caused their removal'. Thompson, *Thomas Gage's Travels*, pp. 68–9, offers eyewitness descriptions of 'this baser sort of people of blackamoors and mulattoes', who provoked both Spanish anxiety ('the Spaniards have feared they would rise up and mutiny against them') and also Spanish (male) lust ('the attire of this baser sort ... is so light and their carriage so enticing that many Spaniards even of the better sort [who are too prone to venery] disdain their wives for them'). Meanwhile, black males were seen as both sexual predators and social subversives: Carroll, *Blacks in Colonial Veracruz*, pp. 90–1.

424 Cope, *Limits of Racial Domination*, pp. 17–18; Rout, *The African Experience*, pp. 105–6; Carroll, *Blacks in Colonial Veracruz*, pp. 30–4, which traces a sustained decline in slave imports after c. 1620; see also pp. 91–2 on *marronnage* in Veracruz. Martin, *Rural Society*, p. 77, notes a spate of slave flights from the Morelos sugar plantations in the early eighteenth century; these would seem to reflect local economic decline, rather than mounting black militancy.

425 Brading, *Miners and Merchants*, pp. 209–10; Brading, *First America*, pp. 225, 297–8, 471–2.

426 Lockhart, *The Nahuas*, pp. 427–36, summarizes a complex argument. As might be expected, the process of philological transformation in Maya Yucatán lagged far behind that of Nahuatl-speaking central Mexico: Restall, *The Maya World*, p. 296.

hacienda, mine and city.[427] The new hacienda communities represented hybrids, initially Indian in terms of language and ethnic identity (the inhabitants were considered 'Indians') but increasingly Hispanic in terms of religion, dress and work. The hacienda thus pioneered the epochal transition from Indian villager to mestizo *campesino*. The mine wrought a similar change, perhaps more thoroughly but on a smaller scale. So, too, did the towns. Mexico City was ringed by a host of Indian satellite communities specializing in the production of goods – pots, pulque, soap, brooms, herbs, flowers, vegetables – which were daily swallowed up in the city's great maw. Within the city, too, although some Indian barrios retained a measure of identity and self-government, patterns of residential segregation blurred over time, as once populous Indian communities, like Texcoco and Tlatelolco, shrank, and as Indian economic activities were merged into the dominant Hispanic urban market economy.[428] By the later seventeenth century the basic polarization in Mexico City was less one of ethnicity than of social class, as the well-to-do elite (perhaps 15 per cent) confronted a plebeian mass (85 per cent).[429]

Mexico City was a special case. Elsewhere, urban acculturation was slower and patchier. The city of Oaxaca swallowed up the neighbouring Indian pueblo of Jalatlaco, its inhabitants became city artisans; and by the later eighteenth century Jalatlaco had lost its Indian character.[430] However, Indian migrants often retained their language – a powerful cultural determinant – even in the barrios of newly established Spanish cities like Querétaro.[431] As a result, seventeenth-century colonial society displayed high levels of

---

[427] MacLeod, 'Forms and Types of Work'. The process was not unilinear: just as economic demand spurred migration and acculturation, so economic depression tended to expel migrants from the commercial sector back to the villages (a process which would be repeated down the centuries to the 1930s and even the 1980s): for example, Martin, *Rural Society*, p. 65, notes how the decline of the Morelos sugar plantations after c. 1690 boosted local village population and production.

[428] Gibson, *Aztecs under Spanish Rule*, ch. 13.

[429] Cope, *Limits of Racial Domination*, pp. 2, 49. In this, Mexico City pioneered what would become a more general polarization between 'plebe' and 'gente decente': Brading, *Miners and Merchants*, p. 20.

[430] Taylor, *Landlord and Peasant*, pp. 20–1.

[431] Super, *La vida en Querétaro*, pp. 179–82. *A fortiori*, the Spanish towns of the heavily Maya southeast – Mérida, Campeche and Valladolid – were ringed with 'satellite [Indian] barrios', most of which were 'structurally identical to any rural Indian pueblo': Farriss, *Maya Society*, p. 104.

bilingualism (chiefly thanks to Indians, who had acquired Spanish as a second language), and it included a ubiquitous class of Indian interpreters and scribes (*nahuatlacos* and *escribanos*, later *tinterillos* – 'inkpots'), who played a key role in the interminable litigation which affected New Spain, not least its Indian communities.[432] As they acquired Spanish, rural Indians also learned to plough with oxen (when they could get them) and to work with metal tools; but they still preferred to use these to raise – and consume – corn rather than wheat. Adherence to the old ways – corn and cornfield, language, dress, even elements of Precolumbian religion – was, of course, strongest in outlying regions and mountain redoubts, where hacienda, city and mine were relatively absent: in Oaxaca and Chiapas, in the interior of Yucatán, and in north-central uplands like the Sierra Gorda and Metztitlán, not to mention the great expanse of the far north, the Gran Chichimeca, where Spanish colonization remained patchy and precarious.[433] Throughout the bulk of Mesoamerica, however, the colonial regime, for all its famous torpor and flaccidity, achieved a degree of social and political integration – and, we might add, peace and political stability – unequalled at least since the days of Teotihuacan.[434] Over the decades and centuries, Spanish rule helped mould a peasant community which was neither a mere chastened survivor of the ancient Mesoamerican village nor yet a carbon copy of the Iberian pueblo, but which represented a new, hybrid, *Mexican* entity, the social analogue of the colony's syncretic religion.

This community possessed – indeed, had to possess – a certain corporate resilience which underwrote its survival and which was symbolically represented by the community land titles.[435] And the colonial regime, like its Tsarist equivalent in pre-revolutionary Russia,

[432] Gruzinski, *Conquest of Mexico*, p. 62; Gibson, *Aztecs under Spanish Rule*, p. 149.

[433] Olivera, *Pillis y macehuales*, p. 159 (oxen); Gibson, *Aztecs under Spanish Rule*, p. 322 (maize); Gruzinski, *Conquest of Mexico*, pp. 182–3 (periphery).

[434] Farriss, *Maya Society*, pp. 129, 174–5, 242, which stresses the connection between the Pax Hispanica and the decline of the old Maya warrior elite; note also Gruzinski, *Conquest of Mexico*, p. 84. Of course, the character of the Pax Teotihuacana remains something of a mystery.

[435] Gruzinski, *Conquest of Mexico*, ch. 3. Ouweneel, *Ciclos interrumpidos*, pp. 264, 267, 290–1, is skeptical about the 'close corporate community'; however, to posit forms of effective collective community action (especially 'resistance') directed against external forces does not have to imply a cosy *gemeinschaftlich* order within; nor is such external action incompatible with a considerable measure of internal stratification, exploitation and feuding.

fostered corporate identity by making the community, through its elected council, responsible for tax and tribute payments, labour obligations, and the maintenance of roads, public buildings and markets. Most day-to-day policing and justice were enacted within the village by Indian authorities, without matters reaching Spanish courts.[436] In Yucatán – something of an extreme case, it is true – 'Spanish civilian authority outside the cities was practically non-existent'.[437] Religious life, too, was often run by Indian laymen, usually grouped in *cofradías*; parish priests were sometimes birds of passage, who irregularly visited outlying villages, or even birds of ill omen, whose sporadic visits were associated with extortion.[438] Ritual autonomy thus mirrored political autonomy. Although by no means formally democratic, village politics were in some respects responsive to public opinion. Elections were held, and voting was real.[439] Indian officials – *gobernadores, regidores* – were certainly capable of oppression: they amassed personal wealth, alienated community land and sometimes exacted heavy tribute payments. Indian communities were not petty egalitarian Utopias. But the scope for oppression was limited, and, over time, the pickings declined. As population fell, Indian officials suffered imprisonment for failing to meet tribute quotas; Indian ambition for office understandably waned.[440] Public office thus tended to become a burden, a duty, a source of communal prestige, rather than a royal road to riches, Spanish style. In Oaxaca, one analysis suggests, prestige within communities accrued according to 'poverty and service', not – as in Spanish towns or even some

---

[436] Gibson, *Aztecs under Spanish Rule*, pp. 179–80; Taylor, *Drinking, Homicide and Rebellion*, p. 74; Farriss, *Maya Society*, pp. 105, 271; MacLachlan, *Criminal Justice in Eighteenth-Century Mexico*, pp. 25–6. Pastor, *Campesinos y reformas*, p. 211, show that Indian authorities were not averse to using the lash (25 lashes for drunks and fornicators; more for adulterers); corporal punishment was thus a familiar feature of Mexican society, readily resorted to by landlords, clerics and officials (both Indian and non-Indian).

[437] Patch, *Maya and Spaniard*, pp. 45–6.

[438] Gruzinski, *Conquest of Mexico*, pp. 237–44; see also Restall, *The Maya World*, pp. 149–52. Taylor, *Magistrates of the Sacred*, chs. 12, 13, analyses cofradías and lay religious elites, noting recurrent conflict between priests and laymen – *cofrades*, sacristans, *fiscales* (quasi-'religious policemen') – over control of both economic resources and symbolic practices. At some rambunctious religious fiestas,Taylor notes, p. 254, the cura was no more than a 'helpless onlooker'.

[439] Taylor, *Landlord and Peasant*, pp. 49–50; Gibson, *Aztecs Under Spanish Rule*, pp. 175–9; Taylor, *Magistrates*, pp. 354–6, 374; Pastor, *Campesinos y reformas*, p. 177; Haskett, *Indigenous Rulers*, ch. 2. See also n. 399.

[440] Gibson, *Aztecs Under Spanish Rule*, pp. 193, 218, 268, 390; Taylor, *Landlord and Peasant*, p. 51–2.

Indian barrios within Spanish towns – according to the self-seeking accumulation of wealth.[441] The ladders of status within these contrasting communities were rigged differently, and would remain so for centuries.[442]

Within the independent Indian communities, office-holding, which often combined lay and religious functions, came to imply the disbursement rather than the accumulation of wealth: a reversion, in some ways, to the ancient logic of the distributive chiefdom, which had been subverted by the onset of powerful states – Mesoamerican as well as Spanish. Those who assumed office both forfeited income and expended their personal wealth on communal projects – economic, legal, ritualistic. Such practices, derivative of ancient Mesoamerican tradition, possibly reinforced the equilibrating mechanisms which operated within communities, inhibiting economic accumulation and social stratification.[443] Though it was no petty egalitarian Utopia, the Indian community was resistant to the forms of accumulation and stratification which Spanish urban society displayed. In crude terms, it did not readily surrender to the embrace of the (capitalist?) market.[444] In addition, there existed a

[441] Whitecotton, *The Zapotecs*, p. 191; see also Pastor, *Campesinos y reformas*, p. 251. Compare Super, 'The Agricultural Near North', which describes a relatively mobile, profit-oriented society; or Martin, *Governance and Society*, p. 46, which portrays Chihuahua as a monetized and market-oriented society, where 'social negotiations [*sic*]...centered on how, and under what conditions, some individuals could command the muscle power of others'.

[442] For a complex analysis of the historical evolution and survival of local religious government in Tlaxcala, see Hugo G. Nutini and Betty Bell, *Ritual Kinship: The Structure and Historical Development of the Compadrazgo System in Rural Tlaxcala* (Princeton, 1980), vol. 1, ch. 10; on the modern – that is, mid-twentieth-century – cargo system, see Cancian, *Economía y prestigio*, chs. 12, 13.

[443] Pastor, *Campesinos y reformas*, pp. 251, 259: 'governing the community was essentially a task of redistributing the surplus produced by the collective economy'; the *cofradía* 'complemented and balanced the possible productive deficit of a family in a bad year and systematically redistributed part of this...among its members, although not in an egalitarian way'; see also Carmagnani, *El regreso de los dioses*, p. 132ff. James B. Greenberg, *Santiago's Sword: Chatino Peasant Religion and Economics* (Berkeley, 1981), pp. 2–12, and Cancian, *Economía y prestigio*, pp. 173–7, review debates concerning the functional role of the (modern) cargo system. As Greenberg, p. 10, following Eric Wolf, points out, the supposed levelling function does *not* imply a 'homogenous distribution of wealth or an absence of class divisions within the community'; rather, it suggests that the cargo system helps to inhibit and mollify such divisions (cf. Ouweneel, *Ciclos interrumpidos*, p. 312). Perhaps the best proof is that the collapse of the cargo system correlates with rapid commercialization, stratification, and political conflict: Frank Cancian, *The Decline of Community in Zinacantan: Economy, Public Life, and Social Stratification, 1960–1987* (Stanford, 1992).

[444] Some market involvement was inevitable – given Spanish fiscal and clerical demands – and even welcome, by way of boosting family income. However, we should not confuse limited

certain diffuse communal memory and sentiment, articulated by the community elders, men and women. The elders were the carriers of custom; they transmitted across generations both the oral record of village traditions (history, myth and heroes) and the material proof of village integrity (saints, shrines and land titles).[445] These in turn underwrote community collective action. For villages proved capable of collective action – most obviously riot and rebellion – which alarmed the Spanish authorities and which, because of its apparently anonymous, leaderless character, mystified them too. To outsiders, villagers often seemed factious, even insolent, especially when compared to docile hacienda peons.[446] The Indians adhere to a 'wicked' form of government, an eighteenth-century priest averred – one in which 'everyone governs' in anarchic fashion; in which respect, he adds, they resemble the turbulent English.[447]

Ostensibly religious institutions and practices were important in sustaining community cohesion – which no doubt helps explain why they were cherished more than the priests who, at least in theory, controlled them. Thus, the *cofradías*, fiestas and cults introduced during the spiritual conquest and subsequently disseminated throughout New Spain afforded villagers opportunities for self-help, collective affirmation and a good deal of fun. During fiestas – which could last days – villagers gave themselves up to collective conviviality and spectacle, involving prolonged drinking bouts, play-acting, even 'transvestism and mock battles'.[448] These events required no clerical supervision; indeed, the Church often frowned on such licentious

---

commercialization – 'penny capitalism', in Sol Tax's famous phrase – with fullblown capitalism, in which market involvement serves the overriding goal of capital accumulation. There are, in other words, quite different scales of market and commercial activity, which obey quite different rationales: see G. A. Cohen, *Karl Marx's Theory of History: A Defence* (Oxford, 1978), p. 81. I return to this question in the final part of this chapter.

[445] Gibson, *Aztecs under Spanish Rule*, p. 193, notes 'a residual community power that survived all colonial pressures'; see also Gruzinski, *Conquest of Mexico*, ch. 3.

[446] Florescano, *Origen y desarrollo*, p. 106; Martin, *Rural Society*, pp. 148, on the preference of (eighteenth-century) Morelos planters for 'permanent resident populations', who 'usually identified themslves as vecinos of a particular estate', and (pp. 167–9, 187–8) the contrasting troubles which the planters experienced with local Indian villages.

[447] Taylor, *Drinking, Homicide and Rebellion*, p. 123. In 1565 Pedro Menéndez de Avilés had proudly and piously slaughtered a French Protestant community in Florida, noting that 'this wicked sect' shared 'similar beliefs' to the Indians, beliefs that were 'probably Satanic in origin': Weber, *The Spanish Frontier*, p. 63.

[448] Taylor, *Drinking, Homicide and Rebellion*, p. 60.

popular exuberance.[449] Thus, all the paraphernalia of the charivari and church ales which cemented communal bonds – and vented social tensions – in early modern Europe had their counterparts in colonial New Spain. And here, too, ostensibly Christian rituals became expressions of secular political values. Outsiders entered carousing communities at their peril; sometimes, outsiders – 'even the king's judges' – were barred from entry for the duration of fiestas.[450] The village church acquired political significance: it stood as proof of full pueblo status, a material guarantee of community autonomy vis-à-vis other pueblos or neighbouring haciendas.[451] The patron saint, too, served as guarantor of the pueblo's well-being; the choice of saint, the moment of settlement, were woven into durable foundation myths – local, Christian, versions of Tenochtitlán's ancient eagle-and-serpent legend.[452]

In the economic realm, autonomy depended on the conservation of communal lands: 'a community might lose a substantial part of its population and still survive as a corporate body, but the loss of lands threatened its very nature and existence'.[453] Village lands assumed a variety of forms: some were corporately owned by the village or by a *cofradía* within the village; occasionally, they were communally worked (or, in the case of woods and pasture, used as commons); but arable land was usually divided into family plots, of which households enjoyed the usufruct. Communally owned land was therefore commoner than communally worked.[454] Indians were familiar with

---

[449] Gruzinski, *Conquest of Mexico*, pp. 242–4, 248, 265–6; Leonard, *Baroque Times*, pp. 160–1, describes Archbishop Aguiar y Seijas (1682–98), 'a twisted Catholic puritan' and mysogynist, who 'relentlessly campaigned against bullfights, cockfights, gambling and the theater', while blessing his own short sight, which prevented him from setting (focused) eyes on women. As Taylor, *Magistrates of the Sacred*, pp. 252–64, shows, such killjoy clerical attitudes became more common during the eighteenth century.

[450] Taylor, *Drinking, Homicide and Rebellion*, p. 61.

[451] Gibson, *Aztecs under Spanish Rule*, p. 297; Taylor, *Magistrates of the Sacred*, p. 42, notes how 'virtually every little pueblo maintained its own church and wanted its own resident priest'; communities vied with each other over the quality of their churches and the efficacy of their patron saints.

[452] Gruzinski, *Conquest of Mexico*, pp. 113, 117–18; Rebecca Horn, 'Gender and Social Identity: Nahua Naming Patterns in Postconquest Central Mexico', in Susan Schroeder, Stephanie Wood and Robert Haskett, eds., *Indian Women of Colonial Mexico* (Norman, Okla., 1997), pp. 105–22, shows how naming practices – that is, the substitution of Spanish/Christian for Indian names – were influenced by patron saints.

[453] Gibson, *Aztecs under Spanish Rule*, p. 297.

[454] Gibson, *Aztecs under Spanish Rule*, pp. 264–8; Taylor, *Landlord and Peasant*, p. 68ff.

private, freehold land, especially that which belonged to *caciques*; its
alienation offered one of the principal means whereby Spanish landlords acquired Indian property.[455] Even when formally guaranteed by
the Crown, village lands were nonetheless at risk, especially as population plummeted during the sixteenth century. Yet their conservation was central to village cohesion. Where they were retained, they
underwote a virtuous circle: their cultivation sustained the village, its
inhabitants, *caciques*, church and *cofradías*, and their defence bred
a certain functional corporate solidarity, as well as a degree of legal
expertise, vested in the local *tinterillo*. Corporate land titles – often
declamatory documents of limited legal cogency – stressed prescriptive right and ancient tradition; village lands were the gift of God,
the fruit of collective struggle, the legitimate reward of a pact with
the Crown,[456] and the inherited responsibility of the current generation. As a typical document declared: 'Spaniards come to seize
what we have justly won ... We urge our sons to know, guard, and
keep the water, woods, streets and houses of the town ... Do not forget ... guard this document'.[457] Given these discursive and organizational resources, villages kept up land disputes through generations,
displaying not only powerful corporate solidarity but also the pervasive legalism of colonial society, which meant that the villages' resort
to the law was by no means futile. Indian litigation with engrossing landlords was assiduous (villagers disputed with *hacendados*
more than hacienda peons did). Viceroys complained of the scale
and intensity of Indian land disputes.[458] In the ample archives of the
General Indian Court, 'the largest proportion of cases and complaints
concerned land'; 'suits were carried on simultaneously in various ju-
risdictions, repeatedly renewed, and piled up costs far in excess of
the value of whatever was in dispute'.[459] But such tenacity went beyond mere book-keeping; it could involve a battle for collective survival; and it achieved results. Indian communities in the Valley of

[455] Lockhart, *The Nahuas*, pp. 174–5; Gibson, *Aztecs under Spanish Rule*, pp. 264–6; Gibson,
Tlaxcala, pp. 85–7; Taylor, *Landlord and Peasant*, pp. 39–40, 54–5, 73–4.
[456] Gruzinski, *Conquest of Mexico*, pp. 115–16.
[457] Gibson, *Aztecs under Spanish Rule*, p. 271.
[458] Taylor, *Landlord and Peasant*, p. 83.
[459] Borah, *Justice by Insurance*, pp. 40, 126, 129. Farriss, *Maya Society*, p. 283, notes the same
Jarndyce vs. Jarndyce phenomenon in Yucatán.

Mexico successfully defended their patrimony against the claims of the colonial capital itself; one dispute between village and hacienda in Querétaro was settled in 1879, after 318 years of contention.[460]

The defence of village land against external threats helped overcome internal divisions, which were common enough: ostensibly feuding, brawling, pueblos might display a sudden solidarity if their fields were threatened. Outsiders (which meant Indians from rival villages as well as Spanish landlords or officials) were viewed with suspicion, and their acquisition of village land was resisted. Land surveys (*vistas de ojo*) inspired displays of collective intimidation, as 'large, menacing crowds of Indians' gathered, obstructed the surveyors, stole their equipment or threw stones.[461] Vigorous village resistance thus conspired with qualified royal paternalism to contest – although neither could halt – the progressive alienation of village land. And communities also engaged in protracted feuds with each other over land and water rights, as well as over questions of political precedence. Thus, while corporate village solidarity could – especially when Indian pueblo was pitted against Spanish *hacendado* – generate a powerful amalgam of ethnic and class loyalties, that same solidarity tended to inhibit broader, regional, supra-communal movements, which might unite peasants or Indians from diverse pueblos. Marx saw the peasants of nineteenth-century France as resembling a sack of potatoes:[462] a collection of discrete units lacking solidarity and organization. The metaphor could be applied to colonial New Spain, with the caveat that here the constituent units were communities rather than families. In most Indian pueblos, above all in central and much of southern Mexico, the primary allegiance was to the community (often the old *altepetl* in new disguise); supposed 'tribal' identity – the sense of being Otomí, Zapotec, Mixtec – probably counted for little.[463] Indeed, one effect

[460] Gibson, *Aztecs under Spanish Rule*, p. 370; González Navarro, *El Porfiriato. La Vida Social*, p. 207.

[461] Taylor, *Landlord and Peasant*, p. 85.

[462] Moore, *Social Origins*, p. 477.

[463] Lockhart, *The Nahuas*, pp. 14–15, 29, 53–6; García Martínez, *Pueblos de la sierra*, pp. 21, 66, 73–7, 156, 268–9; and, for Yucatán, Restall, *The Maya World*, pp. 14–15. Gruzinski, *Conquest of Mexico*, pp. 137–8, 183, discerns supra-local, 'tribal' allegiances (an 'enlarged indigenous conscience') among the Zapotec, Chontal and Mixe of Oaxaca, allegiances which appear absent for the more numerous Nahua. His argument is suggestive rather than conclusive. In central

of the Conquest was to blur such divisions – certainly linguistic divisions – and to encourage the use of Spanish (sometimes Nahuatl) as a *lingua franca* throughout much of the colony.[464] Spaniards, too, tended to see Indians as an undifferentiated ethnic mass, defined by political subjection and tributary status; ethnic niceties passed them by. Only among certain Indian populations of the far south (such as the Maya of inland Yucatán or highland Chiapas) or the far north (notably the Yaquis of Sonora) was collective resistance on the basis of some supra-communal, 'tribal' (i.e., ethnic) identity feasible.[465] In these cases 'tribal' identity had not been triturated by colonial conquest and subjection. Conversely, at the other extreme, and at a later date, among communities which had suffered the loss of both land and autonomy, a new consciousness was gradually formed, in which a broad 'Indian' identity, premised on a common class oppression and divorced from any 'tribal' allegiance, underwrote collective, supra-communal action against Spanish (*gachupín*) landlords and officials. Such nascent sentiments were evident in the two major Mexico City riots of the seventeenth century.[466] This became possible

(Nahua) Mexico the chief challenge to the altepetl/pueblo probably came not from above, but from below, from the calpulli, the old pre-Conquest residential unit which roughly mutated into the Spanish barrio: Horn, *Postconquest Coyoacan*, pp. 20–2, makes rather more of the *calpulli*/barrio and its 'strong sense of micro-patriotism' than Lockhart, *The Nahuas*, pp. 16–17, 43, and Lockhart, *Nahuas and Spaniards*, pp. 40–1. Lockhart does, however, recognize a broad – and diffuse? – 'Nahuatl-speaker patriotism', somewhat analogous to classical Greek notions of a civilized culture surrounded by barbarians: Lockhart, *Nahuas and Spaniards*, p. 55 (cf. Restall, *The Maya World*, p. 15; and n. 465 below). What is clear, however, is that, unlike the primary allegiance to altepetl/pueblo, this diffuse cultural attachment – to the extent that it existed – did not form the basis of regular collective action.

[464] Olivera, *Pillis y macehuales*, p. 135.

[465] Farriss, *Maya Society*, p. 156, argues that the 'Yucatec Maya remained a single cultural and linguistic unit and continued to think of themselves as a single people'; that is, they not only (objectively) shared distinctive cultural traits (perhaps unwittingly) but were also (subjectively) aware of them and acted upon them; yet, Farriss also stresses, p. 149, colonial Maya society was fragmented into 'community' units, hence incapable of supra-communal collective action ('banding together in provinces and subprovinces'), save in respect of religious organization (e.g., pilgrimages). In similar fashion, Restall, *The Maya World*, pp. 14–15, discounts any 'ethnic homogeneity of self-perception' among the Maya, but he then hedges his bets (I think): 'this is not to suggest that the Mayas did not view themselves as distinct in some ethnic sense from non-Mayas'. In the Yucatán case, we should recall that the Maya of the Petén did doggedly resist Spanish rule until 1697 and that the southeastern interior remained a source of Spanish anxiety and Maya resistance well into the national period; sentiments of cultural identity perhaps informed this long saga of resistance. On the Yaquis, see Evelyn Hu-DeHart, *Missionaries, Miners, and Indians: Spanish Contact with the Yaqui Nation of Northwestern New Spain, 1533–1820* (Tucson, 1981); and the comparative observations of Sweet, 'The Ibero-American Frontier Mission', pp. 38–9.

[466] Cope, *Limits of Racial Domination*, pp. 34, 147.

as caste and class merged, as 'Indians' (defined according to colonial caste terminology) came to constitute a *de facto* subordinate class of labourers, sharecroppers and poor tenants. For them, basic socio-economic grievances could be expressed in the name of an oppressed 'Indian' class, transcending individual pueblos; they began to see themselves as the Spaniards saw them. Thus, paradoxically, it was the more acculturated – or 'de-Indianized' – Indians, such as those of the late colonial Bajío, who proved most militant and capable of collective action.[467]

In the main, the emergence of a combined ethnic and class con-sciousness was a phenomenon of the late colony; it depended on the processes of economic and political change set in motion dur-ing the Bourbon era. Under the Habsburgs, the Indian community remained strong and viable, albeit threatened. Outside the far north and south, the village was sufficiently incorporated into colonial society – into colonial economic, legal and administrative systems – for tribal identities to be submerged (arguably, they had never been strong, even in pre-Conquest Mesoamerica) and for loyalty to the community to transcend other loyalties. This meant that the Spanish rulers of New Spain – unlike their Peruvian counterparts – rarely had to reckon with genuine 'Indian' revolts, premised on broad tribal or ethnic allegiances: the Aztecs left no legacy of Indian, pre-Conquest, legitimacy, as the Incas did.[468] In consequence, Mexican intellec-tuals could romanticize Mexico's Aztec past – it was remote, safe, amenable – and weave it into a pretty tapestry of 'proto-national' myth; in the Andes, the Inca past blended with the present and carried threatening connotations.[469] In New Spain, it was the in-dividual village protest – limited in scope but tenacious over time and versatile in its forms – which absorbed most official attention. And to outsiders, the village seemed not only factious (as the priest put it) and feckless (as the colonial stereotype insisted) but also dour, taciturn, introverted and resistant to change. The challenge of the village community, the temptation to split it apart in order

---

[467] Tutino, *From Insurrection to Revolution*, pp. 127–30; Hugh Hamill, Jr., *The Hidalgo Revolt: Prelude to Mexican Independence* (Gainesville, 1966), pp. 48–52.

[468] Brading, *First America*, pp. 341–2, 489–91.

[469] Brading, *First America*, pp. 277–84 (Torquemada), 371 (Sigüenza), 387–8 (Veytia): all – in their often quite different ways – scholars, apologists and myth-makers of Mexico's Aztec (Mexica) heritage.

to release the latent forces of land and labour locked within it, confronted first, Habsburg *hacendados*; later, Bourbon reformers; and finally, nineteenth-century liberals. The history of that confrontation is, perhaps, the major theme running through Mexico history from the Conquest to the 1910 Revolution.

But repeated attempts to split the community and release these latent forces produced dramatic explosions rather than a controlled supply of energy. To the extent that Habsburg landlords and officials treated the peasant community with a certain conservative caution, major conflicts were averted. William Taylor notes 'precious few' peasant insurrections (that is, sustained regional uprisings, as against isolated local revolts) in either central Mexico or Oaxaca during the colonial period, especially before 1700.[470] Localized village tumults were common; but they assumed a distinct, limited form and were readily accommodated within the judicial and administrative framework of the colony. Most rebellions stemmed from specific abuses, usually perpetrated by officials or priests, concerning legal judgements, taxes or church fees. Such abuses appear to have provoked more disputes than land appropriation: evidence that hacienda expansion was limited and that, especially prior to the eighteenth century, expansion took advantage of Indian depopulation. Protests were usually limited to individual communities but were broadly based (women were often prominent) and 'spontaneous', in the sense that organized leadership – which the Spanish authorities were eager to locate and to punish – was strangely lacking. Protests tended, too, to be characterized by a mixture of violence, levity and inebriation. In other words, they closely resembled the village *journées* of early modern Europe.[471] Similarly, rebellious villagers did not mount a basic challenge to the colonial order; instead, they sought redress within that order, invoking rather than repudiating constituted authority, whether of Church or Crown.[472] Only

---

[470] Taylor, *Drinking, Homicide and Rebellion*, p. 113; note also Friedrich Katz, 'Rural Revolts in Mexico', in Katz, *Riot, Rebellion, and Revolution*, p. 5. Kellogg, *Law and the Transformation of Aztec Culture*, pp. 217–18, stresses the capacity of the law to channel and curb discontent.

[471] Cf. E. J. Hobsbawm, *Primitive Rebels* (Manchester, 1959), ch. 7; David Underdown, *Revel, Riot and Rebellion: Popular Politics and Culture in England, 1603–1660* (Oxford, 1987), pp. 96, 106–19.

[472] Taylor, *Drinking, Homicide and Rebellion*, pp. 24, 133–4; Taylor, *Magistrates of the Sacred*, p. 230.

rarely in the Mexican heartland did broader rebellions – potential insurrections – develop, transcending the formidable barriers which demarcated village from village; and these, clustering in the later eighteenth century, indicated the declining legitimacy of authority and presaged the great upheaval of 1810.

The preservation of rural public order was facilitated by the villagers' indifferent weaponry as well as by their deep disunity. Firearms were uncommon; rocks – the scourge of Cortés's conquistadors in 1519–21 – were still the peasantry's chief form of offence, along with whatever agricultural tools (hoes, machetes, axes) came to hand.[473] The same primitive peasant armoury was evident in 1810. The relatively low level of rural violence was part cause, part effect, of Habsburg policy towards the peasantry – a policy which (compared to some analogues) was relatively lenient, even utilitarian. True, the 'ringleaders' of rebellions were gaoled, whipped and occasionally executed. But rebellious communities got off lightly; collective retribution was rare; individual punishment often took a 'useful' form; and redress of grievances often followed revolt (to put it another way: revolts could be effective).[474] This did not necessarily reflect altruism or Christian charity on the part of the authorities. Officials had to show lenience, had to rely on diplomacy as well as repression, because the state's repressive arm was short and spindly. There was no standing army in Habsburg Mexico, only an *ad hoc* civilian militia. The Spaniards' near monopoly of guns and horses facilitated repression, but Habsburg rulers and officials (unlike their Bourbon successors) exploited this monopoly with caution and chose not to crank up the level of social protest and control. In particular, they called upon the Church to mediate and deploy its considerable influence with aggrieved peasants. Just as Franciscan friars processed in the streets of riotous cities, calming the mob, so priests peacefully quelled rural agitation: the bishop of Oaxaca personally brought an end to one of the biggest rural revolts of the Habsburg era, that of Tehuantepec in 1660.[475] Thus, the character, ideology and containment of rural

---

[473] Taylor, *Drinking, Homicide and Rebellion*, pp. 115–16.

[474] Taylor, *Drinking, Homicide and Rebellion*, pp. 120–1; Cope, *Limits of Racial Domination*, pp. 39, 102–3.

[475] 'The Indians of Tehuantepec, who in armed bands had occupied the chief town ... and exhorted the other towns to rise up and kill their opponents, went out to meet the Bishop while still

protest closely paralleled those of urban riot, which was similarly sporadic, limited in scope, and 'naively monarchist': both reflected the genuine political hegemony enjoyed by the Crown, bolstered by the Church, and premised on a certain reciprocity between rulers and ruled.[476]

VII. Acculturation and Resistance: North and South

These generalizations are broadly valid for central and parts of southern Mexico, including the Valley of Mexico, Oaxaca and the Bajío. On the northern and southern peripheries of New Spain, however, where Spanish conquest was more recent or more incomplete, and where Indian acculturation was less pronounced and Indian belligerence more marked, major insurrections ensued, encompassing wide areas and premised upon a more radical repudiation of Spanish rule: Andean-style rebellions, we might say.[477] Several were revolts against, not within, the colonial order, and they were evidence of the distinct patterns of acculturation and resistance which developed in the north and south.

In central Mexico, the Spaniards achieved a swift military and spiritual conquest of the old Aztec empire, a region of densely populated sedentary agriculture. Both political and religious continuities were apparent: the Crown exacted tribute and dispensed justice; the Church enacted rituals which echoed the pre-Conquest past. Though the change was traumatic, it involved one state supplanting another. North and south it was a different story. Here, the Spaniards confronted a congeries of statelets or, more dramatically, acephalic societies (often chiefdoms). Their conquest and incorporation proved

under arms. The Bishop rose through the town in full pontifical robes. In awe, the Indians prostrated themselves on the ground or led the reins of his mule. Women, previously active in the rebellion, took their mantles from their shoulders and spread them over the street so that the Bishop's mule could pass over them': Hamnett, *Politics and Trade*, p. 13. John Tutino, 'Rebelión indígena en Tehuantepec', *Cuadernos Políticos*, 24 (1980), pp. 89–101, offers a *longue durée* analysis of the revolt.

[476] Cope, *Limits of Racial Domination*, pp. 142, 146, offers examples of 'naive monarchism' ('long live the king and death to bad government'); see also Taylor, *Magistrates of the Sacred*, p. 230. Compare Hobsbawm's 'populist legitimism': *Primitive Rebels*, pp. 112, 118.

[477] Compare Steve J. Stern, 'The Age of Andean Insurrection, 1742–1782: A Reappraisal', in Stern, ed., *Resistance, Rebellion, and Consciousness in the Andean Peasant World, Eighteenth to Twentieth Centuries* (Madison, 1987), pp. 34–93.

more difficult, since the Spaniards had to perform the primitive spadework of state- or empire-building, which in central Mexico had been done for them.

The north – the Gran Chichimeca – defied easy conquest. It was large, inhospitable and less richly endowed with population and material resources. It did not lack towns or settled peasant communities;[478] but these were scattered, loosely integrated and resistant to easy exploitation. Where the Spaniards struck silver – at Zacatecas in the sixteenth century or Parral in the seventeenth – the rewards of conquest flowed and the tempo of settlement quickened. Gradually, new Spanish communities, laid out in classic gridiron fashion, came into being: Zacatecas, 1546; Durango, 1563; Santa Fe, 1610; Parral, 1631; Chihuahua, 1709. But such settlements remained small, isolated and threatened. Apart from silver, the chief incentives to expansion were religion and security. During the first two hundred years of the colony Franciscan and Jesuit missionaries pioneered the push to the north, often outstripping their secular counterparts: the Jesuits were prominent in Sonora and Chihuahua, the Franciscans in New Mexico. Not until the eighteenth century (a period we will consider separately) did the state seize the initiative, even to the extent of eliminating the Jesuit missions altogether. Spanish advance thus depended on three institutions: the mine, the mission and the *presidio*, or fort. The last represented – if it is not too grandiose a term – Spanish geopolitical ambitions. Threatened by both hostile Indians and rival powers, the Spaniards sought to place permanent footholds in the sprawling expanses of the north. St Augustine – the only Spanish 'settlement of consequence' in Florida (and the oldest continually inhabited community in the United States) – eked out a remote and precarious existence, 'a muddy garrison town of flammable huts of palmetto', boasting (1600) a population of five hundred, half of them single men; as the governor of Cuba lamented (1673), Florida attracted few settlers, 'only hoodlums and the mischievous'.[479]

---

478 Reff, *Disease, Depopulation, and Culture Change*, pp. 13–14, 41, 57, 61, 78–9, 90, argues for the existence of towns and settled peasant villages (which monarchically minded missionaries tended to disparage) among the Cáhita, Opata, Pima and Acaxee, among others. See also Radding, *Wandering Peoples*, pp. 3, 5, 26, 110 (which shows that some of the people were not in fact wandering).

479 Weber, *The Spanish Frontier*, p. 90. Moorehead, *The Presidio*, offers detailed description of the northern forts.

Although it elicited different responses among the Indian groups of the north, the Spanish advance revealed certain recurrent patterns. In chronological terms, an initial phase of mutual probing gave way (very often) to Indian resistance, Spanish repression and a form of colonial subjugation involving a constant risk of rebellion, and what the Spaniards saw as a kind of pervasive Indian malingering. The northern Indians, complained an early eighteenth-century missionary, 'are vagabonds and layabouts, with even worse vices that, taken together, make them vain, sneaky, cheating, thieves and drunks'.[480] Northern New Spain never enjoyed the long, if flawed, social peace of the centre; Spanish hegemony was, at best, patchy and frequently contested.

Nevertheless – a second recurrent pattern – Spanish attitudes towards the northern Indians were consistent with those displayed in central Mexico. Spanish laymen sought cheap (or free) labour, chiefly for the mines and their ancillary economies but also for the Spaniards' personal upkeep in relatively poor and remote regions like New Mexico.[481] The Crown, which looked to enhance its revenues with a minimum of expenditure, thus allowed local pioneers – the 'subimperialists' of the north – to assume the burdens of conquest and settlement; one attraction of the missions was that they offered 'cost-effective colonization', that is, empire-building on the cheap.[482] The missionaries, for their part, worked to convert and discipline an Indian people whom – following the initial optimism of mass baptism – they came to see as idle, barbarous and backsliding. In doing so, they had to combat not only indigenous mores and religion, but also their lay compatriots, the Spanish miners, settlers and soldiers. For, as in central Mexico, lay and clerical Spaniards frequently competed for access to, and authority over, the Indian population; just as Franciscans and Jesuits competed for the control of bodies, as well as the cure of souls.[483]

---

[480] Deeds, 'Indigenous Reponses', p. 77.

[481] As Viceroy Velasco put it in 1608, 'no-one comes to the Indies to plow and sow but only to eat and loaf': Weber, *The Spanish Frontier*, p. 123. Velasco exaggerated; but there was scant opportunity for Spanish arable farming to flourish in the north, as it did, say, in Puebla.

[482] Robert H. Jackson, 'Introduction', in Jackson and Langer, *The New Latin American Mission History*, p. viii.

[483] Deeds, 'Indigenous Reponses', pp. 77, 95; Weber, *The Spanish Frontier*, pp. 98, 131; Spicer, *Cycles of Conquest*, remains the best overview of the (region now known as the American) southwest.

In the north, too, there were fewer bodies. Historically less populated than central Mexico, the north experienced its demographic collapse, occasioned by European diseases, about fifty years after central Mexico; and the northern population reached it nadir around 1700.[484] Where the Aztecs had ruled an empire of some twenty millions, the northern Mexican 'tribes' (i.e., ethnic groups, linked by a common language, though not a common polity) represented groups of tens of thousands: there were, perhaps, fifty to sixty thousand Mayos and Yaquis in the valleys which bore the same names; perhaps fifty thousand Pueblo Indians in the Río Grande Valley between Taos and Santa Fe.[485] These, furthermore, were the larger groups ('tribes'), characterized by dense village settlements. Other groups, like the Tepehuanes and Tarahumara of the Sierra Madre in Chihuahua, lived in villages or scattered settlements (rancherías), probably organized as chiefdoms; and others, like the Apaches of Arizona or the Seris of coastal Sonora, were non-agricultural peoples, devoted to hunting and fishing and comprising nomadic bands.[486] Thus, though fewer in number than the Indians of central Mexico, the Indians of the north did not constitute a homogeneous type. They were divided not only by social organization but also by language: in the northwest alone – roughly, modern Sonora, Chihuahua, Arizona and New Mexico – there were at least six major linguistic families, each broken into several dialects, often mutually unintelligible; neither Spanish nor Nahuatl afforded a lingua franca, as in central Mexico.[487] Northern Indians, like the Maya, also had a long tradition of mutual conflict: wars, raids, slaving expeditions.[488] In consequence, there was scant cultural cohesion or possibility of multiethnic, cross-'tribal' alliances directed against the Spaniards who, once again, could enlist Indian

[484] Reff, Disease, Depopulation, and Culture Change, ch. 4.
[485] Spicer, Cycles of Conquest, p. 155; see also Radding, Wandering Peoples, pp. 112–15, Reff, Disease, Depopulation, and Culture Change, pp. 211–24, and Gutiérrez, When Jesus Came, who prefers a higher Pueblo figure (80,000). Hu-Dehart, Missionaries, Miners, and Indians, p. 8, suggests a total Indian population, c. 1500, of about half a million in the Mexican northwest.
[486] There is debate concerning the 'chiefdoms' of the Sierra Madre: Deeds, 'Indigenous Responses', pp. 79–80; see also Reff, Disease, Depopulation, and Culture Change, p. 91. On the Seri and Apache, see Spicer, Cycles of Conquest, chs. 8, 9, and pp. 383–4, which roughly categorizes the Apaches as a band society, loosely led by war and peace chiefs; and the Seri as a yet simpler micro-band society, lacking chiefs or 'headmen'.
[487] Spicer, Cycles of Conquest, pp. 10–12.
[488] Reff, Disease, Depopulation, and Culture Change, pp. 64–5.

recruits to fight other Indians.[489] The Concho Indians of Chihuahua became the 'Tlaxcalans of the north'; the Opatas of highland Sonora, who successfully integrated into the colonial order (they mounted only one significant rebellion, in 1696), proved staunch allies of the Spaniards, especially as the Apache threat mounted from the late seventeenth century.[490] Even the Sonoran Yaquis, famous for their martial independence, lent their services to the Spanish elite: twenty-five Yaquis, armed with bows and arrows, enabled the mine owners of Chihuahua to cow protesting miners in 1735.[491]

Patterns varied. Opata collaboration contrasted with Tarahumara belligerence. Yaqui collaboration in the seventeenth century contrasted with Yaqui belligerence in the eighteenth and nineteenth centuries.[492] To some extent these contrasting patterns depended upon individual, conjunctural, factors. The celebrated Italian Jesuit Eusebio Kino, who began to preach among the Upper Pimas in the 1680s, encountered receptive audiences, enjoyed the collaboration of the secular arm and displayed both energy and diplomacy. Although, like all missionaries, Kino sought to impose Spanish and Catholic ways upon a pagan population whose mores he rejected, he did so with a certain relaxed tolerance: he did not strive to extirpate 'witchcraft' and drunkenness; he engaged in long dialogues with Indian *caciques*; and he participated enthusiastically in Indian ceremonies. He was, in the Jesuit manner, a good manager; arguably, he also proselytized at a time when the Pimas, like other northern Indians, reeling from disease, demographic collapse and social dislocation, responded positively to the new organizational opportunities of the mission.[493] As in central Mexico a century before, the mission

---

[489] Thus, in 1610 the Spanish captain Diego Martínez de Hurdaide induced the Yaquis to sue for peace by threatening an attack and 'let[ting] it be known widely that all the Indian nations desiring to settle old scores with the Yaquis would be invited to join the invasion': Hu-Dehart, *Missionaries, Miners, and Indians*, p. 27. Though rare, 'supra-tribal' – or 'inter-ethnic' – alliances were occasionally forged, for example, when groups of 'Xixime, Acaxee, and other *serrano* peoples' joined the Tepehuán rebellion led by the sorcerer (*hechicero*) Quautlatas in 1616: Reff, *Disease, Depopulation, and Culture Change*, p. 273.

[490] Deeds, 'Indigenous Responses', p. 89 (quote); Spicer, *Cycles of Conquest*, pp. 91–101, Radding, *Wandering Peoples*, pp. 16–17, 152–3, 267–8, 280–1 (Opata).

[491] Martin, *Governance and Society*, p. 55.

[492] Hu-Dehart, *Missionaries, Miners, and Indians*, chaps. 3, 4.

[493] Spicer, *Cycles of Conquest*, pp. 118–28, 314–17; Radding, *Wandering Peoples*, pp. 281–3, is more critical of Kino. Reff, *Disease, Depopulation, and Culture Change*, pp. 16, 249–71, stresses Jesuit 'managerial capacity' (rather than technological or other innovations); in part, the black

offered a means to combat anomie and provided a stable foothold in the new colonial order. Yet even Kino could not stand against the inexorable logic of Spanish colonialism. In 1680, the Pueblo Indians launched a massive revolt which sent shock waves throughout the northwest. In 1695, the Upper Pimas rebelled, and, despite Kino's active mediation, the rebellion spread, stimulating Spanish repression. The missionary effort stalled and did not recover momentum until the 1730s, some twenty years after Kino's death.[494]

Many missionaries lacked Kino's mangerial skills. Most were imbued with a sense of rectitude, of Eurocentric dogmatism, and of stern sexual puritanisn, all of which bred conflict.[495] Frequently, the initial Indian reception of the missionaries was favorable and friendly. The missionaries brought new religious ideas and rituals, desirable Spanish goods (axes, liquor, beef) and useful animals.[496] But – along with other Spaniards – they also brought disease, leading to population decline and social upheaval. Immune to disease, the missionaries were seen to possess power; vulnerable, the Indians were receptive to alternative sociocultural messages.[497] As in central Mexico, there was a markedly prudential aspect to Indian conversion (if, indeed, it was conversion at all). The Yaquis, for example, harried by Spanish forces and impressed by the example of the neighbouring Mayos' conversion, invited Jesuit missionaries into their territory early in the seventeenth century.[498] In this case, which was unusual, over a century of relatively peaceful Spanish-Yaqui relations ensued. The Jesuits lived up to expectations: following a rational, quasi-theocratic, project, they converted, taught and organized; they also

robes filled an administrative void created by disease and depopulation; they supplanted the discredited – or dead – shamans and chiefs. Kino's success calls to mind Jesuit policy in Asia, where, instead of 'declar[ing] war' on indigenous culture, the order 'strove to accommodate or "inculturate" the gospel according to the values and expectations of their potential converts': Sweet, 'The Ibero-American Frontier Mission', p. 24.

494 Spicer, *Cycles of Conquest*, pp. 124–8; Radding, *Wandering Peoples*, pp. 282–3; Hu-Dehart, *Missionaries, Miners, and Indians*, p. 56.

495 Sweet, 'The Ibero-American Frontier Mission', pp. 16–31, makes the point, pehaps a little too forcefully. See also Gutiérrez, *When Jesus Came*, pp. 71–3.

496 Sweet, 'The Ibero-American Frontier Mission', pp. 33–5; Reff, *Disease, Depopulation, and Culture Change*, pp. 258–9, argues that cattle represented the major beneficial innovation.

497 Deeds, 'Indigenous Responses', p. 85; Reff, *Disease, Depopulation, and Culture Change*, pp. 263–4.

498 Spicer, *Cycles of Conquest*, pp. 48, 297; Hu-Dehart, *Missionaries, Miners and Indians*, pp. 28–30.

introduced new crops, tools and draught animals; hence agricultural production rose, enabling the region to generate a substantial surplus.[499] In part this was a tribute to Jesuit managerial ability (which seems to have exceeded that of the Franciscans). But it depended primarily on favourable socioeconomic circumstances and the ultimate sanction of force. Both the Yaquis and Mayos lived in fairly compact settlements: no forced 'reduction' was required, and the new mission organization conformed to local tradition. Conversion affected the entire tribe and did not lead to fratricidal sectarian division. Agriculture, already well established, flourished in the fertile river valleys, where the industriousness – as well as the religiosity – of the Yaquis excited the praise of their Jesuit masters.[500] Meanwhile, Sonora lacked a dynamic mining economy, hence Spanish settlement remained limited throughout most of the seventeenth century. The Yaquis and Mayos faced neither the tribulations nor the temptations of Spanish secular rule; the Jesuits exercised a near monopoly of colonial power. By the 1680s, however, the situation began to change: Spanish miners struck silver at Alamos, and Spanish *hacendados* began to acquire land in the depopulated Mayo Valley. The early eighteenth century witnessed growing Spanish settlement, the growth of a market economy and increasing tension between settler and Jesuit. In the 1740s these processes culminated in a Yaqui-Mayo rebellion, the first in a long and bloody cycle which would not conclude until the 1920s.[501]

While the Yaquis and Mayos experienced over a century of relative peace under Jesuit auspices, other northern Indian groups, less suited to the missionary project, proved recalcitrant from the start. In Durango and Chihuahua, the Acaxee, Tarahumara and Tepehuanes mounted recurrent revolts. Each revolt, Reff points out, coincided with a wave of disease (since disease was now endemic, the causal implication of such a coincidence may not be clear).[502] However, this

[499] Spicer, *Cycles of Conquest*, pp. 49, 57–8, 393–4, and Hu-Dehart, *Missionaries, Miners, and Indians*, pp. 37–9, are rather more upbeat than Reff, *Disease, Depopulation, and Culture Change*, pp. 254–9, 266–8.

[500] Hu-Dehart, *Missionaries, Miners, and Indians*, pp. 38–9.

[501] Spicer, *Cycles of Conquest*, p. 51ff.; Radding, *Wandering Peoples*, p. 283; Hu-Dehart, *Missionaries, Miners, and Indians*, p. 56ff.

[502] Reff, *Disease, Depopulation, and Culture Change*, ch. 3. Spanish penetration of the north invariably brought disease and frequently provoked resistance and revolt, hence there is no

protest certainly reflected the Indians' chronic disillusionment that conversion, far from protecting them against deadly disease, seemed instead to spread it: a belief that was empirically grounded and – Spaniards were shocked to find out – actively propagated by 'two very horrible negroes' who travelled the northern sierras in the 1590s, blaming baptism for the spread of disease.[503] The Acaxee rebelled in 1601–2; the Tepehuanes, who first encountered Jesuit missionaries in the 1590s, rose in rebellion in 1616, destroying and desecrating churches, and slaughtering four hundred Spaniards, including several pioneer missionaries. One of the three biggest northern Indian revolts, that of the Tepehuanes was religious and revivalist, led by a prophet and directed against Catholicism as well as Spanish political rule; it appealed to Tepehuanes, Acaxee, Xixime and other Indian groups; and it withstood three Spanish military expeditions and two years of ruthless repression before guttering out, leaving a climate of unrest which simmered well into the 1620s.[504]

Thirty years later, the Tarahumara and Tobosos of Chihuahua, just to the north, mounted their first revolt against Spanish rule. Here, Spanish penetration was well advanced: the big silver strike at Parral (1631) had stimulated settlement, land appropriation and slave-raiding; and the Jesuits, who had first made contact with the Tarahumara back in the 1600s, stepped up their activities in the 1630s. The Tarahumara now faced the twin challenges of both miners/settlers and missionaries. Furthermore, incipient acculturation had left its mark, even if it did not ensure docility. While the Tepehuan rebels of 1616 had harked back to ancient gods and followed prophetic leaders, the Tarahumara of the 1640s and 1650s were led by acculturated Indians, themselves products of the missions, familiar with Spanish ways. Some were 'apostates', lapsed converts; some, like the great Tarahumara leader Tepórame, retained – or at least

---

shortage of plausible correlations. Of course, disease and depopulation alone were not sufficient causes of sustained revolt: central Mexico, also diseased and depopulated, was relatively quiescent. Apart from specific grievances (push factors) – such as economic exploitation or religious oppression – we must take into account the contextual characteristics (the enabling factors) of northern Indian society: remote, scattered, decentralized, often stateless.

[503] Reff, *Disease, Depopulation, and Culture Change*, p. 129.

[504] Reff, *Disease, Depopulation, and Culture Change*, pp. 146–7, 160, 272–3; Spicer, *Cycles of Conquest*, pp. 26–8; on the broader northern impact of the revolt, see Woodrow Borah, 'La defensa fronteriza durante la gran rebelión tepehuana', *Historia Mexicana*, 16/1 (1963), pp. 15–29.

did not repudiate – their Catholicism.[505] But this did not prevent them razing churches and slaying Spaniards. Here, as in Yucatán or Chiapas to the south, the ideological and ritualistic elements of Catholicism could be detached from their institutional apparatus and preserved, alongside older Indian elements; it was the institutional apparatus of the Church which the rebels sought to destroy.

The Tarahumara revolt – comprising three consecutive uprisings – spanned 1648–52. It did not pose so severe a threat as that of the Tepehuanes: the Spanish secular arm was now stronger; and the Tarahumara, given their longer familiarity with Spanish rule, were divided between belligerent rebels and *pacíficos*,[506] who, if they did not necessarily love the Spaniards, at least doubted the wisdom of outright rebellion. Harsh repression rammed home the message. By the 1650s a Roman peace was restored, but the missionary advance had stalled. Not until the 1670s did the Jesuits resume their advance into the highlands of the Sierra Madre, the home of the Upper Tarahumara, where they gradually overcame local suspicions and began to convert and 'congregate' the Indians. Now, the cycle of conversion, settlement, reaction and rebellion was repeated. In the 1680s, as the Jesuits advanced, silver was struck at Cusihuiriáchic. Miners followed the missions into Upper Tarahumara territory; smallpox and measles ravaged the Indian population. In 1690 the biggest of the Tarahumara rebellions erupted and soon spread to encompass the whole newly missionized area of the Sierra. Again, converts lapsed and communities reverted to their old gods. The church bells of the missions, it was said, spread disease among the people. As the fighting spread during the 1690s, the Spanish commanders took preemptive and didactic measures: at Sirupa, Captain Retana attacked a body of presumed rebels, killed sixty of them and displayed some thirty severed heads along the roadside. The Tarahumara responded with killings of their own, and, as their rebellion was ground down,

---

[505] Reff, *Disease, Depopulation, and Culture Change*, pp. 175–6; Spicer, *Cycles of Conquest*, pp. 30–33; Deeds, 'Indigenous Responses', p. 87. Juan Lautaro, leader of the Ocoroni revolt of 1605, was 'a very astute and clever ladino', while the Pima rebellion of 1751 was headed by Luis Oacpicagigua, a landowner, known for his local patronage and largesse, who had been appointed 'captain-general of the Pima nation' by the Spanish authorities: Hu-Dehart, *Missionaries, Miners, and Indians*, p. 26; Radding, *Wandering Peoples*, pp. 286–7.

[506] A pattern (rebels/*pacíficos*, *broncos/mansos*) that would be repeated, for example, in the protracted Yaqui Wars of the nineteenth and twentieth centuries.

they often chose death to surrender. By 1698 the revolt was broken, and Tarahumara armed resistance came to an end. But these and other revolts left their mark on northern colonial society: one where violence was commonplace, men carried guns and renowned Indian-fighters earned positions in the Chihuahuan elite.[507]

The recurrent Tarahumara revolts of the seventeenth century, which contrasted with Yaqui quiescence during the same period, reflected two principal factors: the pressure of Spanish settlement, spurred by mining discoveries; and the character of Tarahumara society, which was traditionally scattered and mobile. Indians who were accustomed to living in isolated *rancherías*, and who seasonally migrated from their summer camps in the highlands to their winter homes in the canyons, resisted Spanish policies of congregation and reduction. The result was sporadic, bitter, but ultimately unsuccessful armed resistance, coupled with progressive retreat into the fastnesses of the sierra. By the early eighteenth century, conquest assumed a more peaceful, quotidian, 'low-intensity' character: Spanish and mestizo settlers and traders penetrated the highland pueblos of the Tarahumara; while Tarahumara migrants were integrated into the Hispanic economy (they built Chihuahua's aqueduct in the 1750s and bugled at the fiesta celebrating Charles III's accession in 1760).[508]

Similar patterns were evident wherever scattered or nomadic populations – such as the Seris or Apaches – confronted the Spanish advance.[509] The Seris of coastal Sonora, who first made violent contact with the Spaniards in the 1660s, resisted reduction and experienced a form of malign neglect for almost a century; it was not until the mid-eighteenth century that they, like the more numerous and threatening Apaches further north, were forced to confront an aggressive, military and secular colonialism. Similarly, in the great expanses of northeastern Mexico (then the provinces of Nuevo León and Coahuila, now the states of the same name) the prevalence of stateless, nomadic or semi-nomadic Indians made Spanish conquest

---

[507] Spicer, *Cycles of Conquest*, pp. 34–5; Martin, *Governance and Society*, p. 75.

[508] Deeds, 'Indigenous Responses', pp. 96–8; Martin, *Governance and Society*, p. 42.

[509] Radding, *Wandering Peoples*, pp. 155, 267–9 (Seris); Spicer, *Cycles of Conquest*, pp. 105–7, 229–30, with the caveat that the pre-Conquest structure of Apache society remains obscure.

difficult and unrewarding.[510] Initial expeditions, mounted in the 1570s, fought with and enslaved the local inhabitants. Scattered settlements were founded, notably Monterrey in 1579. But these scarcely prospered. No major mining strikes occurred in the northeast. The immigration of Tlaxcalan Indians from the south failed to produce a settled, docile, labouring population. Throughout the seventeenth century the local Indians continued to defy Spanish power and to raid Spanish settlements (in 1624 Monterrey itself was directly threatened). Florida, to the far northeast, was no better off: Indian hostility was compounded by French, and later British, aggression, leading Philip III to despair of retaining this remote and unremunerative colony.[511] As the eighteenth century dawned, Spanish colonization of the northeast remained patchy, and Spanish control, never that secure, began to be threatened by the southern push of the Apaches.[512]

A final variant of northern rebellion is offered by the great Pueblo revolt of 1680. Concentrated in the Río Grande Valley, between Santa Fe and Taos, the Eastern Pueblos constituted a dense, sedentary population, familiar with trade and irrigated agriculture.[513] Their vigorous economic – and religious – life did not, however, require a state apparatus, and the Pueblo villages remained autonomous and self-governing, under the rule of war chiefs and religious leaders.[514] Spanish forces under Coronado first made contact with the Pueblos in 1540–1. Hopes of another mining bonanza were soon dashed; the Spaniards took what they wanted – food, goods and women – by force; and in the ensuing fighting they bested the Indians, leaving behind them no permanent Spanish settlement, but a reputation for Spanish ferocity.[515] Fifty years later, more systematic – but no less

[510] Chevalier, *Land and Society*, pp. 181; Thomas R. Hester, 'Texas and Northeastern Mexico: An Overview', in David Hurst Thomas, ed., *Columbian Consequences: Archaeological and Historical Perspectives on the Spanish Borderlands West* (Washington, D.C., 1989), vol. 1, pp. 191–212.

[511] Gibson, *Tlaxcala*, pp. 185–8 (Tlaxcalan diaspora); Weber, *The Spanish Frontier*, pp. 88–9 (Florida).

[512] The southern push of the Apaches was in turn impelled by pressure from Plains Indians – Pawnees, Missouris, Comanches and Wichitas – who had acquired guns from the French: Thomas D. Hall, *Social Change in the Southwest, 1350–1880* (Lawrence, Kans., 1989), p. 104; Weber, *The Spanish Frontier*, pp. 168, 188, 206.

[513] Spicer, *Cycles of Conquest*, pp. 152–3.

[514] Gutiérrez, *When Jesus Came*, pp. 13, 22, 25.

[515] Gutiérrez, *When Jesus Came*, pp. 42–5; Knaut, *The Pueblo Revolt*, pp. 28–30.

violent – Spanish expeditions returned to the Río Grande Valley, playing their part in Oñate's ambitious colonization project.[516] In contrast to the Spanish advance in Chihuahua and Sonora, which was pioneered by the missionaries, the subjugation of New Mexico was initially military and was also more rapid, less piecemeal. But it was scarcely more durable. The Pueblos were subdued but not won over. Missionaries – in this case Franciscans – now entered the territory and a framework of Spanish secular government was established. Parallels with central Mexico abounded: the friars followed the early conquistadors; disease and abuse followed both. Spanish perceptions of the Indians were again simplistic and Eurocentric: kivas were regarded as mosques; they were destroyed and churches were raised on their ruins. The Franciscans performed their mass baptisms and introduced Spanish plays, pictures and ritual. However, through the early seventeenth century, initial mendicant optimism again faded, opening the way to recrimination and coercion.[517]

Spanish settlers, the third party in this triangular relationship, found themselves confronting a hostile environment and people. The first denied the Spaniards rich pickings; the second offered, at best, sullen acquiescence, punctuated by sporadic revolt, in which local shamans often played a leading part. The colonization of New Mexico therefore proceeded slowly. It was also hampered by the familiar story of Spanish Church-State, clerical-secular dissension. Spanish settlers began to expropriate Indian land; Spanish governors strove to extract a surplus – salt, nuts, hides – from a recalcitrant Indian population, who were also put to forced labour. Lay abuses incurred the hostility of the friars, who had their own economic agenda to pursue. Lay critics, in turn, alleged that the Franciscans were too free with the lash, especially as they exerted themselves to stamp out Indian sexual licence and religious

---

[516] Weber, *The Spanish Frontier*, pp. 85–6; Gutiérrez, *When Jesus Came*, pp. 48–55.

[517] Knaut, *The Pueblo Revolt*, pp. xv–xvi, 40, 45, 53–4, 74–6, 83, 98–9, 101, 141, gives ample evidence of Pueblo resentment and resistance, spanning decades; see also Gutiérrez, *When Jesus Came*, pp. 44, 58ff. It is clear, therefore, that the 1680s uprising was not a sudden fall from grace, but a culmination of generations of tension and violence; in this, New Mexico was very different from, say, the Valley of Mexico.

rituals, which survived vigorously. Certainly the Franciscans and their Indian 'spiritual police' resorted to harsh and coercive measures: the stocks, the whip, and worse.[518]

Throughout the mid-seventeenth century this triangular conflict – involving laymen, friars and Indians – continued to simmer. Sometimes it boiled over. Given the weakness of royal authority in such remote regions – New Mexico, Florida – local authorities, lay and clerical, had more latitude, hence more scope to squabble. In New Mexico, successive governors feuded with the Franciscans; excommunications flew like confetti – three governors were excommunicated (one twice), and two were consigned to the Inquisition.[519] The Indians were well aware of their masters' dissension. Meanwhile, Spanish penetration of these northern expanses had addded a new factor to the ancient, ever-shifting Darwinian struggle of Indian tribes, nomadic and sedentary. The new Spanish settlements offered a tempting target to nomadic raiders, especially the Apaches, whose belligerence was further fanned by Spanish slave-raiding. But the Spaniards proved unable to protect their Pueblo charges against the increased Apache depredations of the 1670s. Like disease, the Apaches were a tribulation which the Spaniards brought but could not banish. Coincidentally, the old scourge of drought returned, bringing crop failures. A complex combination of factors thus fuelled Pueblo discontent; the whipping of alleged Indian idolaters afforded a catalyst. In 1672 the Indians of Abó Pueblo rebelled, torched their church, flogged the friar and then axed him to death. Three slaughtered lambs were left at the martyred friar's feet, testimony to the death of the Trinity. This was but the preamble to a massive revolt which broke out in 1680, stretching the whole length of the Eastern Pueblo country and uniting its inhabitants in an unprecedented, supra-village confederation, under the inspired leadership

---

[518] Gutiérrez, *When Jesus Came*, pp. 76–84, 113–27; Knaut, *The Pueblo Revolt*, pp. 45–6, 58–9, 107–8, 111.

[519] Knaut, *The Pueblo Revolt*, pp. 93, 96–8, 105–6, 111–12. Weber, *The Spanish Frontier*, p. 131, notes that similar, if less severe, Church-state conflict affected Florida. On these remote northern marches of the empire paternalist royal authority was at a discount; and Spanish settlers – few in number but desperate for subsistence and income – ruthlessly extorted a surplus from Indian communities, in defiance of local economic and ecological traditions. In short, the parasites devoured the host.

of Popé, a Pueblo shaman, who carried the scars of the Spanish lash.[520]

More than three hundred Spaniards were massacred (they included two-thirds of the missionaries in the region), and the remaining two thousand were sent scurrying south to El Paso. Churches were razed, their bells were broken, their saints defiled. Indian names replaced Christian baptismal ones. The old kivas were rebuilt. No respect for Catholicism, no 'naive monarchism', informed the Pueblo revolt. For the next twelve years the Pueblos retained a brave independence, defying Spanish counterattacks. But the costs were high. Spanish punitive expeditions – initially unsuccessful – wore down the Pueblos; the rebels were forced to abandon their valley homes for retreats in the high mesas; and the rebels' brief unity ended amid internal dissension and fighting. When, in 1692, the Spaniards mounted a sustained campaign to recover the Pueblo territory, they faced a divided people, some of whom submitted, some of whom fought on. It took over a decade of further conflict to restore a semblance of Spanish control; Sante Fe did not fall until 1693. Yet several thousand Pueblos resisted, preferring to retreat into the wilderness beyond the pale of Spanish rule. The subject Pueblo population of the 1700s was therefore perhaps half that of the 1680s.[521]

The Pueblo revolt was notable for its severity, duration and – admittedly transient – success. It was also 'the one instance of effective intertribal organization for the purpose of resisting the Spaniards', for the Western Pueblos (the Hopis of Arizona), who had been no more than superficially conquered and converted, enthusiastically backed the revolt.[522] The revolt won for its protagonists twelve years of independence; it also ensured that, after their bloody reconquest of the pueblos, the Spaniards did not dare repeat the cultural *gleichschaltung* of the 1670s. Catholicism was no longer imposed root-and-branch; native religion lived on, at least clandestinely; and Spanish missionary activity never resumed its pre-1680 level. The *encomienda*

---

[520] Knaut, *The Pueblo Revolt*, pp. 61, 66–9, 157–60, 168–9; Gutiérrez, *When Jesus Came*, pp. 130–2; Weber, *The Spanish Frontier*, pp. 134–6; Hall, *Social Change in the Southwest*, pp. 86–90, reviews interpretations of the revolt.

[521] Knaut, *The Pueblo Revolt*, pp. 172, 180–2; Gutiérrez, *When Jesus Came*, pp. 133–40, 145–6; Weber, *The Spanish Frontier*, pp. 137–41; Spicer, *Cycles of Conquest*, p. 165.

[522] Spicer, *Cycles of Conquest*, p. 168.

was never restored. Revealingly, the Pueblos were the only settled Indian group who repudiated European architectural styles and clung doggedly to pre-Conquest tradition.[523]

The revolt had wider repercussions. Displaced Pueblos now mingled and intermarried with the Navajos (a partially nomadic people living west of the Río Grande), producing an ethnic and cultural mix which remained boldly independent of Spanish control while successfully incorporating useful Spanish innovations: sheep and horses.[524] Spanish conquest of the Western Pueblos – the Hopis – also stalled. The Hopis kept the Spaniards at arm's length; they abandoned Spanish ways (e.g., ceramic motifs) and exercised their right 'to pick and choose from among Spanish ideas and artifacts without the compulsion to adopt any'.[525] Spanish travellers found the Hopis singularly suspicious and inhospitable – traits which not only ensured cultural autonomy but also kept disease at bay, enabling the Hopi population to rise.[526] To the south, the ripples of the Pueblo revolt reached northern Sonora, where in 1695 the Pimas rose up against their Spanish masters and their Opata collaborators; Eusebio Kino was called upon to broker a peace.[527] And coincidentally – the causal links, if any, are hard to discern – the final decades of the seventeenth century saw the first major incursions of the Apaches, fierce nomadic raiders who drove a wedge between the fractious Pueblo territory of New Mexico and the subjugated Tarahumara and

---

[523] George Kubler and Martin Soria, *Art and Architecture in Spain, Portugal and Their American Dominions, 1500 to 1800* (Harmondsworth, 1959), p. 78. On Franciscan post-1680 pragmatism: Jim Norris, 'The Franciscans in New Mexico, 1692–1754: Toward a New Assessment', *The Americas*, 51/2 (1994), pp. 151–72; Weber, *The Spanish Frontier*, p. 141; Gutiérrez, *When Jesus Came*, pp. 157–60, 163, 165–6; John L. Kessel, 'Spaniards and Pueblos: From Crusading Intolerance to Pragmatic Accommodation', in Thomas, *Columbian Consequences*, pp. 127–38.

[524] Hall, *Social Change in the Southwest*, p. 103; Spicer, *Cycles of Conquest*, pp. 211–12.

[525] Spicer, *Cycles of Conquest*, pp. 188–9. See also E. Charles Adams, 'Passive Resistance: Hopi Responses to Spanish Contact and Conquest', in Thomas, *Columbian Consequences*, pp. 77–92.

[526] Reff, *Disease, Depopulation, and Culture Change*, pp. 229–30. An illustration of Hopi hostility is afforded by the story of the intrepid Franciscan Francisco Garcés, reputed by a fellow friar to be an expert in dealing with 'these unhappy, ignorant and rustic people' (i.e., Indians). In the summer of 1776, having successfully trekked and traded his way from California through the Mojave desert to Arizona, Garcés came to the Hopi community of Oraibi, perched atop a mesa near the Grand Canyon, where the inhabitants, 'unlike other Indians whom Garcés had encountered, . . . refused to accept gifts or to give him food, water or shelter'; so, after two nights of sleeping rough and eating corn gruel, Garcés turned around and – on 4 July 1776, as it happened – headed back the way he had come: Weber, *The Spanish Frontier*, pp. 253–4.

[527] Spicer, *Cycles of Conquest*, pp. 124–6; Radding, *Wandering Peoples*, pp. 266–7.

Opata zones of Chihuahua and Sonora to the south.[528] The result-ing 'Apache corridor', stretching from the Río Grande to the Sierra Madre Occidental, represented a major barrier to Spanish coloniza-tion in the northwest from around 1700. By the mid-eighteenth cen-tury the threat had reached Chihuahua, where the Apaches rustled livestock, attacked travellers and forced the abandonment of remote haciendas; 'from the 1750s forward the parish registers of Chihuahua periodically noted the burials of people killed by Indians'.[529] Thus in the west, as in the east, the Bourbon century began with New Spain's northern borders precarious and with the onward march of the fron-tier halted, in places reversed. Here was one of many challenges which the innovative and power-hungry Bourbon rulers confronted.

To the south, the kingdom of New Spain marched with the captaincy-general of Guatemala (which included the province – later the Mexican state – of Chiapas). Thus, the colony's southern frontier was more secure and demarcated than that of the north. And the Indians of the south – Oaxaca, Chiapas, to a lesser extent Yucatán – had been decisively defeated and subjugated by the mid-sixteenth century. Oaxaca, in particular, represented an area of transition be-tween central Mexico, where Indian acculturation proceeded apace and Indian protests tended to be sporadic and localized, and the south, where acculturation proved more superficial and protest – when it occurred – more radical and challenging. Although the conquistadors had overcome initial Indian resistance in Oaxaca by about 1531, the region did not remain tranquil. The Zapotecs of the central region, resentful at Spanish demands for tribute and labour, revolted in 1547–50; the Mixes of the highlands, whose grievances also included forced resettlement, rebelled in 1563, 1570 and 1573.[530] These movements appear to have transcended commu-nities and even 'tribes' (though one must be careful not to infer an

[528] James E. Officer, *Hispanic Arizona, 1536–1856* (Tucson, 1989), p. 33; Spicer, *Cycles of Conquest*, pp. 36–7, 96–8, 127.

[529] Spicer, *Cycles of Conquest*, p. 152; Martin, *Governance and Society*, p. 25.

[530] Alicia M. Barabas, 'Rebeliones e insurreccions indígenas en Oaxaca: La trayectoria histórica de la resistancia étnica', in Alicia M. Barabas and Miguel A. Bartolomé, eds., *Etnicidad y pluralismo cultural. La dinámica étnica en Oaxaca* (Mexico, 1986), pp. 227–36, offers a good overview and discussion; note also Gruzinski, *Conquest of Mexico*, pp. 87, 136; Chance, *Race and Class*, p. 61; and Chance, *Conquest of the Sierra*, p. 23. The late 1540s also saw a serious revolt in the Mixtec highlands, which the Spaniards in part resolved by appeasing the Mixtec *caciques* with lands and honours: Pastor, *Campesinos y reformas*, p. 73.

underlying 'Pan-Indian' allegiance from tactical alliances between different 'tribal' groups: in 1570, Zapotec auxiliaries fought alongside the Spaniards against the insurgent Mixes).[531] In addition, these Oaxacan revolts were steeped in religious revivalism; as such, they represented a more powerful and threatening repudiation of the colonial order than the limited, community-based protests of central Mexico. The rebels of Oaxaca killed friars, revered messianic leaders and foresaw imminent cataclysms.

By the seventeenth century, however, dreams of the millennium had faded. Protests did not cease: Oaxaca knew its share of local protests, and, in 1660, a massive revolt shook the Tehuantepec region of the Isthmus. But the record of that revolt suggests a certain Hispanization of Indian protest.[532] The Isthmus Zapotecs, though formally and facilely conquered back in the 1520s, had retained a large measure of autonomy, under native *caciques*, which the relative economic isolation of the region accentuated.[533] Rebellion did not therefore flow from land disputes or the pressure of Spanish commercial farming. Rather, it was provoked by the conduct of a new heavy-handed, tribute-hungry *alcalde*, who sought to squeeze more than could be tolerated from the depopulated Zapotec pueblos. The *alcalde* had an Indian *cacique* whipped; the Indians – Zapotecs, Chontales and Mixes – slew the *alcalde* and raised some twenty communities in revolt. Their aims were practical and secular (principally the alleviation of the burden of tribute); their ideology was not notably messianic or millennarian; and, perhaps in consequence, their eventual fate was less bleak and bloody. The rebels defied Spanish power for a year, until the bishop of Oaxaca interceded and restored order, eliciting from the rebels protestations of their basic loyalty to Church and Crown. The leaders of the rebellion were executed, but

---

[531] Barabas, 'Rebeliones e insurrecciones', pp. 235–6; Gruzinski, *Conquest of Mexico*, p. 183; Chance, *Conquest of the Sierra*, p. 23. As noted above (n. 254) the question of 'tribes' and 'tribalization' is a vexed one.

[532] On the Tehuantepec revolt, see Hamnett, *Politics and Trade*, pp. 12–13; Tutino, 'Rebelión indígena'; and Barabas, 'Rebeliones e insurrecciones', pp. 237–41, which sees the revolt – especially as it affected the upcountry communities (Nejapa, Villa Alta, Ixtepeji) – as possessing a more radical, messianic and millenarian character, compared to its lowland Tehuantepec form.

[533] Judith Francis Zeitlin, 'Ranchers and Indians on the Southern Isthmus of Tehuantepec: Economic Change and Indigenous Survival', *Journal of Latin American Studies*, 69/1 (1989), pp. 23–60.

the Crown undertook to curb the abuses of Spanish officials in the region. The cycle of protest and response thus followed the classic Habsburg pattern, evident in the lesser cases of village or city riot: endemic abuses, when carried too far, provoked protest which in turn led to an ambiguous official response, part paternalist redress, part exemplary punishment. But the Habsburg regime lacked the means to rule with an iron hand, and repression had to be tempered with conciliation, especially clerical conciliation, which helped shore up a loose hegemony.[534] By the same token, however, the weak, complex and patrimonial character of colonial government ensured that abuses remained endemic, and protests recurrent.

Further south, in the vast, varied, Maya regions of Yucatán and Chiapas, acculturation proceeded fitfully, while abuses were common, especially in Chiapas. In both regions, Spanish settlers were hugely outnumbered by subject Indians, who retained a vigorous culture, still steeped in Precolumbian practices and ways of thought.[535] In Yucatán, the Spaniards showed a 'jittery wariness' of the potential threat of the Indian masses; they took to heart Maya prophecies which foretold the end of Spanish rule.[536] But Spanish fears proved to be exaggerated: following the defeat of the great revolt of 1546–7 the lowland Maya were relatively quiescent; outbreaks of idolatry were sporadically repressed; and the Iztá Maya maintained their independence, deep in the interior of the peninsula, until the 1690s.[537] In northern Yucatán, however, Spanish rule remained secure, if superficial.[538] The countryside remained under Maya control; haciendas

---

[534] Gruzinski, *Conquest of Mexico*, pp. 115–16; Taylor, *Magistrates of the Sacred*, p. 292.

[535] Farriss, *Maya Society*, pp. 64–6, 107–8; Patch, *Maya and Spaniard*, pp. 45–6. Restall, *The Maya World*, pp. 8–9, criticizes Farriss for adopting an excessively 'Gibsonian' – that is, top-down, Spanish, colonial – view of Maya society. While it is true that Farriss (like Charles Gibson) relies extensively on colonial documentation and (unlike Restall) does not form part of the 'new philological' (Lockhartian) approach to Native American history, her pioneering study strikes me (an amateur in these matters, of course) as reasonably balanced. It is worth noting, perhaps, that an informed critic has chided *both* Farriss and Restall for propagating 'the idea that indigenous peoples such as the Maya operated in an autonomous core culture that shared little with the outside world' – a criticism which, whether *historically* valid or not, seems *historiographically* more apposite in respect of Restall than of Farriss: Terry Rugely, *Yucatán's Maya Peasantry and the Origins of the Caste War* (Austin, 1996), pp. xviii–xix.

[536] Farriss, *Maya Society*, pp. 67–8.

[537] Farriss, *Maya Society*, pp. 12–18, 68, 72; Patch, *Maya and Spaniard*, pp. 47–8; Bricker, *The Indian Christ*, pp. 21–4.

[538] Spanish control on the coast was facilitated by Indian depopulation, itself the product of both disease and Indian flight into the remote interior; in Yucatán, the machine of colonial

were few, weak and endebted; Spaniards – lay and clerical – extracted a surplus (foodstuffs and artisanry) directly from a dwindling population of Maya peasant producers. Official abuses were common; egregious offenders were occasionally sanctioned.[539] In this, northern Yucatán reproduced – chronically, in extreme form – elements of sixteenth-century New Spain: a crude, parasitic colonialism, involving direct extraction of surplus and limited acculturation-cum-conversion. Spanish incapacity moderated Spanish oppression, and the Maya faced a large, open frontier to which they could flee. During the hard times of the 1660s, when a louche governor and his clique tightened the screws of extortion, thousands of Maya fled their villages; 'two entire parishes in southern Campeche, Popola and Sahcabchen, containing eight towns, packed up and moved in a bloc across the colonial frontier'.[540] This, it should be stressed, was a migration provoked by depopulation (and a consequent increase in per capita extortion), not by overpopulation and land hunger.[541] As in pre-Conquest days, the political ecology of Yucatán favoured flight, community fission and resettlement, thus inhibiting aggressive centralized state-building; after the mass flights of the 1660s, the Spaniards, parasitically self-interested, realized that 'some degree of self-restraint was necessary in order to preserve the colony's economic base'.[542] Furthermore, in contrast to what occurred in central Mexico, the Spaniards could not rebuild the countervailing 'social bonds' which had provided cultural coherence in the pre-Conquest past; the Church put down shallow roots ('if these Indians had things their way', a *cura* complained, 'they would not even give us an egg for our sustenance'); indeed, Catholic authoritarianism forced the old beliefs underground (sometimes literally), ensuring that heterodoxy

oppression thus possessed an important safety valve (flight) which was less effective in central Mexico: Patch, *Maya and Spaniard*, pp. 21–2; Farriss, *Maya Society*, p. 72.

[539] Farriss, *Maya Society*, pp. 33–5 (haciendas), 42–4, 84–5 (abuses and sanctions).

[540] Farriss, *Maya Society*, p. 79. On Spanish parasitism: Patch, *Maya and Spaniard*, p. 35; Farriss, *Maya Society*, p. 56.

[541] Farriss, *Maya Society*, pp. 79–80.

[542] Farriss, *Maya Society*, p. 85. As the author suggests (p. 78), self-restraint was likely to correlate with permanence: that is, creole families, or *peninsulares* who had put down roots in the colony, had to take the long view; while transient migrants – *peninsular* governors and their clients – looked to get rich quick, hence were more likely to practice rapacious rent-seeking. Some parasites, in other words, took pains to preserve the host; some were prepared to kill it off and move on.

and religious dissent would thrive, ready, when the time was ripe, to legitimize Maya protest.[543]

Chiapas boasted a more turbulent history. The reasons for this divergence, within the southern Maya heartland, are not wholly clear: Chiapas lacked the inviting open frontier of Yucatán; possibly commercial pressures, deriving from cacao, cotton and cochineal production, were more powerful there than in Yucatán.[544] Chiapas also appears to have been racked by more severe conflicts between Spanish elites: *encomenderos*, officials, friars and secular priests.[545] Indeed, the legacy of Las Casas was distinctly ambiguous, for the bishop's campaign in defence of the Indians of Chiapas seems to have provoked Spanish settlers 'to attack autocthonous social and political institutions without quarter'.[546] Whatever the reasons, the Maya of Chiapas proved less quiescent than those of Yucatán, at least during the colonial era. The most serious Yucateco revolt – indeed, the 'one genuine colonial revolt on record' – lasted barely a week and mobilized no more than a thousand rebels.[547] This, the Canek revolt of 1761, constituted no more than a modest interruption of the long, three-century span of social peace – and successful pre-emptive repression – which stretched from the 1540s to the 1840s; directed against the familiar abuses of the *repartimiento*, it was notable more for Spanish paranoia than for Indian militance.[548]

---

[543] Patch, *Maya and Spaniard*, p. 26 (quote). On Maya religious dissent, Farriss, *Maya Society*, pp. 93–4, 309–19; Restall, *The Maya World*, pp. 158–65.

[544] The relative 'caging' of the Chiapaneco – compared to the Yucateco – population should not be exaggerated: see Rodney Watson, 'Informal Settlement and Fugitive Migration Amongst the Indians of Late Colonial Chiapas', in David J. Robinson, ed., *Migration in Colonial Latin America* (Cambrdge, 1990), pp. 238–78. On the diversity and vigour of production in Chiapas, see Antonio Garcia de Leon, *Resistencia y utopía. Memorial de agravios y crónicas de revueltas y profecías acaecidas en la provincia de Chiapas durante los últimos quinientos años de su historia* (2 vols., Mexico, 1985), vol. 1, pp. 50, 59, 68–9, 82; and Wasserstrom, *Class and Society*, pp. 35–6, 37–8.

[545] Wasserstrom, *Class and Society*, pp. 33–4; Gosner, *Soldiers of the Virgin*, pp. 43–6.

[546] Wasserstrom, *Class and Society*, p. 12; see also García de León, *Resistencia y utopía*, pp. 48–9. Spanish rapacity may have partly derived from the character of the Spanish elite in Chiapas, whom Thomas Gage described (in his scarcely objective way) as 'presumptuous and arrogant', combining 'great birth (and) fantastic pride . . . with simplicity, ignorance, misery and penury': Thompson, *Thomas Gage's Travels*, p. 141.

[547] Farriss, *Maya Society*, p. 68.

[548] On the Canek/Quisteil revolt (led by Jacinto Canek of the commmunty of Quisteil, southeast of Mérida), see Farriss, *Maya Socety*, pp. 68–71; Patch, *Maya and Spaniard*, pp. 156–7; Restall, *The Maya World*, pp. 52–3; and Bricker, *The Indian Christ*, ch. 6, which ends (p. 75) with the grisly story of Canek's torture and execution.

In Chiapas, however, sporadic revolts were more common, and a massive rebellion – the southern counterpart of the Great Pueblo Revolt – shook the province in 1712, culminating some thirty years of simmering discontent. Again, territorial dispossession was not the central grievance. Chiapas's Indians had retained land, and Spanish exploiters – *encomenderos*, clerics and officials – sought to extract a surplus by means of tribute payments, tithes, forced labour and (later) the coerced production of crops (such as cacao) or purchase of goods. As the Indian population fell and the Spanish grew, the burden of these exactions increased.[549] In this, the Church played a key role. The Dominicans had lost much of their early paternalist zeal; they had acquired wealth and property; and they faced the competition not only of Franciscans, Mercedarians and Jesuits but also of a more numerous secular clergy. A dwindling productive base thus had to support a growing parasitic elite. The Franciscan bishop Juan Bautista Alvarez de Toledo made 65,000 pesos profit in four years, milking the Indian communities and *cofradías*. A parish priest in Ocosingo received an annual yield of 100 pesos and 30 fanegas of maize, as well as a daily ration of 30 eggs and 2 big strings of fish.[550]

This economic exploitation was greatly compounded by clerical attacks on supposed Indian idolatry. During the late seventeenth century, systematic witch-hunting accompanied the extraction of cash and goods (the association was not wholly coincidental, of course: backsliding idolaters were less likely to honour their obligations to the Church). 'Witches' were arrested; idolatrous paintings were burned; Indians were debarred from certain church rituals and were required to remain standing during High Mass.[551] Such policies proved counterproductive, however, since the disillusioned faithful (who had been, in all probability, genuinely faithful)[552] now sought

---

[549] The Indian population of Chiapas, having slumped during the sixteenth century, continued to decline during the seventeenth, from perhaps 100,000 in 1595 to 87,000 in 1678: Wasserstrom, *Class and Society*, pp. 27, 37–8, 67.

[550] On clerical 'resourcefulness and greed', see Wasserstrom, *Class and Society*, pp. 36–7, 40–2, 56–7; García de León, *Resistencia y utopía*, pp. 50–2, 82; and Gosner, *Soldiers of the Virgin*, pp. 60–3, which lists Dominican revenues.

[551] Bricker, *The Indian Christ*, pp. 55–6; García de León, *Resistancia y utopía*, pp. 66–7, 75–8; Gosner, *Soldiers of the Virgin*, pp. 46, 65–6, 95.

[552] For the rebels' protestations of Catholicism, see Gosner, *Soldiers of the Virgin*, p. 120, and García de León, *Resistencia y utopía*, pp. 79. Bricker, *The Indian Christ*, pp. 68–9, convincingly argues that 'whatever else it may have been, the . . . revolt of 1712 was not an attempt to revive

spiritual solace elsewhere. Indian cults revived, prophets began to appear and a 'climate of expectation' pervaded highland Chiapas. A people tired of arbitrary oppression, suffering demographic decline and social trituration and aware of their enemies' vulnerability (the Indians were apprised not only of local Spanish conflicts but even of the War of the Spanish Succession) began to formulate a radical, millennarian alternative to Spanish rule.[553]

The outcome was the so-called Tzeltal Maya revolt of 1712, one of the most serious uprisings to shake the colony.[554] It embraced some thirty-two communities in the Ciudad Real (San Cristóbal) region, from which a makeshift army of perhaps four thousand was raised. Clearly, this was no isolated village tumult. And, compared to other revolts – such as that of Tehuantepec in 1660 – the 'Tzeltal' insurrection involved a thorough rejection of the colonial order, not least the Church. Indeed, in a fashion distinct from central Mexico but reminiscent of colonial rebellions elsewhere, from the Andes to Africa, the rebels rejected the formal Church hierarchy, while appropriating Christian symbols and inserting them into a radical nativist ideology.[555]

The revolt was preceded by miraculous signs: an image of Saint Sebastian sweated; one of Saint Peter 'emitted rays of life on successive Sundays'; apparitions of the Virgin occurred, stimulating new Marian cults in the favoured communities.[556] Cancuc, the centre of one such cult, became the rebel headquarters; and Sebastián Gómez, a local sacristan-turned-prophet, established himself in almost papal style as its leader, drawing support from Tzeltal, Tzotzil and Zoque Indians.[557] Gómez claimed to derive his authority from Saint Peter himself, whom he had encountered on a recent trip to heaven. Mobilizing existing Indian civil-religious hierarchies (devices which

ancient Maya customs'; 'what the Indians ... rejected was Spanish control of their religious affairs, not the Catholic religion'.

[553] García de León, *Resistencia y utopía*, pp. 78–81.

[554] Herbert S. Klein, 'Peasant Communities in Revolt: The Tzeltal Republic of 1712', *Pacific Historical Review*, 35 (1966), pp. 247–63, offers a useful overview. However, as both Bricker, *The Indian Christ*, pp. 60–1, and García de León, *Resistencia y utopía*, p. 79, point out, the name commonly given to this uprising – the 'Tzeltal Revolt' – is a misnomer, since, of the 32 communities which participated, 3 were Chol(-speaking), 14 Tzeltal and 15 Tzotzil.

[555] García de León, *Resistencia y utopía*, p. 83.

[556] Bricker, *The Indian Christ*, pp. 56–9; Gosner, *Soldiers of the Virgin*, pp. 122–4.

[557] On Gómez: Gosner, *Soldiers of the Virgin*, pp.125–6; Bricker, *The Indian Christ*, p. 60.

the Spaniards had exploited in the interests of indirect rule, but which now revealed their potential for independent, insurrectionary action), Gómez propounded a new syncretic religion which, far from being a reversion to paganism, claimed a higher revelation than the Spaniards' Catholicism. Save for a few Spanish women who were required to dress like Indians and take Indian husbands, all non-Indians – whites, mestizos, mulattos – were to be killed or driven out 'in order that only Indians remain in these lands'. Indians would replace Spanish priests; the latter would be killed along with the Spanish laity; but Indians who contested Gómez's theocratic rule also got short shrift. 'Now', Gómez proclaimed, 'there was neither God nor King and... they must only adore, believe in, and obey the Virgin'. Orthodox belief and ritual – baptism, chalices, crosses, Mariolatry, even anti-Semitism ('the Spaniards were Jews because they did not want to believe in all this') – were appropriated and blended to provide a powerful counterreligion, an Indian Catholicism, which underpinned the rebellion.

This counterreligion, with its reversal of traditional hierarchies and repudiation of established authority, shared with other popular rebellions the quality of 'the world turned upside down'.[558] Subversion did not imply anarchy; on the contrary, the rebels copied the Spanish hierarchy and imposed stern discipline on their people. This was a rebellion which the Church – being both provocation and target – could hardly appease. Rather, the Church advocated root-and-branch repression. In the absence of clerical mediation, such as had succeeded at Tehuantepec, *force majeure* would have to prevail. Suffering the familiar disadvantages of inferior weaponry, local circumscription and eventual internal dissension, the rebellion was bloodily put down, with 'wholesale exiling and executions'.[559] By 1713 a Roman peace had been restored to Chiapas; a Spaniard who arrived soon after noted that the Indians, so recently 'fierce wolves', now showed a lamblike respect for Spaniards and a veneration for the Catholic Church.[560]

---

[558] Bricker, *The Indian Christ*, pp. 62–3; Gosner, *Soldiers of the Virgin*, pp. 142–4; García de León, *Resistencia y utopía*, p. 85. Cf. Christopher Hill, *The World Turned Upside Down: Radical Ideas during the English Revolution* (Harmondsworth, 1975).

[559] Klein, 'Peasant Communities in Revolt', p. 261.

[560] García de León, *Resistencia y utopía*, p. 85.

But this change was the result of coercion, not of conversion nor, it would seem, of reform. The old economic abuses continued in Chiapas; the suppression of Indian ritual did not abate.[561] But the messianic vision survived too. 'The feelings of discontent and expectation which swept Chiapas between 1708 and 1712 reflected a desire to ... transform the multitude of isolated pueblos into a single native community founded upon faith, equality and divine law',[562] and this desire lived on, fuelling powerful Maya insurrections in succeeding centuries: the Caste War of Yucatán of the 1840s, the Tzoztil rebellion of 1869, perhaps even the Zapatista insurrection of 1994. Outer docility masked inner discontent. As a Yucatán *cura* complained: 'the captiousness, malice and dishonesty of the Indians are well recognized ... If royal officials do not stand firm against their feigned humility and other tricks, we Spaniards will never be able to enjoy peaceful possess of our property, especially since they are led by the detestable propositions that they (the Maya) are in their own homeland, that all belongs to them'.[563]

VIII. The Political Economy of New Spain

The Mexican hacienda, we have seen, developed as earlier forms of indirect exploitation of Indian labour declined and as the Indian population itself dwindled. The hacienda responded to individual Spaniards' need for income, and to the authorities' concern to feed the growing cities. In both respects, the hacienda was constituted as a profit-making (or at least profit-seeking) institution. This raises two important questions concerning colonial Mexico: first, the practical consequences for colonial society of its growing reliance on hacienda production; and, second, the theoretical or conceptual implications of hacienda hegemony – to put it simply, was the hacienda a capitalist enterprise operating within a capitalist society? And if it was not, what was it, and what was the character of the society it increasingly dominated?

---

[561] Gosner, *Soldiers of the Virgin*, pp. 156–7; Wasserstrom, *Class and Society*, p. 87ff.
[562] Wasserstrom, *Class and Society*, p. 85.
[563] Farriss, *Maya Society*, p. 283.

It should be stressed at the outset that – notwithstanding a certain traditional, Thomist, aversion to trade – the search for profit was far from being a demeaning 'bourgeois' trait.[564] In colonial Mexico, as in Spain, lineage and profit could happily coexist and no great stigma attached to mercantile fortunes. 'In these provinces', the viceroy stated in 1673, 'the caballero [gentleman] is a merchant and the merchant is a caballero'.[565] Landlords sought profits in order to subsist and – given Spanish aversion to rural residence – to subsist in the cities, above all in the great colonial metropolis of Mexico City.[566] Spanish rulers saw the market – a highly imperfect, manipulated market[567] – as a means whereby to provision those cities; and, of course, the landlords who lived in the cities and who, frequently, organized their provisioning, did not dissent. This did not mean that profit was the *sole* purpose of landowning. The early Spanish settlers lapsed into landowning after initial dreams of military conquest and easy loot evaporated. Thereafter, sprawling acres appealed to seigneurial sensibilities – above all in the frontier expanses of the north but also in areas of brisk, businesslike, commercial agriculture: 'the possession of a rural estate . . . conferred a degree of social power and legitimacy which was unmatched by any other calling'.[568] A landlord might expect his dependents (employees, peons, tenants) to attend upon him when in residence, to grace his days of rural recreation (days of feasting, bullfighting and rodeos), to display a gratifying deference (this might even be written into rental contracts) and even to shoulder arms against threatening villagers, rival landlords or, especially in the north, hostile Indians. The hacienda community was thus bound together by bonds that were personal, ideological and (to a degree that is debated) coercive, as well as simply economic.

---

[564] On the Thomist/Hispanic preference for public office over trade (presented as a demonstrable empirical fact, not a simplistic assumption), see Louisa Schell Hoberman, *Mexico's Merchant Elite, 1590–1660* (Durham, 1991), pp. 156, 224.

[565] Chevalier, *Land and Society*, p. 307.

[566] The reluctance of Spaniards to settle in the countryside supposedly led to a shortage of hacienda overseers and consequent neglect of hacienda farming: Brading, *Miners and Merchants*, p. 6. On Spanish urban bias, see also Farriss, *Maya Society*, pp. 159–61.

[567] Hassig, *Trade, Tribute, and Transportation*, p. 245, characterizes 'the history of market control in [colonial] Mexico . . . [as] one of continual price regulation and continual failure'; likewise Cope, *Limits of Racial Domination*, p. 130: 'colonial authorities were not (to put it mildly) disposed to see free enterprise and public good as synonymous'.

[568] Van Young, *Hacienda and Market*, p. 140; see also Nickel, *Morfología social*, pp. 53–4.

Hacendados figured as 'masters, legislators, judges and magistrates over the hacienda residents'.[569] This did not necessarily make the hacienda a happy 'holistic' community, traditional, organic, bucolic and benign.[570] It was an unequal, exploitative institution, whose internal relations, far from being 'natural' and given, were constructed on the basis of political power, coercion and ideology.

The 'traditional' hacienda thus differed from, say, the 'modern' factory less because of its natural, organic character (which is a piece of reactionary whimsy) than because of its enveloping social role and its distinctive economic *modus operandi*. The rationale of the hacienda, we have stressed, involved profit-seeking. While the acquisition of power and prestige was important, these intangible goods were intimately linked to profit: an unprofitable hacienda would eventually change hands (as many did: hacienda turnover was a colonial fact of life); a losing concern could hardly underwrite seigneurial consumption. On the other hand, political power (office-holding) facilitated profit-making, for officials intervened in the market at every turn, and the courts were jammed with litigation over land.[571]

If the triad of profit, prestige and power thus proves conceptually inseparable, it is necessary nonetheless to stress the central importance of profit, if only to exorcise the mistaken notion (now less readily entertained) that the colonial hacienda represented some kind of

---

[569] Florescano, 'Formation and Economic Structure', p. 167. On the recreational and military side of hacienda life, see Van Young, *Hacienda and Market*, p. 140; Chevalier, *Land and Society*, pp. 149, 151, 154–6, 294, 302, 306.

[570] The (commendable) historiographical reaction against the old *leyenda negra* of Spanish colonial oppression, in which the hacienda, complete with *tienda de raya* and whipping post, played a central and villainous role, has shown a marked tendency to overshoot (as historiographical reactions often do), leading to a new *leyenda blanca*, which depicts the hacienda as a garden of earthly delights (I exaggerate slightly). Interestingly, currents of both romantic nostalgia (the hacienda as a rural idyll) and free market dogma (the hacienda as a rational capitalist enterprise) incongruously mingle in the making of this new stereotype.

[571] On the imbrication of government and market (via litigation, tax-farming and corruption), see Hoberman, *Mexico's Merchant Elite*, pp. 154–5, 160; Horn, *Postcolonial Coyoacán*, pp. 73–4; Gibson, *Aztecs under Spanish Rule*, pp. 292–9; and Nickel, *Morfología social*, pp. 196, which reminds us that powerful landlords not only counted on political back-up but could, when it suited them, spurn political or judicial decisions which went against them. Hacienda turnover is stressed by Super, *La vida en Querétaro*, p. 42; Boorstein Couturier, *La hacienda de Hueyapán*, pp. 47–8 (which notes three changes of ownership in a single year: 1665); Taylor, *Landlord and Peasant*, pp. 140–1; and Van Young, *Hacienda and Market*, pp. 115–17. (Taylor and Van Young focus chiefly on the eighteenth century, when turnover may have accelerated; however, it is clear that in earlier periods too ownership and boundaries recurrently shifted, hence the old myth of a bloated and inert hacienda, lying like a beached whale on the shores of Mexican history, needs to be severely qualified.)

'natural' economy, antagonistic to the market.[572] On the contrary, profit-seeking was fundamental to colonial landownership, lay and ecclesiastical; it determined patterns of economic behaviour, and it demarcated successes from failures. The fact of landlord absenteeism (sometimes construed as evidence of seigneurial fecklessness) did not alter this but merely devolved the daily tasks of management and profit-maximization to administrators and mayordomos. To stress the hacienda's search for profits is not, however, to assert the *capitalist* character of the hacienda, as some have also erroneously assumed.[573] But before broaching that thorny theoretical question, we should give some attention to the practical operations of the hacienda.

The quest for profit in the Mexican colonial market was strongly conditioned by the market's chronic weakness. There are markets and markets: in neoclassical terms, there are markets (mass, industrial, consumer markets) characterized by high elasticity of demand, and markets – like that of colonial, agrarian, Mexico – where demand is low and inelastic.[574] In this respect, the poor communications and

---

[572] Nickel, *Morfología social*, pp. 53–4, 69–70, offers a useful review. His critique of Chevalier – on the grounds that the latter 'denies hacendados rational calculation of their investment' (p. 53) – is somewhat excessive, since Chevalier readily mentions entrepreneurial individuals, such as the landlord and miner Arizmendo Gogorrón, who 'appears in some respects a modern industrialist and businessman' (Chevalier, *Land and Society*, p. 175). The argument – in respect of landlord mentality and *modus operandi* – revolves around the balance between market calculation and other (social, cultural, seigneurial) imperatives; a balance which, unfortunately, it is extremely difficult to measure. As I go on to suggest, however, the question of landlord mentality is really secondary to the bigger question of the rationale of Mexico's political economy as a whole.

[573] Nickel, *Morfología social*, p. 73, asserts the 'rational capitalist calculation' of the hacienda (in respect of tenancy and sharecropping). Ouweneel, *Ciclos interrumpidos*, p. 145, concurs: 'the central Mexican hacienda [was] a modern [*sic*] enterprise, which operated with efficient methods of production'. 'Rational' is, broadly speaking, correct; however, it is not especially informative, since rationality – which has to do with the 'fit' between ends and means – can only be conceptualized within a given framework (in this case economic) which determines the ends. English medieval manors were, broadly speaking, 'rational' in their manner of exploitation (see n. 685) and were not radically different from Nickel's colonial Mexican haciendas. Yet they were by no means 'capitalist' – nor were they 'modern' (whatever that might mean).

[574] As menioned earlier, Cohen, *Karl Marx's Theory of History*, p. 81, offers a neat schematic breakdown of at least six gradations of 'market' activity, ranging from barter ('exchange but not for exchange-value') through forms of 'penny capitalism' to fullblown market exchange geared to capital accumulation. A good empirical example of the contrasting forms of (Spanish and Indian) 'market' engagement is provided by Cynthia Radding, 'Work, Labour and the Market: The Responses of Farmers and Semi–Nomadic Peoples to Colonialism in North-West Mexico', in Paul E. Lovejoy and Nicholas Rogers, eds., *Unfree Labour in the Development of the Atlantic World* (Ilford, 1994), p. 60.

transport of colonial Mexico were crucial. Notwithstanding the innovations of the Spaniards – mules, horses, oxen, carts and the *caminos
reales* (royal roads) – transport remained slow: mules, the basic
draught animals of the colony, plodded about twelve miles a day,
carrying up to two hundred fifty pounds; and, given Mexico's to-
pography and the concentration of population in the centre, they
often plodded up hill and down dale. Tlamemes – human porters –
covered similar distances, the tumpline biting into their calloused
foreheads. Spanish law again tried to curtail abuse of tlamemes, but
protests were common and the system endured, eloquent testimony
to the colony's combination of poor communications and harsh coercion of labour.[575] River transport was negligible; the intricate canal
system of Tenochtitlán decayed, as the lakes were drained.[576] Coastal
traffic was scant, since the coasts were economically peripheral to
the colony. Maritime traffic was therefore reserved for international
trade (of which more in a moment). Thus the cost of bringing grain
into Mexico City frequently doubled its price, while local producers
of goods (such as cheap cotton textiles) were protected by the heavy
costs 'of bringing goods in from outside'.[577] The old topographical
tyranny which had flummoxed the Aztecs was inherited by their conquerors. Indeed, Hassig suggests that the new *caminos reales* were
less efficient than their Aztec counterparts.[578] Poor communications
affected not only transport costs but also market signals. As late as
1802 it took at least three days for a letter to reach Puebla from
Mexico City; San Luis and Oaxaca were a week away, Saltillo and

[575] Hassig, *Trade, Tribute, and Transportation*, pp. 187–207; Chance, *Conquest of the Sierra*, pp. 22,
32, citing abuses and complaints from the Sierra Zapoteca (Oaxaca), where 'the Spaniards
make use of the *macehuales* (Indian commoners) as if they were horses' – not least because
horses and burros could not negotiate the tortuous and slippery mountain tracks.

[576] Hassig, *Trade, Tribute, and Transportation*, pp. 208–11, 218–19.

[577] 'Maize could be moved from outside the Valley to Mexico City only at a price approaching
that of the original maize itself': Gibson, *Aztecs under Spanish Rule*, p. 312. Schwaller, *Origins
of Church Wealth*, p. 41, notes that the cost of shipping tithe goods from beyond the Valley
was prohibitive: 'in general, the cost was so high that only commodities gathered in the Valley
of Mexico were worth bringing into the city'; Toluca – about 35 miles from the capital, as the
crow flies – stood at the outer limit. Brading, *Miners and Merchants*, p. 16, and Van Young,
Hacienda and Market, p. 80, paint a similar picture for late eighteenth-century Mexico. On
cotton textile transport, see Salvucci, *Textiles and Capitalism*, pp. 24 (quoting a Zinapécuaro
entrepreneur), 30, 39, and 41 (where evidence of 'stronger markets' is advanced, not entirely
convincingly).

[578] Hassig, *Trade, Tribute, and Transportation*, p. 260.

Durango two weeks, the distant settlements of New Mexico over two months.[579] International news, of course, came slowly too. The patriotic citizens of Chihuahua celebrated the accession of King Luis I in 1724, unaware that the young king had already died of smallpox months before.[580]

Population decline and Indian patterns of production and consumption further constricted the market. Indians who retained land – and these were many – continued the age-old (but rational) cultivation of corn, chile and beans: they had no need of Spanish crops and only a limited need of Spanish manufactures. Steel machetes were a boon, but other Spanish artefacts remained superfluous. The Maya – the Spaniards complained – remained stubbornly impervious to the appeal of Spanish goods; if they bought tools and trinkets, they passed them down the generations like 'treasured heirlooms'.[581] Indian food, though enriched by European meat and crops, remained simple and parsimonious; and, of course, demand fell commensurate with population.[582] Down to the end of the colony, too, Indians continued to weave basic (cotton) textiles on the simple backstrap looms, frustrating Spanish manufacturers, importers and officials alike.[583] One reponse was the forced sale of goods (*repartimiento de efectos*), which became a major source of Spanish profit and Indian resentment during the eighteenth century, especially in southern zones such as Oaxaca and Chiapas.[584] But forced

---

[579] See Salvucci's 'isochronic map', *Textiles and Capitalism*, p. 95. This suggests a speed of about 30 miles a day, or half that achieved by letters going to and from Venice in the same period (thus, Venice–Nuremberg, which is comparable to Mexico City–Oaxaca, took four days): Fernand Braudel, *Capitalism and Material Life, 1400–1800* (London, 1974), p. 318.

[580] Martin, *Governance and Society*, p. 104.

[581] Farriss, *Maya Society*, p. 45; Restall, *The Maya World*, pp. 106, 179. On Indian/peasant autarky (relative, not absolute, of course), see also Olivera, *Pillis y macehuales*, pp. 156–8; Gibson, *Aztecs under Spanish Rule*, p. 353. Even in the more monetized, mestizo north, poverty was widespread, the ownership of material goods scant, and market demand therefore constricted: Phillip L. Hadley, *Minería y sociedad en el centro minero de Santa Eulalia, Chihuahua (1709–1750)* (Mexico, 1979), p. 93.

[582] Super, *Food, Conquest, and Colonization*, pp. 71–2; Gruzinski, *Conquest of Mexico*, p. 84. As already noted, Indians probably ate more – and even better – after the Conquest than before; Indian abstemiousness is based on contrasts with Spanish consumption.

[583] Salvucci, *Textiles and Capitalism*, pp. 19–20; Daniéle Dehouve, 'El pueblo de indios y el mercado: Tlapa en en siglo XVIII', in Ouweneel and Torales Pacheco, *Empresarios, indios y estado*, p. 91.

[584] Gibson, *Aztecs under Spanish Rule*, pp. 94–5; Wasserstrom, *Class and Society*, pp. 35–6; Pastor, *Campesinos y reformas*, pp. 153–9; Hamnett, *Politics and Trade*, p. 6ff. The *repartimiento de efectos* seems to have been especially abusive in the south, where it was used to extract

consumption had clear limits: until Indians produced profitable cash crops or were paid better money wages (until, some might say, the marginal productivity of their labour had risen), they were bound to constitute an exiguous consumer market.

Indian peasants were not only indifferent consumers of manufactures; they were also active producers of staple foodstuffs. To a substantial degree they fed themselves, constricting domestic demand, and they even entered the market – initially at the behest of the Spanish authorities – competing with haciendas in the production and sale of, chiefly, maize and pulque.[585] Indians also pioneered the production, for the market, of cacao and cochineal; however, with time, Spanish merchants established control over the marketing of these cash crops (the Indians did not, therefore, realize the marginal product of their labour).[586] Although by the seventeenth century haciendas supplied the greater part of New Spain's urban demand, Indian/peasant production remained important, both for major cities like Mexico and Puebla and for commercialized zones like western Morelos.[587] As late as the mid-eighteenth century, by

increasing quantities of profitable goods from the Indians, by means of forced sales: in Oaxaca, silk and cochineal; in Chiapas, cacao; and in Yucatán, cotton textiles and wax (see Patch, *Maya and Spaniard*, pp. 83–92). There seems to be an incipient historiographical trend to rationalize the *repartimiento* – that is, to downplay coercion and to explain the system in terms of broadly free market motivation (as has been done, with some success, in respect of debt–peonage): see Ouweneel, *Ciclos interrumpidos*, p. 328; Pietschmann, 'Agricultura e industria rural indígena', pp. 76–7; and – the clearest statement – Jeremy Baskes, 'Coerced or Voluntary? The *Repartimiento* and Market Participation of Peasants in Late Colonial Oaxaca', *Journal of Latin American Studies*, 28/1 (1996), pp. 1–28. While the phenomenon was no doubt complex and certainly some Indians (e.g., *caciques*) connived in its workings, the argument that the *repartimiento* represented a rational free market solution to problems of deficient credit is contrived, unconvincing and, perhaps, a disingenuous concession to shifting economic fashion. It ignores abundant evidence of coercion; misconceives the nature of colonial political economy (by assuming, *inter alia*, that 'weak' states are not necessarily coercive); and incurs both illogicalities (e.g., the absence of serious revolts – though not of riots and protests – is supposedly evidence of voluntarism!) and inconsistencies (e.g., corrupt officials allegedly did not need to use coercion because they enjoyed a commercial monopoly; yet Indians could at the same time escape official extortion by dealing with rival merchants). As yet, the historiographical consensus, stressing exploitation and 'extra–economic coercion', has been no more than marginally qualified by this modish revisionism.

585 Hassig, *Trade, Tribute, and Transportation*, pp. 240–1; Gibson, *Aztecs under Spanish Rule*, pp. 308–19; Florescano, 'Formation and Economic Structure', p. 179. Ouweneel, *Ciclos interrumpidos*, pp. 117–22, offers a useful comparison of (eighteenth-century) maize and wheat farming: maize, being more labour-intensive and less profitable, suited peasant agriculture (irrespective of cultural norms, which were no doubt important too); haciendas specialized in wheat – at the risk, it seems, of eventual overproduction (p. 170). See also n. 618.

586 Hoberman, *Mexico's Merchant Elite*, pp. 118–20.

587 Garavaglia and Grosso, *Puebla*, pp. 107–9 (mentioning wool, lambs, pigs and pig derivatives such as *chicharrón* – pork scratchings); see also Juan Carlos Garavaglia and Juan

which time hacienda expansion had severely constrained peasant farming, petty producers still provided a quarter of Guadalajara's food supply.[588]

Even where hacienda production dominated the market, it was a highly constricted and regulated market, especially where grain was concerned.[589] Colonial policy favoured the regulation of markets in order, first, to raise revenue and, second, to eliminate fluctuations, shortages and consequent social tension. In this, colonial policy followed old Spanish/European precedents.[590] Speculation in staples was prohibited (like all colonial prohibitions, this was far from absolute in practice). Public granaries (*pósitos*) and markets (*alhóndigas*), initially set up in response to the dearth of the 1570s, became central features of the urban economy, along with public abattoirs.[591] In a city like Guadalajara some two-thirds of the city's grain supply was channelled through the *pósito* in the late colonial period.[592] The cities' food supply was further guaranteed, albeit imperfectly, by agreements struck between city councils and major suppliers, who contracted to deliver grain or meat at fixed prices over a given period. In Mexico City, for example, the meat contract dated back to the earliest years of the colony (since meat, unlike grain, could not be supplied by coerced Indians). Here again the market was regulated – or, better, self-regulated, since the *cabildos* who oversaw the cities' food supply were usually landlords themselves.[593] The result was a market, certainly, but a market hedged about by restrictions, in which producers sought a guaranteed profit on a limited turnover.

Carlos Grosso, 'Indios, campesinos y mercado. La región de Puebla a finales del siglo XVIII', *Historia Mexicana*, 46/2 (1996), pp. 273–5, which cites additional case studies, and Martin, *Rural Society*, p. 42. While it is true that the eighteenth century saw increased commercialization in general, it seems unlikely that Indian producers sprang out of nowhere; rather, they built on established methods and markets.

[588] Van Young, *Hacienda and Market*, p. 86.

[589] Hassig, *Trade, Tribute, and Transportation*, p. 228ff.; Florescano, *Precios del maíz*, pp. 55–8; Thomson, *Puebla de los Angeles*, pp. 101–2, 115, offers a good synopsis of colonial regulation.

[590] Brading, *Miners and Merchants*, p. 236; Super, *Conquest and Colonization*, pp. 39–40. Boyer, *La gran inundación*, p. 69, notes that when, in September 1629, a period of dearth was followed by torrential rains and the flooding of Mexico City, the authorities, fearful of riot, at once raised a loan and began to distribute food to the populace.

[591] Hassig, *Trade, Tribute, and Transportation*, pp. 241–6; Florescano, *Precios del maíz*, ch. 5; Super, *Conquest and Colonization*, pp. 46–50.

[592] Van Young, *Hacienda and Market*, p. 77.

[593] José Matesanz, 'Introducción de la ganadería en Nueva España, 1521–35', *Historia Mexicana*, 14 (1965), pp. 553–4; Van Young, *Hacienda and Market*, pp. 53–4, 71; Israel, *Race, Class, and Politics*, pp. 94–5.

The maximization of production was avoided; political connections counted for as much as economic efficiency. In theory, and to a degree in practice, urban provisioning responded to a kind of moral economy; the 'food bureaucracy' of colonial cities 'was based on the principle that all within the city should have access to good food at a fair price'.[594] Finally, the authorities' demands for revenue further fractured the market. The Church took its tithe; internal customs (*alcabalas*) burdened domestic commerce; international trade was taxed and subjected to tight mercantilist controls which – significantly if not entirely – prohibited intercolonial traffic.[595] As for the Spanish market, Mexico's haciendas could sell nothing except some paltry hides; ironically, the main Mexican agricultural export eventually proved to be an Indian product, cochineal. The haciendas of New Spain, for all their size and (sometimes) grandeur, could not compare, in terms of money-making, with the plantations of the Antilles.[596]

Though haciendas certainly sought profits, they did so, therefore, in a cramped, cumbersome market. Complaints of deficient demand were common, especially prior to the mid-eighteenth century. The Jesuits faced 'inadequate markets' for their goods; hacienda management, their General lamented, 'is a risky investment; some years the yield is bad, while other years it may be good but fetches low prices and lacks outlets'.[597] Even Mexico City's prodigious appetite could be largely satisfied by the haciendas of the Chalco region. There were

594 Super, *Conquest and Colonization*, p. 44; see also Hassig, *Trade, Tribute, and Transportation*, pp. 243–4.
595 Schwaller, *Origins of Church Wealth*, ch. 1; Nickel, *Morfología social*, p. 72; Semo, *History of Capitalism*, pp. 62–3, 85; Hoberman, *Mexico's Mercantile Elite*, pp. 186–96; MacLeod, 'Spain and America', pp. 373–4.
596 In the early seventeenth century, between two-thirds and three-quarters of Mexican exports consisted of bullion; of the remaining third, cochineal (663,000 pesos of exports in 1614) outdistanced indigo (280,000 pesos: a good year) and hides (230,000): Bakewell, *Silver Mining*, p. 228; Hoberman, *Mexico's Merchant Elite*, p. 95; Huguette Chaunu and Pierre Chaunu, *Séville et l'Atlantique, 1505–1650* (8 vols., Paris, 1955–9), vol. 6/2, p. 980ff. In terms of agricultural (as opposed to mining) profits, the real money-spinners of the Americas were the sugar plantations of the Antilles, which Spain had pioneered in the sixteenth century but then relinquished to French and British competitors (in part because of the lure of mainland bullion): 'by 1789', David Brading notes, 'the produce shipped from the French colony of Saint-Domingue came close to equalling the value of the exports of the entire Spanish empire in the New World': 'Bourbon Spain and Its American Empire', in Bethell, ed., *Cambridge History of Latin America*, vol. 1, *Colonial Latin America*, p. 426.
597 Chevalier, *Land and Society*, p. 292.

times when bumper corn harvests had to be burned or when prolific herds of cattle were slaughtered, in prodigal Argentine style, for
their hides and tallow, their carcases being left to rot.[598] Gluts benefited the consumer, of course: Mexico's Indians ate better than their
forebears, especially as population slumped; it is probable, in fact,
that Mexicans ate better than their European counterparts.[599] But
for landlords, gluts meant low profits, even bankruptcy. *Hacendados*
had to contend with these constrictions, with a market which yielded
profits in somewhat grudging, capricious fashion and in which the
arbitrary vicissitudes of weather and politics counted for more than
the logical imperatives of investment and technology.

For Mexico's markets underwent major, unpredictable swings:
long-term swings based on shifting demand and demography, short-
term swings dictated primarily by climatic cycles. In the sixteenth
century, for example, meat became abundant, and grain prices rose.
Hence the prodigal slaughter of cattle and the establishment of public granaries. In the seventeenth century the situation gradually reversed. Maize prices stabilized as Indian and Spanish production
met a falling demand. In the Valley of Mexico some sort of equilibrium was achieved by the 1620s.[600] During the eighteenth century, as population rose and economic activity quickened, food prices
climbed – outstripping wages – and landlords experienced what was,
for them, the most favourable conjuncture of the colonial era. Land
prices rose, landownership became less risky and pastoral farming increasingly gave way to arable. Even then, however, during
the Indian summer of the colonial hacienda, profits were moderate rather than spectacular: 5% was a good annual return, 3% or
4% more usual (*obrajes*, in contrast, might make 9–10%, public
office 10–15%, long-distance trade 30–70%).[601] Bonanzas were rare,

[598] Florescano, *Precios del maíz*, p. 95 (Chalco); Van Young, *Hacienda and Market*, p. 25 (cattle).
[599] Not least because, while in sixteenth-century Mexico population fell and real wages probably
rose, in Europe population grew, inflation increased and living standards declined. Hence
Europeans commented on Mexico's (relatively) high level of consumption: soldiers' rations in
Mexico in the 1580s, for example, were more than double those of soldiers in Spain: Super,
Conquest and Colonization, pp. 20, 29, 61, 71–2. Even wretches in the *obrajes* ate relatively
well: Miño Grijalva, *La protoindustria colonial*, pp. 118–19.
[600] Brading, *Miners and Merchants*, p. 9; Gibson, *Aztecs under Spanish Rule*, pp. 311–12.
[601] Brading, *Miners and Merchants*, p. 216; Tovar Pinzón, 'Elementos constitutivos', pp. 195–6;
Hoberman, *Mexico's Merchant Elite*, p. 55.

bankruptcies common, albeit less common than in earlier times.[602] Bankruptcy, furthermore, stemmed less from any congenital 'aristocratic' prodigality (a vice which was certainly to be found but from which 'bourgeois' entrepreneurs, even corporations, have not always been exempt), than from the hacienda's chronic malaise, a kind of pernicious financial anaemia, the result of low or intermittent profits and limited liquid capital or credit. Not unlike the classic peasant household, the hacienda existed on narrow margins of liquidity;[603] when cash and credit ran out (and credit, supplied by church or merchant, was often the hacienda's vital lifeline), the enterprise was threatened: bankruptcy, sale or partition loomed on the horizon.[604] Even highly capitalized sugar plantations were vulnerable to this cycle.[605] Given the chronic shortage of liquidity, *hacendados* sought to cut money costs just as they sought to boost money income; indeed, amid the enervating constraints of the market, it was often more feasible for *hacendados* to cut costs than to boost income. Autarkic production – in-house production of crops and even manufactures – limited the hacienda's recourse to the external market and staved off bankruptcy. Cost-minimization was as important to the hacienda as profit-maximization. So, colonial haciendas raised their own food, livestock, wood, charcoal and tallow. Some even established their own *obrajes*, producing woolen cloth which provided blankets, sacks and packing material for their workers and tenants; thereby they avoided resort to costly external markets (costly in particular because of high freight charges), and they squeezed a further surplus from their dependents, who paid a big mark-up.[606] In doing so, of

---

[602] Chevalier, *Land and Society*, p. 254; Van Young, *Hacienda and Market*, pp. 117–18.

[603] For all their common autarkic tendencies and limited market engagement, the hacienda and the peasant household differed in one obvious and crucial respect: a failed harvest meant losses – even bankruptcy – for the hacienda, but it meant starvation and worse for the peasant: Gibson, *Aztecs under Spanish Rule*, p. 311.

[604] Chevalier, *Land and Society*, pp. 276–7; Florescano, 'Formation and Economic Structure', pp. 182–4; Brading, *Miners and Merchants*, pp. 100, 215–19; Lindley, *Haciendas and Economic Development*, pp. 35–6.

[605] Martin, *Rural Society*, p. 73; Hoberman, *Mexico's Merchant Elite*, p. 103.

[606] On hacienda autarky, see Florescano, 'Formation and Economic Structure', p. 178; Salvucci, *Textiles and Capitalism*, pp. 58–9; Nickel, *Morfología social*, pp. 69–70; Ouweneel, *Ciclos interrumpidos*, p. 130; and compare Witold Kula, *An Economic Theory of the Feudal System* (London, 1976), pp. 28–35. The sugar plantations of Morelos, in contrast, conformed much more closely to the 'industrial' norm, premised on the principle of comparative advantage: they produced and sold principally sugar; they bought most inputs in the market – including labour (i.e., slaves and free wage labourers); and they achieved significant productivity

course, they constricted the domestic market. The quest for autarky (which, I repeat, represented a rational quest for economic security rather than simple seigneurial gratification) abstracted the hacienda from 'national' and regional markets, and the hacienda's economic rationale was both product of and contributor to the chronic deflation and market weakness of the colony.

Unlike the peasant household, however, the hacienda possessed collateral for loans, as well as mercantile contacts and kinship networks on which its owner could depend. (Indeed, the inseparability of enterprise and kinship was a hallmark of the colony which long survived the colony's demise.)[607] If the hacienda fell on hard times – if crops failed, if a plethora of daughters demanded dowries, if litigation ate up capital – the owner had ready recourse to loans and mortgages. Long-term loans, then, supplemented the short-term credits required to bring the harvest in. Church and commercial lenders thus underwrote many agrarian enterprises; the church tended to supply the longer term credit, merchants the shorter term. Obligations to the Church were further augmented by the tithe, the 10 per cent of production which all producers owed, and the *censo*, a form of mortgage which earmarked a percentage of annual income to a religious institution.[608] *Censos* and chantries were ubiquitous, attesting to the piety of the age, as well as the desire of well-to-do families to find religious 'careers' for their sons and daughters.[609] Hence the

increases: Ward Barrett, *The Sugar Hacienda of the Marquesado del Valle* (Minneapolis, 1970), pp. 65–6, 103–5; compare Chevalier, *Land and Society*, p. 289. However, these were hardly typical colonial haciendas (see Brading, *Miners and Merchants*, p. 13, citing Jean Pierre Berthe): the (domestic) market for sugar was voracious, hence specialization was feasible (see Hoberman, *Mexico's Merchant Elite*, p. 95).

[607] 'The fundamental feature of commercial success was, as with so much of enterprise, the family'; 'the logic of the local credit market suggests that merchants and hacendados sought to establish kinship ties through marital union, since such union permitted sufficient accumulation of capital ... and brought lenders and borrowers together in an institutional setting that insured some regularity and predictability in their credit relations': thus Hoberman, *Mexico's Merchant Elite*, p. 44, on the seventeenth century, and Lindley, *Haciendas and Economic Development*, p. 48, on the eighteenth. For postcolonial case, see David Walker, *Kinship, Business and Politics: The Martínez del Río Family and Mexico, 1824–1867* (Austin, 1986).

[608] Gisela von Wobeser, *El crédito eclesiástico en la Nueva España, siglo XVIII* (Mexico, 1994) offers a useful overview; see also Van Young, *Hacienda and Market*, pp. 182–91; Florescano, 'Formation and Economic Structure', pp. 184–5.

[609] Chevalier, *Land and Society*, pp. 256–7; Farriss, *Crown and Clergy*, pp. 155–6, which quotes a late eighteenth-century observation from the Council of Castile in Madrid: 'it is well known that His Majesty's subjects in the Indies are excessively pious, so that there is scarcely a testament which does not contain a legacy for pious works'.

common colonial spectacle of ostensibly rich estates loaded with debts and obligations, of propertied magnates strapped for ready cash, and of landed fortunes ensnared in 'a tangled web of what modern bankers would call second mortgages, refinanced and discounted loans, surety bonds and defaults'.[610] Once contracted, hacienda loans often limped through the years with the same dogged persistence as hacienda litigation. One consequence was the rapid turnover of landownership, as families bought, sold, parcelled or consolidated their estates according to market and familial vicissitudes (the notion of the static, imperturbable, 'feudal' estate is a myth; though to puncture the myth is not to prove the capitalist character of the colonial estate). Like the *encomenderos* who proceeded them, the landlords of the Habsburg colony frequently failed to establish durable lineages. Bankruptcies and failures outnumbered conspicuous successes.[611] If anything, the tempo of this turnover quickened with the economic growth of the eighteenth century, and did not begin to slow – as hacienda profits rose, as hacienda production achieved greater viability and as swelling mercantile profits found their way into landholding – until the last third of that century.[612]

Thus, although the great estate was, both literally and figuratively, a solid feature of the colonial landscape, individual estates constantly shifted in terms of their size, composition, ownership and profitability.[613] Families came and went, fortunes were made and lost. Wealth from mining, commerce and even manufacturing was repeatedly soaked up in the porous bedrock of the agrarian economy.[614] In part,

---

610 Lindley, *Haciendas and Economic Development*, p. 40. Lindley is discussing the late colonial period; but the broad outlines are valid for the earlier colonial period too: see, for example, Chevalier, *Land and Society*, p. 257; Von Wobeser, *El crédito eclesiástico*, p. 33; Patch, *Maya and Spaniard*, p. 121, which notes that even the modest *estancias* of Yucatán 'were in general deeply in debt'; and Hoberman, *Mexico's Merchant Elite*, p. 102, which rhetorically asks, 'why did seventeenth-century planters borrow so much money?', and lists the reasons: prodigality, 'pious works', drought, market slumps, overinvestment and litigation.

611 Brading, *Miners and Merchants*, pp. 12, 218–19; Van Young, *Hacienda and Market*, p. 117; Boorstein Couturier, *La hacienda de Hueyapán*, pp. 47–8.

612 Martin, *Rural Society*, pp. 72–80, 97ff.; Brading, *Miners and Merchants*, p. 116; Van Young, *Hacienda and Market*, pp. 115–18, 141–68.

613 For illustrative case studies see Boorstein Couturier, *La hacienda de Hueyapán*; Ouweneel, *Ciclos interrumpidos*, pp. 102–17; María Teresa Jarquín Ortega *et al.*, coords., *Origen y evolución de la hacienda en México: Siglos XVI al XX* (Toluca, 1990).

614 According to some, 'the hacienda was a sink through which drained without stop the surplus capital accumulated in the export economy': Brading, *Miners and Merchants*, p. 219; Hoberman, *Mexico's Merchant Elite*, p. 95, somewhat qualifies the picture, noting that 60% of

this reflected the quest for status; but it also reflected the lack of alternative outlets for capital. Trade and mining might yield more cash returns than landholding, but they were risky businesses, and they demanded the right connections.[615] Landholding had its risks, but they were of a different order. Anyway, in an economy where risks were pervasive and risk-aversion was strong, a diversified portfolio made a lot of sense. And, given the close liaison between kinship and capital, the hacienda's injection of vital merchant or mining capital often came with marriage, as merchant wealth allied to landed property, as Spaniard wedded creole. In consequence, the 'landlord class' was a vague and shifting group, which cannot be precisely defined in terms of occupational criteria or family membership. Nor is it easy to determine the pace and governing principles of elite circulation – whether, for example, derogation from the landlord class was as easy and fluid as entry.[616] 'Padre comerciante, hijo caballero, nieto pordiosero' (father a merchant, son a gentleman, grandson a beggar) went the saying, in suggestive, if no doubt exaggerated, fashion;[617] but the fate of third-generation drop-outs tends to remain obscure compared with that of their ascendant ancestors. Even if the landlord class was fluid, however, and even if its membership shifted, these signs of mobility do not denote capitalism, nor do they disqualify us from referring to 'the landlord class' and, indeed, referring to it as the dominant class in the colony. There was no countervailing industrial bourgeoisie, and merchant fortunes, as we have seen, were inextricably mixed with landed. Individual landholding families came and went, but the economic structures and relations associated with the hacienda continued with impersonal inexorability.

merchants who bought into land during the first two-thirds of the seventeenth century continued in trade even after they had become landowners, which suggests (a) that the hacienda was not necessarily seen as a 'sink' and (b) that even if it absorbed capital, it did not necessarily lead to economic ruin.

[615] In neoclassical terms, 'entry' into trade and mining was restricted, with *peninsulares* and political favourites enjoying special advantages; landholding was more readily open to creoles; hence, given the prevailing structure of incentives and opportunities, rich creoles bought into land. 'Culture' (which is sometimes invoked by way of explanation) is not at issue. See McClosky, 'The Economics of Choice', pp. 127–8.

[616] Van Young, *Hacienda and Market*, p. 173; Lindley, *Haciendas and Economic Development*, pp. 46–7.

[617] Hoberman, *Mexico's Merchant Elite*, pp. 223, 232 (which shows that second-generation merchants did regularly assume the honorific title of 'don'), p. 241.

How did these structures and relations operate? The character of the hacienda was determined by its pursuit of profit within the constricted market we have described. The territorial expansion of the hacienda did not represent a simple quest for seigneurial grandeur or for autarky for its own sake. Rather, expansion constituted an economically rational bid for diversified holdings (of water, pasture, woods and varied arable fields) and, ideally, for a local monopoly of land and a local monopsony of markets, which would freeze out competitors, be they rival Spanish landlords, mestizo *rancheros* or Indian peasants, and which would facilitate the acquisition and control of labour – via debts, perks, service tenancies and sharecropping contracts. Diversification enabled landlords to compensate for specific crop failures in any given year and to place different products on the market at different times, thus easing cash flow problems.[618] Monopoly – or, failing that, oligopoly – would help landlords keep prices high even in sluggish markets. Hence the landowner's 'complete scorn' for maximizing production, which was entirely rational in the circumstances.[619]

Indeed, circumstances were such that even more supposedly 'capitalist' entrepreneurs engaged in similar practices. The owners of *obrajes* ruthlessly cut costs by resorting to coercion. They relied on slaves, convicts, endebted workers and dragooned apprentices: 'what often brought labor to the *obrajes* was not the invisible hand of the market but the long arm of the law'. And even when the law sought to correct abuses and encourage free labour recruitment, it largely failed.[620] Thus, in 1620, Puebla's three dozen or so *obrajes* contained 'more than 4,000 Indians shut up in cells and dungeons', toiling in foul conditions.[621] The reason was simple: coerced labour

---

[618] Chevalier, *Land and Society*, pp. 288–9; Lindley, *Haciendas and Economic Development*, pp. 24–5, 27–8; Gibson, *Aztecs under Spanish Rule*, pp. 326–7; Florescano, *Precios del maíz*, pp. 92–7. Risk-aversion may also help to explain why, even though wheat appears to have been more profitable, and less vulnerable to Indian/peasant competition, grain haciendas nevertheless continued to produce maize (there is a related argument: maize may also have been required to feed hacienda workers [the *ración*], hence maize production cut costs and boosted profits): Ouweneel, *Ciclos interrumpidos*, pp. 118, 123. However rational, this is still not the behaviour of a thoroughly profit-maximizing capitalist firm.

[619] The phrase is from Chevalier, *Land and Society*, p. 177, describing a clutch of northern landlord-miners.

[620] Salvucci, *Textiles and Capitalism*, pp. 115, 132.

[621] Miño Grijalva, *La protoindustria colonial*, pp. 77, 84; and p. 135, which illustrates the permanence of such conditions through the colonial period.

was appreciably cheaper than free labour, and manufacturers, like *hacendados*, operated in chronically weak markets and looked to cost-cutting, rather than to technological innovation or production increases, to turn a decent profit. Thus, 'the *obrajes* did not represent proto-industry, much less proto-factories'.[622] Cotton-textile manufacture was also compromised by coercion: Spanish merchants and officials extorted and marketed fabric woven by Indians (often women) in the villages of Yucatán, Oaxaca and Michoacan.[623]

Apart from outright labour coercion, infractions of the free market were legion. Guilds (*gremios*) conspired to regulate artisan apprenticeship and production, with the approval of the authorities.[624] Mexico's mine-owners acquired vast tracts which they declined to exploit. Though – in certain celebrated cases – their investments could dwarf those of landed magnates, the mine-owing class in general could not escape the colony's chronic shortage of capital.[625] One response to market weakness was corporate solidarity. The big merchants of the colony constituted a notoriously tight, endogamous, quasi-official group – colonial *pochteca*, it might be said.[626] Like European guildsmen they did their best to rig prices and eliminate free markets: 'such men excluded competition and monopolized narrow, limited markets. They raised prices by producing fewer goods or by withholding them from the market'.[627] Such behaviour, which characterized the colony's transatlantic merchants above all, was encouraged by the *flota* system, whereby European goods arrived at fixed intervals – naval predators permitting – and were traded in major fairs, as in medieval Europe.[628]

[622] Salvucci, *Textiles and Capitalism*, p. 61.

[623] Miño Grijalva, *La protoindustria colonial*, pp. 43–4; Patch, *Maya and Spaniard*, pp. 83–9; Chance, *Conquest of the Sierra*, pp. 103–5.

[624] Gibson, *Aztecs under Spanish Rule*, pp. 399–401; Semo, *History of Capitalism*, p. 86; Carrera Stampa, *Los gremios*.

[625] Chevalier, *Land and Society*, pp. 176–7; Brading, *Miners and Merchants*, p. 12; Hoberman, *Mexico's Merchant Elite*, pp. 76–7.

[626] Brading, *Miners and Merchants*, pp. 111–13, on the 'peculiar sociology' of colonial trade, which meant that 'many commercial houses owed their survival to...endogamy'; see also Hoberman, *Mexico's Merchant Elite*, pp. 239–40, on mercantile 'clusters', based on marriage and *compadrazgo* (godparenthood).

[627] Richard Boyer, 'Mexico in the Seventeenth Century: Transition of a Colonial Society', *Hispanic American Historical Review*, 57/3 (1977), p. 462.

[628] Brading, *Miners and Merchants*, pp. 95–7, 115–16, which notes how the belated ending of the *flota* system and the associated Cádiz monopoly in 1778 had a 'remarkable' effect, shaking out established merchants and attracting 'a new type of trader, men quite satisfied with small returns taken upon a quick turnover'.

Landlords, manufacturers, artisans, miners and merchants thus displayed certain recurrent characteristics, which in turn were reflections of economic reality, rather than quirky individual attributes. For landlords – the most important single group – conservatism and risk-aversion were logical, as they were for peasant farmers too. Maximizing production – by means of the full exploitation of resources or the introduction of new technology – was futile: markets would be glutted, prices would slump, profits would fall. It was in 'good' years of abundant harvests (such as the 1760s) that landlords were driven to the wall.[629] The art of the colonial landlord (or manufacturer) was the manipulation – often by politico-administrative means – of a limited market and a delicate network of oligopolies. Apparent exceptions, like the rich sugar plantations of Morelos or highly profitable pulque haciendas like the Jesuits' San Nicolás Tlalticahuacan, in fact prove the rule: demand for sugar and pulque was appreciably more elastic than was demand for cereals. In contrast, therefore, a more ruthless, entrepreneurial strategy prevailed; profit- and production-maximization went together. The result was a virtuous 'capitalist' circle, as capital investment increased (the sugar *ingenios* and the slaves who worked them were costly), as profits rose and as a greater degree of specialization ensued, by enterprise or even, in the case of Morelos, by region.[630]

Yet these remained exceptions. Sugar comprised only 1 per cent of New Spain's total agricultural output in the late colony; around the mid-seventeenth century, as the slave trade halted, Morelos's sugar plantations lost momentum and some experienced bankruptcy.[631] Cereals remained the basis of hacienda production. In this sector, weak demand (especially prior to 1750), extensive – rather than intensive – cultivation, and diversification rather than specialization prevailed, making Mexican agriculture very different from the commercial monocultures of the Caribbean. In these crucial respects hacienda and plantation differed, even if both existed to generate

---

[629] Gibson, *Aztecs under Spanish Rule*, pp. 327–8; Florescano, *Precios del maíz*, pp. 92, 99, 113.

[630] Gibson, *Aztecs under Spanish Rule*, pp. 329–31 (pulque); Barrett, *Sugar Hacienda*, pp. 65–6, and the same author's 'Morelos and Its Sugar Industry in the Late Eighteenth Century', in Altman and Lockhart, *Provinces of Early Mexico*, pp. 161–2; additional references to sugar are given in n. 606 above.

[631] Barrett, 'Morelos and Its Sugar Industry', p. 165; van der Meer, 'El Colegio de San Andrés', p. 144; Martin, *Rural Society*, pp. 75–7.

profits.[632] For the Mexican *hacendado*, profits accrued chiefly during times of dearth. As early as the 1550s Spanish landlords were hoarding corn in order to force up prices in Mexico City (even Indian producers were doing the same).[633] Often, nature conspired with the grain farmers. About every ten or eleven years the corn crop failed or was severely reduced: drought or frost (especially the devastating freak autumnal frost) was the usual cause. The result was dearth: in 1533, 1541, 1551–2, 1579–80, 1624, 1695, 1749–50, 1785–6, 1809–10.[634] Then, prices rose to two or three times their normal level; animals died off; disease struck a malnourished population. In times of drought Catholics processed through the populous cities of the central plateau, while in the villages peasants turned to rainmaking wizards and the old rites of Tlaloc were resuscitated.[635]

In such circumstances *hacendados* enjoyed advantages over their lesser (peasant) competitors who, in bad years, not only lacked a surplus to market but even starved for want of subsistence.[636] The *hacendados'* broad and varied acres afforded a degree of insurance against harvest loss, whether from drought or frost; they were less dependent on rainfed fields and better endowed with irrigation; and their capital and credit enabled them to hold back their crops until prices had peaked. In this, hacienda storage facilities (often the enterprise's biggest fixed investment) proved crucial.[637] Landlords held

[632] The classic citation, still worth attention, is Eric R. Wolf and Sidney W. Mintz, 'Haciendas and Plantations in Middle America and the Antilles', *Social and Economic Studies*, 6 (1957), pp. 380–412.

[633] Gibson, *Aztecs under Spanish Rule*, pp. 396–7.

[634] Florescano, *Precios del maíz*, ch. 9, which shows both the relative regularity of dearths and their rough correspondence to the European cycle (pp. 125–9), leading to the tentative conclusion that global climatic forces – possibly related to the sunspot cycle – were at work. Patch, *Maya and Spaniard*, pp. 218–19, also notes an eighteenth-century warming trend which brought recurrent droughts and dearths to the peninsula. On the possible link between sunspot activity and both long- and short-term climatic cycles, see H. H. Lamb, *Climate, History, and the Modern World* (London, 1982), pp. 62–3, 312.

[635] Florescano, *Precios del maíz*, ch. 10; Gibson, *Aztecs under Spanish Rule*, pp. 313–15; Gruzinski, *Conquest of Mexico*, p. 156; Taylor, *Magistrates of the Sacred*, p. 73 ('when the rains were late in coming the old men removed their pants and addressed the clouds with their penises displayed').

[636] Gibson, *Aztecs under Spanish Rule*, p. 311. I discuss the worst dearth of the colonial period – that of 1785–6 – in the following chapter.

[637] Gibson, *Aztecs under Spanish Rule*, pp. 326–7; Florescano, *Origen y desarrollo*, p. 95, and the same author's *Precios del maíz*, pp. 92, 94. Patch, *Maya and Spaniard*, p. 75, offers a contrast with Yucatán, where heat and humidity made long-term grain storage impossible, hence grain production remained largely in Indian hands, at least until the later eighteenth century, 'when

back their crops until the late summer and autumn, when the previous year's harvest had been consumed and the new plants were still maturing in the fields. Standard practice in normal years, this paid extra dividends in times of dearth when prices soared and competitors faltered. Grain sales in Mexico City therefore registered higher figures during bad years than during good years. And, amid dearth, the hacienda prospered, as did the middlemen responsible for financing hacienda operations and marketing crops.[638] Or, at least, some haciendas prospered, for there were always others for whom bad years, possibly coinciding with liquidity crises, spelled bankruptcy. Periodic dearths thus tended to accelerate the turnover of land and, certainly by the later eighteenth century, to stimulate land concentration.[639]

Disaster in the agrarian infrastructure soon transmitted its effects to the rest of the economy. Towns and mining communities faced dearth and a contraction of business (as Engel's law came into effect and dearer food squeezed out other purchases). Unemployment, disease, vagrancy, banditry and, sometimes, riots ensued. The classic example – the Malthusian crisis of 1785–6 – will be considered later. Here, it is the intimate connection between dearth and riot which merits attention. The connection reveals how fundamental – yet, at times, precarious – was New Spain's agrarian base. But riots also revealed something of the nature of urban colonial society. Twice in the seventeenth century Mexico City itself was shaken by major riots, in 1624 and 1692.[640] On both occasions bad harvests, speculation and

food shortages became practically endemic', and the Yucateco landlords began, belatedly, to emulate their central Mexican counterparts.

[638] Florescano, *Origen y desarrollo*, pp. 86, 98–9.

[639] Van Young, *Hacienda and Market*, p. 117, notes that, through much of the eighteenth century, 'the cyclical pattern of sales [of haciendas] corresponds very closely to maize prices and meteorological data'; the pattern is not broken until the last third of the century, when ownership stabilized.

[640] Cope, *Limits of Racial Domination*, ch. 7, provides an excellent account of the 1692 riot; see also Chester L. Guthrie, 'Riots in Seventeenth-Century Mexico City: A Study of Social and Economic Conditions', in *Greater America: Essays in Honor of Herbert Eugene Bolton* (New York, 1968; first pubd. 1945), pp. 243–58; and Rosa Feijoo, 'El tumulto de 1624' and 'El tumulto de 1692' in *Historia Mexicana*, 14 (1964–5), pp. 42–70 and 656–79. Florescano, *Origen y desarrollo*, pp. 75, 78, notes the knock-on effect of dearth, at least for the later eighteenth century; Salvucci, *Textiles and Capitalism*, pp. 151–2, marshals his 'ordinary least squares regression' analyses and concludes that rising maize prices had no effect on textile output; Florescano is in error, Salvucci explains, by assuming 'that the demand for maize was price-inelastic'; whereas, in reality, 'as [maize] prices rose, individuals surely [sic] purchased less maize and

a rapid rise in food prices formed the background – though in 1624 not the immediate cause – of popular protest. Both also showed the inadequacy of Habsburg social control. No standing army existed; at best the viceroy could call on a handful of personal guards and a voluntary militia of armed (Spanish) citizens, whose deployment depended somewhat on the mood of its members. Thus, when the riot reached critical mass, it could wreak considerable material damage (public buildings were torched: in 1692 damage was estimated at 3 million pesos) as well as political embarrassment (in 1624 the viceroy fled his flaming palace in disguise). The precariousness of Spanish authority, at least when a serious challenge developed, thus became evident in the great colonial metropolis as well as the myriad villages of Mexico.

In this respect 1692 was the graver crisis since, although it represented a classic grain riot (part of a global trend in the hungry 1690s),[641] it was also a 'predominantly Indian' movement (1624, in contrast, had involved creole participation and connivance), and it was premised on strong anti-Spanish sentiments – or so, at least, the Spaniards themselves believed.[642] Indian plotters were said to have concocted the uprising well in advance; some of them allegedly planned to oust their Spanish masters and restore their old idols (arguing that 'there was no law other than their old law'); others, however, preferred to appropriate, rather than to destroy, Spanish assets – they would 'keep the nuns to marry with and the priests to teach them the Catholic faith'.[643] Possibly such reports were coloured by Spanish paranoia (the subversive hand of Jews and Portuguese, the

---

compensated, albeit unsuccessfully [sic], by consuming other foodstuffs' (presumably 'unsuccessful compensation' meant going hungry?). Marie ('let-them-eat-cake') Antoinette was, it seems, a neoclassical economist avant la lettre.

[641] Cope, Limits of Racial Domination, pp. 125–6; Martin, Rural Society, pp. 62–3. The 1690s were 'very cold' in Switzerland, and the decade witnessed recurrent harvest failures in England and Scotland, glacial advance in Norway and late grape harvests in French vineyards: Lamb, Climate, pp. 203–30; Emmanuel Leroy Ladurie, Times of Feast, Times of Famine: A History of Climate since the Year 1000 (London, 1972), p. 59. Returning to the theme of sunspots, it could be noted that the decade falls in the middle of the 'Maunder minimum' (1645–1715), when sunspot activity declined, thus (it has been hypothesized) contributing to the 'Little Ice Age': John A. Eddy, 'The "Maunder Minimum": Sunspots and Climate in the Reign of Louis XIV', in Geoffrey Parker and Lesley M. Smith, eds., The General Crisis of the Seventeenth Century (London, 1978), pp. 226–68.

[642] Israel, Race, Class, and Politics, p. 58.

[643] Feijoo, 'El tumulto de 1692', p. 659.

bugbears of the Inquisition, was also discerned behind the tumult).[644] Certainly Mexico City and, to an extent, the colony as a whole, lived with a subliminal fear of caste war, of that apocalyptic moment when the feckless Indian became a vengeful savage, perhaps – in the worst-case scenario – in alliance with insurgent blacks. The Spaniards' 'jittery wariness' of their numerical inferiority was not, therefore, confined to outlying Indian provinces like Yucatán; it affected Mexico City too.[645]

In fact, Spanish fears of generalized insurrection against colonial rule were probably few (Thomas Gage considered the Spaniards positively insouciant in this regard)[646] and certainly exaggerated; but there was a justifiable awareness that specific grievances could provoke short-lived tumults. Riots, whether in city or in village, responded to particular crises, especially associated with dearth or administrative and fiscal abuses, but they rarely challenged the colonial order, which proved capable of accommodating protest (at least until the eighteenth century, when things began to change). Thus, like Church and king mobs in pre-industrial Europe, Mexican rioters exhibited traditional loyalties: 'viva la Iglesia, viva la Fe, viva el Rey, muera el mal gobierno!' (long live Church, Faith and King, death to bad goverment!) was the cry in 1624, and it enabled the Crown, after the event, to take a somewhat relaxed view of proceedings and to grant a general pardon.[647]

The enduring legitimacy of the Crown was matched by that of the Church, especially in the major cities. Though the abuses of specific priests elicited criticism, anticlericalism was weak.[648] Village rioters

[644] Cope, Limits of Racial Domination, pp. 17–18; Boyer, La gran inundación, p. 33.

[645] Farriss, Maya Society, p. 68; Restall, The Maya World, pp. 18, 53, speaks of 'paranoia'.

[646] Thomas Gage, who arrived in Mexico two years after the 1624 riot, depicted blasé Spaniards, careless of the defence of their colony and capital city, 'living fearless of the Indians': Thompson, Thomas Gage's Travels, p. 85. Juan de Ortega y Montañes, viceroy and archbishop of Mexico, writing four years after the 1692 riot, saw 'tranquil[lity] and calm' throughout the colony: Taylor, Magistrates of the Sacred, p. 18.

[647] Feijoo, 'El tumulto de 1624', p. 60; Thompson, Thomas Gage's Travels, p. 86; compare Hobsbawm, Primitive Rebels, pp. 112, 118–20. A similar cry went up in 1692 but, given the circumstances, the Crown was less disposed to be magnanimous: Cope, Limits of Racial Domination, pp. 142, 146.

[648] On respect for the Church: Boyer, Lives of the Bigamists, pp. 216, 220; Taylor, Magistrates of the Sacred, p. 7, who discerns no Enlightenment-driven decline of 'popular devotion and engagement with Christianity'. Indeed, the most notable manifestations of anticlericalism seem to be remote, rural and Indian (hence unrelated to the Enlightenment): e.g, Restall, The Maya World, pp. 158–65. Of course, the forces of both Church and state enforced conformity and ensured that anticlericalism, to the extent that it existed, remained a 'hidden transcript'.

were less respectful of the cloth;[649] but Church properties in Mexico City escaped the fate of its secular buildings and, notably in 1624, the very genesis of the riot illustrated clerical influence over the city population. The affray developed in the context of a dour struggle between the stiffnecked, reformist and mildly anticlerical viceroy (a Bourbon reformer *avant la lettre*) and the no less stiffnecked politically active archbishop.[650] The viceroy, the scourge of highwaymen and other social delinquents, turned his reformist attention to the grain supply, which he sought to rationalize: he cracked down on supposed speculators, one of whom, a friend of the archbishop, was dragged from ecclesiastical sanctuary to face punishment; whereupon excommunication fell upon the viceroy and interdict on the city. Such a schism in the highest political elite, coinciding with dearth, afforded an opening for popular mobilization which, characteristically (though in the circumstances somewhat illogically), took the side of the archbishop. Complicating the issue further, and illustrating, yet again, the familiar coalition of rival colonial interests, the Franciscans inclined to the viceroy's side in opposition to the secular clergy and the Jesuits, with whom the friars were engaged in a protracted struggle for control of Indian parishes in central Mexico.[651] The Audiencia, meanwhile, was divided. Though no clear winner emerged (both viceroy and archbishop soon quit the colony) the episode underlined the high standing of the Church – albeit a divided Church – and the important role it played by way of legitimizing the colonial order.[652]

This role was even more apparent in 1692. For if, in 1624, it was the Church's capacity for mild political subversion which caught the eye,

---

[649] Taylor, *Drinking, Homicide and Rebellion*, pp. 127–8, 137, gives examples of (eighteenth-century) village protests directed against priests; see also Taylor, *Magistrates of the Sacred*, chaps. 14, 17.

[650] Israel, *Race, Class, and Politics*, pp. 145–6; Thompson, *Thomas Gage's Travels*, p. 78; Cope, *Limits of Racial Domination*, pp. 46–7.

[651] Israel, *Race, Class, and Politics*, pp. 97, 147, 206–8, discusses these squabbles.

[652] Farriss, *Crown and Clergy*, pp. 2–4; Taylor, *Drinking, Homicide and Rebellion*, p. 118, captures the complex rationale of clerical legitimation: even if individual priests were unpopular (and Catholic beliefs were tainted with 'idolatrous' and 'superstitious' errors), the Church as an institution enjoyed local roots and an abiding legitimacy – resources which 'good' priests could reliably draw upon. In the later eighteenth century clerical legitimation declined, not so much because priests changed their ways or forfeited their popularity, but because the Bourbon government distanced itself from the Church, thus turning a fairly faithful ally of the Crown into a querulous junior partner (see Taylor, *Magistrates of the Sacred*, and Chapter 2, section II, 'The Bourbon Project').

sixty-eight years later, when popular protest assumed a more radical, ethnic and class character, the Church deployed its undoubted moral strength in the interests of social peace; indeed, it is noteworthy – and to a degree explanatory of that strength – that Church leaders urged a conciliatory approach towards urban rioters, whereas lay officials preferred to use force.[653] On this occasion, however, the officials had their way. The repression which followed the 1692 riot was more severe, involving executions, floggings and sentences of hard labour; the bureaucratic response, too, was more thorough, with subsequent attempts to confine Indians to particular barrios of the city (to create, as it were, urban *reducciones*) and to ban the sale of the demon pulque.[654] Neither policy was carried out effectively; but the attempt suggested a degree of official anxiety commensurate with the greater radicalism of the 1692 riot, a hardening of official attitudes and a preference for secular coercion over clerical mollification which foreshadowed later, Bourbon, methods of government.[655]

IX. The Imperial Liaison

Riot afforded a dramatic manifestation of the *economic* fragility, yet also the underlying *sociopolitical* strength, of the colonial order. When the provisioning of the capital failed, the risk of popular protest grew. It was a situation familiar to the rulers of pre-industrial societies, from ancient Rome to revolutionary France. In Mexico, such protest was easily contained by either clerical mediation or secular force. But at root the problem remained insoluble. Towns, mines and trade all depended on the agrarian infrastructure. Dearth affected all sectors of the economy, since the maize-growing, peasant and hacienda economy constituted the economic base of the whole system. This had been true, of course, of pre-Conquest Mexico too. But now the agrarian base supported a colonial system more extensive and durable than that of the Aztecs. From the Spanish imperial perspective, colonies existed for the benefit – military, psychological,

---

[653] Feijoo, 'El tumulto de 1692', p. 662; Cope, *Limits of Racial Domination*, p. 148.

[654] Cope, *Limits of Racial Domination*, pp. 153–6, 198–9.

[655] Cf. Brading, *Miners and Merchants*, p. 27, and Taylor, *Drinking, Homicide and Rebellion*, p. 122, describing the repression which followed the pro-Jesuit riots of 1767.

above all economic – of the Spanish metropolis and the Habsburg, later Bourbon, dynasty.

Strict mercantilist rules governed colonial commerce as it plied the Atlantic from Seville via the Antilles to Veracruz, or the Pacific from Acapulco to Manila and back. Seville itself acted as the organizing centre of this far-flung network. The Casa de Contratación, initially a simple tax-collecting warehouse, became a multipurpose bureaucracy which taxed and licensed colonial trade, controlled and supplied shipping and, in its capacity as a 'university of the sea', trained pilots, shipfitters and cartographers.[656] All Spanish trade with the New World was – at least in theory – routed through Seville and the Casa. In addition, the principal colonial export – bullion – was subject to close mercantilist control. The Crown regulated the supply of mercury (New Spain had no indigenous supply); it took the royal *quinto* (the fifth of all bullion produced; later, this was reduced to a tenth); and it exacted sizeable tax revenues (tribute, tithe, sales and excise taxes), all of which depended heavily on bullion production for their realization. Together, royal and private shipments of bullion accounted for some three-quarters of American exports to Spain: by the second half of the sixteenth century, American bullion provided the regular, life-sustaining but addictively debilitating injection of monetary stimulants which kept the shambling Hapsburg body politic – and its grand global ambitions – in fitful motion. American silver constituted only a fraction of total Habsburg income (Spain itself carried the principal burden), but it represented the difference between first- and second-class power status.[657] The bullion sector of the colonial economy, which is sometimes depicted as the most typically 'capitalist', was in fact highly regulated, managed and politicized.

So, too, were other trading activities. New Spain exported few goods: only bullion (chiefly silver) amply justified the high costs and risks of the Atlantic passage. Goods with a high weight-to-value ratio

---

656 MacLeod, 'Spain and America', pp. 350–1; MacLachlan and Rodríguez O., *Forging of the Cosmic Race*, pp. 179–80.

657 Bakewell, 'Mining in Colonial Spanish America', p. 151; MacLeod, 'Spain and America', p. 366, reckons that American bullion (Peruvian as well as Mexican) represented, at its peak, about 20% of Crown revenue; Paul Kennedy, *The Rise and Fall of the Great Powers* (London, 1989), p. 68, concurs that American revenue was 'only about one-quarter to one-third of that derived from Castile'.

rarely made the crossing: Cuban sugar could turn a profit in Seville after a 75-day voyage; Mexican sugar, which took 130 days from Veracruz, could not. Only valuable commodities such as cochineal (the colony's second export), indigo and dyewood were exported from Mexico in any quantity, though they ran a distant second to silver. In addition, Mexico acted as an entrepôt for approved colonial trade: silver from Peru; slaves, pitch, dyes and cotton to Peru; Chinese silk shipped from the Philippines (in return for the Spanish silver coinage which came to predominate in Manchu China).[658] But mercantilist principle required that Spanish – rather than colonial – goods circulate in the colonies and, to this end, colonial production of wine, olives, cotton textiles and iron goods was discouraged or prohibited altogether. Similarly, Mexican trade with other Spanish colonies was cut back. Textile exports to Peru were constrained and then banned; by the 1630s, direct trade between Peru and Mexico, the twin axes of Spain's American empire, was prohibited (not wholly effectively).[659] But, like most mercantilist powers, Spain lacked powers of control commensurate with its ambitions for monopoly. Spain also lacked the wherewithal to supply all the colony's needs. Even at the peak of (Habsburg) Spain's exports to the New World, around 1600, many of the goods shipped were re-exports from northern Europe: trade, warfare and government loans all served to divert American profits out of Spain, even to the advantage of Spain's Dutch and English enemies.[660] And as the colonial nexus attenuated during the seventeenth century, the colonies increased both their contraband imports and their domestic production in order to meet the demand which Spain could no longer satisfy.[661]

The central link in this mercantilist system was bullion. If initial hopes of gold had soon been dashed, subsequent discoveries yielded

[658] Imported Chinese silk thus undercut Mexico's nascent silk industry: Miño Grijalvo, *La protoindustria colonial*, p. 57. On Mexican commodity exports, see MacLeod, 'Spain and America', pp. 355, 367–8; and n. 596 above; on colonial trade, Israel, *Race, Class, and Politics*, pp. 99–100; Hobermann, *Mexico's Merchant Elite*, pp. 26–9. Vilar, *A History of Gold and Money*, p. 138, notes how the Mexican (and Spanish) peso 'invaded the whole world (including Africa and Asia)'.

[659] Israel, *Race, Class, and Politics*, pp. 100–1; Hobermann, *Mexico's Merchant Elite*, pp. 214–17.

[660] Hobermann, *Mexico's Merchant Elite*, pp. 268–9; John Lynch, *Bourbon Spain, 1700–1808* (Oxford, 1989), pp. 10–11, 17.

[661] Hobermann, *Mexico's Merchant Elite*, pp. 14–15, 90–1, 188, 219–20.

a rich haul of silver in both Mexico and Upper Peru. Silver never constituted less than 50 per cent of Mexico's exports to Spain; usually it was much more – as high as 95 per cent in the peak year of 1595. Silver strikes in central Mexico in the 1530s were followed by the bonanza at Zacatecas (1548) and points north. Though production fell in the mid-seventeenth century (roughly from 1630 to 1660), the last third of the century saw a revival, which presaged the rapid growth of the eighteenth century.[662] American silver came to play a crucial role not only in Habsburg foreign policy but also in early modern European development – stimulating inflation, market production and trade with Asia.[663] It also played a major role in the colonies themselves. Though silver exports deprived New Spain of desperately needed capital – despite its massive production, Mexico was chronically short of silver coin in the seventeenth century[664] – they quickened the velocity of circulation, stimulated trade and made possible the import of those goods (such as mercury and steel) for which colonial demand was genuine and not mercantilistically contrived. The annual arrival of the fleet at Veracruz would stimulate a bustle of commercial activity, as merchants received consignments and shipped them inland for the great fairs at Jalapa, San Juan de los Lagos, Saltillo and Acapulco.[665] Over decades, too, mining production encouraged agricultural production, artisan and *obraje* manufacturing (chiefly of woollen textiles), and continued European immigration.

But colonial trade, with its heavy dependence on bullion, was precarious. It was vulnerable to both conjunctural crises and structural recessions. The long Atlantic crossing – two-and-a-half months minimum – was risky and arduous. To protect and sustain its valuable American trade, the Crown developed the *flota* system, whereby armed convoys made annual sailings to and from the monopolistic

662 Bakewell, *Silver Mining*, pp. 14–18, 28–9, 31, 195, 241–4.

663 Earl J. Hamilton, *American Treasure and the Price Revolution in Spain, 1501–1650* (Harvard, 1934); Vilar, *A History of Gold and Money*, pp. 76–203.

664 In addition to official remittances, contraband silver was exported in large quantities, especially in the mid-seventeenth century, when one-third of the Mexican silver arriving in Spain was reckoned to be contraband: Hobermann, *Mexico's Merchant Elite*, p. 91. On the silver-producing colonies' dearth of coinage: MacLeod, 'Spain and America', pp. 375–6.

665 Brading, *Miners and Merchants*, p. 97; Manuel Carrera Stampa, 'Las ferias novohispanas', *Historia Mexicana*, 2 (1952), pp. 319–42.

port of Seville. Successful in the later sixteenth century, the *flota* system paralleled the decline of Spain in the seventeenth. Pirates preyed on Spanish shipping; in 1628 the Dutch captain Piet Heyn captured the entire treasure fleet off Matanzas, Cuba, making off with 8 million gold pesos.[666] This incident, which sent tremors through the Spanish empire, was but a dramatic manifestation of a general malaise. The flow of bullion declined; a bankrupt Crown began seizing private remissions of treasure and other goods; colonial taxes were raised, especially to pay for colonial defence; the aggrieved colonists evaded taxes wholesale; and Spanish manufacturers proved increasingly unable to meet colonial demand.[667] In short, the colonial nexus weakened and seemed close to rupture. Prominent Spaniards, like the count-duke of Olivares, anticipating Professor Paul Kennedy, lamented that Habsburg Spain was overextended, debilitated by its global responsibilities and, very likely, 'would have been more powerful without the New World'.[668] To the awesome spatial and temporal distance separating metropolis from colony ('measured in time, the Philippines were much more remote than the moon is today')[669] was now added a mental and economic gulf.

The decline of colonial trade in the seventeenth century, and the alleged recession which went with it, have been the subject of much debate. New Spain's 'century of depression' has been seen as an interestingly colonial variant of Europe's 'general crisis' of the same period.[670] Recent research has qualified the picture and shifted some of the emphases; but it remains true that the weakening of the

[666] MacLeod, 'Spain and America', pp. 367, 372–4; Hobermann, *Mexico's Merchant Elite*, p. 197.

[667] Hobermann, *Mexico's Merchant Elite*, pp. 196–214; Israel, *Race, Class, and Politics*, pp. 29, 99–102; Elliott, 'Spain and America in the Sixteenth and Seventeenth Centuries', pp. 332–5.

[668] Elliott, 'Spain and America in the Sixteenth and Seventeenth Centuries', p. 329; cf. Kennedy, *Rise and Fall of the Great Powers*, ch. 2.

[669] MacLeod, 'Spain and America', pp. 354–5, which shows how transoceanic journeys were affected by winds and currents: Seville–Veracruz took about 75 days, Veracruz–Seville nearer 130; hence, 'in the minds of the people of the times, America was nearer to Spain than Spain was to America'. The Acapulco–Manila leg – 'the longest uninterrupted sea route traveled by Europeans in the sixteenth and seventeenth centuries' – added a further three months to the outward voyage; but the return across the Pacific, in the teeth of monsoons and hurricanes, averaged six months and sometimes took seven or eight: Hoberman, *Mexico's Merchant Elite*, p. 27.

[670] Woodrow Borah, *New Spain's Century of Depression* (Berkeley, 1951); Trevor Aston, ed., *Crisis in Europe, 1560–1660* (New York, 1967); and, for a more recent, revisionist, Iberian perspective: I. A. A. Thompson and Bartolomé Yun Casalilla, eds., *The Castilian Crisis of the Seventeenth Century* (Cambridge, 1994).

colonial liaison had important consequences for the colonial political economy. In particular, the duration and severity of the 'depression' need to be considered. Production at Zacatecas, the pacemaker of sixteenth-century mining, levelled off around the turn of the century; but it did not fall until the 1630s, by which time other northern sources, such as Sombrerete and Parral, were partially compensating for the decline of Zacatecas. This decline, it should be stressed, was temporary and more the result of royal policy than of inherent exhaustion or (an old explanation, now discarded) of labour shortage. As the early Zacatecas veins were depleted, costs rose, and the Crown – always on the look-out for quick returns – gave priority to production at Potosí, in Upper Peru. In the 1630s, therefore, the crucial supply of subsidized mercury (another Crown monopoly) was curtailed. With mercantile credit replacing governmental, the mining industry faced higher costs and had to retrench. Shipments to Spain dropped 'precipitously'; by the 1650s they scarcely equalled those of a century before, when the industry was in its infancy.[671] But this was retrenchment rather than collapse. Lacking mercury, Mexico's miners resorted to smelting, and, within a generation, output had recovered. New strikes were made late in the century, and, from around 1700, the graph of production registers an almost constant increase, thanks largely to the prodigious growth of Guanajuato and (to a lesser degree) San Luis Potosí.[672]

The contraction of mining output and export, even if temporary, had a significant impact on the monetary and mercantile sector of the colony. The chief sufferers were the Crown, which saw its revenues shrink, and Spanish merchants, whose transatlantic profits declined. For the colony itself, the story was different. Silver output declined appreciably less than did silver exports. In other words, the colony retained a larger share of its own most valuable commodity (though, since the volume of silver coin in circulation remained exiguous, the destination of this retained bullion is something of a mystery).[673] But,

---

[671] Brading, *Miners and Merchants*, p. 9; Bakewell, *Silver Mining*, ch. 8, and the same author's 'Mining in Colonial Spanish America', pp. 144–6.

[672] Brading, *Miners and Merchants*, pp. 130–1.

[673] Two possible explanations are increased defence expenditure in the colonies (in the 1620s 'New Spain financed the defence of most of the Caribbean and of the Philippines') and 'conspicuous consumption' by the Mexican elite, e.g., bullion 'being fashioned into ornaments'. Bakewell, *Silver Mining*, pp. 232–3. On clerical hoarding, note Hoberman, *Mexico's Merchant Elite*, p. 81.

as international trade suffered, the colonial economy experienced a degree of emancipation from mercantilist control and a phase of limited import substitution. Manufacturers now catered to a growing domestic demand which Spain – distant and decrepit – could no longer meet. Domestic trade did not therefore decline to the extent of international trade.[674] And inter-colonial trade picked up, as ties to the metropolis atrophied. Mexican manufactures reached Peru and China; grain was shipped from Puebla to Caribbean markets in Cuba and Venezuela, the latter supplying, in return, the cacao which Mexican palates (especially female palates) craved.[675]

The scale of this inter-colonial trade, however, remained small. Much more important was the impact of 'recession' on the domestic economy, especially the bedrock of the agrarian economy.[676] Displaying its characteristic durability, the hacienda responded successfully to the new 'depressed' climate of the seventeenth century. True, some haciendas, closely linked to mining demand, suffered, and even failed; the Morelos sugar plantations, as we have seen, fell on hard times.[677] But hacienda failure was a recurrent story, in good times and bad. Many estates benefited from rising urban demand, which was somewhat enhanced by import-substitution. Between 1570 and 1646, the Spanish population of Mexico City

[674] Thomas Gage, visiting Mexico in the 1620s, noted that 'the cloth of Segovia, which is the best that is made in Spain . . . , is not so much esteemed of nor sent so much from Spain to America by reason of the abundance of fine cloth made in this city of Puebla': Thompson, *Thomas Gage's Travels*, p. 50. See also Israel, *Race, Class, and Politics*, p. 28; Bakewell, *Silver Mining*, pp. 226–8, 235; John Lynch, *Spain under the Habsburgs* (2 vols., Oxford, 1992), vol. 2, p. 212. The thesis of import-substitution manufacturing does not wholly square with the analysis of the *obrajes* presented by Miño Grijalva, *La protoindustria colonial*, pp. 59–62, which suggests growth c. 1570–1620, followed by stagnation (i.e., a rough correlation with silver-mining). However, Miño Grijalva (a) notes regional variations and (b) estimates units of production (*obrajes*), not output (see n. 681 below).

[675] On late sixteenth-century inter-colonial trade: John R. Fisher, *The Economic Aspects of Spanish Imperialism in America, 1492–1820* (Liverpool, 1997), pp. 65–7; Israel, *Race, Class, and Politics*, pp. 99–100; Boyer, 'Mexico in the Seventeenth Century', pp. 463–5, 476, which, along with Hoberman, *Mexico's Merchant Elite*, pp. 217–208, shows how inter-colonial trade increased in defiance of Spanish restrictions. However, the latter took their toll, so that by the mid-seventeenth century, inter-colonial trade had begun to decline: MacLeod, 'Spain and America', pp. 373–4.

[676] MacLeod, 'Spain and America', pp. 373–4, tends to play down inter-colonial trade and concomitant 'Spanish-American [economic] independence and self-sufficiency', suggesting that 'these self-sufficiencies must have been very local in character, regional autarchies of some sort'.

[677] Martin, *Rural Society*, pp. 7, 41–2, 72–3; Israel, *Race, Class, and Politics*, p. 30; Chevalier, *Land and Socety*, p. 180.

nearly tripled, from eighteen thousand to forty-eight thousand.[678] Though the capital was exceptional in terms of population, growth and demand, lesser cities also flourished, adopting the familiar colonial model of which Mexico City was the prototype: the gridiron plan; the clustering of Indian barrios around a Hispanic core; the rich townhouses of the high officials, merchants and landlords; the public buildings, churches and convents; the *obrajes*, markets and granaries; the teeming mass of professionals, minor officials, priests, pedlars, whores and vagrants.[679] As the turbulence of the Conquest period receded, the small, heterogeneous and cosmopolitan towns of the sixteenth century, populated by recent immigrants of various ethnicities, gave way to the more stable, established and homogeneous provincial cities of the seventeenth century.[680]

Urban demand, emanating from these swelling communities, sustained both commercial haciendas and some peasant producers, despite the mines' relative decline. The *obrajes* of Mexico City flourished during the 'depressed' mid-seventeenth century (and declined during the buoyant eighteenth).[681] Pulque flowed into the capital as never before. In the Bajío, the later seventeenth century saw the development of a vigorous ranchero class; in Oaxaca the decline of silk was offset by the growth of cochineal.[682] But more important still, the agrarian economy was only partially linked to the market,

---

[678] Boyer, 'Mexico in the Seventeenth Century', p. 469; the black, mulatto and mestizo population had grown even more rapidly (Boyer, p. 469, citing Benedict, suggests an increase from 16,000 to 106,000, which should be taken with a grain of salt); meanwhile the Indian population, the chief victim of disease, had fallen from perhaps 90,000 to 33,000 (Gibson, *Aztecs under Spanish Rule*, p. 142). The total population of the city thus grew about 50%, from perhaps 120,000 to 180,000; but the Spanish (*ergo*, richer, consuming) population increased from 15% to over 25%.

[679] Super, *La vida en Querétaro*, pp. 12, 16–17; Taylor, *Landlord and Peasant*, pp. 18–19; Gibson, *Tlaxcala*, pp. 124–30; Julia Hirschberg, 'Social Experiment in New Spain: A Prosopographical Study of the Early Settlement of Puebla de los Angeles', *Hispanic American Historical Review*, 59/1 (1979), pp. 1–33.

[680] Hoberman, *Mexico's Merchant Elite*, p. 7; Boyer, 'Mexico in the Seventeenth Century', pp. 463–7.

[681] Salvucci, *Textiles and Capitalism*, p. 138; as Salvucci shows, roughly confirming the analysis of Miño Grijalva, *La protoindustria colonial*, pp. 59–62 (see n. 674), Mexico City *obrajes* appear to have expanded during the seventeenth century, while those of Puebla/Tlaxcala declined; during the eighteenth century both centres experienced decline, while the *obrajes* of the Bajío grew.

[682] Brading, *Haciendas and Ranchos*, pp. 171–2; Super, *La vida en Querétaro*, pp. 37–40; note also Martin, *Rural Society*, pp. 42–4; Taylor, *Landlord and Peasant*, pp. 94, 113–16; Hamnett, *Politics and Trade*, pp. 9–10.

and it could readily withstand deflation. In other words, the sup-posed 'recession' was doubly mitigated: first, by import-substitution in the monetary sector, and, second, by a retreat into subsistence in the – much larger – 'natural' or non-monetary economy.[683] Chevalier's picture of vast estates turning in on themselves and achieving feu-dal self-sufficiency may be exaggerated.[684] But it captures the reality of the seventeenth-century colonial economy better than those pic-tures which stress – overmuch – the newly liberated dynamism of the commercial sector. New Spain successfully weathered the 'depres-sion' as much because of its dogged pre-capitalist (maybe 'feudal'?) tenacity as of its incipient capitalist vigour. Unlike commercial plan-tations, Mexican haciendas always combined subsistence and mar-ket production. As market demand contracted, the internal balance could shift. So long as a modest surplus could be marketed to meet the owner's and the hacienda's demand for cash (or, we should say, for goods which could not be produced on the hacienda; for barter played a role as well as cash purchases), then the enterprise remained viable.

Monetary outlays, furthermore, could be kept low by a variety of stratagems: by maximizing domestic production (e.g., of tools, textiles, furniture, leather goods); by producing basic consumption

[683] I dislike the qualifier 'natural', which seems (semantically) to suggest a system of primitive barter, even egalitarian living-off-the-land. Colonial Mexico was clearly not such a system. However, 'natural' is used by reputable authorities to describe an economy which, while linked to international trade and familiar with money, is weakly monetized, lacking a sizeable internal market, and shot through with market 'imperfections' (e.g., constraints on the free movement of goods and labour): see Ruggiero Romano, 'American Feudalism', *Hispanic American Historical Review*, 64/1 (1984), p. 123, and Kula, *Economic Theory of the Feudal System*, pp. 17, 21, which also suggests that 'natural' may be something of a misnomer ('we use the term "natural" for want of a better one').

[684] Chevalier, *Land and Society*, pp. 4, 41, 49, 66, 291. Chevalier has been the target of a good deal of recent revisionist criticism, chiefly on the grounds that he (i) overestimated the power and scope of the hacienda; (ii) underestimated Indian peasant resistance; (iii) imputed a 'feudal' quest for hacienda autarky, linked to a 'feudal' landlord mentality; and (iv) homogenized Mexico, casting it in the image of the *latifundista* north. A partial defence against all these criticisms would be that Chevalier was attempting an ambitious synthesis at a time when case studies were few and far between. That aside, criticism (iii) seems to me the most telling, especially insofar as Chevalier saw mentality, rather than politico-economic circumstances, as decisive (e.g., pp. 222, 311). However, he did not entirely overlook Indian peasant resistance (cf. pp. 220, 313); and his primary focus – the 'great hacienda' – was clearly signalled in the book's subtitle. He did not homogenize Mexico (the north is analytically separated from the centre and south in chs. 4 and 5); and, in conclusion (p. 307), he stressed the 'bewildering complexity and diversity of this land' – a presciently 'revisionist' observation.

goods – corn, beans, chile, pulque, meat – as well as raw materials, such as leather, timber, wool; by recruiting labour at low or no monetary costs (e.g., by using service tenancies or debt peonage). Since costs could be cut to the bone, even modest sales could produce a viable profit. This flexible, 'feudal' combination of subsistence and market production – not very different from that of the medieval manor during the era of 'high farming'[685] – gave the hacienda its great durability over time, in the face of changing external circumstances. The *obrajes* could, to some extent, cut costs in similar fashion; so, too, could the peasant household, following the principles outlined by Chayanov.[686] These three contrasting colonial institutions thus shared a common capacity to weather depression – cutting costs and marketed output and partially withdrawing from the monetized sector of the economy. A. G. Frank rightly stresses the continuity and survival of the Mexican hacienda from its sixteenth-century birth through the 'depressed' seventeenth century and into the more buoyant eighteenth; however, his model of a supposedly 'capitalist' enterprise is misleading, since, by misconstruing 'capitalism', it exaggerates the scale and significance of the hacienda's participation in the market and thus neglects the very features which made survival possible.[687]

In important respects, therefore, the weakening of the colonial liaison redounded to the colony's benefit – logically enough, since mercantilism was based precisely on the notion of a zero-sum game, in which colonial yields represented metropolitan gains. New Spain's 'depression' was a much more positive, vigorous phase than Old Spain's.[688] To put it in more concrete terms, the Mexican people

[685] M. M. Postan and John Hatcher, 'Population and Class Relations in Feudal Society', in T. H. Aston and C. H. E. Philpin, eds., *The Brenner Debate: Agrarian Class Structure and Economic Development in Pre-Industrial Europe* (Cambridge, 1985), pp. 73–4. The prevalence of (some significant) market relations in feudal economies is now widely accepted, just as the notion of a feudal economy as being closed, autarkic and 'natural' is rejected: for example, Georges Duby, *Rural Economy and Country Life in the Medieval West* (Columbia, S.C., 1968), pp. 260–4, S. H. Rigby, *English Society in the Late Middle Ages* (Basingstoke, 1995), pp. 63–6; R. H. Hilton, 'Capitalism – What's in a Name?', *Past and Present*, 1 (1952), p. 34.

[686] Miño Grijalva, *La protoindustria colonial*, pp. 115–16, notes *obraje* payment in kind or in company store credit. Cf. A. V. Chayanov, *The Theory of Peasant Economy* (Madison, 1986, first pubd. 1925).

[687] Andre Gunder Frank, *Mexican Agriculture, 1521–1630: Transformation of the Mode of Production* (Cambridge, 1979).

[688] Hoberman, *Mexico's Merchant Elite*, p. 5.

benefited rather than suffered from macroeconomic trends in the seventeenth century. By mid-century the demographic decline initiated by the Conquest had been halted, and during the second half of the century Mexico's Indian population grew by nearly a half (though there were considerable regional variations and temporal setbacks). The Spanish population grew faster, aided by natural increase and continued immigration. There were less than 20,000 Spaniards (creoles and Spanish-born) in 1570, some 180,000 in 1646, and 400,000 in 1742. Through these years, the proportion of creoles within the Spanish population rapidly climbed (62%, 92%, 98%). Here lay the basis for the urban demand which in part compensated for the flaccidity of the mining economy.[689]

Only from a *peninsular* perspective, therefore, could the seventeenth century be seen as a period of recession and retreat. By mid-century, Mexico City had, in some respects, usurped the role of Seville as the chief entrepôt controlling transatlantic trade.[690] Certainly the city now dominated lesser colonial centres – even Puebla or Guadalajara – more than it was dominated by Seville, while the north figured as a kind of 'colonial dependency of the central provinces'.[691] With the Spanish colonial bond attenuated, Mexico was constituted by a patchwork of regional economies, loosely stitched together by threads of trade and government.[692] But the attenuation of colonialism – perhaps of the money economy in general – was no catastrophe. On the contrary, demographic recovery suggested an improvement in living standards. Mexico's peasants, Indians and others, probably ate better than most of their European counterparts and almost certainly ate better than their Aztec forebears.[693] The relative social

---

[689] Sánchez-Albornoz, 'The Population of Colonial Spanish America', pp. 28–9; MacLachlan and Rodríguez O., *Forging of the Cosmic Race*, p. 197, following Aguirre Beltrán.

[690] Boyer, 'Mexico in the Seventeenth Century', pp. 455–7, 463; Lynch, *Bourbon Spain*, p. 15, writes (more ambivalently) of a 'diluted dependence' replacing the 'primitive dependence' of the sixteenth century.

[691] Brading, *Miners and Merchants*, p. 18.

[692] MacLeod, 'Spain and America', p. 373; see also Ouweneel, *Ciclos interrumpidos*, pp. 11–13, and Adrian Van Oss, 'Architectural Activity, Demography and Economic Diversification: Regional Economies of Colonial Mexico', *Jahrbuch für Geschichte von Staat, Wirtschaft, und Gesellschaft Lateinamerikas*, 16 (1979), pp. 97–145, which offer useful regional breakdowns.

[693] Gruzinski, *Conquest of Mexico*, pp. 84, 95; Super, *Food, Conquest, and Colonization*, pp. 8, 29, 61, 71–2.

peace of the Mexican countryside in the seventeenth century rested on relative material abundance.

It may also be suggested that the cultural achievement of seventeenth-century Mexico reflected in part the colony's material consolidation and emerging self-identity. Mexico City became the cultural Mecca of Spanish America, apostrophized by a creole poet as the 'Rome of the New World . . . Venice in form, a Tyre in wealth, in artifice a Corinth, a Cairo in trade, Athens in knowledge, in treasure a Thebes'.[694] The University of Mexico – the oldest university in the Americas – had flourished since 1551 and had claims to compete with the best in Europe.[695] A growing creole elite – many of them Jesuit-educated – participated in a diverse and flourishing cultural life. Colleges and convents proliferated; the fortified missions of the sixteenth century, symbols of the spiritual conquest, gave way to the massive city cathedrals of the seventeenth (Mérida, Puebla and, above all, Mexico City), staffed by numerous and affluent cathedral chapters.[696] The priesthood exchanged its militance and millenarianism for a more sedate, urban, intellectual existence. Saints' days, as well as major secular events (such as the arrival of a new viceroy), were celebrated in sumptuous style, with elegant parades in the plaza and anxious jockeying for preeminence among secular and clerical elites. Literature flourished: if the priest Bernardo de Balbuena excelled at the new genre of 'frivolous poems devoted to the luxurious life of the creoles', Sor Juana de la Cruz – no less a product of the rich, educated creole society of Mexico City – devoted her genial talents to music, poetry, religion and philosophy.[697] In literary achievement

---

[694] Brading, *First America*, p. 300, quoting Arias de Villalobos. Practical evidence of this nascent civic patriotism emerged following the great flood of 1629, when plans were mooted – with the approval of King Philip IV – to shift the capital to the higher, dryer plains of Tacuba/Tacubaya, a couple of miles west. The citizens objected; a petition, 'appealing to the new patriotism, begged that the flooded city not be abandoned, because the name of Mexico was renowned throughout the world and, once shifted to another site, it would forever lose its reputation as a great city': Boyer, *La gran inundación*, pp. 38, 125–8. Of course, there were serious economic disincentives too, what might be called the sunk costs.

[695] Brading, *First America*, p. 299; MacLachlan and Rodríguez O., *Forging of the Cosmic Race*, pp. 137–8.

[696] Schwaller, *Origins of Church Wealth*, pp. 60–1.

[697] Jacques Lafaye, 'Literature and Intellectual Life in Colonial Spanish America', in Bethell, ed., *Cambridge History of Latin America*, vol. 2, *Colonial Latin America*, p. 689. Brading, *First America*, pp. 300–1, and Leonard, *Baroque Times*, pp. 55–6, give Balbuena a better

Sor Juana transcended her contemporaries (in a history of Mexican poetry she would merit a chapter rather than a brief mention). But to the social historian she stands as a typical rather than an isolated case, an embodiment of the cultural efflorescence which marked the established colony, especially its burgeoning creole elite. Yet there are hints that this efflorescence spread more widely and was not confined to a narrow metropolitan elite. We find, for example, a yeoman farmer in Morelos – the beneficiary of the mid-seventeenth-century decline of the sugar plantations and thus, in a sense, of the 'century of depression' – who possessed not only six hundred sheep, twenty mules and as many oxen but also 'several paintings' and 'a few books, including a volume of comedies and account of the conquest of the Indies'.[698]

Mexican elite culture remained locked within the prevailing Catholic and Thomist paradigm, policed – with varying degrees of efficiency and brutality – by the Holy Office.[699] Within that paradigm, however, there was scope for innovation and development. Just as

---

write-up. What is clear is that Balbuena's work, with its 'vast profusion of ornamental details', both typified the Mexican Baroque (Leonard, p. 66) and gave poetic expression to a nascent 'civic patriotism', focused on Mexico City (Brading, p. 300). The literature on Sor Juana is extensive: Octavio Paz, *Sor Juana, Or The Traps of Faith* (Cambridge, Mass., 1988) is a hefty, influential, but somewhat literary tome; Nina M. Scott, 'Sor Juana and Her World', *Latin American Research Review*, 29/1 (1994) pp. 143–54, gives a good resumé of recent academic work.

698 Martin, *Rural Society*, p. 44. Perhaps this literate yeoman benefited from the proximity of Mexico City, where the book trade flourished (see Leonard, *Baroque Times*, pp. 163–71). In the distant north, the possessors of modest fortunes, made in mining, might own ample wardrobes, furniture, stables and silverware; but books are conspicuous by their absence, at least in the testamentary record: Hadley, *Minería y sociedad*, pp. 90–3.

699 The old *leyenda negra* of the Inquisition – as a remorseless agent of absolutism and obscurantism – has been seriously qualified, if not altogether subverted, by recent scholarship, notably Alberro, *Inquisición y sociedad*, which illustrates the inefficiency, corruption, nepotism and petty empire-building of the Holy Office – an institution which therefore mirrored more than it moulded colonial society. Statistically, the Inquisition had a limited impact: between 1571 and 1700 it processed only 15 cases a year on average (far less than in Spain); most concerned fairly petty matters of sexual or religious deviance (Alberro, pp. 168, 205–7). However, sentences could be severe: 14% of culprits – notably those guilty of blasphemy, bigamy or magic – were whipped (and the average whipping involved 200 lashes); a similar number suffered exile; some 7% were subject to public shaming (e.g., feathering) and a similar number (of serious male offenders) were sent to the galleys (pp. 192–3, 208). Fewer than 40 victims are known to have perished in the flames, although many more no doubt died of 'illness, old age, desperation or suicide' in the cells of the Inquisition (pp. 172, 192–3, 208). Alberro's portrait of the Inquisition contrasts somewhat with that of Boyer, *Lives of the Bigamists*, p. 232, which depicts a 'fearful, powerful, and often corrupt institution'. At least they agree on the corruption.

Mexican architecture blended European styles with indigenous motifs and materials,[700] so Mexican elite culture achieved a partial
emancipation from Spanish norms. In particular, Mexico's creoles
began, at least by the seventeenth century, to forge a notion of creole and Mexican identity which they set against both Spain's own
self-image and (more important) Spain's pejorative image of the
colony and its creole inhabitants.[701] Balbuena entitled his major
poem *Grandeza mexicana* (Mexican Greatness, 1602); Sor Juana,
along with other seventeenth-century religious writers, celebrated
the spiritual exceptionality of Mexico, in particular its privileged association with the Virgin. Though the Virgin's apparition at Tepeyac
dated back to 1531, it was not until the mid-seventeenth century
that the cult of the Guadalupe became 'official' – sanctioned by the
Church, celebrated in print and in sermons, embodied in altars,
churches and pictures.[702] The cult of the Virgin of Guadalupe thus
provided a basis for an emergent sense of Mexican exceptionality and
nationhood. It also reflected the marked attenuation of the colony's
ties – economic, political, cultural – to Spain, brought about by Mexican development and Spanish decline. This did not go unnoticed in
Spain, of course. The eighteenth century saw the installation of a new
dynasty, the importation of new sociopolitical ideas from Enlightenment France and a dogged attempt by the metropolis to rescind the
relative autonomy which the colony of New Spain had achieved.

X. Theoretical Reprise

Before entering the Bourbon century, a pause for theoretical reflection is in order.[703] It is not essential to attach general (theoretical)

---

[700] Kubler and Soria, *Art and Architecture*, p. 166.

[701] Hoberman, *Mexico's Merchant Elite*, p. 9; Brading, *First America*, ch. 14. This theme is developed in the following chapter.

[702] Brading, *First America*, pp. 300, 353–60; Leonard, *Baroque Times*, pp. 66, 124–9; Poole, *Our
Lady of Guadalupe*, pp. 99–100ff.

[703] And before entering the 'theoretical reprise' a brief health warning may be in order. Some
students of history – readers or practitioners – dislike all theory on principle: they 'do not
recognize the need to construct a model and every attempt in such a direction... calls forth
their indignation' (Kula, *Economic Theory of the Feudal System*, p. 19). In practice, however,
such theoretical know-nothings, in order to remain afloat in the swirling maelstrom of history, usually clutch at tacit assumptions if not arrant prejudices ('common sense' and 'human
nature' are two favourites). Clearly, it is better that historians explicitly define their working

labels to specific historical societies. We can talk of Habsburg Mexico in terms of elites, landlords, priests, peasants, officials and merchants – terms which, though they are not necessarily clear and self-explanatory (what is an elite, a peasant?), are at least amenable to conventional definitions and do not necessarily imply grand causal models.[704] But terms like 'feudalism', 'capitalism', 'mode of production', carry heavy theoretical (including causal) implications. They not only describe; they also seek to explain. They are, of course, the subject of intense debate, theoretical and empirical (so there is a large relevant literature); and they carry implications not only for historical understanding but also for contemporary politics. Was the early hacienda a feudal institution, the recent (twentieth-century) hacienda a feudal relic? Or were haciendas capitalist enterprises *ab initio*, no less at home in twentieth-century Mexico than in seventeenth-century New Spain? If we try to avoid such terms

theories (or models, or 'organizing concepts'), thus making them clear and, perhaps, facilitating debate and comparison. Recently, however, even historians of supposedly theoretical bent have tended to abandon models derived from political economy (especially Marxist grand theory) in favour of the new Foucaultian, postmodern persuasion, which, despite its strident theoretical claims, is notable for its vagueness and vacuity, hence, precisely for its *in*ability to define, clarify and compare. The objections to be made to a *marxistant*, mode-of-production analysis are several (Patch, *Maya and Spaniard*, pp. 1–4, 245–9, offers a perceptive critique). However, there are also several defences, which should be borne in mind as this 'theoretical reprise' proceeds: (i) a political economy – or mode of production – approach does not claim to embrace the totality of human experience, simply a large chunk (see Wolf, *Europe and the People without History*, pp. 401–2); (ii) different modes of production can coexist in a given 'social formation'; (iii) modes do not unfold according to a strict teleological pattern (hence 'marxisant' may be a more accurate description of this approach than 'Marxist'); (iv) this approach does not imply a top-down imposition by masterful European elites on passive Indian subalterns; (v) the fact that Marx was a European does not necessarily mean that the approach is hopelessly Eurocentric (Patch, p. 2, rightly questions the 'unabashedly Eurocentric' views of Braudel; but Braudel is no Marxist, and not much of a systematic model-builder either); (vi) even if political-economy concepts are deficient, they are better than the available alternatives (Divine Providence, the Hegelian World Spirit, modernization theory, neoclassical economics); and (vii) such concepts get us somewhere along the path of historical understanding – they are, in other words, *organizing* rather than *dis*organizing concepts. I would finally add (viii) that the kind of diluted, politico-economic, marxisant-but-not-teleologically-Marxist approach which I am defending has a long lineage by no means all of it Marxist (e.g., Tawney, Pirenne, Sir James Harrington: see H. R. Trevor-Roper, 'Karl Marx and the Study of History', in *Historical Essays* [London, 1958], pp. 289–90). At the end of the day, of course, these theoretical arguments usually depend for their appeal on individual intellectual inclination (and intellectual fashion?) as much as empirical demonstration; and a good deal of history can be usefully studied without recourse to grand theory.

[704] Of course, explanatory theories can be built upon these conventional definitions: for example, Chayanov's theory of peasant production; or elite theory, deriving from Mosca and Pareto.

altogether we (a) absent ourselves from the debate and (b) often allow alternative – and not necessarily superior – terms ('seigneurial', 'quasi-feudal') to slip into our discourse.[705] It is better to confront the problem head on than to try to dodge it.

As already suggested, this discussion concerns modes of production. It is a discussion at a high level of generality (hence annoying to those who dislike departures from empirical detail); and it does not presuppose an *exact* congruence between theoretical modes and actual societies. Theoretical modes are 'ideal types' which are used to make sense of an infinitely complex reality.[706] They facilitate generalization and comparison, both of which are vital historiographical exercises. But they are not exact replicas of historical society. The question remains: how do we construct an 'ideal-type' feudalism or capitalism? 'Feudalism', for my purposes, does *not* connote the specific institutional and juridical structures of medieval Europe (or, some would wish to specify, early medieval France); fiefdoms and vassalage are not essential hallmarks of feudalism.[707] Rather, feudalism connotes a social formation in which the agrarian economy is predominant, markets are limited (but not absent) and a surplus is extracted from 'direct' producers (peasants) by a landed class. The logic of this social formation is such that technology remains simple and changes slowly; that subsistence production coexists with production for the market; that free wage labour is limited in scope; that the mobility of factors of production is scant.[708] These characteristics are not arbitrary: they fit together in a recognizable way. Poor technology inhibits transport and production; thus only a part of production enters the market, and the pull of the market remains relatively weak (compared to capitalist societies, in which production is overwhelmingly geared to market demand).

[705] Here I would applaud Ouweneel's intelligent efforts to evaluate the capitalist character of the hacienda, even if I do not entirely agree with his conclusions: *Ciclos interrumpidos*, p. 102ff.

[706] Weber, *Theory of Social and Economic Organization*, pp. 11–13, 110.

[707] *Pace* Ganshof, Boutruche, and others, I am therefore adopting a broad, as against a narrow definition, of 'feudalism': Julio Valdeón, 'Prólogo', in Charles Parain *et al.*, *El feudalismo* (Madrid, 1992; first pubd. 1972), pp. 10–12.

[708] For comparable formulations see: Kula, *Economic Theory of the Feudal System*, p. 26; Romano, 'American Feudalism', p. 123; Anderson, *Lineages of the Absolutist State*, p. 17; and Peter Kriedte, *Feudalismo tardío y capital mercantil* (Barcelona, 1986), p. 9ff.

Most workers are unfree, but in three different senses.[709] First, some workers are literally coerced: slaves, serfs, peons bound by debt, dragooned Indians.[710] In these cases, 'extra-economic coercion' is required to compel them to work, to prevent them from fleeing. Second – and very important in the Mexican case – workers can be 'unfree' in the sense of lacking any real mobility, even though they may not be legally subject to coercion (they are not prisoners, bondsmen or chattel slaves). As subsistence peasants they are dependent on access to village land, thus they are tied by social and economic bonds to the village. 'Escape' is entirely possible but not necessarily desirable. Their 'escape' from the village may require direct prodding, by state or landlord; in particular, it may require the progressive erosion of village lands, which forces villagers into the embryonic labour market. So long as villagers retain access to subsistence plots they may doggedly (and rationally) refuse to become mobile free wage labourers.[711] Demographic decline – chronic in Mexico through the sixteenth century – obviously enhances this option.

On the hacienda, meanwhile, an alternative immobility may exist. In part, the hacienda community mirrors the peasant village: it

[709] I have found Cohen's disaggregation of the catch-all 'mode of production' (*Karl Marx's Theory of History*, p. 79ff.) useful. Cohen distinguishes between (a) the material mode and (b) the social mode; the latter – which is the focus of discussion here – is in turn divided into (i) purpose (which demands an analysis of markets); (ii) form of surplus labour (compare, for example, the cash nexus and labour rent); and (iii) the 'mode of exploitation', or the 'means whereby the producer is made to perform surplus labour'. Elements of freedom – and unfreedom – enter in to each of these subdivisions: markets can be free (or controlled or non-existent); surplus labour can take the form of direct labour, cash or kind; and, perhaps most important, the 'mode of exploitation' can involve coercion, custom, 'ideological hegemony' or – when labour is entirely 'free' – none of the above. Thus, any discussion of 'free' as against 'unfree' labour demands some sort of disaggregation along these lines.

[710] It is worth recalling that we have tended to downplay their numbers: chattel slavery was of limited and declining importance in Mexico, especially after the sixteenth century; the *encomienda*, whose Indian dependents in some respects resembled serfs, declined from the early seventeenth, as did the *repartimiento*; genuine (coercive) debt-peonage was less extensive than previously thought. Compare Semo, *Origins of Capitalism*, pp. 117–34, and Frédéric Mauro, 'Sistema agrario y régimen de trabajo', *Historia Mexicana*, 38/4 (1989), p. 842, which stress the prevalence of 'extra-economic coercion', especially in the form of debt-peonage.

[711] Again, this is an ideal type; its validity is not vitiated by the fact that many peasant families and communities entered the market to a limited degree, selling goods or labour (compare Kula, *Economic Theory of the Feudal System*, pp. 68–9). The key (empirical) question is the scale and consequences of this market involvement: a villager who occasionally sells his (or his child's) labour in the market is no more a proletarian than a factory worker who grows potatoes in his back garden is, *ipso facto*, a 'peasant'. Again, these are not empty abstractions: the balance of these activities in turn relates to – and sometimes determines – economic calculation, household strategy, investment decisions, social relations and political commitments.

possesses its own subsistence sector – which may be large – as well as its own communal institutions and practices. Irrespective of coercion – such as the classic debt-peonage which approximates to servile bondage – the hacienda peon may also be attached to the hacienda by 'rational' ties of economic self-interest as well as 'affective' ties of family, community and place. Even if outright coercion is absent, the result can be marked immobility, an absence of free-floating labour, hence at best a weak or non-existent labour market, with all that that implies for the entire economy.

Third, the means whereby surplus is extracted from the mass of workers is distinctive. Free wage labourers are paid principally in cash. Subsistence villagers, in contrast, do not pay themselves or their families wages; their *modus operandi* corresponds to that of the peasant household, analysed by Chayanov and others.[712] The peasant household is a self-reproducing enterprise which consumes most of what it produces and, essentially, produces in order to consume. Even if it markets some of its produce, profit-maximization in the market is not the basic goal. Family survival is. Such an enterprise generates only limited purchasing power; cash income is devoted to vital articles which cannot be domestically produced (ironware, salt), to taxes, which accrue to Church, state and/or overlords, and to village corporate activities (fiestas, *cofradías*, cargo obligations). Hacienda peons may be paid a wage, but this, too, generates little purchasing power. A good deal of peon consumption derives from peon production: either staples produced on garden plots, or hacienda (demense) production which is recycled for consumption on the hacienda in the form of rations.[713] Like the peasant household, the hacienda community devotes a good deal of production to its

[712] Chayanov, *Theory of Peasant Economy*; Eric R. Wolf, *Peasants* (Englewood Cliffs, 1966).

[713] Nickel, *Morfología social*, pp. 79–82; Gibson, *Aztecs under Spanish Rule*, p. 252, considers food provision on haciendas in the Valley of Mexico as 'standard and universal', sometimes comprising 50% of peons' remuneration; certainly the *ración* was seen by workers as a crucial perquisite and by landlords as a significant cost (Ouweneel, *Ciclos interrumpidos*, p. 140). Van Young, *Hacienda and Market*, pp. 251–2, similarly describes peons' rations (corn, sometimes beans and meat) as 'virtually universal on rural estates' in the Guadalajara region. Though some enterprises – such as the more market-oriented sugar plantations – bought in food for their slaves and peons (Barrett, *The Sugar Hacienda*, p. 65), haciendas usually produced their own ('even haciendas that did not produce maize for sale customarily raised a supply for their own workers': Gibson, p. 252). Hence, if the hacienda's internal supply failed, maize had to be bought in (Ouweneel, p. 123). Van Young, p. 253, describes how, when the corn harvest failed, haciendas fed their workers wheat, thus curtailing the supply to the cities.

own reproduction. Of course, haciendas must turn a profit in the market to remain viable. But this, as we have seen, may be achieved by cutting money costs as well as boosting money income. If labour can be secured at low or zero cost (either by 'extra-economic coercion' or by letting out plots of surplus land in return for labour) the hacienda thus cuts its wage bill. Profit can then be realized on the basis of the limited production and sale of a cash crop. This contrasts with a capitalist enterprise whose production is geared to the market, whose inputs are genuinely monetized (the workers receive a money wage and do not depend on the enterprise's production for their subsistence), and whose economic environment is characterized by a vigorous domestic market and the free movement of factors of production.

In this respect, the debate between 'circulationists' and 'productionists', which we touched on earlier, can be somewhat resolved: free market circulation in the absence of free labour recruitment is bound to be constrained, since 'deep' markets will be missing. Landlords will continually be trying to turn a profit on a small, constrained, and thus managed market. And they will see no point in innovating. History reveals numerous societies, classical and medieval, European and Asian, in which markets and profits existed but were ancillary to a stodgy agrarian economy which they could not in turn 'revolutionize', technologically or structurally. The market remained an adjunct of that economy; merchant capital could not – to use the appropriate jargon – transform itself into industrial capital. A capitalist society in which free wage labour was not the norm is hard to imagine.[714]

Of course, social formations – which in many analyses are coterminous with countries – are not usually isolated entities. Protagonists of the 'world system' approach rightly point to the importance

---

[714] New World slave plantation societies display several of the attributes of capitalism (market orientation, economic specialization, a degree of technological innovation, even a ruthless rationality). North American slave-owning planters have therefore been hailed as 'hard calculating businessmen', who practised 'a highly capitalistic form of agriculture': R. W. Fogel and S. L. Engerman, *Time On the Cross: The Economics of American Negro Slavery* (2 vols., London, 1976), vol. 1, pp. 73, 129. 'Calculation' is one thing; 'capitalism' another. Conjoining the two – a dubious exercise in the case of the antebellum South – is quite untenable for colonial Mexico, as I try to explain.

of 'international' trade.[715] Foreign demand may elicit increases in production without necessarily fostering free wage labour (classic cases would be the servile estates of Eastern Europe or the slave plantations of the New World). These models are of limited relevance to Habsburg Mexico, however, since the colony's only major export, capable of exerting a powerful effect upon the colonial economy, was silver; and, although Mexican silver (unlike Peruvian) was largely mined by free wage labourers, these were a tiny minority of the labour force, lacking the critical mass required to achieve a capitalist tranformation.[716] The agrarian economy, the very bedrock of the colony, produced few exports and was geared to domestic consumption; so, too, was the small manufacturing sector. Both were tightly constrained by low domestic demand, which in turn reflected low – or non-existent – wages.[717]

One final theoretical clarification is needed. Under 'feudal' conditions, peasants yield up a surplus to landlords and to the state. Landlords expropriate the peasants' surplus in a variety of ways. Strictly feudal dues, the kind of feudal obligations which weighed upon medieval peasants and which, in the case of France, the Revolution triumphantly annulled, had their closest Mexican parallel in the sixteenth-century *encomienda*, which displayed many of the hallmarks of classic feudalism.[718] But other forms of appropriation

[715] Immanuel Wallerstein, *The Modern World-System: Capitalist Agriculture and the Origins of the European World-Economy in the Sixteenth Century* (New York, 1974).

[716] Brading and Cross, 'Colonial Silver Mining'; Bakewell, 'Mining in Colonial Spanish America', pp. 127–8, which gives a Mexican mining labour force (1597) of 9,143, 68% of them free wage labourers (compared to 18% draftees and 14% slaves). A generation later, the mining labour force may have reached 11,000; by the late eighteenth century, when free wage labour had become the norm, the figure had climbed to perhaps 45,000 (less than 1% of the population): Brading, *Miners and Merchants*, pp. 8, 146.

[717] Examples have been given earlier. Romano, 'American Feudalism', pp. 129–30, reminds us that the urban population was a small minority (10–20%, by Romano's reckoning; I would suggest nearer 5–10%); and 'the value of great mining and/or merchant transactions represent [*sic*] only a very small part of all the goods produced'.

[718] The *encomienda*, it will be remembered, came to New Spain via Granada, the Atlantic Islands and the Antilles; it offered a means to control a subject population and support an elite on the basis of supposed reciprocal services; it 'represented a limited form of *señorío* or lordship': J. H. Elliott, *Imperial Spain, 1469–1716* (Harmondsworth, 1983, first pubd. 1970), p. 70. Simpson, *The Encomienda*, p. 63, notes that Cortés 'was...convinced that he could make the encomienda over into something like an orderly society with a feudal basis'. Compare Wallerstein, *The Modern World-System*, p. 93, which sees the established *encomienda* as a 'capitalist enterprise'.

can exist under (broadly defined) 'feudal' conditions: notably, rents, paid in money, kind or labour; and even forms of ostensible wage labour.[719] Peasants also owe obligations to both church and state, in the form of tax, tribute and tithe. Landlords, clerics and governments are all to a degree parasitic upon peasant labour (as Mexico's Spanish elites recognized);[720] and they may compete with each other for shares of the peasants' surplus. According to certain theories, feudalism presupposes the extraction of surplus by a landed class (often, though not invariably, a juridically defined aristocracy); while surplus extraction by the state, usually through the medium of a bureaucracy, is regarded differently, as a hallmark, perhaps, of the so-called Asiatic mode of production. Medieval Europe would be an example of the first, the Ottoman – or Aztec – empire an example of the second.[721]

Eric Wolf has chosen to collapse these two forms into a single 'tributary' mode, arguing that the extraction of a peasant surplus is the defining characteristic of both and that the fact of appropriation by a landed class on the one hand, or by a state bureaucracy on the other, is not in itself crucial.[722] Indeed, these contrasting forms of appropriation may – and often do – coexist, in colonial Latin America, or Manchu China, or the Absolutist states of early modern Europe.[723] The battle to appropriate the peasants' surplus pits landlords against the state (in the Mexican case, *hacendados* against the colonial bureaucracy); sometimes landlords against the church

---

[719] 'Ostensible' because formally money wages were sometimes recycled through the enterprise rather than being released into the wider market; when such payment took the form of 'rations' produced by the enterprise, the result was a form of payment in kind, measured against a monetary standard. As both Chayanov and Kula have stressed, in a typically capitalist economy, wages function alongside price, capital, interest and rent; 'if one brick drops out of the system, the whole building collapses' (or, we might add, if several of the bricks are ill-made and incomplete, the building will again lean and probably topple). In other words, the function of each factor depends on its place in the whole (capitalist) scheme of things; in a different (non-capitalist) scheme of things, factors will behave differently and neoclassical calculations will go astray: Chayanov, *The Theory of Peasant Economy*, pp. 4–5; Kula, *Economic Theory of the Feudal System*, pp. 38–9; and, for a comparable Latin American example, Nils Jacobsen, *Mirages of Transition: The Peruvian Altiplano, 1780–1930* (Berkeley, 1993), p. 313.

[720] 'If the Indian is lacking, so is everything else': Patch, *Maya and Spaniard*, p. 35; see also n. 20 above.

[721] Semo, *History of Capitalism*, pp. xxvii, 27.

[722] Wolf, *Europe and the People without History*, pp. 79–82, 402.

[723] Semo, *History of Capitalism*, pp. xxvii–xxviii; Wolf, *Europe and the People without History*, pp. 81–2; Anderson, *Lineages of the Absolutist State*, ch. 1.

(e.g., *hacendados* against the Franciscans). By the eighteenth century, we see church and state beginning to squabble over their respective parasitic returns. Such battles are waged in the political superstructure, not the socioeconomic infrastructure. They are nevertheless important: they may determine whether a decentralized landlord class or a centralized bureaucratic apparatus rules.[724] But they do not result in any major change in the basic relations of production. Crown and (higher) clergy, official and landlord, figure as competitors for an inelastic peasant surplus, yet also as allies against possible peasant insubordination.[725]

At the most basic level, it is not crucial whether we follow Wolf in analysing colonial Mexico in terms of a single 'tributary' mode; whether we prefer to see Mexico as embracing elements of feudal *and* Asiatic modes;[726] or whether we rest content with a simple, negatively framed, 'pre-' or 'non-' capitalist formulation. (This is the easiest but feeblest response. It has the drawback of being both negative and, to a degree, teleological. Why should a society be defined simply in negative terms, in terms of *what it is not*, or of *what it may yet become*?)[727] All three interpretations, however different in emphasis and semantics, have a crucial common basis. All three deny the capitalist character of colonial Mexico, which has been asserted by Frank and many others.[728] All three argue that the historical passage from colonial to modern Mexico – the story which takes up the greater part of this book – involved a structural transformation of Mexican

---

[724] Compare 'nobiliary revolt[s] against the consolidation of Absolutism' in Europe: Anderson, *Lineages of the Absolutist State*, pp. 53–4.

[725] Hoberman, *Mexico's Merchant Elite*, pp. 183–5, neatly captures this tension, as displayed in the historiography: the 'conflict' model of New Spain stresses the antagonism between a (largely *peninsular*) 'bureaucratic party', composed of 'officials, caciques, and friars', and a (largely creole) 'settlers' party', including 'the secular clergy, landowners, and merchants'; while the 'consensus model' emphasizes the shared solidarity of these elite groups, based on 'joint participation in economic activities' and reinforced 'when confronting the non-elites', e.g., at moments of social protest. In effect, these are contrasting accounts of the same household: the first focuses on squabbles upstairs; the second on troubles in the basement. The 'primacy' of the second is suggested by the fact that below-stairs rumblings usually silence upstairs squabbles (e.g., at the time of the Mexico City riots of 1624 and 1692); and the people in the basement ultimately have the ability to bring the the entire house crashing down (as they nearly did in 1810).

[726] Semo, *History of Capitalism*, p. 150.

[727] 'A feudal economy can much better be defined by what it is not': Romano, 'American Feudalism', p. 123; cf. Braudel, *The Wheels of Commerce*, p. 239.

[728] Frank, *Mexican Agriculture*; Wallerstein, *The Modern World-System*, pp. 92–3, 126–7.

society, a transition from one mode of production to another. This is no trivial or scholastic argument.

We have sketched the theoretical skeleton. How should we put empirical flesh on the bones? The hacienda, we have stressed, sought profits. So did the *obrajes*. Mines and towns were suffused with market relationships. 'Commerce', says Van Young, 'was the glue which held society together and the nexus which held together the various sectors of the economy'.[729] So long as a simple circulationist position is adopted (market production equals capitalism) and so long as the colony's commercial network is seen as determining the character of the colonial economy, then the attribution of capitalism follows, just as it would readily follow for Ancient Rome or seventeenth-century Poland. Or, as some more subtle analysts put it – hedging their bets – enterprises like the hacienda (and we could add the *obrajes*, if not the mines) were *capitalist* in terms of their *external relations of exchange* but *non-capitalist* in terms of their *internal relations of production*.[730] Such a formulation, for all its theoretical eclecticism, is preferable to a blanket attribution of capitalism. But suggesting that the Mexican economy was a rare hybrid – or an inordinately stretched 'transitional' case[731] – is problematic. Mexicans might like to believe 'como México no hay dos' (Mexico is in a class of its own), but this is not a happy position for a comparative historian to adopt. It either calls the very definitional terms into question (it denotes species, as it were, which prove capable of interbreeding with other species!) or it turns Mexico into a genetic freak. If the definitions and theories are

---

[729] Van Young, *Hacienda and Market*, p. 142.

[730] New World slave plantations, which encapsulate this contradiction in extreme terms, were considered an 'anomaly' by Marx. Ciro F. S. Cardoso, focusing on Brazil, thus prefers to avoid either 'feudal' or (worse) 'capitalist' labels and opts for a 'colonial' mode: 'Observaciones', in Parain *et al.*, *El feudalismo*, pp. 97–100; Círo Cardoso and Hector Pérez Brignoli, *Historia económica de América Latina* (2 vols., Barcelona, 1979), vol. 2, pp. 186–9. Steve J. Stern, 'Feudalism, Capitalism, and the World-System in the Perspective of Latin America and the Caribbean', in Cooper *et al.*, eds., *Confronting Historical Paradigms*, pp. 23–83, follows suit. Ernesto Laclau, *Politics and Ideology in Marxist Theory* (London, 1977), p. 48, is dismissive of the idea of 'illegitimately transferring' the 'phenomenon of colonialism' – 'a structural relation between various parts of the world economy' – 'to the level of modes of production'; this criticism carries weight.

[731] Semo, *History of Capitalism*, p. 147, qualifies the combination of market–oriented production and coercive labour as 'an exceptional, anomalous form of capital'; David Goodman and Michael Redclift, *From Peasant to Proletarian: Capitalist Development and Agrarian Transformation* (Oxford, 1981), p. 213, talk of 'a permanent transition'.

wrong (as some outspokenly declare them to be)[732] then we should dispense with them; we should quit talking of capitalism and feudalism and modes of production in favour of some – as yet undeveloped – alternative theory. None exists.

Also, from an empirical standpoint, the asserted prevalence of market relations needs to be questioned: as we have suggested, it is hard to conceive of vigorous markets developing in the absence of free wage labour unless foreign demand supplies the dynamism – which, in the case of Mexico, it generally did not. While free labour was widespread in seventeenth-century Mexico, it was certainly not the norm. The mines probably constituted the biggest concentrations of free labour, especially in the north, yet the number of miners was very small: Zacatecas, at its peak, employed between two thousand and five thousand, and the maximum strength ever attained by the colony's entire mining work force was around fifty thousand; meanwhile, the total Indian population, at its nadir, was a good one and a half million.[733] Hacienda workers were, of course, more numerous (though, even by the later eighteenth century, when haciendas were expanding, villagers still outnumbered hacienda peons by as much as six to one).[734] But even hacienda peons were hardly free wage labourers. They often received payment in kind (rations or access to land), and even when they received money wages, these were often more notional than real. Wages could be used to purchase goods produced on the hacienda; thus, cash did not leave the hacienda, and formal wages concealed further payment in kind. The same was partly true of the *obrajes*.[735] Even on supposedly commercial haciendas, like those of the Jesuits, the bulk of the grain was often consumed *in situ*, and no more than 20 per cent of the workers' wages actually accrued in cash.[736] As late as 1765 (when, it is reckoned, commercialization had made substantial inroads upon hacienda autarky) the manager

[732] Patch, *Maya and Spaniard*, pp. 1–2, 245–9.

[733] Estimates of the total Indian population vary: Cook and Borah favour 750,000 for central Mexico in 1630; to this must be added Yucatán (perhaps 200,000 in 1639: Patch, *Maya and Spaniard*, p. 94), Chiapas and the north. Aguirre Beltrán suggests 1,269,000 for all New Spain in 1646. See Sánchez-Albornoz, 'Population of Colonial Spanish America', p. 4; Semo, *History of Capitalism*, p. 155. On the mining labour force, see n. 716.

[734] Semo, *History of Capitalism*, p. 37, citing José Miranda.

[735] Miño Grijalva, *La protoindustria colonial*, pp. 115–16, 120.

[736] Tovar Pinzón, 'Elementos constitutivos', pp. 152, 172.

of an hacienda near Guadalajara argued that payment in coin was difficult and to be avoided: 'the principles of good estate management demanded payment in food and goods'; 'and this', the manager said in his own words, 'is the general practice, followed by every good administrator'.[737] Indeed, the sheer shortage of coin made cash payments difficult. We have seen that debasement (of Peruvian coin) drove out the good Mexican silver in the course of the seventeenth century. And in the eighteenth century, in the continued absence of banknotes or an official copper currency, silver coins were jealously hoarded for export.[738]

Thus hacienda workers frequently ran up debts. In some cases, no doubt, these reflected coercive mechanisms, designed to tie the worker to the hacienda.[739] This was certainly true of the *obrajes*.[740] But the scale of debt peonage is hard to establish, and, recent scholarship suggests, it may well have been exaggerated. Some workers were owed money by their employers, while some owed large sums which continued to rise and were never settled up.[741] Why would a rational employer advance money to an already entrapped bondsman? Peonage of this kind reflected less draconian coercion than the coinless character of the market. Provincial trade was often conducted on the basis of barter; the quest for credit was ubiquitous.[742] When it came to hacienda employment, 'money served as a measure of value but it hardly ever actually changed hands'.[743] To extend credit to a worker was basically to offer a lien on a modest fraction of hacienda output; if it served to retain the worker (and high debts often correlated with

---

[737] Van Young, *Hacienda and Market*, p. 256. Compare Kula's 'golden rule of good economic management' on Polish estates: 'avoid expenditure in money': *Economic Theory of the Feudal System*, p. 31.

[738] Brading, *Miners and Merchants*, p. 100; Semo, *History of Capitalism*, p. 89; Pfefferkorn, *Sonora*, pp. 304–7, reports that 'no coined money circulates in Sonora' (1750s); 'all products…are paid for according to weight in gold and silver' (and, Pfefferkorn notes, cacao beans continue to circulate as small change).

[739] Nickel, *Morfología social*, pp. 85–6; Semo, *History of Capitalism*, pp. 132–3.

[740] Miño Grijalva, *La protoindustria colonial*, pp. 85–9; Salvucci, *Textiles and Capitalism*, pp. 40, 43–4, 55.

[741] Nickel, *Morfología social*, p. 87; Martin, *Rural Society*, pp. 145–6; Van Young, *Hacienda and Market*, p. 257; Gibson, *Aztecs under Spanish Rule*, p. 255; Taylor, *Landlord and Peasant*, pp. 149–50.

[742] On barter: Semo, *History of Capitalism*, p. 89; Restall, *The Maya World*, p. 182. On credit: Cope, *Limits of Racial Domination*, pp. 112–16; Brading, *Miners and Merchants*, p. 100; Van Young, *Hacienda and Market*, p. 246; Lindley, *Haciendas and Economic Development*, p. 35ff.

[743] Florescano, 'Formation and Economic Structure', pp. 170–1, 178.

trusted workers) it was a sound investment. Such an interpretation of 'debt-peonage' fits the broad historical facts: haciendas, in the main, were not highly coercive institutions; they did not (like slave plantations) rule by repression; they did not experience savage internal uprisings. On the contrary, they needed to provide some reciprocal benefits to their workers. But those benefits – material, social, psychological – did not involve the creation of a mass, wage-earning, free-floating rural proletariat.

Of course, some cash seeped out of the hacienda: to merchants, to tax-collectors (*hacendados* were responsible for paying their Indian workers' tribute) and to the Church. (Here we return to the triangular tussle over the peasant surplus.) But much of that cash was recycled back to the hacienda in the form of investments, credit and purchases of hacienda produce. Merchant capital frequently found its way into land: the hacienda has thus been seen as a kind of sink soaking up the fortunes made in commerce – and in mining.[744] This tendency reflected not simply the seigneurial ambitions of rich merchants and miners, but also the fact that the hacienda was, over time, a pretty sound investment. It could not compete with the more successful mines, but it was a lot safer than the majority of holes in the ground which yielded no profit. Only judicious marriages could sustain a mercantile enterprise through generations (there were no joint-stock companies), hence the most rational course was to plough money into real estate. Manufacturing capital – such as that associated with the Querétaro *obrajes* – often took a similar course. As manufacturers bought into land, they merged with the landlord class: Mexico possessed no discernible – not even an embyronic – industrial bourgeoisie. The *obrajes*, like the hacienda, were run on non-capitalist lines; they relied on bonded labour, static technology, low productivity and a sure profit on a low turnover. Some 'appeared more as the end point of a pastoral latifundium'.[745] They were certainly not industrial, or even proto-industrial, enterprises.[746]

---

[744] Brading, *Miners and Merchants*, pp. 217–19; the image has now migrated from the specialist to the more general literature: Wolf, *Europe and the People without History*, p. 145.

[745] Roberto Sandoval Zarauz, 'Los obrajes de Querétaro y sus trabajadores, 1790–1820', in *Organización de la producción y relaciones de trabajo en el siglo XIX en México* (Mexico, 1979), p. 132.

[746] Salvucci, *Textiles and Capitalism*, p. 43.

Furthermore, the mining and commercial sectors were small and (especially in regard to international trade) heavily controlled by Spaniards. Spanish merchant capital ran the transatlantic traffic, and Spanish officials regularly milked it to their own and the Crown's advantage. Logically, land became the chosen preserve of creole fortunes (and, of course, the sons of Spanish immigrants were automatically creoles). Land had long been the undeniable basis of colonial society. As late as 1810, after some fifty years of mining boom, agricultural production exceeded mineral output in the ratio of nearly four to one. Even manufacturing (which was heavily dependent on hacienda produce: cotton, wool, tallow, leather) yielded nearly double the income of Mexico's celebrated mines.[747] Hacienda and peasant production thus provided the economic basis of colonial society. The low technology and risk-aversion which (rationally, in the circumstances) characterized such production set their stamp upon colonial society as a whole. 'Merchant' capital collaborated with the hacienda but could not transform it. 'Manufacturing' capital followed hacienda principles of economic conduct.[748] There could be no aggressive profit-maximization involving investment, technological innovation and market expansion. The mines and the sugar plantations – both catering to overseas demand – came closest (though the sugar plantations declined in the later seventeenth century, and the great Valenciana mine appalled Humboldt by its primitive technology).[749] They could not, however, shake the entrenched hegemony of the hacienda. And the latter depended on limited and regulated markets, unfree labour and low profits (save for occasional windfalls in time of dearth). This was a *rational*, but not a *rational capitalist* approach. What is more, the agents of economic progress could not

[747] Brading, *Miners and Merchants*, p. 18. The figures are open to question: Richard L. Garner with Spiro E. Stefanou, *Economic Growth and Change in Bourbon Mexico* (Gainesville, 1993), p. 145.

[748] Salvucci, *Textiles and Capitalism*, pp. 38 (technological stasis), 42 (few economies of scale), 43–4 (reliance on coerced or heavily regulated labour). The later eighteenth century saw increases in manufacturing production (cotton textiles, cigars and cigarettes), but it would be rash to see this as a genuine industrial breakthrough. Garner, *Economic Growth*, pp. 141–57, offers a judicious overview. I return to this theme in the following chapter.

[749] On sugar technology, see Barrett, *Sugar Hacienda*, pp. 50–64, 103–4. Martin, *Rural Society*, pp. 81–8, 97ff., shows decline in the Morelos sugar plantations, c. 1680–1750, followed by revival after c. 1760. On mining technology: Humboldt, *Political Essay*, pp. 157–62; Brading, *Miners and Merchants*, pp. 138–9, 166, 262, 288–9.

achieve the dispossession of the peasantry, that process of 'primitive accumulation' which marked the genesis of capitalism in England.[750] A degree of dispossession occurred, but the Mexican peasantry remained numerous and vigorous. Haciendas lacked the incentives to break peasant resistance entirely, and they needed peasant temporary labour during peak times of the year. Hacienda and village coexisted, often mutually hostile, yet often linked by mutual needs and a shared economic rationale.

Meanwhile, the peasants' surplus was appropriated by Crown and landlord: the first via tribute and tithe, the second via rent and labour. We may, with Wolf, see this as a single tributary mode, with the proceeds split between competing elites, one private, one official. Or we may see the Crown's system of appropriation as an example of the Asiatic mode – a continuation, in many respects, of ancient Precolumbian practice and thus especially strong in southern zones, like Yucatán, where the hacienda was weak and official extortion the norm;[751] while the *hacendados'* system, stronger in central and northern Mexico, was more characteristically feudal, despite its quest for profit and avoidance of outright serfdom. Medieval lords, after all, ran extensive domains for profit; French feudalism long survived the demise of serfdom; 'extra-economic coercion' (serfdom and variants) is not diagnostic of feudalism.[752]

Like these comparable agrarian societies, too, colonial Mexico was structurally doomed to underdevelopment. This was not (as Frank and Wallerstein would have us think) the result primarily of Spanish imperialism. Development and imperialism are not inherently incompatible: note the cases of British India and, *a fortiori*, British North America. Some, taking their cue from Marx, would even argue that imperialism, by shattering archaic forms of production and forcing colonies into the global division of labour, advanced the

---

[750] Robert Brenner, 'Agrarian Class Structure and Economic Development in Pre-Industrial Europe', in Aston and Philpin, *The Brenner Debate*, pp. 30–1, 46–54; see also Kriedte, *Feudalismo tardío*, pp. 132–4, 146–7. Marx himself called it 'primary accumulation': Karl Marx, *Capital* (2 vols., London, 1930), vol. 2, p. 790ff., which notes that Adam Smith called it 'previous accumulation'. Take your pick.

[751] Patch, *Maya and Spaniard*, pp. 26–32, 81–93, 96ff.

[752] On the invariancy of serfdom and feudalism: Guy Bois, 'Against the Neo-Malthusian Orthodoxy' and R. H. Hilton, 'A Crisis of Feudalism', in Aston and Philpin, *The Brenner Debate*, pp. 112–13, 124–5; on medieval profit-seeking, see n. 685.

progress of capitalism.[753] Of course, Spanish imperialism was not British imperialism. But the chief differences between New Spain and the Thirteen Colonies derived less from the contrasting characters of the imperial powers (indeed, *ancien régime* mercantilism displayed similar features in both metropolises),[754] than from the divergent patterns of development in the Americas, which in turn were conditioned by resources, population and labour systems, that is, by the colonies' internal relations and forces of production. British North America combined productive, export-oriented slave plantations with family farming, based on mass European immigration. Either way, labour was imported (in the form of slaves, indentured labourers or free workers); the frontier offered free land; and the Indian population was marginalized, not directly exploited.[755] In New Spain agriculture failed to export; the chief source of labour was indigenous; land gravitated into the hands of *latifundistas*; European immigrants were fewer and less given to family farming. As a result, the domestic market remained exiguous, as did capital accumulation; subsistence production and regional autarky prevailed. The relaxation of the imperial nexus in the seventeenth century merely released colonial resources for familiar purposes: bigger and more haciendas, bigger and more churches. To the extent that foreign trade declined – and the 'glue' holding the money economy together weakened – the colonial economy merely fell back on its subsistence resources. The result was readjustment, not trauma or transformation. Foreign trade was ancillary, rather than fundamental, to the political economy of the colony. (For Spain, of course, it was another matter, as the logic of mercantilism required.) As a result, Mexico's economic autonomy did not engender – did not even start to engender – a dynamic transformation. Indeed, change became more evident under the Bourbons in the following century, as the imperial nexus was tightened, as mining revived, and as capital accumulation and peasant dispossession began to accelerate. Even then, we shall see, the

[753] Bill Warren, *Imperialism, Pioneer of Capitalism* (London, 1980).

[754] C. J. Bayly, *Imperial Meridian: The British Empire and the World, 1780–1830* (London, 1989), convincingly argues for an aggressive and successful assertion of centralized imperial power by a British (ancien?) regime which, if not exactly mercantilist, was certainly not yet an exponent of pacific free trade.

[755] Anthony McFarlane, *The British in the Americas, 1480–1815* (London, 1994), especially pp. 313–14.

structures of production in New Spain stymied any real transition to capitalism. Well before the Napoleonic invasion triggered the fall of the Spanish empire, there were signs that the spurt of growth had lost its momentum, that the old hegemony of the hacienda had been maintained, and that, like other agrarian societies, Mexico was doomed to relive the cycle of expansion, crisis (perhaps a Malthusian crisis), then regression.[756] The transition to capitalism – the mutually reinforcing process of proletarianization, capital accumulation and technological innovation – was still a long way off as the colonial era ended. But we have run ahead of our theme. We must first turn to the century of the Bourbons.

---

[756] Tutino, *From Insurrection to Revolution*, ch. 2. The story is told in the next chapter.

TWO. Bourbon New Spain

During the eighteenth century Mexico underwent major social and political changes. Less traumatic than the Conquest, these changes marked a series of new departures, as the Habsburg colony gave way to its Bourbon successor. The colonial siesta – as it has been called – came to an end; and the awakening was as brusque as it was invigorating. The change of dynasty itself, in 1700, was not immediately significant, though over time the Bourbons certainly adopted new policies which helped mould the character of the late colonial era. More important, however, were socioeconomic changes taking place within the colony itself. And, while it would be misleading to conceive of these cumulative changes in excessively teleological terms, as tending inexorably towards the great upheaval of 1810, it is clear that they generated fresh tensions which strained both the 'social contract' linking rulers to ruled within the colony and the 'imperial contract' linking colony to metropolis.[1] In the second case, growing intimacy engendered conflict rather than affection.

Three cycles of change may be discerned and analysed, albeit in brief, schematic terms. They represent changes of progressively shorter duration and external origin; thus the analysis moves from

---

[1] Lynch, *Bourbon Spain*, pp. 331–2 (although Lynch prefers 'colonial compact'). This is not just an 'etic' (*ex post facto*) concept, invented by historians; contemporaries, like Fray Servando Teresa de Mier, would later argue that Spanish misconduct 'had destroyed the social pact or contract that had been established at the time of the Conquest between the Spanish kings and their American subjects': Timothy E. Anna, *The Fall of the Royal Government in Mexico City* (Lincoln, 1978), p. 56.

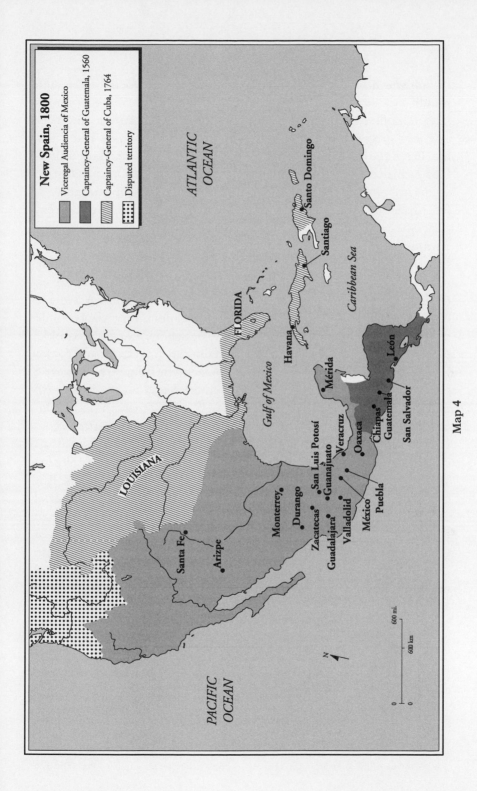

New Spain, 1800

Viceregal Audiencia of Mexico
Captaincy-General of Guatemala, 1560
Captaincy-General of Cuba, 1764
Disputed territory

ATLANTIC OCEAN

Santo Domingo

Santiago

Caribbean Sea

Havana

FLORIDA

León

Mérida

Gulf of Mexico

Chiapas
Guatemala
San Salvador

San Luis Potosí

LOUSIANA

Veracruz

Oaxaca

Monterrey
Durango
Zacatecas
Guanajuato
Guadalajara
Valladolid
México
Puebla

Santa Fe

Arizpe

600 mi.

600 km

N

PACIFIC OCEAN

Map 4

the *longue durée* – which demands a domestic focus – through middle- to short-term factors, often of a political and exogenous kind. The first cycle involved the long-term demographic and economic resurgence of the colony, which dated to the late Habsburg era. From the mid-seventeenth century population picked up, stimulating a process of introverted development (*desarrollo hacia adentro*) which has already been mentioned. This in turn laid the groundwork for the second cycle, the economic growth of the later eighteenth century, when mining came to the fore again. Growth now derived from a combination of factors, some endogenous (population growth, rising demand, falling real wages, the expansion of cities and trade), some exogenous (global demand for Mexican exports, chiefly silver, but also for hides, cochineal, sugar and certain foodstuffs). Mexico thus participated in the quickening of global demand characteristic of the later eighteenth century, as the Bourbons hoped it would.[2] Although the vast agrarian sector remained primarily linked to domestic demand (hence it responded chiefly to the long-term domestic growth of the colony), some areas and enterprises now entered world markets. Thus, they pursued a form of export-led growth (*desarrollo hacia afuera*), following – at a respectful distance – the pattern previously set by Caribbean colonies, British, French and Spanish.[3] In consequence, they began to experience, in milder form, the reflexive 'dependency' which these colonies had known for generations. But export demand made only limited inroads upon pre-existing patterns of production, whether of landlord or peasant. External commerce could not revolutionize the domestic relations of production. When the Bourbon regime entered upon its terminal crisis after 1808, these relations remained essentially unchanged: incremental change did not add up to a structural transformation of colonial society.[4]

---

[2] Richard J. Salvucci, Linda K. Salvucci, and Aslán Cohen, 'The Politics of Protection in Late Bourbon and Early Colonial Mexico', in Kenneth J. Andrien and Lyman L. Johnson, eds., *The Political Economy of Spanish America in the Age of Revolution, 1750–1850* (Albuquerque, 1994), p. 97.

[3] McFarlane, *The British in the Americas*, pp. 226–9, 240–1.

[4] Thus historians now tend to see a certain – economic and demographic – unity in the century following c. 1760, spanning the political rupture of independence: Brading, *Haciendas and Ranchos*, p. 176; Andrien and Johnson, *The Political Economy of Spanish America*, which argues for 'significant socioeconomic continuities over the period approximately 1750 to 1850' and suggests that 'traditional historical periodization and mainstream interpretations of the independence era need revision' (p. vii). However, William Taylor rightly reminds us that independence did constitute a major break, carrying social as well as political implications: 'Between

This was not for want of trying by the Bourbons, especially in the years following the accession of Charles III in 1759. In the last half century of Spanish rule – the third cycle – Mexico was subjected to a raft of reforms, political, administrative, religious and fiscal. These comprised the third – political and conjunctural – chapter in the story of the Bourbon century. The new dynasty aimed to tighten the colonial bond and to extract a bigger and surer surplus from the revitalized colony. The Bourbons fostered trade, hiked taxes and asserted centralized control over both Church and civil society. In doing so, they consciously imitated their French namesakes. For it seemed evident that, if the dynasty did not act with vigour, Spain would fall further behind the rising powers of the period – notably France and Britain – in terms of economic power, military strength and territorial possessions. In particular, Spain's American colonies – distant, ill-protected and under-governed – were vulnerable to these more efficient imperialist rivals, particularly the British, who, during the recurrent imperialist wars of the eighteenth century, saw Spain's American empire as militarily vulnerable and commercially enticing. In the 1740s British fleets descended on Central America and the Spanish Main; Havana, the old entrepôt of Spanish transatlantic trade, fell (temporarily) to the British in 1762.[5] Meanwhile, the great expanses of northern New Spain lay vulnerable to British, French and even Russian advance.[6]

The three cycles sketched here were roughly sequential in time, as well as cumulative in their effects. Demographic recovery and associated economic growth can be dated (depending on the region or sector under consideration) from the mid- or late seventeenth century. Rising mining production, the chief manifestation of *desarrollo hacia afuera*, spanned most of the eighteenth century, though there were marked spurts in the 1730s and 1770s, followed by periods of stagnation.[7] The Bourbon administrative and commercial reforms

Global Process and Local Knowledge: An Inquiry into Early Latin American Social History, 1500–1900', in Olivier Zunz, ed., *Reliving the Past: The Worlds of Social History* (Chapel Hill, 1985), pp. 122–3.

[5] Lynch, *Bourbon Spain*, pp. 136, 139–41, 151–2.

[6] Weber, *The Spanish Frontier*, pp. 285–9.

[7] John Coatsworth, 'The Limits of Colonial Absolutism: The State in Eighteenth-Century Mexico', in Karen Spalding, ed., *Essays in the Political, Economic, and Social History of Colonial Latin America* (Newark, Del., 1982), p. 33; Garner, *Economic Growth*, p. 112.

got under way in the 1760s and were in full flood in the 1780s. Each cycle deserves particular analysis.

I. The Bourbon Economy

Mexico's demographic recovery is clear in broad outline, albeit difficult to explain. The colony's Indian population reached its nadir around 1650, then began to grow (the recovery came some eighty years later in Yucatán, following two troughs, in the early and late seventeenth century).[8] The Indian population of the Valley of Mexico reached a low of 70,000 in the mid-seventeenth century, then climbed to 120,000 in 1742 and 275,000 in 1800. Oaxaca and Morelos followed a similar trajectory.[9] Yucatán's recovery was belated, but between 1730 and 1806 its Indian population more than doubled, from a low point of 130,000, reaching over 280,000, while the non-Indian population trebled, from 34,000 to well in excess of 100,000.[10] Everywhere, growth represented a recovery from the the abnormally low levels of population brought about by epidemic disease. Disease did not disappear: further epidemics – of measles and smallpox – culled the population of the Valley of Mexico at regular intervals: in 1727–8, 1736–41, 1778–80. A quasi-Malthusian crisis, combining dearth, malnutrition and disease took a heavy toll in 1785–6 (Yucatán, again a law unto itself, experienced its own local crisis in 1769–74).[11] But these outbreaks could only check a vigorous revival. Indian resistance to European disease – especially smallpox and measles – had now increased. The Maya rejoiced when the

---

8   Farriss, *Maya Society*, p. 58; Patch, *Maya and Spaniard*, pp. 138–9. The recently missionized and congregated Indians of the far northwest – northern Sonora and the Californias – experienced no demographic rebound; recurrent epidemics, notably measles and smallpox, coupled with social disorganization and oppression, continued to depress population: Robert H. Jackson, *Indian Population Decline: The Missions of Northwestern New Spain, 1687–1840* (Albuquerque, 1994), pp. 163–7.

9   Gibson, *Aztecs under Spanish Rule*, pp. 138–41; Taylor, *Landlord and Peasant*, pp. 29, 32; Martin, *Rural Society*, pp. 55–7.

10 Farriss, *Maya Society*, p. 371; Patch, *Maya and Spaniard*, p. 139.

11 Thomson, *Puebla de los Angeles*, p. 159; Gibson, *Aztecs under Spanish Rule*, pp. 316–7; Farriss, *Maya Society*, p. 61; Patch, *Maya and Spaniard*, pp. 160, 169. On Puebla, see Garavaglia and Grosso, *Puebla desde una perspectiva microhistórica*, pp. 33–5. The crisis of 1785–6 – which I diffidently term 'quasi-Malthusian' in light of Garner's critique of Malthusian interpretations (*Economic Growth*, p. 58) – is discussed later.

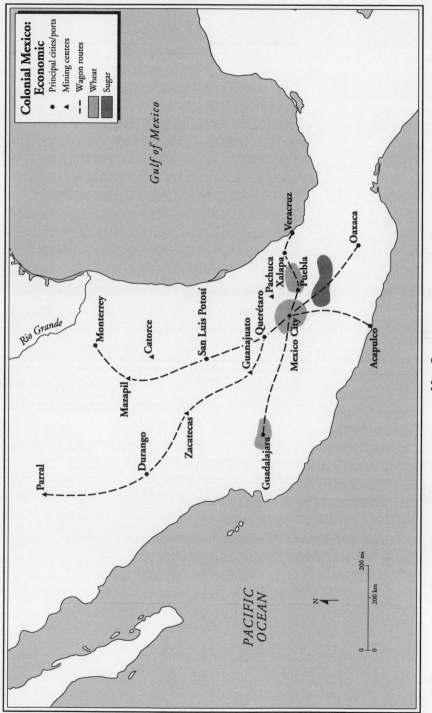

Colonial Mexico: Economic

- ● Principal cities/ports
- ▲ Mining centers
- – – Wagon routes
- Wheat
- Sugar

Gulf of Mexico

Rio Grande

Monterrey
▲Catorce
San Luis Potosí
Mazapil
Zacatecas ▲
Durango ●
Parral

Guanajuato ▲
Querétaro ●
▲Pachuca
Xalapa ●
Puebla
Veracruz ●
Oaxaca ●

Guadalajara ●

Mexico City

Acapulco ●

PACIFIC OCEAN

N

0   200 mi
0   200 km

Map 5

yellow fever epidemic of 1648–50 carried off Spaniards rather than Indians.[12]

Mexico's death rate fell (by 1800 it stood at 33 per thousand, about the same as France's), but the birth rate increased (to 59 per thousand, about two-thirds more than France's).[13] Annual population growth throughout the eighteenth century probably averaged around 1 per cent.[14] Labour shortages, evident since the seventeenth century, may have encouraged faster procreation and larger families; Cook and Borah cite evidence of early marriage, of population 'pushed almost to the limit of procreative capacity'.[15] Yet this trend was not necessarily reversed when, during the eighteenth century, population swelled, labour shortages abated, and real wages began to fall.[16] Then, in a manner anticipatory of some modern Third World societies, impoverishment led, paradoxically, to a further spurt in birth rates, as poor households sought to maximize income and heads of families insured against the vicissitudes of old age by fathering many children at recurrent intervals.[17]

---

[12] Farriss, *Maya Society*, p. 67. Humboldt believed that Mexico's Indians were largely immune to yellow fever but were fatally vulnerable to the *matlazahuatl*, which 'bears some analogy to yellow fever': Humboldt, *Political Essay*, p. 40. The *matlazahuatl* epidemic which broke out in Mexico City in 1736 appears to have been decisive in stimulating the cult of the Virgin of Guadalupe: Poole, *Our Lady of Guadalupe*, pp. 176–7.

[13] Humboldt, *Political Essay*, pp. 35–7.

[14] Garner, *Economic Growth*, p. 17, estimates eighteenth-century population growth at between 0.5 and 1.0% a year; Silvia Marina Arrom, *The Women of Mexico City, 1790–1857* (Stanford, 1985), p. 284, gives an annual growth rate of 1.4% for 1742–1803.

[15] Sherburne F. Cook and Woodrow Borah, *Essays in Population History: Mexico and the Caribbean* (Berkeley, 1974), vol. 2, p. 283. Martin, *Rural Society*, p. 56, notes Chiaramonte's thesis, linking late seventeenth-century population growth to hacienda expansion.

[16] The evidence of population growth, easing of the labour market and falling real wages is widespread, especially for the last quarter of the eighteenth century: Richard L. Garner, 'Prices and Wages in Eighteenth-Century Mexico', in Lyman Johnson and Enrique Tandeter, *Essays in the Price History of Eighteenth-Century Latin America* (Albuquerque, 1990), pp. 73–108, offers a good overview. Eric Van Young, 'A modo de conclusión: El siglo paradójico', in Ouweneel and Pacheco, *Empresarios, indios y estado*, p. 213, estimates a 25% decline in real wages in the second half of the eighteenth century.

[17] Tutino, *From Insurrection to Revolution*, p. 69. Some indications of family strategies can be found in Susan Deans-Smith, *Bureaucrats, Planters, and Workers: The Making of the Tobacco Monopoly in Bourbon Mexico* (Austin, 1992), pp. 177–8, 199, which describes 'entire families' migrating from rural Veracruz to the expanding industrial centre of Orizaba in the late eighteenth century, as well as increased pressure on Mexico City working-class households to find wage labour for their children. Ouweneel, *Ciclos interrumpidos*, pp. 172–4, 252, 317, addresses this – somewhat neglected – factor, but seems keen to relate it to a process of proto-industrialization (along European lines). While industrialization ('proto' or not) played a part, it could not have been a major part, given the pre-industrial character of the Mexican economy; I would place more emphasis on the much broader process of proletarianization, which

Spanish immigration also increased. Renewed colonial prosperity attracted a growing annual quota of migrants, many of them hard-nosed young Spaniards – from Santander and the Basque provinces especially – whose relatives were already established in the colony. Spanish immigration to Mexico City, the main attraction, doubled during the eighteenth century, helping to push the city's population to some 170,000 by 1810.[18] Migration also favoured regions of dynamic growth like the Bajío, as against relatively declining zones, like Puebla and its hinterland.[19] Between 1742 and 1793 – a half century of mining growth – the population of the Guanajuato intendancy increased one and a half times; the city of Guanajuato itself (closely followed by Querétaro) reached 55,000, easily outstripping New York or Boston.[20] Guadalajara, similarly benefiting from the mining boom and the growth of the centre-west, sometimes increased its population by as much as 10 per cent in a single year; by the end of the colonial period it had reached perhaps 40,000, equalling Philadelphia.[21] Thus, as Mexico's total population steadily advanced – from 3.3 million in 1742 to 4.5 million in 1793 and 6 million in 1808 – its demographic centre of gravity moved north and west, through that 'central table land' which, stretching from the Valleys of Puebla and Mexico to the undulating plains of the Bajío, stood 'covered with villages and hamlets like the most cultivated parts of Lombardy'.[22]

The ethnic balance also shifted, though the shifts are hard to calibrate with any confidence. According to certain sources, the ratio of Indians to castes (mestizos and mulattos) to creoles stood at 74:15:10 in 1646 and 62:21:16 in 1742. In the following fifty years these ratios

cast peasants loose from farming and thus made larger (wage-earning) families economically rational.

18 John E. Kicza, *Colonial Entrepreneurs: Families and Business in Bourbon Mexico City* (Albuquerque, 1983), pp. 1–2; Florescano, *Precios del maíz*, p. 171. Europeans comprised only 2% of the city's population (1805), but their influx helped push up the creole population to 48%. Not all Spaniards prospered: poor Spaniards – and creoles – were to be found, for example, toiling in the tobacco factories: Deans-Smith, *Bureaucrats, Planters, and Workers*, pp. 177–8.

19 Brading, *Haciendas and Ranchos*, p. 19; Thomson, *Puebla de los Angeles*, pp. 150, 158; Juan C. Garavaglia and Juan C. Grosso, 'La región de Puebla/Tlaxcala y la economía novohispana (1680–1821)', *Historia Mexicana*, 35/4 (1986), pp. 555, 557.

20 Brading, *Miners and Merchants*, p. 224, 226; Claude Morin, *Michoacan en la Nueva España del siglo XVIII. Crecimiento y desigualdad en una sociedad colonial* (Mexico, 1979), pp. 35, 73; Super, *La vida en Querétaro*, p. 17.

21 Van Young, *Hacienda and Market*, pp. 29–34.

22 Humboldt, *Political Essay*, p. 64.

ostensibly changed very little.[23] It may be, however, that the caste population was underestimated, as mestizos were statistically assimilated to Indians, and that official figures, reflecting the compartmentalized thinking of colonial bureaucrats (especially tax-gatherers), created the illusion of a more rigidly stratified caste system and a more overwhelmingly Indian population than in fact existed.[24] Of course, there were important regional differences. In central Mexico Indians may have comprised a good two-thirds of the population in the late colony; cities like Puebla (a quarter Spanish) or the capital (a half) thus constituted islands of European urbanism amid an ocean of rustic Indians.[25] The south was even more pronouncedly Indian: Indians comprised nearly 90 per cent of the population of Oaxaca and Chiapas and – though the statistics are confusing – about three-quarters of the population of Yucatán.[26] In the Bajío, however, the Indian proportion was about half that of Oaxaca: creoles and castes constituted a majority of the population.[27] To a degree, economic dynamism correlated negatively with Indian population: sleepy Yucatán contrasted with the bustling Bajío.

This correlation, of course, had nothing to do with lazy natives, even though Spanish complaints of Indian indolence remained a staple of colonial discourse.[28] Rather, mining strikes happened to favour (if that is the right word) regions of low Indian population; thereafter, the process of economic growth tended to erode caste barriers. Even

---

[23] MacLachlan and Rodríguez O., *Forging of the Cosmic Race*, p. 197, following Aguirre Beltrán; Brading, *Miners and Merchants*, p. 14.

[24] Gibson, *Aztecs under Spanish Rule*, p. 144; Farriss, *Maya Society*, pp. 65, 107–9.

[25] Garner, *Economic Growth*, p. 47; Thomson, *Puebla de los Angeles*, p. 63; Kizca, *Colonial Entrepreneurs*, p. 3.

[26] Farriss, *Maya Society*, p. 65; Patch, *Maya and Spaniard*, p. 139.

[27] Thus, by the late eighteenth century, 'the Bajío...belonged to mestizo America': Brading, *Haciendas and Ranchos*, p. 19.

[28] 'The Indian by his very nature is given to idleness and slovenliness. There is no incitement that can move him to be employed, nor is he excited by money...he hardly dresses enought to hide his nudity' (Lucas de Gálvez, intendant of Yucatán, 1790): Patch, *Maya and Spaniard*, p. 164. Borah, *Justice by Insurance*, p. 387, paraphrases the tirade of the Bourbon bureaucrat Hipólito Villaroel (1785–7), for whom the Indians were 'lazy, extremely malicious, enemies of truth, untrustworthy, given to riots and disturbance, superficially Christians but really idolaters, outwardly humble but inwardly deceitful, [and] prone to drunkenness, robbery, homicide, rape [and] incest'. Brading, *First America*, p. 476, shows that priests were not necessarily more enlightened; indeed, the later eighteenth century seems to have seen an increase in clerical complaints about Indian sloth, fecklessness and insubordination; Indian towns had become 'seminaries of disputes' and their inhabitants, 'deceitful and lazy', behaved like 'moors without a lord': Taylor, 'Santiago's Horse', p. 169.

in (the city of) Oaxaca, Chance states, the caste system was 'all but obsolete' by the 1790s.[29] Perhaps this is too strong. Other historians have pointed to the continued importance of ethnic barriers, even in the far north: skin colour and 'racial' category still affected marriage patterns, legal standing and perceptions of social worth.[30] The continuation of social discrimination, however, was quite compatible with a progressive erosion of strict political and economic discrimination. Colonial officials found it increasingly difficult to maintain strict caste distinctions. For them, 'Indian' came to denote, above all, a fiscal category, rather than any precise ethnic attribution.[31] Courts, too, grappled with multiple and conflicting claims: was a Chihuahuan bakery worker a Spaniard, as he himself maintained, a mulatto, as his employer stated, or a mestizo, as his fellow workers attested?[32] Priests, responsible for classifying marriage partners, were strongly influenced by the couple's own self-declaration, as well as by their place of origin and the balance of local opinion (which suggested the 'reputational race' of the partners).[33] With economic growth and the progressive dispossession of Indian villages, furthermore, *caste* was increasingly subordinated to *class* as the fundamental determinant of social position and individual 'life chances'. During the later colonial period, Indian *caciques* – well-off, landed and literate – 'grew ethnically closer to Spaniards and castas' and, as the criteria of status shifted, they 'ceased to appeal to the prehispanic past to bolster their legitimacy'.[34] (In this, Mexico – though not, it seems, Yucatán – diverged from Andean America.)[35] At the other end of the spectrum, uprooted Indians tended to merge with castes; as did

---

[29] Chance, *Race and Class*, p. 194.

[30] McCaa, '*Calidad, Clase*, and Marriage'; see also Martin, *Governance and Society*, pp. 128–32.

[31] Salvucci, *Textiles and Capitalism*, p. 18; see also Ouweneel, *Ciclos interrumpidos*, p. 221.

[32] Martin, *Governance and Society*, p. 129.

[33] Cope, *Limits of Racial Domination*, pp. 55–6. Gutiérrez, *When Jesus Came*, p. 198, offers good examples of 'reputational race' (attribution based on what 'a person "appeared to be", "was reputed to be", or "was known to be"'); it should be remembered, however, that Gutiérrez is dealing with the fluid frontier of northern New Spain.

[34] John K. Chance, 'The Caciques of Tecali: Class and Identity in Late Colonial Mexico', *Hispanic American Hstorical Review*, 76/3 (1996), pp. 498–9. For a similar story in the Mixteca, see Pastor, *Campesinos y reformas*, pp. 166–73, 204–7, which sees a process of 'macehualización' – 'plebeianization' – of Indian communities in the Mixteca, as *caciques*/nobles were Hispanized/ladinized, thus forfeiting their social and political power.

[35] On Maya *caciques* (*batabs*) see Farriss, *Maya Society*, pp. 177–80, 237–45; Restall, *The Maya World*, pp. 82–3, 90–2, 97.

the teeming *indios vagos* – proletarians or journeymen – of the Bajío.
The social trajectory of seventeenth-century Mexico City – where
Indians and castes were melded into a multiethnic plebeian mass –
thus prefigured the trend in much of eighteenth-century Mexico at
large.[36] Perceived social attributes (dress, language, life-style) began
to count for more than strict somatic characteristics (indicative of
'Indian race'), and those attributes increasingly depended upon class
position. 'Money whitens', as the old phrase says. Long before the
colonial caste system was formally overthrown, it had suffered severe
erosion. Long after its formal collapse, however, informal discrimination against socially defined Indians remained (and remains).

Demographic and economic growth was intimately linked to the
renewed mining output of the eighteenth century – hence the rapid
relative gains registered by the Bajío and the north. The growth of
the mines conspired with population increase to generate unprecedented demand within the colony; and, although the mines ultimately worked to supply Spain, they no more constituted isolated
economic enclaves now, in the eighteenth century, than they had
during their initial boom beginning in the century of the Conquest.
Thus, the rapid development of a mining centre (like that of Bolaños
after 1747) had an immediate effect on its hinterland: an effect which
might be economically good, in that it stimulated demand for goods
and labour, but ecologically grim, as it brought deforestation and soil
erosion.[37] It is therefore logical to take mining and agrarian growth
as related themes, spanning the eighteenth century.

Mining output grew at between 1.5 and 2 per cent a year throughout the century. Growth was staggered rather than sustained, however. Spurts of growth (1695–1725, 1745–60, 1770–85, 1795–9) al-
ternated with plateaus of stagnation (1725–45, 1760–70, 1785–95);
by the 1800s, rising costs were eating into profits, and major enterprises, like Real del Monte, halted production. Peak production (by
volume) was attained in the 1790s; but maximum returns (the de-
flated value of production) were achieved in the 1770s. During the
last generation of the colony, in other words, mining was losing its

---

[36] Cope, *Limits of Racial Domination*, pp. 22–3; Deans-Smith, *Bureaucrats, Planters, and Workers*,
p. 178.
[37] Lindley, *Haciendas and Economic Development*, p. 13; H. G. Ward, *Mexico* (2 vols., London,
2nd ed., 1829), vol. 1, pp. 468–71, 479–80.

role as the dynamic leading sector of the economy: a trend of great significance for both the 'colonial pact' and the domestic political economy of New Spain.[38]

The causes of this cycle of growth were several, and it is not easy to weigh their relative importance.[39] There were new strikes but also – probably more significant – the assiduous exploitation of old veins and sites, like Sombrerete.[40] While Guanajuato emerged as the pace-maker and record-setter of the late colony, several mining regions contributed, in rolling sequential fashion, to the century-long boom: Pachuca (notably the Real del Monte mine), Bolaños, Chihuahua, San Luis and even, on a small scale, distant Sonora. Growth depended on the application of large quantities of capital, some Spanish, some domestic. Though the aleatory character of mining could never be eliminated,[41] and there were both spectacular bonanzas and (rather more) sorry failures, output and profits tended to accrue according to principles of sound investment and management. Technological innovations, however, were few and modest (in which respect Mexican mining did not differ radically from mining elsewhere, even in industrializing countries). Smelting and refining were improved; gunpowder and windlass hoists were systematically introduced; massive investments were made in new shafts and drainage tunnels (adits).[42] The major enterprises (never above ten in number and still following the pattern of personal economic empires) involved capital of up to a million pesos and a work force of over a thousand apiece; but they were offset by a host of small and middling enterprises, some of them the results of lucky strikes by freelance entrepreneurs.[43] The Crown, greedy for bullion, took steps to encourage mining, especially after the recession of the 1760s:

[38] Garner, *Economic Growth*, ch. 4, is a good resumé; see also Coatsworth, 'Limits of Colonial Absolutism', pp. 26–30; Brading, *Miners and Merchants*, pp. 131, 157.
[39] Brading, *Miners and Merchants*, pp. 156–8.
[40] Ward, *Mexico*, vol. 2, pp. 272–3.
[41] Ward, *Mexico*, vol. 2, p. 274, notes how, thanks to an error of one yard in the construction of a 'crosscut' at Sombrerete, miners hit a huge vein which generated an 11 million peso bonanza for the mine-owners.
[42] Brading, *Miners and Merchants*, pp. 133, 138–40; Hadley, *Minería y sociedad*, p. 159, plays down technological innovation.
[43] Such as Padre Flores, or the muleteer Zúñiga, who made their fortunes at Catorce in the 1780s: Ward, *Mexico*, vol. 2, pp. 241–2, 251–2. On the range of enterprises: Garner, *Economic Growth*, pp. 114, 129.

some zones benefited from tax exemptions; mercury supplies were augmented and subsidized; mining entrepreneurs received privileged status as members of a special corporation which, *inter alia*, gave them access to cheap credit; and a mining college was established in order to improve and disseminate technical knowhow.[44]

Apart from the provision of cheap mercury, however, it does not appear that these direct governmental inputs were responsible for the growth in mining output. In some respects – for example, the Crown's desire to mint all silver into coin – official policy probably hampered production.[45] The authorities did, however, adopt a new, draconian policy in their treatment of labour, not only in the principal and notoriously turbulent Guanajuato district but also in lesser centers like Bolaños, in Chihuahua, and in the booming centre of Pachuca, where Viceroy Gálvez revived and extended the old practice of forced labour. In Guanajuato itself, the newly militarized administration responded to the the troubles of the 1760s (which will be considered separately) by cracking down on the traditionally rowdy miners. With greater social control came a major restructuring of the labour regime, as miners' perks (notably the *partido* or *pepena*) were eliminated;[46] as the returns accruing to labour were cut, to the advantage of profits; and as working conditions palpably deteriorated. The authorities even lent their support – by means of the 1783 mining code, vigorously enforced – to the dragooning of labour.[47] Similar policies had already been attempted at Chihuahua and Pachuca, provoking miners' protests, which met with mixed results.[48]

Although official policy, aimed at the maximization of production, profit and revenue, was not wholly successful, it wrought substantial changes. By the late eighteenth century, forced labour was probably as much an urban and mining phenomenon as it was a rural one; an indication of the hot, hard and often dangerous work which characterized the mines, and which made it difficult to attract sufficient

[44] Brading, *Miners and Merchants*, pp. 140–1, 155–6, 163; Walter Howe, *The Mining Guild of New Spain and Its Tribunal General, 1770–1820* (Cambridge, Mass., 1949).

[45] Brading, *Miners and Merchants*, p. 144; see also Pedro Pérez Herrero, *Plata y libranzas. La articulación comercial del México borbónico* (Mexico, 1988), pp. 121–5, 159.

[46] Brading, *Miners and Merchants*, pp. 147–8, 277; Hadley, *Minería y sociedad*, pp. 168–9, 189.

[47] Brading, *Miners and Merchants*, pp. 147–8, 164, 289.

[48] Martin, *Governance and Society*, pp. 50–6; Ladd, *Making of a Strike*.

numbers of workers at the current (declining) wage rates. A similar pattern of increased growth, enhanced exploitation, and resort to coercion also characterized the *obrajes* of the Bajío.[49] If, in terms of wage rates, the miners still appeared to constitute something of an aristocracy of labour, it was derogated aristocracy, which had exchanged the fractious freedoms and jackpot opportunities of the past for a more regimented and repellent drudgery in the 'caves of Vulcan'.[50] Economic growth did not, therefore, engender a modern proletariat, inured to the time and work-discipline of modern capitalism.[51] On the contrary, the discontents of the miners – and of other urban/industrial workers, such as Mexico City's tobacco workers – simmered through the later Bourbon era, as wages declined, labour discipline increased and sporadic protests broke out.[52] In 1810 Mexico City remained quiet, but the miners of Guanajuato played their part in the great Bajío insurrection of that year.

Bourbon government also gave indirect and unintentional encouragement to the mines by means of its attack on the old commercial monopolists of the colony – specifically the Mexico City merchants' guild, the *consulado* – which had the effect of driving commercial capital into the mining industry. This, of course, was a well-worn route. But the new policy of *comercio libre* ('free trade' – which, we will see, was hardly free) helped the mining zones stump up the capital required for development, especially during the late 1770s and 1780s.[53] Thus, on the basis of global demand, government encouragement and hefty investment, the mines forged ahead: 4 million pesos were minted at the beginning of the eighteenth century, 27 million in 1804. Three-quarters of Mexico's exports were bullion, the

---

[49] Sandoval Zarauz, 'Los obrajes de Querétaro y sus trabajadores', p. 136; Salvucci, *Textiles and Capitalism*, p. 121.

[50] Brading, *Miners and Merchants*, p. 289, citing the Spanish naval captain Francisco Mourelle.

[51] Cf. E. P. Thompson, 'Time and Work-Discipline and Industrial Capitalism', *Past and Present*, 38 (1967), pp. 56–97.

[52] Deans-Smith, *Bureaucrats, Planters, and Workers*, pp. 189, 207, 209, 238, gives examples of tobacco worker protests: some overt and militant (such as the 'paper riot' of 1794), some more covert and discreet.

[53] Brading, *Miners and Merchants*, p. 152. Church credit – a major source for Mexico's landowners – tended not to flow into mining or commerce: Linda L. Greenow, *Credit and Socioeconomic Change in Colonial Mexico: Loans and Mortgages in Guadalajara, 1720–1820* (Boulder, 1983), pp. 10, 69, 78, 88; but cf. Von Wobeser, *El crédito eclesiástico*, pp. 116–17, which presents a different picture. The discrepancy may partly – but cannot wholly – derive from Greenow's focus on Guadalajara.

greater part of it silver.[54] In accordance with the mercantilist logic of the day, Spain was the principal beneficiary: of the 477 million pesos struck in the twenty years after 1784, only 79 million remained in Mexico.[55] What the Crown did not cream off remained in the hands of the new mining entrepreneurs and their mercantile partners: some creole, many Spanish (and, in particular, Basques and Montañeses).[56] A good deal of capital was thus privately recycled to Spain. But, no less important, the capital which remained in the colony followed a circular rather than an ascending path. Now, as in the past, a significant part went into land and buildings, both private and ecclesiastical: it drained into haciendas; it made possible the lavish Churrigueresque churches of the Bajío cities; it funded the dozen or so – reputedly good – portrait painters of Mexico City, headed by the able and entrepreneurial Miguel Cabrera.[57]

Now, too, a larger part was reinvested in the mines, whose appetite for capital was voracious. In this, mining entrepreneurs behaved as rational, profit-seeking – as well as devout, status-seeking – individuals. But the logic of their position told against sustained capital accumulation. Not only were they still organized – or disorganized – in family enterprises, vulnerable to familial vicissitudes (feuds, litigation, profligacy); they also poured capital into an industry which was notoriously risky and incapable of generating sure, sustained returns. With mining and transport technology still in a primitive state, output was constrained by a host of random factors: exhaustion of veins; floods and cave-ins; high – sometimes prohibitive – freight bills;[58] even (in the far north) the threat of

---

[54] Brading, *Miners and Merchants*, p. 96.

[55] Enrique Florescano and Isabel Gil Sánchez, 'La época de las reformas borbónicas y el crecimiento económico, 1750–1808', in *Historia General de México* (Mexico, 1976), vol. 2, p. 270. For a fuller discussion of the resulting shortage of currency in Mexico, see Ward, *Mexico*, vol. 1, pp. 371–81.

[56] Brading, *Miners and Merchants*, pp. 169–70, 201–3, 267–74; see also Kicza, *Colonial Entrepreneurs*, pp. 51–2.

[57] Brading, *First America*, pp. 375–6; Lindley, *Haciendas and Economic Development*, p. 13; 313–15; Kubler and Soria, *Art and Architecture*, p. 315. The great mining magnate Pedro Romero de Terreros, Conde de Regla, who began life as a modest Spanish immigrant and muleteer, carried conspicuous consumption a stage further: 'when his son was christened the whole party walked from his home to church on ingots of silver': Ernest Gruening, *Mexico and Its Heritage* (London, 1928), p. 20.

[58] Shifting refined silver, with its high value-to-weight ratio, was not the main problem; however, only the big, capital-intensive mines could afford to refine on site; others had to ship ore to

Indian attack. Meanwhile, the industry's backward linkages, though important, were insufficient to elicit significant industrialization in the colony. Despite population growth, the output of Mexico's *obrajes* did not register a major increase between 1700 and 1800: demand for textiles was constrained, certainly in the later eighteenth century, by falling real wages, which similarly affected demand for pulque and cigarettes.[59] Thus, despite its ostensible size, the urban market, even in and around Mexico City, was shallow and probably became even shallower after 1780.[60] Demand for basic textiles – often the best barometer of rising living standards[61] – was therefore limited and could be met partly by imports, partly by the production of small, family looms (*trapiches*).[62] In 1800, therefore, Mexico City, with a total population of perhaps 145,000, had less than 13,000 manufacturing workers. Over half (7,000) worked in the tobacco monopoly and about one-eighth in textiles.[63] Clearly, the capital city was no

haciendas de beneficio (refining mills). Inputs presented even greater problems, since mines typically required vast quantities of leather, tallow, forage, timber and – if the amalgamation method of refining was used – mercury, all of which had to be brought in on mule-back or ox-cart, often over rugged country, at great expense: Brading, *Miners and Merchants*, pp. 140–2, 291; Ward, *Mexico*, vol. 2, pp. 247, 255. On the vicissitudes of mining (which prudent mining entrepreneurs foresaw): Boorstein Couturier, *La hacienda de Hueyapán*, pp. 70, 85–6; Brading, *Miners and Merchants*, pp. 176–83, 185–7, 193–4, 197–8.

[59] Contraband imports also hurt Mexican producers: Salvucci, *Textiles and Capitalism*, pp. 140–2, 149–59; on pulque and cigarette consumption, see Juan Pedro Viqueira Albán, *Relajados o reprimidos: Diversiones públicas y vida social en la Ciudad de México durante el siglo de las luces* (Mexico, 1987), pp. 170–1, 188, 197–200, 204.

[60] Garner, 'Prices and Wages', offers a good overview. Nils Jacobsen, 'Livestock Complexes in Late Colonial Peru and New Spain: An Attempt at Comparison', in Nils Jacobsen and Hans-Jürgen Pühle, eds., *The Economies of Mexico and Peru during the Colonial Period, 1769–1810* (Berlin, 1986), pp. 130–1, argues for a stronger domestic market in Mexico than Peru, noting that in 1790 there were 6 cities of over 10,000 population in a 200-mile radius of Mexico City, making a total urban population within that radius of 270,000. That was certainly bigger than Peru's urban population; however, that quarter of a million or so consumers, many of them eking out a bare subsistence, did not necessarily provide the basis for a vigorous domestic industry. A different comparison makes the point: c. 1790 London alone had a population of 860,000, possessed of a higher per capita income, hence capable of exerting a much stronger – and, indeed, transforming – influence on the national economy as a whole: E. A. Wrigley, 'A Simple Model of London's Importance in Changing English Society and Economy, 1650–1750', *Past and Present*, 37 (1967), pp. 44–70.

[61] Thomas G. Rawski, 'Issues in the Study of Economic Trends', in Rawksi *et al.*, eds., *Economics and the Historian*, p. 51.

[62] Salvucci, Salvucci, and Cohen, 'The Politics of Protection', p. 97, reckon that only one-sixth of Mexico's population could afford imported textiles; Salvucci, *Textile and Capitalism*, pp. 141–2, comments on the vigour of late colonial *trapiches*, especially in Querétaro, and p. 19, notes the 'frustration' and 'irritation' of Viceroy Revillagigedo (1791), who found it 'impossible to prevent Indians from making whatever they chose, however numerous the prohibitions'.

[63] Deans-Smith, *Bureaucrats, Planters, and Workers*, pp. 175–7.

industrial powerhouse. Here, and throughout the colony, most urban enterprises were small artisan establishments, employing a handful of workers and using rudimentary technology; the guild system, too, remained entrenched, protecting artisanal production and inhibiting rationalization.[64] Mexican industrialization remained, at best, incipient, at worst, illusory.[65]

Mining profits thus returned to the mine, to the advantage of a circular, mercantilist colonialism, or drained into the hacienda and the Church. The mines constituted a 'growth pole', but the 'growth' they stimulated chiefly involved more of the same – more holes in the ground – rather than any dynamic, qualititative expansion of production. Brief mining bonanzas could make mercantile fortunes, but precisely because of the transport bottlenecks and market imperfections.[66] Bonanzas were less signs of progress than symptoms of backwardness. Mining could not provide the basis for a broader capitalist development, involving expanded (industrial or agrarian) production for an expanded market, enhanced technology, and transformations in the relations of production. Like the merchant capital with which they were intimately associated, the mines could exert a powerful influence upon the agrarian infrastructure, at least in the locality, but that influence was as much conservative as it was transforming. Furthermore, as we have noted, by the later eighteenth century, the dynamism of the mines seemed spent; mining was in 'deep trouble', facing increased costs and lower productivity. Bourbon mining policy proved a short-term fiscal success – it extracted more money from the milch cow of mining – but it was a long-term economic failure.[67]

---

[64] Thomson, *Puebla de los Angeles*, pp. 102–14; Kicza, *Colonial Entrepreneurs*, pp. 209–11; Carrera Stampa, *Los gremios*, p. 270.

[65] Kicza, *Colonial Entrepreneurs*, pp. 26–7; Salvucci, *Textiles and Capitalism*, pp. 52–3, 135; even the more dynamic cotton textile sector (Salvucci, p. 149) failed to achieve an industrial breakthrough (prior to the 1830s and 1840s); rather, 'hand-spinning and hand-loom weaving took place in poor but independent households, employed a rudimentary and static technology, and involved negligible fixed capital costs': Thomson, *Puebla de los Angeles*, p. 239. This picture of manufacturing inertia fits with the broader political-economy analysis of Coatsworth, 'Limits of Colonial Absolutism', pp. 32–3, 37–8.

[66] Ward, *Mexico*, vol. 2, pp. 247, 255.

[67] Coatsworth, 'Limits of Colonial Absolutism', pp. 26–7, 33. Boorstein Couturier, *La Hacienda de Hueyapán*, offers an illustrative study of the (non-transforming) impact of a (massive) mining enterprise.

Meanwhile the agrarian sector, which still remained the solid base of society, confronted new pressures and opportunities. Population growth – the most important factor – heightened demand for staples. The mines required not only foodstuffs but also prodigious quantities of the simple manufactures – tallow and hides, in particular – which were used to light the shafts and load the ore. Other manufactures, such as woollen textiles, saddles, cigars, soap and pulque, as well as construction materials, depended heavily on domestic agrarian production. It is not surprising that, even at the end of the colony, agrarian output considerably exceeded mining and manufacturing production combined (perhaps in the ratio 60:40).[68] Furthermore, the inevitable statistical bias in favour of readily quantifiable, marketable goods undoubtedly underestimates the agrarian share of production.[69]

Now, however, export demand for agrarian products also rose, as a result partly of legitimate Spanish trade, partly of illicit contraband. Of Mexico's average annual exports of 11 million pesos (1796–1820), bullion comprised some 75 per cent; but cochineal provided 12 per cent and sugar 3 per cent. In some years (such as 1775) cochineal exports were almost half as valuable as bullion. Meanwhile, even if aggregate figures do not suggest a major transformation, certain regions, especially in the coastal *tierra caliente*, began to produce new cash crops, especially for the export market: in the lowlands of Guerrero, on the Pacific coast of Jalisco and Colima, in Yucatán and tropical Veracruz, which began to supply cotton to the incipient textile industry of Puebla.[70] In Morelos, the stagnant sugar plantations experienced a 'remarkable recovery' in the second half of the eighteenth century, stimulated initially by domestic demand and then, in the 1790s, by the global demand provoked by the Haitian

---

[68] Brading, *Miners and Merchants*, pp. 17–19. Lindley, *Haciendas and Economic Development*, p. 21, makes the same point, generalizing from Guadalajara: 'Spain's richest colony was fundamentally an agricultural and commercial colony'.

[69] Kicza, *Colonial Entrepreneurs*, p. 91; Van Young, 'A modo de conclusión', p. 210; Pietschmann, 'Agricultura e industria', p. 82.

[70] Brading, *Miners and Merchants*, p. 96 (percentages); Peter Guardino, *Peasants, Politics, and the Formation of Mexico's National State: Guerrero, 1800–1857* (Stanford, 1996), pp. 20–4 (Guerrero); Lindley, *Haciendas and Economic Development*, p. 24 (Jalisco); Morin, *Michoacan*, pp. 32–3, 144–8 (Colima and elsewhere); Patch, *Maya and Spaniard* (Yucatán), p. 142; Salvucci, *Textiles and Capitalism*, p. 146 (Veracruz).

revolution.[71] Like Spanish America as a whole, therefore, Mexico witnessed a shift in its economic activities – its 'growth poles', perhaps – away from the old mining highlands and towards lowland plantations and *estancias*.[72]

As in the past, the agrarian economy reacted to these new influences without changing its basic structures. Technological innovation was scant; unlike Britain or Holland, Mexico experienced no 'agricultural revolution'.[73] However, significant changes-within-continuity can be discerned. If, in the earlier eighteenth century, enhanced demand and opportunity made for greater instability in landholding, as some landlords benefited and some lost out, by the later years the trend was towards land acquisition and concentration (a trend reinforced by the device of the entail, and assisted by windfalls, such as the confiscation of the Jesuit estates in 1767).[74] The trend was also from pastoral to arable farming (evident, for example, in Morelos and west-central Mexico), thus from extensive to more intensive cultivation; since demand for food was rising and the cost of labour was falling.[75] Indeed, the switch from pastoral to arable can be plotted geographically: radiating out from major urban centres like Guadalajara, or pushing the cattle zone north, beyond the booming Bajío, to the northern uplands of San Luis.[76] Even in the

---

[71] Martin, *Rural Society*, p. 98; Pastor, *Campesinos y reformas*, pp. 229, 237, notes the growth of (Spanish) sugar production even in the remote valleys of the Mixteca. The revival of some Morelos sugar plantations, by generating additional demand for water, forced others ('downstream') to switch from sugar to maize and indigo: van der Meer, 'El Colegio de San Andrés', p. 144.

[72] James Lockhart and Stuart B. Schwartz, *Early Latin America: A History of Colonial Spanish America and Brazil* (Cambridge, 1983), pp. 336–44.

[73] Van Young, 'A modo de conclusión', p. 212. See also Morin, *Michoacan*, pp. 252, 254, which concludes that late colonial agriculture 'was extensive rather than intensive'; farming technology remained primitive (tools constituted perhaps 2% of a cereal hacienda's value) and 'no effort was made to save on human labour' (p. 243); productive investment was focused on irrigation. Nevertheless, given cheap labour, abundant land and (a crucial qualification) adequate water, grain farmers could get decent yields compared to their French or Spanish counterparts (pp. 237–40). Brading, *Haciendas and Ranchos*, pp. 65–6, offers a more negative picture of Mexican grain yields, relative to acreage: 'more reminiscent of medieval Europe than of the "age of improvement"'. See also Ouweneel, *Ciclos interrumpidos*, pp. 116, 120–2, 126, which notes wide variations in yields, probably a function of rainfall and irrigation.

[74] Van Young, *Hacienda and Market*, pp. 117–18, 124–6, 308; Brading, *Haciendas and Ranchos*, pp. 63–4, 81–2, 138; Lindley, *Haciendas and Economic Development*, pp. 105–6; Ladd, *Mexican Nobility*, pp. 41–2.

[75] Van Young, *Hacienda and Market*, pp. 205, 249.

[76] Tutino, *From Insurrection to Revolution*, pp. 64, 83–4, 153–4; see also Garner, *Economic Growth*, pp. 60–1.

relative backwater of Yucatán, cattle ranchers responded to growing population and demand by introducing arable crops: maize, rice, sugar – and, we have noted, cotton.[77]

Landlords thus faced a happy combination of strong demand, growing population, rising land values and falling real wages (money wages lagged as prices rose).[78] The incentives to expand production were greater than ever before. Capital from mining and commerce flowed into profitable agriculture: Morelos sugar plantations, Guadalajara wheat haciendas.[79] Notional possessions – the broad, vague titles of the Habsburg era – now acquired economic value and reality, as woods, commons and pastures were fenced off, as dubious claims were aggressively asserted, as squatters and tenants were evicted, or obliged to accept less advantageous rentals. Villages – Indian and others – found their numbers swelling, hence their capacity to market a surplus diminished – which, of course, redounded to the hacienda's benefit. Villages, too, sought to validate old land claims or even to invent plausible new ones; at the same time, as population pressures fissured old, overpopulated pueblos, nascent communities were founded and began the ancient process of carving out their own subsistence holdings. Village therefore squabbled with village, village with landlord, and landlord with landlord, especially in dynamic regions like the Guadalajara hinterland.[80]

[77] Patch, *Maya and Spaniard*, pp. 140–8.

[78] Garner, 'Prices and Wages', in Spalding, *Essays*, pp. 73–108, offers a good resumé, concluding (p. 101) that 'remuneration, whether in cash or kind, for the great mass of the urban and rural workers was largely fixed during the eighteenth century, and the growth in population, especially in the second half of the eighteenth century, gave the employers a distinct and potentially exploitative advantage'. On land values: Martin, *Rural Society*, p. 101 (Morelos); Van Young, *Hacienda and Market*, pp. 177–8 (Jalisco); and Brading, *Haciendas and Ranchos*, pp. 81–2, which notes a 'threefold increase in estate values during the eighteenth century' in the León region of the Bajío. In some remote regions, like the Mixteca of Oaxaca, the outcome was the development, for a first time, of an incipient land market: Pastor, *Campesinos y reformas*, pp. 262–3.

[79] Martin, *Rural Society*, p. 98; Lindley, *Haciendas and Economic Development*, pp. 32, 64; and, for the Bajío, Brading, *Haciendas and Ranchos*, pp. 134–5, and Tutino, *From Insurrection to Revolution*, p. 63.

[80] Van Young, *Hacienda and Market*, pp. 235–6, 321, 340. The Guadalajara region displayed these trends in acute form; but they were evident throughout New Spain. See, for example, Brading, *Haciendas and Ranchos*, pp. 80–1, and Patch, *Maya and Spaniard*, p. 144 (hacienda investment); Farriss, *Maya Society*, pp. 373–4 (hacienda expansion); Morin, *Michoacan*, pp. 269–81 (harsher tenancies); Martin, *Rural Society*, pp. 167–9, and Guardino, *Peasants*, pp. 38–9 (hacienda-village disputes); Taylor, *Landlord and Peasant*, pp. 95–107, and Pastor, *Campesinos y reformas*, pp. 188–90 (inter-village disputes); González Marín, 'Chapingo', pp. 22–3 (inter-hacienda disputes).

Haciendas which had been built up over decades, on the basis of old Habsburg *mercedes*, shrewd purchases, judicious marriages and *de facto* land grabs, now entered a period of unprecedented prosperity but also, it often seemed, of unprecedented litigation, as boundaries and rights to wood, water and pasture were contested. The eighteenth century was therefore littered with such disputes, which affected both the old heartland of the central plateau and the newly developed regions of the centre-west and *tierra caliente*. Landlords also squeezed their tenants: the rancheros of the Bajío, who had prospered on the basis of growing demand *circa* 1680–1740,[81] now came under increasing pressure as rents rose or freehold land was bought up by big *hacendados*. During the later part of the century many independent farmers became dependent tenants, and tenants were reduced to peon status.[82] Morelos experienced a similar trajectory, as *rancheros* lost out to expanding sugar plantations.[83] Within villages, too, population growth and market pressures tended to encourage stratification, especially in regions of economic and demographic growth.[84] *Caciques* (even the occasional *cacica*) capitalized on their access to communal lands – monopolizing, appropriating and renting them out; some Indian commoners rose out of the common ruck, acquiring land, houses and livestock.[85] Even in Yucatán, where market pressures were weaker, the late colony witnessed a process of stratification, as prosperous Maya farmers and stockraisers made their own modest fortunes.[86] The hacienda's demand for land and labour was not, therefore, the only solvent of village society.

The outcome of these several processes was a marked increase in land disputes and rural conflict. In the Guadalajara region, litigation,

[81] Brading, *Haciendas and Ranchos*, pp. 171–2.
[82] Morin, *Michoacan*, pp. 214, 269, 273, 279; Tutino, *From Insurrection to Revolution*, pp. 72–3.
[83] Martin, *Rural Society*, pp. 92–3.
[84] Van Young, *Hacienda and Market*, pp. 285–93; Pastor, *Campesinos y reformas*, p. 263.
[85] Taylor, *Landlord and Peasant*, pp. 60–3; Van Young, *Hacienda and Market*, pp. 286–7, 289–90, which gives examples of prosperous Indians, one of whom, from the Tlajomulco region of Jalisco, despite being propertyless when he married, went on to acquire 18 plots of arable land, 100 horses, 10 cattle and 5 yoke of oxen, while at the same time raising 11 children. It is worth noting the Chayanovian sequel to this success story, however: his widow received half of his estate, his children the other half (divided eleven ways); thus, 'Miguel's small fortune was probably dissipated within a short time after his death' (Van Young, p. 287). Kulakization, in other words, tended to be cyclical; capital accumulation, difficult even at the top, was exceptionally constrained at the bottom.
[86] Patch, *Maya and Spaniard*, p. 193.

threats and violence became 'commonplace', with the 'vast majority' of disputes occurring in the second half of the century.[87] Peasants invaded fields, established squatters' communities and waylaid hacienda workers (who, for reasons of expedience as much as sentiment, tended to identify with their estate and *patrón*). Landlords, in turn, seized, whipped and expelled the culprits, destroyed new settlements, and even razed old communities to the ground.[88] If the litigation and violence were reciprocal, it was the landlords who displayed the greater aggression and capacity. Theirs was an offensive campaign for profit, usually backed by the state; the peasantry fought in defence of precarious subsistence rights and ancient communal identity. This assault on the villages – which, we will see, combined with a more general onslaught upon the Mexican poor, both rural and urban – was particularly evident in regions where enhanced market opportunities impinged upon a rural society in which hacienda and village had contrived to coexist for generations in a climate of limited market activity. Central Jalisco – where, despite hacienda growth and Indian acculturation, half the population still resided in Indian villages – was the classic case. Here, with the expansion of both population and market, the old ground rules changed. Villages had to accept a subordinate role, or sometimes no role at all, within a market-oriented rural economy dominated by the hacienda (in this, Guadalajara's experience in the late eighteenth century prefigured that of Morelos in the late nineteenth). The market economy of the city overrode the moral economy of the subsistence peasant, who might be Indian villager or mestizo tenant.[89]

The Guadalajara region was distinctive (and itself not wholly homogenous).[90] But it represented, in extreme form, trends which were

---

[87] Van Young, *Hacienda and Market*, pp. 279–80, 319–20.

[88] Van Young, *Hacienda and Market*, p. 320; Boorstein Couturier, *La Hacienda de Hueyapán*, pp. 76–9, 82–3.

[89] The notion of the moral economy is now an established (which is not to say uncontroversial) feature of agrarian history: the seminal article is E. P. Thompson, 'The Moral Economy of the English Crowd in the Eighteenth Century', *Past and Present*, 50 (1971), pp. 76–136. For the modern, southeast Asian application of the concept, see Scott, *The Moral Economy*, and the (less-than-persuasive) critique of Samuel Popkin, *The Rational Peasant*; and, for applications to Mexican colonial history (which are allusive more than systematic): Tutino, *From Insurrection to Revolution*, pp. 16–17, 28; Farriss, *Maya Society*, p. 69; Ouweneel, *Ciclos interrumpidos*, pp. 52, 60–1.

[90] Van Young, *Hacienda and Market*, p. 284.

evident throughout much of the late Bourbon colony. If, elsewhere, market demand was less pronounced, less pressing, it still tended to erode subsistence rights and to break down the old relationship which had linked landlord and peasant in an unequal yet durable symbiosis. Or it aggravated official abuses, as local authorities, in league with merchant interests, milked the peasant population. The pattern varied from region to region, but the broad outcome was increased pressure on the peasantry. In populous central Mexico, litigation, protest and occasional revolt marked the later eighteenth century.[91] Here, too, the old symbiosis was breaking down, although its breakdown was less advanced than in the dynamic Guadalajara region. Near Acatlán the Hacienda de Hueyapan benefited from rising demand, associated with the mining boom; it feuded with the local Indian population for control over land, water, woods and cattle; and the Indian protagonists received exemplary punishments – a hundred lashes and six months in a local *obraje* – for their temerity in resisting the hacienda.[92] In Morelos, expanding sugar and indigo production pitted haciendas against villages: Pantitlán against Oaxtepec, Cuahuixtla against Yecapixtla. Litigation dragged on; truces were made and broken; villagers sabotaged plantation aqueducts, and landlords raised posses 'to subdue the angry villagers'.[93] The landlords usually prevailed, but peasant resistance added to the problems of the late colonial sugar industry, arresting its accumulation of land and water.[94] Comparable conflicts and protests spilled over from the central plateau to the surrounding lowlands: to Acayucan, where cotton flourished, and to Papantla, where vanilla production provoked tensions between planters and Indian villagers which would rumble throughout the nineteenth century.[95] Even the

[91] Ouweneel, *Ciclos interrumpidos*, pp. 180, 183–4, graphically depicts the increase in land disputes (villages against haciendas and villages against villages) after c. 1760. See also Brian R. Hamnett, *Roots of Insurgency: Mexican Regions, 1750–1824* (Cambridge, 1986), pp. 79–83, 87–9; Sonya Lipsett-Rivera, 'Puebla's Eighteenth-Century Agrarian Decline: A New Perspective', *Hispanic American Historical Review*, 70/3 (1990), pp. 480–1.

[92] Boorstein Couturier, *La Hacienda de Hueyapán*, pp. 76–9, 82–3.

[93] Martin, *Rural Society*, pp. 109–13 (quote on p. 110).

[94] Martin, *Rural Society*, pp. 113–14.

[95] Hamnett, *Roots of Insurgency*, pp. 79–80; Christon I. Archer, *The Army in Bourbon Mexico, 1760–1810* (Albuquerque, 1977), pp. 94–6; Antonio Escobar Ohmstede, 'La insurgencia huasteca: Origen y desarrollo', in Jean Meyer, coord., *Tres levantamientos populares: Pugachóv, Túpac Amaru, Hidalgo* (Mexico, 1992), pp. 133–48.

outlying sierras, hitherto spurned by commercial landlords, were not immune: at Xichú, in northern Guanajuato, landlords fenced off Indian woodland and pasture, and the Indians responded by tearing down fences and seizing land.[96]

Where the market was weaker, the hacienda offensive was less sustained, the ensuing conflicts more sporadic. In the Maya southeast, the trend was incipient: the haciendas of Yucatán began to meet the Caribbean islands' demand for meat, grain, tallow and cordage; in the hot lowlands of Campeche and Valladolid, planters raised cotton, sugar and rice; while, more generally, growing population stimulated maize production at the expense of livestock.[97] A slow but significant 'transition from estancia to hacienda' became apparent, bringing with it a deterioration in the condition of hacienda labourers and progressive erosion of the *milpas* of the Maya; both trends would accelerate in the nineteenth century, generating severe social conflict.[98]

In Oaxaca, another bastion of the Indian peasantry, the export boom had already started with the growth in cochineal exports, which, reponding to the European textile industry's demands for red dye, peaked in the 1770s. Haciendas were relatively few and weak in Oaxaca, and the labour-intensive production of cochineal was particularly suited to peasant communities.[99] In such circumstances, local elites extracted profits indirectly, inserting themselves between producer and market as political authorities and commercial middlemen. Old patterns of official and mercantile exploitation were (Bourbon reformism notwithstanding) sustained and exacerbated during the later eighteenth century, as *alcaldes*, sponsored by merchant-financiers, compelled cochineal production and forced the sale of Spanish manufactures in return.[100] The outcome was not the

---

[96] Hamnett, *Roots of Insurgency*, pp. 90–1.

[97] Farriss, *Maya Society*, pp. 38, 366–73; Patch, *Maya and Spaniard*, pp. 140–3, 152–3, 173–81; Rugely, *Yucatán's Maya Peasantry*, pp. 13–14, 16–18.

[98] Patch, *Maya and Spaniard*, p. 143 (quote); on the nineteenth century, see Rugely, *Yucatán's Maya Peasantry*, pp. xiv, 63–8, 90, 125–31.

[99] MacLeod, 'Forms and Types of Work', pp. 86–7

[100] Chance, *Race and Class*, p. 147; Hamnett, *Politics and Trade*, pp. 30, 89–92. I have earlier suggested why I do not find the recent revisionist interpretation of the *repartimiento* – as a non-coercive, even consensual, response to market deficiencies – at all convincing: ch. 1, n. 584.

destruction of the peasant community (which would have ended
the cochineal trade), but enhanced exploitation, fresh abuses and
recurrent protests, especially in the cochineal zones of the Mixteca
and the Sierra Zapoteca: villagers from three communities came
together in the Teozacualco revolt of 1774; in 1785, a rebellion
launched at Achiutla 'nearly became a regional uprising'.[101] Even in
distant Chiapas the expansion of the hacienda, especially the cattle
hacienda, pressed upon a peasant population weakened by disease,
taxation and the abortive revolts of the early eighteenth century.[102]
If, therefore, at the upper levels of society, the Bourbon era saw increased competitive market activity, the local impact of commercialization was often very different, being associated with coercion,
monopolization and patrimonial abuses.[103]

Late eighteenth-century Mexico thus displayed the familiar characteristics of a pre-industrial economy undergoing population
growth and apparent boom: profits rose, real wages fell, access to
the means of subsistence became more constricted, social tensions
exacerbated. These were the hallmarks of what John Tutino has
termed agrarian 'compression'; they marked late eighteenth-century
and early nineteenth-century Mexico (as they would again mark late
nineteenth- and early twentieth-century Mexico).[104] They also bear
comparison with phases in pre-industrial Western Europe: notably
the early fourteenth and sixteenth centuries.[105] In simple terms, we
may say, the average Mexican (who was likely to be poor and rural) was better off during the drowsy afternoon of the colonial siesta
(c. 1630–1700) than during the stormy twilight of the Bourbon era
(after 1760). With market and demographic growth, economic opportunities and penalties both increased. Growth divided the current generation (capriciously, it often seemed) into winners and

---

[101] Taylor, *Drinking, Homicide and Rebellion*, p. 126.

[102] García de León, *Resistencia y utopía*, vol. 1, pp. 87–8, 118; Wasserstrom, *Class and Society*,
pp. 87–106.

[103] The point is well made (for Andean America) by Jacobsen, *Mirages of Transition*, pp. 4–5ff.

[104] Tutino, *From Insurrection to Revolution*, pp. 61, 277–8, 356. Tutino repeatedly refers to the
agrarian 'compression' of post-1880, which followed the 'long era of agrarian decompression
from 1810 to 1880' (p. 356). Thus, even if he appears to avoid using the term 'compression'
for pre-1810, the syndrome he describes (p. 61) seems to justify the term; and presumably
post-1810 'decompression' implies a pre-1810 'compression'.

[105] Cf. Kriedte, *Feudalismo tardío*, pp. 12–14.

losers; it also required of that generation investment (i.e., foregone consumption) for the notional benefit of future generations.

Given the colonial relationship, it also implied an additional transfer of resources from periphery to metropolis. Mining, the classic example, could yield rich returns on big investments of labour and capital. But the bulk of the returns accrued to Spain. Landlords, too, invested as never before, favoured by stronger demand and cheaper labour: they built granaries, reservoirs, irrigation canals.[106] As usual in such pre-industrial booms, the spectacular profits of the few (like the fabulously wealthy Fagoaga family of Zacatecas, the Romero de Terreros of Hidalgo or the Bibancos of Bolaños) contrasted with the impoverishment of the many; absolute as well as relative deprivation increased.[107] By the 1800s, Humboldt could view New Spain as a society of unparalleled extremes of wealth and poverty: 'Mexico is the country of inequality. Nowhere does there exist such a fearful difference in the distribution of fortune, civilization, cultivation of the soil, and property'.[108]

'Deprivation' and 'inequality', however, are vague terms. They are too often invested with a retrospective, subjective significance,

---

[106] Ward, *Mexico*, vol. 2, p. 223, decribes the huge reservoir of the Hacienda de Jaral, in northern Guanajuato, built in the 1760s, and observes how the neighbouring pueblo – 3,000 people dependent on the hacienda, lodged in 'mud huts' – 'presents an appearance of wretchedness totally unworthy of its vicinity to the abode of so wealthy a proprietor'. On hacienda investments, see also Van Young, *Hacienda and Market*, p. 211; Brading, *Haciendas and Ranchos*, pp. 80–1; Morin, *Michoacan*, pp. 244, 255; Von Wobeser, *El crédito eclesiástico*, p. 122. Obviously, the shift from pastoral to arable farming, encouraged by population growth, rising food prices and falling real wages, in turn demanded investment in both both irrigation and storage.

[107] Brading, *Miners and Merchants*, pp. 173–91, describes the magnates; on living standards, see Van Young, 'A modo de conclusión', pp. 211, 213–14; and Garner, *Economic Growth*, p. 258, which concludes his statistical analysis of the late colonial economy with the observation that 'for most citizens impoverishment was more of a prospect than was improvement'. Even MacLachlan and Rodriguez O., *Forging of the Cosmic Race*, pp. 334–6, while keen to rebut the black legend ('New Spain, the Western Hemisphere's most successful colony, was a dynamic society enjoying both a stable government and a prosperous economy') accept that, by the later eighteenth century, 'the fantastic wealth of the few contrasted with the expanding ranks of the poor'; however, they see these 'problems' as 'soluble'; and they attribute both the problems themselves and the subsequent failure to solve them, to bad luck and bad (Spanish) government ('European events and Spanish vacillation disrupted the relatively smooth maturation of the Mexican state'). Left to their own devices, the Mexicans would have enacted 'moderate, rational and practical solutions'. The Mexicans thus appear as frustrated Whigs in a would-be Whig interpretation of Mexican history; and the black legend, booted out the front door, sneaks in the back, with the Bourbon reformers – and Bonaparte – recast as the villains.

[108] Humboldt, *Political Essay*, p. 64. Van Young, 'A modo de conclusión', p. 209, quotes Navarro y Noriega (1820) on the striking 'poverty . . . hunger and epidemics' which afflicted most of Mexico.

especially when they are discerned on the eve of a great social upheaval like that of 1810. They need to be broken down and – as
far as space permits – clarified. We have noted the plight of villages which, located in regions of economic dynamism, faced the
increased threat of expansionist haciendas, of internal stratification
or of commercial and official exploitation. The first of these, being
the most novel, direct and damaging, elicited the fiercest response. It
was no coincidence that the central region of Jalisco became a major centre of popular rebellion after 1810 and that communities like
Zacoalco – which had lost six successive court cases against local
hacendados since the 1770s – were in the forefront.[109] They faced a
mortal threat, to which there seemed no redress short of rebellion.
Rebellion in this zone also tended to assume a broader, more radical
form, since it generated a shared Indian solidarity against the common landlord enemy. Paradoxically (we have noted already), Indian
consciousness, which in effect represented a powerful amalgam of
class and ethnic identity, was strongest in regions of commercialization and partial acculturation. More widely, across the plains of
the Bajío, a relatively 'acculturated' Indian population provided the
mass support for Hidalgo's insurrection in 1810.

Protest and rebellion also occurred in regions where the peasant community faced the more familiar, usually more containable,
challenges of tax-collectors, officials and priests. Given that these
pressures were less intense, the courts still offered some respite;
equally, individual protests – even violent revolts – might achieve results, notwithstanding the generally tougher stance adopted by the
Bourbon authorities compared to their Hapsburg predecessors.[110]
Such protests, however, tended to remain tightly circumscribed in
terms of both goals and territory: they were usually concerned with
the specific, often 'traditional' grievances of an individual community; inter-communal alliances were rare, and the authorities could
usually pick off dissident communities using their old combination
of repression and redress. In these regions – Oaxaca, much of the

109 Taylor, 'Banditry and Insurrection', pp. 216–21, 227–9; Van Young, *Hacienda and Market*,
     pp. 281–2.
110 Taylor, *Drinking, Homicide and Rebellion*, pp. 120–4; Tutino, *From Insurrection to Revolution*,
     pp. 140–1.

central plateau – the village survived through the Bourbon era, chastened but still vital; when that era ended amid popular insurgency, the villagers did not play the central revolutionary role which would fall to them a century later, during the 1910 Revolution.[111]

But the grievances of the villagers – the 'external peasantry' – were not the whole story. The hacienda's barrage of physical, paternalist and economic controls tended to keep the 'internal peasantry', the resident peons, relatively docile. Indeed, when times were hard, as they often were in the later eighteenth century, the hacienda's provision of credit, a guaranteed corn ration and maybe a garden plot, were powerful means to ensure obedience. In the Guanajuato region, for example, progressive proletarianization meant that the ratio of *vagos* (landless Indians) to villagers reached an unprecedented 2:1 (for the colony as a whole the ratio was perhaps 1:8).[112] In the face of this emerging labour surplus, landlords could squeeze both workers and tenants. They drove wages down, curtailed access to land, pushed tenants to the risky, outlying, rainfed fields, and, with the switch from pastoral to arable farming, instituted seasonal hiring in place of round-the-year employment. By the 1790s, evictions had become commonplace.[113] In Jalisco, landowners took advantage of the situation to try to reduce their tenants to the status of service tenants, owing labour services like Chilean *inquilinos* (again, we note the recurrent link between 'capitalist' economic growth and pre-capitalist labour relations).[114] Comparable attempts were made to downgrade

---

[111] Tutino, *From Insurrection to Revolution*, pp. 354–7. Tutino, rightly, in my opinion, stresses the material, ecological and socioeconomic causes of agrarian protest. However, some sort of collective learning process – the product, often, of contingent history – also affected popular mobilization (or passivity), by way of creating opportunities, prompting alliances and disseminating ideas: the best study of this process is Guardino, *Peasants* (see pp. 212–14).

[112] Brading, *Miners and Merchants*, p. 228. The 1:8 ratio derives from the intendancy of Mexico, which stretched from the Valley of Mexico down to the Pacific coast and contained a population of a million. Given its size and heterogeneity it can serve as a rough proxy for the colony as a whole; *vagos* may have been more common in the north, but less common in the deep south.

[113] Tutino, *From Insurrection to Revolution*, pp. 64–9, 79–81, 88–9; see also Morin, *Michoacan*, pp. 271, 273.

[114] Van Young, *Hacienda and Market*, p. 233. On *inquilinaje*, see Arnold Bauer, *Chilean Rural Socety from the Spanish Conquest to 1930* (Cambridge, 1975), pp. 50–7, 159–70. Morin, *Michoacan*, p. 278, notes how landlords juggled forms of tenancy (money rents, labour rents and sharecropping), in order to enhance profits and offset risk; the choice of labour system was pragmatic and 'rational' (it did not emanate from some 'feudal' or 'capitalist' psyche); however, collective decisions could have decisive effects on the agrarian political economy – in this case blocking, rather than accelerating, a shift to free wage labour.

the status of tenants and peons in the Querétaro and San Luis regions, where rents were raised, recalcitrant tenants were evicted, and the distribution of rations to the peons was curtailed (a rational, albeit provocative, move by landlords at a time when the price of staples was on the rise).[115]

Such moves did not go unresisted, even by the docile peonage. Landlords, like the Mora family of Celaya, who tried to rationalize their enterprises, stirred up protests and had to resort to force.[116] In reply, some hacienda workers tried – without success – to claim the status of 'Indian' villages, possessed of communal autonomy.[117] Compared to peasant protest, however, peon and tenant resistance was usually less overt and more likely to take the form of non-compliance, poor work, absenteeism and dilatory payments of rent; constrained by the hacienda, peons and tenants resorted to the historic 'weapons of the weak'.[118] The absence of hacienda revolts did not, however, indicate an unsullied hacienda legitimacy. Peon protest erupted, suddenly and violently, when political and agrarian crises coincided in 1808–10.

Meanwhile, throughout the money economy as a whole, wages both urban and rural were depressed: 'all our evidence points in the same direction. In the years before 1810, the labouring classes in Mexico experienced a decline in their standard of living'.[119] Peons and miners were alike affected: rationalizing landlords sought to cut payments in kind just as mine-owners eliminated the shares system in favour of a basic (and depreciating) daily wage. In both cases, workers were driven to defend 'archaic' systems of remuneration (the hacienda *ración*, the miners' *partido*) – not out of any innate

[115] John Tutino, 'Life and Labor on North Mexican Haciendas: The Querétaro-San Luis Potosí' Region: 1775–1810', in Frost, *El trabajo y los trabajadores*, pp. 341, 375.
[116] Brading, *Haciendas and Ranchos*, pp. 198–9; Hamnett, *Roots of Insurgency*, pp. 85–7, notes several severe disputes between coercive landlords and disgruntled peons in the Puebla region.
[117] Tutino, *From Insurrection to Revolution*, p. 83; Hamnett, *Roots of Insurgency*, pp. 88–9. Efforts by hacienda peons, or *gañanes*, to achieve corporate village status – to turn themselves into independent peasants – were not necessarily tactical and instrumental; there is some evidence that the hacienda's 'internal peasantry' (tenants and squatters who farmed hacienda land in return for rent) displayed notions of prescriptive propietorship ('land to the tiller'); José Mora complained that on his hacienda Los Morales, 'some [*gañanes*] acted as if they owned the estate', working when and if they chose: Brading, *Haciendas and Ranchos*, p. 199.
[118] Scott, *Weapons of the Weak*.
[119] Brading, *Haciendas and Ranchos*, p. 199. See also n. 107 above.

archaism of mind, but in a simple attempt to defend their living standards.[120] Usually they failed. A similar logic prevailed in respect of debt peonage. Contrary to common supposition (we have noted), debts often constituted perks or incentives, designed to attract and retain workers; they formed part of a voluntary rather than a coercive labour system. Logically, debts rose in times of labour shortage – they were bid up by workers – and fell, along with real wages, in times of labour abundance. In the late eighteenth century levels of debt appear to have fallen, at least on haciendas (mines and *obrajes* were another matter). In response, hacienda workers sought to defend this pre-capitalist perk in order to maintain their precarious means of subsistence.[121] Landlords, however, had less need to entice workers by advancing them cash, so hacienda credit dried up, especially in the more populous regions of central Mexico. Urban workers, too, faced falling living standards: the wages of textile workers failed to keep pace with rising food prices; and artisans found themselves ensnared in the trammels of merchant-financiers, who were themselves hit by major fluctuations in the market (occasioned by the wars of the 1790s and after) and squeezed by the unbeatable competition of cheap industrial imports.[122]

This generalized fall in income (monetary or material) had macro-economic consequences. In certain circumstances, market expansion and economic growth redound to collective benefit: the rich will get richer, but the poor may also get a little richer too (a good example would be late nineteenth-century Argentina).[123] In other circumstances, the allocation of returns is so skewed that growth is associated with a broad fall in living standards: in late Bourbon Mexico as in late Porfirian Mexico. The difference arises from the structure of the entire political economy: that is, the relative distribution of population, property and power. In Mexico, a rising population confronted an entrenched landlord class, which enjoyed a disproportionate share of resources and considerable – though not

[120] Ladd, *Making of a Strike*, pp. 47–8; Van Young, *Hacienda and Market*, pp. 256–9.

[121] Van Young, *Hacienda and Market*, pp. 249–50; Tutino, *From Insurrection to Revolution*, pp. 59, 71–2, 81, 85–6.

[122] Salvucci, *Textiles and Capitalism*, pp. 124–5; Garner, 'Prices and Wages', p. 101; Tutino, *From Insurrection to Revolution*, pp. 91–4.

[123] H. S. Ferns, *The Argentine Republic, 1516–1971* (Newton Abbot, 1973), p. 89.

absolute – access to political power. Landlords – and employers more generally – could squeeze their workers, relying on a combination of coercion and (more important) a highly favourable, sometimes politically manipulated, labour market. Profits rose, but profits were not usually channelled into further productive investment, since opportunities for such investment were constrained. Save in respect of silver, Mexico was not a major exporter; and a large slice of export earnings was creamed off by the Spanish Crown and Spanish middlemen. Mexican producers – be they *hacendados* or manufacturers – had to rely principally on the domestic market (in this they contrasted with, for example, the planter-entrepreneurs of the Caribbean, who exported the bulk of their production).

Yet as profits rose, real wages and purchasing power declined. Amid apparent boom, the domestic market – never large – contracted further: *alcabala* receipts, which may be taken as a rough indicator of the volume of internal trade, went down; no more than one-sixth of Mexico's population entered the mass consumer market.[124] Engel's law came into play: especially from the 1780s, as food prices rose, popular consumption was squeezed. Wheat – fed to pigs in the early eighteenth century – became too costly for poor consumers in Mexico City; but maize, too, rose in price, as demand outstripped supply and the authorities relinquished control of the grain market to private interests.[125] In Guanajuato, centre of the mining boom, shops now shut on Sundays, since they could no longer sell to the miners and their families; the town's commerce was reportedly 'destroyed' (a piece of commercial hyperbole, no doubt) because of the decline in the miners' purchasing power.[126] The *obrajes* of the Bajío, too, went into decline, as they were hit by foreign competition and cyclical crises (the most severe in 1785).[127] The Bourbon boom, though finally cut short by political crisis in the 1800s, was inherently constrained and incapable of generating sustained growth, especially sustained industrial

[124] See n. 62.

[125] Clara Elena Suárez Argüello, 'Política triguera en el centro de México durante el siglo XVIII', in Ouweneel and Pacheco Torales, *Empresarios, indios y estado*, pp. 107–11.

[126] Brading, *Miners and Merchants*, pp. 276–7. Garner's analysis of *alcabala* (internal customs) receipts for New Spain as a whole (*Economic Growth*, pp. 177–8) reveals irregular growth to the 1780s, then decline until 1810.

[127] Salvucci, *Textiles and Capitalism*, pp. 150–1, 158–9; Super, 'Querétaro Obrajes', pp. 212–13.

growth.[128] Mining faltered; the domestic market shrank; productivity did not match population increase, while population increase drove down wages to the point where Malthusian crisis threatened. Industrialization, as Barrington Moore has pointed out, *solved* the problem of the proletariat – of the swelling, impoverished, landless population – and did not create it.[129] But Bourbon Mexico could not industrialize, nor could it modernize its agrarian infrastructure. It remained a weakly integrated economy, only partially monetized and increasingly milked by a greedy and belligerent metropolis.[130]

This structural bind was dramatically signalled in the 1780s. The lot of Mexico's poor, urban and rural, had never been easy: bare subsistence, punctuated by occasional sprees and recurrent dearths, had been the norm. But it still compared favourably with that of some pre-industrial poor, for example, that of Spain itself (hence the continued flow of immigrants, which attested to the disparity in living standards, at least for Spaniards). But the late eighteenth century witnessed a marked deterioration, characterized by 'ever-increasing impoverishment'.[131] The trend was highlighted, as such trends usually are, by deepening conjunctural crises. The classic case was 1785–6. Then, drought and frost conspired to produce intense privation, disease and mortality. Central Mexico, from Oaxaca through the central highlands up to the Bajío, was deeply affected (the coastal hot country escaped, and the warmer valleys of Puebla and Morelos were spared the worst: such regional variations revealed the economic disarticulation of the colony, which lacked a transport network capable of alleviating such acute regional dearths).[132] In the populous Bajío the death rate soared: by 400 per cent in the city of León. Perhaps

---

[128] Coatsworth, 'Limits of Colonial Absolutism'; Garner, *Economic Growth*, pp. 257–8.

[129] Moore, *Injustice*, p. 135.

[130] Van Young, 'A modo de conclusión', pp. 216–19.

[131] Van Young, *Hacienda and Market*, p. 268.

[132] Florescano, *Precios del maíz*, pp. 142–4, 148, 151; Gibson, *The Aztecs under Spanish Rule*, pp. 316–17; Hamnett, *Politics and Trade*, pp. 63–4; Thomson, *Puebla de los Angeles*, p. 12; Martin, *Rural Society*, pp. 105–6. Morin, *Michoacan*, pp. 142–3, 195–6, notes that wheat (an item of urban, Spanish consumption) was more mobile than corn, hence its price trends were more uniform; prices of corn and beans – the staples of the poor – varied greatly across space as well as time. Thus in June 1792 corn prices in Huétamo, Paracho and Coalcoman – communities about 100 miles distant from each other in Michoacan – were, respectively, 2, 6 and 12 pesos a fanega. This was not unusual: Arij Ouweneel and Catrien C. J. H. Bijleveld, 'The Economic Cycle in Bourbon Central Mexico: A Critique of the Recaudación del diezmo líquido en pesos', *Hispanic American Historical Review*, 69/3 (1989), pp. 486–7.

a fifth of the population of the Guadalajara intendency perished.[133] Even within regions the impact of dearth was not uniform. Landed villages, possessed of an adequate subsistence base, survived better (some crops might be salvaged, depending on the ecological mix; the previous year's grain might be eked out; authorities and *caciques* might take relief measures).[134] Even when such villages suffered, however, they tended to perceive their suffering more as an act of God, requiring Stoic submission, than as a man-made disaster, inviting protest and retribution. Townspeople, too, were hard hit, and they had no subsistence cushion; but they could count on a limited degree of official provisioning.[135] The chief sufferers, therefore, were the rural proletariat and the tenants and sharecroppers who possessed little or poor land: they lacked resources, organization and political clout. Particularly numerous in the Bajío, they suffered and died in their thousands.

All the elements of the classic pre-industrial crisis were present. As shortages developed, prices shot up, to the advantage of landlords who were ready to capitalize on dearth.[136] Crowds flocked to the city where, in the usual paradoxical fashion, grain supplies exceeded those of the countryside. The authorities' capacity to surmount the crisis was scant. Hunger and disease (the familiar diseases of destitution and malnutrition: typhoid, dysentery, pneumonia and influenza) took a huge toll: their victims were piled into anonymous graves. Vagrancy and mendicancy – common enough in the past – reached new proportions. Crowds of beggars roamed the streets of Guadalajara, 'poor, weak, and wasted, like skeletons hardly able to stand on their feet'.[137] Only the providentially bountiful harvest of 1787 resolved the lingering crisis. The Bourbon authorities, of course, did not control the vagaries of the weather and were not directly responsible for the 1785–6 dearth; nor, indeed, can they be blamed for failing to cut

---

[133] D. A. Brading and Celia Wu, 'Population Growth and Crisis: León, 1720–1816', *Journal of Latin American Studies*, 5 (1973), pp. 32–6; Van Young, *Hacienda and Market*, pp. 94–103.

[134] For example, Martin, *Rural Society*, pp. 108–9.

[135] Florescano, *Precios del maíz*, p. 145. Michael C. Scardaville, '(Habsburg) Law and (Bourbon) Order: State Authority, Popular Unrest and the Criminal Justice System in Bourbon Mexico City', *Americas*, 50 (April 1994), pp. 507–9, sees provisioning as part of a broader Bourbon commitment to social welfare and control, which helped offset (urban) class tensions.

[136] Martin, *Rural Society*, p. 107; Gibson, *The Aztecs under Spanish Rule*, p. 316.

[137] Van Young, *Hacienda and Market*, p. 100; see also Florescano, *Precios del maíz*, p. 142ff.

canals through the arid and serrated central highlands. However, the structure of agrarian production which they sustained made recurrent dearth inevitable, and aggravated dearths when they occurred; furthermore, their anticlerical policies curtailed Church charity, and their refusal temporarily to remit tax and tribute payments (now needed all the more to pay the wages of a salaried bureaucracy), bore down hard on the common people. Nor was it a secret that the political authorities and the engrossing, price-gouging landlords were often one and the same or, at least, were joined by political and familial ties. In Puebla, the town councillors allegedly prevented cheap grain from reaching the city: they behaved, as a populist priest put it, not like 'city fathers but (rather) city pirates, as anyone, particularly the poor, would testify'.[138] Thus, dearth inevitably impaired the legitimacy of the ruling elite. When dearth struck again, in 1809–10, coinciding with political crisis, it made a decisive contribution to the great insurgency of Hidalgo.

However, the links between dearth and popular protest were complex and should not be casually assumed. Dearth did not trigger protest in the way that alarm bells set Pavlov's dogs slavering. In the highly urbanized, commercialized and proletarianized Bajío the link seems clear: shortages focused popular attention on local officialdom; the transit and storage of coveted grain supplies afforded obvious coordinates for protest. In the eighteenth-century Bajío, as in eighteenth-century France, dearth and urban unrest went together.[139] In much of the countryside – still the seat of the majority of the population – matters were rather different. William Taylor's careful research reveals no correlation between dearth and village rebellion: 'there is no great bunching of rebellions and famine around a few crucial years'; the 1760s, relatively rebellious years, were also years of relative plenty.[140] For reasons already suggested, villagers were not driven to rebel by sheer hunger: their grievances, whether against oppressive officials or encroaching landlords, responded to

---

[138] Hamnett, *Roots of Insurgency*, p. 91; see also Thomson, *Puebla de los Angeles*, p. 116. On the political – delegitimizing – consequences of dearth, note Florescano, *Precios del maíz*, pp. 172–7.

[139] Charles Tilly, *The Contentious French: Four Centuries of Popular Struggle* (Cambridge, Mass., 1986), pp. 20–3, 113–14, 156–8, 187–92, 221–3.

[140] Taylor, *Drinking, Homicide and Rebellion*, p. 129.

different causes which, save in cases where imprudent officials imposed exactions upon a hungry people, did not connect directly to the vagaries of the harvest. So, too, with hacienda peons, whose dependence on the hacienda was reinforced by shortages. For the village, official abuses were a colonial constant, come rain or shine; hacienda encroachment was also an old, though now much extended, phenomenon.[141] The first elicited protest according to a fairly random pattern (though the evidence suggests it tended to increase during the eighteenth century); the second responded to long-term market trends, mediated through the lottery of litigation. While food riots ignited in immediate, spontaneous fashion, village rebellions smouldered through long years of litigation before flaring up.[142]

When it came to prediction – and repression – these two forms of protest differed. No one could predict where and when dearth would strike, at least until a summer drought or – worse – an early autumn frost blighted the harvest in a particular zone (although a competent colonial statistician could have predicted that such an event would occur about once a decade).[143] Village rebellion, however, was predictable, in that certain communities possessed justifiable reputations for protest and belligerence. It was no surprise to the people of the Guadalajara region that Zacoalco should prove a bastion of the insurgency after 1810, given its long history of litigation and conflict; nor that Izúcar (Puebla) – where hatred of Spaniards 'was intense' – should welcome the insurgent forces of Morelos with open arms in 1811.[144] But the timing of Zacoalco's revolt and Izúcar's welcome was, of course, determined by other factors: political crisis and creole conspiracy, which had nothing to do with either weather or land tenure.

Thus, inasmuch as the insurgency of 1810 linked land-hungry villagers on the one hand, and riotous miners, destitute artisans and impoverished rural labourers on the other, it united two distinct forms

---

[141] There are no time series for the colony; however, Borah, *Justice by Insurance*, p. 128, gives figures of complaints before the General Indian Court in August–September 1784: 32% concern conflicts over land (and 43% property more generally); 26% are directed against secular officials (and only 1% against priests); 12% relate to labour disputes. See pp. 134–8 for particular examples.

[142] E.g., Hamnett, *Roots of Insurgency*, pp. 87–9.

[143] Florescano, *Precios del maíz*, pp. 111–39.

[144] Hamnett, *Roots of Insurgency*, pp. 126, 154.

of protest, the latter strongly conditioned by conjunctural (especially climatic) factors, the former responding to longer term, structural changes associated with the Bourbon boom and the expansion of the commercial hacienda. Nevertheless, all components of the insurgent coalition of 1810 shared certain assumptions which informed their collective protest and which may be loosely summed up under the heading of the 'moral economy'.[145] Villagers rebelled against the apparently arbitrary oppression of state and landlord which, especially as the eighteenth century wore on, posed a profound threat to subsistence rights and communal survival. In much of the south, where the hacienda was weaker, it was the exactions of officials – sometimes priests – which weighed most heavily on the (primarily Indian) peasantry. Here, the old tributary mode survived, but it was increasingly exploited by new Bourbon officials who looked to raise either revenues for the state (that was their formal responsibility) or profits for themselves and their mercantile partners (their informal objective).[146] Either way, the old tributary mode was harnessed to new ends – aggressive state-building or aggressive profiteering. Elsewhere, especially in the Bajío and centre-west, it was hacienda expansion and the more general, insidious effects of agrarian commercialization (such as internal community stratification) which prevailed.[147] The relatively somnolent hacienda of the Habsburg era became the predatory landgrabber of the later Bourbon period; the old symbiosis between hacienda and village progressively eroded. Bishops and *alcaldes* rarely snuffed out entire pueblos (effective parasites do not eliminate their hosts);[148] but haciendas sometimes did, for its was the pueblos' land, water and 'free' labour which they coveted.

---

[145] For references, see n. 89. For a recent, broad formulation, see also Taylor, *Magistrates of the Sacred*, p. 462.

[146] An egregious case of patrimonial profiteering was the forced sale of 'Holy Crusade' (Santa Cruzada) indulgences in Yucatán in the third quarter of the eighteenth century: Patch, *Maya and Spaniard*, pp. 157–8.

[147] Borah, *Justice by Insurance*, p. 383; Van Young, *Hacienda and Market*, ch. 14.

[148] Borah, *Justice by Insurance*, p. 354, offers a somewhat charitable take on Spanish macroparasitism: 'most Spaniards . . . aimed at a continuing, long-term *mise-en-valeur*. The problem was to ensure a regular and moderate form – in short, to restrain excess on the part of unusually greedy individuals . . . and to see to it that that Indians did contribute in what was regarded as proper proportion'. Hence, Borah argues, the need for some paternalist protection of the 'host'.

A range of pressures, of which hacienda was the most potent, thus jeopardized the very survival of the Mesoamerican village, depriving it of its means of subsistence (fields and waters which, apart from their material value, were often invested with ancient telluric tradition)[149] and thrusting its inhabitants across the threshold which separated independent peasants, heirs to millenia of Mesoamerican agrarian culture, from dependent labourers, creatures of the Hispanic hacienda. In such circumstances, peasant protest assumed a forthright moral quality, premised upon a collective rejection of the rationale of agrarian commercialization and an adherence to what indignant Spaniards referred to as 'the rude and thoughtless traditions of their ancestors'.[150] Responding to deep, yet rational, sentiments, such protest was durable, tenacious, not easily bought off or suffocated, and largely impervious to short-term market cycles.

Peasant adherence to the 'moral economy', which granted the village a secure place in the agrarian order and village families access to basic subsistence needs, did not imply a total rejection of the market (as some critics of the 'moral economy' thesis have wrongly assumed). The market was an inescapable fact of life for peasants as well as for peons and urban workers. It was also an ancient fact of life and not necessarily a threatening fact of life. Peasants, as we have seen, participated actively in markets: in Oaxaca, Indian villagers pioneered the commercial cultivation of cochineal; they produced and marketed textiles, *metates*, *mezcal*, pulque and pottery.[151] The potters of Tonalá, near Guadalajara, made handsome profits which enabled their community to grow and prosper.[152] Even groups possessed of a strong ethnic identity and a redoubtable record of resistance, such as the Yaquis of Sonora, adroitly exploited market opportunities to the benefit of their communities.[153] But peasants – and the poor more generally – conceived of limits to the market, as their erstwhile Habsburg rulers had also done. In the countryside, markets – for labour and produce – should supplement and reinforce

[149] Gruzinski, *Conquest of Mexico*, p. 98ff.
[150] Van Young, *Hacienda and Market*, p. 319.
[151] Chance, *Race and Class*, p. 110; Morin, *Michoacan*, pp. 156, 160, 163, 290; Garavaglia and Grosso, *Puebla desde una perspectiva microhistórica*, pp. 107–12.
[152] Taylor, 'Banditry and Insurrection', pp. 240–1.
[153] Hu-Dehart, *Missionaries, Miners, and Indians*, pp. 41–2, 51–2, 59.

the subsistence base, not destroy it;[154] in the city, markets should be regulated, at times suppressed, in order to guarantee a basic right to subsistence. Did not Christian doctrine – and responsible governance – require as much? Unfettered markets, linked to open-ended accumulation by private individuals, brought instability, upheaval and destitution; they were – for rational reasons, unrelated to any inherent mental conservatism – evils to be opposed.

Peasant rebellion thus correlated with areas and periods of rapid agrarian commercialization, unmitigated by a paternalist state and judiciary; areas where families and communities perceived fundamental threats to their livelihood, without adequate legal redress; periods when aggressive profit-seeking – 'a compulsive intensification of primitive accumulation', in the words of García de León[155] – acquired fresh momentum, when the state connived at, and did not mitigate, the process of exploitation, and when, as a result, peasants faced that decisive push across the threshold of subsistence, which would leave them at the mercy of a greedy state and a capricious market. Gradual commercialization (as in the case of Chalco, just east of Mexico City) could be more easily tolerated, albeit with recurrent squabbles and confrontations; official abuses could be checked, especially by the more 'acculturated' communities of central Mexico, which enjoyed some redress at law; epidemics and dearths might be stoically borne, as inscrutable acts of God.[156] These pressures, old, familiar and recurrent, generated sporadic revolts, but not serious insurrections. They did not appear to jeopardize the very existence of the peasant community and the peasant way of life. Insurrection, in contrast, attested to the breakdown of the old moral economy, in city and, *a fortiori*, in countryside; it was fuelled by the deep popular resentments which the new Bourbon order had engendered, with its emphasis on rapid agrarian commercialization, hacienda expansion, mining boom, rising rents, falling wages, wild swings in the price of staples and increasingly oppressive labour systems.

---

[154] As Morin generalizes for the Michoacan peasantry: 'everybody did all they could to achieve self-sufficiency in corn': *Michoacan*, p. 290.

[155] García de León, *Resistencia y Utopía*, vol. 1, p. 89.

[156] John Tutino, 'Agrarian Social Change and Peasant Rebellion in Nineteenth-Century Mexico: The Example of Chalco', in Katz, *Riot, Rebellion, and Revolution*, p. 101; Taylor, *Drinking, Homicide and Rebellion*, pp. 166–7; Isabel Gil Sánchez, 'Trabajadores agrícolas de Tlaxcala en el siglo XVIII', in *Organización de la producción*, p. 115.

II. The Bourbon Project

For, if the underlying sources of change were socioeconomic and impersonal, they were mediated and encouraged by a self-consciously progressive administration which, in contrast to its dynastic predecessor, was determined to accelerate, rather than to brake, such change. Bourbon policies of economic development and political centralization, to which we now turn, simultaneously attacked popular livelihood and liberties – the old, loose, traditional liberties conceded, *faute de mieux*, often enough, by Habsburg patrimonialism. Riots and rebellions were now more savagely repressed: those involved in the 1767 revolts suffered execution, whippings and amputations in 'uniquely cruel' style and on an unprecedented scale.[157] The old give-and-take of Habsburg rule – the necessary corollary of its modest repressive capacity – faded into the past; 'delicate divide-and-rule' policies gave way to exemplary, root-and-branch repression.[158] The mediating role of the parish priest declined, as civilian (and military) officials usurped the role once dominated by the local clergy, who now found themselves caught between querulous parishioners and unsympathetic bureaucrats; in matters of morality and matrimony, secular authority gradually eclipsed clerical.[159] In Yucatán, where Bourbon claims to good (i.e., conscientious, efficient) government were less hollow than elsewhere, the results were still resented more than they were appreciated; for with the new Bourbon officials came 'a new spirit... that violated all the tacit assumptions by which colonial affairs had been managed for centuries'; Maya communities found themselves losing control of their internal affairs, especially financial affairs, losing, too, the 'autonomy that the corrupt and slovenly administration of the old regime had helped to preserve'.[160]

---

[157] Taylor, *Drinking, Homicide and Rebellion*, p. 122; see also Brading, *Miners and Merchants*, pp. 27, 234–5, which considers the 1767 repression as 'a sharp turning-point in Mexico's colonial history', which 'set the pattern for the next forty years'. The Visitador José de Gálvez, the author of this repression, was a stiff-necked martinet, prone to paranoia; nevertheless, his policy reflected a general trend, not just an indvidual whim.

[158] Taylor, *Drinking, Homicide and Rebellion*, p. 122; Pastor, *Campesinos y reformas*, p. 193.

[159] This is the principal thrust of Taylor, *Magistrates of the Sacred*; on the specific question of morality and matrimony, see Seed, *To Love, Honor, and Obey*.

[160] Farriss, *Maya Society*, pp. 358–9. On moral enforcement in the Mixteca of Oaxaca, see Pastor, *Campesinos y reformas*, p. 211.

In the towns as well Bourbon rule was tighter and harsher. The authorities rounded up vagrants and put them to work in the *obrajes* or the tobacco factories, thus satisfying two official desiderata at once: stimulating productive work and keeping tramps off the streets.[161] The factory became a metaphor for social control and plebeian discipline.[162] In the same spirit, the authorities curtailed – or, in Guanajuato, eliminated – the privileges of the urban guilds which, in Bourbon eyes, inhibited economic progress, while promoting festivities (such as the Corpus Christi processions) which were costly, ostentatious and potentially rowdy.[163] More generally, the Bourbon authorities sought to police popular recreation, curbing violence and licence. They cracked down on drinking, gambling and the carrying of illegal arms; they usurped the Inquisition's role as theatre censor, regulated carnival, spurned and finally banned bullfights.[164] The authorities' concern for public morals was nothing new. What was new was the ambitious scale of their intervention, their confident usurpation of ecclesiastical responsibilities and, perhaps, their naive belief that social engineering was working, was indeed producing a more sober, disciplined and tidily dressed populace.[165]

With such policies, we might say, the Bourbons rewrote the social contract, unilaterally and without prior consultation. Bourbon policy, as David Brading sums it up, meant 'power to the wealthy and discipline for the masses':[166] a suitable device for an *ersatz* bourgeois project, designed to achieve a rationalization and commercialization of society, but by dint of state initiative as much as autonomous 'bourgeois' efforts. Such a programme – a 'revolution from above', in Barrington Moore's terminology – sought to recast a recalcitrant

[161] Amparo Ros Torres, 'La fábrica de puros y cigarros de México (1770–1800)', in *Organización de producción*, p. 57; Viqueira Albán, *Relajados o reprimidos*, p. 238.

[162] Deans-Smith, *Bureaucrats, Planters and Workers*, pp. 174, 203–5.

[163] Carrera Stampa, *Los gremios*, pp. 271–5; Brading, *Miners and Merchants*, p. 244; Deans-Smith, *Bureaucrats, Planters, and Workers*, pp. 174; Viqueira Albán, *Relajados o reprimidos*, pp. 158–9.

[164] Viqueira Albán, *Relajados o reprimidos*, pp. 18–19, 43–4, 46, 111, 144, 153–4, 164; we might paraphrase Macaulay and say that the Bourbon authorities sought to ban bull-fighting less for the pain that it gave the bull than for the pleasure it gave the plebs – and the disgust it inspired in enlightened elites.

[165] A 1784 Report on Taverns concluded that Mexico was 'not as dissolute' (*relajado*) as it had been twenty years before (Viqueira Albán, *Relajados o reprimidos*, p. 22); yet similar vices would spur similar reforms, repression and rhetoric for generations to come.

[166] Brading, *Miners and Merchants*, p. 245.

colonial society in the mould of England or France.[167] It was bound to fail. Economic development and political centralization could not be achieved by state fiat; the social archaisms which littered colonial society could not be magicked away by Bourbon prestidigitation. What was true for metropolitan Old Spain (where the Bourbon project was first applied) was even more true of colonial New Spain:

enlightened absolutism, as it developed after 1750, suffered from internal contradictions. Absolute monarchy pressed forward to centralize power, eliminate the archaic, and devise policies capable of transforming the administration of the state and the economy; but it would not, indeed could not, tamper with a traditional social structure dominated by aristocratic and corporate privilege.

Thus, 'in the end, the reforming initiative of the Bourbons resulted in only a superficial resolution of national problems'.[168]

The Bourbon 'revolution from above', to which we now turn, could not succeed in the kind of colonial society we have described: for, despite the stirrings of commercial activity, the administrative zeal of the reformers and the powerful examples of England and France, that society remained too backward, introverted and particularist – in a word, glib but suggestive, too 'feudal'.[169] In taking upon themselves the tasks of a bourgeois revolution – the building of a centralized state, an integrated citizenry and, above all, a commercial economy premised on the free movement of factors of production – the Bourbons assumed tasks beyond their dynastic capacity. They failed, and bequeathed to their republican successors of the nineteenth century the same contradictory, conflict-ridden project; but not before they themselves had fallen victim to the historic danger incurred by 'revolutions from above' – a revolution from below.

The enhancement of tax revenue was a natural consequence of demographic and economic growth (which boosted state income

---

[167] Moore, *Social Origins*. On the Anglo-French model, see Lynch, *Bourbon Spain*, p. 146ff.

[168] William J. Callahan, *Church, Politics and Society in Spain, 1750–1874* (Cambridge, Mass., 1984), p. 4.

[169] 'Feudal' presents a good many problems, not least because of its polysemic character. New Spain retained 'feudal' elements in two different senses: first (in marxisant, socioeconomic terms), the colonial economy remained heavily agrarian, with a large subsistence sector, weak markets and limited free wage labour; second (in liberal juridical terms), colonial society was shot through with patrimonial authorities, corporate interests and particularist privileges. Whatever its faults, 'feudal' is at least preferable – as a portmanteau term, should one be sought – to that even fluffier qualifier, 'traditional'.

without, in this age before transfer payments were invented, augmenting state expenditures). It was also a cardinal objective of Bourbon policy. For only by raising additional revenue could the Bourbons maintain – let alone modernize – their sprawling Atlantic empire. But, again, the extraction of additional revenue provoked popular resentment and strained both the social and the imperial contract. Bourbon fiscal reform, like so many items of Bourbon policy, was first implemented in the peninsula. Driven by the demands of war, successive administrations extended and tightened fiscal exactions, which possibly quintupled during the eighteenth century. But they also looked to squeeze the colonies, whose fiscal contribution had declined in the later Habsburg period.[170] Colonial remittances, above all those of New Spain, therefore increased, at first gradually, then spectacularly. The yield from tribute, levied on Mexico's Indian population, was boosted by population growth. In the 1660s tribute had reached a low of 200,000 pesos annually; by the 1750s it had climbed to 345,000 pesos and by 1779 to around a million. Although tribute returns were now eclipsed by other sources of revenue, they still furnished around 15 per cent of governmental income; tribute, however, fluctuated with the harvest and slumped in years of dearth, like 1778–9 and 1785–6; many communities owed huge arrears of tribute dating back decades.[171]

Economic growth offered a range of alternatives. The royal tenth – the cut taken by the Crown from Mexico's burgeoning bullion production – provided the largest slice of governmental income. But it was supplemented by important sources of revenue, some of them the result of Bourbon fiscal innovation. The new royal tobacco monopoly, established in defiance of popular protest and bureaucratic infighting in the 1760s, yielded 8 million pesos in the 1780s, of which about half was clear profit; this represented as much as

---

[170] Lynch, *Bourbon Spain*, pp. 21, 173–4, 324–7; Garner, *Economic Growth*, pp. 4–5, 25–6, 215ff.

[171] Semo, *History of Capitalism*, p. 43; Garner, *Economic Growth*, p. 226; Hamnett, *Politics and Trade*, pp. 64–5. Gibson, *The Aztecs under Spanish Rule*, pp. 209–11, illustrates the inefficiency of tribute collection – which was vitiated by official fraud, unreliable rolls, shifting categories and exemptions, and widespread evasion ('by universally observed custom, any determined effort to collect tribute was accompanied by an exodus from the community': p. 210). Following the Gálvez visitation (1765–71), however, tribute collection was tightened up, peaking around 1780. Post-1780 tribute returns are open to debate: see Ouweneel and Bijleveld, 'The Economic Cycle', pp. 493, 502–3, and Brading, 'Comments', p. 531.

one-fifth of royal revenue. *Alcabala* (internal customs) receipts contributed a further 3 million.[172] Royal monopolies of salt, playing
cards, gunpowder and pulque were also lucrative (pulque raised
a million pesos annually in the 1780s), if scarcely consistent with
Bourbon pretensions to free market policy. Altogether, New Spain's
contribution to the royal exchequer grew from some 3 million pesos
in 1712 to 6 million in 1765 and over 20 million in 1798; thereafter (although scholars dispute the issue) Crown revenues fluctuated – and
they fluctuated a good deal through the turbulent 1800s – around that
same figure.[173] In addition to regular revenue, however, the Crown
also resorted increasingly to loans and expropriations, as we shall
see. Meanwhile, of the twenty or so million pesos raised in revenue,
about 6 million were devoted to collection and monopoly production, and between 4 and 5 million to other governmental expenses –
administration, the judiciary, defence – within Mexico; 10 million
remained to subsidize expenditures in Europe (which absorbed
6 million) and along the colonial sea-lanes of the Atlantic and
Pacific (4 million). By the late eighteenth century, therefore, Mexico
made a massive contribution to the maintenance of the Spanish
empire; Mexicans contributed 67 per cent more per head in revenue
than Spaniards.[174]

The rise in secular revenue was paralleled by an increase in Church
income too. Tithe receipts, buoyed by a rising tide of population and
production, reached 1.3 million pesos in the 1770s, 1.8 million in the
1780s.[175] Church wealth, however, excited secular envy. In 1767, the

---

[172] Florescano and Gil Sánchez, 'La época de las reformas borbónicas', pp. 220–1; Garner,
Economic Growth, p. 177, and Ouweneel and Bijleveld, 'The Economic Cycle', p. 502, concur
that *alcabala* income peaked c. 1780, then fell. For provincial tax yields, see Garner, *Economic
Growth*, pp. 221–2 (Zacatecas) and Morin, *Michoacan*, pp. 133, 148.

[173] Garner, *Economic Growth*, pp. 216–18, reviews alternative scenarios. The figure of 'about 20
million' follows Humboldt, whose estimate is roughly confirmed by D. A. Brading, 'Facts and
Figments in Bourbon Mexico', *Bulletin of Latin American Research*, 4/1 (1985), pp. 61–4; a much
higher figure (around 50 million c. 1804) is preferred by TePaske, Klein and Coatsworth (see
Brading, p. 61). Readers fascinated by Bourbon fiscal history should also note Richard Garner's
countercritique of the Brading critique, 'Further Consideration of "Facts and Figments in
Bourbon Mexico"', *Bulletin of Latin American Research*, 6/1 (1987), pp. 55–63.

[174] Brading, *Miners and Merchants*, pp. 29–30, and 'Facts and Figments', pp. 63–4. Garner,
Economic Growth, p. 220, following Klein, suggests that by the 1790s Mexico yielded 8 pesos
per capita in taxation compared to 4.8 pesos for Spain itself; however, Klein's figure may be
exaggerated (see n. 173).

[175] Florescano, *Origen y desarrollo*, p. 69, gives figures up to 1790; Ouweneel and Bijleveld, 'The
Economic Cycle', p. 484, goes on until 1809, showing a continued (if irregular) rise in tithe

property of the Jesuits was seized and sold off; in 1804, when war again drained the exchequer, the Crown sequestered ecclesiastical funds (the *obras pías*) to the tune of 40 million pesos. Since most of this huge sum consisted of loans and mortgages, the measure was, in effect, a massive foreclosure, which required the Church's debtors (mostly landlords, miners and merchants) to pay off outstanding loans over a ten-year period. Within four years, 10 million pesos were raised: reluctant contributors included the rich – like the Basque sugar planter Gabriel Yermo – and the not so rich, like the parish priest of Dolores, Father Miguel Hidalgo.[176] Though anticlerical in principle, this drastic, war-induced fiscal expedient hit lay debtors in practice; it was hardly coincidental that, within a few years, many of its victims were to be found among the ranks of the politically disgruntled and dissident.

The revamping of the tax structure required an army of bureaucrats. Monopolies, like the tobacco *estanco*, afforded a sink of patronage into which high-ranking officials – viceroys and visitors-general – could dip to reward their clients and relatives, usually Spaniards, often (in the case of José de Gálvez) fellow-Malagueños.[177] The expanded fiscal machine thus played an important part in the Hispanization of colonial government which aspiring creoles resented. More generally, of course, new or increased taxes were resented. The *estanco* incurred the opposition of both tobacco producers (who, in some regions, were barred from legal production, in others, obliged

income in Puebla and Michoacan; this trend is also evident in Yucatán, where receipts grew from 17,000 pesos a year c. 1750 to more than double that figure in the 1780s and 48,000 pesos in 1809: Farriss, *Maya Society*, p. 368. However, the significance of these figures (did they reflect increased agricultural production or just inflation?) has been the subject of a techical, but bruising, debate: Ouweneel and Bijleveld, 'The Economic Cycle', pp. 479–530, and the same authors, plus D. A. Brading, John Coatsworth and Héctor Lindo-Fuentes, 'Comments', in the same volume, pp. 549–57.

[176] There is an ample literature: Brading, *Miners and Merchants*, pp. 340–1; Brian Hamnett, 'The Appropriation of Mexican Church Wealth by the Spanish Bourbon Government: The "Consolidación de Vales Reales," 1805–9', *Journal of Latin American Studies*, 1 (1969), pp. 85–113; Carlos Marichal, 'La Iglesia y la Corona: La bancarrota del gobierno de Carlos IV y la Consolidación de Vales Reales en la Nueva España', in María del Pilar Martínez López-Cano, coord., *Iglesia, estado y economía. Siglos XVI al XIX* (Mexico, 1995), pp. 241–62; Romeo Flores Caballero, *Counterrevolution: The Role of the Spaniards in the Independence of Mexico* (Lincoln, Neb., 1974), ch. 2; Asunción Lavrín, 'The Execution of the Law of Consolidation in New Spain: Economic Aims and Results', *Hispanic American Historical Review*, 53/1 (1973), pp. 27–49; Margaret Chowning, 'The Consolidación de Vales Reales in the Bishopric of Michoacan', *Hispanic American Historical Review*, 69/3 (1989), pp. 451–78.

[177] Brading, *Miners and Merchants*, p. 37.

to supply the monopoly at fixed prices) and consumers, who faced higher prices for tobacco leaf, cigars, cigarettes and snuff.[178] In Guanajuato, in 1766, this opposition provoked riots, which were severely repressed; a year later, when the expulsion of the Jesuits led to renewed protests, the offices of the *estanco* were sacked. Yet the most pervasive, insidious and effective protest was evasion: illicit cultivation of tobacco, illicit cigar and cigarette manufacture and widespread smuggling. In some remote parts of the colony the authorities never enforced the monopoly; in the heartland, they waged an endless battle against the Hydra of contraband, which flourished despite repeated decapitations.[179]

The story of the *estanco* – a bold, centralizing initiative which yielded cash, though at considerable social cost – epitomized Bourbon fiscal policy. Furthermore, even the cash yield eventually suffered diminishing returns. Total tax revenue reached a plateau in the 1790s. The tribute fluctuated with dearth; the *alcabala* levelled off with the stagnation of the economy; returns from tobacco, aguardiente and pulque declined.[180] By the 1800s Mexico was – certainly compared with its past – an overtaxed and overgoverned society. Fiscal oppression became a staple complaint of the rebels of 1810. By squeezing New Spain as never before, Lynch observes, the Bourbons 'gained a revenue and lost an empire'.[181]

To the Bourbons, Mexico was not overgoverned but, for the first time, properly governed. The dynasty, it has been justly observed, set out to achieve a 'second conquest' of the colonies: to eliminate the inefficiencies of administration and delegations of authority which the Habsburgs, from design or accident, had so long tolerated.[182] A dynasty of French origin, they took as their model of government the French system of centralized administration and, as their model of empire, the rational mercantilism of Colbert, which sought to harness market forces to a tight, state-run, colonial system. Such was

---

[178] Deans-Smith, *Bureaucrats, Planters, and Workers*, pp. 20–9.

[179] Brading, *Miners and Merchants*, p. 27 (riots); Deans-Smith, *Bureaucrats, Planters, and Workers*, pp. 30–3, 226–7 (contraband).

[180] Garner, *Economic Growth*, pp. 177, 216; Ouweneel and Bijleveld, 'The Economic Cycle', p. 502; Morin, *Michoacan*, pp. 127–39.

[181] Lynch, *Bourbon Spain*, p. 21.

[182] Farriss, *Maya Society*, pp. 355–6; John Lynch, *The Spanish American Revolutions, 1808–1826* (London, 1973), pp. 2–7.

the prescription of persuasive Spanish ideologues and policy-makers like Patiño, Campillo and Campomanes, who found a ready audience in reformist kings like Philip V and Charles III, and eager collaborators in colonial bureaucrats like Gálvez, Teodoro de Croix and the count of Revillagigedo.[183] According to their collective project, government would become stronger, the economy more dynamic; the empire would cohere in a more intimate and profitable union, run on mercantilist lines for the benefit of Spain; and it would withstand the commercial and military challenges of rival empires, notably those of Britain and France.

Both internally and externally, this implied a policy of *force majeure*, of progressive militarization. Conversely, though the Bourbons – individually devout – accorded the Church an important role in their reformist project, they required the Church to defer to an enhanced regalism, to serve as a junior partner in the task of renovation; and they frowned, in severe, Jansenist fashion, on the cruder manifestations of popular Iberian religion – baroque ritual, rowdy fiestas, bloody penitences.[184] Typical of Bourbon aims and sensibilities was the visitor-general José de Gálvez, whose sojourn in Mexico (1765–71) laid the basis for the active phase of Bourbon reform in the colony: the establishment of the tobacco monopoly, the expulsion of the Jesuits, the build-up of a regular soldiery, the compilation of an administrative blueprint which would eventually be carried through by another Bourbon paragon, the viceroy Revillagigedo the Younger, in the 1780s. Gálvez even epitomized Bourbon qualities in his own person: a Malagueño lawyer, a parvenu in high social circles, a dedicated servant of the state, a fierce martinet when confronting popular dissidence, and the husband of a French wife, thus *afrancesado* ('Frenchified') by marriage as well as by political and philosophical persuasion.[185] Revillagigedo, the other great architect of Bourbon reform, a creole aristocrat by birth, perhaps fitted the role less neatly. But his commitment to rational, centralizing reform was no less.

[183] Lynch, *Bourbon Spain*, pp. 145–7, 252–4, 258–9; Richard Herr, *The Eighteenth-Century Revolution in Spain* (Princeton, 1958), pp. 56–7, 123.

[184] Viqueira Albán, *Relajados o reprimidos*, pp. 152–60; Taylor, *Magistrates of the Sacred*, p. 14.

[185] Brading, *First America*, pp. 473–8; the fullest biography remains Herbert I. Priestley, *José de Gálvez, Visitor-General of New Spain (1765–1771)* (Philadelphia, 1980; first pubd., Berkeley, 1916).

'The heart of the Viceroy', a clerical critic commented, 'is penetrated with all the maxims which the philosophers of this century have scattered in their books'; on the basis of such far-fetched, alien, *a priori* principles Revillagigedo conceived 'vast projects' and 'kept the entire kingdom in movement with his impetuosity'.[186]

We find, in this Burkean criticism of the rational reformer, a hint of the basic contradiction which, as already mentioned, underlay Bourbon policy. The Bourbons sought to emulate the incipient capitalist dynamism of their Western European neighbours and rivals (Britain was the best example, even if France was the preferred model; the problems of the Spanish Bourbons were in fact also to be found, to a lesser degree, in Bourbon France). Given that the organic forces of Spanish and Spanish-American society would not ensure successful emulation, they had to be urged, prodded and whipped by the central state. Economic dynamism derived from the market, from competition; therefore the state had to clear the ring for competitive market forces. This required a strong, rationalized, centralized state, exercising a monopoly of violence and capable of holding its own in the murderous Grosspolitik of the late eighteenth century. (France's loss of its Canadian and Indian empires and Britain's loss of the Thirteen Colonies were sharp reminders.) To this end, taxes, armies and new structures of government had to be raised. The result was a project premised on notions of the free market but involving a growing and costly bureaucracy, hefty taxation, elaborate regulation of trade and manufacture, and the establishment of powerful monopolies.

Apart from the many practical problems the Bourbon reformers encountered and the many failures they experienced (that is, instances where they could not impose their rational will upon a recalcitrant civil society), this fundamental contradiction lurked even in corners of ostensible success. They sought to emulate a commercially and colonially successful state like the English ('all privileges are odious', stated Campomanes, echoing the antimonopolist sentiments of the seventeenth-century English bourgeoisie), yet they raised up precisely the kind of bureaucratic, monopolistic barriers which the English bourgeoisie – during the revolution of the 1640s and

---

[186] Brading, *Miners and Merchants*, p. 82. The reference is to Revillagigedo the Younger.

after – had successfully dismantled.[187] While Revillagigedo 'kept the entire kingdom in movement' with his 'vast projects', his eighteenth-century contemporary Robert Walpole could confidently act on the old adage *quieta non movere* ('let sleeping dogs lie').[188]

The difference was not simply one of contrasting individual temperaments, but of contrasting sociopolitical systems. In England, the bourgeoisie – commercial, agrarian, incipiently industrial – controlled an inherently dynamic country and empire. It could be left to run the shop. Government intervention in the domestic economy was increasingly limited and largely reflexive. In Spain, both the bourgeoisie and the economic dynamic were weaker (though not absent: the traditional image of late eighteenth-century Spain as a flaccid feudal giant has been qualified).[189] Emulation, even survival, demanded state initiative as, of course, it did in many other 'developing' countries, whose governments played geopolitical catch-up: Hohenzollern Prussia, Meiji Japan, Romanov Russia. In contrast to the pioneer – yet unusual – English model, Spanish economic policy involved extensive state intervention, and political modernization demanded a 'revolution from above'.[190] The Bourbons took upon themselves the paradoxical task of pounding civil society into an acceptance of *laisser-faire* capitalism and rational-legal political authority. Their subjects would be forced to be economically free and cuffed into an acceptance of centralized state authority. The Bourbon project was neither unique nor, in all respects, wildly Utopian. But it was risky and riddled with contradictions, the more so when it was implemented in a colonial context.

---

[187] Farriss, *Crown and Clergy*, p. 95. Cf. Christopher Hill, *The Century of Revolution, 1603–1714* (Edinburgh, 1961), pp. 32–3, and *Reformation to Industrial Revolution*, pp. 91, 96, 131, 181. Hence New Spain, where there existed 'a high degree of state intervention in most aspects of economic life', contrasted sharply with New England: Thomson, *Puebla de los Angeles*, p. 101.

[188] Roy Porter, *English Society in the Eighteenth Century* (London, 1990), p. 98. Or, as Lord Shelburne put it, in terms no Bourbon reformer would have endorsed: 'Providence has so organized the world that very little government is necessary' (Porter, p. 116). That is not to say, of course, that the Georgian state atrophied or that reform was a dead letter (cf. Porter, pp. 105, 107, 121).

[189] Herr, *The Eighteenth-Century Revolution in Spain*, p. 145, 147.

[190] Moore, *Social Origins*, pp. 436–42. Historians have long debated the nature of the Bourbon project; most would now stress the gap between goals and achievements; but while the traditional view (echoed here) stresses dogmatism and authoritarian centralization, revisionist historians have also argued – less persuasively, in my view – for pragmatism and liberal decentralization: see the useful summary in Taylor, *Magistrates of the Sacred*, p. 542.

In the realm of administration, the Bourbon objective – sketched out in the 1760s, finally implemented in the 1780s – was to replace the lax, patrimonial, tax-farming system of the Habsburgs with salaried, centrally appointed, officials, French-style; even French nomenclature (*intendente, subdelegado*) was introduced, in place of the old labels – *alcalde, corregidor*. The administrative map was redrawn to accommodate a dozen intendancies, each possessed of its own treasury (the intendancies of the 1780s were to form the basis of the later states of the Mexican Republic).[191] To the reformers, the old *alcalde* system, with its patrimonial confusion of private and public roles, was inherently corrupt, inefficient and economically retrograde. Apart from being loyally responsive to state policy, salaried officials would also have no need of local trafficking; hence the *repartimiento de mercancías* – the forced sale of goods, the source of much official and mercantile profit and Indian discontent – was abolished, at least in theory (we will turn to practical outcome in a moment).[192] Central administration was also reformed. The Bourbons set up a powerful new council to supervise the colony's finances which, in terms of both income and expenditure, were fast expanding. Conversely, the old audiencias, vestiges of Habsburg conciliar government, declined in importance, in part, and paradoxically, because the Bourbons conceded corporate judicial autonomy to new government agencies, such as the monopolies.[193]

As the bureaucracy swelled, and was progressively Hispanized, an important new colonial entity came into being: the professional military. Hitherto, viceroys had governed with exiguous military backing. In moments of crisis, they drummed up a creole militia – which, of course, gave the creole elites an ultimate veto over viceregal policy: witness the discomfiture of Gelves in 1624. In addition, the colony relied heavily on private levies to counter the threat of rival European imperialists and insurgent Indians, especially in the north. Hence, the recurrent official complaints of the laxity, corruption and patrimonialism of the frontier forts; hence, too, Thomas Gage's insistent refrain, based on early seventeenth-century observations, that New

[191] MacLachlan and Rodríguez O., *Forging of the Cosmic Race*, pp. 268–9.
[192] Brading, *Miners and Merchants*, pp. 44–5; Pastor, *Campesinos y reformas*, pp. 196–7; Florescano y Gil Sánchez, 'La época de las reformas borbónicas', pp. 212–14.
[193] Brading, *Miners and Merchants*, pp. 43, 329, 333–4.

Spain was casually defended and ripe for the picking.[194] A century and more later, the perils were even greater. The northern Indians were more numerous and belligerent (it was while campaigning against them in Sonora that José de Gálvez suffered a mental break-down, 'during which he raved about importing an army of apes from Guatemala to put down Indian insurrection'); but far more threat-ening, from the point of view of Bourbon policy-makers, were the European and, after 1776, the United States challenges.[195]

The Spanish empire had successfully withstood the raids of pi-rates and privateers in the later sixteenth and seventeenth centuries. But, by the eighteenth century, the threat of concerted maritime attack, mounted by a formidable British navy, was of a different order. The fall of Havana (previously thought to be impregnable) shocked the Spanish government (1762). If Havana could fall, so could Veracruz, Spain's only major fortified Atlantic port and the gateway to the rich colony of New Spain.[196] In addition, the sprawl-ing expanses of Spanish North America faced multiple challenges. The burgeoning British colony in the Carolinas threatened Florida, which was cut off from New Spain by the French foothold at the mouth of the Mississippi.[197] Furthermore, Spain's shortage of trade goods – a symptom of economic backwardness and maritime weak-ness – placed Spanish colonists at a serious disadvantage compared to their British and French rivals, who could more easily strike the deals with Indian allies which were the key to successful imperial-ism in North America.[198] Spain's tenuous territorial empire, based on

---

[194] Thompson, *Thomas Gage's Travels*, p. 65; see also Weber, *The Spanish Frontier*, pp. 212–14.

[195] Archer, *Army in Bourbon Mexico*, p. xiii; Weber, *The Spanish Frontier*, p. 248.

[196] Archer, *Army in Bourbon Mexico*, pp. 2–3. The fall of Havana climaxed a series of Anglo-Spanish conflicts in the Americas, which included Admiral Vernon's descent on the Isthmus of Panama and Cartagena (1739–40), recurrent skirmishing on the borders of Florida and contraband trading along the Atlantic littoral from Honduras to the Río de la Plata: Lynch, *Bourbon Spain*, pp. 131–41, 151–2, 317–19.

[197] By 1745 the British population of South Carolina exceeded the Spanish population of Florida by a factor of ten (approximately 20,000 to 2,000); Florida's vulnerability to the west was exemplified by the fate of Pensacola, which in 1719 alone changed hands three times (Spanish-French-Spanish-French): Weber, *The Spanish Frontier*, pp. 166, 179. The Bourbon succession in Spain served to cool Franco-Spanish conflict in the Americas (Spain now settled for a 'quiet containment' of French Louisiana: Weber, p. 184); but, by the same token, it aggravated relations with the British on the Atantic seaboard, where they posed a more formidable threat.

[198] As a Franciscan friar put it: while the Spaniards 'are engaged in vexing the Indians...your Frenchman will take off his shirt to give to them and hold them to their allegiance'; not, of course, because of any Gallic altruism, but because the French had a better supply of cheap shirts: Weber, *The Spanish Frontier*, p. 178.

the ancient traditions of freelance conquest and Catholic conversion, could not compete with the new maritime, migrant and commercial imperialism of the French and, *a fortiori*, the British.[199]

Yet, following the fall of Havana, the Mexican people, elites and commoners, showed no eagerness to join the colours at this time of imperial crisis. No more did they flock to colonize the distant north. For reasons of colonial security, therefore, a standing army was essential; at the same time, Bourbon economic and administrative reforms required a degree of sustained coercion. The first Spanish regular troops arrived, along with Gálvez, in the 1760s: their initial task was the forcible expulsion of the Jesuits, an act replete with political symbolism. Around this nucleus, a new colonial militia was formed, most of it creole and mestizo in make-up (Indians and blacks were not allowed to serve). Like other items of Bourbon policy, however, this military build-up was vitiated by bureaucratic squabbles, official parsimony and the inherent contradictions of colonialism. Arming creoles and mestizos was risky; forced recruitment led to desertion; and the performance of the colonial militia – when it was mobilized during the American War of Independence or sent to confront local insurrections – was desultory.[200] Yet the maintenance of Spanish regular forces in Mexico proved costly and – reformers lamented – suffered diminishing returns, since the troops went native and, over time, acquired all the vices imputed to the degenerate colonial population.[201] The outbreak of the French revolutionary wars found New Spain ill-prepared; by 1796, when Spain joined in the fray against England, there was no alternative but to revive and expand the colonial militia. Desertion and death from illness continued to take a toll, however, and in 1807, desperate for manpower, the Crown made all racial groups liable for military service.

Meanwhile, this progressive military build-up cost the regime, both literally and figuratively. It involved increased taxation and – especially after the 1790s – increased recruitment. Creole elites might be attracted to the colours by the promise of prestige and military

[199] McFarlane, *The British in the Americas*, pp. 180–3, 240–1, suggests contrasts between British and Spanish colonization of the Americas.

[200] Archer, *Army in Bourbon Mexico*, pp. 20, 94–7. On the failings of the conscript militia in the Mixteca (Oaxaca), see Pastor, *Campesinos y reformas*, p. 198.

[201] Archer, *Army in Bourbon Mexico*, ch. 1.

privilege (they benefited from the *fuero militar*, the military's exemption from the civil courts), but the Spanish Crown was leery of creating a creole-dominated military establishment. The common people had no such incentive and, in view of the harsh, disease-ridden nature of life in the ranks, did not readily volunteer. The Bourbon army therefore started Mexico's long tradition of forced recruitment and consequent military demoralization and desertion. The army also exacerbated social tensions in the colony. It became the not-so-strong right arm of Bourbon policy; it rounded up the Jesuits, cracked down on supposed dissidents (like the unfortunate French of the 1790s), put down rural rebellions (often in heavy-handed fashion), repressed city tumults (actual or potential), and patrolled crime-ridden cities. In fact, said critics of the army, the presence of a garrison boosted rather than cut the crime rate; it also inflated prices and led to interminable wrangles with the civil authorities – intendants, *alcaldes*, *cabildos*. Lastly, the army became a focus of rivalry between *peninsulares* and creoles (a topic which we will shortly address).[202]

For all their defects, the military played a key role – and, especially after 1810, a successful role – in the maintenance of Spanish rule in the colony. This involved not only internal repression but also external defence, and it was the external threat which Bourbon rulers and soldiers most feared.[203] Mexico's geopolitical position, we have seen, made it vulnerable to several external challenges: European maritime powers along the Gulf, belligerent Indians in the north, and the burgeoning power of the United States (and, at a further remove, Tsarist Russia) in North America. The Bourbons took steps to protect the strategic Gulf coast, chiefly by reinforcing the defences of the hot, fetid port of Veracruz. Here, at least, nature conspired with Bourbon objectives; if the Tsar could count on Generals January and February, Mexico had the no less formidable Generals Malaria and Yellow Jack (which, though they took a terrible toll of Mexican garrisons, also deterred wary invaders).[204]

The gaping expanses of the north were a different matter. During the great territorial carve-up of the Seven Years War (1756–63)

---

[202] Archer, *Army in Bourbon Mexico*, pp. 90–8, 119–22, 129–32, 249–57.

[203] Not until the 1800s did Spanish fear of internal subversion begin to compete with the age-old fear of external aggression: Archer, *Army in Bourbon Mexico*, pp. 29, 80–6, 90, 105.

[204] Humboldt, *Political Essay*, p. 35.

Spain lost Florida to the British and gained Louisiana (west of
the Mississippi) from the French; characteristically, Florida was
rapidly Anglicized, while Louisiana remained stubbornly French.[205]
The American War of Independence made possible the recovery of
Florida but brought into being a new, expansionist republic in North
America – one, furthermore, born of successful colonial rebellion.[206]
The delimitation of borders produced constant wrangles. France no
longer figured; but Spain and the United States could not agree on
their respective borders along the Gulf and the Mississippi Valley;
and Spain, Britain and Russia laid conflicting claims to the Pacific
northwest. In order to press these claims, Spain established new settlements in Upper California, mapped New Mexico and despatched
naval expeditions as far north as Vancouver Island and the shores of
Alaska.[207] These advances, however, were precarious: the Bourbons
lacked the resources to engage in ambitious empire-building, and,
with the onset of the French revolutionary and Napoleonic wars,
Spain was forced to defer to Britain in the Pacific northwest and to
the United States in Florida. In 1800, by way of a typical geopolitical trade (an Old World throne for a New World colony), Louisiana
was ceded to Napoleon, who – his dreams of North American expansion swiftly dashed – promptly sold it to the United States.[208] The
infant republic thus acquired – on paper – the vast area of the mid-
west (for Thomas Jefferson, Louisiana stretched as far as the Rocky
Mountains), as well as supposed claims to the outlying Spanish ter-
ritories of Florida and Texas.[209] In subsequent years, as New Spain
roiled in rebellion, these claims were pushed: by an American se-
cessionist revolt in West Florida (1810), by the American capture of
Mobile (1813), and by a U.S.-Spanish Treaty (1819) which confirmed

[205] Weber, *The Spanish Frontier*, pp. 198–203. Spanish attempts to integrate Louisiana more tightly
into the Spanish empire – forcing the French, so dissidents complained, to give up claret for
'the wretched wine of Catalonia' – provoked a serious revolt in October 1768; the Spanish
governor was forced to flee, with cries of 'vive le roi, vive le bon vin de Bordeaux' ringing in his
ears. However, this 'brief, bloodless, and boozy' insurrection lasted only a year; a new governor
recovered control, shot the ringleaders of the rebellion and resumed a policy of Hispanization:
Weber, p. 201–2.
[206] Weber, *The Spanish Frontier*, pp. 266–9.
[207] Weber, *The Spanish Frontier*, pp. 252, 265; Gutiérrez, *When Jesus Came*, p. 303.
[208] Weber, *The Spanish Frontier*, pp. 285–91. The old world (Italian) throne, promised to the king
of Spain's brother-in-law, never materialized.
[209] Weber, *The Spanish Frontier*, p. 292.

Spain's loss of Florida and possession of Texas, while fixing the respective western boundaries of the two entities at 42° North (the present Oregon-California state line).[210]

Even within these reduced borders, Spanish control remained tenuous. The eighteenth century witnessed continued migration and settlement, spurred by mining strikes as well as government initiative. But the official resources never matched the scale of the task; Spanish settlement remained patchy;[211] and the very process of expansion provoked strenuous Indian resistance. The Yaquis and Mayos of Sonora, who had lived in relative peace under Jesuit auspices through most of the seventeenth century, came under pressure as Spanish (secular) colonists entered the area in greater numbers, developing the new mines at Alamos (1684) and establishing towns, farms and ranches.[212] The outcome resembled the triangular pattern evident in central Mexico in the wake of the Conquest: Spanish laymen and clerics competed for control of the Indians. The laymen contended that the Jesuits selfishly monopolized Indian labour and resources, and they therefore sought a secularization of the missions; the Jesuits claimed to protect the Indians from rapacious Spanish settlers.

For a time, the Yaquis – and their articulate, 'acculturated' leaders – cleverly played the two camps against each other. As their statement to the viceroy (1739) made clear, they favoured neither outright secularization nor untrammelled theocracy; rather, they sought a genuine measure of independence, political, economic and cultural. This proved impossible. In a tense situation, aggravated by floods and dearth, the Jesuits chose to export grain to the missions of California rather than retain it for local consumption. In 1740 sporadic Yaqui raiding gave way to a major concerted rebellion, in which Mayo, Pima and Yaqui Indians all participated: this was probably the

[210] Weber, *The Spanish Frontier*, pp. 297–300.

[211] The Spanish population of California grew – chiefly by natural reproduction – from 1,000 in 1790 to 3,000 in 1821; by this time that of New Mexico (urban population only) had reached about 15,000, while that of Texas stood at perhaps 4,000: Weber, *The Spanish Frontier*, pp. 195, 265; Gutiérrez, *When Jesus Came*, p. 170. On the somewhat arbitrary basis of current state boundaries, this yields a population density of around one Spaniard to 20–25 square miles. In contrast, the British population of the Carolinas in 1760 was a little over 200,000, a concentration of about two Britons per square mile: McFarlane, *The British in the Americas*, p. 167.

[212] Hu-Dehart, *Missionaries, Miners, and Indians*, pp. 43–4ff.

biggest Indian challenge to Spanish rule in the north since the great Pueblo rebellion of 1680.[213] Though it lasted only a year, the rebellion devastated the area and resulted in heavy casualties on both sides (particularly the rebels'). When, after two major battles, the Indian forces were crushed, the authorities executed their leaders and imposed a draconian regime. Jesuit paternalism – which, like many paternalisms, was often arbitrary and abusive – gave way to secular coercion. After more than a century of relative peace in Yaqui-*yori* relations there ensued nearly two centuries of recurrent conflict. Jesuit mediation disappeared; Spanish (later Mexican) secular control took its place; and the Yaqui people, militarized by their rebellious experience, sustained a belligerent resistance well into the twentieth century.[214]

The Yaqui experience was distinct in that a people who had reached a stable and succesful *modus vivendi* with colonial (especially Jesuit) rule now broke loose. It is likely, indeed, that the very success of the earlier colonial project – its encouragement of economic organization and cultural identity among the Yaqui – made possible their long subsequent resistance. Elsewhere in the north, the colonial-clerical hegemony had proven less stable and successful. Hence the decline of that hegemony counted for less. The Pueblos of New Mexico, who had thrown off Spanish lay and clerical authority in the great revolt of 1680, were reduced to grudging submission in the 1690s. The friars returned, unwelcome, more cautious, perhaps more corrupt.[215] Pueblo idolatry, blasphemy and dissent might be deplored (the Pueblos were still 'heathens underneath and...have a natural antipathy for anything to do with our sacred religion'), but such failings now had to be tolerated.[216] Spanish settlers, lacking mineral wealth and facing the constant threat of Apache raids, lived off Pueblo forced labour, which the friars (again) ineffectually denounced but could not curtail.[217] Meanwhile, the friars' numbers

---

[213] Hu-Dehart, *Missionaries, Miners, and Indians*, pp. 61–70; Spicer, *Cycles of Conquest*, pp. 51–4; Radding, *Wandering Peoples*, pp. 283–4.

[214] Hu-Dehart, *Missionaries, Miners, and Indians*, p. 95ff. *Yori* was the Yaqui term for whites and mestizos.

[215] Gutiérrez, *When Jesus Came*, pp. 311–15.

[216] Gutiérrez, *When Jesus Came*, pp. 157, 161–6, 308 (quoting Viceroy Revillagigedo).

[217] Gutiérrez, *When Jesus Came*, pp. 155, 159–60, 302, 323; and on the Apache threat, pp. 147–8, 158.

dwindled; the Spanish population overtook the Indian; secular officials supplanted priests as the key intermediaries between the colonial state and an Indian population which, though superficially submissive, remained separate, disgruntled, even seditious.[218]

The decline of the missions, and the rise of an exploitative – but not necessarily effectual – secular colonialism, was a recurrent theme of the Bourbon era. The Tarahumara of Chihuahua, for example, had never been thoroughly integrated into colonial society and government. The chief conduit of control and acculturation had been the mission; but when, in accordance with Bourbon policy, the Tarahumara missions were secularized, the Indian communities they had gathered simply melted away (a process encouraged by the recurrent Apache raids of the Bourbon era). The Tarahumara, scattered in remote sierra pueblos, enjoyed a genuine autonomy, ignored by both the government and the gradually swelling white and mestizo population of lowland Chihuahua – at least until the later nineteenth century.[219] The Pima and Seri Indians of Sonora – who had driven Gálvez to distraction in 1769 – similarly escaped the attentions of a distracted colonial state; and the Yuma of Arizona, who rose up and slaughtered Spanish soldiers and missionaries in 1781, also earned themselves the benefits of benign neglect. 'It is necessary', as Viceroy Gálvez pragmatically concluded in 1786, 'to forget those Indians for the moment'.[220]

A rare exception to this story of repression and neglect was Upper California. Desperate to bolster its tenuous northern defences, the Crown encouraged (Franciscan) missionary efforts, led by the diminutive and asthmatic ascetic, Junípero Serra. Serra seemed a throwback to the friars of the early colony; the Californian Indians – scattered, stateless and cautiously friendly to the Spaniards – seemed to be ripe for conversion; and, as in the old days of the spiritual conquest of New Spain, the friars faced no serious competition from European rivals.[221] Thus, despite the ravages of disease and the rapacity of secular Spaniards, the California missions began to take

[218] Gutiérrez, When Jesus Came, pp. 166–70, 310–11.
[219] Spicer, Cycles of Conquest, pp. 36–9.
[220] Spicer, Cycles of Conquest, pp. 128–32; Weber, The Spanish Frontier, pp. 248, 258 (quote).
[221] Weber, The Spanish Frontier, pp. 243, 247, 263.

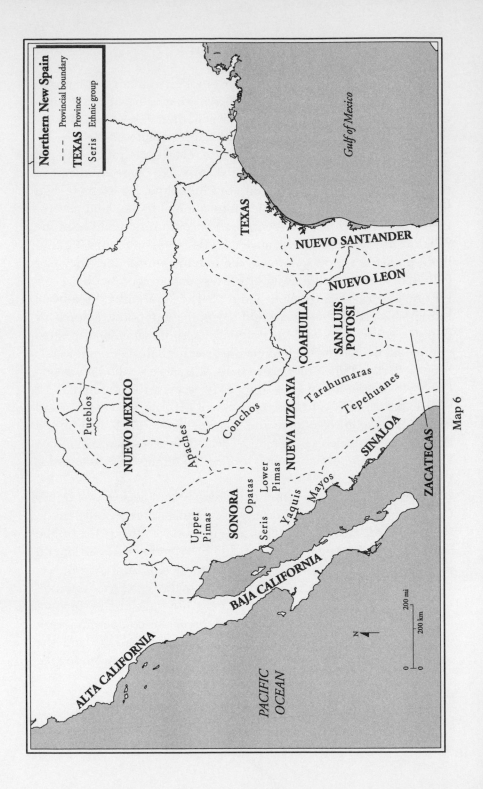

Northern New Spain

- - - Provincial boundary
TEXAS Province
Seris Ethnic group

Gulf of Mexico

TEXAS

NUEVO SANTANDER

NUEVO LEON

COAHUILA

SAN LUIS POTOSI

Tarahumaras

Tepehuanes

NUEVO MEXICO

Pueblos

Conchos

Apaches

NUEVA VIZCAYA

SINALOA

ZACATECAS

Lower Pimas

Opatas

SONORA

Upper Pimas

Seris

Yaquis

Mayos

BAJA CALIFORNIA

ALTA CALIFORNIA

PACIFIC OCEAN

N

0   200 mi
0   200 km

Map 6

root: nine were established by 1784, the year of Serra's death, and twenty by 1821.[222] But this swansong of Franciscan proselytization, reprising old theocratic themes, was profoundly out of tune with Bourbon policy and late colonial reality. It succeeded precisely because California was not a cockpit of great power rivalry; it attracted few Spanish settlers; and Spanish secular power was kept at arm's length by a *cordon sanitaire* of mountains, desert and hostile Indians.[223]

Elsewhere, missions gave way to *presidios*, and coercion took priority over conversion. Spanish imperialism approximated more to its Anglo-French counterpart. The collapse of Jesuit rule in the Yaqui region foreshadowed the general expulsion of the order in 1767 and the progressive secularization of most of the missions of the so-called Commandancy-General of the Internal Provinces – the vast new administrative unit created by Gálvez in the hope of riveting central control upon what is now northern Mexico and the American southwest.[224] Here, as in central Mexico, militarization was a keynote of Bourbon policy. By the 1760s the fort – the presidio – had replaced the mission as 'the way-station into Spanish civilization'.[225] A string of forts was established, stretching from California across to the Gulf of Mexico, manned by some three thousand light dragoons whose organization was designed – with typical Bourbon rationality – to avoid the customary graft and patrimonialism of such frontier garrisons. No less typically, the old vices – embezzled payrolls and corrupt comissaries – persisted.[226] With the fort, too, came settlers, ranchers, miners and other 'Spanish undesirables'.[227] But a modicum of security was attained. Northern towns like Cusihuaráchic, Alamos and

---

[222] In the same period (1784–1821) the Indian mission population rose from 4,650 to over 21,000; however, the total Indian population of California (initially dense in comparison with the rest of northern Mexico and the U.S. southwest) fell from 300,000 to 200,000: Weber, *The Spanish Frontier*, pp. 262–3.

[223] Weber, *The Spanish Frontier*, p. 264.

[224] Weber, *The Spanish Frontier*, pp. 212, 214, 224; Radding, *Wandering Peoples*, p. 44.

[225] Spicer, *Cycles of Conquest*, pp. 332–3; Radding, *Wandering Peoples*, pp. 275–6; Moorehead, *The Presidio*, p. 55ff.

[226] Weber, *The Spanish Frontier*, pp. 217–19.

[227] Spicer, *Cycles of Conquest*, p. 332; Radding, *Wandering Peoples*, pp. 161–206, which offers a good analysis of Spanish penetration of the northwest and the consequent tensions between private and common property rights, indigenous farming and Spanish livestock: a re-run – *mutatis mutandis* – of what had occurred in central Mexico two centuries earlier.

Santa Fe grew, especially as and when mining strikes permitted; the
Spanish population began to outstrip the Indian.[228]

Spatially, if not demographically, however, such towns remained
Hispanic islands in an ocean of sparse, semi-autonomous, Indian
peoples. In particular, nomadic raiders, chiefly Apache and Co-
manche, scoured that ocean like corsairs, defying Spanish power,
inflicting heavy losses on people and livestock.[229] Gálvez, innovative here as elsewhere, hit on a new policy, imitative of French and
English empire-building.[230] Because missionary acculturation had
been abandoned, troublesome Indians, like the Apaches (but not
just the Apaches), would have to be bribed, corrupted and, eventually, exterminated. This was

a frankly cynical policy based on the view that the Apaches could never be civilized and thus [it] represented a very sharp alteration of what had been the
Spanish approach, namely, the belief that all Indians were capable through moral
suasion of changing from barbarians to civilized Christians.[231]

Guns and liquor replaced hymns and Bibles. The Comanches were
played off against the Apaches; premiums were paid for Apache
ears, and Apache prisoners – men, women and children – were sold
into slavery and even shipped to the cane fields of Cuba.[232] In this,
as in so much, Gálvez and the Bourbon reformers were distinctly
modern. But they lacked the resources to keep up with the Yankee
modernizers to the north. Hence, though they achieved a semblance
of peace,[233] they left northern New Spain ill-governed, poorly integrated, and vulnerable to the expansionist efforts of those Yankees'
sons and grandsons.

The attempted militarization of the barbarous north had its counterpart in the Mexican heartland, where government policy could be

[228] Luis Aboites Aguilar, *Norte precario. Poblamiento y colonización en México (1760–1940)*
(Mexico, 1995), pp. 70–5, 80–3; Gutiérrez, *When Jesus Came*, pp. 169–70. Martin, *Governance
and Society*, pp. 24–6, describes a less buoyant Chihuahua.
[229] Weber, *The Spanish Frontier*, pp. 206, 221; Radding, *Wandering Peoples*, pp. 277–9; Aboites,
Norte precario, p. 76; Martin, *Governance and Society*, pp. 25, 108, 122; Gutiérrez, *When Jesus
Came*, pp. 147–8, 309, which notes that by c. 1800 Spaniards in New Mexico were committing
crimes – rape and rustling – disguised as marauding Apaches.
[230] Weber, *The Spanish Frontier*, pp. 227, 230.
[231] Spicer, *Cycles of Conquest*, p. 332.
[232] Weber, *The Spanish Frontier*, pp. 226, 231–2; Gutiérrez, *When Jesus Came*, p. 300.
[233] Weber, *The Spanish Frontier*, pp. 230–3; Aboites, *Norte precario*, p. 41; Radding, *Wandering
Peoples*, p. 268; James E. Officer, *Hispanic Arizona, 1536–1856* (Tucson, 1987), pp. 62–70.

enacted with greater efficacy. The army, regulars and militia, grew in size; military men became viceroys and top officials. Five of the first twelve intendants were military officers (and four of the rest were ex-tax officials). Military power was deployed not only against rebels but also against bandits and common criminals. Early in the eighteenth century the colonial regime had established a new agency – the Tribunal of the Acordada – which constituted a form of autonomous, centralized, police force, dedicated to the extirpation of crime and contraband.[234] But the Acordada was a Mexican and creole innovation. The reforming zealots of the later eighteenth century looked to mechanisms of social control that would be both more efficient and more responsive to the interests of Spain. They deployed the military on the streets of (supposedly) crime-ridden cities like Oaxaca and Guadalajara; in the capital, soldiers controlled the traffic and guarded the entrances to the Alameda, the downtown park, turning away 'anyone of the "clase de mantas" – the beggar, barefoot, naked, or otherwise "indecent" classes'.[235] Indeed, the very lay-out of Mexico City – parks, shops, the Plaza Mayor – was now regulated according to principles of rational order, both practical and symbolic.[236] This concern for social control, which, in turn, mirrored a genuine fear of popular protest, was shared by colonial elites, creole as well as *peninsular*. Town councils (like that of Guadalajara) often appealed for a military presence which the government, its resources stretched, could not easily provide.[237] One outcome was an increase in private paramilitary forces. Landlords in Jalisco armed their trusted retainers against troublesome villagers; the boss of the Bolaños mine raised a body of troops to enforce discipline on his work force.[238]

---

[234] MacLachlan, *Criminal Justice in Eighteenth-Century Mexico*, and for a synopsis, MacLachlan and Rodríguez O., *Forging of the Cosmic Race*, pp. 256–8.

[235] Viqueira Albán, *Relajados o reprimidos*, p. 230; see also Archer, *Army in Bourbon Mexico*, pp. 90–4.

[236] Viqueira Albán, *Relajados o reprimidos*, pp. 231 (well-clipped trees in straight lines), 236–7 (streetlights), 238 (control of vagrants, drunks, stray dogs, horses and mules).

[237] Archer, *Army in Bourbon Mexico*, p. 120.

[238] Taylor, 'Banditry and Insurrection', p. 236; Brading, *Miners and Merchants*, p. 190; see also Martin, *Governance and Society*, pp. 55, 63–4, which gives an example of lynch law in Chihuahua in 1773: an Indian bakery worker, acccused of insulting and stabbing his employer (who, it transpired, had 'given the worker several blows "so that he would mend his ways"'), was tied to the pillory in the plaza and flogged, while the town crier proclaimed to the public that 'he who so behaves shall so pay'; later, a court sentenced the Indian to five years in the *obrajes*.

The progressive militarization of the colony reflected not only fears of social upheaval but also the shifting philosophy of government. Back in the 1660s, the *cabildo* of Guanajuato had favoured the establishment of a Franciscan convent, which they felt would exert a soothing influence on the turbulent miners of the town. A century later, religious tutelage ('ideological hegemony', some might wish to call it) was rejected in favour of open coercion, conducted by the new militia.[239] (In northern mining towns like Chihuahua, religious tutelage had never been strong; strong-arm secular authority was the norm.) Symbolically, too, the Bourbon authorities pruned what they saw as the excesses of Baroque Catholicism: they curtailed popular religious fiestas and promoted secular or dynastic alternatives – the coronations of kings, the births of princes, the (rare) victories of Spanish arms.[240] Even the most basic rites of passage underwent secularization (and, at the same time, 'patriarchalization'): shifting official attitudes towards marriage, which crystallized in the Royal Pragmatic of 1776, conferred greater authority on parents (chiefly fathers), weakening clerical authority and, at the same time, deterring marriages premised on 'the blind passions of youth' in favour of those embodying a due regard for property and status.[241] Thus, across a range of activities – marriage, missions, popular recreation and official ceremony – the state expanded its authority at the expense of the Church. And as the role of the Church receded, so clerical dialogue with the common people became less effective, less politically acceptable. Even in rural Oaxaca, where social tensions were less acute than in the Bajío, clerical mediation gave way to tougher, secular, dictation.[242] 'Where the Habsburgs used priests', Brading concludes, 'the Bourbons employed soldiers'.[243] Prelates, who of course were hardly disinterested observers of this change, warned the secular arm that

[239] Brading, *Miners and Merchants*, p. 276.
[240] Taylor, *Magistrates of the Sacred*, pp. 252–8, 260–3; Brading, *Church and State*, pp. 163–9; Viqueira Albán, *Relajados o reprimidos*, pp. 144–8, describes the official crackdown on the Mexico City carnival which, the author suggests, thus 'lost its force as a mechanism for defending the traditional social equilibrium'. On secular fiestas, see Martin, *Governance and Society*, pp. 103–4, 113, 119; Gutiérrez, *When Jesus Came*, pp. 316–17.
[241] Seed, *To Love, Honor, and Obey*, p. 200ff.; Gutiérrez, *When Jesus Came*, pp. 315–16 (quote).
[242] Taylor, *Drinking, Homicide and Rebellion*, pp. 141–2; the erosion of clerical authority – throughout both the diocese of Guadalajara and the archdiocese of Mexico – is stressed in the same author's *Magistrates of the Sacred*.
[243] Brading, *Miners and Merchants*, p. 27.

'it was principally through the...clergy that the Americans have been and are loyal to God and king': to shake the altar was to undermine the throne.[244]

This brings us to the important question of Bourbon anticlericalism. The Bourbons were not, as we have said, anticlerical in the sense of questioning the Church's right to play a major role in society, still less of impugning the validity of Catholicism. Rather, they were the first in a long line of Mexican anticlericals who, while professing a devout faith, nevertheless sought to curtail the power of the Church, which they conceived to be politically offensive, economically retrograde and, in some respects, culturally stultifying. For them, the Church compromised royal absolutism, obstructed good government and, by virtue of its economic and spiritual influence, inhibited both economic development and educational advance.[245] Their aim was not to eradicate Catholicism, but to clip the Church's wings and make it sing in harmony with secular policy. This stance was justified in terms of a revamped regalism, an appeal to both Divine Right and royal *Realpolitik*.[246]

Accordingly, first in Spain, then in Mexico, the Crown took steps to crimp the influence and autonomy of the Church. The building of new convents and the recruitment of novices were curtailed, and, during 1745–55, parishes were progressively 'secularized' (the Bourbons displayed a distinct preference for the secular over the regular clergy). At times, critics alleged, such secularization was violent and peremptory: 'soldiers were...employed to enforce the measure, so that priories were occupied without warning and friars ordered to leave at once, obliged to set out on foot, carrying little more than their clothes and breviaries'.[247] Clerical privileges at law (the ecclesiastical *fuero*) were cut back, although not eliminated; Church courts were debarred from inflicting corporal punishment.[248] In the north, as we

[244] Brading, *Church and State*, pp. 128–30, citing the archbishop of Mexico, Javier de Lizana (1809)

[245] Farriss, *Crown and Clergy*, pp. 91–2, 101–2.

[246] Farriss, *Crown and Clergy*, pp. 28–32, 39–40, 89–91.

[247] Taylor, *Magistrates of the Sacred*, pp. 78, 83–6; Brading, *Church and State*, p. 62ff.

[248] Brading, *Church and State*, pp. 127–8; Taylor, *Magistrates of the Sacred*, p. 17, notes that the (1795) law bringing the clergy under the jurisdiction of the secular courts alarmed the bishops and cathedral chapters but 'caused only a ripple of discontent among rural pastors, since most of them had little to do with the bishop's court in the first place' (see also p. 420).

have seen, the Jesuit missions were abolished, and, in regions like the Lower Tarahumara, parish priests replaced the friars. Stalwarts of early Habsburg imperialism, the friars incurred Bourbon censure, in both Spain and the colonies, for their supposed demotic coarseness and intellectual backwardness. They were also seen to be dangerously independent, ultramontane and unmanageable. Allegations of mendicant vagrancy and degeneration, too, although tailored to political needs, did not lack basis in fact.[249] Thus, the old battle between regulars and seculars, as old as the colony and the cause of some famous affrays in the past, now swung decisively in favour of the secular clergy. If the militia replaced the Franciscans as guardians of urban tranquillity, secular *curas* now supplanted the friars in many rural parishes. Some were seen an unwelcome interlopers; hence an old legitimacy was squandered. Others, however, became respected members and mentors of the community, and, in that capacity, they often stood out as critics of official abuses and, sometimes, as champions of popular protest.[250]

Bourbon anticlericalism – or, perhaps better, Erastianism – was not uniform or unilinear in its application.[251] It varied from place to place (in the far north, as we have seen, the friars never quit New Mexico, and they pioneered Spanish settlement in distant Upper California); and it experienced spurts and slowdowns – which responded, in part, to the temper of successive viceroys.[252] Economic anticlericalism, too, was a progressive tendency. The *cofradías*, property-owning

---

[249] Brading, *Church and State*, pp. 63, 65, 80–1, which concludes that 'by the beginning of the nineteenth century, the mendicant provinces exhibited clear signs of decay and thus were ripe for reform'.

[250] Notably Miguel Hidalgo. Taylor, *Magistrates of the Sacred*, and Brading, *Church and State*, illustrate the great variety of both clerical conduct – corrupt, abusive, honest, dedicated – and parishioners' responses. Taylor, p. 191, reckons that 'notoriously unpriestly' *curas* constituted about 20% of the total. Brading, pp. 108–9, also stresses the diversity of clerical income (in Michoacan): educated city priests lived high on the hog, while their rural counterparts (often) eked out a bare existence amid their indigent flocks.

[251] Erastianism – the state's project to control, but not to subvert, the Catholic Church – is conceptually closely akin to 'Gallicanism', 'regalism' and 'Jansenism': see Herr, *The Eighteenth-Century Revolution in Spain*, ch. 2; Lynch, *Bourbon Spain*, pp. 187–8, 278–80, and Farriss, *Crown and Clergy*, pp. 101–2.

[252] Thus, Revillagigedo the Elder (1745–55) tried 'to implement secularization [of parishes] with breakneck speed', while his successor, the marquis of Amilpas (1755–60) was more cautious: Brading, *Church and State*, p. 65. Gálvez (visitor-general, 1765–71) was markedly more impetuous and activist than Bucareli (viceroy, 1771–9). The so-called 'pendulum effect', which political scientists have discerned in the successive swings in twentieth-century Mexican administrations, thus appears to follow late colonial precedent.

religious sodalities, were frowned upon as being economically retrograde, perhaps politically questionable, certainly overfond of ostentatious fiestas. 'Countless families of poor subjects are ruined every
year' by the financial demands of *cofradías*, a Crown official complained; after 1796, official registration of *cofradías* was required,
and, in suitably Utilitarian spirit, *cofradía* members were urged to
devote their funds to the 'succour of poor prisoners or the sick
or other useful things for their neighbourhood'.[253] In Mexico City,
Viceroy Revillagigedo the Younger banned the use of arms and uni-
forms in the Holy Week processions, thus ending, by imperial fiat,
a practice which still throve in Seville.[254] In Yucatán, *cofradía* lands
were sold off, to the benefit of local landlords and to the detriment
of local cults.[255] Some Bourbon radicals, like the Puebla intendant
Manuel Flon, sought to go further, floating grand – and prophetic –
schemes for the division and distribution of the Church's massive
landholdings which, they argued, stunted economic development;
and, in 1804, as we will see, a financially pressed government sequestered the Church's chantries and charitable foundations.[256]

More generally, popular (or local) religion came under close official scrutiny:[257] not simply because of the threat it posed to public
order, which has been mentioned; nor because of its idolatrous or di-
abolical character, which now gave less cause for official concern;[258]

---

[253] Brading, *Church and State*, p. 132; Pastor, *Campesinos y reformas*, pp. 259–60, notes the
Physiocratic and Colbertian inspiration behind these measures; while Taylor, *Magistrates of the
Sacred*, pp. 308–11, describes a familiar Bourbon-reformist trajectory (in respect of *cofradías*):
a series of secularizing decrees; an enhancement of secular officfaldom at the expense of parish
priests; a swathe of inspections, reports, and disputes; partial implementation, followed by
partial retreat.

[254] Brading, *Church and State*, pp. 166–7.

[255] Farriss, *Maya Society*, pp. 371–2. Pastor, *Campesinos y reformas*, p. 286, notes a comparable
process of *cofradía* decline and Spanish commercial advance in the Mixteca (Oaxaca).

[256] Brading, *Miners and Merchants*, p. 91; Marichal, 'La Iglesia y la Corona'.

[257] 'Local' may be a safer qualifier, since it is clear that Mexican (like Spanish) Catholicism often served to fortify local patriotisms ('there are many examples of local pride, especially of
villagers boasting about their communities as places privileged by an illustrious past or a
miraculous religious image': Taylor, *Magistrates of the Sacred*, p. 42); hence, Mexico's nascent
sense of national (Guadalupan) providence was underwritten by many mini-patriotisms, similarly sacralized. However, it would be wrong to regard such sentiments as purely 'popular',
since they were shared by many local or provincial elites too; what probably can be said is
that the Bourbon project of secularization was largely an elite project, which was imposed on
society from above (by elites), and from outside (by Spaniards).

[258] Imputations of diabolism continued, but official reactions were now 'decidedly lenient'
(Brading, *Church and State*, p. 159) and campaigns to extirpate idolatry became a thing of
the past (Taylor, *Magistrates of the Sacred*, pp. 66–7).

but because it was associated with drink, degeneracy, sloth, profligacy, backwardness, incivility and superstition – in the eyes not only of secular officials but also of a good many Catholic clerics too.[259] For them, the excessive cult of the saints promoted naive beliefs and irrational practices. At Easter, a critical *cura* noted, Tarascan Indians enacted the Passion of Christ, with one of their community, his 'face, shoulders and body bathed in blood', playing the part of Jesus; but the *cura* dared not intervene for fear of provoking a riot.[260] On a more regular basis, boozy Sundays led to San Lunes – Monday absenteeism (and sometimes further boozing), which harmed public morality and private production alike. True religion would promote, instead, sobriety, thrift, hard work and individual application. Bourbon reformers and Jansenist clergy combined, therefore, in an effort to improve what today's economists would call Mexico's human capital. In doing so, they faced an uphill struggle, but they also established precedents that would be doggedly pursued throughout the nineteenth and twentieth centuries.

The single most dramatic and symbolic act of Bourbon anticlericalism came with the expulsion of the Jesuits in 1767. Like much of Bourbon policy, this derived in part from a misguidedly doctrinaire application of *peninsular* policies to colonial problems. It is true that the Jesuits had carved out sizeable, semi-autonomous fiefs, especially in the far north, where they contested with secular officials, *hacendados* and miners, for control of the Indian population (the Yaqui region being the classic case). Yet allegations of the Jesuit state-within-the-state were somewhat misconceived and redolent of *peninsular* politics – where the court influence of the Order was evident, seen to be evil, and puffed up by international paranoia.[261] In the north of New Spain the Jesuit Order was probably the most effective arm of the colonial state, hence its amputation resulted in a decline, not an enhancement, of Spanish control in that far-flung region. In addition, the expulsion of the Jesuits strained the social

---

[259] Taylor, *Magistrates of the Sacred*, pp. 250–60; Brading, *Church and State*, pp. 163–9. It should be noted that rural parish priests, who had a vested (financial) interest in local fiestas, did not always share their superiors' commitment to reform.

[260] Brading, *Church and State*, p. 163.

[261] On the background, see Farriss, *Crown and Clergy*, pp. 125–31, 137–45; Brading, *Church and State*, pp. 10–11.

fabric of New Spain, compromising the legitimacy of Bourbon reformism at the very outset, in the eyes of both the masses and the
(often Jesuit-educated) creole elites.[262]

The peremptory expulsion order came at a touchy moment, only
a year after anti-tax riots had shaken the cities of the Bajío.[263] The
Order, seven hundred in number, was expelled, and its property was
confiscated and auctioned off.[264] Here, then, was a foretaste of the
great ecclesiastical sell-off which anticlerical reformers advocated
and which the Bourbons and their nineteenth-century liberal successors would eventually implement. It was a bold, risky, enlightenedly
despotic act. In the north, as we have seen, the mission communities largely collapsed. In west-central Mexico the Jesuits' summary
departure left a gaping hole in the provision of charity and education (secular substitutes were introduced, but they scarcely filled
the breach); and it left, too, a legacy of resentment on the part of
both the indigent poor and the educated elite. In Michoacan, over
a hundred Indian villages rose in protest; in Guanajuato, the mob
rioted for three days; in San Luis Potosí miners and Indians took to
the streets, opened the gaol, looted stores and threatened 'to finish
off all Spaniards at once'.[265] Gálvez, author of the policy, sensed a
Jesuit plot to subvert the realm. He reacted in hyper-Bourbon style.
The new regular army and militia were swiftly deployed, and they
exacted a harsh retribution: 85 victims were hung, 73 flogged, 117
banished, 674 gaoled. The hangings were public and exemplary, as
were many lesser punishments. In one pueblo, the scribe who had
recorded the communal vow of resistance had his writing hand severed. This was repression on an unprecedented scale, indicating a
commitment to *force majeure* and an abandonment of the old traditions of Habsburg religio-paternalism. It was, in Brading's words, a
'sharp turning point in Mexico's colonial history'.[266]

---

[262] Brading, *Church and State*, pp. 3–4; MacLachlan and Rodríguez O., *Forging of the Cosmic Race*, pp. 265–7.

[263] Brading, *Church and State*, p. 5; Deans-Smith, *Bureaucrats, Planters, and Workers*, pp. 20–1.

[264] The wealth of the Jesuits – and their (successful) resistance to paying the full tithe – was an old source of complaint and controversy, which tended to inflate estimates of their landed assets (see Brading, *Church and State*, pp. 13–14).

[265] Brading, *Church and State*, p. 5.

[266] Brading, *Miners and Merchants*, p. 27. Forty-five years later, during the War of Independence, the expulsion of the Jesuits would be recalled as an 'evil portent' foreshadowing current up-heavals: Farriss, *Crown and Clergy*, p. 240–1, citing Lucas Alamán.

This transformation even found architectural expression, as the flamboyant Churrigueresque of Bajío churches – 'braggart buildings', as the Spanish reformer Jovellanos called them – gave way to a stern, rational neoclassicism.[267] A similar architectural shift was apparent in Guadalajara and Mexico City.[268] The symbolism is plain, not merely inferential, since the new aesthetic was ordained by the Crown and proselytized by the new Royal Academy of San Carlos (1785): neoclassicism, a genre embodying the rational rigour of the state and repudiating the demotic frippery of the Churrigueresque, was to be the official style of the later Bourbons.[269]

In a variety of ways, therefore, the Bourbon reformers sought to attenuate the bonds – powerful and enduring, despite clerical exploitation and hypocrisy – which linked Church to people; and, in doing so, they flouted the people's strong religious sensibility.[270] The latter was an obstinate fact, the former a risky objective. Like later anticlericals, the Bourbons incurred costly opposition to little purpose. The economic returns to the Crown were limited, the social repercussions serious. For all its faults – and notwithstanding evidence of popular indifference or even Rabelaisian cynicism[271] – the Church enjoyed ample support, and popular Catholicism was more

---

[267] Brading, *First America*, p. 510.

[268] Kubler and Soria, *Art and Architecture*, p. 82; Lindley, *Haciendas and Economic Development*, p. 13. A classic example – both architectural and functional – was the 'beautiful and elegant' state tobacco factory, erected in the capital in 1807: Deans-Smith, *Bureaucrats, Planters, and Workers*, pp. 180–1.

[269] Brading, *Prophecy and Myth*, p. 32.

[270] Farriss, *Crown and Clergy*, pp. 2–3; Taylor, *Magistrates of the Sacred*, pp. 42–3, 244–5, 265–300; Brading, *Church and State*, pp. 18–19, 31. Mexican 'religious sensibility' has not been measured (compare Michel Vovelle's analysis of secularization in eighteenth-century Provence, *Piété baroque et déchristianisation en Provence au XVIIIe siècle* [1973], which is usefully summed up in Robert Darnton, *The Kiss of Lamourette: Reflections in Cultural History* [New York, 1990], pp. 279–90); hence evidence is necessarily 'impressionistic'. Such evidence does, however, suggest a strong religiosity which, far from declining in the eighteenth century, may even have grown (Brading, p. 19, writes of a 'quickening of [the Mexican Church's] Christian life'); in which respect Mexico contrasts with some areas of Western Europe. There is also evidence that Mexican religiosity followed some rough spatial patterns: Brading's 'quickening' seems to have affected Michoacan in particular; and the diocese of Guadalajara appears to have been 'more ardently Catholic in conventional ways' than the archdiocese of Mexico (Taylor, *Magistrates of the Sacred*, p. 42). Coastal and tropical regions – where the institutional church was weak – were reckoned to be comparatively indifferent or irreligious (e.g., Brading, pp. 125, 152): a pattern which endured down to the twentieth century.

[271] Taylor, *Magistrates of the Sacred*, pp. 32, 44, 239, 241–3, 263; Brading, *Church and State*, pp. 152–3, 156–7, which recounts the story of a drunk who declared the Virgin Mary to be a whore and, when reminded that 'God gives us to eat', retorted that 'only his cattle gave him to eat'.

than a match for enlightened reform. Jansenist bishops might be disdained, but local *curas* were often popular, and the recruitment of creole – even Indian – priests was brisk.[272] Above all, the rituals and symbols of popular religion flourished: the cult of the saints, fiestas, retablos, ascetic display, religious art and architecture.[273] Much of the literature of the day was religious; the petitions of the Mexico City working class – the vanguard of the colony's industrial proletariat? – were steeped in Catholic terminology. Mexico showed few signs of the dechristianization which affected (some parts of) eighteenth-century Europe.[274] Like the great tree of Tule, the Church had put down deep roots, which sustained its ancient girth; mighty blows might shake the branches, but they could not budge the trunk; and those who dealt the blows were left with weary arms and broken wills. The destruction of such an ancient organism required gradual, insidious, sapping; a policy that would take time and resources. The Bourbons had neither. By 1810 it was possible for the anti-Spanish insurgents to clothe their nebulous patriotism in clerico-religious terms, to invoke the Virgin of Guadalupe (whose cult the Jesuits had fostered), to assert their American identity (which Jesuit intellectuals had written up), to find many of their popular leaders among the priesthood, and to repudiate both the 'heretic' Spanish viceroy and the ungodly, *afrancesado* regime which he represented.

III. The Imperial Liaison

While benefiting fiscally from the colony's autonomous economic and demographic growth, the Bourbons also sought to boost output (notably of bullion) and to ensure a larger surplus for the metropolis. The aim was to curtail Mexico's economic independence (which had grown apace through the seventeenth century), to stifle the growing contraband trade, and thus to reassert Spanish commercial control.

---

[272] Brading, *Church and State*, pp. 37, 116, which notes that the policy of secularizing parishes also resulted in greater recruitment of Indian and mestizo *curas*. In the late colonial period the majority of parish priests were creoles; in the archdiocese of Mexico perhaps 5% were Indian; but even this number outstripped the number of *peninsulares* (around 3%): Taylor, *Magistrates of the Sacred*, pp. 86–7;

[273] Brading, *Church and State*, pp. 31, 42, 44–5.

[274] Deans-Smith, *Bureaucrats, Planters, and Workers*, pp. 222, 234; Taylor, *Magistrates of the Sacred*, p. 450.

Again, the French – Colbertian – model was influential. Bourbon reform of colonial trade involved a degree of liberalization, hence its title: *comercio libre*, free trade. Yet, like mercantilist strategy in general, this was free trade confined within a dirigiste straitjacket. In accordance with Bourbon policy, narrow commercial monopolies would be broken up and a degree of inter-colonial trade permitted; enhanced competition would re-invigorate the system. However, monopoly gave way only to oligopoly (royal charters were distributed more widely, but such charters were still required for colonial commerce); and inter-colonial trade was still strictly regulated in order to serve (perceived) Spanish interests.[275] In Spain itself, the old Cádiz monopoly, which had run the ricketty *flota* system, was broken, enabling other merchant groups to enter the lucrative colonial trade: in the 1730s, about five merchant ships a year docked at Veracruz, all from Cádiz; fifty years later, the average was well over forty, of which Cádiz contributed fewer than half.[276] Basque and Asturian participation in the American trade increased; and the resurgent Catalan textile industry found a guaranteed market in the Indies.[277] But, as Spanish officials lamented, Catalonia could not compete with Britain, whose cheap textiles began to penetrate the colony in defiance of mercantilist controls: from the 1760s, British (contraband) imports increased, and by the 1790s they had become a flood; from the perspective of Mexican textile manufacturing, Salvucci states, 'British capitalism' now stood 'on a plane with smallpox as an imported agent of efficient destruction'.[278]

In the gradual liberalization of inter-colonial trade, Mexico benefited little and late (not before the mid-1770s). Exports to the Caribbean islands rose, as did trade out of Pacific ports like San Blas; Central and South American products (cotton, cacao, indigo) could now legally enter Mexico, though they were still burdened by

[275] MacLachlan and Rodríguez O., *Forging of the Cosmic Race*, pp. 270–4; Garner, *Economic Growth*, pp. 159–60.

[276] Kicza, *Colonial Entrepreneurs*, p. 49.

[277] Herr, *The Eighteenth-Century Revolution in Spain*, pp. 136–43; Lynch, *Bourbon Spain*, pp. 221–3; Brading, *Miners and Merchants*, pp. 106–7, 115, 117.

[278] Salvucci, *Textiles and Capitalism*, p. 4, which may be a touch hyperbolic. Pfefferkorn, *Sonora*, pp. 43–4, notes British, French and Dutch goods arriving in Sonora after a 700-mile overland trek from Veracruz and Mexico City (c. 1760).

duties.[279] By the 1790s Mexican merchants could freely operate out of Spanish ports. Determined to conserve the fruits of the colonies for Spain, however, the regime cracked down on the mighty illicit trade which linked Mexican exporters (e.g., of cochineal) to European, especially British, markets; and they strove to keep out cheap British imports, notably textiles, which easily undersold Spanish goods.[280] In doing so, they stood against the tide of economic history: contraband could not be eliminated.[281] But Bourbon officials made greater efforts than their predecessors to curtail it. To the extent that they succeeded, they forced up prices for consumers and channelled colonial profits to Spanish merchants. At the same time, Mexican manufactures were deliberately restricted. Mexico's domestic market should serve Spain, Viceroy Revillagigedo the Younger argued; the profitable colonial liaison 'would cease the moment European manufactures and produce are no longer required here'.[282] Mexican artisans, such as those of Querétaro, now faced the dual onslaught of cheap Catalan textiles and even cheaper British contraband.[283] Only in Puebla, where an infant cotton-textile industry, drawing its raw material from plantations in nearby Veracruz, supplanted the old woollen-textile workshops, could Mexican producers somewhat buck the trend of de-industrialization; but even here production was highly sensitive to the vicissitudes of war.[284]

As other imperialist powers found, however, it was not easy to sustain the permanent de-industrialization and 'underdevelopment' of large colonies, especially in a period of endemic warfare. The traditional Mexican textile industry – based on wool and the *obraje* – was only partially curbed; with the British naval blockades of the 1790s, which cut off Spanish supplies, it bounced back. Meanwhile, the

[279] Lindley, *Haciendas and Economic Development*, p. 13; Garner, *Economic Growth*, pp. 159, 161.
[280] Hamnett, *Politics and Trade*, pp. 25–8.
[281] Salvucci, Salvucci, and Cohen, 'The Politics of Protection', p. 97, reckon that, as both Mexican demand for imports and Mexican export of bullion grew, in response to global conditions, so contraband came to constitute half of Mexico's foreign trade.
[282] Brading, *Miners and Merchants*, p. 29; for similar colonialist views, see Stanley J. Stein, 'Bureaucracy and Business in the Spanish Empire, 1759–1804: Failure of a Bourbon Reform in Mexico and Peru', *Hispanic American Historical Review*, 61/1 (1981), p. 22; and Jaime E. Rodríguez O., *The Independence of Spanish America* (Cambridge, 1998), p. 30.
[283] Salvucci, *Textiles and Capitalism*, pp. 154–8.
[284] Salvucci, *Textiles and Capitalism*, pp. 135–6, 146–9, 163; Thomson, *Puebla de los Angeles*, pp. 42–6.

blockade halted the supply of mercury and hampered mining. As in the seventeenth century – albeit on a shorter, 'conjectural', scale – the colony now enjoyed a modest relaxation of colonial control, hence a modest degree of import-substitution industrialization. It was now that Puebla cotton production briefly boomed, and the city's weavers were to be seen sporting 'fine cloth and velvet, gold and silver buckles and buttons'. After 1804, however, imports revived again, and Mexican texile production declined.[285] In the one area where a mass demand for industrial manufactures existed (that of textiles), neither Spanish nor Mexican producers could compete with the British. Bourbon mercantilism therefore depended on the maintenance of an artificial colonial monopoly, but – as the battle of Trafalgar definitively showed – Bourbon maritime power was, despite hefty spending, quite incapable of maintaining such a monopoly.[286]

Within Mexico, too, *comercio libre* brought a switch from regulated monopoly to regulated oligopoly. The Mexico City merchants guild, the *consulado*, a prime beneficiary of Habsburg patrimonialism, which combined extensive commercial and quasi-governmental powers, was stripped of its monopoly privileges. Rival *consulados* were established at Veracruz, Guadalajara and Puebla. The old commercial liaison between Mexico City and Cádiz/Seville, which had dominated transatlantic trade for over two centuries, gave way to a more complex, multistranded network of relationships, linking diverse Spanish ports and mercantile interests to their colonial partners, clients and customers.[287] Thus, Campeche's trade with Havana – 'formerly of a sporadic and frequently clandestine nature' – boomed after 1770.[288] Legitimate (non-contraband) trade increased, to the benefit of Crown revenue.[289] In that these new relationships were

[285] Thomson, *Puebla de los Angeles*, p. 42.

[286] Bourbon naval spending averaged about 18% of total government expenditure between c. 1750 and 1790; however, this sizeable investment, which roughly doubled the number of ships of line, had the paradoxical effect of inducing timidity, for 'the navy was too expensive and too badly led to expose to battle': Lynch, *Bourbon Spain*, pp. 166, 176–8, 312–17 (quote, p. 16). The final debacle of Trafalgar (October 1805) perhaps proved that discretion had indeed been the better part of valour.

[287] Brading, *Miners and Merchants*, pp. 114–15; Garner, *Economic Growth*, p. 189ff.

[288] Patch, *Maya and Spaniard*, pp. 204–5.

[289] The figures are difficult to unravel. It is clear, however, that Mexican exports grew rapidly in the last quarter of the eighteenth century, which coincided with a 'burst of collection of revenue': Garner, *Economic Growth*, pp. 161, 218. *Alcabala* (internal customs) receipts rose from 1.5m pesos a year in the period 1765–77 to 3.2m in 1778–90: Garner, p. 234. For contemporary estimates of the free trade and revenue nexus, see the reports of Carlos de Urrutia and

largely controlled by Spanish merchants (indeed, a key feature of the later Bourbon era was the burgeoning of merchant capital, much of it Spanish),[290] Bourbon policy did nothing to alleviate Mexico's trade dependency; on the contrary, it tended to enhance it, as it was designed to do. But the rewards were not neatly divided along ethnic lines. Creole interests benefited from commercial growth and demand (this point will be developed later); conversely, established Spanish merchants were evicted from their old, featherbedded, patrimonial niches. Antonio Bassoco, for example, a rich merchant-landlord, took a heavy loss as *comercio libre* undercut Spanish prices for his Mexican products.[291] Like others of his kind denied their old monopolistic protection, Bassoco retreated from commerce and bought his way into mining; the mines' late colonial growth thus depended in part on infusions of merchant capital that had been driven out of the cutthroat commercial sector.

The mines also benefited from direct government encouragement. Mining entrepreneurs were now organized in their own corporate association, the Real Tribunal de la Minería (1777), which conferred special judicial privileges. In addition, the Crown supplied cheap mercury and lent support to mining technology and education.[292] Such governmental inputs were hardly decisive, but they further stimulated a resurgent industry; and they indicated, once again, that Bourbon policy was one of enlightened economic despotism, of state-regulated competition, rather than of outright *laisser-faire*. That is, the state encouraged limited areas of *laisser-faire*, within which the beneficial effects of competition were sought; but stout walls – corporatist, colonialist and customary[293] – barred the way to a general and

Humboldt in Enrique Florescano and Isabel Gil Sánchez, *Descripciones económicas de Nueva España, 1784–1817* (Mexico, 1973), pp. 74, 162.

290 Greenow, *Credit and Socioeconomic Change*, p. 153; Morin, *Michoacan*, pp. 163, 183; Pastor, *Campesinos y reformas*, pp. 290–1.

291 Beset by commercial failure, Bassoco turned to usury, thus joining the ranks of a new 'class of professional money-lenders' who emerged in the twilight of the colonial era: Brading, *Miners and Merchants*, p. 126; Greenow, *Credit and Socioeconomic Change*, p. 49.

292 Howe, *The Mining Guild of New Spain*; Garner, *Economic Growth*, pp. 124–40. On the crucial role of mercury, see Kendall W. Brown, 'The Spanish Imperial Mercury Trade and the American Mining Expansion under the Bourbon Monarchy', in Andrien and Johnson, *The Political Economy of Spanish America*, pp. 147–50.

293 It is a recurrent feature of 'enlightened' reformist projects that they encounter opposition not only from privileged elites but also from popular groups, for whom 'custom' can represent a defence against deleterious political and economic rationalization (hence, for example, the miners' defence of the *partido*, or peasant adherence to corporate land tenure). Adherence to

genuine espousal of free trade. In fostering competition, the Bourbons raised up rival corporate interests (such as the *consulados*); in
seeking revenue, they created new monopolies, such as the tobacco
monopoly, an institution which displayed the 'glaring contradictions'
characteristic of Bourbon policy.[294]

In the crucial – and still dominant – agrarian sector, Bourbon policy was short-term in conception and fluctuating in effect. Flirtations
with physiocratic theory – which gave precedence to agriculture –
were never consummated in practice; agriculture remained the
'stepchild' of Bourbon policy.[295] Mexican commodity exports were
subject to arbitrary controls: Spain strove to stimulate the production of strategic goods, like flax and hemp, in defiance of economic
logic; it sought to inhibit Mexico's sugar-refining, thus ensuring that
Mexico's potential as a sugar exporter remained untapped, even in
the wake of the Haitian revolution.[296] Agriculture, like industry, remained subservient to metropolitan needs; and both (which together
comprised some 85 per cent of colonial output) were considered ancillary to mining and commerce, the profitable, Spanish-controlled
sectors of the economy.[297] The Spanish tail wagged the colonial dog,
as was inevitable, given Bourbon imperial policy and Spanish industrial backwardness. No less inevitable was the resentment which
this blatant colonialism inspired within Mexico, as in other colonies
subject to the stiff mercantilism of the eighteenth century.[298] And, if

custom – often instrumental and selective in its form – should not be confused with purblind
popular conservatism. For a suggestive comparative critique of grandiose schemes of 'state-
initiated social engineering', such as the Bourbon reforms, see James C. Scott, *Seeing Like a
State* (New Haven, 1998) (quote from p. 4).

[294] Deans-Smith, *Bureaucrats, Planters, and Workers*, pp. 174–5.

[295] Eric Van Young, 'The Age of Paradox: Mexican Agriculture at the End of the Colonial Period,
1750–1810', in Jacobsen and Pühle, *The Economies of Mexico and Peru*, p. 67 ('stepchild'). On
flirtations with physiocracy: Thomson, *Puebla de los Angeles*, pp. 22, 24. The flirtation seems
to have proceeded further in Spain's Andean realms, where the Bourbon desire to liberate
potentially productive peasants from the dead hand of landlord and official coercion was
more pronounced: Jacobsen, *Mirages of Transition*, p. 88.

[296] Florescano and Gil Sánchez, 'La época de las reformas borbónicas', pp. 229–30, 271.

[297] According to the estimates of José María Quirós (1817), agriculture represented 61% of Mexican production, industry 27% and mining 12%: Florescano and Gil Sánchez, *Descripciones
ecónomicas*, pp. 261–4. Brading, *Miners and Merchants*, p. 18, offers a slightly amended version
(following Fernando Rozenweig): 56%, 29%, 15%.

[298] McFarlane, *The British in the Americas*, pp. 252–61, describes British efforts to increase control
and taxation in North America which, of course, culminated in revolution; yet British North
America was relatively lightly taxed and governed compared to its Spanish counterpart.

this classic colonial division pitted Spanish beneficiaries (merchants and officials) against Mexican victims (creole landlords, manufacturers and tax-payers), Bourbon policy also provoked critics and enemies in other sectors of society. With the loss of Mexico City's commercial monopoly, new mercantile groups flourished, in Veracruz, Guadalajara and lesser towns. The rise of merchant capital became a hallmark of the later Bourbon era. Vigorous and vocal, these new merchant interests challenged both the traditional economic centralization of the colony and the new administrative centralization which the Bourbons were eager to impose. They contributed to a growing sense of regional identity (defined, often enough, in anti–Mexico City terms), which was to underpin the federalism of the early nineteenth century, especially in states like Jalisco and Veracruz.[299] Bourbon policy, while seeking a reinforcement of the central state, thus fostered a diversification and 'thickening' of civil society: a dangerous combination, which was to jeopardize the Bourbon project just as, a hundred years later, it would jeopardize the analogous Porfirian project.

This tentative analogy could be pressed further. The Bourbons fitted within a long tradition of sociopolitical engineers, who, exalting law above custom, sought to fasten their grand, alien, abstract scheme upon the recalcitrant people and terrain of Mexico.[300] Like others within this tradition (we could start with the millenarian Franciscans and work through nineteenth-century liberals to twentieth-century revolutionaries) they found this a thankless, self-defeating task. Some Bourbon bigwigs, like Viceroy Bucareli – a pragmatist, sandwiched between the two ideologues Gálvez and Revillagigedo – remained skeptical throughout. Bucareli soft-pedalled reforms and conciliated the population, especially the creole elite. Like British imperial viceroys, reeling from the impact of the Indian Mutiny, he considered radical reform to be dangerous and provocative. In similar fashion, the *oidor* Blas de Basaraz, ordered

---

[299] Greenow, *Credit and Socioeconomic Change*, p. 163; Hamnett, *Politics and Trade*, pp. 98–103. Kicza, *Colonial Entrepreneurs*, p. 94, sees the relationship between Mexico City and Veracruz merchants as less conflictual. Morin, *Michoacan*, p. 20, offers a lyrical example of provincial – *michoacano* – patriotism; for the Guadalajara region, see Brian Connaughton, *Ideología y sociedad en Guadalajara (1788–1853)* (Mexico, 1992), pp. 43, 108.

[300] Taylor, *Magistrates of the Sacred*, pp. 13–14, offers a neat summary.

by Gálvez to mete out exemplary punishment to the Indian rebels of Papantla in 1767, tempered repressive policy with pragmatic conciliation.[301] Such caution was justified. Too many Bourbon officials were more naively optimistic, more myopically zealous. Hence, in the main, the enlightened Bourbons, like the millenarian Franciscans who had preceded them and the liberals and revolutionaries who would follow, experienced more setbacks than they did success. That is not to say that they were ineffectual; they had a profound impact on Mexico's history; but they did not achieve their ambitious objectives and, in the process of falling short, they provoked resentment and recrimination.[302]

The new Bourbon bureaucracy of supposedly loyal and efficient salaried officials soon acquired the faults of its predecessor. The dozen intendants, paid a decent salary, conformed to the bureaucratic norm: they were keen, innovative, loyal to the central government – and therefore usually unpopular. The lower tier of *subdelegados*, the crucial intermediaries between state and people, received a cut of the tribute revenue; in consequence, like the *alcaldes mayores* whom they replaced, the *subdelegados* grafted, extorted and served as the clients and allies of powerful local interests, landlords and merchants. In Oaxaca they connived at mercantile exploitation of the Indian peasantry; in Morelos they speculated in the grain trade; around Lake Chapala they collaborated with expansionist landlords; at Papantla and Acayucan, in Veracruz, they became the targets of popular protest.[303] Bureacratic salaries were too small, local temptations too enticing, for the *subdelegados* to achieve the kind of impersonal, Weberian-style bureaucracy to which the Bourbons aspired. Such aspirations could achieve limited success: the General Indian Court, which processed Indians' complaints, was

[301] Brading, *Miners and Merchants*, pp. 46–7 (Bucareli), though for a less flattering view, see Pastor, *Campesinos y reformas*, p. 193; Felipe Castro Gutiérrez, 'Del paternalismo autoritario al autoritarismo burocrático: Los éxitos y fracasos de José de Gálvez (1764–1767)', in Jaime E. Rodríguez O., ed., *Mexico in the Age of Democratic Revolutions, 1750–1850* (Boulder, 1994), p. 30. Compare, too, the viceregal prevarications over the *repartimiento* in Yucatán: Patch, *Maya and Spaniard*, pp. 164–5.

[302] Taylor, *Magistrates of the Sacred*, p. 542, n. 7, offers a concise review of recent debates.

[303] Garner, *Economic Growth*, p. 233 (graft); Patch, *Maya and Spaniard*, p. 166 (*subdelegados*); Pastor, *Campesinos y reformas*, pp. 273–5 (Oaxaca); Martin, *Rural Society*, p. 117 (Morelos); Taylor, 'Rural Unrest in Central Jalisco', p. 227 (Lake Chapala); Hamnett, *Roots of Insurgency*, pp. 78–80 (Oaxaca, Papantla and Acayucan); Stein, 'Bureaucracy and Business'.

partially reformed; the policing and provision of public charity in Mexico City were tightened up; the tobacco monopoly was run with a dour efficiency worthy of Mr Gradgrind.[304]

Frequently, however, Bourbon bureaucracy was cannibalized by old Habsburg patrimonial practices – which, we might say, more faithfully reflected the character of colonial society, with its profound ethnic, class and regional differences, its cellular, corporative and particularist tendencies. The state, in other words, lacked the power and autonomy to refashion civil society – although it could certainly shake up civil society in the process. Abuses, such as illegal forced labour and the old *repartimiento* of goods, persisted, despite enlightened official prohibitions.[305] Reformist intendants, like Manuel Flon of Puebla, found their efforts 'contested, contradicted, and resisted' by lower officials, justices and *caciques* (again, more recent parallels spring to mind).[306] And even those at the top – sometimes those most earnest for reform – succumbed to the lure of profit: in Puebla, Flon illegally built up a small economic empire based on landholdings and flour mills; José de Gálvez, chief architect of the Bourbon administrative reforms, was a notorious nepotist.[307]

Resistance to reform was strongest in the sprawling, serrated countryside of the colony. If the cities were, to an extent, politically malleable, the countryside proved the graveyard of enlightened reformism, both Bourbon and later liberal. In the cities, at least, Bourbon officialdom could indulge its penchant for public works and public order. Taxes were raised and police were put on the streets. An incipient system of state welfare – evident in orphanages, hospitals, the official pawnshop – began to supplant religious charity, at least in Mexico City; bureaucrats delighted in the 'beautiful

---

[304] Borah, *Justice by Insurance*, p. 296; Scardaville, '(Habsburg) Law'; Deans-Smith, *Bureaucrats, Planters, and Workers*, ch. 6.

[305] Hamnett, *Politics and Trade*, pp. 150–1; Borah, *Justice by Insurance*, pp. 133–4, 150–1; Pastor, *Campesinos y reformas*, pp. 273–5; Chance, *Conquest of the Sierra*, pp. 103–10; Patch, *Maya and Spaniard*, pp. 165–6. These examples are heavily drawn, as might be expected, from southern Mexico (Oaxaca and Yucatán especially): a zone of relatively weak haciendas, where the direct exploitation of Indian peasant communities by Spanish officialdom prevailed.

[306] Brading, *Miners and Merchants*, pp. 78–9.

[307] Thomson, *Puebla de los Angeles*, p. 78; Brading, *First America*, p. 478. Borah, *Justice by Insurance*, pp. 385–7, illustrates, in the career of the late colonial 'career bureaucrat' Hipólito Villarroel, an ambiguous – but perhaps not unusual? – combination of enlightened ideas, reformist drive, virulent ethnocentrism (even racism) and personal corruption.

and elegant' neoclassical building of the tobacco monopoly, where six thousand uniformed workers laboured in light and airy conditions.[308] In Guanajuato, the intendant Riaño boasted in 1792, his new ordering of urban society (involving the dissolution of the guilds, the reform of the grain supply, the redrawing of administrative boundaries) had tamed the once factious plebs of the city and created a peaceful, orderly obedient community, through which, he crowed, 'I walk...without any other defence than my cane of office and my hat'.[309] Eighteen years later, Riaño was shot in the head while fruitlessly defending the Guanajuato public granary – a new, typically Bourbon, neoclassical pile, hastily turned into a royalist fortress – against the insurgent hordes of Hidalgo.

In these urban contexts the Bourbon political achievement was real, if precarious. In much of the countryside, however, it was yet more superficial and elusive. Rather than establish a loyal, financially sound, efficient bureaucracy, which could bind the colony to Spain in a tight, profitable union, the Bourbons in fact created a more costly, rapacious, corrupt, Spanish and, above all, illegitimate official class. In the process, they alienated many in colonial society: the old *alcaldes* and their commercial partners, ousted by reform; the Church and the merchants of the Mexico City *consulado* (both 'prime victims of reforming zeal');[310] the Jesuits and the Jesuit-educated, the devout, and the beneficiaries of both Church credit and Church charity; tax-payers, both Indian tributaries and urban consumers; miners, rioters and rebels who felt the smack of firm government as never before. Resentment therefore spanned a wide swathe of colonial society and was not the monopoly of any one group, class or region. Indians, mestizos, creoles and even some Spaniards chafed under the new administration; the rich were levied as well as the poor. Regions, especially those which combined economic dynamism with hostility to central direction, began to display proto-federalist tendencies. Socioeconomic change coupled with political centralization proved to be potent stimuli of protest in the years before 1810, as they would in the years before 1910. And all this the Bourbons attempted in an

[308] Deans-Smith, *Bureaucrats, Planters, and Workers*, pp. 180–1, 205; see also Scardaville, '(Habsburg) Law'.
[309] Brading, *Miners and Merchants*, pp. 244–5.
[310] Brading, *Miners and Merchants*, p. 119.

era of mounting great power rivalry and recurrent global warfare. 'In a corrupted age', as the Marquess of Halifax, a first-hand witness of the debacle of British absolutism, observed, 'the putting the world in order would breed confusion'; so, too, the Bourbons, even as they pursued a risky and expensive foreign policy, sought to put their colonial world in order, generating severe tensions and provoking recurrent popular protests.[311]

If popular grievances ran deep, intra-elite conflicts were also significant. A key feature of the Bourbon era – and a key cause of the eventual break with Spain – was the growing hostility between native Spaniard (*peninsular*) and American-born Spaniard (*criollo*, or creole), which Bourbon policy exacerbated. So, at least, runs the conventional view. *Peninsular*-creole friction, of course, was nothing new. During the seventeenth century major disputes had flared up – in Mexico City in 1624, in Puebla in the 1640s – in which this tension was apparent.[312] There had also been long-running factional battles, fuelled by the same antagonism, between secular and regular clergy, between viceroys and bishops, and between rival mendicant factions. This conflict, we have seen, was overlaid with crude stereotypes, typical of colonial relationships, which served to sharpen the division. In the eyes of the European, the creole was – like the Indian whose American birthplace he shared – idle, feckless and decadent. Creole friars were – to their more severe European brothers – dissolute and worldly. Even American flora and fauna were inferior, tainted by their New World origins. Such prejudices – some as old as the colony – were now reinforced, as prejudices often are, by learned writers and pseudo-scientists: the French naturalist, the comte de Buffon, and the 'renegade Dutch cleric', Cornelius de Pauw, who built an edifice of ethnocentrism on the twin foundations of climatic determinism and American exceptionality.[313] According to

---

[311] The Marquess of Halifax, *Complete Works* (ed., John Kenyon; Harmondsworth, 1969), p. 231. Richard Garner, a sober economic historian, concludes, on the basis of contemporary reports (c. 1805), that Mexico's 'social order was on the verge of disintegration' (*Economic Growth*, p. 246); this view should be set against the hypothesis – currently in vogue? – that the collapse of colonial rule derived largely or primarily from the external shock of 1808 – the Napoleonic invasion of Spain, which subverted a fairly stable, even consensual, colonial system.

[312] Brading, *Church and State*, p. 27; Israel, *Race, Class, and Politics*, pp. 84–94; Leonard, *Baroque Times*, pp. 42–3.

[313] Brading, *First America*, pp. 428–32 (quote p. 429).

de Pauw, American dogs could not bark; American women were in-
fertile; American men were 'deficient in ardour, often impotent, and
much given to sodomy'.[314] If these were ancient Indian deficiencies,
creoles nurtured in the enervating tropics soon acquired them too.
Nature conspired with nurture to produce a feckless creole elite,
seigneurs with 'white hands' who were 'reared to think of themselves
as gentlemen and were generally unfit for any trade or form of productive work'.[315] Spain's Bourbon administrators, keen to shake up
the flaccid colony, readily subscribed to such notions. The prejudices
of Gálvez, like those of many lesser officials, 'would have done credit
to an Algerian colon'; what is more, they were translated into policy,
as Gálvez aggressively promoted *peninsulares* and froze out supposedly feckless creoles – from the courts, the military, the bureaucracy
and the Church.[316] So strong and pervasive were these notions – of
creole incapacity and contrasting Spanish efficiency – that, it has
been suggested, they came to colour subsequent historiography: the
subjective prejudices of the Spanish colonial mentality insidiously
become 'objective' evaluations of creole socio-psychological make-
up.[317]

To the creole, of course, the European appeared as a privileged interloper, enjoying political power out of all proportion to
his talent, his local expertise and (often) his material assets. The
creoles, too, produced their intellectual champions, who celebrated
the history, culture and achievements of New Spain, rebutting
European slights. In doing so, they harked back to the Aztecs, appropriating them for a distinctive Mexican culture, which embraced
Indian, mestizo and creole; they defended contemporary Indians
from charges of inherent inferiority; they eulogized the flora, fauna
and natural landscape of the Americas; and they fostered devotion

---

[314] Brading, *First America*, p. 430: note that the sodomy charge reprised an old Spanish prejudice first levelled against native Americans at the time of the Conquest: Todorov, *Conquest of
America*, p. 150; Díaz, *Conquest of New Spain*, pp. 222, 225; Pagden, *Hernán Cortés*, p. 37.

[315] Brading, *First America*, p. 574, quoting the notorious criollophobe, Juan López de Cancelada.

[316] Brading, *Miners and Merchants*, pp. 38, 111.

[317] See the comments of Lindley, *Haciendas and Economic Development*, pp. 115–16. Certainly, a
great deal of modern Latin American historiography (and some political 'science') has been
blighted by glib 'attitudinal' explanations – that is, 'explanations' of events and processes
which rely on reified (and often imaginary) ingrained attitudes (feudal, fatalistic, violent,
personalist, macho, authoritarian, etc.). Stuart Sutherland, *Irrationality: The Enemy Within*
(Harmondsworth, 1992), pp. 191–6, offers a perceptive critique of such 'dispositional' explanations of human behaviour.

to the Virgin of Guadalupe, the official patroness of Mexico, symbol of the Mexican people's divine favour, whose cult flourished during the Bourbon years.[318] Lay publicists played their part in the creole counterblast, but the most vocal and telling critics of European ethnocentrism were the Jesuits, trained intellectuals whose expulsion typified Spanish colonial tyranny, while at the same time generating a diaspora of disgruntled patriots. Clavijero, the most influential, took on Buffon and de Pauw directly: the Mexican climate, he argued, was benign, and its animals were prolific; the Aztecs had built a civilization 'greatly superior to that which the Phoenicians and Carthaginians found in our Spain'; Nahuatl was 'as euphonious a language as German or Polish'; and, if the Indians of Bourbon New Spain were degenerate, this derived from oppression and denial of education: 'who', Clavijero asked, 'would recognize in the contemporary Greeks, groaning under the rule of the Ottoman Turks, the descendants of Plato and Pericles?' Clearly, affirmations of creole 'proto-patriotism' could easily spill over into anticolonial subversion.[319] Patriotic protestations of Mexico's distinctive worth – of its human and material resources, of its rich culture, history and landscape – did not necessarily embody a demand for independence; but they certainly challenged European prejudice and authority, pointing up the stifled potential of the colony and, implicitly at least, advocating a measure of Mexican autonomy, of colonial 'home rule'.

Peninsular-creole rivalry, however, should not be exaggerated or reified. For centuries, *peninsulares* had monopolized the viceroyship (though not the Audiencias, the *cabildos* or the cathedral chapters, all of which contained a strong creole presence). Most, but by no means all, bishops had been *peninsulares*. However, there had been *peninsular* bishops, like Palafox of Puebla, who had sided with creole interests against *peninsular* officials and mendicants;[320] equally, the early Jesuits, mostly *peninsulares*, had been vocal champions of

[318] The discovery, in 1790, beneath the main square of Mexico City, of the Aztec *piedra de sol*, the great stone-carved calendar wheel, was a providential find for creole Aztecófilos: Brading, *First America*, pp. 462–4; note also pp. 447–8 (South American creole apologists) and, regarding the creole origins and espousal of Guadalupanismo, Poole, *Our Lady of Guadalupe*, pp. 1–2, 10–11, 82, 106, 127ff.

[319] On Clavijero: Brading, *First America*, pp. 450–62.

[320] Brading, *First America*, pp. 230–2, which argues that Palafox's partiality towards creoles stemmed from his 'profound sense of aristocratic rights', which he believed would provide a surer foundation for colonial rule than corrupt officialdom.

the creole elite, who were often generous benefactors as well as erstwhile pupils of the Order. Thus, while factional divisions within the
colony were partially drawn along *peninsular*-creole lines, the resulting factions were far from ethnically homogeneous; ethnic identities were cross-cut by those of class, region and family. For, as
recent research has tended to stress, *peninsulares* and creoles often collaborated closely, even during the Bourbon era. The complex cycle whereby merchant capital (often Spanish) sustained hacienda production (often creole), in terms of both short-term credit
and long-term investment, required persistent economic collaboration, frequently reinforced by bonds of marriage and *compadrazgo*.
The spectacle of Spanish merchants marrying creole heiresses was a
colonial commonplace.[321] Given the nature of the *peninsular*-creole
distinction it invited constant blurring. Though these were ascriptive
identities, determined by birth, they were not sustained by caste-
like endogamy; quite the reverse. 'In many cases', Brading writes,
'the division between gachupín and creole was soon resolved into
little more than a distinction of generations: creole lawyers were
often the sons of gachupín merchants and gachupín merchants were
equally often the sons-in-law of creole miners'.[322]

Economic and familial collaboration was much more marked –
albeit less spectacular and historically newsworthy – than overt conflict. The battle for office in Church and state, which certainly divided *peninsular* and creole and which, under the Bourbons, swung
in favour of the former, was thus offset by the alliance for profit which
joined the two in powerful local oligarchies. If a strong 'clannish con-
fraternity' united *peninsulares* – especially *peninsular* bureaucrats –
in New Spain,[323] no less powerful sentiments linked local oligarchies,
peninsular and creole, in collective opposition to peasants and urban
plebs (who themselves spanned the ethnic spectrum)[324] and, sometimes, in regional opposition to Mexico City. Hamnett suggests that
we view the late colonial elite in terms not of a strict European/creole
dichotomy, ascriptively determined by birth, but rather of acquired

---

[321] Brading, *Miners and Merchants*, pp. 312–13; Greenow, *Credit and Socioeconomic Change*,
   pp. 118, 143.
[322] Brading, *Miners and Merchants*, pp. 303–4.
[323] Brading, *Miners and Merchants*, p. 214.
[324] Hence, since the sixteenth century, a class of impoverished Spaniards existed: Cope, *Limits
   of Racial Domination*, p. 21; Deans-Smith, *Bureaucrats, Planters, and Workers*, p. 178; Pastor,
   Campesinos y reformas, p. 335.

interests, which separated the 'Mexican or resident elite' – those, European as well as creole, who were 'deeply rooted in New Spain by virtue of their financial, professional, and matrimonial commitments' – and the 'bureaucratic elite', transient European officials, army officers and clerics, who were essentially colonial birds-of-passage.[325] The picture is therefore complex but familiar, particularly in respect of certain colonial societies:[326] individuals, families and groups were 'cross-pressured' by conflicting interests: a loosely class allegiance was cross-cut by ethnic ties, and vice versa. Creoles and mestizos might share anti-*gachupín* sentiments; but elite creoles and Europeans had a common interest in order, property and profit. As the War of Independence showed, pressing circumstances would dictate which allegiance prevailed, and when.

Bourbon policy, by reinforcing metropolitan political control and commercial hegemony, tended to favour the *peninsular* interest: the Jesuits were expelled (1767), the *obras pías* were expropriated (1804), the courts and audiencias were Hispanized, and the new intendancies and other bureaucratic posts (e.g., in the tobacco monopoly) went disproportionately to *peninsulares*: nine out of the first twelve intendants were European Spaniards. But there were creole beneficiaries of Bourbon rule too: those enriched by the boom in mining and real estate; and recipients of direct administrative favours, such as the miners' guild, the new creole officer class and creole merchants who capitalized on the opportunities of *comercio libre*. Equally, there were Spanish victims: priests, members of the Mexico City *consulado* and officials ousted in the administrative overhaul of the 1780s.[327]

IV. Towards Independence

In summary, the Bourbon era saw a marked erosion of the implicit social contract which linked rulers and ruled, elites and masses,

---

[325] Hamnett, *Roots of Insurgency*, p. 19; see also Luis Villoro, *El proceso ideológico de la revolución de Independencia* (Mexico, 1986), pp. 22–34.

[326] Compare the American Revolution, which cannot be viewed as a simple 'struggle against an external power', but which involved emerging cleavages within the colony, hence a series of disputes 'not only over "home rule" but also...over "who would rule at home"': McFarlane, *The British in the Americas*, pp. 266–7, citing Carl Becker.

[327] On the Hispanization of officialdom, see Brading, *Miners and Merchants*, pp. 33–44, 53, 64; on creole survival, pp. 325–6 (militia), 331 (miners' guild); and *peninsular* victims, pp. 119, 341–2. See also Taylor, *Magistrates of the Sacred*, pp. 400–1, 421.

landlord and peasant; it also witnessed new tensions in the colonial contract which bound Mexico to Spain.[328] These tensions were not terminal. For all their differences, creole and *peninsular* had overriding common interests, especially when popular rebellion threatened the internal social contract. Creole 'nationalism' was far from requiring the establishment of a Mexican nation: it sought, rather, a relaxation of metropolitan control, a greater measure of home rule.[329] But with the political and international crisis of 1808 – an abrupt, conjunctural event – these tensions were suddenly aggravated, and the *peninsular*-creole distinction acquired a fresh, somewhat artificial, clarity – artificial because the two sides were still by no means clearly demarcated or clearly polarized by contrasting political stances. In 1808 the colonial contract snapped; then, after a pause of only two years, the social contract was violently annulled. First the legitimacy of the colonial tie foundered, then the legitimacy of the colonial social order. But these dual crises, though initially complimentary, were in many respects antithetical: they tended to cancel each other out. The colonial rupture triggered social upheaval; but the latter, in turn, made for a renewal of the colonial tie. Creole-*peninsular* differences were superficial compared with the common stake which both ethnic elites had in the social order. Creoles in Guanajuato genuinely deplored the massacre of Spaniards by the insurgent populace: 'our interests and wealth were mixed with theirs', one declared, 'and indeed depended upon them absolutely. In their misfortune we were all involved'.[330] Conversely, the plebeian class solidarity which, uniting Indians and castes, had been incipiently evident in the Mexico City riots of the seventeenth century, now became more widespread, especially in regions of greater mobility, miscegenation

---

[328] As contemporaries recognized: recall Mier's comment (n. 1 above); and the assorted writings of Bishop Abad y Queipo, a Spanish prelate resident in Mexico from 1784 who, in Brading's words, 'frame[d] the first real analysis of colonial society', lamenting Bourbon anticlericalism, social inequality, Spanish privilege and the plight of a rural population who 'groan under the weight of indigence, ignorance and abjection': Brading, *Church and State*, pp. 228–34.

[329] MacLachlan and Rodríguez O., *Forging of the Cosmic Race*, pp. 294–5, 301–3; Jaime Rodríguez O., 'From Royal Subject to Republican Citizen: The Role of the Autonomists in the Independence of Mexico', in Rodríguez O., *The Independence of Mexico and the Creation of the New Nation*, pp. 19–43.

[330] José María de Septién y Montero, 'on behalf of the [largely creole] town council', quoted in Brading, *Miners and Merchants*, p. 319.

and commercialization.[331] In the face of a dual, social-colonial crisis like that of 1810, when plebeian protest exploded, the need to maintain social order united *peninsular* and creole more than the dispute over the colonial order divided them. As we will see, it was creole arms and creole repression which, above all, achieved the defeat of the popular rebels and the reassertion of social control.

The Bourbon project was implemented in a period when domestic Mexican tensions, mentioned earlier, were paralleled by global change and upheaval – the 'democratic revolution' which spanned the last third of the eighteenth century and beyond.[332] While European (especially British) economic growth exerted a strong influence on the Atlantic trade, European (especially French) ideas permeated Spain's colonies, and the example of revolution – North American, then French – cast a long shadow. For some historians, the diffusion of Enlightenment ideas in Mexico, as in the rest of Spanish America, generated dissent and rebellion. Bourbon officials were not the only people seduced by Enlightenment values, and these values contained the potential for political dissidence as well as political reform or scientific progress. According to this view, Montesquieu, Voltaire and Rousseau became the intellectual gravediggers of the colonial order.[333] Certainly their ideas circulated, affording a basis for a critique of that order: on the one hand, Enlightenment thinkers stressed natural rights and even popular sovereignty, which fundamentally challenged any colonial and absolutist system of government; on the other hand, thinkers like Montesquieu, emphasizing the utility of ancient liberties and intermediate powers, offered a more traditional, a more English, perhaps even a more Spanish, critique of despotism.[334] In response, the colonial regime took steps

---

[331] Cope, *Limits of Racial Domination*, p. 22; Taylor, *Magistrates of the Sacred*, p. 177; Brading, *Haciendas and Ranchos*, p. 47; Hamnett, *Roots of Insurgency*, pp. 12–13; Hamill, *The Hidalgo Revolt*, pp. 50–2.

[332] R. R. Palmer, *The Age of the Democratic Revolution: Political History of Europe and America, 1760–1800* (2 vols., Princeton, 1959–64); and, for an interesting fiscal-financial-climatic interpretation of the period, see David Hackett Fischer, *The Great Wave: Price Revolutions and the Rhythms of History* (Oxford, 1996), pp. 142–56. Rodríguez O., *Mexico in the Age of Democratic Revolutions*, is, despite its title, resolutely Mexicocentric in focus.

[333] Charles C. Griffin, 'The Enlightenment and Latin American Independence', in Arthur P. Whitaker, ed., *Latin America and the Enlightenment* (Ithaca, 1961, first pubd. 1942), pp. 120–1.

[334] Griffin, 'The Enlightenment', pp. 123–4; Rodríguez O., 'From Royal Subject', pp. 22–5, and *The Independence of Spanish America*, pp. 46–7.

to curb intellectual dissent. The Inquisition was roused from its recent torpor and, late in life, began to root out political dissidence
as well as religious heresy (Hidalgo, along with other leaders of the
insurgency, was among its victims).[335] More important, the secular
authorities, keen to impose social control while usurping erstwhile
clerical functions, cracked down on political and intellectual dissent: the Mexico City theatre came under close scrutiny; a 1790 play,
México segunda vez conquistado (Mexico twice conquered), which
treated the martyrdom of the Aztec prince Cuauhtémoc at the hands
of the conquistadors, was banned after one performance.[336]

Theatrical performances might be banned, but subversive ideas
were as difficult to keep out of the colony as contraband textiles.
There was a constant flow of 'officials, merchants, emigrants and
scientists' who came from Spain to Mexico, bringing books in their
sea-chests and ideas in their heads.[337] Foreigners – British, North
American, above all, French – brought news and information; a
British exile, fleeing Australia in 1796, passed through California,
where he 'delighted the governor with first-hand tales of the
French Revolution'.[338] Indeed, ideas of popular sovereignty and self-
government were reinforced by the examples of the American and
French Revolutions (though the French Revolution also inspired
conservative fear and Catholic loathing);[339] and the international
wars which flowed from these revolutions made the maintenance
of ideological control all the more difficult. Just as trade policies
fluctuated, so did official censorship. In 1791, the Spanish government, alarmed by the French Revolution, tightened its controls
on the press; a year later these were relaxed, allowing 'news from
France and revolutionary propaganda to pour into Spain', whence
they took flight to the New World.[340] Bans and denunciations also

[335] Hamill, *The Hidalgo Revolt*, pp. 3–5, 65–7; Viqueira Albán, *Relajados o reprimidos?*, p. 115.
Brading's evidence – 132 cases from the diocese of Michoacan, spanning the years 1740–
1803 – displays an Inquisition still chiefly concerned with bigamy, blasphemy and witchcraft;
it is not clear, however, whether the sample is representative (see *Church and State*, pp. 155–6).

[336] Viqueira Albán, *Relajados o reprimidos?*, pp. 111–14.

[337] Roland D. Hussey, 'Traces of French Enlightenment in Colonial Hispanic America', in
Whitaker, *Latin America and the Enlightenment*, pp. 28–9.

[338] Hussey, 'Traces', pp. 31–2.

[339] Arthur P. Whitaker, 'The Dual Role of the Enlightenment in Latin America', in Whitaker,
Latin America and the Enlightenment, p. 19; Griffin, 'The Enlightenment', p. 136.

[340] MacLachlan and Rodríguez O., *Forging of the Cosmic Race*, p. 295.

had ambiguous effects. In Mexico, as in Spain, proscriptions – of Rousseau, for example – gave 'subversive' authors free publicity.[341]

Meanwhile, as already mentioned, the colony experienced the maturation of a form of 'creole patriotism', an assertion of Mexican values and symbols which implicitly – and occasionally explicitly – challenged Spanish rule and *peninsular hauteur*. Mexico's Aztec past became an object of study and veneration (hence the appeal of Cuauhtémoc's martrydom); Mexican 'proto-patriots' not only rebutted Spanish ethnocentric prejudices but also stressed the economic potential of New Spain, thwarted by colonial mercantilism. By means of scientific groups and institutes, they sought to realize this potential: the Basque Society of Friends of the Country (sociedad de amigos del país) had a significant Mexican following, and its Mexico City membership almost equalled that of Madrid.[342] Alongside this rational, enlightened, 'developmental' nationalism (which was closely akin to official Bourbon philosophy),[343] there flourished the more traditional, symbolic and popular religious nationalism which found its chief expression in the figure of the Virgin of Guadalupe. This extensive cult blended traditional Catholic values with more subversive, popular, anti-Spanish sentiments; its assertion of the divine privilege and special mission of the Mexican people transcended class and ethnic divisions and fostered a sense of nationhood which was incompatible with tight (though perhaps not loose) imperial control.

However, we should not succumb to the sirens of Guadalupanismo – nor exaggerate the ideological and symbolic causes of Mexican independence in general. Like most sociopolitical symbols, the Virgin of Guadalupe was versatile and slippery. She was espoused by popular rebels, by creole reformers and – it is important to note – by Spanish officials (the cult had been officially recognized by the papacy in 1754).[344] In 1819 the viceroy invoked the Virgin of

---

[341] Hussey, 'Traces', pp. 24–5, 36.

[342] MacLachlan and Rodríguez O., *Forging of the Cosmic Race*, pp. 289–90. The Spanish scientist-miner Fausto de Elhuyar, a protegé of the Society, spent 25 years in Mexico, 'promoting the natural sciences...(and) improving mining methods': Whitaker, 'The Dual Role', pp. 14–15. On the Society's origins, see Herr, *The Eighteenth-Century Revolution in Spain*, pp. 154–5.

[343] Whitaker, 'The Dual Role', pp. 5–6.

[344] On the polyvalence of Guadalupanismo: Taylor, *Magistrates of the Sacred*, pp. 26, 55, 458, 462. Brading, *Church and State*, pp. 16–17, charts the official legitimation of the cult. Poole, *Our Lady of Guadalupe*, convincingly shows that the cult began to prosper in the

Guadalupe when Lake Texcoco threatened to flood the capital. The Guadalupe cult, in other words, was not inherently subversive; it became an adjunct to subversion in particular cases, just as it became an adjunct to order and orthodoxy in others. The notion that the independence wars were fought beneath the rival banners of the (creole/mestizo) Virgin of Guadalupe and the (*peninsular*) Virgin de los Remedios is simplistic.[345] The Virgin of Guadalupe may have afforded creole and popular patriots a powerful symbol, but they did not monopolize that symbol and, like most powerful symbols (be they saints, national flags, 'foundation myths' or local heroes), this one was subject to a good deal of competitive invocation by rival factions. And, one may hypothesize, if the insurgents had not hit upon this particular symbol, they would have found others – less efficacious, perhaps, but still capable of stirring emotions and offering iconic inspiration.

In similar fashion, we should question the more extreme claims of *ideengeschichte*, when it promotes (Enlightenment) ideas as first movers of Mexican independence. The Enlightenment was a big and contradictory bundle of ideas; some were heartily endorsed by the Bourbon Crown; some (such as religious toleration) were repudiated by the champions of independence. Some – associated with scientific and geographical inquiry – were politically neutral.[346] Of course, ideas played a part in the struggle to come, but the struggle derived from a concatenation of causes, structural and conjunctural, among which 'ideas' played a secondary role.

This can be seen in the tortuous narrative of events which spanned the thirty years *circa* 1790–1820. The stirrings of creole nationalism became evident in a series of plots and would-be rebellions which affected the colony in the 1790s and 1800s. In 1793 a 'seditious

mid-seventeenth century as a vehicle of criollismo; during the eighteenth century its scope and acceptance widened, as it was espoused by Indians and castes, and given the official imprimatur of Rome.

[345] Hamnett, *Roots of Insurgency*, pp. 15–16.

[346] Some (Foucaultians?) would vehemently contest this judgement. Two rather different issues are at stake: the grand ontological question whether science in general can be objective, transcending political interests (to which I, unlike the Foucaultians, would reply, yes); and the more specific, empirical – and relevant – question whether *Enlightenment* science could be 'neutral', in the sense of lacking any necessary connection to or elective affinity with particular political ideologies. Again, I would reply, yes; for, as Whitaker ('The Dual Role', pp. 5–6) points out, 'in one of its most important aspects – the zeal for the promotion of useful knowledge – the Enlightenment was ardently supported in circles that were politically and socially conservative', *especially* in Latin America.

conspiracy' was scotched in Guadalajara. In 1799 young lower-class creoles hatched an abortive plot in Mexico City.[347] None of these seriously troubled Spanish control: they did not garner mass support, nor did they even win over significant sections of creole opinion. Foreign ideas and examples might generate a diffuse atmosphere of heterodoxy, but they were not the prime determinants of effective political action. Ideas acquired efficacy at the right political moment, when sociopolitical conflict broke out of the confines imposed by the colonial state; when, quite suddenly, new political vistas opened and new political options presented themselves. Then, belligerent social actors naturally justified their demands and rallied their followers by ideological appeals – to the Rights of Man or to the Virgin of Guadalupe. 'Hidden transcripts' then became public;[348] old ideas acquired revolutionary potential. But 'transcripts' and ideas waited on events;[349] they possessed no inner transforming power. For, just as the Virgin was a flexible, fungible symbol, so, too, the ideas of the Enlightenment or the French Revolution were capable of diverse application. The Bourbon reformer was as much a creature of the Enlightenment as the liberal patriot (conversely, many patriots were Catholic traditionalists, bitterly hostile to French 'atheism'). The Church, too, was affected by Enlightenment values: the old emphasis on sin, penitence and retribution gave way to a more optimistic temper, which stressed divine love, human potential and social well-being.[350]

Spain and Mexico therefore fought out their colonial battle within an intellectual arena pervaded by Enlightenment notions, and these notions could, on occasion, supply appropriate war-cries; but the

---

[347] Lindley, *Haciendas and Economic Development*, p. 90; Hamill, *The Hidalgo Revolt*, p. 93. Farris, *Crown and Clergy*, p. 199, also mentions 'the first scheme discovered in Mexico for separation from Spain in 1794'.

[348] Terminology taken from James Scott, *Domination and the Arts of Resistance*.

[349] This is not easy to prove – or disprove. However Taylor, *Magistrates of the Sacred*, p. 455, stresses the contingency attached to clerical rebellion ('insurgent pastors were not mainly young radicals who acted if they were oppressed by the upper clergy or swayed by French and Ango-American liberal ideas'); he notes, too, that royalists were more anticlerical than patriots (p. 455) and that the patriot leader Morelos, who does not appear to have imbibed much by way of liberal philosophy, stoutly 'represented hmself as an orthodox believer and loyal priest, not a renegade' (p. 467). Intellectual heterodoxy, in other words, fails to explain patriotic rebellion.

[350] Taylor, *Magistrates of the Sacred*, pp. 19, 451. This, Taylor also notes, p. 452, brought an iconographic shift, as the gory Christs beloved of Baroque artists and sculptors gave way to 'more serene, idealized representation[s] of his body that anticipated the resurrection'.

battle derived from the old contradictions of rulers and ruled, rich and poor, which had been severely aggravated by the social and political trends of the late eighteenth century and were now catalysed by the conjunctural crisis of 1808–10. Notions of popular sovereignty, in particular, acquired a particular resonance since in Mexico, unlike Chile or the Río de la Plata, the independence movement displayed a radical, popular and egalitarian dimension right from the start.[351]

The petty conspiracies of the 1790s, we have seen, came to nothing. The dearth and destitution of 1785–86 had not generated widespread popular protest (as some simplistic theories might lead one to expect). But a decade later the story was different. Around the turn of the century a series of political and economic shocks, radiating from the epicentre of Napoleonic Europe, began to shake the colony. These were more than external jolts: they struck at the basis of the colonial compact, thus initiating a battle for local control in Mexico which at once laid bare – and accentuated – the profound tensions pullulating within colonial society.

After 1793, Spanish communications with Mexico were repeatedly interrupted by war. The interdiction of Spanish manufactures at first stimulated Mexican production (especially of textiles), but between 1802 and 1805 Spanish transatlantic trade revived, only to be dashed again with Trafalgar and Napoleon's Continental System.[352] In the interim, Spain sought to protect its colonial markets by allowing neutral ships to carry Spanish goods to the Americas: a further telling admission of imperial failure. The outcome was a series of commercial vicissitudes, which gave the urban/mercantile/manufacturing sector a rough ride, and a progressive decline in both Spanish mercantilist control and (as foreign imports flooded in) Mexican manufacturing output. Since this coincided with stagnation in the mining sector, regions of mining and manufacturing experienced hardship, unemployment and commercial collapse; external crisis therefore broke upon a society undergoing severe stress.[353]

At the same time, Spain, engaged in recurrent and costly wars, turned the fiscal screw. From the 1760s, the growth of government

---

[351] Lynch, *Spanish American Revolutions*, p. 295.

[352] Garner, *Economic Change*, pp. 163–4; Thomson, *Puebla de los Angeles*, pp. 111–12.

[353] Garner, *Economic Change*, p. 246ff.; Thomson, *Puebla de los Angeles*, pp. 47–52; Ladd, *Mexican Nobility*, p. 93; Super, 'Querétaro obrajes', pp. 210–13.

spending fast outstripped the value of bullion production.[354] The total tax yield of New Spain began to climb; during the war-torn 1790s it soared, as the Crown hiked taxes, issued bonds and imposed the first direct levies on the nobility.[355] A massive forced loan was demanded from the miners' guild; the *cofradías* had to make their funds available to the state; the selling price of an aristocratic *mayorazgo* (entail) went through the roof.[356] Worse still, the Royal Law of Consolidation, which had been applied in Spain in 1798, was extended to New Spain in 1804.[357] The law confiscated the Church's chantries and charitable foundations and put them on the auction block. Whereas in Spain the measure had both yielded income and thrown Church lands on to the market (thus meeting two Bourbon objectives), in Mexico the outcome was different: here, the Church had accumulated vast financial assets, which made it the chief banker, especially the chief investment banker, of the colony; the confiscation of its capital required the Church to foreclose on loans and sell off properties on which it held liens.[358]

The potential effects were sweeping. According to the bishop of Michoacan some two hundred thousand property-owners throughout Mexico depended on Church loans which were now at risk. Landowners, merchants, miners, farmers and shopkeepers protested. Nevertheless, the government pressed on. Between 1805 and 1809 the Law of Consolidation yielded over 10 million pesos (about one-quarter of the imputed wealth of the Church): despite

[354] Bullion production as a percentage of taxation fell from some 250% in the 1760s to 135% in 1790–4 and 44% in 1800–4: Coatsworth, 'Limits of Colonial Absolutism', p. 42.

[355] Kicza, *Colonial Entrepreneurs*, pp. 43–5, estimates a doubling of taxation (in real terms) between the 1750s and 1780s, and a further tripling by the 1800s. See also MacLachlan and Rodríguez O., *Forging of the Cosmic Race*, p. 296.

[356] Garner, *Economic Change*, pp. 238–40; Farriss, *Maya Society*, pp. 360–4; Pastor, *Campesinos y reformas*, pp. 200–1; Ladd, *Mexican Nobility*, pp. 90–1.

[357] For citations, see n. 176 above.

[358] In Querétaro, the measure was seen as 'a savage capital levy which would effectively ruin most landowners': Brading, *Church and State*, p. 223, citing the creole *corregidor*. In Nueva Galicia (Jalisco-Zacatecas) the Consolidation 'had the effect of all but eliminating Church loans and the level of borrowing... decreased dramatically in the years immediately following the program': Greenow, *Credit and Socioeconomic Change*, p. 26. Like the expulsion of the Jesuits in 1767, therefore, the Consolidation was an example of a Spanish (*peninsular*) policy which, when arbitrarily exported to Mexico, caused far greater disruption and resentment than it had in Spain: Brading, *Church and State*, pp. 222–3; Ladd, *Mexican Nobility*, p. 98. And, although the imperial crisis of summer 1808 led the viceroy to suspend the measure, the damage had already been done (Hamnett, *Politics and Trade*, p. 121).

their vigorous protests and tenacious haggling, influential nobles found themselves compelled to make substantial payments to the Crown. Haciendas were sold off; bankruptcies proliferated. After 1808 the ensuing instability conspired with poor harvests – the worst since 1785–6 – to ravage Mexican agriculture. Dearth and speculation preyed on the countryside.[359] The Crown got its money, with which to prosecute an abortive war. But it offended the Church (the Consolidation was compounded by lesser fiscal demands);[360] and, more important, it alienated a large section of the Mexican propertied class – not all of them opulent grandees. As the Tehuacan town council complained, the measure shook popular faith in the idea of a 'just monarch directing his people toward prosperity and happiness'.[361] The reservoir of royal legitimacy was running dangerously low.

In the wake of these fiscal blows came the dramatic political bouleversement of 1808, as Napoleon invaded Spain, deposed the Bourbon dynasty (Charles IV had just abdicated in favour of his son Ferdinand VII), and imposed his brother Joseph Bonaparte as king.[362] Throughout the Spanish empire rulers and ruled had to come to terms with this new decapitated imperial order. As in Spain itself, local movements – often centred on town councils (*cabildos*) and hence representative of creole elites – now claimed to represent legitimate political authority. Although notions of popular sovereignty were sometimes involved, the main thrust of the movement was traditional and restorative. The creole elites of the *cabildos* constituted rivals of the *peninsular* bureaucracy, strong in the Audiencias; but the creoles did not advocate a repudiation of Spain; rather, they legitimized their authority in the name of the Spanish Crown and the Bourbon dynasty, the victim of Napoleonic subversion. They sustained the fabric of royal law and government and adhered to the

---

[359] On the 1809–10 dearth: Florescano, *Precios de maíz*, pp. 152–3, 178–9; Brading, *Miners and Merchants*, pp. 32–3 (Guanajuato); Martin, *Rural Society*, pp. 117–18 (Morelos); Thomson, *Puebla de los Angeles*, pp. 116–25. Given both the ecological diversity and the structural disarticulation of the Mexican economy, some regions – including Jalisco and the Valley of Mexico – were much less seriously affected by the 1809–10 dearth: Hamnett, *Roots of Insurgency*, pp. 116–22; Tutino, *From Insurrection to Revolution*, pp. 147, 175–6.

[360] Brading, *Church and State*, p. 8.

[361] Flores Caballero, *Counterrevolution*, p. 23.

[362] Lynch, *Bourbon Spain*, pp. 419–21.

ancient contract which, supposedly, linked the colony to the Crown (that is, to the dynasty and not to any alien, imposed French puppet). Essentially, this was an assertion of *de facto* home rule within a loose but legitimate colonial federation, constituted under monarchical auspices.[363] While 'home rule' might carry liberal and progressive connotations, there was much to the creole project which was conservative, in the strict sense of the word. The monarchy, the imperial tie, and, above all, the social, political and religious order within the colony would be conserved, not subverted, by home rule, by the assumption of power by respectable, loyal and patriotic elites. The philosophical premises of this position traced back through Natural Law thinkers to the traditional contractualism of medieval Spain; and there were precedents in colonial history – such as the seventeenth-century debate over the Union of Arms – which anchored creole autonomist claims within local tradition too.[364]

The then viceroy, Iturrigaray, concurred. Despite the opposition of *peninsular* officials in the Audiencia and elsewhere, he appeared to sanction this assertion of creole power. He convened a series of *cabildos abiertos* ('open' town meetings), at which elite representatives hotly debated the course which the colony should follow. Some *peninsular* officials, keen to cement the imperial tie, spoke in favour of recognizing the Seville Junta (which inaccurately claimed to represent the provincial juntas of the metropolis); some creole spokesmen called instead for a junta representative of all Mexico; many, both *peninsulares* and creoles, preferred to wait and see.[365] The crisis of 1808 thus began to acquire an ethnic (creole/*peninsular*) character, which a barrage of speeches, broadsheets and sermons sustained and emphasized. Yet, in terms of social reality within the colony, the *peninsular*-creole division was blurred and complex; the imperial crisis served, as crises often do, to lend a spurious exactitude, born of polemic and partisanship, to this murky polarity. Indeed, even as the elites, *peninsular* and creole, wrangled among themselves, rumours

---

[363] Rodríguez O., 'From Royal Subject', pp. 25–7; Rodríguez O., *Independence of Spanish America*, pp. 53–4.

[364] Luis Villoro, 'La revolución de la independencia', in Daniel Cosío Villegas, coord., *Historia General de México* (Mexico, 1976), vol. 2, pp. 318–19; MacLachlan and Rodríguez O., *Forging of the Cosmic Race*, pp. 302–3.

[365] MacLachlan and Rodríguez O., *Forging of the Cosmic Race*, pp. 304–5; Anna, *Fall of the Royal Government*, p. 38; Ladd, *Mexican Nobility*, pp. 107–8.

of popular dissidence – alarming even if exaggerated – began to circulate. The common people were reported to be restive (they were certainly hungry); they shirked hard work; they talked, it was said, of independence, of republics, of Indian monarchies, even of 'Our King Bonaparte'.[366] Although exaggerated, such rumours suggested that the politico-colonial crisis might soon acquire social implications; that the battle for power might not be confined within narrow elite circles. And so it turned out, unusually for Latin America.

The creole challenge met a swift and extreme *peninsular* response. In September 1808 the *peninsular* landlord Guillermo de Yermo, backed by the *peninsular* merchants of the capital, launched a near-bloodless coup and deposed the viceroy. In his place they put the octogenarian field marshal Pedro de Garibay. Similar *peninsular* coups were mounted in provincial cities like Oaxaca and Guadalajara.[367] This was the signal for a draconian assertion of *peninsular* power; a dramatic – even desperate – bid by the *peninsulares* to fasten their control on the restless colony, to preserve Spanish hegemony and to protect their own skins and fortunes. Like the Algerian *colons* of the 1960s (the parallel has already been suggested) they sought to impose their own local control in default of metropolitan authority. The parallel is apt for, it should be noted, the architects of the *peninsular* coup were precisely those old, entrenched European interests which had been prejudiced by Bourbon policy: the Audiencia, whose power had been eclipsed by the intendants; the Mexico City *consulado*, whose interests had suffered from the new policy of *comercio libre*; and the landlord victims of the 1804 Consolidation Law, who included Yermo himself.[368] For them, 1808 was an opportunity not only to dish the creoles but also to reassert the power and privilege they had lost as a result of the Bourbon reforms. They at once set about reversing the recent moves towards home rule. Creole political representation was curbed and creole military forces disbanded; there was a spate

[366] Christon I. Archer, '"La revolución desastrosa": Fragmentación, crisis social y la insurgencia del cura Miguel Hidalgo', in Meyer, *Tres levantamientos populares*, p. 117 (quote); Van Young, 'Quetzalcóatl', 'in Rodríguez O., *The Independence of Mexico*, pp. 109–10ff.; Hamnett, *Politics and Trade*, pp. 128–9 (more work-shy Indians).

[367] Lynch, *Spanish American Revolutions*, pp. 304–5; Hamnett, *Politics and Trade*, pp. 121–2ff.

[368] Anna, *Fall of the Royal Government*, pp. 51–2, 54; Brading, *Miners and Merchants*, pp. 340–2; Ladd, *Mexican Nobility*, pp. 99, 110, which adds that 'as a family man, Yermo despised the viceroy's posturing among Creole sycophants at cockfights, theater parties and balls'.

of arrests and courts martial (a couple of prominent creole leaders died in gaol); the police acquired fresh powers; a curfew was imposed. The dilatory rule of law was replaced by summary justice.[369] In consequence, the lines of ethnic division became etched ever more deeply; but the path towards creole home rule – even outright independence – now being trodden in Buenos Aires and Caracas was, in Mexico, barred by *peninsular* intransigence.[370]

Such intransigence prompted an uneasy alliance between creole elites on the one hand and the Indian and mestizo people on the other. The elites needed popular support if they were to challenge European hegemony; the people had their own – albeit diffuse, disparate – grievances. In particular, the people were now suffering the effects of another major dearth, reminiscent of that of 1785–6. In 1808–9 drought produced a 'great mortality' among Mexico's livestock and decimated the harvest, especially in the Bajío and centre-north.[371] Food prices tripled. As in the past, agrarian crisis soon affected the rest of the economy: mining and manufacturing faltered and unemployment rose. The muletrains which carried maize to the public granaries travelled under military escort. Dearth also aggravated old agrarian conflicts and led – it would seem – to a spate of peasant land invasions in the Puebla, Guanajuato and San Luis regions.[372]

Creole elites, indignant and threatened, now sought to capitalize on these social tensions. In 1809, officers of the militia based at Valladolid, Michoacan, hatched a plot which sought to wrest power from the *peninsulares* and establish a form of creole home rule, within the framework of the Spanish empire. This reassertion of creole autonomism, of the political project of 1808, acquired fresh significance when the plotters made contact with local groups,

---

[369] Farriss, *Crown and Clergy*, pp. 206–7; Ladd, *Mexican Nobility*, p. 110; Hamnett, *Politics and Trade*, pp. 122–4.

[370] Anna, *Fall of the Royal Government*, p. 55; Lynch, *Spanish American Revolutions*, pp. 35–6, 51–7, 194–6.

[371] Hamnett, *Roots of Insurgency*, p. 116. See also n. 359 above.

[372] Anna, *Fall of the Royal Government*, pp. 23–4; Garner, *Economic Growth*, pp. 266–7, shows maize prices more than tripling between 1808 and 1810 (from 12 to over 38 reales per fanega). The 1810 price is therefore the highest of the entire period 1700–1810; and the three-year cycle, 1808–1809–1810 (12→ 22.60→ 38.30 reales/fanega) closely parallels that of the catastrophic dearth of 1784–1785–1786 (11.32→ 22.77→ 36.92). Archer, '"La revolución desastrosa"', p. 119 (muletrains); Hamnett, *Roots of Insurgency*, pp. 90–3 (land disputes and seizures).

including the powerful Indian *cacique* Rosales, and sought to enlist popular support by promising the abolition of the tribute.[373] The plot was scotched; the local bishop pooh-poohed such vain efforts at subversion.[374] A year later, however, a similar alignment produced the Hidalgo rebellion, the *fons et origo* of the Mexican insurgency, and thus of the independent nation of Mexico.

V. The Insurgency

Miguel del Hidalgo y Costilla was the parish priest of Dolores, on the northeastern fringes of the Bajío. A heterodox *cura* (like many of his kind), he owned a modest property, lived in sin, flirted with new ideas (hence his brush with the Inquisition) and performed a central role in the community, which went beyond spiritual tutelage to include economic organization and innovation (he stimulated pottery, silk production and viticulture in the town).[375] As priest and petty entrepreneur, he enjoyed close links with the common people; as a member of the provincial elite, he rubbed shoulders with the creole landlords, merchants and officers who resented both *peninsular* political domineering and Bourbon fiscal exactions (Hidalgo and several of his cronies had suffered from the Law of Consolidation). Local allies included Ignacio Allende, a macho military officer, Mariano Abasolo, a creole officer and landlord, the Aldama brothers, modest provincial merchants, and Miguel Domínguez, the *corregidor* of Querétaro. These, it should be stressed, were not opulent creole magnates. They did not possess sprawling estates, huge fortunes or high offices (Domínguez, the *corregidor*, eventually sided with the government). Rather, they were members of a modest provincial elite, a Mexican 'country party', which, located on the borders of the Mexican heartland, was suspicious of Mexico City and central officialdom and possessed of vaguely progressive and patriotic ideas.[376]

---

[373] Hamill, *The Hidalgo Revolt*, pp. 97–9; Hamnett, *Roots of Insurgency*, p. 125.

[374] Archer, '"La revolución desastrosa"', p. 115, citing Abad y Queipo. Not that the bishop was unaware of the grave social and political tensions of the time: Brading, *Church and State*, pp. 229–34.

[375] Hamill, *The Hidalgo Revolt*, ch. 3; Carlos Herrejón, 'Hidalgo, razones personales', in Meyer, *Tres levantamientos populares*, pp. 161–72.

[376] Brading, *Miners and Merchants*, p. 344; Tutino, *From Insurrection to Revolution*, p. 134. The 'country party' in seventeenth-century England was constituted by 'that indeterminate unpolitical but highly sensitive miscellany of men who had mutinied not against monarchy

In that the rich creole aristocracy represented a different group, and remained largely marginal to the Hidalgo conspiracy, it is misleading to see the conspiracy as a simple bid for creole supremacy over the *peninsulares*. Here, and throughout the independence movement, complex motives intertwined. Anti-*peninsular* feeling ran strong, exacerbated by recent events, and it formed a vital link between the provincial creole elite and the local Indian and mestizo masses. But many creoles spurned the revolt, and most – including several members of the original Hidalgo conspiracy – would have no truck with social subversion. Thus they faced an agonizing dilemma: they needed mass support to combat the *peninsulares*; but they shared with the *peninsulares* a justifiable fear of mass insurrection. Indeed, they had personal ties to *peninsular* officials like intendant Riaño, who knew Hidalgo and esteemed him as a learned theologian of 'gentle disposition'.[377]

The Hidalgo conspiracy had many of the characteristics of a protest by middling, 'out' groups, who resented recent policies and events, and who displayed the perennial sensitivity of peripheral elites, hostile to the demands and pretensions of central government. It was significant that outlying regions – Michoacan, the Bajío – outstripped the cities of central Mexico (such as Mexico City or Puebla) in such elite protest; throughout the independence struggle and well into the nineteenth century it was the periphery – states such as Michoacan, Guerrero, Oaxaca and the north – which would recurrently produce movements and rebellions in opposition to the power of the centre, represented by the City and Valley of Mexico. Furthermore, as regards the colonial tie, Hidalgo and his allies did not envisage a complete rupture. They stood within the tradition of creole patriotism and autonomism, and they sought to establish a creole government which would rule in the name of Fernando VII.[378] In

(they had long clung to monarchical beliefs) nor against economic archaism...but against the vast, oppressive, ever-extending apparatus of parasitic bureaucracy': Hugh Trevor-Roper, *Religion, the Reformation, and Social Change* (London, 1984; first pubd. 1967), pp. 73–4, 87–8; and for a case study, Peter Clark, *English Provincial Society from the Reformation to the Revolution: Religion, Politics and Society in Kent, 1500–1640* (Hassocks, 1977), pp. 3–4, 49–50, 120–1ff., 388, 406–7.

377 Brading, *Church and State*, p. 111. On the reaction of the colonial aristocracy: Ladd, *Mexican Nobility*, p. 112; and the creole dilemma: Hamnett, *Roots of Insurgency*, p. 128.

378 While pledging loyalty to Fernando VII – and even striking coins carrying his image, Hidalgo also promised to expel the *peninsulares*: a palpable ambivalence – a 'yawning contradiction', in

doing so, they denied the legitimacy of the imposed, *afrancesado* regime of Joseph Bonaparte, and they flaunted traditional patriotic and religious symbols, notably the Virgin of Guadalupe.

In all this, the conspirators followed precedents established in 1808–9, not only in Mexico but elsewhere in Spanish America. In one crucial respect, however, they innovated. They rallied the Indian and mestizo masses to their cause; as, indeed, they had to if they were seriously to challenge a tough Spanish regime which clung to power more tenaciously in Mexico than, for example, in the Río de la Plata. Buenos Aires witnessed the swift ouster of its Spanish rulers, after which the *rioplatense* revolution became a basis for the spread of subversion to Chile and ultimately Peru (Venezuela, in northern South America, performed a similar subversive role).[379] If the South American independence movements conformed to a loose domino theory, that of Mexico was self-contained; it was fought on the basis of domestic resources, which meant that rebellious elites required the backing of rebellious masses. As a result, the sequence of events proved to be dramatic, violent and, for elites of all persuasions, profoundly worrying. Mexico, it seemed, might go the way of Saint-Domingue.[380]

When word came that the authorities had got wind of the conspiracy, an armed insurrection began, signalled by Father Hidalgo ringing the bell of the Dolores parish church. Traditionally, the church bell was the tocsin of the community, just as the church tower was its principal material and psychological landmark;[381] and this particular

Van Young's words ('Quetzalcóatl', p. 121) – which has generated divergent views concerning his goals. Hamill, *The Hidalgo Revolt*, pp. 122–3, 130, 191, suggests that independence was Hidalgo's goal from the outset; Rodríguez O., 'From Royal Subject', pp. 30–1, clings to the 'home rule' thesis ('the Hidalgo revolt began as a criollo movement for autonomy'). The latter thesis can (just about) be reconciled with the call to expel the *peninsulares*: the insurgent Luis Bernardo López, for example, pledged allegiance to the king, reassured alarmed creoles and promised that nothing would change in Mexico, save for the expulsion of the *peninsulares*; moreover, *peninsulares* who remained in Spain and 'defend[ed] themselves against the French and defend[ed] the King are and will be our brothers' (Hamill, *The Hidalgo Revolt*, pp. 129–30; compare Van Young, 'Quetzalcóatl', p. 212, n. 29). In practical terms, of course, a *peninsular*-free Mexico would no longer be a colony, but a separate kingdom; and insurgents (like Allende) who believed – and, *a fortiori*, historians who still believe – that the absolutist Fernando VII would sanction such an outcome would seem to be guilty of a certain credulity.

[379] Lynch, *Spanish American Revolutions*, chs. 3, 6.

[380] Where, in 1801, after a long and bloody struggle, the black insurgents of Toussaint l'Ouverture had overthrown the French slavocracy and established the Republic of Haiti: Archer, '"La revolución desastrosa"', p. 124, citing Bishop Abad y Queipo.

[381] Van Young, 'Quetzalcóatl', p. 119.

bell-ringing, the so-called Grito de ('Cry of') Dolores, has since assumed national mythopoeic status, with its annual re-enactment by the president of Mexico on the night of 15/16 September, national independence day. Hidalgo's local followers, most of them campesinos, responded to the call, and they formed the nucleus of a popular host of peasants, peons, artisans and miners which swelled in size as the rebels tramped from Dolores to San Miguel, then to Celaya and Guanajuato. Within a couple of weeks a ragged army of some eighty thousand stood at the gates of Guanajuato, where the Spanish intendant gathered the frightened *gachupines* inside the stout walls of the *alhóndiga*, the new, sternly classical, city granary. Outside, the creole leaders were hard put to control their tumultuous horde. Allende and his fellow creole militiamen were vastly outnumbered by the hastily recruited popular levies. Discipline was lax, weaponry was primitive and hatred of the *gachupines* ran deep. On 28 September the *alhóndiga* was attacked; amid bloody fighting, an intrepid lad rushed forward and put a torch to the wooden doors; the mob broke in, and the defenders – Spaniards and creoles alike – were massacred. Guanajuato, the third largest city in Spanish America, was plundered for two days.[382]

Most of the Bajío was now engulfed in popular insurrection. Hidalgo led – nominally, at least – an army of eighty thousand. But such precipitate growth and success could not be sustained. The colonial authorities, jolted by the events at Guanajuato, recruited and propagandized hard. Landlords raised military contingents, and bishops denounced the rebellion, excommunicated its leaders and drew dire parallels with the great Haitian slave revolution of the 1790s (the slave-owners of Veracruz, already alarmed, needed no such warning).[383] At the end of October, Hidalgo led his army south towards the Valley of Mexico. At Monte de las Cruces, between Toluca and the capital, they were met by a small force of loyalist troops which, in a desperate day-long encounter, severely mauled

---

[382] Hamill, *The Hidalgo Revolt*, pp. 137–41; Brading, *Miners and Merchants*, pp. 343–4. Guanajuato's population – between 40,000 and 50,000 – placed it third after Mexico City and Lima, hence not far behind Philadelphia and about the same as Sheffield.

[383] Hamill, *The Hidalgo Revolt*, pp. 125–6, 151–2; Hamnett, *Roots of Insurgency*, p. 153 (slave-owners). Within two years, Hidalgo's call to arms had provoked a tenacious slave revolt in the Córdoba region of Veracruz: Carroll, *Blacks in Colonial Veracruz*, pp. 99–100.

the rebel forces, above all by the use of artillery.[384] But loyalist losses
were heavy; perhaps two hundred out of a force of over two thousand limped back to Mexico, which now awaited the onslaught of
Hidalgo's hordes, the well-to-do fearing a repeat of the Guanajuato
massacre, the 'dangerous classes' anticipating a lucrative opportunity to loot.[385] The would-be looters waited in vain. Though far from
defeated, Hidalgo's ill-armed levies had suffered heavy losses and numerous desertions, which perhaps halved their numbers. They also
became acquainted with the firepower of professional troops, which
counterbalanced the insurgents' numerical superiority.[386] The check
at Monte de las Cruces also deepened divisions that had opened up
within the rebel leadership, as respectable creoles like Allende saw
their limited, autonomist, political rebellion degenerating into un-
controllable class and ethnic warfare and their original legitimist
aims yielding to more radical yet inchoate demands – for independence, land reform, even Indian supremacy. For, as the rebellion
spread, it drew upon old traditions of popular messianism which,
even when they were couched in traditional monarchical terms,
carried connotations of social upheaval, of caste war, of the 'world
turned upside down'. 'Long live the king', proclaimed such traditional
monarchists; but, they went on, 'death to the Spaniards', an exhorta-
tion which they implemented recurrently, ruthlessly and sometimes
with a certain ritual sadism.[387] 'Boys, now we have cannons to kill all
the *gachupines* who have usurped our America for so long', a rabble-
rousing *cura* from Temascaltepec, east of Mexico City, (allegedly) declared to his flock; '... long live Our Lady of Guadalupe, and death
to the *gachupines* and their lackey friends'.[388]

---

[384] Hamill, *The Hidalgo Revolt*, pp. 126, 178; Christon Archer, 'Bite of the Hydra: The Rebellion
of Cura Miguel Hidalgo, 1810–1811', in Jaime Rodríguez O., ed., *Patterns of Contention in
Mexican History* (Wilmington, Del., 1992), pp. 88–9.
[385] Anna, *Fall of the Royal Government*, pp. 71–2.
[386] Anna, *Fall of the Royal Government*, p. 71, reckons that only about a thousand of Hidalgo's
80,000 troops had guns; and that casualties may have reached 40,000; Archer, 'Bite of the
Hydra', pp. 89–90, expresses some justified skepticism concerning reported (i.e., official,
royalist) casualty figures.
[387] On creole disenchantment: Hamill, *The Hidalgo Revolt*, pp. 148, 170–5, 200; on popular xeno-
phobia: Hamill, *The Hidalgo Revolt*, pp. 142–3, 149, 182–3; Van Young, 'Quetzacóatl', p. 111;
Lynch, *Spanish American Revolutions*, p. 310.
[388] The *cura*, who had organized a foundry to cast the necessary cannons, also enunciated a
rough cost-benefit analysis of independence: 'now that Spain is finished, we won't have brandy,
Brittany cloth, and other things ... but we'll still have our *charape* [and] homespun': Taylor,
Magistrates of the Sacred, p. 459. *Charape* was an alcoholic drink, extracted from maguey,

Violence and social radicalism, however, produced its own resolute opposition. In this, creoles and property-owners were prominent, but there were also popular groups who shunned or opposed Hidalgo's rebellion. Throughout the insurgency, the cities of New Spain remained relatively tranquil.[389] True, the Guanajuato mob had ably seconded the rural invaders when the city was sacked; there had been a brief riot at Aguascalientes; and other mining towns, like Zacatecas, were thought to be at risk of the rebellious mob. Rebel sympathizers organized clandestinely, flyposting on the streets of Mexico City, channelling intelligence to the rebels in the field.[390] But covert subversion never became overt insurrection. The major cities of central Mexico, above all Mexico City, remained calm, in part because they were tightly policed,[391] but in part, too, because urban grievances were less pronounced, urban groups enjoyed less collective solidarity, and the legitimacy of the urban authorities was less eroded. These authorities not only deployed guns and artillery, they also maintained a rudimentary system of provisioning, which alleviated the worst effects of dearth. In addition, city-dwellers lacked the tight corporate organization and, perhaps, the emotive popular symbols which underpinned revolt in the countryside. Never noted for their social turbulence, the cities of central Mexico remained 'islands in the storm', as the insurgency lashed at their shores.[392]

hence akin to pulque. As for the *cura*'s improvised artillery, the conversion of church organs into bullets and iron railings into cannons seems to have been a feature of the insurgency: Pastor, *Campesinos y reformas*, p. 415.

[389] Eric Van Young, 'Islands in the Storm: Quiet Cities and Violent Countrysides in the Mexican Independence Era', *Past and Present*, 118 (1988), pp. 130–55.

[390] Virginia Guedea, 'Las sociedades secretas durante el movimiento de independencia' in Rodríguez O., *The Independence of Mexico*, pp. 49–52; note also Anna, *Fall of the Royal Government*, pp. 71–2 (elite fear of the city mob).

[391] The new viceroy, Francisco Javier de Venegas, who took office just as Hidalgo raised the standard of revolt, was a tough and able career soldier; building on recent Bourbon precedents (see Scardaville, '(Habsburg) Law', pp. 510–11), he created a Junta of Police and Public Safety and introduced a system of internal passports for the Valley of Mexico: Anna, *Fall of the Royal Government*, pp. 81–2; see also Christon I. Archer, '"Viva Nuestra Señora de Guadalupe!" Recent Interpretations of Mexico's Independence Period', *Mexican Studies/Estudios Mexicanos*, 7/1 (1991), pp. 162–3.

[392] Van Young, 'Islands in the Storm', which, in addition to the factors already mentioned (strict policing, regulated food supply, urban anomie), notes that Mexico City became a haven for refugees from the countryside who, one may assume, were neither well-disposed towards the insurgents nor likely to initiate popular protest. As a result, the metropolitan population grew, from perhaps 137,000 in 1803 to 169,000 in 1811. Thanks to the insurgency, therefore, the city 'may have surpassed the enormous Aztec capital on whose foundations it rested': Arrom, *Women of Mexico City*, p. 7.

The same was true of some rural areas: the insurgency was not uniformly popular. We will attempt some sort of regional break-down shortly. Here, it is the – negative – response of the people of central Mexico, urban and to some degree rural, which is notable. The masses of central Mexico did not readily respond to Hidalgo's appeal as his army headed south. The villagers of the Valley of Mexico – such as those around San Angel – were 'overcome with teror and dread' as Hidalgo's host approached.[393] In Puebla and Tlaxcala, Indian *caciques* protested their loyalty to king, viceroy, and 'Our Most Sacred Mother . . . Mary of Guadalupe', deploring the 'scandalous and detestable acts' of Hidalgo.[394] In part, perhaps, this was prudential rhetoric (at a moment of crisis declarations of the appropriate 'public transcript' offered a form of insurance); in part, it reflected the ancient – and rational – peasant suspicion of outsiders, especially those bearing arms. But there were also deeper, structural reasons why the mass recruitment of the Bajío could not be so easily achieved elsewhere, and why the pattern of insurgency was highly variable.

The insurgency varied by time and place: structure and contingency were interwoven, as in any great revolution.[395] Repulsed at Monte de las Cruces, denied the ready cooperation of the central Mexican peasantry, Hidalgo's insurgency lost its momentum. The viceroy refused his demand for the surrender of Mexico City. Enigmatically, the rebels backed off and veered north towards Querétaro.[396] On 7 November 1810 seven thousand loyalist troops – trained militiamen commanded by the able Félix Calleja – confronted Hidalgo's diminished army at Aculco, sixty miles northwest of the capital. The weaponry which had been amassed to resist a notional French invasion was now turned against Mexico's rebellious populace, with devastating effect.[397] The rebels broke and fled; Hidalgo, leading a reduced force, retreated to the more promising locale of the

---

[393] Hamill, *The Hidalgo Revolt*, p. 176.

[394] Hamill, *The Hidalgo Revolt*, p. 177.

[395] Cf. Guardino, *Peasants*, p. 45.

[396] Archer, 'Bite of the Hydra', pp. 90–1, explains the rebels' retreat in terms of internal divisions (especialy creole elite defections) and military-logistical failings. See also Anna, *Fall of the Royal Government*, pp. 71–2. Hamill, *The Hidalgo Revolt*, p. 178, argues that 'the retreat from the gates of Mexico [City] . . . was of no great importance in determining the fate of the insurrection. The retreat was a symptom rather than the cause of defeat'.

[397] Anna, *Fall of the Royal Government*, pp. 72–3; Hamill, *The Hidalgo Revolt*, pp. 180–1.

Bajío and centre-west. Here, the rebels could count on greater local support (we will shortly consider why), and, in cities like Valladolid and Guadalajara, they resumed their persecution of the *peninsulares*. Now, however, mob fury was replaced by clinical executions – of 60 *peninsulares* at Valladolid, 350 at Guadalajara (most were knifed or macheted on the outskirts of the city: the massacre began, perhaps significantly, on 12 December, the feast day of the Virgin of Guadalupe).[398] More constructively, Hidalgo promulgated laws protecting Indian landholding and abolishing tribute, slavery and certain excise taxes. Meanwhile, supportive rebellions gathered pace: to the west, in the hilly terrain of Tepic; to the south, in the hot country of Michoacan and Guerrero; and in pockets of the centre (Puebla, Tlaxcala) and of the northeast around San Luis Potosí (where, as in the French Revolution, rumour inflated rebel numbers and instilled, among elites and authorities, a kind of contagious 'great fear').[399]

But Spanish recruitment was also proceeding apace. Local militias, often recruited by landlords, reinforced the regular army and, although they were numerically dwarfed by the insurgents and their calibre was open to question, these royalist force possessed the weaponry and basic military organization which their opponents chronically lacked. Led by the capable and confident Calleja, a royalist army of some 8,000 made for Guadalajara. Hidalgo's forces perhaps numbered 36,000, but of these less than a thousand possessed firearms, and such artillery as they had was old and unreliable. Apart from a small nucleus – perhaps 200 – of ex-militiamen, this was a disorganized host, equipped with machetes, pikes and clubs. At the battle of Calderón Bridge, fought near Guadalajara on 17 January 1811, the rebels broke, ran and were massacred. They suffered between 6,000 and 7,000 casualties to the royalists' 150.[400] The subsequent dispersal of Hidalgo's army was as rapid as its inital mustering. Retreating northwards, Hidalgo himself was stripped of his command by his disgruntled creole lieutenants; Allende wrestled with

[398] Hamnett, *Roots of Insurgency*, p. 134.

[399] Hamill, *The Hidalgo Revolt*, p. 185; Hamnett, *Roots of Insurgency*, pp. 77–100, 136–48; Tutino, *From Insurrection to Revolution*, pp. 158–64, 184–7; Escobar Ohmstede, 'La insurgencia huasteca', pp. 140–4; Van Young, 'Islands in the Storm', p. 139 ('great fear').

[400] Archer, '"La Causa Buena": The Counterinsurgency Army of New Spain and the Ten Years' War', in Rodríguez O., *The Independence of Mexico*, p. 91, n. 25; Hamill, *The Hidalgo Revolt*, pp. 201–2.

his conscience pondering 'whether it would be moral...to poison Hidalgo in order to avoid even greater evils'.[401] The insurgent army broke up, as contingents sought safe refuges: in the mountains of the Bajío, in Zacatecas, in San Luis, even in distant Texas. But Calleja's army pressed on in pursuit, even though its strength was sapped by the 'whores and heat' which accompanied northern campaigning.[402] Rebel leaders were successively defeated, caught or amnestied. In March 1811 Hidalgo was run to ground near Monclova (Coahuila). After a show trial and defrocking he was executed and his dismembered head sent to Guanajuato, where for ten years it adorned the *alhóndiga*, the site of the rebels' first bloody triumph.[403]

The defeat and death of Hidalgo did not, however, end the insurgency. The rebels perceived the folly of big conventional campaigns, and they now mounted decentralized guerrilla operations against the Spanish authorities. A roster of leaders suggests the geographical scope and social heterogeneity of the insurgency: the muleteer-priest José María Morelos fought on in the hot country of Michoacan and Guerrero, where he counted on the support of members of the provincial elite such as the Bravo and Galeana families; a congeries of Indian revolts affected the region around Lake Chapala, some of them (Zacoalco, Mezcala) proving obdurately resistant to royalist repression; Indian rebels also controlled the fastnesses of the Sierra Gorda; the Rayón brothers and Albino García remained active in the Bajío; Julián Villagrán, the *cacique* of Huichapán, led his family, clan and Indian supporters in the region north of Querétaro; and the Osorno family – another provincial clan – operated in northern Puebla and the pulque-rich plains of Apam, which became the focus of a sustained insurgency in 1811–12.[404]

Of these, Morelos was the most militarily successful and politically significant. Like Hidalgo, whose pupil he had been, Morelos was a parish priest who enjoyed a close rapport with the local

[401] Lindley, *Haciendas and Development*, p. 70.
[402] Hamill, *The Hidalgo Revolt*, p. 207.
[403] Hamill, *The Hidalgo Revolt*, p. 216.
[404] Archer, 'Bite of the Hydra', pp. 92–3, notes the shift from conventional to guerrilla warfare, which Calleja correctly perceived 'as similar to the mode used by the provinces of Spain with respect to the French' after 1808. Hamnett, *Roots of Insurgency*, p. 136ff., offers a good review of the patriot leaders and their rebellions.

peasantry, in his case the peasantry of the remote coastal hot country of Michoacan. Like Hidalgo, too, he was a heterodox priest of entrepreneurial bent; early in life he had worked as an *arriero* (muleteer); as *cura* of the poor, rough, parish of Carácuaro he traded in grain, livestock and rum, while fathering two children.[405] Unmoved by the initial revolt of 1810 – he had contributed to the royal war chest in 1808 – Morelos was, it seems, driven to rebel by the excommunication and execution of his old mentor, Hidalgo.[406] Unlike Hidalgo, however, Morelos exerted greater control over his popular levies and thus secured and retained the support of important local elites. Raising the standard of revolt in November 1810, Morelos promptly decreed the abolition of slavery and caste distinctions (apart from Indians, the Pacific *tierra caliente* had a large black and mulatto population). But, in addition, Morelos won and retained the support of local creole elites, such as the Bravo and Galeana families, resentful (it would seem) of central authority and of the powerful Spanish merchants who controlled the cotton trade of the region.[407] Mindful of the lessons of Hidalgo's revolt, Morelos strove to contain ethnic and class tensions: he stressed the common American identity of the rebels, creoles, castes and Indians alike and their common opposition to the Godless, *afrancesado*, 'Machiavellian' Spaniards; he attracted to his camp members of the moderate creole opposition who had been alarmed by the wanton violence of the Bajío insurgency; and he blended religion and patriotism in a powerful amalgam, exemplified by his war-cry, 'the true religion and the patria'.[408]

As Hidalgo's fortunes fell, those of Morelos rose. From his secure southwestern base,[409] Morelos launched major campaigns into the Mexican heartland. In 1811 his forces crossed Oaxaca, winning support from communities which had suffered the abuses of the *repartimiento* system. By the winter of 1811–12 he was ready to invade southern Puebla, and it seemed as if the military initiative had

405 Taylor, *Magistrates of the Sacred*, pp. 463–4. Wilbert H. Timmons, *Morelos: Priest, Soldier, Statesman of Mexico* (El Paso, 1963), is a worthy but somewhat dated biography.

406 Taylor, *Magistrates of the Sacred*, p. 465.

407 Timmons, *Morelos*, p. 47; Guardino, *Peasants*, pp. 56–7 (creole elites), 65–6 (mulattos).

408 Taylor, *Magistrates of the Sacred*, p. 466.

409 Between 1810 and 1815 the insurgents led by Morelos gained control of modern-day Guerrero and established 'an organized and functioning government' in the region – something, of course, which Hidalgo had failed to do in Jalisco or the Bajío: Guardino, *Peasants*, p. 68.

again switched to the insurgents. But Morelos failed to press the advantage; he declined to attack the panic-stricken city of Puebla; and he turned back to the west, assuming a defensive position in the southern town of Cuautla (Morelos). The Puebla region became the scene of scattered guerrilla operations, while Cuautla withstood a costly three-month siege at the hands of the redoubtable Calleja.[410] Both sides suffered heavy losses from fighting and disease until, in May 1812, the weary rebels broke out and the no less weary royalists allowed them to disperse and regroup. Later in 1812, Morelos led a second thrust eastwards, into Puebla and Veracruz, but now the royalist garrisons were stronger, and the rebels were again forced to retreat to their southwestern bastions in Guerrero and Oaxaca. By the end of 1812 the main rebel threat to the central highlands had been conjured, and royalist commanders were able to embark on counterinsurgency operations which successfully limited – but could not eliminate – the local guerrillas.[411]

Morelos pulled back to the west coast, where in the summer of 1813 he captured and razed the Pacific port of Acapulco 'as a warning to the gachupines'.[412] Flushed with victory, he now convened an insurgent congress, which met in the small, hot, provincial town of Chilpancingo (Guerrero). The congress – more a hand-picked junta than a popular assembly – boldly proclaimed the independence of Mexico and named Morelos generalísimo and chief of the executive of the new nation. The monarchism and autonomism which had characterized most of the early insurgency now gave way to a forthright nationalism. A year later (October 1814) the congress convened at Apatzingán and promulgated a prolix, liberal, federal and republican constitution.[413] With these two political declarations the literati of the revolution – many of them middle-class *letrados*, nurtured on Enlightenment thinking and profoundly influenced by the examples of the French Revolution and the Spanish Cortes de

[410] Anna, *Fall of the Royal Government*, pp. 86–7; Timmons, *Morelos*, pp. 64–72; Hamnett, *Roots of Insurgency*, pp. 157–61.

[411] Hamnett, *Roots of Insurgency*, pp. 165–8.

[412] Hamnett, *Roots of Insurgency*, pp. 169–70; Timmons, *Morelos*, p. 82.

[413] Lynch, *Spanish American Revolutions*, pp. 315, 317. On the character and evolution of Morelos's political thought, see Brading, *Church and State*, pp. 244–5, and Taylor, *Magistrates of the Sacred*, pp. 466–7.

Cádiz – gave a new twist to the insurgency. Spanish intransigence in Mexico undercut the appeal of home rule within the empire, while it exacerbated the old hatred of the *gachupines*. At the same time, Bourbon collaboration with Napoleon tarnished the monarchy. The result was an outright, articulate independence movement, the vehicle of Mexico's middle-class intellectuals and professionals, as well as of its restive provincial elites, who now enunciated a new discourse: 'the Kingdom became the Nation, and the subject became the citizen'.[414]

Meanwhile, events in Spain offered the last best chance for a negotiated home rule solution. In response to the Napoleonic invasion, Spain's Central Junta convened an elected Cortes (parliament), which met in Cádiz between 1810 and 1813. The Cortes, representing both the Spanish electorate and the provinces of Spanish America, introduced liberal reforms (press freedom, the abolition of tribute and the Holy Office) and conceded *de facto* home rule to the colonies. These provisions were embodied in the new Constitution of 1812, which set up a constitutional monarchy. Elections – of an indirect, even incestuous, kind – were held throughout Mexico in the summer of 1810,[415] and Mexican delegates crossed the Atlantic to Cádiz, where they participated in the framing of the 1812 Constitution and argued eloquently for free trade, equal opportunity and colonial

---

[414] Guardino, *Peasants*, p. 68.

[415] Nettie Lee Benson, ed., *Mexico and the Spanish Cortes, 1810–1822* (Austin, 1966), in which Charles R. Berry, 'The Election of the Mexican Deputies to the Spanish Cortes, 1810–1822', p. 14, observes that, 'since only municipal council members of the provincial capitals participated', the initial selection of Mexican representatives to the Cortes 'could be called an election only by a broad interpretation of the word'. See also Rodríguez O., *Independence of Spansh America*, pp. 61–2. After the promulgation of the Constitution of Cádiz in 1812, although the electoral process retained a three-tiered indirect character (voters chose electors at parish, district and provincial levels), elections were conducted on the basis of a broader (male) franchise: Berry, pp. 18–19, states that Indians and mestizos had the right to vote, so long as they 'had a place of residence and an honest occupation' (domestic servants did not count under this heading); Virginia Guedea, 'The First Popular Elections in Mexico City, 1812–13', in Jaime Rodríguez O., ed., *The Evolution of the Mexican Political System* (Wilmington, Del., 1993), pp. 51–2, eliminates *castas* from the electorate (in principle), while noting that, in practice, they sometimes voted, 'appearance' and 'colour' notwithstanding: proof that 'the old model – the caste society – was no longer corresponding to reality', in political as well as in socioeconomic terms. In short, elections were genuine, if somewhat limited; they still compared pretty favourably with, say, their pre-1832 English equivalents; and, generalized throughout Mexico, they represented a genuine political transformation – in the words of Antonio Annino, 'a silent but profound revolution': 'Cádiz y la revolución territorial de los pueblos mexicanos, 1812–21', in Annino, ed., *Historia de las elecciones en Iberoamerica, siglo XIX* (Buenos Aires, 1995), p. 177; see also Rodríguez O., *Independence of Spanish America*, p. 94.

self-government.[416] While Morelos fought for outright independence
in the Mexican south, deputies like José Miguel Ramos Arizpe flew
the flag for Mexican home rule in Cádiz.

But both failed. The Spanish military authorities in Mexico ignored constitutional niceties when it suited them: they flouted the
provisions for free speech and when, in November 1812, a clutch
of creoles was elected to the city council – amid popular jubilation
and subversive sloganeering – the viceroy promptly annulled the election.[417] A tenuous constitutionalism, constantly checked by a viceroy
who 'functioned as if he were at the head of a military dictatorship',
survived until 1814, when, following Napoleon's defeat, the restoration of King Ferdinand VII scuppered the constitutional experiment
in both Spain and the colonies.[418] As metropolitan reform collapsed,
so, too, the Mexican insurgency faltered. In December 1813 Morelos's
attack on Valladolid (Michoacan) was beaten off by Calleja. In May
1814 Oaxaca fell to the royalists.[419] Insurgent leaders were picked
off; the survivors fell to bickering among themselves; and Morelos's
authority wilted. The rump congress which proclaimed the new Constitution at Apatzingán in November 1814 represented an embattled
minority; not surprisingly their Constitution – a liberal, *letrado* challenge to a restored royal absolutism – remained a dead letter.[420] A year

---

[416] W. Woodrow Anderson, 'Reform as a Means to Quell Revolution', in Benson, *Mexico and the Spanish Cortes*, pp. 188–9; Timothy Anna, 'The Independence of Mexico and Central America', in Leslie Bethell, ed., *The Cambridge History of Latin America*, vol. 3, *From Independence to c. 1870* (Cambridge, 1985), pp. 73–4.

[417] Guedea, 'The First Popular Elections', pp. 55–7; Nettie Lee Benson, 'The Contested Mexican Election of 1812', *Hispanic American Historical Review*, 26 (1946), pp. 336–50.

[418] Anna, 'The Independence of Mexico', pp. 76–7. The story is told in greater detail in Rodríguez O., *Independence of Spanish America*, pp. 103–6.

[419] Restored to authority in Oaxaca, where trade and hacienda production had been devastated by fighting and peon flight, the royalists – acting at the behest of the local merchants' lobby – sought to restore the *repartimiento* system of forced commerce, designed to extract commodities (especially cochineal) from the Indians: an indication (a) of how politico-colonial conflict (royalists vs patriots) intertwined with ethnic-economic divisions (merchants vs Indians); and (b) of how difficult it therefore becomes to imagine a decorous and peaceful transition to 'home rule' (see Hamnett, *Politics and Trade*, pp. 139–44). In crudely schematic terms: peaceful transitions to home rule (e.g., Canada) depend on the prior existence of class or ethnic relations in which coercion and antagonism are at a discount, hence the withdrawal of impe-rial authority does not substantially affect such relations and can therefore be contemplated with equanimity; in Mexico, in contrast, the colonial nexus was intertwined with such rela-tions, hence could not be broken – or progressively attenuated – without provoking severe repercussions within colonial society.

[420] Morelos himself – who played only a small part in the creation of the Constitution – regarded it as 'mal por impracticable' ('bad by virtue of being unworkable'): Taylor, *Magistrates of the*

later Morelos himself, covering the retreat of the itinerant congress, was run to ground near Puebla and, like his mentor and predecessor Hidalgo, was tried, defrocked and executed.[421]

Many lesser captains of the insurgency were also eliminated: Albino García was executed – by the sanguinary royalist officer Agustín Iturbide – in June 1812, and Julián Villagrán, 'the emperor of the Huasteca', met a similar fate in June 1813.[422] The island fortress of Mezcala, in Lake Chapala, which had held out against repeated royalist assaults for five years, surrendered, on honourable terms, in November 1816.[423] Guerrillas – and bandits – still prowled the countryside of Guanajuato, Jalisco, Michoacan, Veracruz, Zacatecas and the hot country of Guerrero.[424] Several – like Juan Alvarez, Gordiano Guzmán and Guadalupe Victoria (of Guerrero, Michoacan, and Veracruz respectively) – would emerge as the provincial caudillos of independent Mexico. Collectively, they were a redoubtable force, who controlled extensive tracts of country, and could throw a scare into major towns – Querétaro, Jalapa, Puebla, even Mexico City – with

Sacred, p. 467 (admittedly, the quote derives from Morelos's interrogation while a prisoner of the Inquisition – hardly a 'transparent speech situation'). Villoro, *El proceso ideológico*, p. 119, following José Miranda, stresses the French constitutional models (of 1793 and 1795) which supposedly inspired the Constitution of Apatzingṭn; compare MacLachlan and Rodríguez O., *Forging of the Cosmic Race*, p. 328, who assert that 'the new Mexican charter was modeled on . . . the Spanish Constitution of 1812'.

[421] Timmons, *Morelos*, pp. 156–63. Morelos was, in effect, successively tried by the Church, the Inquisition, and the (colonial) state; in the course of which ordeal he appeared to recant, at least to the extent of furnishing information about the continued insurgency – prompted, it seems, less by physical intimidation or political remorse than by fear for his immortal soul.

[422] On García and Villagrán, see Hamnett, *Roots of Insurgency*, pp. 138–9, 180–82; Archer, '"La Causa Buena"', p. 91; Villoro, *El proceso ideológico*, p. 104; Brading, *First America*, pp. 637–8.

[423] On the remarkable story of Mezcala, see Taylor, 'Rural Unrest in Central Jalisco', pp. 221–5, and Christon I. Archer, 'Politicization of the Army of New Spain during the War of Independence, 1810–21', in Rodríguez O., *Evolution of the Mexican Political System*, pp. 27–8.

[424] Hamnett, *Roots of Insurgency*, pp. 183–97. The distinction between 'guerrillas' and 'bandits' (thus, between political rebels and freelance criminals) is often blurred, especially in times of endemic civil war. The distinction often depends on the perspective of the observer – most obviously and systematically with the authorities' blanket attribution of 'banditry' to all forms of popular rural insurgency, protest and dissidence (a phenomenon which Escobar Ohmstede, 'La insurgencia huasteca', p. 145, dates to the 1810s). However, even 'civil society' had its contrasting viewpoints, depending not only on class and ethnicity but also on locality: a popular insurgent-cum-'social bandit' need only cross a range of hills to be perceived as an interloping bandit. Time, too, could affect perceptions (as well as reality): bandits, possessing skills which are functional to popular rebellion, can experience sudden rehabilitation when peace and normality give way to to insurgency; conversely, the receding tide of popular revolution usually leaves some washed-up rebels who, by way of survival, mutate into mercenary (distinctly 'unsocial') bandits.

sudden, bold raids.[425] Even after 1815, the insurgency was not beaten and, indeed, could not be beaten.[426] But, given their 'atomization', the insurgents could not defeat Calleja's royalist army in the field.[427] The result was a weary stalemate. Between 1815 and 1820, therefore, Spain's rule endured; like an ageing prize-fighter, groggy and punch-drunk, the viceregal regime stayed shakily on its feet and refused to go down; and the scattered insurgents could not mount a knock-out blow. When the insurgent Francisco Javier Mina launched a bold filibustering expedition from the United States in 1816, he confronted a militarized colonial regime and a war-weary population, and his quixotic effort came to nothing.[428]

In this, once again, Mexico was somewhat unusual. Most of Spanish America had by now won its independence. Of mainland Spanish America, only Peru, a comparable centre of powerful Spanish vested interests and a dense, restless, indigenous peasantry, remained under Spanish rule, that rule being accepted by property-owners, European and creole alike, as a necessary guarantee against popular upheaval and caste war. Thus, in Mexico, the counterinsurgency was to a considerable extent the work of creole elites who – perhaps not surprisingly – placed their lives and property above their commitment to independence. (They were also attracted by the *fuero militar*, the judicial privilege enjoyed by the military who, along with the clergy, were exempt from civil jurisdiction.)[429] Creole officers like

[425] Archer, '"La Causa Buena"', pp. 99–100.

[426] Anna, *Fall of the Royal Government*, p. 73, discerns the 'final defeat of the...rebel forces' in 1816 (see also the same author's 'Independence of Mexico', p. 81). However, there remained plenty of insurgents (and bandits) in the field, whom the royalists could not quell; hence Archer's image of a hydra which, in Calleja's own words, 'the more you cut off its heads, the more it is reborn', seems a more convincing picture: 'Bite of the Hydra', p. 69 (see also '"La Causa Buena"', pp. 102–3). Such debates – which are of obvious relevance to the broader question of the legitimacy of the colonial regime – took place among the royalist commanders themselves: General José de la Cruz, military commander in western Mexico, president of the Audiencia, and 'student of guerrilla warfare and counterinsurgency', questioned royalist propaganda which, in 1815, dismissed the insurgents as no more than 'small gangs of bandits' when, in fact, 'the insurrection raged unchecked along the frontiers of the provinces of Guanajuato, Valladolid, and Nueva Galicia' and, in Cruz's own words, 'the whole kingdom knows that large rebel gatherings are taking place'. Cruz also produced his own variant on the hydra metaphor: how, he pondered, could one defeat a rebellion 'that renews itself and grows like grass?': Archer, 'Politicization of the Army', pp. 21, 32.

[427] The word is Villoro's, *El proceso ideológico*, p. 105.

[428] Villoro, *El proceso ideológico*, pp. 122–3; Rodríguez O., *Independence of Spanish America*, p. 193.

[429] Neill Macaulay, 'The Army of New Spain and the Mexican Delegation to the Spanish Cortes', in Benson, *Mexico and the Spanish Cortes*, pp. 136–7, 140, 149.

Agustín Iturbide were ruthless in their repression of the rebels. Commanding in the Bajío, Iturbide engaged in the whole gamut of counterinsurgency tactics: the taking of hostages, the forced concentration of populations, the enactment of exemplary punishments. The Spanish authorities encouraged creole military recruitment and repression. Calleja organized vigilante groups in the Bajío, officered by the local well-to-do, whose task it was to combat insurrection and 'contain the excesses of the lower orders'.[430] Fear of 'the lower orders' ran deep, especially after the initial uprising of 1810. The president of the Audiencia of New Galicia, based in the strife-torn city of Guadalajara, responded to Hidalgo's earlier excesses by arbitrarily executing batches of suspects, choosing his victims by lot. Even the possession of kitchen knives became a capital offence.[431]

All this had serious implications for the colonial nexus, which, as Calleja frankly admitted, was now largely sustained by *force majeure*.[432] This involved increased taxation, a major military build-up and widespread forced recruitment. Arbitrary taxes were levied, compounding old fiscal grievances, both creole and popular, and driving landlords, merchants and artisans to ruin.[433] Yet, as mining production slumped, government debt rose inexorably.[434] Between 1810 and 1820 the (royalist) military payroll nearly tripled, from some thirty to nearly ninety thousand men: men who had to be fed and billeted, and whose daily conduct – carousing, thieving, vandalizing, philandering – gave offence to civilians of all classes.[435] The majority of this new military establishment was Mexican-born (many were reluctant conscripts, whom even savage floggings could not deter from desertion); but some twenty thousand Spanish veterans

---

[430] Brian Hamnett, 'Royalist Counterinsurgency and the Continuity of Rebellion: Guanajuato and Michoacán, 1813–1820', *Hispanic American Historical Review*, 62 (1982), p. 25.

[431] Lindley, *Haciendas and Economic Development*, p. 92.

[432] 'The Empire of Spain is a giant...whose conservation depends on physical force' (Calleja): Anna, *Fall of the Royal Government*, p. 74 (see also pp. 89, 138–9); Archer, 'Bite of the Hydra', pp. 84, 92–3.

[433] John Jay TePaske, 'The Financial Disintegration of the Royal Government of Mexico during the Epoch of Independence', in Rodríguez O., *The Independence of Mexico*, pp. 63–84; Ladd, *Mexican Nobility*, pp. 147–9, cites contemporary estimates and complaints, suggesting that the collapse of credit and disappearance of circulating money were the most serious blows.

[434] In 1809 24.7 million pesos of silver were minted; in 1810 18 million; in 1811 9 million; and in 1812 4 million: Hira de Gortari, 'La minería durante la guerra de independencia y los primeros años del México independiente', in Rodríguez O., *The Independence of Mexico*, pp. 132–3.

[435] Anna, *Fall of the Royal Government*, pp. 83–4 (figures); Archer, ' "La Causa Buena" ', p. 100 (conduct).

were also deployed in Mexico, where they combined harsh repression with haughty racism, further aggravating anti-Spanish sentiments.[436] The popular classes, who had never much loved the Spaniards, now grew to hate the *gachupines* more than ever. The creoles, who itched for home rule but feared popular subversion, became increasingly aware of their pivotal role in maintaining – by force of arms – a colonial regime which they disliked. And the regime itself lost its residual legitimacy: the progressive secularization and militarization of society which the Bourbons had initiated now gathered speed; priests were executed by the dozen and martial rule replaced civilian.[437] Even during its brief liberal incarnation, between the establishment of the 1812 Constitution and the restoration of Ferdinand VII in 1814, the Spanish metropolitan regime failed to extend liberal guarantees to New Spain. Spanish liberalism was for *peninsular* consumption rather than export to the restive colonies.[438] And Spanish claims to civilized superiority were daily refuted by the work of firing squads, practising the 'exemplary terror' recommended by Spanish commanders.[439] The result, by 1815, was a Roman peace, premised on repression and exhaustion, tempered by judicious amnesties.[440] But this, as soon became clear, was no basis for stable colonial rule.

---

[436] Villoro, *El proceso ideológico*, pp. 138–40, 147–8. The Spanish veterans also found themselves employing the same kind of counterinsurgency methods which the Napoleonic armies had used against them in recent years: Archer, ' "La Causa Buena" ', p. 93. Spanish abuses enabled patriot polemicists – like Fray Servando Teresa de Mier – to harp on old historical themes redolent of Hispanophobia: Calleja's recapture and repression of Guanajuato recalled Pedro Alvarado's slaughter of the Aztec nobility, while General Cruz now ravaged Michoacan as Nuño de Guzmán had done three centuries before: Brading, *First America*, p. 592.

[437] Archer, ' "La Causa Buena" ', p. 94; Archer, 'Bite of the Hydra', p. 92; Berry, 'The Army of New Spain', pp. 143–5. On the execution of priests (which necessitated the final abolition of the *fuero eclesiástico* – clerical immunity to criminal prosecution), see Farriss, *Crown and Clergy*, pp. 210–36 (which, p. 219, cites a – probably exaggerated – figure of 125 priests executed between 1810 and 1815). Taylor, *Magistrates of the Sacred*, pp. 453, 491–7, records 11 *known* executions, out of a total number of ('reputed') insurgent priests of around 145. The real number presumably lies between these extremes, probably closer to Taylor's estimate.

[438] Farriss, *Crown and Clergy*, p. 223; Villoro, 'La revolución de independencia', pp. 338–9.

[439] Archer, ' "La Causa Buena" ', p. 94, quoting General Cruz's preferred means of dealing with the 'vile scum' who had risen with Hidalgo.

[440] Juan Ruiz de Apodaca, who succeeed Calleja as viceroy in September 1816, was more disposed to conciliate and boasted of issuing 30,000 amnesties in two years. However, conciliation complemented – and in no sense supplanted – a continued reliance on repression which, in turn, attested to the continued vigour of the insurgency: Hamnett, 'Royalist Counterinsurgency', pp. 42–5; Archer, 'The Counterinsurgency Army', pp. 101–5.

Before the dramatic events of 1820–21 and the final debacle of Spanish colonialism in Mexico are considered, it is worth pausing to review the dynamics of the insurgency: a movement which, although it failed directly to overthrow Spanish rule, drastically weakened the colonial regime, transformed sociopolitical relations in Mexico, and provided the backdrop not only for the elite secession of 1820–21 but also for the ensuing independent regime – the 'Bourbon Republic' – of 1821–54.[441] Like any mass revolution – albeit in this case a failed revolution – the insurgency embraced different groups, localities and interests. Often, closer inspection of particular cases reveals bewildering variations; the grand popular struggle for independence, the foundation myth of the modern Mexican nation-state, seems to fragment into a multitude of petty feuds and quarrels. According to Hamnett's careful study, 'the revolutionary movement launched by Hidalgo and led subsequently by Morelos briefly transformed scattered, sporadic local conflicts into the semblance of a national movement'; but 'when the official leadership receded, the revolutionary movement fragmented into its component elements' – varied, isolated and incoherent.[442] The motives of participants remain obscure; their own understanding of the historical events they witnessed can only be conjectured. For some authors, therefore, the popular insurgency becomes an almost meaningless, stochastic sequence of events. The Indians, it has been said, rallied to whichever leader pitched the first appeal to their impressionable minds; an interpretation which, though hard either to prove or to refute, seems both condescending and questionable.[443]

The recent historiography of the 1810 insurgency, like that of the 1910 Revolution, has adopted a local, regional and 'bottom-up' approach, which, rightly, accentuates variation and complexity – at the level of the colony, the region, even the individual community.[444]

---

[441] This revisionist description – now, perhaps, an orthodoxy – suggests that the caesura of independence (1821) was less dramatic than previously supposed; and that basic continuities – especially socioeconomic continuities – spanned the period c. 1750–1850 (see n. 4 above). There are arguments for and against, which cannot be reviewed here; it is hoped that a follow-up volume will address them.

[442] Hamnett, *Roots of Insurgency*, p. 202.

[443] Lynch, *Spanish American Revolutions*, p. 311.

[444] Hamnett, *Roots of Insurgency*, illustrates regional diversity; Guardino, *Peasants*, gives examples of variations within communities (see pp. 4, 49, 53).

But this trend should not be allowed to convert the insurgency (or the Revolution) into an aimless shambles. Certain patterns were evident within the complex skein of events and processes. Like any great revolution, the insurgency involved a supreme political crisis, marked by the clash of rival ideologies, visions and sovereignties. Some Mexicans eagerly entered the fray; some were forced to define their allegiances by the prick of circumstances; many contrived to remain neutral observers – although, quite often, 'neutrality', in the sense of non-participation, appears to have masked sympathy for the insurgents, inhibited by draconian Spanish coercion.[445]

By decapitating the Spanish monarchy, Napoleon's invasion provoked a crisis of legitimacy, removed the supreme arbiter which was the monarch and drove a wedge between Mexico's ruling elites; in this, Napoleon's adventurism had profound effects – in Mexico as in Italy, Germany or the Low Countries – and it would be wrong to consider it a mere 'trigger', a random spark put to an already smouldering powderkeg.[446] However, it is even more wrong to endow this external cause with supreme explanatory power or to suggest that, but for the random roll of the geopolitical dice in Europe, Spain would have continued to rule a contented empire for generations to come.[447] For New Spain was not contented; pressures had been

---

[445] For examples of popular neutrality and clerical mediation between the warring parties, see Taylor, *Magistrates of the Sacred*, pp. 451, 458–9, 462.

[446] Unfortunately, we historians readily amplify our etiological vocabulary ('causes', 'factors', 'determinants', 'influences', 'catalysts', 'triggers') without being able to differentiate between these concepts, save in gross terms (e.g., a 'cause' is more important than a 'trigger'): James D. Fearon, 'Causes and Counterfactuals in Social Science', in Philip Tetlock and Aaron Belkin, eds., *Counterfactual Thought Experiments in World Politics* (Princeton, 1996), p. 39. One 'counterfactual' approach to the dilemma is to consider what might have happened had Napoleon not invaded Spain: would Mexico have remained a loyal colony (and if so, for how long)? I incline to the view that a prolonged colonial relationship was unlikely; and, given the nature of Spanish regime, a decorous transition to 'home rule' also seems improbable.

[447] As MacLachlan and Rodríguez O., *Forging of the Cosmic Race*, pp. 294–5, seem to suggest. Rodríguez O., *Independence of Spanish America*, pp. 240–1, argues that a rapprochement between metropolis and colonies was still eminently feasible as late as 1814, but – something of a concession to the 'Bad King John' theory of history? – 'the king opted to rely on force to restore royal order in the New World' and the opportunity was lost. The argument seems to me to *over*estimate the role of Fernando VII (important though that certainly was) and to *under*estimate the sociopolitical obstacles to rapprochement, in both Spain and Spanish America. It is worth noting, as a coda, that Spain clung to her remaining colony – Cuba – for a further eighty years, in the face of sustained opposition, and was only finally dislodged by *force majeure*.

accumulating for a couple of generations; and, while the timing of the explosion depended on external factors, the potential for upheaval existed (in a way that it had not, say, a century earlier), and, barring some prescient Spanish statesmanship (a commodity not much in evidence), some sort of explosion was quite likely.[448]

However, the pressures pullulating within Mexican society took many forms; hence, at the local level – which was usually the crucial level[449] – the crisis of 1808 unleashed a gamut of conflicts and commitments: those of class, ethnicity, faction and generation. Regions and communities polarized according to old divisions: peasant against landlord, village against village, clique against clique. Sometimes straight socioeconomic divisions determined alignments; sometimes ethnic ties were paramount; but often, factional – what may be called 'Namierite' – divisions carried more weight, pitting against each other groups which were indistinguishable in terms of their socioeconomic categories.[450] An 'in' faction (e.g., royal officials or privileged merchants) aligns with the regime; their rival 'outs' flirt with rebellion. Viewed at a national or regional level such splits assumed the 'court-and-country' character, mentioned earlier: provincial ('country') elites mobilized against central ('court') officialdom. Hence the insurgency counted on the support of some provincial elites: in the Bajío, Allende, Aldama and Abasalo ('all three landowning sons of Basque merchants'); in Guerrero the propertied Bravo and Galeana families.[451] At the local level, too, the factional splits which chronically affected village communities often assumed new political labels – royalist or insurgent – which

---

[448] It is a telling point that the succession crisis of 1700 – which led to the prolonged War of the Spanish Succession (1700–1714) – did not provoke major upheaval in Spain's American colonies: 'the political moment had not arrived when a conjuncture of this kind would raise thoughts of liberation' (Lynch, *Bourbon Spain*, p. 53). A century later, things were different.

[449] Tip O'Neill's dictum, 'all politics is local politics', is particularly valid for rural Mexico (which was still the bulk of Mexico): see Guardino, *Peasants*, p. 41; Hamnett, *Roots of Insurgency*, p. 53. For a good example of local redefinition of 'national' issues, see Martin's analysis of how, in response to the crisis of 1808, the 'citizens of Yautepec [Morelos] quickly grafted political controversies onto their own longstanding disputes': *Rural Society*, pp. 190–1.

[450] By 'Namierite' (from Lewis Namier, the celebrated historian of British eighteenth-century politics) I refer to political allegiances premised on clientelism and patronage, to the exclusion, more or less, of class, ethnic and ideological loyalties.

[451] MacLachlan and Rodríguez O., *Forging of the Cosmic Race*, p. 310; Guardino, *Peasants*, pp. 56–7.

failed to correspond to any clear socioeconomic polarization.[452] Revolt could also take on generational significance, as it was often the
work of younger men (and women), keen to steal a march on their elders and betters.[453] Thus, like other great revolutions (France, 1789;
Mexico, 1910), the insurgency drew upon the reservoir of innumer-
able, ostensibly petty, local squabbles, which fed into and swelled
the national crisis. But the absence of a coherent shared programme
or a 'vanguard party' did not prevent the movement from having a
decisive impact; nor does the multiplicity of events and actors make
rational analysis and generalization impossible.

As already suggested, the insurgency possessed a distinct regional
pattern. The Bajío was the seat of the great initial uprising captained
by Hidalgo and characterized by explosive, sometimes 'expressive',
violence. On the one hand, the revolt was whistled up by disgruntled provincial elites – especially those of the peripheral northern
Bajío – who espoused the familiar creole project of colonial self-
government, of home rule. Major landlords and officials opposed
the revolt *ab initio*, and most well-to-do creoles were, at best, neutral. When Hidalgo sought a new intendant to govern Guanajuato,
none of the four creole *regidores* (town councillors) would consent.
Only two prominent Guanajuato creoles joined the rebellion.[454] As
the violence spread, creole leaders like Allende were appalled and
waverers increasingly shifted to the royalist side; hence the initial
creole-*peninsular* division (easily exaggerated anyway) tended to give
way to a more pronounced class division, between rich and poor,
propertied and propertyless.

[452] It is often difficult to know whether local polarizations were purely 'factional' and 'Namierite',
   i.e., based on simple clientelism and the Hobbesian struggle for power and profit, or, in fact,
   masked deeper class or ethnic divisions. For example, did the 'rabid' and 'peaceful' factions
   discerned by colonial officials within communities in Guerrero (Guardino, *Peasants*, p. 30)
   correspond to plebeians and elites, or to Indians, castes and creoles, or did they defy any
   such 'deeper' classification? Sometimes – for example, when one faction expelled another,
   alleging its 'agachupinado' (pro-Spanish) character, evidenced by its 'close identification with
   colonial authorities and merchants' (Guardino, *Peasants*, p. 53) – a presumption of a 'deeper'
   rationale may be made; but we should be aware that, from the colonial period down to the
   present, local factions have been adept at smearing their opponents and invoking 'deeper'
   justifications (social, political, cultural) for what might in fact be naked 'Namierite' power
   politics. Catholic-Protestant disputes in modern Chiapas may be a case in point.
[453] Christon Archer, 'Banditry and Revolution in New Spain, 1790–1821', *Bibliotheca Americana*,
   1/2 (1982), pp. 59–88.
[454] Hamill, *The Hidalgo Revolt*, p. 146; Brading, *Miners and Merchants*, p. 344.

By the same token, popular violence acquired a momentum of its own, which the rebellion's leaders, Hidalgo especially, were hard put to control.[455] Haciendas were ransacked, *gachupines* slaughtered. The leadership could mitigate but not halt these impolitic acts. But these acts also tell us something about the nature of the insurgency; they enable us to make cautious inferences about motives, especially when formal statements of aims are lacking. Rebel proclamations and policies offer some guide, of course. Hidalgo, for example, decreed the end of slavery and tribute (his local rival, the ill-fated intendant Riaño, also declared the abolition of tribute, in a vain attempt to appease popular opposition).[456] Slavery was a weak and decaying institution (there were perhaps 10,000 slaves in a population of over 6 million), but the abolition of tribute – along with the mitigation of Bourbon taxes on liquor and tobacco – promised some respite for Indians and castes alike. Yet the tribute-paying population of the Bajío, the seat of the rebellion, was proportionately less than that of central Mexico, where the rebels encountered a mixed response. In Guerrero, too, the Chilapa region – home to 'large numbers of Indian peasants in corporate villages' – was staunchly royalist; in Oaxaca, the bulk of the Indian peasantry spurned the insurgency, even when Morelos raised the standard of revolt in their region.[457] Promises of agrarian reform – the division of the great estates, the protection of peasant villages – later became important, as Hidalgo recruited followers in the Guadalajara region; but this was not a crucial source of support in the Bajío, where day labourers and sharecroppers outnumbered peasant villagers; nor did it figure prominently in rebellious Guerrero.[458]

Thus, in the Bajío itself, it was the sheer insecure, impoverished quality of rural (and, to a degree, urban) life which affected the majority of the popular classes, the latter embracing tenants, sharecroppers and peons, as well as urban artisans and miners. The main trends of the late colonial economy – falling real wages, tougher

---

[455] Archer, ' "La revolución desastrosa" ', p. 125; Hamill, *The Hidalgo Revolt*, pp. 148–9.

[456] Hamill, *The Hidalgo Revolt*, pp. 136, 139. Viceroy Venegas attempted a similar populist ploy a couple of weeks later: Anna, *Fall of the Royal Government*, p. 69.

[457] Guardino, *Peasants*, pp. 21, 52; Taylor, 'Banditry and Insurrection', pp. 229–30.

[458] Hamill, *The Hidalgo Revolt*, p. 196; Van Young, *Hacienda and Market*, pp. 292, 353; Guardino, *Peasants*, pp. 48, 66.

tenancy arrangements, recurrent agrarian crises – had been compounded by official policy (repression of labour and vagrancy, the
curtailment of clerical charity). The year 1809 was one of dearth, with
corn prices between two and four times higher than normal. The vicissitudes of international trade, meanwhile, hit the manufacturing
sector. Similar factors – economic instability, tax increases, mercantile exploitation – stimulated protest on the Pacific coast of Guerrero
and the Acayucan region of southern Veracruz, both centres of peasant cotton production.[459] (We may contrast Indian communities like
Tonalá and Tlajomulco, in Jalisco, which, though highly commercialized and litigious, eschewed rebellion, being 'prosperous . . . districts
that were less disturbed by the economic and political changes of
the late eightenth century', and whose inhabitants – precisely because they were both prosperous and litigious – were able to protect
their interests in the colonial courts.)[460]

It seems clear, therefore, that the prevalence of popular rebellion
in the Bajío was closely related to the region's pattern of socioeconomic development: one that had been rapid, sometimes traumatic,
and scarcely cushioned by deft political management. While it would
be simplistic – and theoretically dubious – to attribute the 1810 insurrection to the 'development of capitalism', nevertheless it was hardly
coincidental that it was the pacemaker of the Bourbon economy
which took the lead in terms of popular insurgency after 1810.[461]
But it was a perverse capitalism, compounded by extreme economic
vicissitudes and aggressive colonial (fiscal) parasitism, both greatly
exacerbated by recurrent warfare.

Hidalgo's programme offered no structural solutions to the plight
of the Bajío poor. No wholesale expropriation of haciendas was
promised. Elsewhere, sporadic, 'informal' agrarian reform occurred,
as peasants, taking advantage of the insurgency, seized land or refused to pay rents: at Mezquitic (San Luis Potosí), Zacoalco (Jalisco),
Tlastitaca (Morelos) and Tulancingo (Hidalgo) – where, in 1812, 'an
army of 4,000 "Indians" was said to have seized control of a major

[459] Guardino, *Peasants*, pp. 22–3, 34, 40–1; Hamnett, *Roots of Insurgency*, p. 80; in Oaxaca, the
region which most welcomed – or least spurned – Morelos was the cochineal-producing zone
of the Mixteca: Taylor, 'Banditry and Insurrection', p. 230.

[460] Taylor, 'Banditry and Insurrection', pp. 237–43.

[461] Tutino, *From Insurrection to Revolution*, pp. 61ff.

estate belonging to the Condesa de Regla'.[462] It cannot be said, however, that agrarian unrest – evidenced in outright land seizures – was the defining characteristic of the insurgency. In some (insurgent) areas it was largely absent; in others it was overshadowed by alternative forms of popular protest. In the Bajío, for example, rebels pillaged haciendas and killed hacienda *administradores* (*peninsulares* especially), but – and here the brevity of the rebellion was no doubt important – they undertook no grand *reparto de tierras*.[463] Meanwhile, the hated *gachupines* came to stand as scapegoats for the entire Bajío ruling class, political and economic, European and creole. Creoles did not entirely escape popular aggression, but European Spaniards suffered disproportionately.

A similar discrimination was evident in Guerrero. In part, this reflected the prominent – and resented – role of *gachupín* officials and entrepreneurs, the latter including landlords, merchants and manufacturers. In Querétaro, for example, the *obrajes* were dominated by Spaniards who reputedly exploited their workers while flaunting their excessive – and ill-gotten – wealth.[464] In coastal Guerrero, 'anti-Spanish prejudice' became the central feature of the insurgency; rebels distinguished between *peninsulares* and creoles; the creoles were 'consciously excluded ... from being identified as enemies of the movement', while the persecution of the *peninsulares* was immediate and popular.[465] Of course, the official ideology of the insurgency,

---

[462] Tutino, *From Insurrection to Revolution*, pp. 160–4, 176, 180; Guardino, *Peasants*, p. 66; Hamnett, *Roots of Insurgency*, pp. 30, 91; Taylor, 'Banditry and Insurrection', pp. 216–17; Archer, '"Viva Nuestra Señora de Guadalupe!"', p. 149; Eric Van Young, 'Moving Towards Revolt: Agrarian Origins of the Hidalgo Rebellion in the Guadalajara Region', in Katz, *Riot, Rebellion, and Revolution*, p. 183 (quote).

[463] Van Young, 'Moving Towards Revolt', pp. 183–4; note also Hamnett, *Roots of Insurgency*, pp. 181, 198; and, for Guerrero, Guardino, *Peasants*, p. 66, which illustrates Morelos's caution. During the 1810 insurgency, as in the 1910 Revolution, peasant leaders had to be careful about proclaiming a distribution of land which might result in their forces rushing home to collect their share. A precipitate land reform would also alienate sympathetic landlords and, perhaps, jeopardize insurgent income. The absence of an 'official' land reform cannot therefore be taken as guaranteed proof of the absence of popular agrarianism or land hunger, especially in the case of revolts which, like Hidalgo's, were short-lived.

[464] Sandoval Zarauz, 'Los obrajes de Querétaro', p. 132.

[465] Guardino, *Peasants*, p. 61. This evidence of Indian discrimination contrasts with Anna's (unsubstantiated) assertion that the Indian insurgents evenhandedly massacred *peninsulares* and creoles alike, since 'in the Indians' minds all whites comprised the ruling class': *Fall of the Royal Government*, p. 65. Van Young, 'Quetzalcóatl', p. 121, also notes that *peninsulares* 'were attacked and killed with such ferocity', while creoles 'were for the most part exempted from such treatment'; but he somewhat muddies the waters by then quoting Jan Szeminski

propounded by disaffected creole elites, stressed the culpability of
the *gachupines* for Mexico's ills. The Bajío poor, rising up in a mood
of long-standing resentment, either internalized this ideology – and
conceived of the *gachupines* as the true villains and appropriate targets – and/or chose to invest their plebeian violence with a broader
legitimacy by focusing on *peninsular* victims. Just as popular participants in the French Wars of Religion pursued their vendettas
and aired their rancours through the medium of religious passion
and symbolism, so the canaille of the Bajío channelled their social
antagonisms through the officially approved filter – the insurgent
'public transcript' – of ethnicity.[466] Nevertheless, popular hatred of
the *gachupines* was 'real' (I am not at all arguing for popular idiocy,
'false consciousness', or 'some irremediable superego lacunae' which
impelled the plebs to irrational acts of violence).[467] Such hatred reflected forms of colonial and ethnic oppression which were endemic,
which had gathered strength in the late colonial period and which
would be further reinforced by Spanish repression after 1810: arbitrary taxation, tribute, mercantile extortion, discrimination against
castes and Indians, the dragooning of labour and the derogation of
the Church.

Here, expressive and instrumental aspects of popular violence in-
termingled. Even if the insurgency often lacked coherent goals and
solutions, it did not want for powerful motivating sentiments (which,
I should also add, did not make the insurgents 'primitive' or 'prepolitical', as compared with more 'modern' protestors; for the latter,
too, may also draw heavily upon symbolic and expressive sources
of inspiration, such as nationalism). The historian of the insurgency
must therefore capture something of the *mentalité*, as well as the material grievances, of the rebels. The rebellion was characterized by
'excessive, almost ritual violence', inflicted particularly (though not
solely) upon the *gachupines*.[468] This violence – stabbings and stonings

---

(an Andeanist) to the effect that 'Indian rebels understood the term "Spaniard" (*español*) to
include *all* whites, whether of New or Old World origin'.

[466] Scott, *Domination and the Arts of Resistance;* cf. Natalie Zemon Davis, *Society and Culture in
Early Modern France: Eight Essays* (Stanford, 1975), ch. 6.

[467] Van Young, 'Origins of the Hidalgo Insurrection', p. 181.

[468] Eric Van Young, 'Who Was That Masked Man Anyway? Popular Symbols and Ideology in
the Mexican Wars of Independence', in *Rocky Mountain Council on Latin American Studies.
Annual Meeting* (Las Cruces, 1984), vol. 1, p. 20; note also Van Young, 'Moving Towards Revolt',

above all – reflected not only the crude weaponry of the rebels but also the fury with which they rose up and exacted vengeance on their perceived enemies: officials, landlords and merchants in particular. At Atemajac (Jalisco) Indians 'executed' a Spanish traveller – using his own lance and sword – 'because they said he was a gachupín'.[469] At Tecpan (Guerrero), twelve Spaniards were publicly beheaded, at which 'even the women demonstrated great pleasure'.[470] Of course, this popular reaction responded to years of exploitation, the product of economic change and political 'reform'. Bourbon officialdom, we have seen, was more pervasive and demanding; so, too, was the burgeoning merchant class (the link between insurrection and mercantile penetration seems to be crucial).[471] And there was method in this mayhem: destroying official archives made the subsequent collection of taxes and tribute difficult, if not impossible, while killing a few officials or merchants no doubt served as a salutary warning to those who remained.[472] The sudden conversion of once (fairly) docile castes and Indians into sanguinary insurgents invited not only elite repression but also elite reflection. Even in defeat, popular insurrection left an important legacy: 'once broken, traditional bonds and popular obedience could not be reestablished'; the landlords of independent Mexico found, after 1821, that they confronted a more belligerent, organized and militant peasantry, for whom the epithet 'bandit' now became commonplace.[473]

Despite the ethnic violence and social radicalism of the insurgency, its ideology was predominantly traditional and suffused with Catholic, conservative, even royalist values. Like the Sicilian mob, the masses of the Bajío rose up against the authorities in the name

p. 181 ('a great deal of savagery'); Hamnett, *Roots of Insurgency*, p. 32 ('hideous deaths'); and Taylor, 'Banditry and Insurrection', p. 218, on the insurgents' 'reign of terror' around Zacoalco.

[469] Taylor, 'Banditry and Insurrection', pp. 218–19.

[470] Guardino, *Peasants*, p. 61.

[471] Hamnett, *Roots of Insurgency*, pp. 26–30, 68, 80, 138, 145; Guardino, *Peasants*, pp. 40–1, 55.

[472] Guardino, *Peasants*, p. 74.

[473] Archer, ' "La revolución desastrosa" ', pp. 126–7; Escobar Ohmstede, 'La insurgencia huasteca', p. 145; Rugely, *Yucatán's Maya Peasantry*, pp. 40–4, 52–7, while noting the relative absence of outright rebellion in Yucatán, cites evidence of the Maya 'now acting with a new aggressiveness and self-assurance': for example, shunning church, refusing to pay taxes and clerical fees and casting off their deferential manners. On post-Independence peasant militancy: John H. Coatsworth, 'Patterns of Rural Rebellion in Latin America: Mexico in Comparative Perspective', in Katz, *Riot, Rebellion, and Revolution*, pp. 38, 50, 55.

of the king; like Pugachev's Cossack horde, they pledged allegiance to the *true* king – Ferdinand VII, *El Deseado* ('The Longed-For One') – whom they conceived as being a prisoner of bad advisers and French invaders,[474] a king who they sometimes believed had escaped to Mexico, where he lived a mysterious, masked existence. According to captured Indian rebels in the Bajío, the king had appeared near their village, riding in a dark coach, and he had 'enjoined them, through the headman (*gobernador*) of their village, to kill the viceroy and all other European-born Spaniards and divide their property among the poor'.[475] A woman from Cuautla (Morelos) reported that the king, disguised in a silver mask, was travelling with Hidalgo.[476] Popular messianic hopes, which had been evident in several popular movements prior to 1810, were here channelled into the unlikely figure of a reactionary Bourbon prince: a tribute to the appeal of popular monarchism (a 'naive monarchical legitimism', in Van Young's phrase) and thus, perhaps, to the residual legacy of an earlier royal paternalism.[477]

But other figures, some scarcely more appropriate, also excited messianic hopes. Some – like Hidalgo himself, who was thought by some to be able to raise his followers from the dead – were priests; a couple were Indian-messiahs, carriers of an ancient ethnic *revanchisme*.[478] But the latter were unusual (and not very effective).[479] Compared with Andean America, Mexico produced few genuinely Indian messianic or revivalist movements, pledged

[474] Jean Meyer, 'Introducción', in Meyer, *Tres levantamientos populares*, pp. 17–8.

[475] Van Young, 'Quetzalcóatl', p. 110.

[476] Van Young, 'Quetzalcóatl', p. 110; Van Young, 'Who Was That Masked Man, Anyway?', p. 18.

[477] Van Young, 'Quetzalcóatl', p. 111.

[478] Van Young, 'Quetzalcóatl', pp. 109, 123; Eric Van Young, 'Millennium on the Northern Marches: The Mad Messiah of Durango and Popular Rebellion in Mexico, 1800–15', *Comparative Studies in Society and History*, 28 (1986), pp. 385–413; Enrique Florescano, *Memoria mexicana. Ensayo sobre la reconstrucción del pasado: Época prehispánica* (Mexico, 1987), pp. 492–500. Gruzinski, *Man-Gods*, illustrates the pedigree of such phenomena.

[479] With the exception of Hidalgo, whose 'messianic' status is debatable, the messiahs of insurgent Mexico made little progress, compared with non-messianic leaders (such as Morelos), or with their nineteenth-century Brazilian counterparts: see Isaura de Queiroz, 'Messiahs in Brazil', *Past and Present*, 31 (1985), pp. 62–86. The two best-known Indian messiahs arose in Durango and Tepic – peripheral regions with a legacy of Franciscan evangelization, which may be significant (Taylor, 'Rural Unrest in Central Jalisco', pp. 232–3, notes a correlation between prior Franciscan influence and insurgency): see Van Young, 'Quetzalcóatl', p. 118. However, the impact of these northern messiahs on mainstream events was scant.

to the restoration of a Precolumbian past.[480] For whereas in Upper Peru the Inca tradition lived on, represented by known descendants of the Inca royal line, in Mexico such traditions were weak or non-existent, especially in the colonial heartland. Indian culture had been closely fused with Catholic, Iberian culture; popular protest, like popular culture more generally, assumed hybrid forms, neither specifically 'Indian' nor 'Spanish'. (Hence, insurgent elites and plebeians were often united by a common discursive repertoire: Catholic, patriotic, initially monarchist.)[481] No Aztec prince rose up to claim the mantle of sovereignty. Rather, messianic hopes were vested in the unlikely figure of Ignacio Allende, a well-to-do creole militia officer, who 'was seen by many Indians as a great avenger and killer of *gachupines*, social equalizer, abolisher of tributes and fixer of prices, and even as an agrarian reformer'.[482] Here, material demands and messianic hopes interwove: Allende (rather than, say, Hidalgo) probably became the brief beneficiary of this unlikely apotheosis because he fitted the kingly role (he was white, relatively young, martial in bearing and, above all, secular – he was not a priest). Hence he could be raised to regal status, and his elevated figure could legitimize the popular struggle.

Popular royalism consorted with popular religion. By the eighteenth century, outright 'paganism' was rare in Mexico, confined to the remote northern and southern peripheries. Even covert idolatry had faded, such that the clergy of Bourbon Mexico were less preoccupied by the idolatrous backsliding of their Indian flocks than their Habsburg predecessors had been.[483] If paganism had retreated, rationalism and unbelief had made scant progress. The vast

---

[480] It was precisely because the threat of Aztec revivalism was minimal that Mexican elites – creole and mestizo – could comfortably assimilate Aztec myths, heroes and motifs, and turn them to patriotic purposes; or that rich aristocrats could boast of their Aztec lineage: Brading, *First America*, pp. 580–1; Villoro, *El proceso ideológico*, pp. 82, 155–6; Ladd, *Mexican Nobility*, p. 21.

[481] Guardino, *Peasants*, p. 58. Brading makes a similar point: while the great revolt led by Tupac Amaru – a descendant of the Incas – in Upper Peru (1780–1) assumed the form of a caste war, in which 'the Indian peasantry began to attack all Spaniards and their property, whether European or American', the Mexican insurgency was premised on Catholic and patriotic – rather than caste – allegiances (hence, it 'resembled the Spanish resistance to the French invasion' of 1808): *First America*, pp. 487, 564.

[482] Van Young, 'Quetzalcóatl', pp. 124–5.

[483] Taylor, *Magistrates of the Sacred*, pp. 18, 48.

majority of Mexicans – of all classes – were Catholics, even if their Catholicism was frequently of the distinctive, hybrid, 'folk' variety.[484] The insurgency reflected this pervasive Catholicism. Rebel contingents proudly carried banners of the Virgin of Guadalupe (a powerful symbol which linked popular religion to the more cerebral proto-patriotism of creole intellectuals); the insurgent leader Félix Fernández changed his name to Guadalupe Victoria; the official seal of the Congress of Chilpancingo incorporated the name of the Virgin.[485] In the eyes of the insurgents the Spanish viceroy Venegas was an irreligious heretic, the French invaders of Spain were carriers of atheism. 'We are', Morelos boasted to the bishop of Puebla, 'more religious than the Europeans'. 'O Serene Princess', devout children in Mexico City sang to the Virgin, 'save us from Napoleon and the French nation'.[486] Thus, the Napoleonic invasion of Spain offered an ideal opportunity to link popular patriotism and religion in opposition to an alien liberalism: it compounded popular hatred of the *afrancesado* Bourbon regime which, in the eyes of the poor, was associated with the bad times of the 1780s and 1800s, the flouting of religion, the flaunting of an enhanced secular authority and the disciplining of labour. As Hidalgo excoriated the *gachupines* of Guadalajara: 'they are only Catholics through policy, their true god is money'.[487] Or, in a common variation on this theme – which also suggests popular appropriation of a 'public transcript' – 'all the gachupines are Jews'.[488]

484 Taylor, *Magistrates of the Sacred*, pp. 7, 450, on the weakness of unbelief. Florescano, *Memoria mexicana*, p. 486, mentions 'profane dances, songs and entertainments' which, proliferating in both town and country, reflected the 'new winds' blowing from Enlightenment Europe. The evidence is thin, however; it is partly generated by the fusty paranoia of the Inquisition; and it may, in fact, reflect an old Rabelaisian anticlericalism, rather than enlightened unbelief. More research is required.
485 Florescano, *Memoria mexicana*, pp. 503–9; Villoro, *El proceso ideológico*, p. 101; Matt S. Meier, 'María insurgente', *Historia Mexicana*, 23/2 (1974), pp. 466–82.
486 Lynch, *Spanish American Revolutions*, p. 314; Dorothy Tanck de Estrada, 'Los catecismos políticos: De la revolución francesa al México independiente', in Solange Alberro *et al.*, coords., *La revolución francesa en México* (Mexico, El Colegio de México, 1992), p. 69.
487 Brading, *Miners and Merchants*, p. 347.
488 Villoro, *El proceso ideológico*, p. 83. After the Spanish intendant of Guanajuato was slain, his body was allegedly 'stripped...and exhibited...to prove that he did not have a tail', as Jews were reported to have: Hamill, *The Hidalgo Revolt*, p. 137. (Later, similar stories circulated about Protestants.) See also Taylor, *Magistrates of the Sacred*, p. 459; Guardino, *Peasants*, p. 63, which, plausibly, explains this equation of *peninsulares* with Jews in terms of (a) Spain's old tradition (i.e., 'public transcript') of anti-Semitism, directed against *conversos*; and (b) the

The strength of traditional Catholicism within insurgent ideology was matched by the prominent role of priests in the ranks of the insurgents. Apart from the central figures – Hidalgo and Morelos – some four hundred priests are known to have figured in the rebellion, the majority of them secular clergy.[489] They included José María Mercado, *cura* of Ahualulco (Jalisco), who led 'a few rancheros and 600 Indians armed with sticks and garrotes' in a successful expedition against the Pacific port of San Blas; José Antonio Díaz, who transported the cannons of San Blas to Hidalgo at Guadalajara; José Manuel Herrera, *cura* of Chiautla (Puebla), who became vicar general of Morelos's forces; José Sixto Verduzco, of Tuzantla, who vied for leadership of the revolution in Michoacan; and Marcos Castellanos, who inspired the rebel resistance on the island redoubt of Mezcala, in Lake Chapala.[490] In response, the authorities – already tarred with the anticlerical brush – cracked down on troublesome priests, curtailed clerical judicial immunity and resorted to the widespread execution of rebel *curas* (again, Hidalgo and Morelos were only the most prominent of up to 125 priests who suffered execution). Soon, there were clerical rebels who proclaimed their readiness to 'die for ecclesiastical immunity': an anticipation of the powerful Church rights movements which would affect nineteenth-century Mexico. Popular rebellion, as the conservative Lucas Alamán lamented, involved 'a monstrous union of religion and assassination'.[491]

Yet, as in comparable later conflicts, the Church was divided. Although many *curas* were active on the rebel side, most remained neutral, and many supported the authorities. The *cura* of San Angel dutifully reported that his flock – the inhabitants of eleven villages

peninsulares' reputation for greed and commercial sharp practice. The Mexican proclivity for denouncing European Spaniards – the original carriers of Catholicism – as backsliding heretics and Jews was not new: see above, p. 149.

[489] Farriss, *Crown and Clergy*, p. 198–9; Taylor, *Magistrates of the Sacred*, pp. 453–4, lists 145 insurgent priests (106 'confirmed' rebels, 39 'alleged supporters'), two-thirds of whom (97) were parish priests, who in turn comprised about 10% of Mexico's 1,027 *curas*. The majority came from four regions: the Bajío, the Jalisco/Michoacan highlands, the hot country of Michoacan, Guerrero and Puebla, and the highlands of Mexico State. Not suprisingly, this roughly conforms to the geography of the insurgency.

[490] Hamnett, *Roots of Insurgency*, pp. 133, 135, 154, 186, 189–90.

[491] Lucas Alamán, *Historia de Méjico* (Mexico, 1968), vol. 2, pp. 243–4; Fariss, *Crown and Clergy*, pp. 201, 211, 231.

south of Mexico City – were terrified by the approach of Hidalgo's ragtag army.[492] In some communities, the parish priest was a target of popular hostility: at San Miguel Mezquitic (San Luis Potosí), for example, where an insurgent community confronted a rich, entrepreneurial *cura*.[493] Some royalist *curas* went beyond sermonizing: in Jalisco Father Alvarez, 'el cura chicharronero', earned his nickname ('the pork scratchings priest') by burning alive rebels and rebel sympathizers.[494] Not surprisingly, the rebels, too, killed their quota of priests (though fewer, it seems, than their royalist enemies did).[495] Thus, like rural Mexico itself, the lower priesthood was divided, affording leaders and martyrs to both sides. Insurgent priests provided a crucial source of leadership, but the insurgents also demonstrated that God-fearing Catholics were quite capable of butchering priests who stood across the sociopolitical divide. Folk Catholicism did not require unconditional respect for the cloth: it was a system of beliefs, rituals and symbols, rooted in rural clans and villages, rather than a set of binding ecclesiastical rules and tenets.

This became abundantly clear with the Catholic hierarchy's response to the insurgency. While the parish priests were divided, the bishops – even noted reformists like Abad y Queipo – were, to a man, hostile to the insurgency. Like the bishop of Guadalajara, they fled at the approach of rebel forces and their Virgin of Guadalupe banners; like the bishop of Oaxaca they preached against rebellion, raised funds for the royalists and even served in the militia. From the pulpit and in pamphlets the Church hierarchy declaimed against the rebels, stressed the virtues of Christian peace and declared their support for 'Religion, King, and Country'.[496] Thus rebel and royalist propaganda often echoed each other. The rebels (we have seen) did not enjoy a monopoly of the Virgin of Guadalupe, let alone other

[492] Hamill, *The Hidalgo Revolt*, p. 176.

[493] Tutino, *From Insurrection to Revolution*, pp. 161–4. Lesser disputes between communities and *curas*, often focusing on Church fees, were legion; even Morelos had had his problems: Taylor, *Magistrates of the Sacred*, p. 464.

[494] Taylor, *Magistrates of the Sacred*, p. 454, and the same author's 'Rural Unrest in Central Jalisco', p. 221.

[495] Fariss, *Crown and Clergy*, pp. 218–19; Taylor, *Magistrates of the Sacred*, pp. 458–9, 462–3, notes that the royalists' anticlericalism – even sacrilege – exceeded the insurgents'.

[496] Hamnett, *Roots of Insurgency*, p. 133; Hamnett, *Finance, Trade and Politics*, pp. 134–5; Hamill, *The Hidalgo Revolt*, pp. 152–64, 168.

Catholic symbols; the excommunicate Hidalgo was branded a fallen Lucifer, a disciple of Machiavelli, a traitorous ally of the French – epithets similar to those which the rebels hurled at their royalist opponents.[497] This congruence reflected, of course, a set of common popular – to some extent national – symbols, to which both sides laid claim. Rebels and royalists alike sought to tap popular Catholicism, investing their own cause with traditional, legitimist symbols, while equating their opponents with treason and heresy. In doing so, the rebels denied – or disguised – the strong currents of educated, *letrado* liberalism which fed their autonomist and patriotic cause; while the royalists, too, chose to overlook the no less powerful liberal, secularizing and antipopular ethos which had coloured Bourbon policy for over a generation. On both sides, revolutionary circumstances obliged political elites to bid for popular support, to compromise with deeply rooted popular sentiments and to qualify some of their elite ideology. Equally, a popular insurgency which was fundamentally conservative in terms of many of its symbols and ideas nevertheless proved genuinely revolutionary, in that it challenged the holders of power and, in some regions, toppled them too: a paradox which lies at the heart of many major revolutions.[498]

However, the insurgency could not be carried through to a revolutionary conclusion. Hidalgo's army briefly dominated the Bajío, suffered defeat, then broke up into scattered guerrillas and bandits. Morelos, though more successful at forging a coherent force, left a legacy of division. In the Bajío, the relative absence of a solidary, village-based peasantry made prolonged resistance impossible; conversely, where such a peasantry existed (for example, at Mezcala, in Jalisco) its tenacious struggle failed to galvanize broad collective support in the region. Instead, local rebellions remained local; insurgent pueblos (like Zacoalco) existed cheek-by-jowl with peaceful communities (like Tonalá); hence the insurgents were gradually worn down and picked off. The old colonial divide-and-rule strategy could still work.[499] Meanwhile, in the wake of the insurgency

[497] Villoro, *El proceso ideológico*, pp. 75–6; Connaughton, *Ideología y sociedad*, pp. 116, 126.
[498] Alan Knight, *The Mexican Revolution* (Cambridge, 1986), vol. 1, pp. 161, 314, citing Laurence Stone.
[499] 'In the event of a mob or riot', the intendant of Puebla, Manuel Flon advised, 'it is easier to pacify one village than many. Rarely if ever do they unite in such affairs...on the contrary,

(and, again, in the wake of the Revolution a hundred years later) the Bajío degenerated into bloody bandit campaigns: with Albino García after 1810 and José Inés Chávez García after 1910. Banditry, indeed, became a notable legacy of the declining insurgency, which it generously bequeathed to independent Mexico.[500] In contrast, coherent and sustained popular rebellions such as Mexcala's prefigured the durable peasant movements of the ninteenth century and Revolution; but, during the turbulent 1810s, these could not achieve the critical mass required to detonate the entire rural class structure. In many regions – notably the Valleys of Mexico, Toluca and Oaxaca – the colonial order, based on the authority of *hacendado*, *cacique*, and official, remained loosely intact, sustained by a residual legitimacy, an effective resort to coercion and a local fear of rebellious outsiders. In certain regions too (San Luis, Chihuahua), where the hacienda dominated a sparse population, landlords could drum up support for the royalist cause and even lead their peons into battle.[501]

Rebellion therefore remained geographically limited, capable of undermining but not overthrowing the colonial regime. It racked the Bajío and parts of the centre-west, from Jalisco through to Guerrero; it troubled but could not subvert the central highlands; it bypassed much of the underpopulated north and the Indian tributary zone of the southeast – Oaxaca, the Isthmus of Tehuantepec and beyond. Meanwhile, creoles who had initially flirted with rebellion recoiled in horror and threw their weight behind the authorities. Creole and *peninsular* sank their politico-ethnic differences and joined in a close, expedient, but loveless embrace, an embrace, however, in which the creole elite, now possessed of unprecedented military muscle, was the dominant partner.[502] The insurgency therefore placed the colonial regime in pawn to the creoles who, in the main, sought

the neighbouring villages are those that usually provide help to contain the riot': Guardino, *Peasants*, p. 28 (English slightly changed). Taylor, 'Rural Unrest in Central Jalisco', pp. 217–18, 237, 240, illustrates contrasting community responses.

[500] Taylor, 'Rural Unrest in Central Jalisco', pp. 214–15; Hamnett, *Roots of Insurgency*, pp. 164–5, 180–2, 209.

[501] Tutino, *From Insurrection to Revolution*, pp. 152–8; Jan Bazant, *Cinco haciendas mexicanas* (Mexico, 1975), p. 101, cites the case of the Hacienda de Bocas (San Luis), whose administrator led 180 peons – kitted out in distinctively coloured shirts – in support of Calleja's royalist army; he went on to lose his life at the siege of Cuautla in 1812.

[502] On creole political preferences, tactics and leverage: Hamill, *The Hidalgo Revolt*, pp. 170–5; Hamnett, *Politics and Trade*, pp. 137–8; Brading, *Miners and Merchants*, pp. 344–6.

autonomy – whether 'home rule' or outright independence – under orderly creole auspices.

This made possible the strange events of 1821, whereby Mexico finally attained its independence. Early in 1820 a military coup in Spain toppled Bourbon absolutism and restored the liberal Constitution of 1812. Spanish liberalism had now acquired a new militancy: the government sought to curtail Church property, to suppress the monastic orders, to eliminate clerical and military judicial privileges (*fueros*) and to broaden the franchise.[503] Spain, the erstwhile defender of corporate privilege and Catholicism, now emerged as the enemy of these powerful vested interests, the pillars of colonial society. Church and army felt threatened, as did the narrow urban oligarchies of New Spain. Within weeks of the promulgation of these measures the creole elite rose in rebellion. It was a brief, modest, swiftly successful rebellion. It called for independence, the defence of Church, property and corporate privilege, and the establishment of a constitutional monarchy. Its programme, the Plan of Iguala (February 1821), embodied three so-called guarantees: Religion, Union, Independence (that is: official Catholicism, equality of creoles, castes and Spaniards before the law, and independence from Spain). Hence it declared itself the 'Trigarantine' army. Although, as a sop to popular interests and liberal values, the rebels proposed the abolition of caste barriers, they had no intention of subverting the social order. On the contrary, the Trigarantine captain, Agustín de Iturbide, a well-to-do, second-generation creole, an ambitious plotter, and a royalist military officer of sanguinary and corrupt reputation, was typical of the propertied elites who now rebelled against Spain, chiefly in order to protect (and enhance) their positions of social and political privilege.[504] Long-standing creole wealth, buttressed by newfound creole political and military power, now came into its own. In Oaxaca, for example, the creole leader Murguía, who had represented the region at the abortive Congress of Chilpancingo in 1813 and had subsequently come to terms with the

---

[503] The abolition of the clerical *fuero* generalized a war-time expedient of 1812, whereby insurgent priests had been denied judicial immunity (not least in the cases of Hidalgo and Morelos): Farriss, *Crown and Clergy*, pp. 214, 220, 247. See also Macaulay, 'The Army of New Spain', pp. 140, 148–9.

[504] Hamnett, *Revolución y contrarrevolución*, pp. 307–8; Archer, ' "La Causa Buena" ', pp. 107–8.

restored royalist regime, called the tune; elsewhere, creole *cabildos*
seized local power, displaying a confidence and capacity they had
lacked ten years earlier. The Church, of course, was warmly sympathetic. Iturbide's rebellion was seen as a crusade, its leader a new
Moses sent by God to deliver his people. Prelates who had fallen foul
of *peninsular* liberalism were high in the counsels of the rebellious
movement; some cultivated Iturbide's imperial ambitions, envisag-
ing an independent Mexican monarchy under the divine aegis of the
Virgin of Guadalupe.[505]

In general terms, therefore, Mexico's creole elite perceived that
it could now secure independence – hence the enjoyment of local
power, privilege and property, untrammelled by metropolitan control and *gachupín* arrogance – without the attendant risks of social upheaval, which had bedevilled earlier essays in creole self-
assertion. The forces of the popular movement were at a low ebb;
those few rebels who remained under arms, like Vicente Guerrero
and Guadalupe Victoria, were either ignored or co-opted into the
rebel movement as junior partners. But Spain, the guarantor of order
and property in 1810–15, now, in 1820–21, appeared as a meddle-
some liberal metropolis, driven by imperial pretensions which more
than ever outstripped its imperial capacity. Hence, a decade after
the Hidalgo rebellion, Mexican independence was championed – as
Lucas Alamán put it – 'by the same people who until then had been
opposing it'.[506] After a decade of civil war, the creole elite possessed
sufficient military strength to impose its political will; the royalist
army, largely officered by creoles, wilted, and Spanish commanders, despairing of successful resistance, bowed to the inevitable.
Through the early summer of 1821, as Iturbide's Trigarantine army
marched triumphally through the Bajío, Viceroy Apodaca tried in
vain to repeat the counterinsurgency measures of Calleja.[507] But
this was no simple insurgency; it was also an army mutiny and
an elite declaration of independence. By August, when the new
Spanish captain-general O'Donojú sailed into Veracruz harbour,

[505] Villoro, *El proceso ideológico*, p. 197 (Moses); Brading, *Church and State*, pp. 250–1; Farriss,
     Crown and Clergy, pp. 248–51; Connaughton, *Ideología y sociedad*, pp. 151, 154.
[506] Lynch, *Spanish American Revolutions*, p. 320. Ladd, *Mexican Nobility*, p. 125, places greater
     emphasis on the liberal-aristocratic content of the Trigarantine rebellion.
[507] Anna, *Fall of the Royal Government*, pp. 213–16.

only Veracruz, along with Acapulco and Mexico City, remained in royalist hands. O'Donojú acquiesced: by the Treaty of Córdoba (24 August 1821) he gave unilateral (though qualified) recognition to Mexico's independence, roughly on the terms of the Plan of Iguala. What is more, he was at once accommodated within the new national administration.[508] On 24 September Iturbide's forces entered Mexico City, almost three hundred years to the day after Cortés's conquest of Tenochtitlán.

Thus Spain – which witheld recognition of Mexico's independence for a further fifteen years – succumbed to the classic syndrome of decolonizing powers. By clinging to power, the metropolis provoked popular opposition, which it managed to defeat, though not destroy. But in doing so it strengthened indigenous elites who, once their sociopolitical control was well established, seized power and evicted their colonial masters. In the process, the popular elements which, in fighting for emancipation, had gravely weakened imperial rule were now pushed to the margin. The potential for popular revolution was dissipated, and – in Mexico as elsewhere – national independence took the form of a political, rather than a social, revolution. The political regime changed, but much of the old socioeconomic order remained intact. Meanwhile, the popular insurgency, though unsuccessful, left a rich legacy of myths, ideals and organization; and the destruction of royal legitimacy left a hollow at the heart of the new regime. The key question facing Mexico's new rulers was how the old colonial society, agitated and mobilized as never before, could be governed under the new postcolonial political dispensation.

---

[508] O'Donojú did not profit from his preferment – he died of pleurisy ten days later: Anna, *Fall of the Royal Government*, pp. 222, 224–5.

Select Bibliography

Aboites Aguilar, Luis, *Norte precario. Poblamiento y colonización en México (1760–1940)* (Mexico, 1995).

Aguirre Beltrán, Gonzalo, *Población negra de México* (Mexico, 1972).

Alberro, Solange, *Inquisición y sociedad en México, 1571–1700* (Mexico, 1988).

Altman, Ida, and Lockhart, James, eds., *Provinces of Early Mexico: Variants of Spanish American Regional Evolution* (Los Angeles, 1976).

Anderson, Perry, *Lineages of the Absolutist State* (London, 1979).

Andrien, Kenneth J., and Johnson, Lyman L., eds., *The Political Economy of Spanish America in the Age of Revolution, 1750–1850* (Albuquerque, 1994).

Anna, Timothy, *The Fall of the Royal Government in Mexico City* (Lincoln, 1978).

Anna, Timothy, 'The Independence of Mexico and Central America', in Leslie Bethell, ed., *The Cambridge History of Latin America*, vol. 3, *From Independence to c. 1870* (Cambridge, 1985), pp. 51–94.

Archer, Christon I., *The Army in Bourbon Mexico, 1760–1810* (Albuquerque, 1977).

Arrom, Silvia Marina, *The Women of Mexico City, 1790–1857* (Stanford, 1985).

Bakewell, Peter, 'Mining in Colonial Spanish America', in Leslie Bethell, ed., *Cambridge History of Latin America*, vol. 2, *Colonial Latin America* (Cambridge, 1984), pp. 105–52.

Bakewell, P. J., *Silver Mining and Society in Colonial Mexico: Zacatecas, 1546–1700* (Cambridge, 1971).

Barrett, Ward, *The Sugar Hacienda of the Marquesado del Valle* (Minneapolis, 1970).

Benson, Nettie Lee, ed., *Mexico and the Spanish Cortes, 1810–1822* (Austin, 1966).

333

Boorstein Couturier, Edith, *La hacienda de Hueyapán, 1550–1936* (Mexico, 1976).

Borah, Woodrow, *Justice by Insurance: The General Indian Court of Colonial Mexico and the Legal Aides of the Half-Real* (Berkeley, 1983).

Borah, Woodrow, *New Spain's Century of Depression* (Berkeley, 1951).

Boyer, Richard, *La gran inundación. Vida y sociedad en la ciudad de México (1629–1638)* (Mexico, 1975).

Boyer, Richard, *Lives of the Bigamists: Marriage, Family and Community in Colonial Mexico* (Albuquerque, 1995).

Brading, D. A., 'Bourbon Spain and Its American Empire', in Leslie Bethell, ed., *Cambridge History of Latin America*, vol. 1, *Colonial Latin America* (Cambridge, 1984), pp. 389–440.

Brading, D. A., *Church and State in Bourbon Mexico: The Diocese of Michoacán, 1749–1810* (Cambridge, 1994).

Brading, D. A., *The First America: The Spanish Creole Monarchy and the Liberal State, 1492–1867* (Cambridge, 1991).

Brading, D. A., *Haciendas and Ranchos in the Mexican Bajío: León, 1700–1860* (Cambridge, 1978).

Brading, D. A., *Miners and Merchants in Bourbon Mexico, 1763–1810* (Cambridge, 1971).

Brading, D. A., *Myth and Prophecy in Mexican History* (Cambridge, 1984).

Braudel, Fernand, *Civilization and Capitalism, Fifteenth-Eighteenth Centuries*, vol. 2, *The Wheels of Commerce* (London, 1982).

Braudel, Fernand, *Civilization and Capitalism, Fifteenth-Eighteenth Centuries*, vol. 3, *The Perspective of the World* (London, 1985).

Braudel, Fernand, *The Mediterranean and the Mediterranean World in the Age of Philip II* (vol. 1, London, 1972).

Bricker, Victoria Reifler, *The Indian Christ, The Indian King: The Historical Substrate of Maya Myth and Ritual* (Austin, 1981).

Burkhart, Louise, *The Slippery Earth: Nahua-Christian Moral Dialogue in Sixteenth-Century Mexico* (Tucson, 1989).

Carmagnani, Marcelo, *El regreso de los dioses: La reconstitución de la identidad étnica en Oaxaca, siglos XVII y XVIII* (Mexico, 1988).

Carrera Stampa, Manuel, *Los gremios mexicanos* (Mexico, 1954).

Carroll, Patrick J., *Blacks in Colonial Veracruz: Race, Ethnicity and Regional Development* (Austin, 1991).

Cervantes, Fernando, *The Devil in the New World* (New Haven, 1994).

Chance, John K., *Conquest of the Sierra: Spaniard and Indian in Colonial Oaxaca* (Norman, Okla., 1989).

Chance, John K., *Race and Class in Colonial Oaxaca* (Stanford, 1978).

Chayanov, A. V., *The Theory of Peasant Economy* (Madison, 1986, first pubd. 1925).

Chevalier, François, *Land and Society in Colonial Mexico* (Berkeley, 1970, first pubd. 1963).

Chipman, Donald E., *Nuño de Guzmán and the Province of Pánuco in New Spain (1518–1533)* (Glendale, 1967).

Clendinnen, Inga, *Ambivalent Conquest: Maya and Spaniard in Yucatán, 1517–1570* (Cambridge, 1987).

Clendinnen, Inga, *Aztecs* (Cambridge, 1991).

Cline, S. L., *Colonial Culhuacan, 1580–1600: A Social History of an Aztec Town* (Albuquerque, 1986).

Cohen, G. A., *Karl Marx's Theory of History: A Defence* (Oxford, 1978).

Connaughton, Brian, *Ideología y sociedad en Guadalajara (1788–1853)* (Mexico, 1992).

Cook, Noble David, *Born to Die: Disease and the New World Conquest, 1492–1650* (Cambridge, 1998).

Cook, Sherburne F., and Borah, Woodrow, *Essays in Population History: Mexico and the Caribbean* (vol. 2, Berkeley, 1974).

Cook, Sherburne F., and Borah, Woodrow, *The Indian Population of Central Mexico, 1531–1610* (Berkeley, 1960).

Cope, R. Douglas, *The Limits of Racial Domination: Plebeian Society in Colonial Mexico City, 1660–1720* (Madison, 1994).

Corcuera de Mancera, Sonia, *El fraile, el indio y el pulque. Evangelización y embraiguez en la Nueva España (1523–1548)* (Mexico, 1991).

Crosby, Alfred W., *The Columbian Exchange: Biological and Cultural Consequences of 1492* (Westport, 1972).

Deans-Smth, Susan, *Bureaucrats, Planters, and Workers: The Making of the Tobacco Monopoly in Bourbon Mexico* (Austin, 1992).

Dusenberry, William H., *The Mexican Mesta: The Administration of Ranching in Colonial Mexico* (Urbana, 1963).

Elliott, J. H., *Imperial Spain, 1469–1716* (Harmondsworth, 1983, first pubd. 1970).

Elliott, J. H., 'Spain and America in the Sixteenth and Seventeenth Centuries', in Leslie Bethell, ed., *Cambridge History of Latin America*, vol. 1, *Colonial Latin America* (Cambridge, 1984), pp. 149–206.

Elliott, J. H., 'The Spanish Conquest and Settlement of America', in Leslie Bethell, ed., *Cambridge History of Latin America*, vol. 1, *Colonial Latin America* (Cambridge, 1984), pp. 149–206.

Farb, Peter, *Man's Rise to Civilization as Shown by the Indians of North America from Primeval Time to the Coming of the Industrial State* (New York, 1968).

Farriss, N. M., *Crown and Clergy in Colonial Mexico, 1759–1821: The Crisis of Ecclesiastical Privilege* (London, 1968).

Farriss, Nancy M., *Maya Society under Colonial Rule: The Collective Enterprise of Survival* (Princeton, 1984).

Florescano, Enrique, 'The Formation and Economic Structure of the Hacienda in New Spain', in Leslie Bethell, ed., *Cambridge History of Latin America*, vol. 2, *Colonial Latin America* (Cambridge, 1984), pp. 153–88.

Florescano, Enrique, *Memoria mexicana. Ensayo sobre la reconstrucción del pasado: Época prehispánica* (Mexico, 1987).

Florescano, Enrique, *Origen y desarrollo de los problemas agrarios de México, 1500–1821* (Mexico, 1976).

Florescano, Enrique, *Precios del maíz y crisis agrícolas en México (1708–1810)* (Mexico, 1969).

Florescano, Enrique, and Gil Sánchez, Isabel, *Descripciones económicas de Nueva España, 1784–1817* (Mexico, 1973).

Florescano, Enrique, and Gil Sánchez, Isabel, 'La época de las reformas borbónicas y el crecimiento económico, 1750–1808', in *Historia General de México* (vol. 2, Mexico, 1976).

Florescano, Enrique, ed., *Haciendas, latifundios, y plantaciones en América Latina* (Mexico, 1975).

Frost, Elsa Cecilia, Meyer, Michael C., and Vázquez, Josefina Zoraida, eds., *El trabajo y los trabajadores en la historia de México* (Mexico, 1979).

Garavaglia, Juan C., and Grosso, Juan C., *Puebla desde una perspectiva microhistórica. Tepeaca y su entorno agrario: Población, producción e intercambio (1740–1870)* (Mexico, 1994).

García de León, Antonio, *Resistencia y utopía. Memorial de agravios y crónicas de revueltas y profecías acaecidas en la provincia de Chiapas durante los últimos quinientos años de su historia* (2 vols., Mexico, 1985).

García Martínez, Bernardo, *Los pueblos de la sierra: El poder y el espacio entre los indios del norte de Puebla hasta 1700* (Mexico, 1987).

Garner, Richard L., with Stefanou, Spiro E., *Economic Growth and Change in Bourbon Mexico* (Gainesville, 1993).

Gerhard, Peter, *A Guide to the Historical Geography of New Spain* (Cambridge, 1972).

Gibson, Charles, *The Aztecs under Spanish Rule: A History of the Indians of the Valley of Mexico, 1519–1810* (Stanford, 1964).

Gibson, Charles, *Tlaxcala in the Sixteenth Century* (Stanford, 1967, first pubd., 1952).

Gosner, Kevin, *Soldiers of the Virgin: The Moral Economy of a Colonial Maya Rebellion* (Tucson, 1992).

Greenleaf, Richard E., *The Mexican Inquisition of the Sixteenth Century* (Albuquerque, 1969).

Greenow, Linda L., *Credit and Socioeconomic Change in Colonial Mexico: Loans and Mortgages in Guadalajara, 1720–1820* (Boulder, 1983).

Gruzinski, Serge, *The Conquest of Mexico* (Cambridge, 1993).

Gruzinski, Serge, *Histoire de Mexico* (Paris, 1996).

Gruzinski, Serge, *Man-Gods in the Mexican Highlands: Indian Power and Colonial Society, 1520–1800* (Stanford, 1989).

Guardino, Peter, *Peasants, Politics, and the Formation of Mexico's National State: Guerrero, 1800–1857* (Stanford, 1996).

Gutiérrez, Ramón A., *When Jesus Came the Corn Mothers Went Away: Marriage, Sexuality and Power in New Mexico, 1500–1856* (Stanford, 1991).

Hadley, Phillip L., *Minería y sociedad en el centro minero de Santa Eulalia, Chihuahua (1709–1750)* (Mexico, 1979).

Hall, Thomas D., *Social Change in the Southwest, 1350–1880* (Lawrence, Kans., 1989).

Hamill, Hugh, Jr., *The Hidalgo Revolt: Prelude to Mexican Independence* (Gainesville, 1966).

Hamnett, Brian, *Politics and Trade in Southern Mexico, 1750–1821* (Cambridge, 1971).

Hamnett, Brian, *Roots of Insurgency: Mexican Regions, 1750–1824* (Cambridge, 1986).

Haskett, Robert, *Indigenous Rulers: An Ethnohistory of Town Government in Colonial Cuernavaca* (Albuquerque, 1991).

Hassig, Ross, *Trade, Tribute, and Transportation: The Sixteenth-Century Political Economy of the Valley of Mexico* (Norman, Okla., 1985).

Herr, Richard, *The Eighteenth-Century Revolution in Spain* (Princeton, 1958).

Hoberman, Louisa Schell, *Mexico's Merchant Elite, 1590–1660: Silver, State and Society* (Durham, 1991).

Hoberman, Louisa Schell, and Socolow, Susan Migden, eds., *Cities and Society in Colonial Latin America* (Albuquerque, 1986).

Horn, Rebecca, *Postconquest Coyoacán: Nahua-Spanish Relations in Central Mexico, 1519–1650* (Stanford, 1997).

Howe, Walter, *The Mining Guild of New Spain and Its Tribunal General, 1770–1820* (Cambridge, Mass., 1949).

Hu-Dehart, Evelyn, *Missionaries, Miners, and Indians: Spanish Contact with the Yaqui Nation of Northwestern New Spain, 1533–1820* (Tucson, 1981).

Humboldt, Alexander Von, *Political Essay on the Kingdom of New Spain* (Norman, Okla., 1988; first pubd in this ed., abridged by Mary Maples Dunn, 1972; first pubd. 1811).

Israel, J. I., *Race, Class, and Politics in Colonial Mexico, 1600–1670* (Oxford, 1975).

Jackson, Robert H., *Indian Population Decline: The Missions of Northwestern New Spain, 1687–1840* (Albuquerque, 1994).

Jacobsen, Nils, and Pühle, Hans-Jürgen, eds., *The Economies of Mexico and Peru during the Colonial Period, 1769–1810* (Berlin, 1986).

Jarquín Ortega, María Teresa, *Origen y evolución de la hacienda en México: Siglos XVI al XX* (Toluca, 1990).

Johnson, Lyman, and Tandeter, Enrique, eds., *Essays in the Price History of Eighteenth-Century Latin America* (Albuquerque, 1990).

Katz, Friedrich, ed., *Riot, Rebellion, and Revolution: Rural Social Conflict in Mexico* (Princeton, 1988).

Kellogg, Susan, *Law and the Transformation of Aztec Culture, 1500–1700* (Norman, Okla., 1995).

Kicza, John E., *Colonial Entrepreneurs: Families and Business in Bourbon Mexico City* (Albuquerque, 1983).

Knaut, Andrew L., *The Pueblo Revolt of 1680* (Norman, Okla., 1995).

Kobayashi, José María, *La educación como conquista (empresa franciscana en México)* (Mexico, 1985).

Kriedte, Peter, *Feudalismo tardío y capital mercantil* (Barcelona, 1982).

Kubler, George C., *Mexican Architecture of the Sixteenth Century* (2 vols., New Haven, 1948).

Kula, Witold, *An Economic Theory of the Feudal System* (London, 1976).

Ladd, Doris, *The Making of a Strike: Mexican Silver Workers' Struggles in Real del Monte, 1766–1775* (Lincoln, 1988).

Ladd, Doris M., *The Mexican Nobility at Independence, 1780–1826* (Austin, 1976).

Lafaye, Jacques, *Quetzalcóatl y Guadalupe. La formación de la conciencia nacional en México* (México, 1991; first pubd. 1974).

Landa, Diego de, *Yucatán Before and After the Conquest* (New York, 1978, first pubd. 1937).

Langer, Erick, and Jackson, Robert H., eds., *The New Latin American Mission History* (Lincoln, 1995).

Leonard, Irving, *Baroque Times in Old Mexico: Seventeenth-Century Persons, Places, and Practices* (Ann Arbor, 1966).

Lindley, Richard B., *Haciendas and Economic Development: Guadalajara, Mexico, at Independence* (Austin, 1983).

Liss, Peggy, *Mexico under Spain, 1521–1556: Society and the Origins of Nationality* (Chicago, 1975).

Lockhart, James, *The Nahuas after the Conquest: A Social and Cultural History of the Indians of Central Mexico, Sixteenth Through Eighteenth Centuries* (Stanford, 1992).

Lockhart, James, *Nahuas and Spaniards: Postconquest Central Mexican History and Philology* (Stanford, 1991).

Lockhart, James, and Otte, Enrique, *Letters and People of the Spanish Indies: The Sixteenth Century* (Cambridge, 1976).

Lockhart, James, and Schwartz, Stuart B., *Early Latin America: A History of Colonial Spanish America and Brazil* (Cambridge, 1983).

Lynch, John, *Bourbon Spain, 1700–1808* (Oxford, 1989).

Lynch, John, *Spain under the Habsburgs* (2 vols., Oxford, 1992).

Lynch, John, *The Spanish American Revolutions* (London, 1973).

MacLachlan, Colin, *Criminal Justice in Eighteenth-Century Mexico: A Study of the Tribunal of the Acordada* (Berkeley, 1974).

MacLachlan, Colin, and Rodríguez O., Jaime, *The Forging of the Cosmic Race: A Reinterpretation of Colonial Mexico* (Berkeley, 1980).

MacLeod, Murdo J., 'Aspects of the Internal Economy of Colonial Spanish America: Labour; Taxation; Distribution and Exchange', in Leslie Bethell, ed., *Cambridge History of Latin America*, vol. 2, *Colonial Latin America* (Cambridge, 1984), pp. 219–64.

MacLeod, Murdo J., 'Forms and Types of Work and the Acculturation of the Colonial Indians of Mesoamerica: Some Preliminary Observations', in Elsa Cecilia Frost, Michael C. Meyer, and Josefina Zoraida Vázquez, eds., *El trabajo y los trabajadores en la historia de México* (Mexico, 1979), pp. 75–91.

MacLeod, Murdo J., 'Spain and America: The Atlantic Trade, 1492–1720', in Leslie Bethell, ed., *Cambridge History of Latin America*, vol. 1, *Colonial Latin America* (Cambridge, 1984), pp. 341–88.

Martin, Cheryl English, *Governance and Society in Colonial Mexico: Chihuahua in the Eighteenth Century* (Stanford, 1996).

Martin, Cheryl English, *Rural Society in Colonial Morelos* (Albuquerque, 1985).

McFarlane, Anthony, *The British in the Americas, 1480–1815* (London, 1994).

Melville, Eleanor G. K., *A Plague of Sheep: Environmental Consequences of the Conquest of Mexico* (Cambridge, 1994).

Meyer, Jean, coord., *Tres levantamientos populares: Pugachóv, Túpac Amaru, Hidalgo* (Mexico, 1992).

Miño Grijalva, Manuel, *La protoindustria colonial hispanoamericana* (Mexico, 1993).

Morin, Claude, *Michoacan en la Nueva España del siglo XVIII. Crecimiento y desigualdad en una sociedad colonial* (Mexico, 1979).

Nickel, Herbert J., *Morfología social de la hacienda mexicana* (Mexico, 1988).

Olivera, Mercedes, *Pillis y macehuales. Las formaciones sociales y los modos de producción de Tecali del siglo XII al XVI* (Mexico, 1978).

Ouweneel, Arij, *Ciclos interrumpidos. Ensayos sobre historia rural mexicana, siglos XVIII–XIX* (Toluca, 1998).

Ouweneel, Arij, and Torales Pacheco, Cristina, *Empresarios, indios y estado. Perfil de la economía mexicana (siglo XVIII)* (Amsterdam, 1988).

Padden, R. C., *The Hummingbird and the Hawk: Conquest and Sovereignty in the Valley of Mexico, 1503–1541* (New York, 1970).

Pagden, Anthony, ed., *Hernán Cortés, Letters from Mexico* (New Haven, 1986).

Palmer, Colin A., *Slaves of the White God: Blacks in Mexico, 1570–1650* (Cambridge, Mass., 1976).

Pastor, Rodolfo, *Campesinos y reformas: La Mixteca, 1700–1856* (Mexico, 1987).

Patch, Robert W., *Maya and Spaniard in Yucatán, 1648–1812* (Stanford, 1993).

Paz, Octavio, *Sor Juana, or the Traps of Faith* (Cambridge, Mass., 1988).

Peña, José F. de la, *Oligarquía y propiedad en Nueva España (1550–1624)* (Mexico, 1983).

Pérez Herrero, Pedro, *Plata y libranzas. La articulación comercial del México borbónico* (Mexico, 1988).

Phelan, John L., *The Millennial Kingdom of the Franciscans in the New World* (Berkeley, 1956).

Poole, Stafford, *Our Lady of Guadalupe: The Origins and Sources of a Mexican National Legend, 1531–1797* (Tucson, 1995).

Powell, Philip Wayne, *Soldiers, Indians and Silver: The Northwards Advance of New Spain, 1550–1600* (Berkeley, 1952).

Radding, Cynthia, *Wandering Peoples: Colonialism, Ethnic Spaces, and Ecological Frontiers in Northwestern Mexico, 1700–1850* (Durham, 1997).

Reff, Daniel T., *Disease, Depopulation, and Culture Change in Northwestern New Spain, 1518–1764* (Salt Lake City, 1991).

Restall, Matthew, *The Maya World: Yucatec Culture and Society, 1550–1850* (Stanford, 1997).

Ricard, Robert, *The Spiritual Conquest of Mexico* (Berkeley, 1966, first pubd. 1933).

Rodríguez O., Jaime, *The Independence of Spanish America* (Cambridge, 1998).

Rodríguez O., Jaime, ed., *The Evolution of the Mexican Political System* (Wilmington, Del., 1993).

Rodríguez O., Jaime, ed., *The Independence of Mexico and the Creation of the New Nation* (Los Angeles, 1989).

Rodríguez O., Jaime, ed., *Mexico in the Age of the Democratic Revolutions, 1750–1850* (Boulder, 1994).

Rugely, Terry, *Yucatán's Maya Peasantry and the Origins of the Caste War* (Austin, 1996).

Salvucci, Richard J., *Textiles and Capitalism in Mexico: An Economic History of the Obrajes, 1539–1840* (Princeton, 1987).

Sánchez-Albornoz, Nicolás, 'The Population of Colonial Spanish America', in Leslie Bethell, ed., *Cambridge History of Latin America*, vol. 2, *Colonial Latin America* (Cambridge, 1984), pp. 3–36.

Schroeder, Susan, Wood, Stephanie, and Haskett, Robert, eds., *Indian Women of Colonial Mexico* (Norman, Okla., 1997).

Schwaller, John Frederick, *Origins of Church Wealth in Mexico: Ecclesiastical Revenues and Church Finances, 1523–1600* (Albuquerque, 1985).

Seed, Patricia, *To Love, Honor, and Obey in Colonial Mexico: Conflicts over Marriage Choice, 1574–1821* (Stanford, 1988).

Semo, Enrique, *The History of Capitalism in Mexico: Its Origins, 1521–1763* (Austin, 1993).

Semo, Enrique, coord., *Siete ensayos sobre la hacienda mexicana, 1780–1880* (Mexico, 1977).

Simpson, Lesley Byrd, *The Encomienda in New Spain: The Beginnings of Spanish Mexico* (Berkeley, 1982, first pubd. 1950).

Spalding, Karen, ed., *Essays in the Political, Economic, and Social History of Colonial Latin America* (Newark, Del., 1982).

Spicer, Edward E., *Cycles of Conquest: The Impact of Spain, Mexico and the United States on the Indians of the Southwest, 1553–1960* (Tucson, 1962).

Spores, Ronald, *The Mixtec Kings and Their People* (Norman, Okla., 1967).

Stern, Steve J., *The Secret History of Gender: Women, Men, and Power in Late Colonial Mexico* (Chapel Hill, 1995).

Super, John C., *Food, Conquest, and Colonization in Sixteenth-Century Spanish America* (Albuquerque, 1988).

Super, John C., *La vida en Querétaro durante la Colonia, 1531–1810* (Mexico, 1983).

Taylor, William B., *Drinking, Homicide and Rebellion in Colonial Mexican Villages* (Stanford, 1979).

Taylor, William, B., *Landlord and Peasant in Colonial Oaxaca* (Stanford, 1972).

Taylor, William B., *Magistrates of the Sacred: Priests and Parishioners in Eighteenth-Century Mexico* (Stanford, 1996).

Taylor, William, and Pease, Franklin, eds., *Violence, Resistance and Survival in the Americas: Native Americans and the Legacy of the Conquest* (Washington, D.C., 1994).

Thomas, David Hurst ed., *Columbian Consequences: Archaeological and Historical Perspectives on the Spanish Borderlands West* (vol. 1, Washington, D.C., 1989).

Thomas, Hugh. *The Conquest of Mexico* (London, 1993).

Thompson, J. Eric S., ed., *Thomas Gage's Travels in the New World* (Norman, Okla., 1985; first pubd this edition, 1958; first pubd. 1648).

Thomson, Guy P. C., *Puebla de los Angeles: Industry and Society in a Mexican City, 1700–1850* (Boulder, 1989).

Timmons, Wilbert H., *Morelos: Priest, Soldier, and Statesman of Mexico* (El Paso, 1963).

Tutino, John, *From Insurrection to Revolution in Mexico: Social Bases of Agrarian Violence, 1750–1940* (Princeton, 1986).

Van Young, Eric, *Hacienda and Market in Eighteenth-Century Mexico: The Rural Economy of the Guadalajara Region, 1675–1820* (Berkeley, 1981).

Vilar, Pierre, *A History of Gold and Money* (London, 1984).

Villoro, Luis, *El proceso ideológico de la revolución de Independencia* (Mexico, 1986).

Viqueira Albán, Juan Pedro, *Relajados o reprimidos: Diversiones públicas y vida social en la Ciudad de México durante el siglo de las luces* (Mexico, 1987).

Wachtel, Nathan, 'The Indian and the Spanish Conquest', in Leslie Bethell, ed., *Cambridge History of Latin America*, vol. 1, *Colonial Latin America* (Cambridge, 1984), pp. 207–48.

Wachtel, Nathan, *The Vision of the Vanquished: The Spanish Conquest through Indian Eyes, 1520–1570* (Hassocks, 1977).

Wallerstein, Immanuel, *The Modern World-System: Capitalist Agriculture and the Origins of the European World-Economy in the Sixteenth Century* (New York, 1974).

Ward, H. G., *Mexico* (2 vols., London, 2nd ed., 1829).

Warren, J. Benedict, *The Conquest of Michoacan: The Spanish Domination of the Tarascan Kingdom in Western Mexico, 1521–1530* (Norman, Okla., 1985).

Wasserstrom, Robert, *Class and Society in Central Chiapas* (Berkeley, 1983).

Weber, David J., *The Spanish Frontier in North America* (New Haven, 1992).

Weber, Max, *The Theory of Social and Economic Organization* (New York, 1964).

Weckman, Luis, *La herencia medieval de México* (Mexico, 1996, first pubd. 1984).

Whitaker, Arthur P., ed., *Latin America and the Enlightenment* (Ithaca, 1961, first pubd. 1942).

Whitecotton, Joseph W., *The Zapotecs: Princes, Priests, and Peasants* (Norman, Okla., 1984, first pubd. 1977).

Wobeser, Gisela von, *El crédito eclesiástico en la Nueva España, siglo XVIII* (Mexico, 1994).

Wolf, Eric R., *Europe and the People without History* (Berkeley, 1982).

Wolf, Eric R., *Sons of the Shaking Earth* (Chicago, 1972).

Zorita, Alonso de, *The Lords of New Spain* (London 1973).

Index

Abad y Queipo, Bishop, 284 n.328, 326
Abasolo, Mariano, 296, 315
Abó, 139
Absolutism, 192, 242
Acapulco, 176 n.669, 306, 331
Acatlán, 224
Acaxee, 128, 133, 134
Acayucan, 224, 276, 318
acculturation, 13, 23, 29, 70, 73, 83, 102–16, 143, 228, 239; defined, 74 n.266, 102 n.369; linguistic, 114, 123
accumulation, 95, 118
Achiutla, 226
Actopan, 65
Aculco, Battle of, 302
Africa, 83, 95
agrarian reform, 318–19
Aguascalientes, 301
Ahualulco, 325
Alamán, Lucas, 330
Alamos, 133, 255, 272
Alaska, 254
alcabala, 232, 244, 272
alcaldes mayores, 55, 57, 276, 278
Algiers, 8
Allende, Ignacio, 296, 300, 303–4, 315, 316, 323

altepetl, 65, 108, 122
Alvarado, Pedro de, 4, 10
Alvarez, Juan, 309
anticlericalism, 170, 263, 264, 268, 324
Antilles, 15, 24, 158
Apaches, 66, 82, 130, 131, 136, 137, 139, 141, 142, 256, 257, 260
Apam, 304
Apodaca, Viceroy, 330
architecture, 185, 268
Argentina, 77, 159, 231
Arizona, 130, 140
army, 71, 250, 252, 253, 259, 261, 311–12
articulation of modes of production, 92, 187
artisans, 93, 218, 231
Asiatic Mode of Production, 87, 193, 199
Atemajac, 321
audiencias, 54, 171, 250, 293, 294
Augustinians, 75; *see also* friars
autarky, *see* hacienda rationale
Aztecs, 1, 48, 94 n.337, 103, 107–8, 124, 154, 192, 280

Bajío, the, 26, 28, 30, 62, 67, 87, 124, 179, 209, 210, 212, 215, 220, 222, 228, 233, 234, 235, 237,

343

nationalism, proto-, *see* patriotism, proto-
New Galicia, 7, 8, 9, 16, 21, 86
New Laws, 18
New Mexico, 8, 9, 10, 37, 55, 60, 71, 128, 139, 155, 254, 255 n.211, 256
New York, 209
nepantlism, 41, 104
Nezahualpilli, 107
nobility, 59
Nombre de Dios, 67
North America, British, 199–200, 251, 274 n.298
Nueva Vizcaya, 55
Nuevo León, 25, 55, 136
Nuevo México, *see* New Mexico

Oaxaca, 1, 4, 9, 11, 13, 15, 21, 28, 30, 33, 34, 39, 80, 81, 86, 93, 94, 96, 103, 115, 116, 117, 142–4, 154, 179, 206, 210–11, 225, 238, 261, 262, 276, 294, 297, 305, 308, 317, 328, 329
obrajes, 17, 87, 88, 98, 159, 160, 164–5, 178 n.674, 179 n.681, 181, 194, 195, 196, 197, 215, 217, 232, 271
Ocosingo, 147
O'Donojú, Juan, 330–1
officials, royal, *see* crown, bureaucracy
oidores, 54, 57
Ojuelos Pass, 70
Old South (United States), 109
Olid, Cristóbal de, 6
Olivares, Count-Duke of, 176
Olmos, Andrés de, 33
Oñate family, 59, 138
Opatas, 67, 128, 131, 141
Orizaba, 208 n.17
Ortega, Juan de, 10
Osorno family, 304
Otomíes, 10, 34, 65, 70, 103
Ottoman Empire, 192, 281
oxen, 161

Pacheco, Gaspar, 4
Pachuca, 63, 213
Palafox, Arhcbishop, 281
Pames, 72
Pánuco, 4
Papantla, 224, 276
Parral, 63, 69, 128, 134
Pascal, Blaise, 38
Patambán, 40
Patch, R., 107
paternalism, 100; of Crown, 26, 30, 54, 84, 109, 277–8; of landlords, 97, 98, 100
patriarchy, 262
patrimonialism, 245, 259
patriotism, proto-, 114, 183, 281, 284
Patronato Real, 32, 54
Pauw, Cornelius de, 279, 281
peasants: community, 73 n.262; economy, 160; strategy, 90, 94, 239 n.154
Peláez de Barrio, 37
peninsulares, 182, 253, 279–83, 284, 293, 297, 303, 305, 316, 319, 328
Peru, 8, 19, 65, 174, 178, 217 n.60, 298, 310, 322–3
peonage, *see* debt peonage
peones acasillados, *see* gañanes
Petén, 9
Peter of Ghent, 1, 32
peyote, 106
Philadelphia, 209
Philip II, 57, 60
Philip III, 137
Philip IV, 43
Philip V, 247
Philippines, 55, 174, 176, 177 n.673
pigs, 24
Pimas, 67, 128, 131, 132, 135, 255, 257
piracy, 6, 251
Plains Indians, 70, 134 n.512
Plan of Iguala, 329
Poland, 194
polygamy, 13, 29